Controversies in Constitutional Law

Collections of Documents and Articles on Major Questions of American Law

General Editor

Paul Finkelman

University of Tulsa School of Law

A ROUTLEDGE SERIES

Contents of the Collection

Children and the Law

Volume 3

Child vs. State

Edited with introductions by

Janet W. Steverson
Northwestern School of Law
of Lewis and Clark College

ROUTLEDGE
New York/London

Published in 2002 by
Routledge
711 Third Avenue
New York, NY 10017

Published in Great Britain by
Routledge
2 Park Square, Milton Park
Abingdon, Oxfordshire OX14 4RN

Routledge is an imprint of the Taylor & Francis Group.

First issued in paperback 2011

10 9 8 7 6 5 4 3 2

Library of Congress Cataloging-in-Publication Data

Children and the law / edited with introductions by Janet W. Steverson.
p. cm. — (Controversies in constitutional law)
Includes bibliographical references.
Contents: v. 1. The State as Child Protector — v. 2. The State and the Schooling of Children — v. 3. Child vs. State.
ISBN 0-415-93803-1 (set : alk paper) — ISBN 0-415-93804-X (vol. 1 : alk. paper) — ISBN 0-415-93805-8 (vol. 2 : alk. paper) — ISBN 0-415-93806-6 (vol. 3 : alk. paper)
1. Children—Legal status, laws, etc.—United States. 2. Parent and child (Law)—United States. 3. Juvenile justice, Administration of—United States. I. Steverson, Janet W. II. Series.
KF479.A75 C478 2002
346.7301'35—dc21 2002020626

ISBN13: 978-0-415-93806-8 (hbk)
ISBN13: 978-0-415-51280-0 (pbk)

Contents

Series Introduction

This ongoing series, *Controversies in Constitutional Law,* provides teachers, scholars, and students convenient access to the debates and scholarly literature surrounding major questions of constitutional law. Each set of books—from two to four volumes—consists of four elements: an extended introduction to the issue by the editor; reprints of the significant cases and briefs on the subject; congressional testimony, and other primary documents on the issue; and a selection of the best scholarly articles on the subject. By conveniently gathering all this material in one place, each set of volumes allows users to become familiar quite quickly with the arguments and positions surrounding a particular constitutional controversy.

Scholars and students interested in constitutional law and public policy are often overwhelmed by the sheer amount of material published on controversial subjects. The topics in *Controversies in Constitutional Law* are timely, politically significant, and intellectually compelling. They are the issues that bring the legal academy, courts, politicians, and general public together—although not always in harmony.

Many scholars are barely able to keep up with the material in their own fields. Yet there is a need to learn about issues beyond our own specialties. A new course may require an introduction to a problem; our own research may lead us to a new issue. The series *Controversies in Constitutional Law* is designed to meet these needs, enabling scholars and teachers to come up to speed quickly on the topics in each volume.

This series also serves students at all levels of higher education. Students often encounter controversial topics without the background in how the problem developed. These volumes provide such a background. The important cases are reprinted in full; the introductions provide students with a map of the issues; the briefs, congressional testimony, and scholarly articles give convenient access to the arguments and debates.

The volumes bring together in one place a wide variety of sources and materials that are unlikely to be found in any one library. The primary documents include cases, briefs, testimony from legislative committee hearings, and, on occasion, executive branch publications. Few law libraries, university libraries, or public libraries will have all these materials. The secondary literature comes from the scholarly literature of law, history, political science, economics, criminology, and other relevant fields. Some of the articles also may be from serious nonacademic journals.

The related government publications, briefs, and congressional testimony are particularly important. Too often scholars overlook them. There is a tendency to focus on court opinions—what the Supreme Court said. Obviously this is important for understanding doctrine, but briefs, especially amicus briefs, are also an important source of information about the larger constitutional controversy the case represents. The politics of a case are often more apparent in these briefs than in either the oral arguments or the Court's opinion. Similarly, congressional hearings illustrate the social, philosophical, and political dimensions of these questions.

The goal of limiting each collection—two to four focused volumes—and the occasional inability to secure a reasonable copyright permission fee for some important articles often forces hard and judicious choices. Important articles that are not reprinted here are listed in the further reading sections at the end of the introductions.

The ongoing series *Controversies in Constitutional Law* provides in one single place comprehensive introductions to topics that will satisfy most lawyers, scholars, and students. By combining cases, briefs, legislative debates, and testimony from committee hearings with secondary articles, it is hoped to facilitate access to the issue presented in each set of volumes.

Paul Finkelman

Volume Introduction

This volume continues the discussion started in volume two concerning the way in which the Supreme Court differentiates between the nature of the rights afforded to adults under the Constitution and those afforded to children. This volume, however, concentrates on the rights of children outside of the school context. Similar to the first volume, the materials again focus on the rights of the children, the interests and rights of the parents, and the interests of the state. Unlike the first volume, however, where the parents were most often pitted against the state, with the state ostensibly advancing the interests of the child, the issues in this area most often pit the child against the state, with the state arguably attempting to protect the interests of the parents. In an attempt to inform the reader concerning the variety of issues in this area, the first article in the volume gives an overview of the Supreme Court's treatment of children, with a specific focus on free speech, search and seizure, abortion and the death penalty.

Part two then hones in on the general medical rights of children, with a particular emphasis on the controversial subjects of contraception and abortion. Under common law it is typically found that the parent's consent to medical treatment of her/his child was both necessary to, and sufficient for, such medical treatment. When, however, a state's restrictions upon a child's ability to consent to her/his own treatment implicate that child's constitutional rights, the courts must determine whether the state's interests are strong enough to uphold the restriction. The first article explores this issue with regard to children's medical rights generally. The next focuses specifically upon contraception by presenting the case of *Carey v. Population Services International*, where the Supreme Court protected a minor's right to receive contraceptive devices.

The final three articles in part two all focus on abortion. The first of these articles outlines the current boundaries of a minor's constitutional right to an abortion without parental consent or notification. In general, the U.S. Supreme Court has held that a state may constitutionally require a minor to notify her parents of her decision to abort, or to obtain her parent's consent for an abortion, as long as the state provides a method by which the minor may bypass the consent or notice requirement by petitioning a court for permission to abort. The next two articles present differing viewpoints as to the correctness of the limits placed by the Supreme Court upon the minor's right to an abortion.

Part three moves away from a minor's medical rights and into the minor's freedom of movement or travel. In an attempt to cut down on the perceived rise in juvenile crimes, many states and locales have enacted juvenile curfew laws that limit the movement of minors, with such limits generally encompassing the late night hours. The first two articles in part three adopt differing stances concerning the general constitutionality of juvenile curfew laws. The next two articles then focus specifically on the District of Columbia's curfew law and debate the constitutionality of that law.

Janet W. Steverson

JUVENILENESS: A SINGLE-EDGED CONSTITUTIONAL SWORD

*William S. Geimer**

I. Lorena Tinker, Constitutions, and Rhetoric

On January 9, 1987, I did a lot of thinking about constitutions. Along with my classmates in a language and cultural exchange program,[1] I was leaving the Plaza de la Revolucion in Managua, Nicaragua. We had just witnessed the signing of the Nicaraguan Constitution. As we discussed the balance of substance and rhetoric in that document, an older member of the group began to ask me about the courses I taught. When I mentioned a seminar in Juvenile Law, she said: "Oh, maybe you might have heard of our case." She was Lorena Jeanne Tinker, mother of the first named plaintiffs in *Tinker v. Des Moines Independent Community School District*,[2] and I had indeed heard of her case. *Tinker* is the starting point for virtually every judicial discussion of the first amendment rights of children. Through my friendship with Lorena Tinker, I was able to interview her children, John and Mary Beth, whose suspension from school for wearing black armbands in the early days of U.S. involvement in Vietnam triggered the landmark decision protecting student speech.

A premise of this Article is that the United States Supreme Court's application of the Bill of Rights to issues involving young people has been both curious and counterproductive. Supreme Court cases have been characterized by declarations, often accompanied by

---

* Associate Professor of Law, Washington and Lee University. B.S., East Tennessee State University, 1962; J.D., University of North Carolina, 1969. The author expresses thanks to law student William Morrisey for research assistance.

[1] We studied Spanish and lived with a Nicaraguan family for a month in the northern city of Esteli under the auspices of Nuevo Instituto de Centro America (NICA).

[2] 393 U.S. 503 (1969).

soaring rhetoric,[3] that the constitutional guarantee at issue is indeed available to juveniles. However, the Court also employs what I call "juvenileness" to reach the conclusion that the young person loses. The few cases that do not follow this pattern are those arising in highly controversial areas where well-organized, well-financed groups of adults argue on either side of the issue. In these cases, the juvenile is little more than a tool in an adult struggle.[4] Thus, "juvenileness" is a single-edged sword which cuts through a young person's constitutional rights.

Law in general, and constitutional law in particular, is often referred to in metaphorical terms of attack and defense. The metaphor of the double-edged sword is used to remind us that the weapons we use for protection may also be dangerous to us. That is, the principles we employ to further our case may also be utilized by the opposition to their advantage. Moreover, legal principles announced in the Constitution may be described as a bulwark or shield against governmental encroachment on individual liberty. Even though using the law as a sword when it is supposed to be only a shield is frowned upon,[5] Justice Black thought the students were

---

[3] *See, e.g., id.* at 511. *See also In Re* Gault, 387 U.S. 1 (1967) (15-year-old boy arrested for making obscene telephone calls entitled to constitutional due process guarantees of notice, right to counsel, and freedom from self-incrimination). *Gault* is widely viewed as the landmark case that opened the way for imposition of adult criminal due process standards in juvenile delinquency proceedings. *See, e.g.*, Ceresi, In Re Gault*: A Constitutional Celebration*, 36 VA. B. NEWS, August, 1987, at 17. I view it as much less significant. *See* Geimer, *Ready to Take the High Road? The Case for Importing Scotland's Juvenile Justice System*, 35 CATH. U.L. REV. 385, 390-92 (1986).

[4] The most highly visible current examples are abortion and the death penalty. *See infra* notes 64-96 and accompanying text. There are earlier examples. In the landmark decision Brown v. Board of Education, 347 U.S. 483 (1954), adults chose children and their education rather than adult housing and employment as the most vulnerable place to attack racial discrimination. Professor Mnookin provides an excellent account of this enlistment of very young children in a laudable cause they did not control. *See* R. MNOOKIN, IN THE INTEREST OF CHILDREN 7-10 (1985). He concludes: "How many children were unconsenting footsoldiers sent off to war by judges and parents fighting to save this nation's soul? Subsequent generations owe them a great deal." *Id.* at 10.

[5] The Supreme Court's opinion in Taylor v. Illinois, 108 S. Ct. 646 (1988), is illustrative. In that case, the Court approved preclusion of defense evidence in a criminal trial in the face of a constitutional claim of the right to put on evidence. The Court stated that "the Compulsory Process Clause provides [a defendant] with an effective weapon, but it is a weapon that cannot be used

being given a sword by the majority in *Tinker*.[6] With the exception of those cases where adult interests are directly at stake, Supreme Court decisions in the two decades following *Tinker* have left the Constitution as no shield for juveniles, but rather as a sword for custodians and protectors of juveniles to combat deviation from adult-imposed norms. Given the apparent unconcern of most juveniles and their parents,[7] the sword has but a single edge and currently poses no threat to those who employ it.

This sword, which cuts through constitutional protections ostensibly granted, is the concept of "juvenileness." Juvenileness is, in one sense, contextual. That is, juveniles live their lives in places and situations where adults have "legitimate interests" to be balanced against juveniles' assertions of right. Juveniles are also largely without the power to acquire property, a capability intimately related to the law of rights. Their expectation of privacy is negligible since they live, work, and learn in places owned by others. They depend on outside funding for fora in which to express their views. It is hardly surprising that adults, who control home, school, workplace, and courts, exaggerate their legitimate interests whenever the exercise by juveniles of their constitutional rights appears to conflict with adult orthodoxy.[8]

---

irresponsibly." *Id.* at 653. "Whenever a lawyer makes use of the sword provided by the Compulsory Process Clause, there is some risk that he may wound his own client." *Id.* at 657. *See generally* Ball, *Law Natural: Its Family of Metaphors and Its Theology*, 3 J. LAW & RELIGION 141 (1985).

[6] *Tinker*, 393 U.S. at 525 (Black, J., dissenting).

[7] There is, of course, no definitive data on the level of concern by parents and students for the current state of juvenile constitutional law. If the case of Doe v. Renfrow, 475 F. Supp. 1012 (N.D. Ind. 1979), *aff'd in part and remanded in part*, 631 F.2d 91 (7th Cir. 1980), *cert. denied*, 451 U.S. 1022 (1981), is representative, however, the level is not high. *Renfrow* was an action on behalf of a junior high school girl who was subjected to a nude search after a drug sniffing dog was brought into the school and alerted on her. She had no contraband, but had been playing earlier with her own dog, which was in heat. *Id.* at 1017. Several hundred parents and patrons of the school system intervened in the lawsuit *on behalf of the defendant school officials*. *Id.* at 1015.

[8] The orthodoxy to which reference is made, and to which young people are generally required to subscribe, includes but is not limited to chauvinistic assumptions that the economic and political organization of this nation is superior to that of any other, and that its military activities are always justified. *See, e.g.*, TENN. CODE ANN. § 49-6-1205 (1983) (requirement that "free enterprise" be taught in public schools); N.Y. EDUC. LAW § 801 (McKinney 1988) (requirement that

Juvenileness is, in another sense, philosophical. That is, it consists of a set of assumptions about young people—some demonstrably false, some occasionally accurate, some half-valid. When unjustifiably exaggerated, these assumptions serve adult orthodoxy and the status quo in the same manner as the "legitimate interest" balancing of the contextual component. The catalog of assumptions includes the following:

> 1. Children are "immature" and must be protected by adults from all sorts of things, including one another.
> 2. Children are incapable of making responsible decisions. They are also incapable of making any meaningful contribution to the solution of real world problems, even those like war and divorce—created by adults but having an impact on children.

Children, in short, are to be "prepared for adulthood" by adults. The Constitution is not to be interpreted in a manner that would hinder that enterprise.[9] The employment of juvenileness to cut

---

patriotism be taught in public schools). That the role of the Supreme Court is to support whichever litigant represents obeisance to traditional authority is documented in a prophetic article by Professor Robert A. Burt. *See* Burt, *The Constitution of the Family*, 1979 SUP. CT. REV. 329, 338-42.

[9] The substance of the philosophical component of juvenileness will emerge from the post-*Tinker* cases to be analyzed *infra*. Here is an introductory sampler: "Children, by definition, are not assumed to have the capacity to take care of themselves. They are assumed to be under the control of their parents, and if parental control falters, the State must play its role as *parens patriae*." Schall v. Martin, 467 U.S. 253, 265 (1984) (justifying pretrial detention of juveniles). "The State's interest in protecting a young person from harm justifies the imposition of restraints on his or her freedom even though comparable restraints on adults would be constitutionally impermissible." H.L. v. Matheson, 450 U.S. 392, 422 (1980) (Stevens, J., concurring) (quoting Planned Parenthood of Cent. Missouri. v. Danforth, 428 U.S. 52, 102-03 (1976) (Stevens, J., concurring in part and dissenting in part)) (approving statute requiring parental notification of impending abortion). *See also infra* notes 64-75 and accompanying text.

Although there are doubtless children who fit these generalizations, there is evidence that juveniles are capable of greater participation in society than our laws afford them. *See* E. BOULDING, CHILDREN'S RIGHTS AND THE WHEEL OF LIFE 13-18 (1979). There is even evidence that adolescence itself is a relatively new invention of adults, brought about by factors having little to do with the capacities of teenagers. *See* L. EMPEY, AMERICAN DELINQUENCY: ITS MEANING AND CONSTRUCTION 70-72 (1982). The purpose of this Article is not to undertake resolution of this matter, but to suggest that the monolithic, paternalistic approach of the courts may simply be a control mechanism rather than a reflection of an honestly held belief that children are helpless or irresponsible.

through constitutional guarantees is most apparent when young people claim protection of the first and fourth amendments, and this Article focuses principally on those cases. However, other examples of the practice are plentiful respecting other guarantees.[10]

Why the Court continues to insist that the Bill of Rights is facially applicable to juveniles is a mystery. The ingredients of juvenileness could easily form the rationale of a definitive opinion holding that, until adulthood, juveniles are committed to the sound discretion of adults, protected officially by the sound discretion of those bastions of orthodoxy, the state legislatures and the United States Congress. Such a pronouncement would have the virtue of candor, would enhance the integrity of constitutional discourse, and would more accurately reflect reality.

II. Juveniles and the First Amendment: *Tinker* to *Bethel* to *Hazelwood*

A. *John and Mary Beth Tinker: The Case From the Litigants' Perspective*

The reflections of John and Mary Beth Tinker a generation after their historic case comprise an appropriate starting point for challenging juvenileness as a controlling constitutional factor. They dispute the assumption that children are incapable of considering important issues and making decisions apart from the dictates of adults. They contend, contrary to a view implicit in the *Tinker* dissent,[11] that they were fully capable of understanding that people were dying in Vietnam and of determining that they would make

[10] *See, e.g.*, McKeiver v. Pennsylvania, 403 U.S. 528 (1971) (though liberty at stake, no right to jury trial); Ingraham v. Wright, 430 U.S. 651 (1977) (eighth amendment applicable to corporal punishment of adult prisoners but not school children); *In re* T.D., 81 Ill. App. 3d 369, 401 N.E.2d 275 (1980), and *In re* Eric J., 25 Cal. 2d 522, 601 P.2d 549, 159 Cal. Rptr. 317 (1979) (because the purpose of confinement is different, juveniles may be imprisoned longer than adults for the same conduct without violating equal protection clause).

[11] *See*, Tinker v. Des Moines Indep. Community School Dist., 393 U.S. 503, 516 (1969) (Black, J., dissenting) (reference to Tinkers' father as "minister without a church" who was paid by American Friends Service Committee, and to the mother of co-plaintiff Chris Eckhardt as an official of the Women's International League for Peace and Freedom). Professor Burt likewise concludes that one reason for Justice Black's dissent was his belief that the armbands more reflected the parents' views than those of the children. Burt, *supra* note 8, at 349-50.

a gesture of mourning and opposition to the war.[12] Mary Beth said: "I made my own decision. Dad tried to dissuade me but respected my right to express myself."[13] John concurred: "The degree of autonomy was very high. People who pose the autonomy question usually assume my parents were both 100% for it. Not so, although both were involved against the Vietnam war. What Mary Beth and I did was more than autonomy. We truly acted independently."[14]

The Tinkers also remind us of another point relevant to the coming analysis of the few cases in which juveniles prevail. Even though adults underestimate the capabilities of young people and seldom listen to what they have to say, adults are still willing to use youth—sometimes to further the adult agenda, sometimes even to try to empower young people.

For example, Mary Beth Tinker reported that in the period following the Supreme Court's decision she became cynical about the importance of legal victories. That is because the legal system had improperly focused on student rights issues and not war issues.[15] John put the matter eloquently: "The wearing of the armbands was against the Vietnam war continuing. The ACLU [American Civil Liberties Union] took it up as a students' rights case and won on that. But civil liberties don't mean much if you continue to kill people every day."[16]

Of course, the Tinkers speak as adults recalling a childhood experience with the law. Their adult lives are characterized by compassionate endeavors entirely consistent with the concerns that prompted them to wear the armbands.[17] To what extent this is attributable to their independent development, the influence of their

---

[12] According to John, the particular gesture of wearing black armbands was the idea of Herbert Hoover, eighth cousin of the former President. "The group didn't think anyone would notice them, but no better idea came up, so we decided to do it." Interview with John Tinker in Fayette, Missouri (December 26, 1987).

[13] Interview with Mary Beth Tinker in Fayette, Missouri (December 26, 1987).

[14] Interview with John Tinker in Fayette, Missouri (December 26, 1987).

[15] Interview with Mary Beth Tinker in Fayette, Missouri (December 26, 1987).

[16] Interview with John Tinker in Fayette, Missouri (December 26, 1987).

[17] Mary Beth is a registered nurse, working with paraplegics in St. Louis. John has engineering and computer skills he planned to offer to war-torn Nicaragua in January, 1988. Letter from Lorena Jeanne Tinker to William S. Geimer (December 26, 1987).

parents, or the positive effect of having their rights respected by the legal system cannot be known. John observed: "I like to think my life has a stability of which the armband case was a part."[18] If there was any benefit to the Tinkers from their experience with the law, few young people today will be able to share it.

B. *Meaningful Standard to Meaningless Illusion*

Tinker became a valuable precedent because it set a meaningful standard for permissible interference with speech. The burden was placed on putative censors to demonstrate that John and Mary Beth's symbolic speech would "materially and substantially" interfere with the requirements of appropriate discipline in the operation of the school.[19] The words are not precise, but they are the stuff from which courts have traditionally been able to fashion workable limits on government. Also important is the virtual absence of juvenileness consideration in the decision. Apart from the previously noted gratuitous suggestion by Justice Black that the students were not acting autonomously,[20] the decision evidences little of the philosophical component of juvenileness. Indeed, *Tinker*'s "soaring rhetoric" passages implicitly put children on an equal footing with adults.[21] The contextual component of juvenileness was of course involved since the armbands were worn at school, but the conduct of the students was so minimal that the legitimate interests of school administrators and other students would have been difficult to articulate plausibly in a manner that would permit the government to win the balancing game.[22]

Two recent decisions have dismantled *Tinker* without formally pronouncing the end of first amendment rights for juveniles. They

[18] Interview with John Tinker in Fayette, Missouri (December 26, 1987).

[19] Tinker v. Des Moines Indep. Community School Dist., 393 U.S. 503, 509 (1969) (citing Burnside v. Byars, 363 F.2d 744, 749 (1966) (children's first and fourteenth amendment rights were violated when school officals would not allow them to wear "freedom buttons" while attending school)).

[20] *See supra* note 6 and accompanying text.

[21] "It can hardly be argued that either students or teachers shed their constitutional rights to freedom of speech or expression at the schoolhouse gate." *Id.* at 506. "In our system, students may not be regarded as closed-circuit recipients of only that which the State chooses to communicate. They may not be confined to the expression of those sentiments that are officially approved." *Id.* at 511.

[22] *Id.* at 508-09 (armbands were silent, passive expression of opinion which did not interfere with the work of the school or the rights of other students).

are *Bethel School District No. 403 v. Fraser*[23] and *Hazelwood School District v. Kuhlmeier*.[24] The contextual and philosophical components of juvenileness are apparent in both cases.

Bethel, which considered a sexually suggestive speech at a high school assembly,[25] is a blatant defense of the power of adults to insist that children engage only in mainstream speech. Although the speech was not directly in conflict with adult orthodoxy in the way that the Tinkers' was, the Court approved of penalties imposed by the school on the speaker, Mathew Fraser.[26] Fraser was disciplined for violating a rule modeled after the *Tinker* test, and the majority opened its defense of the school officials with the rhetoric of *Tinker*; however, the majority's rationale had nothing to do with the armband case. Instead, juvenileness was enlisted in service of orthodoxy in a manner that prepared the way for a more direct assertion of the primacy of orthodoxy in *Hazelwood*.

Fraser's speech was given at school. Contextual juvenileness is supplemented by relatively few *direct* references to the philosophical underpinnings of juvenileness. Nevertheless, the majority opinion betrays the clear assumption that what is being dealt with is "childish" speech, that fact being so apparent that elaboration is not necessary. Indeed, most of us might also conclude that the speech was "childish," even if we had some difficulty distinguishing its level of childishness from the adult speech recently protected by the Court in *Hustler Magazine, Inc. v. Falwell*.[27]

---

[23] 478 U.S. 675 (1986).

[24] 108 S. Ct. 562 (1988).

[25] The speech was:

> I know a man who is firm—he's firm in his pants, he's firm in his shirt, his character is firm—but most . . . of all, his belief in you, the students of Bethel, is firm.
>
> Jeff Kuhlman is a man who takes his point and pounds it in. If necessary, he'll take an issue and nail it to the wall. He doesn't attack things in spurts—he drives hard, pushing and pushing until finally—he succeeds.
>
> Jeff is a man who will go to the very end—even the climax, for each and every one of you.
>
> So vote for Jeff for A.S.B. vice-president—he'll never come between you and the best our high school can be."

Bethel, 478 U.S. at 687 (Brennan, J., concurring in the judgment).

[26] The penalties were slight, including a two-day suspension. *Id.* at 678. Lower courts had held for Fraser. *Id.* at 679.

[27] 108 S. Ct. 876 (1988). *Hustler* magazine published an ad parody depicting

The majority opinion in *Bethel* does contain some indications that it was also grounded in philosophical juvenileness. Chief Justice Burger referred to Fraser as "this confused boy."[28] And there is a second, almost throwaway, basis for the decision found in a state's interest in "protecting minors from exposure to vulgar and offensive spoken language."[29] Further, the *Bethel* Court introduced a new twist on juvenileness that was later employed in *Hazelwood* to inter *Tinker*: "disassociation." Building on the assumption that juvenile speech has no merit, the Court concluded that a school has the right to penalize speech as a means of disassociating itself from it.[30]

While the Court in *Bethel* referred to protecting other students, it did not find that punishing Fraser's speech was "necessary to avoid material and substantial interference with school work or discipline," the *Tinker* standard.[31] Indications to the contrary in the concurring opinion of Justice Brennan were doubtless written in an attempt to limit the scope of the holding.[32] The underpinning of *Bethel* is not *Tinker*, but rather a simple ode to orthodoxy. The new *Bethel* test balances first amendment rights against a countervailing societal interest in teaching students the boundaries of

---

evangelist Jerry Falwell as a drunkard whose first sexual encounter was with his mother in an outhouse. *Id.* at 878. In protecting *Hustler* from an end run around the constraints of libel law through the tort of intentional infliction of emotional distress, the Court sought to preserve a long tradition of political commentary, often done in poor taste. *Id.* at 881.

In *Bethel*, probably because high school political offices are universally viewed by students and administrators alike as meaningless, no mention was made of the fact that Fraser's speech was political. On the contrary, the Court observed "[U]nlike the sanctions imposed on the students wearing armbands in *Tinker*, the penalties imposed in this case were unrelated to any political viewpoint." *Bethel*, 478 U.S. at 685.

There are, of course, significant differences between *Hustler* and *Bethel*. Critical to the decision in the former was the public figure status of Falwell. *Hustler Magazine, Inc.*, 108 S. Ct. at 880. Still, one may entertain doubts that Fraser's speech would have been tolerated even if he had likened his friend Kuhlman to a public figure such as, for example, a candidate for the national presidency.

[28] *Bethel*, 478 U.S. at 683.

[29] *Id.* at 684.

[30] *Id.* at 685.

[31] Tinker v. Des Moines Indep. Community School Dist., 393 U.S. 503, 509 (1969).

[32] *Bethel*, 478 U.S. at 688 (Brennan, J., concurring in the judgment).

socially appropriate behavior.[33] If this "test" were honestly a test, one might wonder how the values embodied in free speech could possibly *lose* such a balancing contest. Here, in the words of the Court, is how:

> [P]ublic education must prepare pupils for citizenship in the Republic. . . . It must inculcate the habits and manners of civility as values in themselves conducive to happiness and as indispensable to the practice of self-government in the community and the nation.[34]
>
> Surely it is a highly appropriate function of public school education to prohibit the use of vulgar and offensive terms in public discourse. Indeed, the "fundamental values necessary to the maintenance of a democratic political system" disfavor the use of terms of debate highly offensive or threatening to others. Nothing in the Constitution prohibits the states from insisting that certain modes of expression are inappropriate and subject to sanctions. The inculcation of these values is truly the "work of the schools."[35]
>
> [S]chools must teach by example the *shared values of a civilized social order*.[36]

The degree of the Court's elevation of civility to the status of glue of our democracy causes one to wonder if it is speaking of the same first amendment, or even the same country that has nurtured a host of uncivil malcontents, including Gary Trudeau and Larry Flynt.[37]

Justice Stevens confined his dissenting opinion to the strong argument that Matthew Fraser was denied procedural due process—fair notice that the speech would be considered a violation of the school rule.[38] In passing, however, Justice Stevens also made the

---

[33] *Id.* at 683-85.

[34] *Id.* at 681 (quoting C. BEARD & M. BEARD, NEW BASIC HISTORY OF THE UNITED STATES 228 (1968)).

[35] *Id.* at 683 (citing *Tinker*, 393 U.S. at 508).

[36] *Id.* (emphasis added).

[37] Flynt is the publisher of *Hustler* magazine. Trudeau authors the "Doonesbury" cartoon strip, which is occasionally censored or moved to the editorial pages in some newspapers.

[38] *Bethel*, 478 U.S. at 693-96 (Stevens, J., dissenting).

point that Fraser was in a better position to determine whether an audience of his contemporaries would be offended than is a group of Supreme Court Justices at least two generations and three thousand miles removed from the scene of the crime.[39] This quite accurate observation highlights the point that *Bethel* is not about protecting children, disrupting schools, or even prohibiting speech that is outside the mainstream of *juvenile* orthodoxy.[40] Rather, it is about the use of juvenileness language to justify efforts to make sure that kids do not say what adults do not like to hear.

Using *Bethel* as a bridge, *Hazelwood* completed the evisceration of *Tinker*. In *Hazelwood*, the principal of a Missouri high school censored two pages of the school newspaper because he did not like an article dealing with three students' experiences with pregnancy and another dealing with the impact of divorce on the students at the school.[41] Before he had obtained the assistance of legal counsel and two federal courts in the construction of an acceptable *post-hoc* rationale for the censorship, the principal gave the students two reasons for it. The first was the now familiar protectionist part of juvenileness: the articles were "too sensitive" for "our immature audience of readers."[42] The second was simply a transparent assertion of the right to censor. The articles were "inappropriate, personal, sensitive and unsuitable for the newspaper."[43]

The Supreme Court majority added the respectable, though far from obvious, conclusion that the paper, as a project of the journalism class, had not been converted to a public forum[44] and that

---

[39] *Id.* at 692.

[40] Fraser maintained the support of a majority of his schoolmates after the speech. Although one of the penalties levied on Fraser was his removal from the list of candidates for graduation speaker at the school's commencement exercises, he was elected anyway by write-in vote of his fellow students. Aided by an injunction from the district court, Fraser gave a speech at that event. *Id.* at 679.

[41] Hazelwood School Dist. v. Kuhlmeier, 108 S. Ct. 562, 565-67 (1988).

[42] *Id.* at 577 (Brennan, J., dissenting).

[43] *Id.*

[44] There is room for reasonable differing about whether a newspaper that was a part of the journalism curriculum had been converted into a public forum, thereby increasing the showing required to justify content based censorship. It is possible to create a public forum inadvertently without being required to do so. *See* Madison Joint School Dist. v. Wisconsin Employment Relations Comm., 429

the stories did not meet acceptable journalistic standards.[45] Yet the Court also dressed up and endorsed the protectionist reasoning of the principal. Compare the principal's comments with the Court's assertion that "[i]t was not unreasonable for the principal to have concluded that such frank talk was inappropriate in a school-sponsored publication distributed to 14-year-old freshmen and presumably taken home to be read by students' even younger brothers and sisters."[46] Because the paper was school-sponsored, the Court was also able to throw in the newly found right of the school to disassociate itself from the student speech.[47]

Building, on the shaky foundation of the principal's actual reasoning, the Court constructed in place of *Tinker* a new and meaningless standard: "[E]ducators do not offend the First Amendment by exercising editorial control over the style and content of student speech in school-sponsored expressive activities so long as their actions are reasonably related to legitimate pedagogical concerns."[48]

Future court opinions may contain less of the rhetoric of juvenileness. Under the tests stated in *Bethel* and *Hazelwood*, a simple statement that deviation from orthodoxy is the reason for the punishment or censorship of juvenile speech may be sufficient.

U.S. 167, 174-76 (1976) (public meeting of board of education could not exclude statements by teachers who were not members of the teachers' union concerning contract negotiations even though negotiation of collective bargaining agreements was ordinarily conducted privately and only by designated union officials). Whether the Hazelwood paper, ironically titled *The Spectrum*, was *intended* as a public forum is an open question also. The paper published a statement that only speech that materially and substantially interfered with discipline could be prohibited. *Hazelwood*, 108 S. Ct. at 569 n.2. A school board policy also committed it not to restrict free expression or diverse viewpoints within the rules of responsible journalism. The policy also referred, however, to the curricular status of school publications. *Id.* at 568-69.

[45] One of the claims of poor journalism arose from a belief that the parents of a child named in the divorce story should have been permitted to respond to unfavorable comments made by their daughter. The school presented an expert witness who testified to the effect that the divorce story did not meet journalistic standards of fairness and balance. *Id.* at 572 n.8. The record does not reveal whether the expert witness was aware, as the censoring principal was not, that the name of the student making the allegations had been deleted from the final version of the article. *Id.* at 566.

[46] *Id.* at 571-72.

[47] *Id.* at 570 (citing *Fraser*, 478 U.S. at 685).

[48] *Id.* at 571.

Hazelwood, for example, concludes that a contrary decision would undermine the school's mission of inculcating "shared values of a civilized order," as well as preparation of students for professional training and assisting "normal" adjustment to one's environment.[49]

III. Juveniles and the Fourth Amendment: No Privacy Left?

The right of adults to be free from unreasonable searches and seizures has taken quite a beating from the Supreme Court in recent years.[50] A decision restricting the right in juveniles was hardly unexpected. *New Jersey v. T.L.O.*,[51] however, was remarkable in the scope of its assault on juvenile privacy, raising the question of why the fourth amendment was not simply held to be inapplicable in the school setting.

Mr. Choplick, assistant vice principal of a New Jersey high school, conducted a search of 14-year-old T.L.O.'s purse—an historically recognized enclave of privacy in a public world. The object of the search was evidence to impeach her denial of a report that she had violated a school rule against smoking in the lavatory.[52] The actual fruits of the search, evidence of possession and sale of marijuana, were sought to be used against her in a proceeding which could result in loss of her liberty.[53]

The Supreme Court upheld the search, discarding the concept of probable cause and fashioning a new juvenile fourth amendment standard of reasonableness under all the circumstances.[54] Given the

---

[49] *Id.* at 570 (citing *Fraser*, 478 U.S. at 685, and Brown v. Board of Educ., 347 U.S. 483, 493 (1954)).

[50] *See, e.g.*, Massachusetts v. Sheppard, 468 U.S. 981 (1984) (good faith exception to fourth amendment exclusionary rule); Michigan v. Long, 463 U.S. 1032 (1983) (police may search any area in vehicle where suspect might reach to obtain a weapon even though suspect is out of vehicle and not within reach of a weapon at time of search); Illinois v. Gates, 462 U.S. 213 (1983) (lowering standard for issuance of search warrants); United States v. Ross, 456 U.S. 798 (1982) (no warrant requirement for automobile searches).

[51] 469 U.S. 325 (1985).

[52] *Id.* at 328.

[53] *Id.* at 328-29.

[54] *Id.* at 341. The Court elaborated:

> Under ordinary circumstances, a search of a student by a teacher or other school official will be "justified at its inception" when there are reasonable grounds for suspecting that the search will turn up

complete unreasonableness of this search,[55] the student should have won under the new test if the test is something more than blind sanctioning of official conduct. Secreted in the interstices of this "test," however, is substantive juvenileness sufficient to guarantee the outcome. The Court declared that reasonableness was to be assessed by the now familiar "balancing" of public against private interests.[56]

Individuals, young and old, almost always lose the balancing game. The contest is particularly hopeless for young people because adult orthodoxy in the schools does not include instilling appreciation and respect for the rule of law or the value to the community of having the government leave its citizens alone. Once again, the philosophical as well as contextual components of juvenileness in service of orthodoxy leave the students nothing to weigh in the balance. Because of their immaturity and need to be prepared for adulthood, children are not to question those in legitimate authority. Comparison of *T.L.O.* with its most nearly analogous adult counterpart, *Terry v. Ohio*,[57] is illustrative. Even the hardworking

---

> evidence that the student has violated or is violating either the law or the rules of the school.

Id. at 341-42 (footnotes omitted).

[55] The search was patently unreasonable because, *inter alia*, it was completely unnecessary. Mr. Choplick's conduct would have been perfectly lawful had he advised T.L.O. of the offense of which she was accused, given her an opportunity to say what she wished about it, informed her that he elected to believe the report of a teacher that T.L.O. was smoking, and proceeded to impose the appropriate penalty for the infraction. *See* Goss v. Lopez, 419 U.S. 565 (1975) (students facing suspension from school qualified for protection under the due process clause of the fourteenth amendment). In addition, even under its new standard, in order to conclude that cigarettes in T.L.O.'s purse would constitute evidence that she had earlier been smoking, the Court was forced to resort to the liberal relevance standard of the Federal Rules of Evidence. *T.L.O.*, 469 U.S. at 345. This was truly not the Court's finest hour.

[56] *Id.* at 339-40.

[57] 392 U.S. 1 (1968). In *Terry*, a plainclothes police detective, on a city beat which he had patrolled for many years, observed three men behaving suspiciously. The detective, concerned that the three were planning a daylight robbery, approached two of the men and identified himself as a police officer. When the men did not respond, the detective performed a pat-down search and felt what he thought was a revolver in the coat pocket of one of the men. He then conducted a more thorough search of the men's clothing and discovered that each man carried a concealed gun. The two men were arrested and convicted of carrying concealed weapons. *Id.* at 5-8. On appeal, the Supreme Court affirmed the

cop on the beat was not entitled to such automatic respect from adults that he could avoid the requirement of articulating a reasonable, individualized suspicion as a legal predicate for his conduct of a limited pat-down search in the interest of his own safety.[58] In contrast, what the New Jersey Supreme Court found to be only a "good hunch"[59] was enough to justify Mr. Choplick's search of T.L.O.'s purse. Surely, a school's overriding interest in keeping its bathrooms smoke-free did not justify a departure from prior law; more likely the decision was necessitated by the status of the parties to the dispute.

The question then is why does the Court bother to make a facial guarantee only to render it meaningless in the application? Professor Rosenberg offers the view that a flat declaration of fourth amendment inapplicability to school searches might evoke widespread criticism, would be at odds with prior relevant precedent, and would be an invitation to lawlessness in the schools because teachers cannot be trusted with power equal to that afforded parents.[60]

The extent to which the Court's decision in *T.L.O.* will produce a functionally similar result remains to be seen. The intrusion was so extensive and the justification so flimsy in *T.L.O.* that lawlessness in the schools may occur anyway. But perhaps school officials will continue to feel themselves restrained to some extent and perhaps that alone explains the Court's choice. Sometimes officials perceive the scope of constitutional limitations announced in the occasional lower court victories for young people[61] to be broader

---

convictions because "[the detective] had reasonable grounds to believe that [the men were] armed and dangerous. . . . The policeman carefully restricted his search to what was appropriate to the discovery of the particular items he sought." *Id.* at 30.

[58] *Id.* at 27-30.

[59] State *ex rel.* T.L.O., 463 A.2d 934, 942 (N.J. 1983).

[60] Rosenberg, New Jersey v. T.L.O.: *Of Children and Smokescreens*, 19 FAM. L.Q. 311, 416-17 (Fall 1985). This Article does not undertake a detailed analysis of the many shortcomings of *New Jersey v. T.L.O.* in ignoring relevant precedent and distorting fourth amendment jurisprudence. An excellent treatment of those matters may be found in Rosenberg, *supra*; *see also* Gardner, *Student Privacy in the Wake of* T.L.O.: *An Appeal for an Individualized Suspicion Requirement for* Valid Searches and Seizures in the Schools, 22 GA. L. REV. 897 (1988).

[61] *See, e.g.*, State v. Mora, 307 So. 2d 317 (La. 1975) (on facts similar to

than they are. Litigating on behalf of young people in the mid-1970s, I occasionally had more success than I deserved as a matter of law because school officials worried about *Wood v. Strickland*,[62] permitting school officals to be held personally liable for willful constitutional violations, and about *Goss v. Lopez*,[63] requiring a minimal amount of administrative due process before even brief suspensions. Neither case has turned out to be anything for officials to fear, but none of the parties could be sure at the time.

With these vaguely perceived legal limits lurking in the background, most teachers and school officials have exercised the broad discretion granted them in a highly responsible manner. Most, after all, are in the profession because they like kids. Whether any substantial change would result if their discretion were officially unbridled is unknown. But if the breadth of the holding in *T.L.O.* is completely understood in the school districts, we may yet learn.

IV. Juveniles on the Adult Battleground: Abortion and the Death Penalty

When adolescents are involved in cases having an impact on controversial adult disputes, curious things happen to juvenileness. Disputes over a woman's right to an abortion and over the state's right to kill prisoners provide a litigational battlefield with well organized, highly motivated troops on both sides. Because juveniles are ancillary to the principal conflict, we find that litigants take positions and the courts fashion rules that are inconsistent with what we have seen in the cases previously discussed.

A. *Abortion*

Since 1973, adults opposed to all abortions and those who want the right to abortion absolutely unfettered have had to conduct

---

those in *T.L.O.*, teacher's search of student's belongings held unreasonable and marijuana found declared inadmissible); People v. Flowers, 23 Mich. App. 523, 179 N.W.2d 56 (1970) (parent may not consent to search of child's room).

[62] 420 U.S. 308 (1975) (school officals are entitled to a qualified good-faith immunity for damages, but are not immune where they knew or should have known that their actions would violate a student's constitutional rights).

[63] 419 U.S. 565 (1975) (students facing suspension from school for misbehavior entitled to notice and a hearing under the due process clause of the fourteenth amendment).

their judicial combat within the constraints of *Roe v. Wade*.[64] Naturally, questions about the legal status of pregnant teenagers have become a part of this struggle. To date, the results for young people have been mixed, though sometimes strikingly different from those in the first and fourth amendment areas.

In 1974, over the governor's veto and after heavy lobbying by adult organizations, Massachusetts passed a law requiring that minors seeking an abortion notify their parents and obtain written consent from both or from a superior court judge.[65] The court challenges to this law and to similar statutes in other states were carried on by adults involved in the struggle over the larger issue.[66] The child plaintiffs were recruited and their individual interests, apart from the interest in obtaining an abortion, were not controlling.

The results in the law of teenage abortion have been interesting. The Supreme Court, having authored one of the most controversial decisions of a decade in *Roe v. Wade*, and also having fashioned the doctrine of juvenileness as a means of imposing second class constitutional status on young people, has sought fidelity to both the case and the doctrine. Currently, the *Roe* case has a slight edge.

The Court has denied parents an absolute veto over the child's abortion decision.[67] Later, it also invalidated parts of the Massachusetts law discussed above.[68] The Court reaffirmed its juvenileness pronouncements, specifically naming by analogy cases citing immaturity as a justification for limiting first amendment rights.[69] Yet,

---

[64] 410 U.S. 113 (1973) (fourteenth amendment due process clause grants woman absolute right to abortion in first trimester of pregnancy).

[65] R. MNOOKIN, IN THE INTEREST OF CHILDREN 167 (1985).

[66] *Id.* at 167-73 (ACLU, an abortion clinic physician, and a group of parent intervenors were the major players in Massachusetts).

[67] Planned Parenthood of Cent. Missouri v. Danforth, 428 U.S. 52 (1976). Unsurprisingly, the law at issue also affected adults. Physicians were required to obtain written consent of a parent or guardian before terminating the pregnancy of an unmarried minor. *Id.* at 58. The Court balanced Missouri's interest in safeguarding the family unit and parental authority against the minor's privacy right. The minor's *Roe v. Wade* interest prevailed, though the Court specifically noted that its ruling was not intended to allow for all minors to consent to abortions. *Id.* at 75.

[68] Bellotti v. Baird, 443 U.S. 622 (1979).

[69] *Id.* at 635-39.

on the basis of the "unique" nature of the abortion right, the Court required that states provide a process by which, without notifying her parents, a child seeking an abortion may demonstrate to a court either that she is mature enough to make the decision on her own or that the abortion is in her best interest.[70] It is truly remarkable that a child is afforded the opportunity at the same time to free herself from the legal disability imposed by chronological age and to win a "balancing of interests" contest with parents and the state. I am aware of no other constitutional context in which the juvenile is so fortunate. I doubt the Court believes juveniles to be more mature or less in need of protection when deciding whether to have an abortion than when delivering or hearing speeches at high school assemblies. I can only conclude that the situation exists because at the moment the "pro-choice" adults have the judicial upper hand over the "pro-life" adults.

A case clearly illustrating that abortion is an adult battle is *H.L. v. Matheson*,[71] which challenged a Utah statute requiring parental notification by the physician performing an abortion on a minor. In this case, the minor plaintiff's attorney pushed the court too far and may have subordinated his client's interest in obtaining an abortion to the pro-choice battle to keep the government absolutely out of the process. The litigation strategy apparently was to make no showing of the plaintiff's "maturity" and to contend that the reason for wishing to avoid notification of parents was irrelevant.[72] This choice may have closed off the possibility that the trial court would relieve her of the notification requirements on individualized grounds, forcing the court instead to review the facial constitutionality of the statute.

The Supreme Court upheld the "notification but not veto" provisions of the Utah statute, finding support of parental authority

---

[70] *Id.* at 642-44.

[71] 450 U.S. 398 (1981).

[72] This strategy was employed at a hearing on H.L.'s request to represent all unmarried pregnant minors impeded by the statute. H.L. was the only witness and gave monosyllabic answers to her attorney's questions. *Id.* at 401-03. The attorney resisted cross-examination about H.L.'s reasons for not desiring to notify her parents, contending that they were "irrelevant to the Constitutional issue." *Id.* at 403 nn.7-8. The colloquy reported suggests strongly that the adults representing H.L. had elected to pitch their case on an unbending assertion that she had a right to be treated in all respects as an adult.

and family integrity to be legitimate state interests.[73] Because of the posture of the case, the lengthy opinion does not deal with what happened to H.L., whether she was mature or not, or the nature or adequacy of her desire not to inform her parents.[74] The adults on H.L.'s side may have been trying to help her, use her, or both. The adults who prevailed upon the Utah legislature to enact the notification statute may have been interested in family integrity or they may have sought only another means to limit the number of abortions. But it appears in any event that the paramount consideration of the protagonists may have been the adult, not the juvenile, agenda.[75]

B. *The Death Penalty*

The Supreme Court's recent decision in *Thompson v. Oklahoma*[76] reveals much about the changing uses of juvenileness when adult issues are on the line. *Thompson* was a direct constitutional challenge to the right of states to execute those who were juveniles at the time of their crimes.[77] A five to four plurality determined

---

[73] *Id.* at 409-11. Justice Powell, who authored *Bellotti*'s requirement that a child be permitted to show that she is mature enough to make the abortion decision on her own or that it is nevertheless in her best interest, *Bellotti*, 443 U.S. at 643-44, concurred with the majority in *H.L.*, observing that the requirements remain undisturbed given H.L.'s inflexible trial level stance. *H.L.*, 450 U.S. at 413-20 (Powell, J., concurring).

[74] In my view, the most telling indication that this litigation was principally an adult matter is the Court's notation that: "The record does not reveal whether appellant proceeded with the abortion." *Id.* at 401 n.4.

[75] A recent case shows the adult struggle over juvenile abortion to be a close one, although the "pro-choice" position prevailed. Zbaraz v. Hartigan, 763 F.2d 1532 (7th Cir. 1985), *aff'd* per curiam, 108 S. Ct. 479 (1987). In *Zbaraz*, the litigants challenged a 1983 Illinois statute requiring a 24-hour waiting period for minors after consent to abortion had been given. The Supreme Court had struck down a similar requirement for adult women by a 6-3 majority in Akron v. Akron Center for Reproductive Health, 462 U.S. 416 (1983). The court of appeals in *Zbaraz* found that a mandatory waiting period after parental notification or consent was unconstitutional because it did not significantly further the state's interest in promoting parental consultation and because such a requirement unduly burdened a minor's right to have an abortion.

[76] 108 S. Ct. 2687 (1988).

[77] Thompson, who was fifteen at the time of the offense, was certified by the juvenile court to stand trial as an adult, convicted of the murder of his former brother-in-law and sentenced to death. Thompson v. State, 724 P.2d 780, 782 (Okla. Crim. 1986), *cert. granted*, Thompson v. Oklahoma, 479 U.S. 1084 (1987),

that Oklahoma could not constitutionally execute William Wayne Thompson, but shed little light on the capital punishment debate. Juvenileness is employed in all three opinions written in the case.[78] The components of juvenileness, however, show up in surprising places and are used in interesting ways.

It was difficult to forecast what the Court would do in *Thompson* because the usual positions of the litigants in juvenile cases were reversed. The State of Oklahoma minimized or abandoned the protective generalizations of juvenileness and instead argued that teenage killers should be executed just like adults.[79] Conversely, advocates for Thompson had to adopt all the juvenileness rhetoric about immaturity, lack of capacity to appreciate reality, and inability to make informed decisions that, in other contexts, had been the basis for denial of rights to juveniles. Those were exactly the positions taken by Thompson and his amici curiae, many of whom do not support the results in the cases they cited.[80]

---

vacated, Thompson v. Oklahoma, 108 S. Ct. 2687 (1988). Three co-defendants, separately tried and sentenced to death, were older than Thompson. Brief for Petitioner at 5, Thompson v. Oklahoma, 108 S. Ct. 2687 (1988) (No. 86-6169). At trial, the prosecutor characterized Thompson as older than his chronological age and therefore fit for the death penalty. Thompson v. State, 724 P.2d 780, 784 (Okl. Crim. 1986), *cert. granted*, Thompson v. Oklahoma, 479 U.S. 1084 (1987), *vacated*, Thompson v. Oklahoma, 108 S. Ct. 2687 (1988).

[78] The plurality opinion, delivered by Justice Stevens, employed juvenileness language to justify the finding that children's irresponsible conduct is less morally reprehensible than similar adult conduct. *Id.* at 2698. In her concurring opinion, Justice O'Connor referred to "[t]he special qualitative characteristics that justify legislatures in treating [juveniles] differently from adults . . . ." *Id.* at 2709. Justice Scalia's dissenting opinion, joined by Chief Justice Rehnquist and Justice White, is critical of the plurality's generalization that adolescents are less mature and responsible than adults as justification for establishing the rule that no person under 16 years of age when the crime was committed can be executed. *Id.* at 2718-19.

[79] Oklahoma did ultimately concede that there was some age below which the eighth amendment forbade executing children, and suggested 14. Thompson v. Oklahoma, 108 S. Ct. 2687, 2695, n.28 (1988).

[80] Thompson cited the juvenileness language of Bellotti v. Baird, 443 U.S. 622, 635 (1979), *see supra* notes 69-70 and accompanying text, and Schall v. Martin, 467 U.S. 253, 265 (1984), *see supra* note 9 and accompanying text. Brief of Petitioner at 27-28, Thompson v. Oklahoma, 108 S. Ct. 2687 (1988) (No. 86-6169). Comparison of two amici briefs illustrates the tension generated by the application of prior law to the juvenile death penalty issue. The briefs of the Child Welfare League of America, Children's Defense Fund, National Association

Though they may appear strange, these positions are of course logically consistent. The adult eighth amendment does not encompass the right to be free from the death penalty.[81] Child advocates here understandably do not want their clients treated like adults. Yet the question is made more interesting by the adult eighth amendment's inclusion of the right to individualized consideration by the sentencer of a virtually unlimited list of mitigating factors, including age, as a basis for a sentence other than death.[82] Thompson asked the Court to generalize as to all who may claim the age factor.[83]

Thompson also urged that the real question before the Court was whether to compel the United States to join the majority of "civilized nations" which do not kill their children.[84] Evidence on

---

of Social Workers and others relied on the same juvenileness pronouncements advanced by Thompson. In tone, however, it simply referred the Court back to its own rulings without necessarily endorsing them. *See* Brief Amici Curiae of Child Welfare League of America, at 17-32, Thompson v. Oklahoma, 108 S. Ct. 2687 (1988) (No. 86-6169). The National Legal Aid and Defender Association and other organizations not primarily involved with children were less hesitant to embrace the juvenileness assumptions formulated in the Court's earlier opinions. *See* Brief Amici Curiae of National Legal Aid and Defender Association, at 16-17, Thompson v. Oklahoma, 108 S. Ct. 2687 (1988) (No. 86-6169).

[81] The adult eighth amendment, measured by "evolving standards of decency," has been held to permit execution of some but not all who commit murder. *See* Gregg v. Georgia, 428 U.S. 153 (1976); Proffitt v. Florida, 428 U.S. 242 (1976); Jurek v. Texas, 428 U.S. 262 (1976); Woodson v. North Carolina, 428 U.S. 280 (1976) (sanctioning death penalty when sentencers properly consider mitigating factors).

[82] On this matter, the Court has been relatively consistent since it established the principle in Lockett v. Ohio, 438 U.S. 586 (1978) (eighth and fourteenth amendments require that sentencers not be precluded from considering any mitigating factors the defendant proffers against imposition of death penalty). An earlier attempt by Oklahoma to execute a juvenile was thwarted on *Lockett* grounds. *See* Eddings v. Oklahoma, 455 U.S. 104 (1982) (eighth and fourteenth amendments require that sentencers may not refuse to consider, as a matter of law, any relevant mitigating evidence against imposition of death penalty). And a recent decision reaffirms disapproval of state procedures that limit consideration of individualized mitigating factors. *See* Hitchcock v. Dugger, 107 S. Ct. 1821 (1987) (disapproving judge's exclusion of mitigating factors not provided in Florida statute on rationale of *Lockett* and *Eddings*).

[83] No member of the Court accepted the position urged by Thompson and various amici that the relevant age was 18. Thompson v. Oklahoma, 108 S. Ct. 2687, 2700 (1988).

[84] More than 80 nations, including most western European nations, have either

that issue was in part responsible for the conclusion of Justice Stevens, writing for Justices Brennan, Marshall, and Blackmun, that "evolving standards of decency that mark the progress of a maturing society,"[85] have simply evolved far enough to prohibit execution of anyone under age sixteen at the time of his crime.[86]

The Court's usual method of determining eighth amendment boundaries at a given time also includes a canvass of the attitude of state legislatures toward the issue in question. In *Thompson*, the Court, in performing this function, was impressed with an array of statutes drawing the line between childhood and adulthood at age sixteen or less.[87] It recognized and cited with enthusiastic approval the tenets of philosophical juvenileness supporting the statutes and denying rights and responsibilities to juveniles.[88] Further, the plurality found that juvenileness undermines the two basic legal

---

abolished the death penalty or forbidden its use on children. Hartman, *"Unusual" Punishment: The Domestic Effects of International Norms Restricting the Application of the Death Penalty*, 52 U. CIN. L. REV. 655, 666 (1983), cited in Brief Amici Curiae of Child Welfare League of America, at 61-62, Thompson v. Oklahoma, 108 S. Ct. 2687 (1988) (No. 86-6169). The plurality considered this data relevant to its constitutional analysis. Thompson v. Oklahoma, 108 S. Ct. 2687, 2696 (1988).

[85] Thompson v. Oklahoma, 108 S. Ct. 2687, 2691 (1988).

[86] *Id.* at 2698.

[87] "The line between childhood and adulthood is drawn in different ways by various States. There is, however, complete or near unanimity among all 50 States and the District of Columbia in treating a person under 16 as a minor for several important purposes." *Id.* at 2692. The plurality referred to appendices compiled by amici organizations and listing hundreds of statutes dealing with everything from the right to vote to the right to gamble. *Id.* at 2701-06.

[88] *Id.* at 2693 n.23. This lengthy and remarkable footnote contains the paternalistic generalizations which in *Bethel*, *Hazelwood*, and *T.L.O.* supported a ruling against the child. Here, however, the plurality asserts that the collection of statutes:

> reflects [the] basic assumption that our society makes about children as a class; we assume that they do not yet act as adults do, and we act in their interest by restricting certain choices we feel they are not yet ready to make with full benefit of the costs and benefits attending such decisions. It would be ironic if these assumptions that we so readily make about children as a class—about their inherent differences from adults in their capacity as agents, as choosers, as shapers of their own lives—were suddenly unavailable in determining whether it is cruel and unusual to treat children the same as adults for purposes of inflicting capital punishment.

Id.

justifications accepted for the death penalty: retribution and deterrence.[89] After examining the attitudes of juries and the infrequency of juvenile death sentences and executions, the plurality concluded that "the imposition of the death penalty on a fifteen-year-old offender is now generally abhorrent to the conscience of the community."[90]

Had Justice O'Connor voted to make the plurality a majority, *Thompson* would represent a small but significant victory for adult death penalty opponents, whose acknowledged judicial strategy is to chip away at the penalty's application. Justice O'Connor, however, chose to write separately, concurring only in the judgment. Part of her indecision rested on an inability to make a determination about the proper application of juvenileness to the issue. Citing juvenileness language from *Hazelwood* and other cases discussed in this Article, she acknowledged that legislatures have recognized the relative immaturity of adolescents and the Court has permitted them to administer age-discriminatory laws premised on that assumption of immaturity.[91] But, in citing abortion cases, Justice O'Connor noted that the Court has recognized differing levels of maturity within an age group.[92] For opaque reasons boiling down to the *possibility* that there is a national consensus against executing fifteen-year-old felons,[93] and a *possibility* that the Oklahoma

[89] *Id.* at 2699.

[90] *Id.* at 2697.

[91] *Id.* at 2709.

[92] *Id.*

[93] *Id.* Justice O'Connor alleged that there is a need for more data before a determination can be made that juries oppose execution of 15-year-olds. She asks particularly for data on how many times juries have been asked to impose death sentences on them, and how many times prosecutors have exercised their discretion not to seek death though the statutory requirements are met. *Id.* It may be a little late for concern about the actual administration of the death penalty as a means of informing the Court's "evolving standards" analysis. The information Justice O'Connor desired on prosecutorial discretion probably does not exist. The Court has pointedly heretofore not been concerned with the exercise of prosecutorial discretion. *See, e.g.*, Gregg v. Georgia, 428 U.S. 153, 224-26 (1976) (White, J., concurring). Further, the Court has turned aside attacks on the death penalty stemming from studies about how it works, without repudiating the studies' findings. *See* McCleskey v. Kemp, 107 S. Ct. 1756, 1769 (1987); Lockhart v. McCree, 476 U.S. 162, 168 (1986). There has been little incentive to gather the data that Justice O'Connor wants.

legislature's intent was not clear, she resolved the ambivalence about juvenileness by voting with the plurality.

There is no ambivalence about the dissenting opinion of Justice Scalia, joined by Chief Justice Rehnquist and Justice White. The tone is mean-spirited[94] and the reasoning is occasionally specious,[95] but on the juvenileness question Justice Scalia stands where one usually finds child advocates. In his view, the law permitted and required individualized consideration of the maturity of Thompson, he was afforded that, and therefore there is no barrier to executing him.[96]

The generalized protectionist assumptions of philosophical juvenileness are usually employed to deny rights to juveniles. When juveniles find themselves caught in the adult controversy over abortion, those assumptions are sometimes not employed. But on the adult capital punishment battlefield, the abandonment of these assumptions can mean death for the juvenile. What to do with juvenileness in cases where adult interests are directly at stake is a question to which the Court has yet to fashion a clear answer.

Conclusion

Some may legitimately ask what all the fuss is about. As long as the majority of adults exercise their discretion humanely and the

---

[94] Justice Scalia seemed particularly disturbed that Justice O'Connor's opinion would require legislatures to face squarely the issue of executing juveniles, and that as a result they might not have the political will to approve the practice:

> What the concurrence proposes is also designed, of course, to make it more difficult for all States to enact legislation resulting in capital punishment for murderers under 16 when they committed their crimes. It is difficult to pass a law saying explicitly "15-year-olds can be executed," just as it would be difficult to pass a law saying explicitly "blind people can be executed," or "white-haired grandmothers can be executed," or "mothers of two-year-olds can be executed."

Thompson v. Oklahoma, 108 S. Ct. 2687, 2721 (1988) (Scalia, J., dissenting).

[95] The three opinions take issue with one another on the proper interpretation of the action of state legislatures relevant to the death penalty for juveniles. Many of the conflicting interpretations are those upon which reasonable people might differ. The most egregious failure of Justice Scalia, however, is his cavalier dismissal from the "national consensus" inquiry, of the 14 jurisdictions without capital punishment at all. *Id.* at 2717. It is difficult to give any credit to an argument that these jurisdictions have not made the lesser included determination that 15-year-olds are not to be executed.

[96] *Id.* at 2714.

majority of kids does not complain, why should the law accommodate deviant behavior and viewpoints in the young? For my part, a sufficient answer comes not from harking back with nostalgia to the Age of Enlightenment and the Founding Fathers, but from observation of today's students.

For the past few summers, it has been my privilege to teach a course in Law and Contemporary Social Problems to a group of bright, college bound high school seniors drawn from public and private schools in all parts of the nation. It is fascinating to watch them encounter diversity for the first time. An example is our consideration of the eighth amendment and corporal punishment in the schools. The eyes widen on the students who cannot imagine a school where teachers hit kids, while a bemused "What's the big deal?" expression comes over those who experience violence every day. Orthodoxy may vary somewhat from place to place, but questioning it or examining the reasons for it is apparently not part of our educational experience and the courts help to ensure that.

Later, many of these good, intelligent, decent kids come to law school. They often encounter the greatest difficulty just understanding what conflict is about—what advocacy is, why people are passionate about their beliefs. If and to the extent the law's treatment of unorthodox young people contributes to this state of affairs, the law does us all a disservice.

I would not like to see the definitive opinion withdrawing the Constitution, sword or shield, from juveniles. Rather, for the sake of adults and young persons both, I would that the Matthew Frasers, Cathy Kuhlmeiers, and T.L.O.s of the future experience the positive power of the law, as did John and Mary Beth Tinker.

NOTES & COMMENTS

Acknowledging the Hypocrisy: Granting Minors the Right to Choose Their Medical Treatment

INTRODUCTION

Traditionally, minors have been considered dependents of their parents and who do not have any legal rights.[1] Specifically, they are dependent on their parents until they reach the age of majority. As such, a minor is legally unable to provide or withhold consent to medical procedures.[2] That legal incapacity to give informed consent has resulted in numerous cases where a minor has been subjected to medical treatment that was against his or her wishes or was unable to obtain treatment that a parent has chosen to withhold.[3]

Legislatures and courts have carved out exceptions to this rule during the past century. For example, a minor may obtain adult legal status, despite his or her age, through the statutory process of emancipation.[4] Once emancipated, the minor is bestowed with both the rights and responsibilities of adulthood.[5] The United States Supreme Court created another exception by extending the fundamental right of privacy and bodily integrity to minors with respect to terminating a pregnancy[6] and obtaining contraception.[7] In

---

1 *See* Susan D. Hawkins, Note, *Protecting the Rights and Interests of Competent Minors In Litigated Medical Treatment Disputes*, 64 FORDHAM L. REV. 2075, 2076 (1996) (surveying the history of children's legal rights); *see also* Jay C. Laubscher, Note, *A Minor of 'Sufficient Age and Understanding' Should Have the Right to Petition for the Termination of the Parental Relationship*, 40 N.Y.L. SCH. L. REV. 565, 568 (1996) (discussing the common law background and constitutional rights of minors).

2 *See* Hawkins, *supra* note 1, at 2079-80.

3 *See infra* notes 148-151 and accompanying text.

4 *See infra* Part III.A.

5 *See generally* Laubscher, *supra* note 1, at 577-80.

6 *See* Planned Parenthood v. Danforth, 428 U.S. 52 (1976) [hereinafter Danforth].

7 *See* Carey v. Population Services International, 431 U.S. 678 (1977).

the state law context, many states have enacted statutes that allow minors to obtain treatment for sexually transmitted diseases and alcohol and substance abuse, regardless of age, without parental knowledge or consent.[8] A few states have completely eliminated the parental consent requirement for medical treatment and now allow a "mature minor" to make his or her own medical treatment decisions.[9]

Part I of this note discusses the traditional legal status of children and the impact of parental and state interests, rooted in constitutional law, on that status.[10] Part II examines the common law, legislative, and court created exceptions to the traditional legal disabilities of minors.[11] The legal requirement for informed consent prior to receiving medical treatment and an adolescent's ability to give informed consent are discussed in Part III.[12] Part IV discusses the process that physicians should undertake in allowing their adolescent patients to participate in deciding their medical treatment.[13] Also considered are alternatives to litigation for resolving any conflicts that arise and, if and when courts are involved in the dispute, the proper role of judges.[14] The facts above support the proposition that the current exception to traditional dependency doctrine is inconsistent with the best interests of the minor. Specifically, the exceptions undermine the minor's interests because they create a paradox that denies mature minors, capable of making responsible decisions, the legal ability to make medical decisions,[15] but grants immature minors

---

[8] *See* Janine P. Felsman, Note, Eliminating Parental Consent and Notification for Adolescent HIV Testing: A Legitimate Statutory Response to the AIDS Epidemic, 5 J.L. & POL'Y 339, 353-54 (1996).

[9] *See* Nancy Batterman, *Under Age: A Minor's Right to Consent to Health Care*, 10 TOURO L. REV. 637, 641 (1994).

[10] *See infra* notes 17-56 and accompanying text.

[11] *See infra* notes 59-147 and accompanying text.

[12] *See infra* notes 148-189 and accompanying text.

[13] *See infra* notes 192-227 and accompanying text.

[14] *See infra* notes 228-243 and accompanying text.

[15] For example, requiring parental consent for withholding medical treatment. *See infra* notes 167-171.

the ability to make critical life decisions.[16]

I. THE LEGAL STATUS OF CHILDREN

Throughout most of United States history, children were regarded as chattel, lacking any legal rights.[17] The law focused instead on the rights of parents with respect to their children.[18] Since minor children was completely dependent on their parents, they were under a legal disability.[19] This legal disability precluded minors from establishing their own domicile, from entering into binding contracts, from consenting to any type of medical, dental, or psychiatric treatment, from bringing a civil action, from making a will, and from conveying real property.[20] The view that children are more than mere property is a relatively new concept.[21]

The Industrial Revolution marked the beginning of a shift in society's perception of children.[22] Child labor laws and compulsory education laws were enacted as a way to protect children from the effects of industrialization.[23] However, despite these progressions, the common law continued to regard minors as mentally incompetent, and

---

16 For example, allowing a minor to terminate her pregnancy without parental consent. *See infra* Part III.B.

17 *See* Hawkins, *supra* note 1, at 2076.

18 *Id.*

19 *See* Laubscher, supra note 1, at 568.

20 *Id.* at 568-69 (listing these and other traditional legal disabilities of children).

21 *See* Lynne Marie Kohm & Maria E. Lawrence, *Sex at Six: The Victimization of Innocence and Other Concerns Over Children's "Rights,"* 36 BRANDEIS J. FAM. L. 361, 369 (1997-98) (describing the historical background on the law and society's perception of childhood).

22 *See* Hawkins, *supra* note 1, at 2076.

23 *Id. See also* DAVID J. ROTHMAN, CONSCIENCE AND CONVENIENCE: THE ASYLUM AND ITS ALTERNATIVES IN PROGRESSIVE AMERICA 205-12 (1980) (discussing the influence of the progressives on the adoption of child welfare measures including labor and education laws).

thus applied a legal presumption of incapacity.[24]

The presumption of incapacity was prevalent in both civil and criminal law.[25] For instance, a minor could not be held liable for an intentional tort, because it was presumed that he or she was unable to formulate the requisite intent.[26] Criminal law presumed that young children were unable to formulate the necessary *mens rea* element of a crime and therefore, could not be held culpable.[27] These beliefs continued basically unchanged until the Twentieth Century.[28]

During the second half of the Twentieth Century, many courts and legislatures altered or removed some of the traditional legal disabilities placed on minors.[29] For example, both tax and criminal law, have "recognized that children under the age of eighteen should sometimes be treated as adults."[30] The United States Supreme Court's declaration that "constitutional rights do not mature and come into being magically only when one attains the state-defined age of majority,"[31] ushered in a new era in children's legal rights.

Despite this expansion of children's legal rights, a minor still needs the express or implied consent of his or her parents or guardians in order to receive medical treatment.[32] The notion that children do

---

24 *See generally* Jennifer Fouts Skeels, *In Re E.G.: The Right of Mature Minors In Illinois to Refuse Lifesaving Medical Treatment*, 21 LOY. U. CHI. L.J. 1199, 1209 (1990) (explaining the presumption of incapacity with respect to minors).

25 *Id.*

26 *Id.*; *see, e.g.*, Cardwell v. Bechtol, 724 S.W.2d 739, 745 (Tenn. 1987).

27 *See generally* Fouts Skeels, *supra* note 24, at 1209; *see also* WAYNE R. LAFAVE & AUSTIN W. SCOTT, JR., CRIMINAL LAW (2d ed. 1986). The criminal law follows the "Rule of Sevens" for determining capacity of minors to form the required *mens rea*. *Id.*

28 *See* Hawkins, *supra* note 1, at 2076.

29 *See* Laubscher, *supra* note 1, at 569 (discussing the changes in the law relative to children).

30 *Id.*

31 *See* Planned Parenthood v. Danforth, 428 U.S. 52, 74 (1976) (recognizing that minors possess constitutional rights). *See also* discussion *infra* notes 79-90 and accompanying text.

32 *See* Felsman, *supra* note 8, at 347-48 (describing the common law requirement of parental consent and notification).

not have the cognitive capacity, experience, and maturity necessary to make complicated life-choices continues to permeate this area of the law.[33] In addition, there is a belief that parents, in consultation with the child's physician, will make the correct treatment decision; treatment that is in the child's best interest.[34]

A. The Parents' Interest

The presumption that parents will act in the best interest of their children is rooted in our constitutional law.[35] In *Pierce v. Society of Sisters*[36] and *Prince v. Massachusetts,*[37] the United States Supreme Court recognized that a fundamental right, embodied in the due process clause of the Fourteenth Amendment, is the parents' "liberty interest in the custody and management of their children, [and] a corresponding duty to provide care."[38] Furthermore, in *Meyer v. Nebraska* the Supreme Court held that parents have an implicit constitutional right to freedom from state intervention in family matters.[39] The basis for the *Meyer* Court's decision rested on

---

33 *Id.* at 347-48; *see also* Bellotti v. Baird, 443 U.S. 622, 634 (1979).

34 *See* Richard E. Redding, *Children's Competence to Provide Informed Consent for Mental Health Treatment*, 50 WASH. & LEE L. REV. 695, 697-98 (1993) (arguing that the assumption that parents always act in the child's best interest is invalid).

35 *See* Elizabeth J. Sher, Note, *Choosing for Children: Adjudicating Medical Care Disputes Between Parent and the State*, 58 N.Y.U. L. REV. 157, 171-72 (1983).

36 268 U.S. 510 (1925) (holding that a state law mandating parents to send their children to public schools interfered with the parents' liberty to control their children's education).

37 321 U.S. 158 (1944) (recognizing that religious freedom and parental autonomy are important, but not without limitation and thus, holding that the state, as *parens patriae*, could restrict parental control by prohibiting child labor).

38 *See* Isabel Traugott & Ann Alpers, *In Their Own Hands: Adolescent's Refusal of Medical Treatment*, 151 ARCHIVES OF PEDIATRICS & ADOLESCENT MEDICINE 922, 923-24 (1997) (discussing the presumption of parental decision making); *see also* Sher, *supra* note 35, at 170-72 (explaining the basis for parental autonomy in child rearing).

39 262 U.S. 390, 399 (1923) (invalidating a Nebraska law, enacted during World War I when anti-German feelings were strong, which banned the teaching of foreign languages in public schools).

society's acceptance of the premise that parents should be able to make choices for their child, without state intrusion, and that parents typically act in their child's best interests.[40]

This deference to parental authority is driven by two presumptions. First, courts believe that "parents possess what a child lacks in maturity, experience, and capacity for judgment required for making life's difficult decisions."[41] Second, lawmakers presume that the "natural bonds of affection" cause parents to act in their child's best interests.[42] Thus, parents, as decision-makers for their children, are given wide latitude in authorizing their medical care and treatment.[43]

B. The State's Parens Patriae Interest

Despite the widely held belief that parents will act in their child's best interest, parental authority is not absolute.[44] In fact, if a parent is not acting in the best interest of the child the state may intervene.[45] The authority for state intervention is based on the doctrine of *parens patriae*.[46]

---

40 *See* Sher, *supra* note 35, at 169, 171-72.

41 *See* Parham v. J.R., 442 U.S. 584, 602 (1979). *But see* Jennifer L. Rosato, *The Ultimate Test of Autonomy: Should Minors Have a Right to Make Decisions Regarding Life-Sustaining Treatment?*, 49 RUTGERS L. REV. 1, 78-79 (1996) (arguing these presumptions do not apply to life-sustaining treatment).

42 *See Parham*, 442 U.S. at 602; *see also* Sher, *supra* note 35, at 171-72. For example, the Supreme Court has articulated that an "important justification for state deference to parental control over children is that '[t]he child is not the mere creature of the State; those who nurture him and direct his destiny have the right, coupled with the high duty, to recognize and prepare him for additional obligations.'" *Bellotti*, 443 U.S. at 637 (quoting Pierce, 268 U.S. at 602).

43 *See* Traugott & Alpers, *supra* note 38, at 924.

44 *See, e.g.*, *Prince*, 321 U.S. at 166.

45 *See generally* Sher, *supra* note 35, at 157 (contrasting the competing interests of parents and the state in medical treatment of minors); *see also* Traugott & Alpers, *supra* note 38, at 924 (arguing that the best interest of the child should always prevail, even if in opposition with the parents and the state's interest).

46 "'*Parens patriae*' literally 'parent of the country,' refers traditionally to [the] role of [the] state as sovereign and guardian of persons under legal disability, such as juveniles. It is the principle that the state must care for those who cannot take care of

Although the history of the *parens patriae* doctrine is a somewhat ambiguous,[47] it has come to mean that the state has an obligation and a right to protect the interests of its legally disabled citizens, those who can not protect themselves, including children.[48] The Supreme Court validated the *parens patriae* concept in *Prince v. Massachusetts*.[49] In *Prince*, the Court stated that "neither rights of religion nor rights of parenthood are beyond limitation. Acting to guard the general interest in youth's well being, the state as *parens patriae* may restrict the parent's control by requiring school attendance, regulating or prohibiting the child's labor, and in many other ways."[50] Some of the state's interests that support *parens patriae* include preservation of human life, ensuring a productive and self-perpetuating society, and, at the same time, conserving the state's resources.[51]

The state typically evokes its *parens patriae* authority with respect to children when parents have jeopardized or threatened their child's health and safety.[52] Based on the belief that a child has the "might to live and to grow up with a sound mind in a sound body,"[53] the state will exercise its authority and intervene in the parent-child relationship.[54] In the medical arena, the state is mostly likely to

---

themselves, such as minors who lack proper care and custody from their parents." BLACK'S LAW DICTIONARY 1114 (6th ed. 1990).

47 *See In re* Gault, 387 U.S. 1, 16 (1967) (stating that the meaning of *parens patriae* is "murky and its historic credentials are of dubious reliance.").

48 *See* Sher, *supra* note 35, at 170; *see also* Hawkins, *supra* note 1, at 2084.

49 321 U.S. at 165 (holding that a state's authority over the conduct of children exceeds its authority to control the conduct of adults).

50 *Id.* at 166. *See also* Schleifer v. Charlottesville, 159 F.3d 843 (4th Cir. 1998) (holding municipal curfew law over parental objections constitutional).

51 *See* Hawkins, *supra* note 1, at 2085; *see also* Rosato, *supra* note 41, at 70.

52 *See generally* Walter Wadlington, *David C. Baum Memorial Lecture: Medical Decision Making For and By Children: Tensions Between Parent, State, and Child*, 1994 U. ILL. L. REV. 311, 322-23 (1994) (explaining relevance of child abuse reporting statutes to medical treatment cases); *see also* Hawkins, *supra* note 1, at 2084.

53 *In re* Clark, 185 N.E.2d 128, 132 (Ohio 1962).

54 *See* Laura M. Plastine, Comment, *"In God We Trust": When Parents Refuse Medical Treatment for Their Children Based Upon Their Sincere Religious*

intervene when the child is suffering from a serious and potentially life-threatening illness or injury, not when the child has a minor childhood illness.[55] Thus, the parent's right to raise their children is not absolute and must give way when the child's life is at risk.[56]

II. RIGHTS CURRENTLY AFFORDED ADOLESCENTS DESPITE THEIR TRADITIONAL LEGAL DISABILITIES

It is clear that both parents and the state have legitimate interests in the welfare of children. However, it is unclear where the child fits in. In today's society it is not uncommon for an adolescent to exclaim to their parent or teacher "Don't tell me what to do. I *know* my rights." In reality, the expansion of minors' legal rights has been minimal, and in fact, these rights are still limited.[57]

A. Emancipation

Emancipation is the "legal process by which a child is released from the control and authority of his [or her] parent."[58] Most children are automatically emancipated from their parents upon reaching the age of majority, which in most jurisdictions is eighteen.[59] However,

---

Beliefs, 3 SETON HALL CONST. L.J. 123, 139 (1993) (exploring the right of the state to override parental religious-based objections to their children's medical treatment).

55 *Id.* at 139-41 (exploring the parental right to engage in faith-healing even when a child's life is endangered).

56 *Id.*

57 *See* Laubscher, *supra* note 1, at 569.

58 *See* 1 HOMER H. CLARK, JR., THE LAW OF DOMESTIC RELATIONS IN THE UNITED STATES 548 (2d ed. 1987). *See also* Carol Sanger & Eleanor Willemsen, *Minor Changes: Emancipating Children in Modern Times*, 25 U. MICH. J.L. REFORM 239, 240 (1992) (discussing use of statutory emancipation by parents as a way of coping and dealing with troubled adolescents).

59 *See* Robert F. Weir & Charles Peters, *Affirming the Decisions Adolescents Make About Life and Death*, THE HASTINGS CENTER REP., Nov. 11, 1997, at 29, 33. *See also* Dana F. Castle, *Early Emancipation Statutes: Should They Protect Parents as Well as Children?*, 20 FAM. L.Q. 343, 348-49 nn.35-36 (1986). After the Twenty-sixth Amendment was enacted, granting the right to vote to eighteen-year-olds, many jurisdictions lowered the age of majority from twenty-one to eighteen. Today, forty-four

there are several processes by which an adolescent who has not yet reached his or her eighteenth birthday may be emancipated from his or her parents or guardian and thus, have the rights (and responsibilities) of adulthood conferred upon him or her.[60] First, in many states, minors are automatically emancipated if they enter military service and marry.[61]

Second, many states have statutes that allow minors who meet the requirements set forth therein to be emancipated from their parents.[62] For instance, in California, if a minor can demonstrate that he or she: "(1) is at least fourteen years of age; (2) able to manage his or her own affairs; (3) lives separate and apart from parents with either parental consent or acquiescence; and (4) receives income derived from legal activity,"[63] the minor may be legally emancipated.[64] The court is ultimately left with the discretion to deny an emancipation request if it believes doing so would be in the minor's best interest.[65] One factor this and other statutes do not require a judge to consider is whether the minor is actually competent to live on his or her own.[66] Instead, the focus is on the minor's independence from his or her parents.[67]

---

jurisdictions have a statutory age of majority of eighteen. *Id. See, e.g.*, CAL. FAM. CODE § 7002 (West 1994); MICH. COMP. LAWS ANN. § 722.4 (West 1993 & Supp. 1995); MO. REV. STAT. § 452.340.3 (1993); N.J. STAT. ANN. § 9:17B-3 (West 1976); N.C. GEN. STAT. § 50-13.4(c) (1994); W. VA. CODE § 2-3-1 (1992).

60 *See generally* Laubscher, *supra* note 1, at 578-80; John C. Polifka, *The Status of Emancipated Minors in Iowa: The Case For a Clearly Drafted Statute*, 44 DRAKE L. REV. 39, 45-48 (1995) (arguing emancipation statutes are preferable to common law); Batterman, *supra* note 9, at 641.

61 *See, e.g.*, CAL. FAM. CODE § 7002; *see also* Redding, *supra* note 34, at 712; Laubscher, *supra* note 1, at 578.

62 *See, e.g.*, ALASKA STAT. § 09.55.590 (Miche Supp. 1994); CAL. FAM. CODE §§ 7000-143 (West Supp. 1994); KAN. STAT. ANN. §§ 38-108 to -110 (1993); MICH. COMP. LAWS. ANN. §§ 722.4-.4e (West 1993).

63 *See* Polifka, *supra* note 60, at 45.

64 CAL. FAM. CODE § 7120 (West Supp. 1994).

65 *See* Polifka, *supra* note 60, at 45.

66 *See* Rosato, *supra* note 41, at 28.

67 *Id.*

Finally, some states recognize a common law right to emancipation.[68] In these states, minors petition the court, and "[t]heir status is judicially determined on a case-by-case basis."[69] The factors enumerated in emancipation statutes tend to be the same ones considered by judges in common law states.[70] For example, in New York, a common law emancipated minor is one whose parents have surrendered control over the child's behavior and personal affairs.[71] As a result, the doctrine is typically discussed in cases regarding the payment of child support.[72]

For the minor whose petition for an emancipation decree is granted he or she is bestowed with all of the rights and responsibilities of an adult.[73] Besides being free from the control and authority of their parents, emancipated minors are able to enter into binding contracts, sue in their own names, establish their own residences, retain their own earnings, receive public assistance, consent to their own medical treatments, execute either living wills or proxy directives.[74]

B. Abortion and Personal Health Rights

The United States Supreme Court has recognized that the

---

68 *Id.* at 43 (stating that Iowa is a common law emancipation state); *see also* Batterman, *supra* note 9, at 645-46.

69 *See* Polifka, *supra* note 60, at 43.; *see also* Smith v. Seibly, 431 P.2d 719 (Wash. 1967) (recognizing that emancipation of minors may occur even in the absence of a statute).

70 *See generally* Batterman, *supra* note 9, at 641. Courts will look at whether the minor is living separate and apart from his or her parents; self-supporting; managing his or her own financial affairs; and if emancipating the minor is in his or her best interest. *Id.*

71 *See* Batterman, *supra* note 9, at 645-46.

72 *Id.* at 646.

73 *See* Sanger, *supra* note 58, at 240-41 (explaining that because such minor's attain legal adulthood prior to reaching the age of majority, such emancipated minors may engage in adult acts, such as signing binding contracts, keeping their own property, and disobeying their parents).

74 *See generally* Polifka, *supra* note 60, at 47; Redding, *supra* note 34, at 712; Batterman, *supra* note 9, at 647-48; Rosato, *supra* note 41, at 34-35.

Constitution grants minors a right to privacy.[75] The reach of these decisions, however, have been primarily limited to the areas of reproductive rights and limited personal health care issues.[76] The first major step was taken by the Supreme Court in *Planned Parenthood v. Danforth*,[77] which extended the fundamental privacy right to choose abortion to unmarried, minor women.[78]

In *Danforth*, the Supreme Court was considering the constitutionality of a Missouri statute that required written parental consent before an unmarried woman under the age of eighteen could have an abortion.[79] Since the right to choose an abortion flows from a fundamental right to privacy the applicable standard for evaluating the effect of the Missouri statute was strict scrutiny.[80] In its analysis the Court first recognized that minors do have constitutional rights[81] and declared that the statute imposed an unconstitutional burden on the minor's privacy right.[82] According to the Court, this burden was a result of the Missouri legislature granting a third party "an absolute,

---

75 *See* Jan C. Costello, *Making Kids Take Their Medicine: The Privacy and Due Process Rights of De Facto Competent Minors*, 31 LOY. L.A. L. REV. 907, 908 (1998) (forwarding that the right to privacy includes, but is not limited to the right to protect bodily integrity and to make health care decisions).

76 *See* Fouts Skeels, *supra* note 24, at 1213.

77 428 U.S. 52 (1976).

78 *See generally* Katherine M. Waters, *Judicial Consent to Abort: Assessing a Minor's Maturity*, 54 GEO. WASH. L. REV. 90, 94-95 (1985); Rosato, *supra* note 41, at 16 (commenting on the Supreme Court's deferential position on minor's abortion rights).

79 *Danforth*, 428 U.S. at 74.

80 *See* Roe v. Wade, 410 U.S. 113, 153 & 155 (1973). *Roe* established that the right of privacy is broad enough to encompass abortion and reiterated that the right of privacy is a fundamental right triggering strict scrutiny analysis. *Id.* at 153. A regulation that limits fundamental rights will only survive strict scrutiny if there is a compelling state interest and the regulation is "narrowly drawn to express only the legitimate state interests at stake." *Id.* at 155.

81 *See Danforth*, 428 U.S. at 74. The *Danforth* Court recognized that "constitutional rights do not mature and come into being magically only when one attains the state-defined age of majority. Minors, as well as adults, are protected by the Constitution and possess constitutional rights." *Id.*; *see also* Fouts Skeels, *supra* note 24, at 1210.

82 *See Danforth*, 428 U.S. at 74.

and possibly arbitrary, veto over the decision of the physician and his patient to terminate the patient's pregnancy, regardless of the reason for withholding the consent."[83] The Court then examined whether the parents' interest may nevertheless outweigh the minor's right of privacy.[84] However, the Court concluded "[a]ny independent interest the parent may have in the termination of the minor daughter's pregnancy is no more weighty than the right of privacy of the competent minor mature enough to have become pregnant."[85]

Nevertheless, the Supreme Court placed a limitation on the minor's fundamental right to choose an abortion.[86] The Court stated: "[O]ur holding . . . does not suggest that every minor, regardless of age or maturity, may give effective consent for termination of her pregnancy."[87] Thus, the *Danforth* Court established that only mature minors could choose an abortion without parental consent.[88] How a minor's maturity was determined was left unanswered.[89] Justice White's dissent criticized the majority's lack of detail in their opinion and stated that states are entitled to protect minors "from their own immature and improvident decisions; and there is absolutely no reason expressed by the majority why the State may not utilize that method here."[90]

The next major decision about a minor's fundamental right to choose an abortion was enunciated in *Bellotti v. Baird* (Bellotti II).[91] The *Bellotti* Court held that states must provide an alternative to parental consent for a minor's seeking an abortion.[92] Accordingly,

---

[83] *Id.*

[84] *Id.* at 75.

[85] *Id.*

[86] *Id.*

[87] *Danforth*, 428 U.S. at 75.

[88] *See* Waters, *supra* note 78, at 95.

[89] *Id.*

[90] *See Danforth*, 428 U.S. at 95 (White, J. dissenting).

[91] 443 U.S. 622 (1979). In Bellotti v. Baird, 428 U.S. 132 (1976), the Court remanded the case to the Massachusetts Supreme Judicial Court to construe a statute which regulated minors' abortions. *Id.* at 151-52.

[92] *Bellotti*, 443 U.S. at 643.

states must afford a minor an alternative procedure in which she can demonstrate that she is "mature enough and well enough informed to make her abortion decision."[93] It is important to note that the burden was on the minor to rebut the presumption that she is incompetent of making decisions about her medical care.[94] If the court does not believe that the minor is mature enough, the judge may still grant the minor the right to have an abortion without parental consent or notification, as long as it would be in the minor's best interest.[95]

Another pivotal case involving minors and their privacy was *Carey v. Population Services International.*[96] In *Carey*, the Supreme Court addressed a minor's access to contraception.[97] At issue in *Carey* was a New York statute which prohibited the distribution of non-medical contraceptives to persons sixteen or older, and entirely prohibited distribution to children under sixteen.[98] Reiterating the principle that the right to privacy extends to minors as well as adults, the Court found the statute unconstitutional because the state failed to show a significant interest that outweighs the minors right to privacy.[99]

In addition to reproductive rights, minors have been granted minimum rights in other areas of personal health.[100] These laws are

---

[93] *Id.*

[94] *See* Costello, *supra* note 75, at 909-10; *see also* Satsie Veith, *The Judicial Bypass Procedure and Adolescents' Abortion Rights: The Fallacy of the "Maturity" Standard*, 23 HOFSTRA L. REV. 453, 455 (1994).

[95] *See Bellotti*, 443 U.S. at 650.

[96] 431 U.S. 678 (1977).

[97] *Id.*

[98] Individuals sixteen years of age and older were able to receive contraceptives from a licensed pharmacist. *Id.* at 681-82; *see also* Hawkins, *supra* note 1, at 2097-98.

[99] *See Carey*, 431 U.S. at 694-96; *see also* Hawkins, *supra* note 1, at 2098; Jessica A. Penkower, *The Potential Right of Chronically Ill Adolescents to Refuse Life-Saving Medical Treatment - Fatal Misuse of the Mature Minor Doctrine*, 45 DEPAUL L. REV. 1165, 1182-83 (1996).

[100] *See* Penkower, *supra* note 99, at 1178 (including sexually transmitted diseases, alcohol and substance abuse, and psychiatric care).

often referred to as age of consent laws[101] and usually involve medical decisions relating to treatment of sexually transmitted diseases, alcohol, and substance abuse.[102] These statutory exceptions to the common law rule requiring parental consent for medical treatment of minors evolved due to the increase of sexually transmitted diseases among adolescents and the perception that adolescents would not seek treatment if they needed to first inform their parents.[103] Neither the minor's maturity or decision-making capacity were factors in the passing of these laws.[104] Further, the laws focus upon a minor's right to consent to treatment, not his or her right to refuse treatment.[105] Statutes that permit minors to obtain alcohol and substance abuse treatment, and mental health care were enacted on the same premise.[106]

C. The Mature Minor Doctrine

The "mature minor" doctrine is a relatively new legal concept which allows some minors to consent to medical treatment without parental consent.[107] However, only a few states have recognized this doctrine, and the Supreme Court has yet to declare it applicable to

---

101 *See generally* Redding, *supra* note 34, at 712; Rosato, *supra* note 41, at 30-31.

102 *See, e.g.*, UTAH CODE ANN., § 26-6-18 (1999) (permitting minors to consent to treatment for sexually transmitted diseases without parental consent); N. Y. PUB. HEALTH LAW § 2305(2) (McKinney 1993) (authorizing diagnosis, treatment and prescription of persons under 21 years of age infected with, or exposed to, sexually transmissible diseases without parental consent); N. Y. MENTAL HYG. LAW § 21.11 (McKinney Supp. 1994) (allowing treatment of minors for substance abuse problems without parental consent if "such treatment is necessary for the best interests of the child"); N.J. STAT. ANN. § 9:17A-4 (West 1993); VA. CODE ANN. § 54-325-2.D (1992); *see also* Felsman, *supra* note 8, at 354.

103 *See* Penkower, *supra* note 99, at 1178; *see also* Felsman, *supra* note 8, at 342-45.

104 *See* Penkower, *supra* note 99, at 1178.

105 *See* Rosato, *supra* note 41, at 31.

106 *Id.*

107 *See* Batterman, *supra* note 9, at 641.

medical treatment decisions outside of reproductive rights.[108]

In an early case, *In re Green,*[109] physicians sought to perform a spinal fusion to sixteen year old Ricky Green, who suffered from severe curvature of the spine with accompanying paralytic scoliosis.[110] However, there was no evidence that the condition was life threatening or that it was necessary to immediately perform the operation.[111] Ricky's mother, however, refused to consent to the procedure since blood transfusions would be necessary.[112] Although Ricky was initially excluded from the decision-making process, the Supreme Court of Pennsylvania stated that it would be "most anomalous to ignore Ricky in this situation when we consider the preference of an intelligent child of sufficient maturity"[113] and remanded the matter, holding that Ricky's personal choices should be considered.[114]

Several years later, the Tennessee Supreme Court recognized in *Cardwell v. Bechtol* the mature minor exception to parental consent for medical treatment.[115] *Cardwell* involved an action against an

---

108 *Id.*; *see also* Hawkins, *supra* note 1, at 2100-01. *See, e.g.*, ARK. STAT. ANN. § 20-9-602(7) (Michie 1991) (granting "[a]ny unemancipated minor of sufficient intelligence to understand and appreciate the consequences of the proposed surgical or medical treatment or procedures" the legal ability to consent to said treatment); NEV. REV. STAT. § 129.030(2) (1991) (stating if a minor "understands the nature and purpose of the proposed examination or treatment and its probable outcome, and voluntarily requests it" his or her consent alone is sufficient). State appellate courts in Georgia, Illinois, Maine, Michigan, Missouri, and Tennessee have held that life-sustaining medical treatment may be withheld or withdrawn from adolescents. *See* Weir, *supra* note 59, at 29 (arguing that adolescents are capable of making health care decisions and that advance directives should be used by adolescents to allow them to participate in their treatment).

109 *In re* Green, 292 A.2d 387 (Pa. 1972), *aff'd*, 307 A.2d 279 (Pa. 1973).

110 *Id.* at 388.

111 *Id.*

112 *Id.*

113 *See In re* Green, 292 A.2d at 392.

114 *Id. But see* Commonwealth v. Nixon, 718 A.2d 311 (Pa. Super. 1998) (holding mature minor doctrine does not allow a mature minor to refuse medical treatment in life-threatening situations).

115 724 S.W.2d 739 (Tenn. 1987); *see also* Joan-Margaret Kun, *Rejecting the Adage "Children Should Be Seen and Not Heard" — The Mature Minor Doctrine*, 16

osteopath who had treated Sandra Cardwell, without the consent of her parents, five months prior to her eighteenth birthday.[116] The Court noted that several Tennessee laws "recognize[d] the varying degrees of responsibility and maturity of minors [fourteen] years and older"[117] and also considered the "Rule of Sevens"[118] which presumes different levels of capacity depending on the age of the minor.[119] The court concluded that a mature minor exception to parental consent *does exist*, however, it affirmed the jury's verdict that Sandra did not have capacity to consent and did not effectively consent to treatment.[120]

Two years later, the Illinois Supreme Court in *In re E.G.*, recognized that minors have a common law right to refuse medical treatment.[121] E.G. was a seventeen and a half-year-old girl with acute nonlymphatic leukemia who needed blood transfusions to treat the disease.[122] Both E.G. and her mother were Jehovah's Witnesses and refused to consent to the treatment because of their belief that receiving a blood transfusion violates the Bible's prohibition against consuming blood.[123] The Illinois State Attorney General sought a judicial determination that E.G. was medically neglected and in need of treatment. The trial court agreed and appointed a temporary

PACE L. REV. 423, 430-32 (1996).

[116] 724 S.W.2d at 742-43.

[117] *Id.* at 745.

[118] *Id.* "The Rule of Sevens" presumes different levels of capacity depending on the age of the child. *Id.* According to the Rule a child under the age of seven lacks capacity. *Id.* Between the ages of seven and fourteen there is a rebuttable presumption of lack of capacity. *Id.* For children between the ages of fourteen and twenty-one there is a rebuttable presumption of capacity. *Id.* *See also* Kun, *supra* note 115, at 431.

[119] *Cardwell*, 724 S.W.2d at 745.

[120] *Id.* at 756.

[121] 549 N.E.2d 322 at 328 (Ill. 1989).

[122] *Id.* at 323; *see also* William D. Brewster, Casenote, *In Re E.G., A Minor: Death Over Life: A Judicial Trend Continues as the Illinois Supreme Court Grants Minors the Right to Refuse Life-Saving Medical Treatment*, 23 J. MARSHALL L. REV. 771, 772-73 (1990).

[123] *See In re* E.G., 549 N.E.2d at 323; *see also* Brewster, *supra* note 122, at n.14 (citing J. PENTON, APOCALYPSE DELAYED: THE STORY OF JEHOVAH'S WITNESSES 153 (1985)) "[Jehovah's] Witnesses believe that taking blood transfusions is contrary to the teachings of Genesis 9:4, Leviticus 3:17, and Acts 15:29". *Id.*

guardian to make E.G.'s treatment decisions.[124] On appeal the appellate court held that E.G. was a mature minor and her constitutional right to exercise her religion permitted her to refuse blood transfusions.[125]

The State appealed to the Illinois Supreme Court, which in turn granted certiorari.[126] Since the United States Supreme Court had not recognized that either adults or minors have a constitutional right to refuse life-saving medical treatment, the court based its decision on case law and Illinois statutes to conclude that a minor, with judicial approval, could refuse medical treatment.[127] The court stated that in the absence of a statute, a trial judge should determine "whether a minor is mature enough to make health care choices on her own."[128] However, the court stated that the right must be balanced against four state interests: "(1) the preservation of life; (2) protecting the interests of third parties; (3) prevention of suicide; and (4) maintaining the ethical integrity of the medical profession."[129] Since E.G. was no longer a minor, the court did not remand the case to the trial court.[130]

The Maine Supreme Judicial Court has also recognized that a minor has a right to refuse life-sustaining procedures.[131] In *In re Swan*, Chad Swan was involved in a car accident nine months before his eighteenth birthday that left him in a persistent vegetative state.[132] The court found clear and convincing evidence that on more than one occasion prior to the accident, Chad had expressed his desire not to be kept on life-sustaining equipment, and therefore, his prior statements were controlling.[133] Thus, Chad's parents were allowed to determine

124 *See* Brewster, *supra* note 122 at 773-74.

125 *In re* E.G., 515 N.E.2d 286, at 290-91(Ill. App. Ct. 1987).

126 *In re* E.G., 549 N.E.2d 322 at 323 (Ill. 1989).

127 *Id.* at 325, 328.

128 *Id.* at 327.

129 *Id.* at 328.

130 *Id.*

131 *See In re* Swan, 569 A.2d 1202 (Me. 1990) (per curiam).

132 *Id.* at 1203.

133 *Id.* at 1204-05. *See also* Rosato, *supra* note 41, at 40-41.

whether or not to re-insert a gastronomy tube.[134] The court's decision also noted the common law presumption of competency for persons fourteen years and older,[135] that persons attain capacity at different ages,[136] and the Illinois Supreme Court's decision in *In re E.G.*.[137]

Most recently the Massachusetts Appeals Court considered whether a superior court judge erred in entering an order authorizing blood transfusions to a seventeen-year old Jehovah's Witness.[138] In a pro-adolescents' rights decision, the court vacated the lower court's order.[139] Because Rena was no longer hospitalized the court concluded the issue was moot and did not remand the case for additional proceedings.[140] Clearly defining the applicable test,[141] the court placed particular emphasis on evaluating the minor's maturity.[142] In addition, the court directed judges to also consider the minor's wishes, if applicable, his or her religious convictions, and to receive testimony directly from the minor.[143] Accordingly, the *Rena* decision grants minors the right to determine their medical treatment and if their decision is contested by their parents or physician, they have judicial recourse.

Thus, the mature minor doctrine seeks to balance the privacy interests of the minor with the legitimate interests of the state and the parents.[144] However, critics have argued that the doctrine is vague

---

[134] *Swan*, 569 A.2d at 1206.

[135] *Id.* at 1205.

[136] *Id.*

[137] *Id.*

[138] *See In re* Rena, 705 N.E. 2d 1155 (Mass. 1999).

[139] *Id.*

[140] *Id.* at 1157.

[141] *Id.* at 1157 (stating " (1) the patient's expressed preferences, if any; (2) the patient's religious convictions, if any; (3) the impact on the patient's family; (4) the probability of adverse side effects from the treatment; (5) the prognosis without treatment; and (6) the present and future incompetency of the patient in making that decision").

[142] *Id.*

[143] *Id.*

[144] *See* Waters, *supra* note 78, at 90; Kohm & Lawrence, *supra* note 21, at

and ambiguous and fails to provide judges with clear guidelines for determining maturity.[145] Furthermore, other states have refused to adopt the mature minor doctrine.[146] As a result, minors in only a few states may rely on the mature minor doctrine to exercise their privacy right to decide their own medical treatment.[147]

III. THE NEED FOR CONSISTENCY: EXTENDING PRIVACY RIGHTS AND THE RIGHT OF SELF-DETERMINATION TO ADOLESCENTS' MEDICAL TREATMENT

In Massachusetts, a sixteen-year-old boy ran away from home to avoid chemotherapy treatment despite his parents' consent.[148] In California, a fifteen year old girl fled her home after being physically forced to succumb to chemotherapy, despite both her parents' and her

376.

145 *See* Waters, *supra* note 78, at 92, 98; *see also* Brewster, *supra* note 122, at 779 (arguing that the court's holding in *In re* E.G. was incorrect, because it did not adequately consider precedent case law, ignored the fact that blood transfusions were in E.G.'s best interest, and did not recognize the differences between abortion cases and blood transfusions); Rosato, *supra* note 41, at 22 (criticizing the courts that apply the mature minor doctrine for being too broad based in analysis).

146 *See, e.g.*, Novak v. Cobb County-Kennestone Hospital Authority, 849 F.Supp. 1559 (N.D. Ga., 1994); *In re* Long Island Jewish Medical Center, 557 N.Y.S.2d 239 (N.Y. Sup. Ct. 1990) (holding minor could not refuse blood transfusions due to lack of maturity, despite minor being only one month shy of his eighteenth birthday and refusing to adopt a mature minor doctrine); Commonwealth v. Nixon, 718 A.2d 311 (Pa. 1998) (holding parents' have a duty to override their child's refusal of medical treatment in life-threatening situations, despite child's mature minor status); O.G. v. Baum, 790 S.W.2d 839 (Tex. Ct. App. 1990) (distinguishing *In re E.G.* on the basis that the minor did not testify and that Texas did not have a mature minor standard); *see generally* Kun, *supra* note 115, at 439-41.

147 *See* discussion *supra* Part II.C.

148 *See* Traugott & Alpers, *supra* note 38, at 922-23; Hawkins, *supra* note 1, at 2075. In 1994, Billy Best of Norwell, Massachusetts ran away to Texas to avoid chemotherapy because "[he] could not stand going to the hospital every week" and felt like the medicine was killing him instead of curing him. *See* Traugott & Alpers, *supra* note 38, at 923. After being persuaded to return home through the media, Billy and his parents chose alternative therapy. *Id.* at 923.

lack of consent.[149] Another fifteen-year old who, with parental consent, chose to discontinue his medication and decline a third liver transplant, was forcibly removed by police from his home and hospitalized.[150] Another fifteen year old, suffering from end-stage cystic fibrosis, was placed on a ventilator despite his repeated wishes against life-prolonging measures, such as intubation and mechanical ventilation.[151]

The laws throughout this country are inconsistent with respect to a minor's ability to make his or her own medical decisions.[152] Depending on the state, a minor may be able to obtain an abortion or treatment for sexually transmitted diseases, but that same minor may not be able to choose the course of treatment for cancer.[153] Further, a minor as young as fourteen years old may be declared emancipated, based on financial independence, and may subsequently make his or her own medical decisions.[154] However, a terminally ill minor who has his or her family's support cannot refuse medical treatment.[155]

---

149 *See* Traugott & Alpers, *supra* note 38, at 923; Hawkins, *supra* note 1, at 2075. Lee Lor, a Hmong refugee, and her parents believed that "surgically removing the cancer would cause it to recur in someone else" and that Lee would be unable to fill her traditional role in Hmong society if the treatment resulted in infertility. *See* Traugott, *supra* note 38, at 923. A court order resulted in the forcible removal of Lee from her home and submission to chemotherapy, which Lee described as "torture." *Id.* at 923.

150 *See* Traugott & Alpers, *supra* note 38, at 923. Benny Agrelo was eight years old when he underwent his first liver-transplant. Five years later the a second liver transplant was performed. *Id.* Following this procedure Benny, which his mother's approval, decided to discontinue his medication therapy based on the desire to have "a few months of health" instead of "long-term survival with pain." *Id.* At fifteen Benny's doctors wanted to perform a third transplant and Benny and his mother refused, resulting in a court order to hospitalize Benny. *Id.* Eventually a judge ruled that Benny could return home without resuming his medication. Benny died two months later. *Id.*

151 *See* Weir, *supra* note 59, at 30. C.G. was hospitalized four times during his last year of life and repeatedly stated that he knew he did not have much longer to live and did not want to be on a ventilator. *Id.*

152 *See* Sher, *supra* note 35, at 159.

153 *See, e.g.*, Kun, *supra* note 115, at 424-25 (discussing the case of Billy Best who ran away from home after two and one-half months of chemotherapy and learning from doctors that four more months of treatment was required).

154 *See supra* note 62 and accompanying text.

155 *See supra* notes 149-150 and accompanying text.

A. Informed Consent

A patient must give informed consent before a physician may proceed with treatment.[156] This common law doctrine requires a physician to explain to the patient the diagnosis, treatment options, the risks and benefits of each option, and prognosis.[157] If a physician fails to explain these issues and fails to obtain the consent of the patient, he or she may be liable for an intentional tort of battery.[158] This doctrine resulted from common law out of respect for individual autonomy[159] and continues to allow "individuals the freedom to make certain choices about their lives that comport with their own values."[160]

The right to be informed about medical treatment and to consent to or refuse treatment is a fundamental right, afforded only to adults.[161] As early as 1891, the United States Supreme Court declared in *Union Pacific Railway Company v. Botsford*[162] that "[n]o right is held more sacred, or is more carefully guarded, by the common law, than the right of every individual to the possession and control of his

---

156 *See* Penkower, *supra* note 99, at 1170 (discussing the doctrine of informed consent as it applies to adults); *see also* Hawkins, *supra* note 1, at 2093-94; Rosato, *supra* note 41, at 10-14.

157 *See* Penkower, *supra* note 99, at 1170; *see also* Hawkins, *supra* note 1, at 2093.

158 *See* Hawkins, *supra* note 1, at 2094 (explaining the common law doctrine of informed consent and one's right to make treatment decisions).

159 *See* Hawkins, *supra* note 1, at 2094; *see also* Penkower, *supra* note 99, at 1169-70; Redding, *supra* note 34, at 704-05; Rosato, *supra* note 41, at 10-11.

160 *See* Penkower, *supra* note 99, at 1169.

161 *See* Andrew Popper, *Averting Malpractice By Information: Informed Consent in the Pediatric Treatment Environment*, 47 DEPAUL L. REV. 819, 821-22 (1998) (suggesting initiation of a broad survey to learn what occurs when children are informed about treatment decisions); *see also* Julie A. Koehne, *Witnesses on Trial: Judicial Intrusion Upon the Practices of Jehovah's Witness Parents*, 21 FLA. ST. U. L. REV. 205, 207 (1993) (arguing that Jehovah's Witnesses should be able "to adhere to the principles of their chosen faith and raise their children accordingly without interference from courts").

162 141 U.S. 250 (1891).

own person, free from all restraint or interference of others."[163] The *Botsford* court specifically held that an individual could not be forced to submit to unwanted medical treatment.[164] The Court has affirmed this right in more recent cases, including the so-called "right to die case": *Cruzan v. Director, Mo. Dep't of Health.*[165] Although some have declared that *Cruzan* finally established a constitutional right to die,[166] the Court only stated that "a competent person has a constitutionally protected liberty interest in refusing unwanted medical treatment."[167] Thus, a patient who may give consent to a treatment plan may also withhold consent and either forego all treatment or seek alternative methods.[168]

On the contrary, when it comes to treatment decisions for minors, the right of informed consent does not rest with the adolescent patient, it rests with his or her parents or legal guardians.[169] If a parent refuses "necessary" treatment, the state can challenge that decision, claiming neglect, and can obtain both temporary legal custody and the authorization to make treatment decisions for the minor child.[170] The minor's wishes and desires are virtually ignored.[171] Occasionally, the parents will agree with the physicians on the preferred course of treatment, but the minor will disagree.[172] When the minor's choice is different than that of his or her parents and physician, litigation is unlikely because there is not a legal

---

[163] *Id.* at 251.

[164] *Id.* at 257.

[165] 497 U.S. 261, 269 (1990) (stating that value of bodily integrity is embodied in the doctrine of informed consent). *See also* Rochin v. California, 342 U.S. 165, 175 (1952) (holding that forced stomach pumping is "offensive to human dignity."); Schmerber v. California, 384 U.S. 757, 772 (1966) (stating that the "integrity of an individual's person is a cherished value in our society.").

[166] *See* Penkower, *supra* note 99, at 1172 & n.40.

[167] *See Cruzan*, 497 U.S. at 278.

[168] *See* Penkower, *supra* note 99, at 1170.

[169] *See* Hawkins, *supra* note 1, at 2079.

[170] *Id.*

[171] *Id.* at 2080.

[172] *See supra* note 148 and accompanying text.

process that allows a minor to challenge the parent's consent.[173] Thus, when an unemancipated minor needs medical treatment, with the exception of an abortion or treatment for a sexually transmitted disease, the premise that minors are incapable of making informed decisions and that adults know best prevails.[174]

B. Adolescents Are Capable of Making Informed Decisions

Crucial to successful medical treatment is the consent, cooperation, and participation of the patient.[175] The medical community, as well as some legal scholars, have realized that minors should be allowed to participate in determining what course their medical treatment should take and that minors are in fact capable of doing so.[176] In fact, researchers have found "that children often are capable of making important life decisions in a rational matter, including decisions about medical and psychological treatment."[177] Further, if a minor is included in the decision-making process and provides informed consent for his or her treatment the effectiveness of the treatment will improve.[178]

---

173 *See* Hawkins, *supra* note 1, at 2080 (hypothesizing that even if a mechanism existed courts would probably not consider the case on the basis that minors lack legal standing and parents have ultimate authority over their children).

174 *See, e.g.*, Parham v. J.R., 442 U.S. 584, 603 (1979) (stating "most children, even in adolescence, simply are not able to make sound judgments . . . including their need for medical care or treatment. Parents can and must make those judgments."); *see also* Popper, *supra* note 161, at 833 (discussing results of a survey of pediatricians in which more than half agreed that "parental anxiety or other factors . . . cause many parents to consent . . . without fully exploring the alternatives and risks of treatment").

175 *See* Michael A. Grodin & Joel J. Alpert, *Informed Consent and Pediatric Care*, *in* CHILDREN'S COMPETENCE TO CONSENT, 93 at 94 (Gary B. Melton et. al. eds., 1983); *see also* Redding, *supra* note 34, at 709 (stating that "[c]linicians agree treatment outcomes are poor when children are forced to receive treatment").

176 *See* Redding, *supra* note 34, at 708; *see also* Hawkins, *supra* note 1, at 2118-19; Weir, *supra* note 59, at 31.

177 *See* Redding, *supra* note 34, at 707.

178 *See* Redding, *supra* note 34, at 709 (discussing the impact of recent research on the traditional views of children's competence); *see also* Popper, *supra* note 161, at 826 (stating that "the rate and quality of healing and recovery is higher with

Recognizing the discrepancies in statutory and case law, the American Academy of Pediatrics Task Force ("the Task Force") issued guidelines for physicians who treat minors.[179] The Task Force declared that if the procedure is either elective surgery or treatment and the minor is thirteen years of age or older, the minor's written consent should be obtained.[180] In addition, the Task Force suggested that children older than seven years of age should be provided an opportunity to also consent or assent to treatment.[181] In determining whether a child between seven and thirteen years old is able to comprehend the implications of undergoing or foregoing a medical procedure, the Task Force instructs pediatricians to consider the child's "age, disease, severity, prognosis, risks, and proposed benefits of therapy," as well as expert opinions concerning the adolescent "patient's level of intelligence, reasoning ability, and emotional state."[182]

Adolescents as young as twelve years of age are capable of understanding the nature of their medical problems.[183] Some

informed patients than with those who do not understand the nature of their treatments").

[179] *See* American Academy of Pediatrics, Task Force on Pediatric Research, Informed Consent, and Medical Ethics, *Consent*, 57 PEDIATRICS 414, 415 (1976); *see also* Weir, *supra* note 59, at 32 (discussing the Pediatric Bill of Rights, adopted by the National Association of Children's Hospitals in 1974, which states any minor "who is of sufficient intelligence to appreciate the nature and consequences of the proposed medical care and if such medical care is for his own benefit, may effectively consent to such medical care in doctor-patient confidentiality"); The United Nations Convention on the Rights of the Child, G.A. Res. 44/25, U.S. GAOR, 44th Sess., Supp. No. 49 at 166, U.N. Doc. A/44/736 (1989), *revised by* U.N. doc. A/RES/44/25/Corr.1 (1990), *reprinted in* 28 I.L.M. 1456 (1989). "States Parties shall assure to the child who is capable of forming his or her own views the right to express those views freely in all matters affecting the child, the views of the child being given due weight in accordance with the age and maturity of the child." *Id.* President Clinton signed the Convention in 1995, however, the United States Congress has not ratified the Convention.

[180] *See* Grodin & Alpert, *supra* note 175, at 95 (detailing the proclamations of the American Academy of Pediatrics).

[181] *Id.*

[182] *Id.*

[183] *See generally* Redding, *supra* note 34, at 708; Grodin, *supra* note 175, at 96-97; Weir, *supra* note 59, at 31; Traugott & Alpers, *supra* note 38, at 924. The variation in an agreed upon age of competency lends further support for the need to evaluate a minor's competence on an individual basis. *See* Rosato, *supra* note 41, at 51.

professionals are concerned that adolescent patients, who by nature are seeking to establish their independence and individualism, may choose a course of treatment that is not within their best interests in an effort to gain the acceptance of their peers or defy their parents.[184] However, this is not true of all adolescents.[185] Thus, it is imperative for physicians to put aside preconceived notions of adolescent nature and focus on the individual adolescent patient's maturity and capacity.[186]

The problem however, is that the courts continue to rely on "traditional assumptions about children's abilities, and idealistic views about the role of parents in making decisions for their children."[187] Thus, if the physician follows the Task Force guidelines[188] and respects the adolescent patient's choice to refuse treatment the state may still intervene and consent to the procedure against the wishes of the patient and parents.[189]

IV. When The Adolescent Should Decide

Since adolescents are capable of making competent decisions, the question becomes whether it is appropriate for them to do so and what limitations, if any, should be placed on their decision-making

[184] *See* Grodin & Alpert, *supra* note 175, at 96; *see also* Traugott & Alpers, *supra* note 38, at 924.

[185] *See* Grodin & Alpert, *supra* note 175, at 96-97.

[186] *Id.* at 96-97. Grodin and Alpert also point out that the type of illness is a critical factor in determining the significance to be placed on a minor's articulated desire. *Id.* at 97. Thus, the more chronic disease the more likely that the minor is capable of making an informed, competent decision, based on a significant history of dealing with the illness. *Id.*

[187] Redding, *supra* note 34, at 705 and discussion of United States Supreme Court cases at 705-06.

[188] *But see* Popper, *supra* note 161, at 822. "In practice, however, 'few children are asked if they agree . . . to having a blood test, or to being given a drug, or to having an operation.'" *Id.* (quoting George Rylance, *Making Decisions with Children: A Child's Rights to Share in Health Decisions Can No Longer Be Ignored*, 312 BRIT. MED. J. 794, 794 (1996)).

[189] *See supra* notes 148-152 and accompanying text.

process. Many children's rights advocates believe that a presumption of competence should be extended to adolescents, allowing them to make medical treatment decisions unless proven incompetent.[190] Changing this exception and extending the fundamental right of informed consent and bodily integrity to adolescents will grant greater autonomy and freedom to the minor and will place the burden on those who wish to abridge these rights.[191]

Medical decisions are premised on the belief that the treatment chosen will promote the best interests of the patient. Supposedly, this will mean that the expected benefits of treatment will outweigh the possible harms.[192] Thus, in making the decision several factors, such as the quality and duration of life, the adverse effects and duration of therapy, and the likelihood of success, will be important variables in deciding what form of treatment is best for the individual adolescent.[193] Values and cultural perspectives will also play a very important role in determining the appropriate course of treatment.[194] For some adolescent patients, quality of life, during what is inevitably the end-stages of a terminal illness may be more important than extended treatment with limited benefits.[195] Other adolescent patients may place a higher value on the ability to play and interact with peers instead of being hospitalized.[196]

The ability to cure a minor's illness is also an important factor in considering whether to order treatment regardless of objections by the parents or the minor.[197] There is currently an indication that the

---

[190] *See* Hawkins, *supra* note 1, at 2129 (putting forth the ideas of children's rights advocates Hillary Rodham Clinton and Henry Foster's position "that the presumption that children are incompetent should be set aside"). *See also* Weir, *supra* note 59, at 36 (advocating for a rebuttable presumption of competence in adolescents between fourteen and seventeen).

[191] *See* Weir, *supra* note 59, at 39.

[192] *See* Traugott & Alpers, *supra* note 38, at 924.

[193] *Id.* at 925.

[194] *Id.*

[195] *Id.*

[196] *Id.*

[197] *See* Plastine, *supra* note 54, at 150.

courts will be more willing to respect the adolescent patient's or the parents' choice if the child is suffering from an incurable affliction.[198] For instance, in *Newmark v. Williams*,[199] the Supreme Court of Delaware held that Colin Newmark was not a neglected child under Delaware law, and the State could not intervene and compel treatment because the egregious facts of Colin's case outweighed the State's authority to intervene in the parent-child relationship.[200] Colin suffered from a deadly form of pediatric cancer and the proposed course of treatment offered less than a 40% chance of "success."[201] Although Colin was too young to be involved in deciding what treatment would be utilized,[202] his parents, practicing Christian Scientists,[203] desired to treat their son spiritually through prayer

198 *See, e.g.*, Newmark v. Williams, 588 A.2d 1108 (Del. 1991); *See In re* Philip B., 156 Cal. Rptr. 48 (Cal. Ct. App. 1979), *cert. denied*, 445 U.S. 949 (1980) (upholding parents' constitutional right of parental autonomy by respecting their decision to withhold cardiac surgery for their twelve year old child who was suffering from a congenital heart deformity and Down's syndrome); *In re* Green, 292 A.2d 387 (Pa. 1972) (upholding wishes of parents who refused blood transfusions for child with paralytic scoliosis); *In re* D.P., No. 91950 (Santa Clara County Juv. Ct. July 3, 1986) (holding that fourteen year old cancer patient who refused blood transfusions could not be kept in the hospital against her will). *But see In re* Sieferth, 127 N.E.2d 820 (N.Y. 1955) (declining to order surgery to correct child's cleft palate and harelip when there was no serious threat to child's life or health).

199 588 A.2d 1108.

200 *Id.* at 1118. The Court focused on the nature of the proposed treatment, stating that it was "highly invasive, painful, involved terrible temporary and potentially permanent side effects, posed an unacceptably low chance of success, and a high risk that the treatment itself would cause death." *Id.*

201 *See id.* at 1109-10. Colin was only three years old when diagnosed with Burkitt's Lymphoma. *Id.*

202 Although Colin was unable to make his own treatment decisions, this case illustrates that the courts are not going to order treatment over objections of those legally authorized to give consent if the illness is incurable. Should the laws be expanded to grant adolescents the right to give or with hold consent this premise would likely apply. *Id.* at 1118.

203 The First Church of Christ, Scientist, was founded in 1879 by Mary Baker Eddy and teaches its members that diseases and sickness are manifestations of the mind that can be overcome by praying and drawing closer to God. *See* Janna C. Merrick, *Christian Science Healing of Minor Children: Spiritual Exemption Statutes, First Amendment Rights, and Fair Notice*, 10 ISSUES L. & MED. 321, 325 (1994); *see also*

instead of with chemotherapy.[204] In contrast, when a minor's condition is life threatening, but curable, courts have declared minors neglected when parents withhold consent for treatment.[205] Further, the courts will intervene even in situations where the minor's affliction is not life threatening.[206] Thus, the courts will be less likely to intervene and order medical treatment as "the level of bodily invasion rises and the prognosis dims."[207]

A. The Physician's Role

The physician has a key role in the decision-making process, and that role should begin long before choosing or implementing the course of treatment.[208] The physician must educate both the adolescent and his or her family about treatment options and expected outcomes and negotiate a treatment plan that is acceptable to everyone

---

Elizabeth A. Lingle, *Treating Children by Faith Colliding Constitutional Issues*, 17 J. LEGAL MED. 301, 306 (1996).

[204] *See Newmark*, 588 A.2d at 1109.

[205] *See, e.g.*, People ex rel. D.L.E., 645 P.2d 271 (Colo. 1982) (holding that when parents refuse medical treatment for their child on religious grounds, the state can meet its burden by demonstrating that the child suffers from a life-threatening, but curable condition); *In re* Ivey, 319 So. 2d 53 (Fla. Dist. Ct. App. 1975) (ordering blood-transfusions for a child whose life was endangered by the parents refusal to consent to the procedure); *In re* McCauley, 565 N.E.2d 411 (Mass. 1991) (holding that life-saving blood transfusions were in the best interest of the child and outweighed the parents' constitutional objections).

[206] *See, e.g.*, *In re* Eric B., 235 Cal. Rptr. 22 (Cal. Ct. App. 1987) (ordering periodic monitoring of child to detect possible reoccurrence of cancer over parents' religious objections); *In re* Karwath, 199 N.W.2d 147 (Iowa 1972) (ordering surgical removal of child's tonsils and adenoids over father's religious objections); *In re* Sampson, 317 N.Y.S.2d 641 (N.Y. Fam. Ct. 1970), *aff'd*, 323 N.Y.S.2d 253 (N.Y. App. Div. 1971), *aff'd*, 278 N.E.2d 918 (N.Y. 1972) (ordering child to undergo a risky surgical procedure that would partially correct, but not cure, child's non-life-threatening facial deformity, over his mother's religious objections); *In re* Gregory S., 380 N.Y.S.2d 620 (N.Y. Fam. Ct. 1976) (upholding state intervention where mother refused medical and dental care for child suffering from cavities, fractured teeth, and an umbilical hernia); Mitchell v. Davis, 205 S.W.2d 812 (Tex. Civ. App. 1947) (holding that mother's faith in spiritual healing was not a defense to a prosecution for child neglect where mother refused to provide medical treatment for son's arthritic knee).

[207] *See* Plastine, *supra* note 54, at 149.

[208] *See* Traugott & Alpers, *supra* note 38, at 925.

involved.[209] Thus, the physician's first task is to provide the adolescent patient, as he or she would any patient, with information about his or her diagnosis, the nature of the recommended procedure including the risks, and the prognosis if the procedure is performed as well as other alternative medical treatments.[210] However, the physician must simultaneously determine the "adolescent's decision-making capacity by determining whether he or she understands the recommended therapy, the alternatives, the risks and the benefits, and the likely consequences of refusal."[211] Based on the close relationship with the adolescent patient and daily experience with adolescents with same or similar conditions, the physician is the most qualified to determine whether the minor is capable of making an informed and competent decision.[212] Should a dispute arise between the parents' and the adolescent's choice of treatment, the physician should act as a negotiator to facilitate a compromise.[213] In doing so, the physician should use the same criteria to evaluate the parents' decision, and assess the overall relationship between the adolescent and his or her parents.[214] As a negotiator, the physician must listen to and acknowledge the adolescent patient's concerns.[215] By carefully listening to the adolescent patient's reasons for refusal or for choosing one therapy over another, the physician will be better able to address and alleviate the concerns, which may actually lead to the adolescent accepting a beneficial treatment that he or she was originally

---

209 *Id.*

210 *See* Penkower, *supra* note 99, at 1170. *See also supra* notes 157-160 with accompanying text.

211 *See* Traugott & Alpers, *supra* note 38, at 925.

212 *See* Waters, *supra* note 78, at 113-14 (suggesting that "trained and qualified medical professionals can best determine an individual minor's maturity and best interests"). The United States Supreme Court has upheld medical-review procedures in other areas. *See, e.g.*, Parham v. J.R., 442 U.S. 584, 607 (1979) (conditioning parental decision to commit a child to a state's mental hospital on an independent review by the state's hospital authorities).

213 *See* Traugott & Alpers, *supra* note 38, at 925.

214 *Id.*

215 *Id.* at 926.

unwilling to undergo.[216]

When the conflict is severe, hospital ethics committees can assist in this process.[217] All hospitals are required by the Joint Commission on Accreditation of Healthcare Organizations to implement process for resolving patient care disputes.[218] It is suggested that such committees include an expert in adolescent medicine, such as an adolescent psychiatrist or psychologist, and if a non-Western culture is involved, a representative of that community.[219] If the dispute can be resolved at this level, child welfare officials or courts will not need to become involved.[220]

As discussed above, the best interests of the adolescent patient will control, however, non-medical factors may be as important as medical factors in determining what is the best interest of the adolescent patient, especially if the adolescent places great weight on them.[221] Thus, the physician should consider the quality of life as well as the duration of life when determining what is in the adolescent patient's best interest.[222]

The cultural perspective of the patient and his or her family is also a crucial factor that must be considered.[223] The *Lor* case[224]

---

216 *Id.* Adolescents tend to be particularly concerned with peer acceptance. *Id.* For instance, a refusal to undergo chemotherapy treatment, may be, in part, out of concern for physical appearance at an important upcoming social occasion. *Id.*

217 *See* Traugott & Alpers, *supra* note 38, at 926.

218 *Id.*

219 *Id.*; *see also* Rosato, *supra* note 41, at 13-14 (discussing how treatment decisions "shape the definition of one's entire life").

220 *Id.*; *see also* Redding, *supra* note 34, at 739. With respect to mental health treatment Redding suggests that a clinician and attorney work as a team to determine whether a minor is capable of giving consent; the attorney guarding the legal rights of the child and the clinician assessing the child's ability to consent. *Id.* This system may also work in other medical situations, although it may be more cumbersome than necessary. *Id.* at 739-40

221 *See* Traugott & Alpers, *supra* note 38, at 926.

222 *Id. See also supra* note 208 and accompanying text.

223 *See* Traugott & Alpers, *supra* note 38, at 925.

224 See sources cited *supra* note 149 and accompanying text for a discussion of the Lor case.

illustrates how non-Western cultures may have different views about the adolescent's best interest.[225] In cases such as this one, the physician should consider whether the adolescent embraces the values of his or her culture and whether non-Western treatment may be a viable alternative.[226] Above all, the physician should maintain a sense of neutrality, by not imposing his or her beliefs and value system on the adolescent and, instead, should respect the views of the informed adolescent.[227]

B. The Court's Role

Involvement of the court in the treatment decision may only further exacerbate the situation between the adolescent, family, and physicians. However, until adolescents in all jurisdictions are afforded the constitutional right to give informed consent, and even once this right is granted, it may, at times be necessary to resort to litigation and involve judges in the decision-making process.[228] When agreement cannot be reached regarding an adolescent's medical treatment, either the physician, hospital, or state may request the court to authorize treatment, or empower a third party with the right to consent on behalf of the patient.[229]

When deciding who gets to choose the course of medical treatment, the judge "should not assume that a broad parental autonomy right dictates the outcome."[230] Instead, the judge should focus on the best interests of the adolescent patient, granting more weight to the adolescent's wishes, while not ignoring the positions of the physicians, the state, and the parents.[231] In fact, many, if not all,

---

[225] *See* Traugott & Alpers, *supra* note 38, at 925.

[226] *Id.*

[227] *Id.*

[228] *Id.* at 926.

[229] *Id.*

[230] *See* Sher, *supra* note 35, at 184.

[231] *See* Traugott & Alpers, *supra* note 38, at 926; *see also* Rosato, *supra* note 41, at 50 (arguing the "judge's initial and most important determination will be whether the minor demonstrated his maturity by clear and convincing evidence").

of the factors the physician needs to assess in determining the adolescent patient's ability to consent should also be considered and weighed by the judge.[232]

In evaluating a case, the courts should utilize experts in adolescent medicine in order to obtain a reliable understanding of the particularities of the adolescent's case.[233] These experts should interview the patient and offer testimony both about the decision-making capabilities of the typical adolescent and this particular individual.[234] If based on all of the testimony, the court concludes that the adolescent is capable of making an informed decision, the adolescent's choice should be respected.[235] If the adolescent is not capable of making such a decision, the alternative would be to determine which treatment option would be in the adolescent patient's best interest.[236]

The judicial bypass procedure authorized in *Bellotti*[237] is an alternative method which allow adolescents to seek the medical treatment they desire.[238] In a judicial bypass hearing the judge would determine if the minor has the maturity and capability to consent to treatment.[239] This type of legal proceeding most likely would occur if the parents and adolescent were in conflict as to the preferred course

---

[232] *See supra* Part V.A. Professor Rosato also argues that a state's interest should only prevail if "treatment is nonexperimental and when a significant probability exists that the condition or disease will be cured or that the major symptoms of the condition will be alleviated in the foreseeable future." *See* Rosato, *supra* note 41, at 50, 68-69, & 83-87. This argument would result, for example, in court ordered blood transfusion of a Jehovah's Witness if such treatment would save his or her life. Similarly, the court would have been forced to reach a different conclusion in the *Swan* case. *See* discussion *supra* notes 131-137 and accompanying text. *See also* Rosato, *supra* note 41, at 87-94.

[233] *See* Traugott & Alpers, *supra* note 38, at 926.

[234] *Id.*

[235] *Id.*

[236] *Id.*

[237] *See* Bellotti v. Baird, 443 U.S. 622, 643 (1979); *see also supra* note 93 and accompanying text.

[238] *See* Traugott & Alpers, *supra* note 38, at 926-27.

[239] *Id.* at 927.

of treatment and neither the hospital nor state intervened first.[240] Such a mechanism would place the burden on the adolescent patient to take legal action in order to have his or her choice considered.[241] In cases where the adolescent is seriously ill this may be a very difficult, if not impractical, option.[242] Thus, a more practical approach would be to allow the physician to assess the adolescent's decision-making capacity, as discussed above, and only resort to a court procedure in the most extreme cases.[243]

CONCLUSION

The exceptions that the Supreme Court and legislatures have made with regard to an adolescent's ability to consent to medical treatment are inconsistent with the traditional legal doctrine that a minor is incapable of giving consent. However, research has shown that adolescents are in fact as capable of making complex decisions as adults.[244] In light of this fact, the law should give way to the trend established in the areas of emancipation and abortion and embrace the mature minor doctrine.

Under the current scheme, a presumably immature minor may still obtain an abortion. Furthermore, if the minor opts to have the child, she has legal authority to make medical decisions for the child, regardless of the fact that she is prohibited from making any medical treatment choices for herself. In contrast, a mature adolescent, who has dealt with the complexities of an incurable illness, does not have a legal voice in deciding treatment. In addition, the inconsistencies that exist make it extremely difficult to know whether a court will intervene and to what extent.[245] What has happened is the legislature

---

240 *Id.*

241 *Id.*

242 *Id.*

243 *See* Traugott & Alpers, *supra* note 38, at 927.

244 *See* Redding, *supra* note 34, at 707-09.

245 *See* Sher, *supra* note 35, at 159.

and courts have reacted to specific teen "crises," such as pregnancy and sexually transmitted disease, and have not actually carved out these consent exceptions because they believe minor's have a right to privacy or self-determination.[246]

These inconsistencies make it clear that there is a need to reevaluate whether adolescents should be allowed to consent to medical care. Based on the Supreme Court's declaration that minors have constitutional rights, including the right to privacy,[247] and minors ability to make complex decisions a rebuttable presumption of competency should be granted to adolescents. This presumption of capacity should only be challenged if there is strong evidence that the adolescent is actually incompetent to make such important decisions. The adolescent's physician should play the paramount role in assessing the adolescent's decision-making ability. Where conflict arises that the physician is incapable of resolving through negotiation with the adolescent and the adolescent's parents, a hospital ethics committee would be the next appropriate dispute resolution method. The courts should only be used as a last resort in resolving conflict. The few states that have recognized the mature minor doctrine have realized that age is an arbitrary method of determining capacity. It is time that the rest of the legal community also acknowledge this obvious principle. By creating this rebuttable presumption adolescents will finally enjoy their rights of informed consent, bodily integrity, self-determination, and privacy to the fullest extent.

Christine M. Hanisco

---

[246] *See* Walter J. Wadlington, *Consent to Medical Care for Minors*, *in* CHILDREN'S COMPETENCE TO CONSENT 57, 73 (Gary B. Melton et. al. eds., 1983); *see also* Rosato, *supra* note 41, at 29.

[247] *See* discussion *supra* notes 73-99 and accompanying text.

CAREY, GOVERNOR OF NEW YORK, ET AL. *v.* POPULATION SERVICES INTERNATIONAL ET AL.

APPEAL FROM THE UNITED STATES DISTRICT COURT FOR THE SOUTHERN DISTRICT OF NEW YORK

No. 75-443. Argued January 10, 1977—Decided June 9, 1977

Section 6811 (8) of the New York Education Law makes it a crime (1) for any person to sell or distribute any contraceptive of any kind to a minor under 16; (2) for anyone other than a licensed pharmacist to distribute contraceptives to persons 16 or over; and (3) for anyone, including licensed pharmacists, to advertise or display contraceptives. In appellees' action against appellant state officials challenging the constitutionality of § 6811 (8), a three-judge District Court declared the statute unconstitutional in its entirety under the First and Fourteenth Amendments insofar as it applies to nonprescription contraceptives, and enjoined its enforcement as so applied. *Held:* The judgment is affirmed. Pp. 682-703; 707-708; 713-716.

398 F. Supp. 321, affirmed.

MR. JUSTICE BRENNAN delivered the opinion of the Court with respect to Parts I, II, III, and V, finding that:

1. Appellee Population Planning Associates (PPA), a corporation that makes mail-order sales of nonmedical contraceptive devices from its North Carolina offices and regularly advertises its products in New York periodicals and fills mail orders from New York residents without limiting availability of the products to persons of any particular age, has the requisite standing to maintain the action not only in its own right but also on behalf of its potential customers, *Craig* v. *Boren*, 429 U. S. 190, and therefore there is no occasion to decide the standing of the other appellees. Pp. 682-684.

2. Regulations imposing a burden on a decision as fundamental as whether to bear or beget a child may be justified only by compelling state interests, and must be narrowly drawn to express only those interests. Pp. 684-686.

3. The provision prohibiting distribution of nonmedical contraceptives to persons 16 or over except through licensed pharmacists clearly burdens the right of such individuals to use contraceptives if they so desire, and the provision serves no compelling state interests. It cannot be justified by an interest in protecting health insofar as it applies

to nonhazardous contraceptives or in protecting potential life, nor can it be justified by a concern that young people not sell contraceptives, or as being designed to serve as a quality control device or as facilitating enforcement of the other provisions of the statute. Pp. 686–691.

4. The prohibition of any advertisement or display of contraceptives that seeks to suppress completely any information about the availability and price of contraceptives cannot be justified on the ground that advertisements of contraceptive products would offend and embarrass those exposed to them and that permitting them would legitimize sexual activity of young people. These are classically not justifications validating suppression of expression protected by the First Amendment, and here the advertisements in question merely state the availability of products that are not only entirely legal but constitutionally protected. Pp. 700–702.

MR. JUSTICE BRENNAN, joined by MR. JUSTICE STEWART, MR. JUSTICE MARSHALL, and MR. JUSTICE BLACKMUN, concluded in Part IV that the provision prohibiting distribution of contraceptives to persons under 16, as applied to nonprescription contraceptives, cannot be justified as a permissible regulation of minors' morality in furtherance of the State's policy against promiscuous sexual intercourse among the young. Pp. 691–699.

(a) The right to privacy in connection with decisions affecting procreation extends to minors as well as to adults, and since a State may not impose a blanket prohibition, or even a blanket requirement of parental consent, on the choice of a minor to terminate her pregnancy, *Planned Parenthood of Missouri* v. *Danforth,* 428 U. S. 52, the constitutionality of a blanket prohibition of the distribution of contraceptives to minors is *a fortiori* foreclosed. Pp. 693–694.

(b) The argument that sexual activity may be deterred by increasing the hazards attendant on it has been rejected by the Court as a justification for restrictions on the freedom to choose whether to bear or beget a child. *Eisenstadt* v. *Baird,* 405 U. S. 438, 448; *Roe* v. *Wade,* 410 U. S. 113, 148. Moreover, there is substantial doubt whether limiting access to contraceptives will in fact substantially discourage early sexual behavior. When a State, as here, burdens the exercise of a fundamental right, its attempt to justify that burden as a rational means for the accomplishment of some state policy requires more than the unsupported assertion (appellants here having conceded that there is no evidence that teenage extramarital sexual activity increases in proportion to the availability of contraceptives) that the burden is connected to such a policy. Pp. 694–696.

(c) That under another provision of the statute a minor under 16 may be supplied with a contraceptive by a physician does not save the challenged provision, especially where appellants asserted no medical necessity for imposing a limitation on the distribution of nonprescription contraceptives to minors. Pp. 697–699.

MR. JUSTICE WHITE concluded that the prohibition against distribution of contraceptives to persons under 16 cannot be justified primarily because the State has not demonstrated that such prohibition measurably contributes to the deterrent purposes that the State advances as justification. Pp. 702–703.

MR. JUSTICE POWELL concluded that the prohibition against distribution of contraceptives to persons under 16 is defective both because it infringes the privacy interests of married females between the ages of 14 and 16 and because it prohibits parents from distributing contraceptives to their children, thus unjustifiably interfering with parental interests in rearing children. Pp. 707–708.

MR. JUSTICE STEVENS concluded that the prohibition against distribution of contraceptives to persons under 16 denies such persons and their parents a choice which, if available, would reduce exposure to venereal disease or unwanted pregnancy, and that the prohibition cannot be justified as a means of discouraging sexual activity by minors. Pp. 713–716.

BRENNAN, J., announced the Court's judgment and delivered an opinion of the Court (Parts I, II, III, and V), in which STEWART, MARSHALL, BLACKMUN, and STEVENS, JJ., joined; in all but Part II of which WHITE, J., joined; and in Part I of which POWELL, J., joined; and an opinion (Part IV), in which STEWART, MARSHALL, and BLACKMUN, JJ., joined. WHITE, J., *post,* p. 702, POWELL, J., *post,* p. 703, and STEVENS, J., *post,* p. 712, filed opinions concurring in part and concurring in the judgment. BURGER, C. J., dissented. REHNQUIST, J., filed a dissenting opinion, *post,* p. 717.

Arlene R. Silverman, Assistant Attorney General of New York, argued the cause for appellants. With her on the briefs were *Louis J. Lefkowitz,* Attorney General, and *Samuel A. Hirshowitz,* First Assistant Attorney General.

Michael N. Pollet argued the cause for appellees. With him on the brief was *Steven Delibert.**

*Briefs of *amici curiae* urging affirmance were filed by *Melvin L. Wulf,*

MR. JUSTICE BRENNAN delivered the opinion of the Court (Parts I, II, III, and V), together with an opinion (Part IV), in which MR. JUSTICE STEWART, MR. JUSTICE MARSHALL, and MR. JUSTICE BLACKMUN joined.

Under New York Educ. Law § 6811 (8) (McKinney 1972) it is a crime (1) for any person to sell or distribute any contraceptive of any kind to a minor under the age of 16 years; (2) for anyone other than a licensed pharmacist to distribute contraceptives to persons 16 or over; and (3) for anyone, including licensed pharmacists, to advertise or display contraceptives.[1] A three-judge District Court for the Southern District of New York declared § 6811 (8) unconstitutional in its entirety under the First and Fourteenth Amendments of the

Judith M. Mears, and *Rena Uviller* for the American Civil Liberties Union; and by *Harriet F. Pilpel* and *Eve W. Paul* for the Planned Parenthood Federation of America et al.

[1] Section 6811 (8) provides:

"It shall be a class A misdemeanor for:

. . . . .

"8. Any person to sell or distribute any instrument or article, or any recipe, drug or medicine for the prevention of contraception to a minor under the age of sixteen years; the sale or distribution of such to a person other than a minor under the age of sixteen years is authorized only by a licensed pharmacist but the advertisement or display of said articles, within or without the premises of such pharmacy, is hereby prohibited."

After some dispute in the District Court the parties apparently now agree that Education Law § 6807 (b) (McKinney 1972) constitutes an exception to the distribution prohibitions of § 6811 (8). Section 6807 (b) provides:

"This article shall not be construed to affect or prevent:

. . . . .

"(b) Any physician . . . who is not the owner of a pharmacy, or registered store, or who is not in the employ of such owner, from supplying his patients with such drugs as the physician . . . deems proper in connection with his practice . . . ."

The definition of "drugs" in Education Law § 6802 (7) (McKinney 1972) apparently includes any contraceptive drug or device. See nn. 7, 13, and 23, and text, *infra,* at 697–699. See also 398 F. Supp. 321, 329–330, and n. 8.

Federal Constitution insofar as it applies to nonprescription contraceptives, and enjoined its enforcement as so applied. 398 F. Supp. 321 (1975). We noted probable jurisdiction, 426 U. S. 918 (1976). We affirm.

I

We must address a preliminary question of the standing of the various appellees to maintain the action. We conclude that appellee Population Planning Associates, Inc. (PPA) has the requisite standing and therefore have no occasion to decide the standing of the other appellees.[2]

PPA is a corporation primarily engaged in the mail-order retail sale of nonmedical contraceptive devices from its offices in North Carolina. PPA regularly advertises its products in periodicals published or circulated in New York, accepts orders from New York residents, and fills orders by mailing contraceptives to New York purchasers. Neither the advertisements nor the order forms accompanying them limit availability of PPA's products to persons of any particular age.

Various New York officials have advised PPA that its activities violate New York law. A letter of December 1, 1971, notified PPA that a PPA advertisement in a New York college newspaper violated § 6811 (8), citing each of the three challenged provisions, and requested "future compliance" with the

---

[2] In addition to PPA, the plaintiffs in the District Court, appellees here, are Population Services International, a nonprofit corporation disseminating birth control information and services; Rev. James B. Hagen, a minister and director of a venereal disease prevention program that distributes contraceptive devices; three physicians specializing in family planning, pediatrics, and obstetrics-gynecology; and an adult New York resident who alleges that the statute inhibits his access to contraceptive devices and information, and his freedom to distribute the same to his minor children. The District Court held that PPA and Hagen had standing, and therefore found it unnecessary to decide the standing of the other plaintiffs. *Id.*, at 327–330.

The appellants here, defendants in the District Court, are state officials responsible for the enforcement of the Education Law provisions.

law. A second letter, dated February 23, 1973, notifying PPA that PPA's magazine advertisements of contraceptives violated the statute, referred particularly to the provisions prohibiting sales to minors and sales by nonpharmacists, and threatened: "In the event you fail to comply, the matter will be referred to our Attorney General for legal action." Finally, PPA was served with a copy of a report of inspectors of the State Board of Pharmacy, dated September 4, 1974, which recorded that PPA advertised male contraceptives, and had been advised to cease selling contraceptives in violation of the state law.

That PPA has standing to challenge § 6811 (8), not only in its own right but also on behalf of its potential customers, is settled by *Craig* v. *Boren,* 429 U. S. 190, 192–197 (1976). *Craig* held that a vendor of 3.2% beer had standing to challenge in its own right and as advocate for the rights of third persons, the gender-based discrimination in a state statute that prohibited sale of the beer to men, but not to women, between the ages of 18 and 21. In this case, as did the statute in *Craig,* § 6811 (8) inflicts on the vendor PPA "injury in fact" that satisfies Art. III's case-or-controversy requirement, since "[t]he legal duties created by the statutory sections under challenge are addressed directly to vendors such as [PPA. It] is obliged either to heed the statutory [prohibition], thereby incurring a direct economic injury through the constriction of [its] market, or to disobey the statutory command and suffer" legal sanctions. 429 U. S., at 194.[3] There-

[3] Appellants contend that PPA has not suffered "injury in fact" because it has not shown that prosecution under § 6811 (8) is imminent. *Steffel* v. *Thompson,* 415 U. S. 452, 459–460 (1974) is dispositive of this argument. PPA alleges that it has violated the challenged statute in the past, and continues to violate it in the regular course of its business; that it has been advised by the authorities responsible for enforcing the statute that it is in violation; and that on at least one occasion, it has been threatened with prosecution. The threat is not, as in *Poe* v. *Ullman,* 367 U. S. 497, 508 (1961) (plurality opinion), "chimerical." In that

fore, PPA is among the "vendors and those in like positions [who] have been uniformly permitted to resist efforts at restricting their operations by acting as advocates for the rights of third parties who seek access to their market or function." *Id.*, at 195. See also *Eisenstadt* v. *Baird,* 405 U. S. 438, 443–446 (1972); *Sullivan* v. *Little Hunting Park,* 396 U. S. 229, 237 (1969); *Barrows* v. *Jackson,* 346 U. S. 249, 257–260 (1953). As such, PPA "is entitled to assert those concomitant rights of third parties that would be 'diluted or adversely affected' should [its] constitutional challenge fail." *Craig* v. *Boren, supra,* at 195, quoting *Griswold* v. *Connecticut,* 381 U. S. 479, 481 (1965).[4]

II

Although "[t]he Constitution does not explicitly mention any right of privacy," the Court has recognized that one aspect of the "liberty" protected by the Due Process Clause of the Fourteenth Amendment is "a right of personal privacy, or a guarantee of certain areas or zones of privacy." *Roe* v. *Wade,* 410 U. S. 113, 152 (1973). This right of personal privacy includes "the interest in independence in making certain kinds of important decisions." *Whalen* v. *Roe,* 429 U. S. 589, 599–600 (1977). While the outer limits of this aspect of privacy have not been marked by the Court, it is clear that among

---

case, the challenged state law had fallen into virtual desuetude through lack of prosecution over some 80 years, and plaintiffs alleged no explicit threat of prosecution. Here, PPA has been threatened with legal action, and prosecutions have been brought under the predecessor of § 6811 (8) as recently as 1965. See, *e. g., People* v. *Baird,* 47 Misc. 2d 478, 262 N. Y. S. 2d 947 (1965).

[4] Indeed, the case for the vendor's standing to assert the rights of potential purchasers of his product is even more compelling here than in *Craig,* because the rights involved fall within the sensitive area of personal privacy. In such a case potential purchasers "may be chilled from . . . assertion [of their own rights] by a desire to protect the very privacy [they seek to vindicate] from the publicity of a court suit." *Singleton* v. *Wulff,* 428 U. S. 106, 117 (1976).

the decisions that an individual may make without unjustified government interference are personal decisions "relating to marriage, *Loving* v. *Virginia,* 388 U. S. 1, 12 (1967); procreation, *Skinner* v. *Oklahoma ex rel. Williamson,* 316 U. S. 535, 541–542 (1942); contraception, *Eisenstadt* v. *Baird,* 405 U. S., at 453–454; *id.,* at 460, 463–465 (WHITE, J., concurring in result); family relationships, *Prince* v. *Massachusetts,* 321 U. S. 158, 166 (1944); and child rearing and education, *Pierce* v. *Society of Sisters,* 268 U. S. 510, 535 (1925); *Meyer* v. *Nebraska,* [262 U. S. 390, 399 (1923)]." *Roe* v. *Wade, supra,* at 152–153. See also *Cleveland Board of Education* v. *LaFleur,* 414 U. S. 632, 639–640 (1974).

The decision whether or not to beget or bear a child is at the very heart of this cluster of constitutionally protected choices. That decision holds a particularly important place in the history of the right of privacy, a right first explicitly recognized in an opinion holding unconstitutional a statute prohibiting the use of contraceptives, *Griswold* v. *Connecticut, supra,* and most prominently vindicated in recent years in the contexts of contraception, *Griswold* v. *Connecticut, supra; Eisenstadt* v. *Baird, supra;* and abortion, *Roe* v. *Wade, supra; Doe* v. *Bolton,* 410 U. S. 179 (1973); *Planned Parenthood of Central Missouri* v. *Danforth,* 428 U. S. 52 (1976). This is understandable, for in a field that by definition concerns the most intimate of human activities and relationships, decisions whether to accomplish or to prevent conception are among the most private and sensitive. "If the right of privacy means anything, it is the right of the individual, married or single, to be free of unwarranted governmental intrusion into matters so fundamentally affecting a person as the decision whether to bear or beget a child." *Eisenstadt* v. *Baird, supra,* at 453. (Emphasis omitted.)

That the constitutionally protected right of privacy extends to an individual's liberty to make choices regarding contraception does not, however, automatically invalidate every state regulation in this area. The business of manufacturing and selling contraceptives may be regulated in ways that do not infringe protected individual choices. And even a burdensome regulation may be validated by a sufficiently compelling state interest. In *Roe* v. *Wade,* for example, after determining that the "right of privacy . . . encompass[es] a woman's decision whether or not to terminate her pregnancy," 410 U. S., at 153, we cautioned that the right is not absolute, and that certain state interests (in that case, "interests in safeguarding health, in maintaining medical standards, and in protecting potential life") may at some point "become sufficiently compelling to sustain regulation of the factors that govern the abortion decision." *Id.,* at 154. "Compelling" is of course the key word; where a decision as fundamental as that whether to bear or beget a child is involved, regulations imposing a burden on it may be justified only by compelling state interests, and must be narrowly drawn to express only those interests. *Id.,* at 155–156, and cases there cited.

With these principles in mind, we turn to the question whether the District Court was correct in holding invalid the provisions of § 6811 (8) as applied to the distribution of nonprescription contraceptives.

III

We consider first the wider restriction on access to contraceptives created by § 6811 (8)'s prohibition of the distribution of nonmedical contraceptives to adults except through licensed pharmacists.

Appellants argue that this Court has not accorded a "right of access to contraceptives" the status of a fundamental aspect of personal liberty. They emphasize that *Griswold* v. *Connecticut* struck down a state prohibition of the *use* of contraceptives, and so had no occasion to discuss laws "regulating their manufacture or sale." 381 U. S., at 485. *Eisenstadt* v. *Baird,* was decided under the Equal Protection Clause, holding that "whatever the rights of the individual to access to contraceptives may be; the rights must be the same for the unmarried and the married alike." 405 U. S., at 453. Thus appellants argue that neither case should be treated as reflecting upon the State's power to limit or prohibit distribution of contraceptives to any persons, married or unmarried. But see *id.*, at 463–464 (WHITE, J., concurring in result).

The fatal fallacy in this argument is that it overlooks the underlying premise of those decisions that the Constitution protects "the right of the individual . . . to be free from unwarranted governmental intrusion into . . . the decision whether to bear or beget a child." *Id.*, at 453. *Griswold* did state that by "forbidding the *use* of contraceptives rather than regulating their manufacture or sale," the Connecticut statute there had "a maximum destructive impact" on privacy rights. 381 U. S., at 485. This intrusion into "the sacred precincts of marital bedrooms" made that statute particularly "repulsive." *Id.*, at 485–486. But subsequent decisions have made clear that the constitutional protection of individual autonomy in matters of childbearing is not dependent on that element. *Eisenstadt* v. *Baird,* holding that the protection is not limited to married couples, characterized the protected right as the "*decision* whether to bear or beget a child." 405 U. S., at 453 (emphasis added). Similarly, *Roe* v. *Wade,* held that the Constitution protects "a woman's *decision* whether or not to terminate her pregnancy." 410 U. S., at 153 (emphasis added). See also *Whalen* v. *Roe, supra,* at 599–600, and n. 26. These decisions put *Griswold* in proper perspective. *Griswold* may no longer be read as holding only that a State may not prohibit a married couple's use of contraceptives. Read in light of its progeny, the teaching of *Griswold* is that the Constitution protects individual decisions in matters of childbearing from unjustified intrusion by the State.

Restrictions on the distribution of contraceptives clearly burden the freedom to make such decisions. A total prohibition against sale of contraceptives, for example, would intrude upon individual decisions in matters of procreation and contraception as harshly as a direct ban on their use. Indeed, in practice, a prohibition against all sales, since more easily and less offensively enforced, might have an even more devastating effect upon the freedom to choose contraception. Cf. *Poe* v. *Ullman*, 367 U. S. 497 (1961).

An instructive analogy is found in decisions after *Roe* v. *Wade, supra*, that held unconstitutional statutes that did not prohibit abortions outright but limited in a variety of ways a woman's access to them. *Doe* v. *Bolton*, 410 U. S. 179 (1973); *Planned Parenthood of Central Missouri* v. *Danforth*, 428 U. S. 52 (1976). See also *Bigelow* v. *Virginia*, 421 U. S. 809 (1975). The significance of these cases is that they establish that the same test must be applied to state regulations that burden an individual's right to decide to prevent conception or terminate pregnancy by substantially limiting access to the means of effectuating that decision as is applied to state statutes that prohibit the decision entirely. Both types of regulation "may be justified only by a 'compelling state interest' . . . and . . . must be narrowly drawn to express only the legitimate state interests at stake." *Roe* v. *Wade, supra*, at 155.[5] See also *Eisenstadt* v. *Baird*, 405 U. S., at 463 (WHITE, J., concurring in result). This is so not because there is an independent fundamental "right of access to contraceptives," but because such access is essential to exercise of the constitutionally protected right of decision in matters of childbearing that is the

[5] Contrary to the suggestion advanced in MR. JUSTICE POWELL's opinion, we do not hold that state regulation must meet this standard "whenever it implicates sexual freedom," *post*, at 705, or "affect[s] adult sexual relations," *post*, at 703, but only when it "burden[s] an individual's right to decide to prevent conception or terminate pregnancy by substantially limiting access to the means of effectuating that decision." *Supra*, this page. As we observe below, "the Court has not definitively answered the difficult question whether and to what extent the Constitution prohibits state statutes regulating [private consensual sexual] behavior among adults," n. 17, *infra*, and we do not purport to answer that question now.

underlying foundation of the holdings in *Griswold, Eisenstadt* v. *Baird,* and *Roe* v. *Wade.*

Limiting the distribution of nonprescription contraceptives to licensed pharmacists clearly imposes a significant burden on the right of the individuals to use contraceptives if they choose to do so. *Eisenstadt* v. *Baird, supra,* at 461–464 (WHITE, J., concurring in result). The burden is, of course, not as great as that under a total ban on distribution. Nevertheless, the restriction of distribution channels to a small fraction of the total number of possible retail outlets renders contraceptive devices considerably less accessible to the public, reduces the opportunity for privacy of selection and purchase,[6] and lessens the possibility of price competition.[7] Cf. *Griswold* v. *Connecticut,* 381 U. S., at 503 (WHITE, J., concurring in judgment). Of particular relevance here is *Doe* v. *Bolton, supra,* in which the Court struck down, as unconstitutionally burdening the right of a woman to choose abortion, a statute requiring that abortions be performed only in accredited hospitals, in the absence of proof that the requirement was substantially related to the State's interest in protecting the patient's health. 410 U. S., at 193–195. The same infirmity infuses the limitation in § 6811 (8). "Just as in *Griswold,* where the right of married persons to use contraceptives was 'diluted or adversely affected' by permitting a

---

[6] As MR. JUSTICE POWELL notes, *post,* at 711, the prohibition of mail-order sales of contraceptives, as practiced by PPA, is a particularly "significant invasion of the constitutionally protected privacy in decisions concerning sexual relations."

[7] The narrow exception to § 6811 (8) arguably provided by New York Educ. Law § 6807 (b) (McKinney, Supp. 1976–1977), see n. 1, *supra,* which permits a physician "who is not the owner of a pharmacy, or registered store" to supply his patients with "such drugs as [he] . . . deems proper in connection with his practice" obviously does not significantly expand the number of regularly available, easily accessible retail outlets for nonprescription contraceptives, and so has little relevance to our analysis of this aspect of § 6811 (8).

conviction for giving advice as to its exercise, . . . so here, to sanction a medical restriction upon distribution of a contraceptive not proved hazardous to health would impair the exercise of the constitutional right." *Eisenstadt* v. *Baird,* 405 U. S., at 464 (WHITE, J., concurring in result).

There remains the inquiry whether the provision serves a compelling state interest. Clearly "interests . . . in maintaining medical standards, and in protecting potential life," *Roe* v. *Wade,* 410 U. S., at 154, cannot be invoked to justify this statute. Insofar as § 6811 (8) applies to nonhazardous contraceptives,[8] it bears no relation to the State's interest in protecting health. *Eisenstadt* v. *Baird, supra,* at 450–452; 463–464 (WHITE, J., concurring in result).[9] Nor is the interest in protecting potential life implicated in state regulation of contraceptives. *Roe* v. *Wade, supra,* at 163–164.

Appellants therefore suggest that § 6811 (8) furthers other state interests. But none of them is comparable to those the Court has heretofore recognized as compelling. Appellants argue that the limitation of retail sales of nonmedical contraceptives to pharmacists (1) expresses "a proper concern that young people not sell contraceptives"; (2) "allows purchasers to inquire as to the relative qualities of the varying products and prevents anyone from tampering with them"; and (3) facilitates enforcement of the other provisions of the statute. Brief for Appellants 14. The first hardly can justify the statute's incursion into constitutionally protected rights, and

---

[8] We have taken judicial notice that "not all contraceptives are potentially dangerous." *Eisenstadt* v. *Baird,* 405 U. S., 438, 451, and n. 9 (1972). See also *id.,* at 463–464 (WHITE, J., concurring in result).

[9] Indeed, in light of other provisions of both federal and state law that comprehensively regulate hazardous drugs and devices, see, *e. g.,* 21 U. S. C. §§ 351–360, especially § 353 (b); N. Y. Educ. Law §§ 6800–6826 (McKinney 1972 and Supp. 1976–1977), especially § 6810, it is unclear what health-related interest the State could have in nonprescription contraceptives. *Eisenstadt* v. *Baird, supra,* at 452.

in any event the statute is obviously not substantially related to any goal of preventing young people from selling contraceptives.[10] Nor is the statute designed to serve as a quality control device. Nothing in the record suggests that pharmacists are particularly qualified to give advice on the merits of different nonmedical contraceptives, or that such advice is more necessary to the purchaser of contraceptive products than to consumers of other nonprescription items. Why pharmacists are better able or more inclined than other retailers to prevent tampering with prepackaged products, or, if they are, why contraceptives are singled out for this special protection, is also unexplained.[11] As to ease of enforcement, the prospect of additional administrative inconvenience has not been thought to justify invasion of fundamental constitutional rights. See, *e. g., Morrissey* v. *Brewer,* 408 U. S. 471 (1972); *Goldberg* v. *Kelly,* 397 U. S. 254 (1970).

IV [12]

A

The District Court also held unconstitutional, as applied to nonprescription contraceptives, the provision of § 6811 (8) prohibiting the distribution of contraceptives to those under

[10] Nothing in New York law limits the employment of minors who work as sales clerks in pharmacies. To the extent that minors employed in other retail stores selling contraceptive products might be exposed "to undesirable comments and gestures," Brief for Appellants 3–4, or otherwise corrupted by exposure to such products, minors working as sales clerks in pharmacies are exposed to the same hazards.

[11] As the District Court pointed out, while these interests are insufficient to justify limiting the distribution of nonhazardous contraceptives to pharmacists, other restrictions may well be reasonably related to the objective of quality control. We therefore express no opinion on, for example, restrictions on the distribution of contraceptives through vending machines, which are not before us in this case. See 398 F. Supp., at 336.

[12] This part of the opinion expresses the views of JUSTICES BRENNAN, STEWART, MARSHALL, and BLACKMUN.

16 years of age.[13] Appellants contend that this provision of the statute is constitutionally permissible as a regulation of the morality of minors, in furtherance of the State's policy against promiscuous sexual intercourse among the young.

The question of the extent of state power to regulate conduct of minors not constitutionally regulable when committed by adults is a vexing one, perhaps not susceptible of precise answer. We have been reluctant to attempt to define "the totality of the relationship of the juvenile and the state." *In re Gault,* 387 U. S. 1, 13 (1967). Certain principles, however, have been recognized. "Minors, as well as adults, are protected by the Constitution and possess constitutional rights." *Planned Parenthood of Central Missouri* v. *Danforth,* 428 U. S., at 74. "[W]hatever may be their precise impact, neither the Fourteenth Amendment nor the Bill of Rights is for adults alone." *In re Gault, supra,* at 13.[14] On the other hand, we have held in a variety of contexts that "the power of the state to control the conduct of children reaches beyond the scope of its authority over adults." *Prince* v. *Massachusetts,* 321 U. S. 158, 170 (1944). See *Ginsberg* v. *New York,* 390 U. S. 629 (1968). See also *McKeiver* v. *Pennsylvania,* 403 U. S. 528 (1971).

---

[13] Subject to an apparent exception for distribution by physicians in the course of their practice. See n. 1, *supra,* and *infra,* at 697–699, and n. 23.

[14] Thus minors are entitled to constitutional protection for freedom of speech, *Tinker* v. *Des Moines School Dist.,* 393 U. S. 503 (1969); *West Virginia Bd. of Education* v. *Barnette,* 319 U. S. 624 (1943); equal protection against racial discrimination, *Brown* v. *Board of Education,* 347 U. S. 483 (1954); due process in civil contexts, *Goss* v. *Lopez,* 419 U. S. 565 (1975); and a variety of rights of defendants in criminal proceedings, including the requirement of proof beyond a reasonable doubt, *In re Winship,* 397 U. S. 358 (1970), the prohibition of double jeopardy, *Breed* v. *Jones,* 421 U. S. 519 (1975), the rights to notice, counsel, confrontation, and cross-examination, and not to incriminate oneself, *In re Gault,* 387 U. S. 1 (1967), and the protection against coerced confessions, *Gallegos* v. *Colorado,* 370 U. S. 49 (1962); *Haley* v. *Ohio,* 332 U. S. 596 (1948).

Of particular significance to the decision of this case, the right to privacy in connection with decisions affecting procreation extends to minors as well as to adults. *Planned Parenthood of Central Missouri* v. *Danforth, supra,* held that a State "may not impose a blanket provision . . . requiring the consent of a parent or person *in loco parentis* as a condition for abortion of an unmarried minor during the first 12 weeks of her pregnancy." 428 U. S., at 74. As in the case of the spousal-consent requirement struck down in the same case, *id.,* at 67–72, "the State does not have the constitutional authority to give a third party an absolute, and possibly arbitrary, veto," *id.,* at 74, " 'which the state itself is absolutely and totally prohibited from exercising.' " *Id.,* at 69. State restrictions inhibiting privacy rights of minors are valid only if they serve "any significant state interest . . . that is not present in the case of an adult." *Id.,* at 75.[15] *Planned Parenthood* found that no such interest justified a state requirement of parental consent.[16]

[15] This test is apparently less rigorous than the "compelling state interest" test applied to restrictions on the privacy rights of adults. See, *e. g.,* n. 16, *infra.* Such lesser scrutiny is appropriate both because of the States' greater latitude to regulate the conduct of children, *Prince* v. *Massachusetts,* 321 U. S. 158 (1944); *Ginsberg* v. *New York,* 390 U. S. 629 (1968), and because the right of privacy implicated here is "the interest in independence in making certain kinds of important decisions," *Whalen* v. *Roe,* 429 U. S. 589, 599–600 (1977), and the law has generally regarded minors as having a lesser capability for making important decisions. See, *e. g., Planned Parenthood,* 428 U. S., at 102 (STEVENS, J., concurring in part and dissenting in part).

[16] *Planned Parenthood,* however, "does not suggest that every minor, regardless of age or maturity, may give effective consent for termination of her pregnancy. See *Bellotti* v. *Baird,* [428 U. S. 132 (1976)]. The fault of [the particular statute considered in *Planned Parenthood*] is that it imposes a special-consent provision, exercisable by a person other than the woman and her physician, as a prerequisite to a minor's termination of her pregnancy . . . without a sufficient justification for the restriction." *Id.,* at 75.

Since the State may not impose a blanket prohibition, or even a blanket requirement of parental consent, on the choice of a minor to terminate her pregnancy, the constitutionality of a blanket prohibition of the distribution of contraceptives to minors is *a fortiori* foreclosed. The State's interests in protection of the mental and physical health of the pregnant minor, and in protection of potential life are clearly more implicated by the abortion decision than by the decision to use a nonhazardous contraceptive.

Appellants argue, however, that significant state interests are served by restricting minors' access to contraceptives, because free availability to minors of contraceptives would lead to increased sexual activity among the young, in violation of the policy of New York to discourage such behavior.[17] The argument is that minors' sexual activity may be deterred by increasing the hazards attendant on it. The same argument, however, would support a ban on abortions for minors, or indeed support a prohibition on abortions, or access to contraceptives, for the unmarried, whose sexual activity is also against the public policy of many States. Yet, in each of these areas, the Court has rejected the argument, noting in *Roe* v. *Wade*, that "no court or commentator has taken the argument seriously." 410

[17] Appellees argue that the State's policy to discourage sexual activity of minors is itself unconstitutional, for the reason that the right to privacy comprehends a right of minors as well as adults to engage in private consensual sexual behavior. We observe that the Court has not definitively answered the difficult question whether and to what extent the Constitution prohibits state statutes regulating such behavior among adults. See generally Note, On Privacy: Constitutional Protection for Personal Liberty, 48 N. Y. U. L. Rev. 670, 719–738 (1973). But whatever the answer to that question, *Ginsberg* v. *New York*, *supra*, indicates that in the area of sexual mores, as in other areas, the scope of permissible state regulation is broader as to minors than as to adults. In any event, it is unnecessary to pass upon this contention of appellees, and our decision proceeds on the assumption that the Constitution does not bar state regulation of the sexual behavior of minors.

U. S., at 148. The reason for this unanimous rejection was stated in *Eisenstadt* v. *Baird:* "It would be plainly unreasonable to assume that [the State] has prescribed pregnancy and the birth of an unwanted child [or the physical and psychological dangers of an abortion] as punishment for fornication." 405 U. S., at 448. We remain reluctant to attribute any such "scheme of values" to the State.[18]

Moreover, there is substantial reason for doubt whether limiting access to contraceptives will in fact substantially discourage early sexual behavior. Appellants themselves conceded in the District Court that "there is no evidence that teenage extramarital sexual activity increases in proportion to the availability of contraceptives," 398 F. Supp., at 332, and n. 10, and accordingly offered none, in the District Court or here. Appellees, on the other hand, cite a considerable body of evidence and opinion indicating that there is no such deterrent effect.[19] Although we take judicial notice, as did the

---

[18] We note, moreover, that other provisions of New York law argue strongly against any conclusion that the deterrence of illegal sexual conduct among minors was an objective of § 6811 (8). First, a girl in New York may marry as young as 14, with the consent of her parents and a family court judge. N. Y. Dom. Rel. Law §§ 15-a, 15 (2), 15 (3) (McKinney 1964 and Supp. 1976-1977). Yet although sexual intercourse by a married woman of that age violates no state law, § 6811 (8) prohibits distribution of contraceptives to her. Second, New York requires that birth control information and services be provided to recipients of certain welfare programs, provided only that they are "of childbearing age, including children who can be considered sexually active." N. Y. Soc. Serv. Law § 350 (1)(e) (McKinney 1976); cf. 42 U. S. C. § 602 (a)(15)(A) (1970 ed., Supp. V). See also N. Y. Soc. Serv. Law § 365-a (3)(c) (McKinney 1976); cf. 42 U. S. C. § 1396d (a)(vii)(4)(C) (1970 ed., Supp. V). Although extramarital intercourse is presumably as contrary to state policy among minors covered by those programs as among others, state law requires distribution of contraceptives to them and prohibits their distribution to all others.

[19] See, *e. g.*, Settlage, Baroff, & Cooper, Sexual Experience of Younger Teenage Girls Seeking Contraceptive Assistance for the First Time, Family Planning Perspectives 223 (fall 1973); Pilpel & Wechsler, Birth Control,

District Court, *id.*, at 331–333, that with or without access to contraceptives, the incidence of sexual activity among minors is high,[20] and the consequences of such activity are frequently devastating,[21] the studies cited by appellees play no part in our decision. It is enough that we again confirm the principle that when a State, as here, burdens the exercise of a fundamental right, its attempt to justify that burden as a rational means for the accomplishment of some significant state policy requires more than a bare assertion, based on a conceded complete absence of supporting evidence, that the burden is connected to such a policy.[22]

Teenagers and the Law: A New Look 1971, Family Planning Perspectives 37 (July 1971); Stein, Furnishing Information and Medical Treatment to Minors for Prevention, Termination and Treatment of Pregnancy, Clearinghouse Review 131, 132 (July 1971); Reiss, Contraceptive Information and Sexual Morality, Journal of Sex Research 51 (Apr. 1966). See also Note, Parental Consent Requirements and Privacy Rights of Minors: The Contraceptive Controversy, 88 Harv. L. Rev. 1001, 1010, and n. 67 (1975); Jordan, A Minor's Right to Contraceptives, 7 U. Calif. Davis L. Rev. 270, 272–273 (1974).

[20] See, *e. g.*, *id.*, at 271–273; Kanter & Zelnick, Sexual Experience of Young Unmarried Women in the United States, Family Planning Perspectives 9 (Oct. 1972).

[21] Although this is not the occasion for a full examination of these problems, the following data sketchily indicate their extent. According to New York City Department of Health statistics, filed with the Court by the American Civil Liberties Union as *amicus curiae*, in New York City alone there were over 6,000 live births to girls under the age of 17 in 1975, as well as nearly 11,000 abortions. Moreover, "[t]eenage motherhood involves a host of problems, including adverse physical and psychological effects upon the minor and her baby, the continuous stigma associated with unwed motherhood, the need to drop out of school with the accompanying impairment of educational opportunities, and other dislocations [including] forced marriage of immature couples and the often acute anxieties involved in deciding whether to secure an abortion." Note, Parental Consent Requirements and Privacy Rights of Minors: The Contraceptive Controversy, 88 Harv. L. Rev. 1001, 1010 (1975) (footnotes omitted). See also Jordan, *supra*, n. 19, at 273–275.

[22] Appellants argue that the statement in *Ginsberg* v. *New York*, 390

B

Appellants argue that New York does not totally prohibit distribution of contraceptives to minors under 16, and that accordingly § 6811 (8) cannot be held unconstitutional. Although § 6811 (8) on its face is a flat unqualified prohibition, Educ. Law § 6807 (b) (McKinney, Supp. 1976–1977), see nn. 1, 7, and 13, *supra,* provides that nothing in Education Law §§ 6800–6826 shall be construed to prevent "[a]ny physician . . . from supplying his patients with such drugs as [he] . . . deems proper in connection with his practice." This narrow exception, however, does not save the statute. As we have held above as to limitations upon distribution to adults, less than total restrictions on access to contraceptives that significantly burden the right to decide whether to bear children must also pass constitutional scrutiny. Appellants assert no medical necessity for imposing a medical limitation on the distribution of nonprescription contraceptives to minors. Rather, they argue that such a restriction serves to emphasize to young people the seriousness with which the State views the decision to engage in sexual intercourse at an early age.[23] But this is only another form of the

U. S., at 641, that "it was not irrational for the legislature to find that exposure to material condemned by the statute is harmful to minors," is authority that the burden is appellees' to prove that there is no connection between the statute and the asserted state policy. But *Ginsberg* concerned a statute prohibiting dissemination of obscene material that it held was not constitutionally protected. In contrast § 6811 (8) concerns distribution of material access to which is essential to exercise of a fundamental right.

[23] There is considerable doubt that appellants accurately identify the legislative purposes in enacting Educ. Law §§ 6807 (b) and 6811 (8). Section 6811 (8) (formerly Educ. Law § 6804–b and before that Penal Law § 1142 (2)) was first enacted in 1965 as a modification, apparently in response to *Griswold* v. *Connecticut,* 381 U. S. 479 (1965), of former Penal Law § 1142, titled "Indecent articles." 1965 N. Y. Laws, c. 637. This statute, which dated back at least to § 318 of the Penal Code of

argument that juvenile sexual conduct will be deterred by making contraceptives more difficult to obtain. Moreover, that argument is particularly poorly suited to the restriction

---

1881, 1881 N. Y. Laws, c. 676, had made it a misdemeanor for any person to distribute or advertise "any instrument or article, or any drug or medicine, for the prevention of conception." Section 6807 (b), on the other hand, generally excepts the distribution of drugs by a physician in the course of his practice from all the licensing requirements and restrictions imposed on the practice of pharmacy by Education Law §§ 6800–6826 (subject to certain provisos not here relevant). Such a provision, in one form or another and bearing several different numbers, has been included in the article concerning the practice of pharmacy since that article was first incorporated in the Education Law in 1927, see former Education Law § 1361, 1927 N. Y. Laws, c. 85, and before that a similar provision was included in the statutes regulating pharmacy in the Public Health Law. See, *e. g.*, Public Health Law of 1893, § 187, 1893 N. Y. Laws, c. 661. Thus, § 6807 (b) and its predecessors long predate the inclusion of § 6811 (8) in the Education Law.

Even more significantly, when § 6811 (8) was first enacted as Penal Law § 1142 (2), it was not subject to the physicians' exception of § 6807 (b). Rather, it was apparently subject to a different physicians' exception, former Penal Law § 1145 (§ 321 of the Penal Code of 1881), which provided:

"An article or instrument, used or applied by physicians lawfully practicing, or by their direction or prescription, for the cure or prevention of disease, is not an article of indecent or immoral nature or use, within this chapter. The supplying of such articles to such physicians or by their direction or prescription, is not an offense under this chapter."

This was interpreted by the New York Court of Appeals to permit a physician "in good faith" to use contraceptives to treat "a married person to cure or prevent disease," but not to permit "promiscuous advice to patients irrespective of their condition." *People* v. *Sanger,* 222 N. Y. 192, 194–195, 118 N. E. 637, 637–638 (1918), appeal dismissed for lack of jurisdiction, 251 U. S. 537 (1919) (*per curiam*). See also *People* v. *Byrne,* 99 Misc. 1, 163 N. Y. S. 682 (1917); *People* v. *Baird,* 47 Misc. 2d 478, 262 N. Y. S. 2d 947 (1965).

In light of this history, it appears that insofar as the legislature had § 6807 (b) in mind at all when it transferred the prohibition of distribu-

appellants are attempting to justify, which on appellants' construction delegates the State's authority to disapprove of minors' sexual behavior to physicians, who may exercise it arbitrarily,[24] either to deny contraceptives to young people, or to undermine the State's policy of discouraging illicit early sexual behavior. This the State may not do. Cf. *Planned Parenthood of Central Missouri* v. *Danforth,* 428 U. S., at 69, 74.[25]

---

tion of contraceptives to those under 16 from the Penal Law to the Education Law, it thought of that section as at most a narrow exception, analogous to § 1145, permitting physicians, "in connection with [their] practice," to treat or prevent disease, rather than, as appellants assert, intending that §§ 6807 (b) and 6811 (8) be read together as establishing a scheme under which contraceptives would be freely available to those under 16, but limiting the distribution function to physicians. The legislative history of attempts in 1972 and 1974 to modify § 6811 (8), to which appellants refer, supports this construction. The legislators debating those bills seem to have thought of § 6811 (8) as a flat prohibition of the distribution of contraceptives to minors, and made no reference to § 6807 (b).

[24] In *Doe* v. *Bolton,* 410 U. S. 179, 196 (1973), we doubted that physicians would allow their moral "predilections on extramarital sex" to interfere with their medical judgments concerning abortions. Here, however, no *medical* judgment is involved at all; the State purports to commission physicians to engage in *moral* counseling that can reflect little other than their private views on the morality of premarital sex among the young. It seems evident that many physicians are likely to have views on this subject to a significant degree more permissive or more restrictive than those of the State, the minor, or the minor's parents. Moreover, nothing in § 6807 (b) suggests that the role of the physician is limited to such "counseling." The statute does nothing more than to permit the physician to provide his patients with such drugs or devices as he "deems proper." Such "absolute, and possibly arbitrary" discretion over the privacy rights of minors is precisely what *Planned Parenthood* condemned. 428 U. S., at 74.

[25] In cases involving abortions, we have emphasized that the decision to terminate a pregnancy is properly made by a woman in consultation with her physician. See, *e. g., Roe* v. *Wade,* 410 U. S. 113, 153, 164 (1973); *Planned Parenthood of Central Missouri* v. *Danforth,* 428 U. S.,

V

The District Court's holding that the prohibition of any "advertisement or display" of contraceptives is unconstitutional was clearly correct. Only last Term *Virginia Pharmacy Bd.* v. *Virginia Citizens Consumer Council,* 425 U. S. 748 (1976), held that a State may not "completely suppress the dissemination of concededly truthful information about entirely lawful activity," even when that information could be categorized as "commercial speech." *Id.,* at 773. Just as in that case, the statute challenged here seeks to suppress completely any information about the availability and price of contraceptives.[26] Nor does the case present any question left open in *Virginia Pharmacy Bd.;* here, as there, there can be no contention that the regulation is "a mere time, place, and manner restriction," *id.,* at 771, or that it prohibits only misleading or deceptive advertisements, *ibid.,* or "that the transactions proposed in the forbidden advertisements are themselves illegal in any way. Cf. *Pittsburgh Press Co.* v. *Human Relations Comm'n,* [413 U. S. 376 (1973)]." *Id.,* at 772–773. Moreover, in addition to the "substantial individual and societal interests" in the free flow of commercial information enumerated in *Virginia Pharmacy Bd., supra,* at 763–766, the

at 75. No such suggestion, however, has been made concerning the right to obtain or use contraceptives. See *Griswold* v. *Connecticut, supra; Eisenstadt* v. *Baird,* 405 U. S. 438 (1972). The reason, of course, is that the abortion decision necessarily involves a medical judgment, *Roe* v. *Wade, supra,* at 164, while the decision to use a nonhazardous contraceptive does not. *Eisenstadt* v. *Baird, supra,* at 463–464 (WHITE, J., concurring in result). See also n. 24, *supra.*

[26] The prohibition of advertising and display of contraceptives is invalid as to prescription as well as nonprescription contraceptives, at least when the advertising is by persons who are licensed to sell such products. *Virginia Pharmacy Bd.* v. *Virginia Citizens Consumer Council,* 425 U. S. 748 (1976).

information suppressed by this statute "related to activity with which, at least in some respects, the State could not interfere." 425 U. S., at 760. Cf. *Bigelow* v. *Virginia,* 421 U. S. 809 (1975).

Appellants contend that advertisements of contraceptive products would be offensive and embarrassing to those exposed to them, and that permitting them would legitimize sexual activity of young people. But these are classically not justifications validating the suppression of expression protected by the First Amendment. At least where obscenity is not involved, we have consistently held that the fact that protected speech may be offensive to some does not justify its suppression. See, *e. g., Cohen* v. *California,* 403 U. S. 15 (1971).[27] As for the possible "legitimation" of illicit sexual behavior, whatever might be the case if the advertisements directly incited illicit sexual activity among the young, none of the advertisements in this record can even remotely be characterized as "directed to inciting or producing imminent lawless action and . . . likely to incite or produce such action." *Brandenburg* v. *Ohio,* 395 U. S. 444, 447 (1969). They merely state the availability of products and services that are not only entirely legal, cf. *Pittsburgh Press Co.* v. *Human Relations Comm'n,* 413 U. S. 376 (1973), but constitutionally protected. Cf. *Bigelow* v. *Virginia, supra.*[28] These arguments

[27] Indeed, as the Court recognized in *Virginia Pharmacy Bd.,* much advertising is "tasteless and excessive," and no doubt offends many. 425 U. S., at 765.

[28] Appellants suggest no distinction between commercial and noncommercial speech that would render these discredited arguments meritorious when offered to justify prohibitions on commercial speech. On the contrary, such arguments are clearly directed not at any commercial aspect of the prohibited advertising but at the ideas conveyed and form of expression—the core of First Amendment values. Cf. *Linmark Associates, Inc.* v. *Willingboro, ante,* at 96–97.

therefore do not justify the total suppression of advertising concerning contraceptives.[20]

Affirmed.

THE CHIEF JUSTICE dissents.

MR. JUSTICE WHITE, concurring in part and concurring in the result.

I join Parts I, III, and V of the Court's opinion and concur in the result with respect to Part IV.*

Although I saw no reason in *Eisenstadt* v. *Baird,* 405 U. S. 438 (1972), to reach "the novel constitutional question whether a State may restrict or forbid the distribution of contraceptives to the unmarried," *id.,* at 465 (concurring in result), four of the seven Justices participating in that case held that in this respect the rights of unmarried persons were equal to those of the married. Given *Eisenstadt* and given the decision of the Court in the abortion case, *Roe* v. *Wade,* 410 U. S. 113 (1973), the result reached by the Court in Part III of its opinion appears warranted. I do not regard the opinion, however, as declaring unconstitutional any state law forbidding extramarital sexual relations. On this assumption I join Part III.

I concur in the result in Part IV primarily because the State has not demonstrated that the prohibition against distribution of contraceptives to minors measurably contributes to the deterrent purposes which the State advances as justification for the restriction. Again, however, the legality of state laws forbidding premarital intercourse is not at issue here; and, with MR. JUSTICE STEVENS, "I would describe as

[20] We do not have before us, and therefore express no views on, state regulation of the time, place, or manner of such commercial advertising based on these or other state interests.

*There is no need for present purposes to agree or disagree with the Court's summary of the law expressed in Part II.

'frivolous' appellees' argument that a minor has the constitutional right to put contraceptives to their intended use, notwithstanding the combined objection of both parents and the State," *post,* at 713.

In joining Part V of the Court's opinion, I should also say that I agree with the views of MR. JUSTICE STEVENS expressed in Part II of his separate opinion.

MR. JUSTICE POWELL, concurring in part and concurring in the judgment.

I agree that Population Planning Associates has standing to maintain this action, and therefore join Part I of the Court's opinion. Although I concur in the judgment of the Court, I am not persuaded that the Constitution requires the severe constraints that the Court's opinion places upon legislative efforts to regulate the distribution of contraceptives, particularly to the young.

I

The Court apparently would subject all state regulation affecting adult sexual relations to the strictest standard of judicial review. Under today's decision, such regulation "may be justified only by compelling state interests, and must be narrowly drawn to express only those interests." *Ante,* at 686. Even regulation restricting only the sexual activity of the young must now be justified by a "significant state interest," a standard that is "apparently less rigorous" than the standard the Court would otherwise apply. *Ante,* at 693 n. 15. In my view, the extraordinary protection the Court would give to all personal decisions in matters of sex is neither required by the Constitution nor supported by our prior decisions.

A

The cases on which the Court relies for its "compelling interest" standard do not support the sweeping principle it adopts today. Those cases generally involved direct and substantial interference with constitutionally protected rights. In *Griswold* v. *Connecticut,* 381 U. S. 479 (1965), the Court invalidated a state statute prohibiting the use of contraceptives and making it illegal for physicians to give advice to married persons regarding contraception. The statute was viewed as one "operat[ing] directly on an intimate relation of husband and wife and their physician's role in one aspect of that relation," *id.,* at 482, and "seek[ing] to achieve its goals by means having a maximum destructive impact upon that relationship," *id.,* at 485. In *Roe* v. *Wade,* 410 U. S. 113 (1973), the Court reviewed a Texas statute imposing severe criminal sanctions on physicians and other medical personnel who performed nontherapeutic abortions, thus effectively foreclosing the availability and safety of this desired service. And just last Term, in *Planned Parenthood of Central Missouri* v. *Danforth,* 428 U. S. 52 (1976), we invalidated Missouri's requirement of spousal consent as a state-imposed "absolute obstacle to a woman's decision that *Roe* held to be constitutionally protected from such interference." *Id.,* at 71 n. 11.

The Court relies on *Planned Parenthood, supra,* and *Doe* v. *Bolton,* 410 U. S. 179 (1973), for the proposition that "the same test must be applied to state regulations that burden an individual's right to decide to prevent conception or terminate pregnancy by substantially limiting access to the means of effectuating that decision as is applied to state statutes that prohibit the decision entirely." *Ante,* at 688. But neither of those cases refers to the "compelling state interest" test. In *Bolton,* the Court invalidated procedural requirements of the Georgia abortion statute that were found not "reasonably related" to the asserted legislative purposes or to the "patient's needs." 410 U. S., at 194, 199. *Planned Parenthood* involved—in addition to the "absolute obstacle" referred to above—the Missouri requirement of prior written consent by the pregnant woman. Despite the fact that Missouri normally did not require written consent for other surgical procedures, the Court sustained this regulation without requiring any demonstration of compelling state interests. The Court recognized that the decision to abort "is an important, and often a stressful one," and the State thus constitutionally could assure that the woman was aware of the significance of the decision. 428 U. S., at 67.

In sum, the Court quite unnecessarily extends the reach of cases like *Griswold* and *Roe.* Neither our precedents nor sound principles of constitutional analysis require state legislation to meet the exacting "compelling state interest" standard whenever it implicates sexual freedom. In my view, those cases make clear that that standard has been invoked only when the state regulation entirely frustrates or heavily burdens the exercise of constitutional rights in this area. See *Bellotti* v. *Baird,* 428 U. S. 132, 147 (1976). This is not to say that other state regulation is free from judicial review. But a test so severe that legislation rarely can meet it should be imposed by courts with deliberate restraint in view of the respect that properly should be accorded legislative judgments.

B

There is also no justification for subjecting restrictions on the sexual activity of the young to heightened judicial review. Under our prior cases, the States have broad latitude to legislate with respect to adolescents. The principle is well settled that "a State may permissibly determine that, at least in some precisely delineated areas, a child . . . is not possessed of that full capacity for individual choice" which is essential to the exercise of various constitutionally protected interests. *Ginsberg* v. *New York,* 390 U. S. 629, 649–650 (1968) (STEWART, J., concurring in result). This principle is the premise of our prior decisions, ostensibly reaffirmed by the plurality, *ante,* at 692, holding that "the power of the state to control the conduct of children reaches beyond the scope of its authority over adults." *Prince* v. *Massachusetts,* 321 U. S. 158, 170 (1944).

Restraints on the freedom of minors may be justified "even though comparable restraints on adults would be constitutionally impermissible." *Planned Parenthood of Central Missouri* v. *Danforth, supra,* at 102 (STEVENS, J., concurring in part and dissenting in part).[1]

New York has exercised its responsibility over minors in areas falling within the "cluster of constitutionally protected choices" relating to sex and marriage. *Ante,* at 685. It has set an age limitation below which persons cannot marry without parental consent, N. Y. Dom. Rel. Law §§ 15, 15–a (McKinney 1964 and Supp. 1976–1977), and has established by statute the age at which a minor is legally recognized as having the capacity to consent to sexual activity, Penal Law § 130.05 (3) (a) (McKinney 1975). See also Penal Law §§ 130.25, 130.30, 130.35 (McKinney 1975). These provisions highlight the State's concern that its juvenile citizens generally lack the maturity and understanding necessary to make decisions concerning marriage and sexual relationships.

Until today, I would not have thought it was even arguably necessary to review state regulation of this sort under a standard that for all practical purposes approaches the "compelling state interest" standard. At issue in *Ginsberg* v. *New York, supra,* for example, was the question of the constitutionality on its face of a New York criminal obscenity statute which prohibited the sale to minors of material defined to be obscene on the basis of its appeal to them whether or not it would be obscene to adults. The Court recognized that "the State has

---

[1] MR. JUSTICE STEVENS recently provided the following examples, deeply rooted in our traditions and law:

"Because he may not foresee the consequences of his decision, a minor may not make an enforceable bargain. He may not lawfully work or travel where he pleases, or even attend exhibitions of constitutionally protected adult motion pictures. Persons below a certain age may not marry without parental consent. Indeed, such consent is essential even when the young woman is already pregnant." 428 U. S., at 102.

an interest 'to protect the welfare of children' and to see that they are 'safeguarded from abuses' which might prevent their 'growth into free and independent well-developed men and citizens.'" 390 U. S., at 640–641, quoting *Prince* v. *Massachusetts, supra,* at 165. Consequently, the "only question remaining" in that case was "whether the New York Legislature might rationally conclude, as it has, that exposure to the materials proscribed by [the statute] constitutes such an 'abuse.'" 390 U. S., at 641. Similarly, the relevant question in any case where state laws impinge on the freedom of action of young people in sexual matters is whether the restriction rationally serves valid state interests.

II

With these considerations in mind, I turn to the specific provisions of the New York statute limiting the distribution of contraceptives.

A

New York has made it a crime for anyone other than a physician to sell or distribute contraceptives to minors under the age of 16 years. Educ. Law § 6811 (8) (McKinney 1972). This element of New York's program of regulation for the protection of its minor citizens is said to evidence the State's judgment that the health and well-being of minors would be better assured if they are not encouraged to engage in sexual intercourse without guidance. Although I have no doubt that properly framed legislation serving this purpose would meet constitutional standards, the New York provision is defective in two respects. First, it infringes the privacy interests of married females between the ages of 14 and 16, see *ante,* at 695 n. 18, in that it prohibits the distribution of contraceptives to such females except by a physician. In authorizing marriage at that age, the State also sanctions sexual intercourse between the partners and expressly recognizes that once the marriage relationship exists the husband and wife are presumed to possess the requisite understanding and maturity to make decisions concerning sex and procreation. Consequently, the state interest that justifies a requirement of prior counseling with respect to minors in general simply is inapplicable with respect to minors for whom the State has affirmatively approved marriage.

Second, this provision prohibits parents from distributing contraceptives to their children, a restriction that unjustifiably interferes with parental interests in rearing their children. Cf. *Ginsberg* v. *New York*, 390 U. S., at 639 and n. 7. "[C]onstitutional interpretation has consistently recognized that the parents' claim to authority in their own household to direct the rearing of their children is basic in the structure of our society. 'It is cardinal with us that the custody, care and nurture of the child reside first in the parents, whose primary function and freedom include preparation for obligations the state can neither supply nor hinder.'" *Ibid.*, quoting *Prince* v. *Massachusetts*, *supra*, at 166. See *Wisconsin* v. *Yoder*, 406 U. S. 205, 231–233 (1972); *Pierce* v. *Society of Sisters*, 268 U. S. 510, 534–535 (1925); *Meyer* v. *Nebraska*, 262 U. S. 390, 399–401 (1923). Moreover, this statute would allow the State "to enquire into, prove, and punish," *Poe* v. *Ullman*, 367 U. S. 497, 548 (1961) (Harlan, J., dissenting), the exercise of this parental responsibility. The State points to no interest of sufficient magnitude to justify this direct interference with the parental guidance that is especially appropriate in this sensitive area of child development.[2]

[2] The particular provision at issue makes it a crime for "[a]ny person to sell or distribute any instrument or article, or any recipe, drug or medicine for the prevention of contraception to a minor under the age of sixteen years . . . ." Educ. Law § 6811 (8) (McKinney 1972). For the reasons stated in the text, this provision unjustifiably infringes the constitutionally protected interests of parents and married female minors, and it is invalid in those two respects. Although the prohibition on distribution might be sustained as to other individuals if the restrictions on

But in my view there is considerably more room for state regulation in this area than would be permissible under the plurality's opinion. It seems clear to me, for example, that the State would further a constitutionally permissible end if it encouraged adolescents to seek the advice and guidance of their parents before deciding whether to engage in sexual intercourse. *Planned Parenthood,* 428 U. S., at 91 (STEWART, J., concurring). The State justifiably may take note of the psychological pressures that might influence children at a time in their lives when they generally do not possess the maturity necessary to understand and control their responses. Participation in sexual intercourse at an early age may have both physical and psychological consequences. These include the risks of venereal disease and pregnancy, and the less obvious mental and emotional problems that may result from sexual activity by children. Moreover, society has long adhered to the view that sexual intercourse should not be engaged in promiscuously, a judgment that an adolescent may be less likely to heed than an adult.

Requiring minors to seek parental guidance would be consistent with our prior cases. In *Planned Parenthood,* we considered whether there was "any significant state interest in conditioning [a minor's] abortion [decision] on the consent of a parent or person *in loco parentis* that is not present in the case of an adult." 428 U. S., at 75. Observing that the minor necessarily would be consulting with a physician on all aspects of the abortion decision, we concluded that the Missouri requirement was invalid because it im-

---

parental distribution and distribution to married female minors could be treated as severable, the result "would be to create a program quite different from the one the legislature actually adopted." *Sloan* v. *Lemon,* 413 U. S. 825, 834 (1973). I therefore agree with the Court that the entire provision must be invalidated. See *Dorchy* v. *Kansas,* 264 U. S. 286, 291 (1924); *Dollar Co.* v. *Canadian C. & F. Co.,* 220 N. Y. 270, 279, 115 N. E. 711, 713 (1917).

posed "a special-consent provision, exercisable by a person other than the woman and her physician, as a prerequisite to a minor's termination of her pregnancy and [did] so without a sufficient justification for the restriction." *Ibid.* But we explicitly suggested that a materially different constitutional issue would be presented with respect to a statute assuring in most instances consultation between the parent and child. *Ibid.*, citing *Bellotti* v. *Baird,* 428 U. S. 132 (1976). See *Planned Parenthood, supra,* at 90–91 (STEWART, J., concurring).

A requirement of prior parental consultation is merely one illustration of permissible regulation in this area. As long as parental distribution is permitted, a State should have substantial latitude in regulating the distribution of contraceptives to minors.[3]

B

New York also makes it a crime for anyone other than a licensed pharmacist to sell or distribute contraceptives to adults and to minors aged 16 or over. The only serious justification offered by the State for this prohibition is that it is necessary to facilitate enforcement of the limitation on distribution to children under 16 years of age. Since the Court invalidates that limitation today, the pharmacy restriction lacks any rational justification. I therefore agree with the Court that § 6811 (8)'s limitation on the distribution of nonprescription contraceptives cannot be sustained.

But even if New York were to enact constitutionally permissible limitations on access for children, I doubt that it could justify the present pharmacy restriction as an enforcement measure. Restricting the kinds of retail outlets that may dis-

[3] As long as access is available through parents, I perceive no constitutional obstacle to state regulation that authorizes other designated adults—such as physicians—to provide relevant counseling.

tribute contraceptives may well be justified,[4] but the present statute even prohibits distribution by mail to adults. In this respect, the statute works a significant invasion of the constitutionally protected privacy in decisions concerning sexual relations. By requiring individuals to buy contraceptives over the counter, the statute heavily burdens constitutionally protected freedom.[5]

III

I also agree with the Court that New York cannot lawfully prohibit all "advertisement or display" of contraceptives. But it seems to me that the Court's opinion may be read too broadly. It flatly dismisses, as justifications "classically" irrelevant, the State's contentions that the indiscriminate advertisement of contraceptive products in some settings could be unduly offensive and could be viewed by the young as legitimation of sexual promiscuity. I agree that these jus-

[4] Absent some evidence that a restriction of outlets to registered pharmacists heavily burdens the constitutional interests of adults, there would be no basis for applying the standard of review articulated in *Griswold* and *Roe*. See Part I, *supra*. Indeed, in the absence of such evidence there would be no reason to set aside a legislative judgment that enforcement of constitutionally permissible limitations on access for minors, see Part II–A, *supra*, warrants a reasonable limitation on the means for marketing contraceptives. Without some limitations on the number and type of retail outlets it would be difficult—if not impossible—to effectuate the state interest in assuring that minors are counseled before purchasing contraceptive devices. As pharmacists are licensed professionals, the State may be justified in relying on them to act responsibly in observing regulations applicable to minors.

[5] It is not a satisfactory answer that an individual may preserve anonymity as one of a number of customers in a retail outlet. However impersonal the marketplace may be, it does not approach the privacy of the home. There may be some risk that mail distribution will occasionally permit circumvention of permissible restrictions with respect to children, but this does not justify the concomitant burden on the constitutional rights of adults.

tifications cannot support a complete ban on advertising, but I see no reason to cast any doubt on the authority of the State to impose carefully tailored restrictions designed to serve legitimate governmental concerns as to the effect of commercial advertising on the young.[6]

MR. JUSTICE STEVENS, concurring in part and concurring in the judgment.

For the reasons stated in Parts I, II, and III of the opinion of the Court, which I join, I agree that Population Planning Associates, Inc., has standing to challenge the New York statute and that the grant to licensed pharmacists of a monopoly in the distribution of nonmedical contraceptives is unconstitutional. I also agree with the conclusion that New York's prohibition against the distribution of contraceptives to persons under 16 years of age is unconstitutional, and with the Court's conclusion that the total suppression of advertising or display of contraceptives is invalid, but my reasons differ from those set forth in Part IV of MR. JUSTICE BREN-

[6] The State argues that unregulated commercial advertisement of contraceptive products would be viewed by the young as "legitimation" of—if not an open invitation to—sexual promiscuity. The Court simply finds on the basis of the advertisements in the record before us that this interest does not justify total suppression of advertising concerning contraceptives. The Court does leave open the question whether this or other state interests would justify regulation of the time, place, or manner of such commercial advertising. *Ante*, at 702 n. 29. In my view, such carefully tailored restrictions may be especially appropriate when advertising is accomplished by means of the electronic media. As Judge Leventhal recently observed in that context: "[T]here is a distinction between the all-out prohibition of a censor, and regulation of time and place of speaking out, which still leaves access to a substantial part of the mature audience. What is entitled to First Amendment protection is not necessarily entitled to First Amendment protection in all places. *Young* v. *American Mini Theatres, Inc.*, 427 U. S. 50 . . . (1976). Nor is it necessarily entitled to such protection at all times." *Pacifica Foundation* v. *FCC*, 181 U. S. App. D. C. 132, 157, 556 F. 2d 9, 34 (1977) (dissenting opinion).

NAN's opinion and I wish to add emphasis to the limitation on the Court's holding in Part V.

I

There are two reasons why I do not join Part IV. First, the holding in *Planned Parenthood of Missouri* v. *Danforth,* 428 U. S. 52, 72–75, that a minor's decision to abort her pregnancy may not be conditioned on parental consent, is not dispositive here. The options available to the already pregnant minor are fundamentally different from those available to nonpregnant minors. The former must bear a child unless she aborts; but persons in the latter category can and generally will avoid childbearing by abstention. Consequently, even if I had joined that part of *Planned Parenthood,* I could not agree that the Constitution provides the same measure of protection to the minor's right to use contraceptives as to the pregnant female's right to abort.

Second, I would not leave open the question whether there is a significant state interest in discouraging sexual activity among unmarried persons under 16 years of age. Indeed, I would describe as "frivolous" appellees' argument that a minor has the constitutional right to put contraceptives to their intended use, notwithstanding the combined objection of both parents and the State.

For the reasons explained by MR. JUSTICE POWELL, I agree that the statute may not be applied to married females between the ages of 14 and 16, or to distribution by parents. I am not persuaded, however, that these glaring defects alone justify an injunction against other applications of the statute. Only one of the three plaintiffs in this case is a parent who wishes to give contraceptives to his children. The others are an Episcopal minister who sponsors a program against venereal disease, and a mail-order firm, which presumably has no way to determine the age of its customers. I am satisfied, for the reasons that follow, that the statute is also invalid as applied to them.

The State's important interest in the welfare of its young citizens justifies a number of protective measures. See *Planned Parenthood of Central Missouri* v. *Danforth, supra,* at 102 (STEVENS, J., concurring in part and dissenting in part). Such special legislation is premised on the fact that young persons frequently make unwise choices with harmful consequences; the State may properly ameliorate those consequences by providing, for example, that a minor may not be required to honor his bargain. It is almost unprecedented, however, for a State to require that an ill-advised act by a minor give rise to greater risk of irreparable harm than a similar act by an adult.[1]

Common sense indicates that many young people will engage in sexual activity regardless of what the New York Legislature does; and further, that the incidence of venereal disease and premarital pregnancy is affected by the availability or unavailability of contraceptives. Although young persons theoretically may avoid those harms by practicing total abstention, inevitably many will not. The statutory prohibition denies them and their parents a choice which, if available, would reduce their exposure to disease or unwanted pregnancy.

---

[1] Only two other States have adopted similar legislation. Family Planning, Contraception and Voluntary Sterilization: An Analysis of Laws and Policies in the United States, Each State and Jurisdiction, A Report of the National Center for Family Planning Services 76 (1971) (DHEW Pub. No. (HSA) 74-16001). This publication contains a comprehensive survey of state laws in this area. The authors were aware of "no case in which either a doctor or a layman has been successfully prosecuted under any criminal statute for providing contraceptive information or services to a minor or has been held liable for damages for providing contraception to a minor without parental consent." *Id.,* at 70. This survey also indicated that "the clear trend is toward the removal of all such barriers to the sale and distribution of contraceptives." *Id.,* at 59. By 1971 there were 34 States with no law restricting or regulating distribution of contraceptives, *ibid.,* and 33 States with no restrictions on advertising or display. *Id.,* at 60.

The State's asserted justification is a desire to inhibit sexual conduct by minors under 16. Appellants do not seriously contend that if contraceptives are available, significant numbers of minors who now abstain from sex will cease abstaining because they will no longer fear pregnancy or disease.[2] Rather appellants' central argument is that the statute has the important *symbolic* effect of communicating disapproval of sexual activity by minors.[3] In essence, therefore, the statute is defended as a form of propaganda, rather than a regulation of behavior.[4]

Although the State may properly perform a teaching function, it seems to me that an attempt to persuade by inflicting harm on the listener is an unacceptable means of conveying a message that is otherwise legitimate. The propaganda technique used in this case significantly increases the risk of unwanted pregnancy and venereal disease. It is as though a State decided to dramatize its disapproval of motorcycles by forbidding the use of safety helmets. One need not posit a constitutional right to ride a motorcycle to characterize such a restriction as irrational and perverse.

Even as a regulation of behavior, such a statute would be defective. Assuming that the State could impose a uniform

---

[2] Appellants make this argument only once, in passing. See Brief for Appellants 20. In the District Court, appellants candidly admitted that "there is no evidence that teenage extramarital sexual activity increases in proportion to the availability of contraceptives. . . ." See 398 F. Supp. 321, 332. Indeed, appellants maintain that it is a "fact that youngsters will not use contraceptives even where available . . . ." Reply Brief for Appellants 5.

[3] The fact that the State admittedly has never brought a prosecution under the statute, *id.*, at 2, is consistent with appellants' position that the purpose of the statute is merely symbolic.

[4] Appellants present no empirical evidence to support the conclusion that the State's "propaganda" is effective. Simply as a matter of common sense, it seems unlikely that many minors under 16 are influenced by the mere existence of a law indirectly disapproving of their conduct.

sanction upon young persons who risk self-inflicted harm by operating motorcycles, or by engaging in sexual activity, surely that sanction could not take the form of deliberately injuring the cyclist or infecting the promiscuous child. If such punishment may not be administered deliberately, after trial and a finding of guilt, it manifestly cannot be imposed by a legislature, indiscriminately and at random. This kind of government-mandated harm, is, in my judgment, appropriately characterized as a deprivation of liberty without due process of law.

II

In Part V of its opinion, the Court holds that New York's total ban on contraceptive advertising is unconstitutional under *Bigelow* v. *Virginia,* 421 U. S. 809, and *Virginia Pharmacy Bd.* v. *Virginia Citizens Consumer Council,* 425 U. S. 748. Specifically, the Court holds that all contraceptive advertising may not be suppressed because *some* advertising of that subject may be offensive and embarrassing to the reader or listener. I also agree with that holding.

The Court properly does not decide whether the State may impose any regulation on the content of contraceptive advertising in order to minimize its offensive character. I have joined Part V of the opinion on the understanding that it does not foreclose such regulation simply because an advertisement is within the zone protected by the First Amendment.

The fact that a type of communication is entitled to some constitutional protection does not require the conclusion that it is totally immune from regulation. Cf. *Young* v. *American Mini Theatres, Inc.,* 427 U. S. 50, 65–71 (opinion of STEVENS, J.). An editorial and an advertisement in the same newspaper may contain misleading matter in equal measure. Although each is a form of protected expression, one may be censored while the other may not.

In the area of commercial speech—as in the business of exhibiting motion pictures for profit—the offensive character of the communication is a factor which may affect the time, place, or manner in which it may be expressed. Cf. *Young* v. *American Mini Theatres, Inc., supra.* The fact that the advertising of a particular subject matter is *sometimes* offensive does not deprive all such advertising of First Amendment protection; but it is equally clear to me that the existence of such protection does not deprive the State of all power to regulate such advertising in order to minimize its offensiveness. A picture which may appropriately be included in an instruction book may be excluded from a billboard.

I concur in the judgment and in Parts I, II, III, and V of the Court's opinion.

MR. JUSTICE REHNQUIST, dissenting.

Those who valiantly but vainly defended the heights of Bunker Hill in 1775 made it possible that men such as James Madison might later sit in the first Congress and draft the Bill of Rights to the Constitution. The post-Civil War Congresses which drafted the Civil War Amendments to the Constitution could not have accomplished their task without the blood of brave men on both sides which was shed at Shiloh, Gettysburg, and Cold Harbor. If those responsible for these Amendments, by feats of valor or efforts of draftsmanship, could have lived to know that their efforts had enshrined in the Constitution the right of commercial vendors of contraceptives to peddle them to unmarried minors through such means as window displays and vending machines located in the men's room of truck stops, notwithstanding the considered judgment of the New York Legislature to the contrary, it is not difficult to imagine their reaction.[1]

---

[1] As well as striking down the New York prohibitions of commercial advertising and sales to persons under 16, the Court holds invalid the State's requirement that all sales be made by licensed pharmacists. Whatever New York's reasons for this particular restriction on distribution—and several can be imagined—I cannot believe that it could significantly impair

I do not believe that the cases discussed in the Court's opinion require any such result, but to debate the Court's treatment of the question on a case-by-case basis would concede more validity to the result reached by the Court than I am willing to do.[2] There comes a point when endless and ill-considered extension of principles originally formulated in quite different cases produces such an indefensible result that no logic chopping can possibly make the fallacy of the result more obvious. The Court here in effect holds that the First and Fourteenth Amendments not only guarantee full and free debate *before* a legislative judgment as to the moral dangers to which minors within the jurisdiction of the State should not be subjected, but goes further and absolutely prevents the representatives of the majority from carrying out such a policy *after* the issues have been fully aired.

No questions of religious belief, compelled allegiance to a secular creed, or decisions on the part of married couples as to procreation, are involved here. New York has simply decided that it wishes to discourage unmarried minors under 16 from having promiscuous sexual intercourse with one another. Even the Court would scarcely go so far as to say that this is not a subject with which the New York Legislature may properly concern itself.

That legislature has not chosen to deny to a pregnant woman, after the *fait accompli* of pregnancy, the one remedy

---

the access to these products of a person with a settled and deliberate intention to procure them.

[2] I cannot, however, let pass without comment, the statement that "the Court has not definitively answered the difficult question whether and to what extent the Constitution prohibits state statutes regulating [private consensual sexual] behavior among adults." *Ante*, at 688 n. 5, 694 n. 17. While we have not ruled on every conceivable regulation affecting such conduct the facial constitutional validity of criminal statutes prohibiting certain consensual acts has been "definitively" established. *Doe* v. *Commonwealth's Attorney*, 425 U. S. 901 (1976). See *Hicks* v. *Miranda*, 422 U. S. 332, 343-344 (1975).

which would enable her to terminate an unwanted pregnancy. It has instead sought to deter the conduct which will produce such *faits accomplis*. The majority of New York's citizens are in effect told that however deeply they may be concerned about the problem of promiscuous sex and intercourse among unmarried teenagers, they may not adopt this means of dealing with it. The Court holds that New York may not use its police power to legislate in the interests of its concept of the public morality as it pertains to minors. The Court's denial of a power so fundamental to self-government must, in the long run, prove to be but a temporary departure from a wise and heretofore settled course of adjudication to the contrary. I would reverse the judgment of the District Court.

Abortion Rights of Minors, Parental Consent, and Parental Notification

CAROLYN PUZELLA
Family Law, February 1997

Question Presented

Does an unemancipated minor female have a constitutional right to an abortion without first obtaining parental consent?

Short Answer

Yes, although not without limitations. The United States Supreme Court has extended the constitutional right of a woman to choose to have an abortion to unemancipated minor females. Although the Court has recognized that parental consent requirements further both the parental right to raise children free of state interference and legitimate state interests in protecting the minor's vulnerability, health and safety, minors nevertheless have a limited privacy right in the choice of whether to have an abortion. A state statute requiring parental consent before an unmarried minor can have an abortion would violate the minor's constitutionally protected right to privacy.

The Court has held that a state may require the minor to seek parental approval if an alternative method is provided, such as judicial waiver or bypass, to permit the minor to express her choice in the event her parents do not consent. Such an alternative is deemed necessary to protect those minors who cannot obtain parental consent and who either are mature enough to make the decision on their own, or who are immature and incapable of making such a decision when having an abortion would be in their best interest. Provision for judicial waiver also ensures that the minor's fundamental right to choose an abortion is not unduly burdened by the State.

The Constitutional Framework

In the landmark decision of *Roe v. Wade,* 410 U.S. 113 (1973), the Court recognized that this fundamental right of privacy is broad enough to encompass a woman's decision to terminate her pregnancy. In 1976 the Court held that a Missouri statute violated the constitutionally protected right to privacy in requiring the written consent of a parent as a condition to abortion when the woman desiring abortion was unmarried, under the age of eighteen, and in the first twelve weeks of her pregnancy. *Planned Parenthood of Central Missouri v. Danforth,* 428 U.S. 52 (1976). The *Danforth* Court reasoned that, since the State itself cannot regulate the abortion decision during the first trimester, the State lacks the constitutional authority to give a third party an absolute, and possibly arbitrary, veto over the decision of the physician and his/her patient to terminate the patient's pregnancy. "Constitutional rights do not mature and come into being magically only when one attains state-defined age of majority. Minors, as well as adults, are protected by the Constitution and possess constitutional rights." *Id.,* at 74.

The *Danforth* Court recognized that the State has broader authority to regulate the activities of children than of adults. But when the minor and the nonconsenting parent are so fundamentally in conflict and the "very existence of the pregnancy already has fractured the family structure," *id.* at 75, providing a parent with the absolute power to overrule a determination of the physician and her minor patient to terminate the patient's pregnancy does not further any significant state interest in safeguarding the family unit or in enhancing parental authority and control. The *Danforth* Court emphasized, however, it did not mean to suggest that every minor, regardless of age or maturity, has the power to give effective consent for termination of her pregnancy. *Id.*

Three years later, in *Bellotti v. Baird,* 443 U.S. 622 (1979) *(Bellotti II),* the Court reconsidered the constitutionality of a statutory parental-consent requirement. Reaffirming its decision in *Danforth,* the *Bellotti II* Court held that a State may not constitutionally impose a *blanket* provision requiring consent of a parent as a condition of abortion for an unmarried minor. The Court noted that the potentially severe detriment facing a pregnant woman is not mitigated by her minority; and that unwanted motherhood may be exceptionally burdensome for a minor, considering the probability of her limited education, employment skills, financial resources, and emotional maturity. *Id.* at 642.

However, the *Bellotti II* Court refused to equate the constitutional rights of children with those of adults. The Court gave three reasons for this refusal: the special vulnerability of children; their inability to make critical decisions in an informed, mature manner; and the importance of the parental role in child rearing. *Id.* at 634. The Court recognized the State's strong and legitimate interest in the welfare of its young citizens, whose immaturity, inexperience, and lack of judgment may sometimes impair their ability to exercise their rights wisely. *Id.* at 634-639. Accordingly, the Court stated that the State may reasonably determine that parental consultation often is desirable and in the best interest of the minor, and that parental notification and consent requirements are not unconstitutional *per se. Id.* at 640. But the Court concluded that if a State decides to require a pregnant minor to obtain one or both parents' consent to an abortion, then it must also provide an alternative procedure, such as judicial proceedings, by which authorization for the abortion can be obtained.[1] *Id.* at 643. The Court explained *(id.* at 644-645):

> "A pregnant minor is entitled to a proceeding to show either: (1) that she is mature enough and well enough informed to make her abortion decision, in consultation with her physician, independently of her parents' wishes; or (2) that even if she is not able to make this decision independently, the desired abortion would be in her best interests."

In order to protect the minor's fundamental right to seek an abortion and not unduly burden her decision, the bypass procedure must ensure that the provision requiring parental consent does not in fact amount to an "absolute, and possibly arbitrary veto." *Id.*[2]

Bellotti II supplied the basic requirements for future statutes that would provide alternative judicial proceedings to minors who wished to obtain authorization for abortion. Two recent Supreme Court decisions—*Hodgson v. Minnesota*, 497 U.S. 417 (1990), and *Ohio v. Akron Center for Reproductive Health*, 497 U.S. 502 (1990) *(Akron II)*—discuss the nature

1. The alternative procedure discussed in the case is a judicial proceeding, but the Court did not mean to suggest that a State could not delegate the alternative procedure to a juvenile court or an administrative agency or officer. Id. at 643.

2. The Court held the Massachusetts statute unconstitutional because it permitted judicial authorization to be withheld from a minor who was found to be mature and fully competent to make the decision independently, and because it required parental notification in every instance without affording the pregnant minor an opportunity to receive an independent determination that she was mature enough to consent or that an abortion would be in her best interest. Id. at 651.

and type of judicial proceeding necessary to comport with due process as indicated in *Bellotti II*.[3]

In *Hodgson*, a Minnesota statute required a mandatory 48-hour delay between notification of *both* parents and performance of the abortion, but allowed for a judicial bypass if the minor could convince the judge that she was mature and capable of giving informed consent. *Hodgson*, 497 U.S. at 422. It was clear to the Court that the requirement that both parents be notified, whether or not they had assumed responsibility for the upbringing of the child, furthered no legitimate state interest in the family situation and could lead to detrimental effects on the minor. *Id.* at 438-440, 450. The 5-4 majority upheld the constitutionality of the statute, however, on the ground that any constitutional infirmity in the two-parent notification requirement was removed by the judicial bypass option. *Id.* at 455.

In *Akron II*, an Ohio statute required that an unemancipated minor's physician give notice to one of her parents prior to performing an abortion. However, the statute provided for a judicial bypass procedure through which a minor could obtain a waiver of the notice if she presented clear and convincing evidence that she was mature enough to make the decision herself, that one of her parents had abused her, or that the notification was not in her best interest.[4] *Akron II*, 497 U.S. at 507-508. The Court upheld the statute, finding that it comported with *Bellotti II* on parental notice and did not impose an unconstitutional or undue burden on a minor seeking an abortion. *Id.* at 519. The Court reasoned that, because of the close relationship between the physician and the patient, parental notification logically should be the physician's responsibility; that notification by the physician does not place any greater burden on the minor, while furthering the valuable purpose of providing important medical data to the physician through parents; and that the notification procedure may facilitate better advice given from parent to child. *Id.* at 518-519.[5]

3. See generally Sue Ganske Graziano, *Parental Notification and a Minor's Right to an Abortion After Hodgson & Akron II*, 17 Ohio N.U.L. Rev. 581 (1991); Christopher M. Kelly, Tracy D. Knox, Randolph R. Rompola, *Hodgson and Akron II: The Supreme Court's New Standard for Minor's Abortion Statutes*, 66 Notre Dame L. Rev. 527 (1990).

4. The judicial bypass procedure also included a provision allowing the minor to proceed with the abortion without either parental or judicial consent if the court did not act within five days of the hearing.

5. The Court also found that imposing a "clear and convincing burden of proof" on the minor during the judicial proceeding was appropriate to advance the state interest in insuring that immature minors do not make the choice to have an abortion. *Id.* at 516.

SEEKING SOLOMON'S WISDOM: JUDICIAL BYPASS OF PARENTAL INVOLVEMENT IN A MINOR'S ABORTION DECISION

Teresa Stanton Collett*

TABLE OF CONTENTS

---

*Professor of Law, South Texas College of Law, Houston, Texas. The author testified in favor of Senate Bill 30 before legislative committees in both houses of the Texas Legislature, served on the Texas Supreme Court Rules Advisory Special Subcommittee on Implementation of Family Code Chapter 33, and represented the Texas Coalition for Parents' Rights in amicus briefs to the Texas Supreme Court in *In re Doe* and *In re Doe 2*. The author also represented the legislative sponsors of Senate Bill 30 in an amicus brief presented to the Texas Supreme Court in *In re Doe 4 (II)*. Portions of this article have been drawn from those briefs.

I. INTRODUCTION

On January 1, 2000, the Parental Notification Act, chapter 33 of the Texas Family Code, went into effect. This Act requires a physician to provide forty-eight hours notice to the parent, guardian or managing conservator of any unemanicipated minor seeking an abortion prior to performing the procedure in Texas.[1] Notice must be given by the physician rather than a member of his or her staff.[2] In cases where the doctor has made reasonable attempts to contact a minor's parent but been

[1]*See* TEX. FAM. CODE ANN. § 33.002(a)(1) (Vernon Supp. 2000).

[2]*See id.* In *H.L. v. Matheson*, the Supreme Court upheld a Utah notice statute which required the physician to notify the parents because the physician often could obtain a better medical history of the minor from her parents and was in the best position to provide full medical information to the parents so that the parents could provide good medical advice to their child. 450 U.S. 398, 411–12 (1981). This position was reaffirmed in *Ohio v. Akron Center for Reproductive Health*. 497 U.S. 502, 518 (1990); *cf.* Mazurek v. Armstrong, 520 U.S. 968 (1997) (per curiam) (upholding as constitutional a statute that restricts the performance of abortions to licensed physicians).

unsuccessful, the doctor may perform the abortion forty-eight hours after providing notice to the parent by certified mail.[3]

The minor may petition a court for an order permitting her to consent to the abortion without such notification if she believes that she is sufficiently mature and well informed to make the decision without parental notification; that parental notification is not in her best interest; or that notification may lead to physical, sexual, or emotional abuse.[4] While Texas statutes permit minors to make a limited number of medical decisions without parental involvement,[5] the general rule is that a parent must consent to all medical procedures performed on a minor due to the legal incapacity of minors.[6] The judicial bypass process contained in chapter 33 represents the first time that Texas courts have been asked to consider bypassing parental involvement in decisions relating to the medical care of minors, absent any showing that the parent cannot be contacted[7] or has unreasonably refused to consent to life-sustaining care.[8]

During the first six months the Act has been in effect, Texas appellate courts have been called upon to interpret the judicial bypass provisions of chapter 33[9] numerous times. To date, the Texas Supreme Court has issued

---

[3]*See* TEX. FAM. CODE ANN. § 33.002(b). Several statutes upheld by the United States Supreme Court provide for constructive notice by certified mail. An Ohio statute's constructive notice by mail provision, where the physician was not able to contact the parent after a "reasonable effort," provided an adequate method of insuring that the notice requirement to the parent did not overly impose upon the doctor's schedule. *See Akron Ctr. for Reprod. Health*, 497 U.S. at 519. A Montana statute permitting constructive notice by certified mail after reasonable effort was upheld in *Lambert v. Wicklund*, 520 U.S. 292, 293 (1997) (per curiam).

It is interesting that notice by mail under this Act is shorter than the general rule of civil procedure.

> Whenever a party has the right or is required to do some act . . . within a prescribed period after the service of a notice or other paper upon him and the notice or paper is served upon him by mail [or by telephonic document transfer], three days shall be added to the prescribed period.

TEX. R. CIV. P. 21a (emphasis added).

[4]*See* TEX. FAM. CODE ANN. § 33.003(i).

[5]*See id.* § 32.003(a) (Vernon 1996 & Supp. 2000).

[6]*See id.* § 151.003(a)(6).

[7]*See id.* § 32.001 (Vernon 1996).

[8]*See.* O.G. v. Baum, 790 S.W.2d 839, 841 (Tex. App.—Houston [1st Dist.] 1990, no writ) (finding parental authority limited where a parent has unreasonably refused to consent to life sustaining care).

[9]*See* TEX. FAM. CODE ANN. §§ 33.003–.004 (Vernon Supp. 2000).

eight rulings in five cases by way of twenty-three separate opinions,[10] and there is reason to believe that the court will continue to be called upon to provide guidance regarding the proper interpretation and application of this Act.[11]

This Article provides a brief description of the current federal constitutional law regarding parental involvement laws, a summary of the historical experience with judicial bypass proceedings in other states, a discussion of the Texas judicial bypass process as it has been interpreted by the Texas Supreme Court, and an explanation of the statutory basis for bypassing parental notification of a minor's decision to obtain an abortion. The appendix to this Article contains an annotated series of suggested questions that may be used in evaluating whether minors meet the statutory grounds.[12] Only through knowledgeable and careful review of minors' applications to bypass parental notification can Texas courts achieve the proper balance between the liberty interest of the minor in deciding whether to continue or abort her pregnancy and the constitutional right of parents to be involved in decisions regarding their minor daughters' medical care.

A. The Landscape of Federal Constitutional Law

Laws requiring parental notification or consent prior to the performance of an abortion upon a minor, collectively known as "parental involvement laws," are the product of widespread agreement that parents should be involved in their minor daughter's decision to continue or terminate an unplanned pregnancy. Neither abortion rights activists nor pro-life

---

[10]*See In re* Doe 5, No. 00-0636 (Tex. June 28, 2000) (affirming lower courts without opinion); *In re* Doe (II), 19 S.W.3d 346 (Tex. 2000) (six opinions); *In re* Doe 4 (II), 19 S.W.3d 337 (Tex. 2000) (two opinions); *In re* Doe 4, 19 S.W.3d 322 (Tex. 2000) (three opinions); *In re* Doe 3, 19 S.W.3d 300 (Tex. 2000) (per curiam) (five opinions); *In re* Doe 1, 19 S.W.3d 300 (Tex. 2000) (one opinion published, three to follow); *In re* Doe 2, 19 S.W.3d 278 (Tex. 2000) (three opinions); *In re* Doe, 19 S.W.3d 249 (Tex. 2000) (four opinions).

[11]*See In re Doe 3*, 19 S.W.3d at 318 (Hecht, J. dissenting).

[12]Not every suggested question will be appropriate for each minor seeking to bypass parental involvement. Each minor's circumstances and claims will be unique and should be explored through individualized questions by the court. *See In re Doe 1 (II)*, 19 S.W.3d at 359 (finding that responses to a uniform checklist of questions are not required to establish that minor has thoughtfully considered her options). However, many issues will be common to all minors seeking an abortion without parental knowledge, and the suggested questions provide a basis for exploring the common issues.

advocates dispute this point.[13] The national consensus on this issue is illustrated by the fact that there are parental involvement laws on the books in forty-three of the fifty states.[14] Of these forty-three, the laws of thirty-

---

[13]*See* NARAL Publications: *Factsheet: The Child Custody Protection Act Threatens Young Women's Health*, (Jan 10, 2000) <http://www.naral.org/mediaresources/fact/ccpa_womenshealth.html>. "Adolescents should be encouraged to seek their parents' advice and counsel when facing difficult choices regarding abortion and other reproductive health issues." *Id.* "Planned Parenthood encourages young women to involve their parents when they become pregnant and consider an abortion." *'Child Custody Protection Act' Endangers Young Women*, PR NEWSWIRE, May 13, 1998 (statement by Gloria Feldt, President of Planned Parenthood).

> [P]hysicians should strongly encourage minors to discuss their pregnancy . . . with their parents. . . . Physicians should explain how parental involvement can be helpful and that parents are generally very understanding and supportive. . . . If a minor expresses concerns about parental involvement, the physician should try to ensure that the minor's reluctance is not based on any misperceptions about the likely consequences of parental involvement.

Council on Ethical and Judicial Affairs, American Medical Association, *Mandatory Parental Consent to Abortion*, 269 JAMA 82, 83 (1993) (opposing laws that mandate parental involvement on the basis that such laws may expose minors to physical harm, or compromise the minor's need for privacy on matters of sexual intimacy).

[14]*See* ALA. CODE §§ 26-21-1 to -8 (1992 & Supp. 1999); ALASKA STAT. §§ 18.16.010–030 (Michie 1998); ARIZ. REV. STAT. ANN. § 36-2152 (West 1993 & Supp. 1999); ARK. CODE ANN. §§ 20-16-801 to -808 (Michie 2000); CAL. HEALTH & SAFETY CODE § 123450 (West 1996 & Supp. 1999); COLO. REV. STAT. ANN. §§ 12-37.5-101 to -108 (West Supp. 1999); CONN. GEN. STAT. ANN. § 19(a)-601 (West 1997); DEL. CODE ANN. tit. 24, §§ 1780–1789B (1997); FLA. STAT. ANN. § 390.01115 (West Supp. 2000); GA. CODE ANN. §§ 15-11-110 to -118 (Harrison 1998); IDAHO CODE § 18-609(6) (1997); 750 ILL. COMP. STAT. 70/1-70/99 (West 1999); IND. CODE ANN. §§ 16-18-2-267, 16-34-2-4 (West 1997); IOWA CODE ANN. §§ 135L.1–8 (West 1997 & Supp. 2000); KAN. STAT. ANN. § 65-6705 (1992 & Supp. 1999); KY. REV. STAT. ANN. § 311.732 (Michie 1995 & Supp. 1998); LA. REV. STAT. ANN. § 40:1299.35.5 (West 1992 & Supp. 2000); ME. REV. STAT. ANN. tit. 22, § 1597-A (West 1992 & Supp. 1999); MD. CODE ANN., HEALTH-GEN. § 20-103 (1996); MASS. ANN. LAWS ch. 112, § 12s (Law. Co-op. 1991 & Supp. 2000); MICH. STAT. ANN. §§ 25.248 (101)–(109) (Law. Co-op. 1999 & Supp. 2000); MINN. STAT. ANN. § 144.343 (West 1998); MISS. CODE ANN. §§ 41-41-51 to -63 (1993 & Supp. 1998); MO. ANN. STAT. §§ 188.015, 188.028 (West 1996 & Supp. 2000); MONT. CODE ANN. §§ 50-20-201 to -215 (1999); NEB. REV. STAT. §§ 71-6901 to -6909 (1996); NEV. REV. STAT. §§ 442.255–.257 (2000); N.J. STAT. ANN. §§ 9:17A-1 to -1.12 (West 1993 & Supp. 2000); N.M. STAT. ANN. §§ 30-5-1 to -3 (Michie 2000); N.C. GEN. STAT. §§ 90-21.6 to .10 (1999); N.D. CENT. CODE §§ 14-02.1 to 03.1 (1997); OHIO REV. CODE ANN. § 2919.12 (Anderson 1996); 18 PA. CONS. STAT. ANN. § 3206 (West 1983 & Supp. 2000); R.I. GEN. LAWS § 23-4.7-6 (1996); S.C. CODE ANN. §§ 44-41-30 to -37 (Law. Co-op. 1985 & Supp. 1999); S.D. CODIFIED LAWS § 34-23A-7 (Michie 1994 & Supp. 1999); TENN. CODE ANN. § 37-10-301 to -304 (1996 & Supp. 1999); TEX. FAM. CODE ANN. § 33.001–.004 (Vernon Supp. 2000); UTAH CODE ANN. § 76-7-304 (1999); VA. CODE ANN. § 16.1-241(D) (Michie 1999 &

seven states are in effect today.[15] While nine of these states have laws that are substantially ineffectual in assuring parental involvement in a minor's decision to obtain an abortion,[16] parents in the remaining twenty-six states are effectively guaranteed the right to parental notification or consent in most cases.[17]

This consensus in favor of parental involvement is also reflected in the decisions of the federal courts. *Planned Parenthood v. Danforth* was the first of a series of United States Supreme Court cases dealing with parental involvement laws.[18] In this opinion, Justice Stewart wrote, "There can be little doubt that the State furthers a constitutionally permissible end by encouraging an unmarried pregnant minor to seek the help and advice of her parents in making the very important decision whether or not to bear a child."[19] Three years later in *Bellotti v. Baird* (*Bellotti II*), the Court acknowledged that parental consultation is critical for minors considering abortion because "minors often lack the experience, perspective, and

---

Supp. 2000); W. VA. CODE §§ 16-2F-1 to -8 (1998); WIS. STAT. ANN. § 48.375 (West 1997); WYO. STAT. ANN. § 35-6-118 (Michie 1999).

[15]The implementation of seven state statutes has been enjoined by courts in the face of claims of state or federal constitutional infirmity. *See* Planned Parenthood v. Lawall, 180 F.3d 1022, 1033 (9th Cir. 1999); Foe v. Vanderhoof, 389 F. Supp. 947, 959 (D. Colo. 1975) (having been corrected by new legislation, but new legislation has been attacked in court); Glick v. McKay, 616 F. Supp. 322, 327 (D. Nev. 1985), *aff'd*, 937 F.2d 434 (9th Cir. 1991); Valley Hosp. Ass'n v. Mat-Su Coalition for Choice, 948 P.2d 963, 972 (Alaska 1997); American Acad. of Pediatrics v. Lungren, 940 P.2d 797, 800 (Cal. 1997); State v. Presidential Women's Ctr., 707 So. 2d 1145, 1151 (Fla. Dist Ct. App. 1998);

[16]*See* CONN. GEN. STAT. ANN. § 19(a)-601 (stating that the abortion provider need only discuss the possibility of parental involvement); DEL. CODE ANN. tit. 24, § 1783(a) (allowing notice to a licensed mental health professional not associated with an abortion provider); KAN. STAT. ANN. § 65-6705(j) (allowing a physician to bypass parental notice in cases where the physician determines that an emergency exists that threatens the "well-being" of the minor); ME. REV. STAT. ANN. tit. 22, § 1597-A(2) (allowing a minor to give informed consent after counseling by the abortion provider); MD. CODE ANN., HEALTH-GEN. § 20-103(c) (allowing a physician to determine that parental notice is not in the minor's best interest); OHIO REV. CODE ANN. § 2919.12 (stating that notice may be given to a brother, sister, step-parent, or grandparent if certain qualifications are met); UTAH CODE ANN. § 76-7-304 (stating that a physician need notify only if possible); W. VA. CODE § 16-2F-1 (stating physician not affiliated with an abortion provider may waive the notice requirement); WIS. STAT. ANN. § 48-375 (stating that the notice may be given to any adult family member).

[17]The guarantee is qualified by the fact that every state with an effective parental involvement law has judicial bypass of parental involvement for mature and well-informed minors and minors for whom the court determines that abortion is in their best interest.

[18]428 U.S. 52 (1976).

[19]*Id.* at 91 (Stewart, J., concurring).

judgment to recognize and avoid choices that could be detrimental to them."[20] The *Bellotti II* Court also observed that "[parental] consultation is particularly desirable with respect to the abortion decision [since it is] one that for some people raises profound moral and religious concerns."[21] More recently, in *Planned Parenthood v. Casey* Justices O'Connor, Kennedy, and Souter observed that parental consent and notification laws "are based on the quite reasonable assumption that minors will benefit from consultation with their parents and that children will often not realize that their parents have their best interests at heart."[22]

Notwithstanding the acknowledged value of parental involvement in a minor's decision to obtain an abortion, the Supreme Court has placed some limits on the traditional authority of parents to decide whether to consent to medical intervention on behalf of their minor children.[23] In *Planned Parenthood v. Danforth* the Supreme Court struck down a parental consent statute similar to an earlier Texas statute,[24] observing that "the State does not have the constitutional authority to give a third party an absolute, and possibly arbitrary, veto over the decision of the physician and his patient to terminate the patient's pregnancy, regardless of the reason for withholding the consent."[25] The Court retained this rule in *Bellotti II*, while providing

---

[20]443 U.S. 622, 635 (1979) (plurality opinion) (*Bellotti II*).

[21]*Id.* at 640.

[22]505 U.S. 833, 895 (1992) (plurality opinion).

[23]Many state cases represent the traditional authority of parents to make medical decisions for their minor children. *See In re* Eric B., 235 Cal. Rptr. 22, 29 (Ct. App. 1987) (requiring the medical monitoring of a child following court-ordered chemotherapy treatments over renewed parental objections); Newmark v. Williams, 588 A.2d 1108, 1120 (Del. 1991) (upholding parents' rejection of chemotherapy in favor of prayer treatment where survival was not assured even with medical intervention); *In re* Green, 292 A.2d 387, 392 (Pa. 1972) (dismissing court-ordered medical intervention for 17-year-old poliomyelitis patient suffering from 94% curvature of the spine on basis that condition is not considered life-threatening); Powers v. Floyd, 904 S.W.2d 713, 718 (Tex. App.—Waco 1995, writ denied) (failure to obtain minor's consent to abortion in 1974 did not constitute battery since parent consented); Moss v. Rishworth, 222 S.W. 225, 226 (Tex. Comm'n App. 1920, judgm't adopted) (battery to operate on child absent parent's consent).

[24]In 1981, the state attorney general issued an opinion that Proposed Parental Consent and Notification Statute, House Bill 578, would be unconstitutional unless amended to include a bypass procedure for in cases where abortion is found to be in the minor's best interest as well as a bypass for mature minors. *See* Op. Tex. Att'y Gen. No. MW-346 (1981).

[25]428 U.S. at 74. The Court observed that "[a]ny independent interest the parent may have in the termination of the minor daughter's pregnancy [was] no more weighty than the right of privacy of the competent minor mature enough to have become pregnant." *Id.* at 75.

guidance to state legislatures regarding the requirements for a constitutional parental consent statute:

> We therefore conclude that if the State decides to require a pregnant minor to obtain one or both parents' consent to an abortion, it also must provide an alternative procedure whereby authorization for the abortion can be obtained.
>
> A pregnant minor is entitled in such a proceeding to show either: (1) that she is mature enough and well enough informed to make her abortion decision, in consultation with her physician, independently of her parents' wishes; or (2) that even if she is not able to make this decision independently, the desired abortion would be in her best interests.[26]

Thus, a parental consent statute must contain some process for bypassing parental involvement in cases involving well-informed, mature minors, or in cases where the abortion is found to be in the best interest of the minor.

It has been recognized that parental notification laws do not empower parents to veto any decisions by their minor daughters.[27] In *Hodgson v. Minnesota*, Justice Stevens observed that "[a]lthough the Court has held that parents may not exercise 'an absolute, and possibly arbitrary, veto' over [the] decision [by a minor to terminate her pregnancy], it has never challenged a State's reasonable judgment that the decision should be made after notification to and consultation with a parent."[28] Nonetheless, the United States Supreme Court has explicitly declined to rule on the question of whether a judicial bypass process is required to preserve the constitutionality of notification statutes, absent a case presenting such a statute.[29] Lower federal courts are split on this issue.[30]

---

[26]*Bellotti II*, 443 U.S. at 643–44 (footnotes omitted) (plurality opinion).

[27]*See Danforth*, 428 U.S. at 74.

[28]497 U.S. 417, 445 (1990) (citations omitted) (quoting *Danforth*, 428 U.S. at 74).

[29]*See* Ohio v. Akron Ctr. for Reprod. Health, 497 U.S. 502, 510 (1990); *see also* Lambert v. Wicklund, 520 U.S. 292, 295 (1997) (per curiam); *Bellotti II*, 443 U.S. at 654 n.1 (Stevens, J., concurring) ("[T]his case [does not] determin[e] the constitutionality of a statute which does no more than require notice to the parents, without affording them or any other third party an absolute veto."); Planned Parenthood v. Camblos, 155 F.3d 352, 361–67 (4th Cir. 1998) (reviewing extensively Supreme Court precedent on this issue).

[30]The United States Court of Appeals for the Fifth Circuit has never ruled on this question. The most recent and thorough opinion on the issue held that bypass was not required in all notification statutes. *See Camblos*, 155 F.3d at 373 (4th Cir. 1998). However, the United State Courts of Appeals for the Sixth, Seventh, and Eighth Circuits have ruled to the contrary. *See*

In part due to this unresolved constitutional question and in part due to varied political judgments about the desirability of legally requiring parental involvement in a minor's decision to obtain an abortion,[31] the Texas legislature chose to include judicial bypass in the Parental Notification Act codified as chapter 33 of the Texas Family Code.

B. Experience with Bypass Proceedings in Other States

Some opponents of the Parental Notification Act dismiss the judicial bypass process as too political, warning that courts will refuse minors' requests in an arbitrary and capricious manner.[32] Yet empirical evidence

---

Planned Parenthood, Sioux Falls Clinic v. Miller, 63 F.3d 1452 (8th Cir. 1995), *cert. denied sub nom.* Janklow v. Planned Parenthood, Sioux Falls Clinic, 517 U.S. 1174 (1996); Akron Ctr. for Reprod. Health v. Slaby, 854 F.2d 852 (6th Cir. 1988), *rev'd on other grounds sub nom.* Ohio v. Akron Ctr. for Reprod. Health, 497 U.S. 502 (1990); Indiana Planned Parenthood Affiliates Ass'n v. Pearson, 716 F.2d 1127, 1138 (7th Cir. 1983).

[31]"Three Texas polls since 1995 showed that at least 70 percent of those surveyed favored parental notification or consent." Sylvia Moreno, *73% in Texas Poll Back Abortion-Notification Law: Legislature Set to Debate Bill on Parental Notice*, THE DALLAS MORNING NEWS, Mar. 3, 1997, at 1A, *available in* 1997 WL 2650941. According to a Harte-Hanks Communications, Inc. survey conducted in April 1995, 73% of those surveyed favored passage of parental notification laws. *See Poll Finds 73% of Texans Back Parental Notification for Abortions*, THE DALLAS MORNING NEWS, Apr. 30, 1995, at 41A, *available in* 1995 WL 7489419. A 1992 Texas Abortion Rights Action League survey revealed 74% of all Texans support the even stronger measure of requiring parental *consent* prior to the performance of an abortion on a minor. *See* Ken Herman, *74% Support Consent Rule for Abortions*, THE HOUSTON POST, July 3, 1992, at A31; *see also* Anne Marie Kilday, *Poll Finds Texans Favor Parent Consent Rule: But 59% Want State to Let Abortion Law Alone*, THE DALLAS MORNING NEWS, July 3, 1992, at 38A, *available in* 1992 WL 7126785. In 1989, 70% of those surveyed favored passage of parental *consent* laws. Wayne Slater, *Most in Texas Poll Back Abortion in Certain Cases: Parental Consent for Minors Widely Supported*, THE DALLAS MORNING NEWS, Feb. 21, 1989, at 1A, *available in* 1989 WL 6165972 (reporting results of a poll conducted January 21 through February 23, 1989 by the Public Policy Resources Center at Texas A&M University). *But see* Kate McLaughlin & Bill Price, *Notifying Parents About Abortions: An Advocate and an Opponent of a Bill Before the Texas Legislature Debate the Merits of Requiring that a Parent Be Informed Before a Daughter Under 18 Can Have the Procedure*, THE DALLAS MORNING NEWS, Apr. 13, 1997, at 1J, *available in* 1997 WL 2661372 and 1997 WL 2661373; James Kimberly, *Texans Want Parents Told of Abortions, Poll Indicates*, HOUSTON CHRON., Mar. 13, 2000, at 1A, *available in* 2000 WL 4285672 (reflecting decline in public support due to the ability of the minor to bypass parental notification through a judicial order).

[32]*See Cruel Laws: Lawmakers, Texans Must Oppose Harmful Abortion Bill*, HOUSTON CHRON., Mar. 23, 1999, at 18A, *available in* 1999 WL 3980649.

> Forcing teens to seek a judge's ruling necessarily will politicize this private, medical issue. In a county like Harris, where approving an abortion could be political

from other states suggests just the opposite. For example, testimony received by the Texas House of Representatives' Committee on State Affairs revealed that approximately 16,000 petitions for judicial bypass have been heard by Massachusetts courts since 1981, yet only thirteen of these petitions have been denied, and eleven of those denials were overturned on appeal.[33] An earlier study of the Massachusetts experience

---

> suicide for a Republican jurist, some judges will rule based on career interests rather than the best interests of girls. Some judges flat oppose abortion and will rule accordingly, again ignoring the well-being of pregnant teens. Finally, the entire process is a license to re-victimize girls impregnated through rape or incest.

Id.; *see also Hearings on Tex. H.B. 623 Before the House Comm. on State Affairs*, 76th Leg., R.S. 13 (Apr. 19, 1999) (tapes available from the Office of the House Comm. Coordinator and content is from private transcripts of those tapes) (questioning by Representative Debra Danberg of the impartiality and judicial independence of state judges in Harris County); Debate on Tex. S.B. 30 on the Floor of the House, 76th Leg., R.S. 3 (May 22, 1999) (tapes available from the House Comm. Coordinator and content is from private transcripts of those tapes). The following exchange took place between Representatives David Swinford and Senfronia Thompson:

> REP. THOMPSON: Mr. Swinford, wouldn't you agree that a lot of our judges are elected by special interest groups?
>
> REP. SWINFORD: Oh I don't know. Probably.
>
> REP. THOMPSON: And don't you think they're not free to exercise judicial discretion when called upon particularly in situations like this?
>
> SWINFORD: Well, you know I would be, if I was a judge, I would really dislike this bill because I'd hate to make that decision. But he's got a different thing to do than a minister. A minister is to take care of the flock.

Id.; *see also* Debate on Tex. S.B. 30 on the Floor of the House, 76th Leg., R.S. 3 (May 22, 1999) (testimony of Representative Ken Yarborough) (expressing concern that experienced judges will decline to hear bypass cases from fear of political consequences) (tapes available from the Office of the House Comm. Coordinator and content is from private transcripts of those tapes); *In re* Doe (II), 19 S.W.3d 346, 353 (Tex. 2000) (noting that some legislators voiced concerns that the bypass provision would be too onerous to provide a real option for minors wanting to avoid parental notice).

[33]*See Hearings on Tex. H.B. 623 Before the House Comm. on State Affairs*, *supra* note 32, at 21–22 (testimony of Ms. Jamie Sabino, chair of the Mass. Judicial Consent for Minors Lawyer Referral Panel) (tapes available from the Office of the House Comm. Coordinator and content is from private transcripts of those tapes). This is consistent with earlier reported studies of the Massachusetts bypass. A survey of Massachusetts cases filed between 1981 and 1983 found that every minor that sought judicial authorization to bypass parental consent received it, except for one, who went to a neighboring state to secure an abortion rather than appeal. *See* ROBERT H. MNOOKIN, IN THE INTEREST OF CHILDREN: ADVOCACY, LAW REFORM, AND PUBLIC POLICY 239 (Robert H. Mnookin ed., 1985). A subsequent study found that orders were refused to only 1 of 477 girls seeking judicial authorization from Massachusetts courts between December 1981

revealed that the average hearing lasted only 12.12 minutes, and "more than 92 percent of the hearings [were] less than or equal to 20 minutes."[34]

Legislative committees also heard anecdotal evidence of similar ease in obtaining a bypass in Nebraska. During the hearing before the Texas Senate Committee on Human Services, Senator Florence Shapiro, the Senate sponsor, recounted a conversation with an attorney in Nebraska who worked with local affiliates of Planned Parenthood. "[I]n all the years that she's [represented minors seeking to judicially bypass parental involvement, there was only] one minor child, one, that was turned down, not only by the district court, but also by the court of appeals."[35]

These experiences are not unique. Based upon a review of bypass petitions filed in Minnesota from August 1, 1981 to March 1, 1986, a federal trial court determined that of the 3573 bypass petitions filed, six were withdrawn, nine were denied, and 3558 were granted.[36] News reports of the early experience under the Virginia statute requiring parental notification suggest equal readiness of the courts to allow minors to bypass their parents. Out of eighteen requests for judicial bypass, "[a]ll but one of the requests were granted eventually."[37]

The statistical record of approvals in some other states is troubling in so far as it suggests that courts may merely be going through the motions of making a judicial determination, rather than giving adequate consideration to the issues inherent in excluding parents from medical decisions regarding their minor children. For example, the finding that the average hearing lasts only 12.12 minutes in Massachusetts may evidence that the Massachusetts courts have severely overcrowded dockets and are unable to take the time necessary to explore the maturity or best interest of the minors seeking to avoid parental involvement. It may reflect abbreviated judicial inquiry due to inadequate knowledge of the issues surrounding teen pregnancy and abortion procedures, or the brevity and outcome of

---

and June 1985. *See* Susanne Yates & Anita J. Pliner, *Judging Maturity in the Courts: The Massachusetts Consent Statute*, 78 AM. J. PUB. HEALTH 646, 647 (1988).

[34]Yates & Pliner, *supra* note 33, at 648.

[35]The Parental Notification Act: *Hearings on Tex. S.B. 30 Before the Senate Human Servs. Comm.*, 76th Leg., R.S. 24 (Mar. 10, 1999) (transcript available from Senate Staff Servs. Office).

[36]*See* Hodgson v. State, 648 F. Supp. 756, 765 (D. Minn. 1986).

[37]Ellen Nakashima, *Fewer Teens Receiving Abortions in Virginia: Notification Law to Get Court Test*, WASH. POST, Mar. 3, 1998, at A1, *available in* 1998 WL 2470790 ("In Virginia, since the law took effect, 18 teenagers have gone to a judge, who determines whether the girl is mature enough to make her own decision about abortion. All but one of the requests were granted eventually.").

these hearings may reflect a de facto conclusive presumption that abortion is always in the best interest of the minor. The first two possible reasons are inexcusable in light of the gravity of the decision before the courts,[38] and the third is medically unsound[39] and constitutionally untenable.[40]

Members of the Texas Supreme Court recently suggested that legislative awareness of the ease of obtaining a bypass in other states evidenced legislative intent that bypasses be granted routinely by Texas courts.[41] However, thorough review of the legislative history of the Texas Act indicates that most legislative statements regarding the experiences of other states were intended to be descriptive, rather than normative, and that Texas courts were expected to do more than rubber-stamp bypass

---

[38]*See* Planned Parenthood v. Casey, 505 U.S. 833, 852 (1992) (plurality opinion).

> Abortion is a unique act. It is an act fraught with consequences for others: for the woman who must live with the implications of her decision; for the persons who perform and assist in the procedure; for the spouse, family, and society which must confront the knowledge that these procedures exist, procedures some deem nothing short of an act of violence against innocent human life; and, depending on one's beliefs, for the life or potential life that is aborted.

Id.

[39]*See* Stanley K. Henshaw, *Unintended Pregnancy and Abortion: A Public Health Perspective, in* A CLINICIAN'S GUIDE TO MEDICAL AND SURGICAL ABORTIONS 11, 20 (Maureen Paul et al. eds., 1999) (stating that mortality rates for abortions performed at 16-20 weeks is 9.3% and 12% for those performed after 20 weeks compared to a mortality rate of 6.5% due to complications attendant to pregnancy and childbirth). An example of where a court could reasonably determine that obtaining a secret abortion would not be in the best interest of a minor would be where the minor has delayed acknowledging her pregnancy until the fifth or sixth month of pregnancy, with the medical risks of abortion equaling those attendant to childbirth. *See id.*

[40]*See* Bellotti v. Baird, 443 U.S. 622, 648–49 (1979) (plurality opinion) (*Bellotti II*).

> Yet, an abortion may not be the best choice for the minor. The circumstances in which this issue arises will vary widely. In a given case, alternatives to abortion, such as marriage to the father of the child, arranging for its adoption, or assuming the responsibilities of motherhood with the assured support of family, may be feasible and relevant to the minor's best interests.

Id. at 642–43.

[41]*See* Brief Amici Curiae of State Senator Florence Shapiro and State Representative Dianne White Delisi, *In re* Doe 4 (II), 337 S.W.2d (Tex. 2000) (No. 00-0317). The supreme court discussed the brief in *In re Doe (II)*. 19 S.W.3d 346, 352–53 (Tex. 2000).

applications. This is made clear in an amicus brief filed by the Act's sponsors with the court in *In re Doe 4 (II)*.[42]

> Legislators were unanimous in their characterization of the bypass as "rare" or exceptional. The examples of cases involving use of the judicial bypass given by legislators during committee hearings or floor debate involved young girls facing dire circumstances. Senator Gallegos expressed repeated concern about girls who would be hospitalized or die due to abuse by parents who became outraged at the news of their daughter's pregnancy. Members of the House State Affairs Committee discussed use of the bypass in the context of the incest victim's needs. Representative Gray, in laying out House Bill 5 in committee, provided an even more detailed example of cases where bypass should be granted by discussing a hypothetical ten-year-old victim of incest. On the second reading of the Committee Substitute for Senate Bill 30 in the House of Representatives, Representative Gray offered a further example of bypass being appropriate in cases where "one parent may be in prison [and] another one may be on the streets with their own health problems." In the House floor debate Representative Giddings gave the example of a mother who had agreed to require her daughter to have sex with the mother's new husband. At the third, and final reading, of Senate Bill 30, Representative Delisi voiced a continuing concern that victims of incest, or physical abuse receive protection, and her belief that [Senate Bill] 30 advanced that goal. Each of these examples involve extraordinary circumstances presenting a real and present danger that a minor will be grievously harmed if a parent learns she is pregnant.[43]

The presumption of searching judicial review prior to the granting of a bypass is also reflected in the fact that the fiscal note accompanying the

---

[42]Brief Amici Curiae of State Senator Florence Shapiro and State Representative Dianne White Delisi, *In re Doe 4 (II)* (No. 00-0317). Nine senators and forty-seven representatives subsequently joined the sponsors in support of the brief. *See In re Doe (II)*. 19 S.W.3d at 352 n.6.

[43]Brief Amici Curiae of State Senator Florence Shapiro and State Representative Dianne White Delisi at 20–22, *In re Doe 4 (II)* (No. 00-0317) (footnotes omitted).

Texas legislation assumed that fifty percent of all applications would be denied and appealed.[44]

II. OVERVIEW OF TEXAS JUDICIAL BYPASS PROCESS

Under the Parental Notification Act, if a girl wishes to obtain an abortion without notification of a parent, she may seek judicial authorization to bypass parental involvement.[45] This process is initiated by filing a verified application stating that the applicant is an unemancipated minor who is pregnant and wishes to obtain an abortion without notifying either of her parents.[46] She must indicate whether she is seeking to avoid parental involvement because she is sufficiently mature and well informed to make the decision alone, because parental involvement is not in her best interest, or because notifying a parent may lead to physical, sexual, or emotional abuse.[47] The application and verification page also require the minor to provide her birthdate, whether she has retained counsel, whether she has previously sought judicial bypass of parental involvement in decisions regarding this pregnancy, and the means by which she can be contacted immediately and confidentially.[48]

Upon receipt of the application, the statute requires courts to appoint a guardian ad litem and an attorney ad litem to represent the girl.[49] While both the statute and the Texas Supreme Court Parental Notification Rules permit these offices to be combined in one person,[50] the potential for an impermissible conflict of interest is substantial.[51] The primary duty of the guardian ad litem is to seek a court ruling consistent with the guardian's

---

[44]*See* FISCAL NOTE, Tex. S.B. 30, 76th Leg., R.S. (1999).

[45]*See* TEX. FAM. CODE ANN. § 33.003 (Vernon Supp. 2000).

[46]*See* TEX. PARENTAL NOTIFICATION R. 2.1(c). For an extended discussion of the Texas Supreme Court Parental Notification Rules, see Ann Crawford McClure et al., *A Guide to Proceedings Under the Texas Parental Notification Statute and Rules*, 41 S. TEX. L. REV. 755 (2000).

[47]*See* TEX. PARENTAL NOTIFICATION R. 2.1(c)(1)(C); *see also* TEX. FAM. CODE ANN. § 33.003(m).

[48]*See* TEX. PARENTAL NOTIFICATION R. 2.1(c).

[49]*See* TEX. FAM. CODE ANN. § 33.003(e); *see also* TEX. PARENTAL NOTIFICATION R. 1.8 cmts. 3, 4.

[50]*See* TEX. FAM. CODE ANN. § 33.003(e).

[51]*See* TEX. DISCIPLINARY R. PROF'L CONDUCT 1.06, *reprinted in* TEX. GOV'T CODE ANN., tit. 2, subtit. G app. A (Vernon Supp. 1997) (TEX. STATE BAR R. art. X, § 9) (governing conflict-laden representation of present clients). *See generally* Nancy J. Moore, *Conflicts of Interest in the Representation of Children*, 64 FORDHAM L. REV. 1819 (1996) (discussing conflicts of interests arising in the representation of minors).

assessment of the best interest of the minor.[52] The attorney ad litem is obligated to seek the objective desired by the client, regardless of his or her assessment of the consistency of that objective with the minor's best interest.[53] The potential for these duties to come into direct conflict, necessitating withdrawal and replacement within the very short time periods permitted for adjudication of the minor's application, suggests that the better practice is to appoint two individuals to serve in these distinctive roles.[54]

The court must hear and rule on the application by five o'clock p.m. on the second business day after the application is filed, subject to any postponement sought by the minor.[55] Court rules suggest that the hearing be held in chambers, or some other location that assures the confidentiality

---

[52]*See* Dawson v. Garcia, 666 S.W.2d 254, 265 (Tex. App.—Dallas 1984, no writ); Pleasant Hills Children's Home of the Assemblies of God, Inc. v. Nida, 596 S.W.2d 947, 951 (Tex. Civ. App.—Fort Worth 1980, no writ); *cf.* TEX. FAM. CODE ANN. § 107.001 (Vernon Supp. 2000) (stating that a guardian ad litem shall be appointed to represent the best interests of a child in a suit to terminate parental rights); *id.* § 31.004 (Vernon 1996) (stating that a guardian ad litem shall be appointed to represent the interests of the minor in an emancipation hearing); *id.* § 51.11 (Vernon 1996) (stating that a guardian ad litem shall be appointed to protect the interests of a child in a juvenile court proceeding).

[53]*See* TEX. DISCIPLINARY R. PROF'L CONDUCT 1.02 (a). *See generally* James K. Genden, *Separate Legal Representation for Children: Protecting the Rights and Interests of Minors in Judicial Proceedings*, 11 HARV. C.R.-C.L. L. REV. 565 (1976); Martin Guggenheim, *The Right to be Represented But Not Heard: Reflections on Legal Representation For Children*, 59 N.Y.U. L. REV. 76 (1984); Jonathan O. Hafen, *Children's Rights and Legal Representation—The Proper Roles of Children, Parents, and Attorneys*, 7 NOTRE DAME J.L. ETHICS & PUB. POL'Y 423 (1993); Sarah H. Ramsey, *Representation of the Child in Protection Proceedings: The Determination of Decision-Making Capacity*, 17 FAM. L.Q. 287 (1983). The most recent and comprehensive exploration of these issues appears at *Special Issue, Ethical Issues in the Legal Representation of Children*, 64 FORDHAM L. REV. 1281 (1996).

[54]*See In re* Doe 2, 19 S.W.3d 278, 290 (Tex. 2000) (Owen, J., concurring). "In view of the very short time constraints within which section 33.003 proceedings must be conducted and the complex layer that conflicts and waiver issues could add, I think it imprudent for courts to appoint the same individual as attorney and ad litem." *Id.* A similar point was made to the Texas Supreme Court Rules Advisory Special Subcommittee on Implementation of Family Code Chapter 33. *See* Letter from Robert J. Gieb, Esq. to Bob Pemberton, Rules Attorney for the Supreme Court of Texas (Dec. 7, 1999) (on file with the author). "Section 2.3 (b) allows the attorney ad litem and the guardian ad litem to be the same person. To have the same person as both attorney ad litem and guardian ad litem produces an irreconcilable conflict." *Id.*

[55]*See* TEX. FAM. CODE ANN. § 33.003(h). The brevity of this time period led one trial court to sua sponte declare the Act unconstitutional as a violation of fundamental due process and the Texas Constitution's separation of powers clause. *See In re* Doe 2, 19 S.W.3d at 280. The Texas Supreme Court reversed on the basis that the issue was not properly before the court. *See id.* at 284.

of the proceedings.[56] In camera hearings have the added advantage of reducing the formality of the proceedings, which may reduce any anxiety the girl may feel about appearing before a judge. The hearing is closed to the public.[57] "If the minor appeals, or if there is evidence of past or potential abuse of the minor, the hearing must be transcribed instanter."[58]

III. EX PARTE NATURE OF THE HEARINGS

Under the Texas statute and court rules, the case is captioned "Jane Doe" with a cause number[59] hearings are closed and attended only by the girl, her representatives, and witnesses on her behalf;[60] and strict confidentiality surrounds the proceedings.[61] In reflecting upon these aspects of the bypass procedure, Justice Enoch of the Texas Supreme Court observed:

> Unlike virtually any other judicial proceeding I am aware of, this proceeding is not only "non-adversarial," but notice to the very persons (besides the minor) likely to have the most interest in the outcome of the hearing—the parents who stand not to be notified of their minor child's decision—is prohibited. And the secrecy of the

---

[56]*See* TEX. PARENTAL NOTIFICATION R. 2.4(b).

[57]*See id.* 2.4(c).

[58]*Id.* 2.4(d).

[59]*See id.* 1.3(b).

[60]*See id.* 2.4(c).

[61]*See* TEX. FAM. CODE ANN. § 33.003(k)–(l) (Vernon Supp. 2000). The level of confidentiality afforded by the statute has been the subject of judicial concern. *See* Texas Parental Notification Rules, Explanatory Statement. This extraordinary level of confidentiality has also generated sharp public criticism. *See Judicial Accountability: The Secret Won't Get Out*, AMARILLO GLOBAL NEWS, Dec. 29, 1999; *Secret Judges, Texas Supreme Court Ignores Constitutional Questions*, HOUSTON CHRON., Dec. 22, 1999, at A34, *available in* 1999 WL 24271619. The breadth of the Act's confidentiality requirements are a product of political compromise, rather than constitutional mandate. *Compare* Tex. S.B. 30, 76th Leg., R.S. § 33.003(i) (1999) (Introduced Version), Senate Comm. Substitute Tex. S.B. 30, 76th Leg., R.S. § 33.003(j)–(k) (1999), *and* House Comm. Substitute Tex. S.B. 30, 76th Leg., R.S. § 33.003(k)–(l) (1999), *with* TEX. FAM. CODE Ann. § 33.003(k)–(l). The constitutional requirement is merely anonymity. Notification statutes must only take "reasonable steps to prevent the public from learning of the minor's identity." Ohio v. Akron Ctr. for Reprod. Health, 497 U.S. 502, 513 (1990); *see also* State *ex rel.* Cincinnati Post v. Court of Appeals, Second Appellate Dist., 604 N.E.2d 153, 156 (Ohio 1992) (noting that the state constitutional requirement of open courts required public access to the results of judicial bypass cases so long as disclosure did not compromise anonymity of the minor).

> proceeding assures that the hearing will be entirely one-sided."[62]

Justice Enoch is correct in his observation that judicial bypass proceedings are sui generis. In no other American judicial proceeding do the courts deprive an individual of a constitutional right without notice or opportunity to be heard at some point in the proceeding. Certainly there is no American precedent for a proceeding that precludes participation by an affected individual and that is structured in such a way to minimize the possibility that the individual subsequently learns of the deprivation of his or her interest or rights. Yet this is exactly the case in judicial bypass proceedings with regard to a parent's right to direct the medical care of his or her minor daughter.

The constitutional dimension of a parent's right to be involved in a minor's decision to continue or abort a pregnancy has been generally

---

[62] *In re* Doe, 19 S.W.3d 249, 258 (Tex. 2000) (Enoch, J., concurring). A similar process has led at least one trial judge in Nebraska to observe:

> There is nobody on the other side, unless a judge takes it on himself. Now I know of no other case that is like that, where it is truly one-sided. If after that one-sided hearing, the judge finds that the girl is mature and can give an informed consent, then the judge is *required* to authorize the abortion physician to perform the abortion.

JOSEPH W. MOYLAN, *No Law Can Give Me the Right to Do What is Wrong*, *in* LIFE AND LEARNING V: PROCEEDINGS OF THE FIFTH UNIVERSITY FACULTY FOR LIFE CONFERENCE 234, 235 (Joseph W. Koterski ed., University Faculty for Life 1995) (emphasis omitted) (explaining Judge Moylan's decision to resign from a bench in the juvenile court he had occupied for more than twenty years). The judicial bypass process in Nebraska has "no adversarial aspect" as noted by that state's supreme court. *See* Orr v. Knowles, 337 N.W.2d 699, 706 (Neb. 1983). "This statute does not provide that the state or anyone else will contest the minor's claim that she is mature enough to make the abortion decision herself. Rather, she will present evidence, and the judge will then make the decision as to her maturity." *Id.*; *see also* Wallace J. Mlyniec, *A Judge's Ethical Dilemma: Assessing a Child's Capacity to Choose*, 64 FORDHAM L. REV. 1873, 1891–92 (1996).

> Because such a scenario does not involve judges' employing normal rules concerning proof in the litigation process, the result of these hearings is practically preordained: no opposing party challenges the evidence and the court, thus, bases its finding regarding the minor's maturity either on the one-sided evidence presented, or on idiosyncratic biases.

Mlyniec, *supra*.

accepted by the United States Supreme Court,[63] and at least one federal appellate court has recognized this right as the basis for a cause of action under 42 U.S.C. § 1983 against government officials for violating a parent's constitutional rights.[64] Notwithstanding this recognition, the United States Supreme Court has never addressed the question of what process is due parents of a minor prior to depriving those parents of their right to guide their minor daughter in deciding how to respond to an unplanned pregnancy. This lack of judicial consideration may be due to the difficulties and disincentives facing any parents seeking to assert their rights.

The first hurdle a parent must overcome is the question of standing. Prior to the pregnancy of their minor daughter, parents cannot know with certainty that their rights will even be affected by the statute.[65] If the

---

[63]*See* Hodgson v. Minnesota, 497 U.S. 417, 445–49 (1990). However, this right does not outweigh the right of a mature, well-informed minor to seek an abortion without parental consent. *See* Planned Parenthood v. Danforth, 428 U.S. 52, 75 (1976).

[64]*See* Arnold v. Board of Educ., 880 F.2d 305, 318 (11th Cir. 1989) (reversing the trial court's dismissal of section 1983 claims by parents of two teens who asserted that their constitutional right to direct the upbringing of their children was violated by public school employees coercing the minors into keeping the girl's pregnancy a secret in order to assure the girl obtained an abortion). A similar claim was recently settled in Pennsylvania. *See* Robert Sanchez, *District, Parents Settle Abortion Suit*, PHILADELPHIA INQUIRER, Mar. 16, 2000, at B5 *available in* 2000 WL 10276575.

[65]Such an action assumes that the parents would have standing to challenge the bypass provisions. The issue of a parent's right to challenge the judicial bypass provisions of a parental involvement law as unconstitutional has never been placed directly before the courts. However, the Supreme Court has rejected the standing of a parent seeking to defend the general constitutionality of a parental involvement law. *See* Diamond v. Charles, 476 U.S. 54, 69 (1986). In *Diamond v. Charles*, the United States Supreme Court reviewed an appeal by a father who had intervened on the side of the state in a case challenging Illinois statutes regulating abortion. *Id.* The district court found the statutes to be unconstitutional, and this ruling was affirmed by the Seventh Circuit. *See id.* at 61. Illinois decided not to pursue the case beyond the Seventh Circuit. *See id.* at 56. The father who had been permitted to intervene in the district court claimed that he had standing to appeal the adverse judgment of the intermediate appellate court on several grounds. *See id.* at 66–67. He argued, in part, that he had standing due to his interest in ensuring that his daughter not be prescribed an abortifacient without receiving the information that would have been required had the statutes been held constitutional. *See id.* at 67. The Court disposed of this claim by noting that he had not shown that his daughter was a minor or incapable of asserting her own interest. *See id.* Further, the Court ruled that the father could not use the Court to compel Illinois to retain a legal framework that it had decided to abandon by virtue of its acquiescence in the lower courts' decisions. *See id.* at 65; *cf.* Ruiz v. Estelle, 161 F.3d 814, 829 (5th Cir. 1998) (discussing the *Diamond* case in the context of the standing jurisprudence of the Fifth Circuit), *cert. denied*, 526 U.S. 1158 (1999).

parents know of their minor daughter's pregnancy, this knowledge may be sufficient to preclude standing in states with parental-notification statutes, even where the parents do not know of their daughter's intention to obtain an abortion. In states with parental-consent statutes, parents who know of their daughter's pregnancy and intention to obtain an abortion may still confront the argument that they lack standing because their right to provide guidance is limited to guidance in the best interest of the minor and that the minor's best interest will be determined during the bypass hearing. While a similar argument was rejected by the United States Supreme Court with regard to a parent's right to commit a minor child for psychiatric care,[66] no court has considered such an argument in the context of abortion.

If a parent learns of the abortion after completion of bypass proceedings, there are substantial disincentives to seeking judicial relief. Parents who learn of the secret abortion after the fact will likely be dealing with feelings of rejection and anger at being excluded from their daughter's decision. They may forego any action since, unlike the return of misappropriated property taken through an illegitimate proceeding,[67] there can be no restoration of their right to guide their daughter in responding to the pregnancy. Nor is there any financial incentive to file suit since the officials depriving the parents of their right in almost all cases are cloaked in some form of governmental immunity.[68] To the contrary, there is some financial risk to a parent. At least one court has imposed the costs of litigation upon a parent seeking to defend a parental involvement statute.[69]

In states where the statute requires parental consent, challenging the bypass process is risky since the court might strike the judicial bypass proceedings entirely, rendering the statute unconstitutional under *Planned*

---

[66]*See* Parham v. J.R., 442 U.S. 584, 602 (1979).

[67]*See* United States v. James Daniel Good Real Property, 510 U.S. 43, 56 (1993) (stating that due process requires, absent exigent circumstances, pre-deprivation notice and hearings to determine the legality of a home seizure).

[68]*See generally* TEX. CONST. art. I, § 2; TEX. FAM. CODE ANN. § 33.006 (Vernon Supp. 2000) (guardian ad litem immunity). *Compare* Morris v. Dearborne, 181 F.3d 657, 665–66 (5th Cir. 1999) (discussing the extent of qualified immunity afforded government officials performing discretionary functions in the context of allegations of parental abuse), *with* Riley v. Camp, 130 F.3d 958, 987 n.9 (11th Cir. 1997) (Kravitch, J., concurring in part and dissenting in part) (holding that a state social worker may be liable for depriving a parent of the "right to guide her own child through adolescence without undue state interference" where the social worker denied the mother access to her daughter and affirmatively assisted the adult boyfriend in obtaining access to the girl after which he engaged in conduct constituting statutory rape).

[69]*See Diamond*, 476 U.S. at 70 n.22.

Parenthood v. Danforth.[70] In states with parental notification statutes, while it is not clear that judicial bypass is constitutionally required,[71] there is some risk that any determination that the bypass is constitutionally flawed may result in the entire statute being found unconstitutional.[72] In either case, those truly committed to insuring involvement of parents in medical decisions affecting their daughters could "win the battle" of establishing the lack of due process afforded parents in these secret proceedings, while "losing the war" by returning to a situation like that of Texas prior to the passage of the Parental Notification Act, which minors could obtain abortions with no parental knowledge or involvement.

The inherent advantages of parental involvement in the medical care of their children and the constitutional dimension of parents' right to guide the medical care of their minor children,[73] compounded by the inadequacy of any *ex parte* proceeding in arriving at a complete understanding of the circumstances surrounding the minor's application for judicial intervention,[74] counsels great caution in granting applications to bypass parental notification.

IV. STATUTORY BASES FOR BYPASISNG PARENTAL NOTIFICATION

The Parental Notification Act provides three bases for bypassing parental notification of a minor's intention to obtain an abortion.[75] First, the court must determine if the minor is mature and sufficiently well informed to make the decision to obtain an abortion without parental notice.[76] If so, the court must grant the bypass.[77] Immature or ill informed minors may still bypass parental notification if the court finds that notification of a parent is not in the minor's best interest.[78] Inherent in the "best interest" analysis, yet listed as a separate basis for bypass in the Texas act, is where notification may lead to physical, sexual, or emotional

[70] 428 U.S. 52 (1976).

[71] *See* Bellotti v. Baird, 443 U.S. 622, 643–44 (1979) (plurality opinion) (*Bellotti II*).

[72] *See* cases cited *supra* note 30.

[73] *See infra* notes 140, 216–72 and accompanying text.

[74] *See supra* text accompanying notes 61–65.

[75] *See* TEX. FAM. CODE ANN. § 33.003(i) (Vernon Supp. 2000); *see also* TEX. PARENTAL NOTIFICATION R. 2.5(b), (c). However, "[u]nder Rule 2.5(b), once a court concludes that an application should be granted on a single ground, it need not address other grounds." *Id.* cmt. 5.

[76] *See* TEX. FAM. CODE ANN. § 33.003(i).

[77] *See id.*

[78] *See id.*

abuse.[79] The information needed by the court in determining whether to grant or deny a bypass varies depending upon the basis asserted by the minor. Each of these bases is explored separately below.

A. *Mature and Sufficiently Well Informed*

The first basis for granting judicial bypass of parental notification listed in the Texas statute is in cases where "the minor is mature and sufficiently well informed to make the decision to have an abortion performed without notification to either of her parents or a managing conservator or guardian."[80] This standard is an adaptation of the first requirement for a constitutionally-sound parental consent law under *Bellotti v. Baird.*[81] As the Texas Supreme Court has acknowledged, this standard has two prongs that should not be conflated.[82]

1. Establishing Maturity

The first prong requires a finding that the girl is mature enough to make the decision to obtain an abortion independent of parental knowledge.[83] As the *Bellotti II* court recognized, maturity is difficult to define.[84] The closest the United States Supreme Court has come to providing a definition of maturity is in its reference to the "experience, perspective and judgment" that should guide reasoned decision-making in this context.[85]

---

[79]*See id.*

[80]*Id.*

[81]443 U.S. 622, 643 (1979) (plurality opinion) (*Bellotti II*).

[82]*See In re* Doe, 19 S.W.3d 249, 254 (Tex. 2000).

[83]*See Bellotti II*, 443 U.S. at 643.

[84]*Id.* at 643–44 n.23. "Not only is it difficult to define, let alone determine, maturity, but also the fact that a minor may be very much an adult in some respects does not mean that his or her need and opportunity for growth under parental guidance and discipline have ended." *Id.*

[85]*Id.* at 635. In response to this amorphous definition, state courts have looked at various facts in deciding whether a minor is sufficiently mature to obtain an abortion without parental involvement. Facts considered to be relevant include: the girl's age, whether she lives with her parents or alone, whether she has worked, who she consulted with concerning the pregnancy, and whether she plans to use contraception in the event she plans to continue to be sexually active after the abortion. *See* H.B. v. Wilkinson, 639 F. Supp. 952, 953–54 (D. Utah 1986); *In re* Anonymous 2, 570 N.W.2d 836, 839 (Neb. 1997); *In re* Anonymous 1, 558 N.W.2d 784, 788 (Neb. 1997); *In re* Doe I, 566 N.E.2d 1181, 1184 (Ohio 1990).

One commentator has summarized the approach of the courts as follows:

> Trial courts keep proceedings confidential and seal records, thus rendering direct insight into a judge's rationale inaccessible. Few cases reach the appellate courts. Those cases that have received appellate review suggest that trial judges intuit maturity

The Texas Supreme Court provided more definitive guidance in its discussion of the "mature and sufficiently well informed" standard in *In re Doe*:

> Thus, we conclude that a minor is "mature and sufficiently well informed to make the decision to have an abortion without notification to either of her parents" when the evidence demonstrates that the minor is capable of reasoned decision-making and that her decision is not the product of impulse, but is based upon careful consideration of the various options available to her and the benefits, risks, and consequences of those options.[86]

Under this standard, a minor seeking to establish that she is mature must show that she is capable of "reasoned decision-making" and that she has given "thoughtful consideration to her alternatives" in responding to her unplanned pregnancy.[87] Evidence that her decision to obtain an abortion is based upon impulse would support denial of the application to bypass parental notification.[88]

While abortion rights activists may bristle at the suggestion that a female of any age would choose abortion impulsively, the concern that teens do not respond in the same manner as adults to unplanned pregnancies is supported by the overrepresentation of teens among those obtaining abortions after the first trimester,[89] as well as the explanation for this overrepresentation offered by abortion providers.

> from their perceptions of the children's demeanor while testifying. Such cases also indicate that judges evaluate the coherence of the child's response to questions concerning child rearing, abortion procedures and risks, adoption, and the child's postoperative plans.

Mlyniec, *supra* note 62, at 1889 (citations omitted).

[86]*In re* Doe, 19 S.W.3d at 255 (quoting Tex. Fam. Code Ann. § 33.003(h) (Vernon Supp. 2000)) (citing *In re* Anonymous, 711 So. 2d 475, 477 (Ala. Civ. App. 1998); *In re Anonymous 2*, 570 N.W.2d at 838–39; *In re Anonymous 1*, 558 N.W.2d at 788; *In re* Doe, 485 S.E.2d 354, 356 (N.C. Ct. App. 1997)).

[87]*In re* Doe, 19 S.W.3d at 256. Evidence of the minor's age, educational background or academic performance, and history of participation in extra-curricular activities is relevant, but not determinative of maturity. *See id.* at 257.

[88]*See id.* at 255.

[89]"More than one third of all abortions after 12 weeks are obtained by teenagers." Susan Dudley, National Abortion Federation, *Facts About Abortion, Abortion After 12 Weeks* (visited Oct. 9, 2000) <http://www.prochoice.org/default8.htm>.

> Teens face not only state regulatory hurdles, but also delays in recognizing that they are pregnant and taking decisive action. For example, they may: understand little about how their bodies work and therefore may not recognize signs of pregnancy; become pregnant before they have begun to menstruate or before their menstrual periods are regular, so they don't have the signal of a missed period; believe a variety of myths, such as "You can't get pregnant the first time"; or keep rape or sexual abuse a secret, denying the possibility of pregnancy.
>
> When such young women do realize they are pregnant, they may panic, fearing their parents will never forgive them or that their parents will force them out of the house. They may hide the pregnancy in secret shame, or spend weeks wishing and hoping it isn't true, or that it will go away. Of course, when the pregnancy does not go away, the realities of the situation gradually become evident.[90]

One of the most recently published medical text on abortion provides an additional explanation of why teens delay in seeking abortions.

> Some adolescents fantasize that a baby can fix a relationship and bring them love. The fantasy usually lasts as long as the boyfriend is still seeing her and her parents do not know about the pregnancy. If the partner becomes frightened and changes his mind or her parents find out, reality sets in.[91]

The characterization of pregnant teens as often in denial about their pregnancies and subsequently panicked by their situation is supported by testimony received by the Texas Senate Human Services Committee.[92]

---

[90]*Id.*

[91]Anne Baker et al., *Informed Consent, Counseling, and Patient Preparation*, *in* A CLINICIAN'S GUIDE TO MEDICAL AND SURGICAL ABORTIONS 25, 31–32 (Maureen Paul et al. eds., 1999).

[92]*See Hearings on Tex. S.B. 27, 30, 65, 83 Before the Senate Human Servs. Comm.*, 76th Leg., R.S. 8 (Mar. 10, 1999) (statement of Natalie Wolk) (transcript available from the Senate Staff Services Office). ("The teenagers I see [as a counselor at Planned Parenthood of Houston] are very, very scared."); *id.* at 11 (statement of Dave Kittrell) ("I also know that if they [pregnant teens] perceive that they're going to be embarrassed or have difficulty obtaining parental consent, for whatever their reasons are, these people are in distress, they're in crisis and I, I personally, as a physician, certainly want them to involve their parents."); *id.* at 18 (statement of Margot

Both denial and panic can be strong barriers to reasoned decision making, even for mature adults. For minors, many of whom have not previously been called upon to make serious and irreversible decisions, these emotions can dominate their thinking and render them incapable of accurately assessing the different ways of responding to an unplanned pregnancy. Only through maturity can these emotions be set aside and options be considered in light of the woman's "experience, perspective, and judgment."

2. Establishing that a Minor is Sufficiently Well Informed

Even where the minor is mature, the statute requires more before a bypass of parental notification may be granted. A minor must also be "sufficiently well informed" about her options in dealing with her pregnancy prior to receiving a court order allowing her to consent to an abortion without parental involvement. The Texas Supreme Court has interpreted this to require the following:

> First, she must show that she has obtained information from a health-care provider about the health risks associated with an abortion and that she understands those risks. That would include an understanding of the risks

---

Clarke) ("[pregnant teens] struggle with a sense of being cornered, or hope desperately that it will just go away"); *see also id.* at 21 (statement of Margaret Romberg Carter) ("I could not bring myself to go and discuss my being pregnant with my parents, even though I was raised in a very, very loving family, very supportive family.").

See Texas Family Planning Association, *Voluntary Survey of Minors Seeking Abortion Care*, submitted in support of testimony by Peggy Romberg, Hearing before the Senate Human Services Committee, March 10, 1999.

Some of the reasons minors stated for not involving a parent (verbatim):

> "Because I was too scared to tell anyone and I was against the procedure until it was my problem."
>
> "I did not involve my parents because they are unreasonable. My dad would've tried to put my boyfriend in jail."
>
> "My parents have high expectations for me."
>
> "They would not take it well."

Id. Published studies confirm that adolescents who seek to avoid parental involvement are often concerned about parental disappointment. *See* Mary S. Griffin-Carlson & Kathleen J. Mackin, *Parental Consent: Factors Influencing Adolescent Disclosure Regarding Abortion*, 28 ADOLESCENCE 1, 4 (1993).

> associated with the particular stage of the minor's pregnancy.
>
> Second, she must show that she understands the alternatives to abortion and their implications. As with any medical procedure, part of making an informed decision is knowing the available alternatives. A minor should be able to demonstrate that she has given thoughtful consideration to her alternatives, including adoption and keeping the child. She should also understand that the law requires the father to assist in the financial support of the child. She should not be required to justify why she prefers abortion above other options, only that she is fully apprised of her options.
>
> Third, she must show that she is also aware of the emotional and psychological aspects of undergoing an abortion, which can be significant if not severe for some women. She must also show that she has considered how this decision might affect her family relations. Although the minor need not obtain this information from licensed, professional counselors, she must show that she has received information about these risks from reliable and informed sources, so that she is aware of and has considered these aspects of the abortion procedure.[93]

In order to fairly evaluate evidence related to these three showings, it is important that judges and lawyers become educated on the issues of teen pregnancy and abortion.

a. Information Obtained from a Health Care Provider

The first required showing is that the minor has received information regarding risks related to abortion from a health-care provider.[94] While the minor may not be required to obtain information from a particular health-care provider or consult with or review materials prepared by an advocacy

[93] *In re* Doe, 19 S.W.3d at 256–57 (citation omitted). In *In re* Doe (II), the court noted without elaboration that the statute did not require that a minor be "fully informed." 19 S.W.3d 346, 352 (Tex. 2000). It is unclear what this dicta means in the context of existing Texas law requiring the informed consent of a patient prior to any surgical procedure. It seems unlikely that the court would allow a minor to consent to a secret abortion with less knowledge than an adult would be entitled to, yet that is one possible reading of Justice O'Neill's comment.

[94] *See In re Doe*, 19 S.W.3d at 256.

or religious group,[95] she must establish that "she has obtained information on the relevant considerations from reliable sources of her choosing that enable her to make a thoughtful and informed decision."[96] In cases where a girl has voluntarily consulted with a pro-life group, yet decided to obtain an abortion, courts of other states have recognized such voluntary consultation as some evidence of maturity.[97]

In addition to showing that she has consulted with a health care provider, the minor must establish that she understands the risks attendant to abortion. A general listing of the risks is contained in a brochure on teen pregnancy and parental notification prepared by the Texas Department of Health (TDH) pursuant to a last minute amendment to the Parental Notification Act.[98] The TDH brochure, which is written for teens and is

---

[95]*See id.* at 257. The court does not offer a definition of an "advocacy" group. It appears to encompass organizations like Texas Abortion & Reproductive Rights Action League, Texas Right to Life, Greater Dallas Coalition for Reproductive Freedom, and Greater Austin Right to Life. However, it is unclear whether organizations that both provide health-care services and engage in advocacy are included. *See id.* at 265 (Owen, J., concurring).

For example, there are sound arguments for describing affiliates of Planned Parenthood Federation of America as "advocacy" groups. Their involvement in abortion-related litigation is evidenced by the frequency with which they appear as a plaintiff. A search on Oct. 9, 2000 of the "allfeds" Westlaw database for federal cases with "Planned Parenthood" in the case caption resulted in 255 cases. The same search in the "allstates" Westlaw database resulted in 113 cases. In Texas, abortion is the primary service provided to pregnant women by Planned Parenthood. Planned Parenthood of Dallas lists no prenatal services other than pregnancy testing on its webpage. However, it lists abortion or pregnancy termination. Planned Parenthood of Dallas and Northeast Texas, *Medical Services* (visited Oct. 9, 2000) <http://www.ppnet.org/Category/Medical.htm>. The only website of a Texas Planned Parenthood affiliate to list prenatal care as a service is Planned Parenthood of Houston and Southeast Texas. Of the 6027 pregnancy-treatment-related visits by clients in the 1997-98 fiscal year, only 562 were for prenatal care. The remaining 5465 visits were for abortion procedures. *See* Planned Parenthood of Houston and Southeast Texas, *Who Are Our Clients*? (visited March 6, 2000) <http://www.pphouston.org/aboutpp.htm>. An organization where all, or even 9 of every 10 pregnancy-related visits results in abortion procedures is unlikely to be a disinterested or reliable provider of information regarding all of a girl's options in dealing with an unplanned pregnancy.

[96]*In re Doe*, 19 S.W.3d at 257.

[97]*See Ex parte* Anonymous, 595 So. 2d 497, 499 (Ala. 1992). The minor's "decision to seek advice from a group opposed to abortion in order to get a broader perspective on the issue demonstrates maturity." *Id.* Because this determination will only be made in the context of an application to obtain an abortion without parental notification, it is unnecessary to require that the minor establish that she has obtained information from a source that expresses a preference for abortion over childbirth. *Cf.* Harris v. McRae, 448 U.S. 297, 326 (1980) (holding a state may express preference for childbirth over medically necessary abortions in funding decisions).

[98]TEX. FAM. CODE ANN. § 33.011 (Vernon Supp. 2000). The brochure *So You're Pregnant, Now What?* is available via the internet at <http://www.tdh.state.tx.us/bvs/> (visited Oct. 9,

available on the Internet, lists the risks of abortion as hemorrhage, infection, incomplete abortion, perforation of the uterus, sterility, hysterectomy, injury to the bowel and/or bladder, the need for abdominal surgery to correct an injury, and, in rare cases, death.[99] The brochure includes all of the risks identified by the Texas Medical Disclosure Panel[100] for abortion, with the risks ordered from the most to the least frequently occurring.[101] The brochure also warns readers of a possible link between abortion and breast cancer, as well as the possibility of severe emotional distress related to obtaining an abortion.[102] A medical text on induced abortion lists all the risks identified by TDH, plus unrecognized ectopic pregnancy,[103] cervical injury,[104] anesthesia complications,[105] amniotic fluid embolism,[106] and cervical cancer.[107]

These risks can be divided into immediate complications, which, if experienced, will occur during or within three hours of the abortion; delayed complications; which will manifest themselves after three hours, but within twenty-eight days of the procedure; and late complications, which will only become recognizable later.[108] Immediate complications include uterine perforation, hemorrhage, unrecognized ectopic pregnancy, cervical injury, anesthesia complications, and amniotic fluid embolism.[109]

2000). Click on "Induced Abortions" at the bottom of the page for the online version of the educational booklet.

[99]*See* Texas Department of Health, *So You're Pregnant, Now What?*, 11–12 (1999).

[100]*See* 25 TEX. ADMIN. CODE § 601.1 (1995) (Tex. Dep't of Health); *Texas Medical Disclosure Panel* (visited Oct. 9, 2000) <http://www.tdh.state.tx.us/hfc/tmdp.htm>.

[101]*See id.* Texas Department of Health, *supra* note 99, at 11–12.

[102]*See id.* at 13. For an expanded discussion on the legal aspects related to the link between abortion and breast cancer, see John Kindley, *The Fit Between the Elements for an Informed Consent Cause of Action and the Scientific Evidence Linking Induced Abortion with Increased Breast Cancer Risk*, 1998 WIS. L. REV. 1595 (1998). The legal dimension of psychological injuries related to abortion are explored in Thomas R. Eller, *Informed Consent Civil Actions for Post-Abortion Psychological Trauma*, 71 NOTRE DAME L. REV. 639 (1996). Additional information about post abortion syndrome can be obtained from The Elliott Institute, P.O. Box 7348, Springfield, IL 62791-7348 or via their website at <http://www.afterabortion.org> (visited on Oct. 9, 2000).

[103]*See* David A. Grimes, *Sequelae of Abortion*, *in* MODERN METHODS OF INDUCING ABORTION 95, 99–100 (David T. Baird et al. eds., 1995).

[104]*See id.* at 100.

[105]*See id.*

[106]*See id.* at 101.

[107]*See id.* at 105.

[108]*See id.* at 98.

[109]*See id.* at 98–101.

One of the most common delayed complications is infection,[110] especially with incomplete abortions.[111] Late complications may include sterility and other reproductive sequelae,[112] as well as emotional distress.[113]

To protect the minor from adverse effects of delayed complications, it is critical that she be able to recognize any symptoms or warning signs. For example, infection is "one of the more common complications of abortion."[114] The actual rate of occurrence is unknown because it is a delayed complication, and only about one-third of all abortion patients keep their appointments for post-operative checkups.[115] Two recognized experts on abortion have described infection and its gravity in the following manner:

> The risk of death from postabortion sepsis [or infection] is highest for young women, those who are unmarried, and those who undergo procedures that do not directly evacuate the contents of the uterus. . . . A delay in treatment allows the infection to progress to bacteremia, pelvic abscess, septic pelvic thrombophlebitis, disseminated intravascular coagulopathy, septic shock, renal failure, and death.[116]

The warning signs of infection typically begin within the first forty-eight to ninety-six hours after the abortion and can include fever, pain, pelvic tenderness, and elevated white blood count.[117] Caught early, most

---

[110]*See id.* at 101.

[111]*See id.*

[112]*See id.* at 102–03.

[113]*See id.* at 103–04.

[114]*Id.* at 101.

[115]*See* Henshaw, *supra* note 39, at 20.

[116]Phillip G. Stubblefield and David A. Grimes, *Current Concepts: Septic Abortion*, NEW ENGLAND J. MED., Aug. 4, 1994, at 310, 310. Dr. Stubblefield provided expert testimony in *Carhart v. Stenberg*. 11 F. Supp. 2d 1099, 1116 (D. Neb. 1998) (stating that Dr. Stubblefield was a most persuasive and helpful expert). Dr. Grimes has written extensively on abortion procedures and is one of four editors of a recent medical text dealing with induced abortion. *See generally* A CLINICIAN'S GUIDE TO MEDICAL AND SURGICAL ABORTIONS (Maureen Paul et al. eds., 1999).

[117]*See* E. Steve Lichtenberg et al., *Abortion Complications: Prevention and Management, in* A CLINICIAN'S GUIDE TO MEDICAL AND SURGICAL ABORTIONS 197, 206 (Maureen Paul et al. eds.,1999).

infections can be treated successfully with oral antibiotics.[118] Ignored and left unattended, the girl's future fertility and even her life are at risk.[119]

The statistical probability of a girl experiencing any of these complications varies depending upon the type of abortion performed and the length of her pregnancy. Recognizing this, the *Doe* Court required more than a mere showing that the minor understands the general risks attendant to any abortion.[120] Rather, before judicial bypass can be granted, the minor must establish that she understands the information regarding the health risks related to the particular type of abortion to be performed at her particular stage of pregnancy.[121] Adherence to this "particularity" requirement is important to insure that the girl adequately comprehends the potential consequences of the decision she seeks to make.

There is no question that "[t]he choice of abortion method greatly influences safety."[122] The choice of abortion method is largely determined by the duration of the pregnancy.[123] While the rate of abortion-related complications varies with the method of abortion selected, the frequency and severity of complications increase for all methods as the pregnancy progresses.[124] Failure to accurately determine the stage of the pregnancy prior to performing an abortion increases the risk of complications.[125]

---

[118]*See id.* at 206–07.

[119]*See* Stubblefield & Grimes, *supra* note 116, at 310.

[120]*See In re* Doe, 19 S.W.3d 249, 256 (Tex. 2000).

[121]*See id.*

[122]Grimes, *supra* note 103, at 105.

[123]Charlotte Ellertson & Carolyn Westhoff, *Procedure Selection, in* A CLINICIAN'S GUIDE TO MEDICAL AND SURGICAL ABORTIONS 63, 63 (Maureen Paul et al. eds., 1999). "Although medical, acceptability, and logistical factors are important, the most fundamental determinant of the set of abortion options open to a woman and her provider is the duration of the pregnancy to be terminated." *Id.*

[124]*See* Grimes, *supra* note 103, at 105 ("[N]ational health statistics have shown conclusively that early abortions are safer than later procedures.").

[125]*See* Lichtenberg, *supra* note 117, at 200. An example of the harm suffered due to inaccurate dating of the pregnancy was provided in the testimony of Dr. Michael Love, an ob-gyn who had previously performed abortions:

> My golf partner has recently taken care of a lady who underwent a legal abortion, if you will, only to find out that she was much further along. And in the course of the events, she had to go to Brackenridge, where he became her provider, had to take her to surgery and repair her multi-lacerated uterus, because the [abortion] provider had not come about with the correct estimated gestational age.

Patient information regarding the date of their last menstrual period is often inaccurate, as are the results of dating a pregnancy through physical examination.[126] "Patient anxiety, obesity, and uterine retroversion may increase the difficulty of estimating gestational age."[127]

A teenager experiencing an unplanned pregnancy is likely to be very anxious about her circumstances and therefore at increased risk of inaccurate dating of the pregnancy. This problem can be minimized by use of an ultrasound. Ultrasonographic evaluation is "of clinical value" for all pregnancies estimated to be in the first trimester[128] and standard practice for pregnancies exceeding twelve weeks.[129] In those cases where ultrasound has been performed, insuring that the minor had the opportunity to view the ultrasound results is consistent with the concept of informed consent as articulated by the United States Supreme Court in *Planned Parenthood v. Casey*.[130]

The Parental Notification Act: *Hearings on Tex. S.B. 30 Before the House State Affairs Comm.*, 76th Leg., R.S. 23 (April 19, 1999) (statement by Michael Love) (tapes available from the Office of the House Comm. Coordinator and content is from private transcripts of those tapes).

[126]*See* Steven Goldstein et al., *Documenting Pregnancy and Gestational Age*, *in* A CLINICIAN'S GUIDE TO MEDICAL AND SURGICAL ABORTIONS 39, 40–42 (Maureen Paul et al. eds., 1999).

[127]Lichtenberg, *supra* note 117, at 200.

[128]*See* NATIONAL ABORTION FEDERATION, CLINICAL POLICY GUIDELINES 13 (1999).

[129]*See* Lichtenberg, *supra* note 117, at 200; *cf.* NATIONAL ABORTION FEDERATION, *supra* note 128, at 13 (requiring ultrasonography for pregnancies estimated to be more than 14 weeks from the last menstrual period).

[130]505 U.S. 833, 882 (1992) (plurality opinion) (discussing the Pennsylvania statutory requirement that women be offered the opportunity to view materials on fetal development).

> In attempting to ensure that a woman apprehend the full consequences of her decision [including the consequences of abortion to the fetus], the State furthers the legitimate purpose of reducing the risk that a woman may elect an abortion, only to discover later, with devastating psychological consequences, that her decision was not fully informed.

Id.

The wisdom of requiring women to understand these consequences is illustrated by the testimony of Ms. Linda Gartman before the Texas Senate Human Services Committee:

> In 1983 I went to a women's clinic in Fort Worth to confirm a pregnancy. The test was positive. This was late in the afternoon on a Thursday afternoon, and my test was positive and she scheduled me for an appointment the following morning. The following morning I asked the nurse when she came in, how developed the baby would be. She said I was about twelve weeks pregnant and that it was only a mass of cells, that you couldn't tell what it was. I asked her if she was sure and she said yes. This was all the counsel that I received. No one informed me of any side effects or

Once the gestational age of the fetus has been determined, the physician may present the minor with various alternatives in terminating the pregnancy. Until recently, surgical abortions by suction curettage during the first trimester were generally considered safer than "medical" abortions induced through the use of various drugs.[131] However, new drug

---

> risks that would be involved, as he [a physician who testified immediately prior to Ms. Gartman] was talking about with a hysterectomy, they tell you all the risks that are about that you may, that may occur. I had none of that, I didn't even get to see the doctor, I didn't get to talk to him, I was never examined by him to see how far along I was. After I recovered from the abortion I was in a lot of pain because of the procedure, and they sent me home. I was very weak, I was very ill, but they sent me home, they didn't keep me there. The following Monday, three days later, I had to go back, I was running fever, I had infection, I had an incomplete and botched abortion. They had not gotten everything and, and they had to do the procedure again. This was not an easy thing to do, it wasn't an easy thing to do in the first place, and in the second place, then to have to turn around and have to do it again was very traumatic. Later the nurse told me that she was wrong, or that they were wrong, I was not [twelve] weeks, I was [seventeen] weeks. From that point on there was a huge void in my heart. I became depressed, and in 1991 my daughter was having her first baby, this is my grandbaby and she invited me to see the sonogram, she was 12 weeks pregnant. I couldn't believe my eyes, I'd never seen a sonogram, I wanted to be happy for her, and to be excited for her, and I was in shock, I couldn't believe my eyes, couldn't believe what I was seeing, it was a tiny baby, complete body, had everything it needed except time in the womb. It was fully developed, it was doing flips inside her womb. It was precious, I could see her silhouette of her face. And I had to, I had to be happy, but I wanted to run out of there screaming. And inside I've been screaming ever since. I was depressed for years. I hated myself, my self-esteem went down. I wanted to die. Abortion is not an easy choice. There are circumstances for it and we have the right to choose. We certainly need to have all the facts, and we need the truth up front, so that we can make that choice, and make sure that, that's what we wanna do. If we had to wait 24 hours I might have talked to someone, to receive counsel on choosing life, I might have changed my mind. We have the right to all the facts. Legalized abortion was intended to protect women but believe me, it does not. If has been 15 years and I still mourn for my child. Please don't allow these laws to be such that they could take our children, our minors, without our consent, and perform an abortion on them. I know how I suffered emotionally and I can't, as an adult, and I can't image how they might be traumatized by this when they're having to do this alone and in secret, without anyone in their family knowing, and being able to go to them.

Hearings on S.B. 65 Before the Senate Human Servs. Comm., 76th Leg. R.S. 16–17 (Mar. 10, 1999) (statement by Linda Gartman) (tapes available from the Office of the House Comm. Coordinator and content is from private transcripts of those tapes).

[131] *See* Grimes, *supra* note 103, at 105.

> In the first trimester, suction curettage remains the gold standard against which other methods should be compared. While prostaglandins can successfully induce medical

combinations have been developed that appear to avoid or minimize many of the adverse side effects experienced by women seeking medical abortions in the 1970s and 1980s.[132] Proponents of medical abortions suggest that this method will allow women to end their pregnancies in the privacy of their own homes and avoid surgery.[133] Nonetheless, at this point in time in the United States, medical abortions are primarily limited to research protocols with many practical questions still unanswered.[134] The experimental nature of medical abortions suggests that courts should be very reluctant to authorize minors to avoid parental notification in cases where the girl proposes to obtain a medical abortion, rather than a surgical one.

The skill and experience of the abortion provider influence the realization of any risks related to a particular method of abortion. As with all medical procedures, one of the most important guarantees of patient safety is the professional competence of the physician and those who assist him or her. While it is important that minors seeking abortions be apprised of the risk of immediate complications, if experienced, these complications should be recognized and responded to by medical personnel at the abortion facility prior to the girl's departure. Therefore, it is of vital importance that the minor seeking to avoid parental notification establish that she had adequately considered the qualifications of the abortion provider she intends to use.[135] It is important that the physician be licensed, in good standing with the Texas Board of Medical Examiners, and that he have admitting privileges at a local hospital not more than

---

> abortions, the incidence of incomplete abortion, severe pain, nausea and vomiting are usually prohibitive.
>
> In contrast, medical abortion with mifepristone plus prostaglandin has been shown to have very low complication rates.

Id.

[132]*See* Ellertson & Westhoff, *supra* note 123, at 63.

[133]*See id.* at 64.

[134]*See id.* at 65. For example, American women obtaining a medical abortion typically self-administer the drugs and experience the abortion at home. *See id.* In Europe, the drugs are only administered in a clinical setting to allow medical intervention if a woman begins to experience adverse side effects. *See id.*

[135]The United States Supreme Court has acknowledged the superior ability of parents to evaluate and select appropriate healthcare providers. *See* Bellotti v. Baird, 443 U.S. 622, 641 n.21 (1979) (plurality opinion) (*Bellotti II*).

twenty minutes away from the location where the abortion is to occur.[136] If the abortion is to occur in a clinic,[137] the clinic should be licensed by the Texas Department of Health and have no history of violations of the licensing requirements.[138]

Two of the many advantages of parental involvement in a minor's decisions regarding an unplanned pregnancy are that parental notification enables a parent to assist in the selection of the physician performing the abortion and to monitor his or her daughter's recovery after the abortion. The Texas Legislature heard extensive testimony regarding dangerous and unnecessary delays by minors in seeking treatment related to post-abortion

---

[136]*See* National Abortion Federation, *Having an Abortion? Your Guide to Good Care* (visited Jan. 1, 2000) <http://www.prochoice.org/pregnant/goodcare.htm>.

[137]The majority, 81.4%, of resident abortions were performed in abortion clinics. Seventeen and one-half percent were performed in physicians' offices, and 0.9% were performed in hospitals and ambulatory surgery centers. *See* Texas Department of Health, Bureau of Vital Statistics, *Induced Terminations of Pregnancy by Facility and Length of Gestation, 1998* tbl. 37 (visited June 16, 2000) <http://www.tdh.state.tx.us/bvs/stats98/ANNR_HTM/98t36_38.htm>.

[138]This information is available from the Texas Department of Health via its toll-free telephone number, 1-888-973-0022. *See* 25 TEX. ADMIN. CODE § 139.6 (1999) (Tex. Dep't of Health). This service is in response to section 245.023 of the Texas Health & Safety Code which provides:

> The department on request shall make the following information available to the public:
>
> (1) the status of the license of any abortion facility;
>
> (2) the date of the last inspection of the facility, any violation discovered during that inspection that would pose a health risk to a patient at the facility, any challenge raised by the facility to the allegation that there was a violation, and any corrective action that is acceptable to the department and that is being undertaken by the facility with respect to the violation; and
>
> (3) an administrative or civil penalty imposed against the facility or a physician who provides services at the facility, professional discipline imposed against a physician who provides services at the facility, and any criminal conviction of the facility or a physician who provides services at the facility that is relevant to services provided at the facility.

TEX. HEALTH & SAFETY CODE ANN. § 245.023 (Vernon Supp. 2000).

Additional provisions protect the identity of callers who inquire about particular clinics, as well as the identity of abortion clinic employees. *See id.*; *see also* 25 TEX. ADMIN. CODE § 139.6.

complications when the parent did not know of the abortion.[139] Prior to authorizing a minor to bypass parental notification and obtain a secret abortion, the court must be convinced that the minor understands the risks related to the particular type of abortion to be performed at her particular stage of the pregnancy, that she can identify symptoms of post-abortion complications, and perhaps most importantly, that the girl will obtain a post-operative examination and promptly seek medical attention prior to that examination if there are any signs that she is experiencing complications.

b. Alternatives to Abortion

The second showing required prior to granting a bypass based upon a finding that a minor is mature and sufficiently well informed to obtain an abortion without parental notification, is that the minor understands the

---

[139]*See* The Parental Notification Act: *Hearings on Tex. S.B. 30 Before the Senate Human Servs. Comm.*, *supra* note 35, at 6 (statement of Senator Florence Shapiro) (transcript available from the Senate Staff Servs. Office); *id.* at 13–17 (statement of Veronica Moore).

> I know from my own personal experience—I have dealt with septic abortion. And it was a young lady that I cared for. She chose to go to one of the local reproductive clinics here in town, obtain their services, and if it were not for her parents knowing about what happened and caring for her, she probably would have died, because by the time I was notified about her, she already had an elevated temperature of 104, she was obtunded, didn't know who she was, where she was, and if not for the concern of her parents who were able to bring her to the emergency room for treatment and subsequent surgery, there is a strong possibility that she would have died, much as the 15-year-old girl who died at Ben Taub hospital in the mid 90's.

The Parental Notification Act: *Hearings on Tex. S.B. 30 Before the House State Affairs Comm.*, *supra* note 125 (statement by Michael Love) (tapes available from the Office of the House Comm. Coordinator and content is from private transcripts of those tapes).

> [Amy] obtained an abortion on Friday, suffered terrible complications, and subsequently died on Sunday. Because [her] parents did not know, they delayed taking her to hospital until she was unconscious. [Her] parents were originally told [their daughter] died of septic shock syndrome, but [a] friend who knew of the abortion told them after [Amy's] death. They then confirmed [her death] was due to [a] botched abortion, but [they] were misled because of [Amy's] right to privacy. [Healthcare providers explained that they initially refused to discuss the abortion as the cause of death because of their concern for Amy's right to privacy.]

Id. (statement by Leslie French) (tapes available from the Office of the House Comm. Coordinator and content is from private transcripts of those tapes) (recounting the story of her friend "Amy" who was fifteen, and pregnant).

alternatives to abortion and their implications.[140] This requirement was the focus of the Texas Supreme Court's opinions in *In re Doe (II)*.

> [T]he courts' fundamental inquiry is whether the minor has thoughtfully considered her alternatives. This inquiry must focus not on whether the minor has recited a generally recognized list of benefits or consequences in order to justify her decision. Instead, the inquiry must take into account whether the minor has considered and weighed her alternatives in light of her particular circumstances. When a minor has established that she has engaged in a rational and informed decision-making process and concluded that realistic concerns foreclose her alternatives, she cannot be denied the statutory bypass for failing to list general benefits that others might see.[141]

The Court stresses the individualized nature of the judicial inquiry and the requirement that the girl make an informed decision. It is commonly understood that a minor responding to an unplanned pregnancy has the options of obtaining an abortion; continuing the pregnancy to term and raising the child, either alone or with the assistance of others; or placing the child with another family through adoption. Less commonly understood are the implications of these options and the resources available to support her if the minor continues her pregnancy.

i. Continuing the Pregnancy to Term

In deciding whether to continue her pregnancy, a minor must understand both the health risks attendant to pregnancy and the availability of resources to help her with the medical, educational, and economic aspects of her decision.

(1) Health Risks Related to Pregnancy and the Importance of Prenatal Care

It is often stated that abortion is safer than childbirth.[142] Setting aside any objections arising from the lack of reliable information on the

---

[140] *See In re* Doe (II), 19 S.W.3d 346, 352 (Tex. 2000).

[141] *Id.* at 360.

[142] *See, e.g.*, National Abortion Federation, *Teenage Women, Abortion and the Law* (visited June 24, 2000) <http://www.prochoice.org/facts/teens.htm> ("Although the risk of complication is not as high as that of childbirth, it does rise with every week of pregnancy beyond eight weeks.").

complications from abortion, even with the limited information currently available, this statement is not true for abortions late in the pregnancy.[143] It is important that minors choosing abortion, particularly without the guidance of a parent, understand this fact.

It is also important that girls understand that most of the risks related to continuing their pregnancies are preventable by proper prenatal care.

Primary prevention of maternal deaths, such as those associated with ectopic pregnancy and some cases of infection and hemorrhage, is possible. However, some complications that can occur during pregnancy cannot be prevented, such as pregnancy-induced hypertension, placenta previa, retained placenta, and thromboembolism. Nevertheless, more than half of all maternal deaths can be prevented through early diagnosis and appropriate medical care of pregnancy complications.[144]

Teen mothers who adopt good dietary habits; take vitamins; avoid smoking, drugs and alcohol; and promptly obtain prenatal care experience no greater problems with their pregnancies than adult mothers.[145] Some

---

[143]*See* Henshaw, *supra* note 39, at 20.

> An important risk factor for mortality is gestational age. According to CDC [(Center for Disease Control)] calculations, for the period 1972-1987 mortality ranged (per 100,000 abortions) from 0.5 at less than 9 weeks to 2.9 at 13-15 weeks, 9.3% at 16-20 weeks, and 12% at more than 20 weeks.
>
> . . . .
>
> Between 1987 and 1991 in the United States morality due to complications of pregnancy and childbirth (excluding ectopic pregnancy and induced and spontaneous abortion) was 6.5 per 100,000 births, compared with 0.6 per 100,000 abortions. Thus the mortality risk associated with pregnancy and childbirth is approximately 10 times that associated with induced abortion. After 20 weeks there is no statistically significant difference between the risks of terminating a pregnancy by abortion and continuing the pregnancy.

Id. (footnotes omitted). The author fails to explain the conclusion that mortality rates of 9.3% for abortions performed 16 to 20 weeks, or mortality rates of 12% for abortions performed after 20 weeks do not differ significantly from the 6.5 mortality rate associated with pregnancy and childbirth. *See id.*

[144]*See* Center for Disease Control, *Maternal Mortality—United States, 1982-1996*, 47(34) MORBIDITY AND MORTALITY WKLY. REP. 705–07 (visited July 1, 2000) <http://www.cdc.gov/epo/mmwr/preview/mmwrhtml/00054602.htm>.

[145]*See* E. Hopkins, *Pregnancy Complications Not Higher in Teens*, 15 OB-GYN NEWS, May 1980.

reports even suggest that such teens may experience healthier pregnancies than those of older women.[146]

A study encompassing all Texas women giving birth to their first child in 1995 shows that teen mothers are less likely to give birth prematurely than mothers of thirty-plus years.[147] Their babies are less likely to be underweight, less than 2500 grams, at birth than those of mothers' thirty-plus years and only slightly more likely than babies born to mothers age thirty to thirty-nine.[148] Teens were less likely than any other age group to have twins or other multiple births, with the complications related to multiple births.[149] Less than one percent of all babies born to teen mothers suffered from any of the twenty-two congenital anomalies that may afflict newborns tracked by the study.[150] On average, teen mothers and their babies fared better than mothers of thirty-plus years and their babies and almost as well as mothers in their twenties and their children.[151]

This was true even though teen mothers were often found to delay seeking prenatal care until late in the pregnancy,[152] and when they did obtain care, it was more likely to be inadequate.[153] There is little doubt that those teens who sought early prenatal care and received adequate

---

[146]*See* Monica T. Smoot, *Delayed Childbearing: Increased Maternal Age at First Birth and Its Association with Labor and Delivery Outcomes* tbl. 7 (visited July 1, 2000) <http://www.tdh.state.tx.us/bvs/reports/sreport2.ppf>. Of thirteen common complications of labor and delivery, mothers age 10-19 consistently ranked below other age groups, with the exception of seizures during labor and precipitous labor. Of all first time mothers giving birth in Texas in 1995, teen mothers had the lowest percentage of premature ruptures of the membranes, placenta previa, prolonged labor, breech birth or malpresentation, and cephalopelvic disproportion. Their experience rate of hemorrhaging, "other excessive bleeding," placenta abruption, and cord prolapse were no higher than any other age group and equal to the lowest percentage of any age group. *See id.*

[147]*See id.* at tbl. 4.

[148]*See id.* at tbl. 5.

[149]*See id.* at tbl. 6.

[150]*See id.* at tbl. 10.

[151]*See id.* at tbls. 7–10.

[152]*See* Constance M. Wiemann et al., *Factors Associated with Adolescents' Risk of Late Entry into Prenatal Care*, 29 FAM. PLAN. PERSP. 273 (1997). Of all first-time mothers ages 10-19 in 1995, 64.6% obtained prenatal care in the first trimester, 27.2% began in the second trimester, 5.5% delayed until the third trimester, and 2.6% received no prenatal care at all. *See* Smoot, *supra* note 146, at tbl. 2. Teens delay seeking prenatal care much longer than older women. *See* Wiemann et al., *supra*. A study of 533 pregnant teens under the age of eighteen obtaining care at the Adolescent Obstetrics Clinic at the University of Texas Medical Branch at Galveston revealed that 47% enter prenatal care after the first twelve weeks of gestation. *See id.*

[153]*See* Smoot, *supra* note 146, at tbl. 2.

medical attention profited both in terms of their own medical well-being, as well as that of their children. In order to maximize a girl's chances of a healthy pregnancy, delivery, and baby, it is important that she obtain prenatal care as early in the pregnancy as possible.

(2) Medical Care and Support During Pregnancy

Medical care and a variety of other services are available to assist pregnant teens who continue their pregnancies. Medicaid provides coverage for many teens who have no private insurance for expenses related to pregnancy and childbirth.[154] For those who are uninsured but do not qualify for Medicaid, there are additional state programs that may provide assistance. A listing of the services available for particular locations can be obtained by contacting the Family Health Services Information and Referral Line[155] or through use of the online directory maintained by the Texas Department of Health and Human Services.[156]

Churches and other private organizations often know of doctors and health care organizations that provide free prenatal and delivery services.[157] These organizations can often assist with maternity clothes, emergency or long term housing, prenatal and childcare education, and post delivery

---

[154] *See* Center for Disease Control, *Insurance Coverage of Unintended Pregnancies Resulting in Live Born Infants—Florida, Georgia, South Carolina, and Oklahoma 1996*, 48 MORBIDITY AND MORTALITY WKLY. REP. 4, 5 (Feb. 12, 1999) <http://www.cdc.gov/epo/mmwr/preview/mmwrhtml/00056474.htm>. "For unmarried white women, Medicaid was the main source (68.3%-85.4%), followed by [private care insurance] (7.5%-27.4%) and other sources (4.1%-7.2%) . . . . For unmarried black women, payment sources were Medicaid (71.9%-88.3%), [private care insurance] (10.3%-19.7%), and other sources (1.4%-8.4%)." *Id. But see* William D. Mosher & Christine A. Bachrach, *Understanding U.S. Fertility: Continuity and Change in the National Survey of Family Growth, 1988-1995*, 28 FAM. PLAN. PERSP. 1 (Jan.–Feb. 1996) ("About one-third of teenage, black and never-married mothers relied on Medicaid for payment for their most recent delivery in 1982 and 1988.").

[155] *See* Texas Department of Health, *Family Health Services Information & Referral Line* (visited Oct. 7, 2000) <http://www.tdh.state.tx.us/mch/babylove.htm>. The toll free telephone number for referral to local services is 1-800-422-2956.

[156] *See* Texas Health and Human Services Commission, *Finding Help in Texas* (visited Oct. 7, 2000) <http://www.hhsc.state.tx.us/tirn/findhelp.htm>.

[157] Information about various crisis pregnancy centers can be obtained by calling toll free 1-888-550-7577 or online at <http://www.pregnancycenters.org>, <http://www.bethany.org>, or <http://www.heartbeatinternational.org/pages.html>. The Roman Catholic Church sponsors Project Gabriel, a program of spiritual and material support for pregnant women. Information about this project can be found at <http://www.holyspiritcatholic.com/adul&famlife/project_gabriel.htm> or <http://216.205.119.34/gabriel%20project.htm>. For teens contemplating adoption, many of these services are provided by the adoption agency. *See* Adoption Services Associates (visited Oct. 7, 2000) <http://www.asasatx.org/parents.htm>.

needs like baby clothes and furniture. A girl choosing to place her child with another family through adoption frequently will be provided all necessary services through the adoption agency or professional assisting her.[158] Beyond meeting the physical and material needs of the teen mother, and perhaps more importantly, many of these organizations include women who experienced pregnancy as a teenager and therefore can relate directly to the current experiences of the minor and provide much needed emotional support.

(3) Continuing Her Education

The effects of an unmarried teenager continuing her pregnancy are not limited to merely medical changes. It is often assumed that teen mothers are destined to be high school drop-outs, and this assumption has some historical basis. In the past, pregnant teens either had to delay continuing their education or accept transfers to alternative schools for unwed mothers. Now, pregnant girls are encouraged to stay in school. The effect of this change is evidenced by the results of a recent study which found that childbearing before the age of eighteen had no effect on the educational attainment for white women and only decreased schooling for black women by one year.[159]

Texas has made a particularly strong effort to assure the availability of educational opportunities for pregnant and parenting teens. They may either continue their education at the school they presently attend,[160] or choose to attend an alternative school offering more flexible scheduling and greater individualization of the pace of study. Programs for pregnant and parenting teens offered on regular campuses typically are part of the Pregnancy, Education and Parenting Program (PEP) established in section 29.085 of the Texas Education Code.[161] Schools offering the PEP program provide several valuable services to pregnant teens, including:

> (1) individual counseling, peer counseling, and self-help programs; (2) career counseling and job readiness training;

---

[158] *See* Adoption Services Associates, *Birth Parent Services* (visited Oct. 7, 2000) <http://www.asasatx.org/services.htm>.

[159] *See* David H. Klepinger et al., *Adolescent Fertility and the Educational Attainment of Young Women*, 27 FAM. PLAN. PERSP. 23 (Jan.–Feb. 1995).

[160] *See* TEX. EDUC. CODE ANN. § 29.085 (Vernon 1996); *see also* Region 20 Education Service Center, *Pregnancy, Education and Parenting: Life Skills Program for Student Parents Pregnancy, Education, and Parenting (PEP) Program* (visited Oct. 7, 2000) <http://www.esc20.k12.tx.us/pep/default.htm>.

[161] *See* TEX. EDUC. CODE ANN. § 29.085.

> (3) day care for the students' children on the campus or at a day-care facility in close proximity to the campus; (4) transportation for children of students to and from the campus or day-care facility; (5) transportation for students, as appropriate, to and from the campus or day-care facility; (6) instruction related to knowledge and skills in child development, parenting, and home and family living; and (7) assistance to students in the program in obtaining available services from government agencies or community service organizations, including prenatal and postnatal health and nutrition programs.[162]

In the 1999-2000 school year, 271 schools offered PEP programs to over 20,000 Texas students.[163]

Alternative schools represent another strategy for pregnant or parenting teens in completing their high school education.[164] These schools are limited to students who choose to pursue their education in this setting and by law must be separate from programs designed for disciplinary placement.[165] These schools allow pregnant and parenting teens to attend school with other young parents. Typically instruction is offered in the evenings, and some programs may include weekend instruction. Childcare is often provided on these campuses, and the curriculum includes instruction in parenting and child development.[166] Alternative education programs are available in all districts in Texas.

It is important that girls responding to unplanned pregnancies understand that these programs exist and that they offer a wide range of support to teens who want to continue their pregnancy. School counselors can provide information about the programs available at a particular school and throughout the school district. Not knowing these programs exist may lead a minor to mistakenly believe that the price of continuing her pregnancy is her education or that abortion is her only option.

(4) Economic Support from the Father

---

[162] *Id.*

[163] *See* Region 20 Education Service Center, *Pregnancy, Education, and Parenting Program: Historical Perspective* (visited June 24, 2000) <http://www.esc20.k12.tx.us/pep/history.htm>.

[164] *See* TEX. EDUC. CODE ANN. § 29.081(d)(1)(E) (defining the term "student at risk of dropping out of school" to include students who are pregnant or parenting).

[165] *See id.* § 37.008(a)(3) (1996).

[166] *See id.* § 29.085.

The sexual partner of the minor wanting to continue her pregnancy is another potential source of support. As the Texas Supreme Court noted in *In re Doe*, state "law requires the father to assist in the financial support of the child."[167] This obligation continues until the child turns eighteen and graduates from high school.[168] While the father may be limited in his present ability to assist in supporting the child, particularly if he is also a minor, his ability will change over time, and he may become an important source of support for the child.[169] Even in cases where the father's income does not allow for substantial contributions to the child's support, by acknowledging paternity the father makes it easier for a child to receive benefits derived through him, such as health care coverage and dependent's or survivor's benefits from the Veterans Administration or the Social Security Administration.

Early acknowledgement of the paternity is also associated with healthier pregnancies. This is true in part because physicians can obtain a complete medical history for both parents allowing the doctors to better anticipate any medical conditions the baby may experience *in utero* or at birth. Even for children who do not evidence any inherited conditions at birth, having access to a full medical history of both parents can facilitate diagnosis and treatment later in life.[170]

A study by the Texas Department of Health found that unmarried mothers with an acknowledgment of paternity were more likely to obtain prenatal care early, less likely to experience medical risk factors during the pregnancy, and more likely to deliver their babies full term than those

---

[167] 19 S.W.3d 249, 256 (Tex. 2000) (citing TEX. FAM. CODE ANN. § 154.001 (Vernon 1996)); *see also* TEX. CONST. art. XVI, § 28 (allowing for garnishment of wages for court-ordered child support payments).

[168] *See* TEX. FAM. CODE ANN. § 154.001(a)(1) (Vernon Supp. 2000).

[169] *See* Annie E. Casey Foundation, *The Right Start: Conditions of Babies and Their Families in America's Largest Cities* (visited Oct. 7, 2000) <http://www.aecf.org/kidscount/rightstart/text_front.pdf>.

> Data from the Census Bureau indicate that only 3 percent of mothers ages 15 to 17 received child-support payments in 1995. Data from the March 1998 Current Population Survey show that only 56 percent of males ages 16 to 19 had any earned income in 1997 and that the average annual income for those who worked was slightly less than $5,000.

Id. (citations omitted).

[170] *See* Office of the Attorney General—State of Texas, *Child Support Program* (visited Oct. 18, 2000) <http://www.oag.State.tx.us/child/mainchil.htm#paternity>.

mothers whose partners did not acknowledge paternity.[171] This study suggests that even in cases where the father is unable to provide financial support, his willing involvement in the pregnancy is desirable in many cases.

A mother who wants the father to assist in supporting the child can contact the Office of the Texas Attorney General for help in establishing paternity and obtaining child support.[172] Refusal of the father to acknowledge paternity and provide the necessary support has legal consequences. In cases where the father is unwilling or has failed to support the child, absence of support by the birth father allows for the termination of his parental rights regardless of his desires.[173] This can be advantageous in cases where the mother subsequently marries and her husband wishes to adopt the child or where the mother decides to place the child with another family for adoption.

ii. Raising the Child or Placing the Child with Another Family through Adoption

If the minor decides to continue her pregnancy, at some point she must decide whether to raise the child by herself, to raise the child with the assistance of others, or to place the child with another family through adoption. This decision, however, need not be made at any particular point in the pregnancy. Voluntarily relinquishment of a child for adoption remains an option at all times during the pregnancy and even thereafter if a mother is overwhelmed by the demands of parenthood. Even in cases where the pregnant minor is certain she wants to place the child with another family through adoption, Texas law forbids the signing of an affidavit of Voluntary Relinquishment of Parental Rights by the birth

---

[171] *See* Monica T. Smoot, *Acknowledgment of Paternity and Its Effect on Unmarried Mothers and Birth Outcomes* (visited Oct. 7, 2000) <http://www.tdh.state.tx.us/bvs/reports/paternty.htm> (finding that "[u]nmarried mothers were less likely to experience a medical risk factor when the father acknowledged paternity").

[172] *See* Office of Attorney General—State of Texas, *Child Support Program* (visited Oct. 7, 2000) <http://www.oag.state.tx.us/child/mainchil.htm> (listing a summary of services available).

[173] *See* Lehr v. Robertson, 463 U.S. 248 (1983) (stating that the failure of the putative father to establish a relationship with the child supported the state's refusal to set aside the adoption for failure of notice to the putative father where the state had no actual knowledge of his identity and putative father could have established paternity by registering with state paternity registry).

parents until at least forty-eight hours have passed from the time of the child's birth.[174]

While the percentage of teenagers becoming pregnant outside of marriage has increased dramatically in the past generation,[175] the percentage of teen mothers choosing to place their children with other families through adoption has declined.[176]

"When they become pregnant, very few teens choose to place their children for adoption. In a 1995 survey, 51% of teens that become pregnant give birth; 35% seek abortions; 14% miscarry. Less than 1% choose to place their children for adoption."[177]

From 1952 to 1988, the percentage of premarital births resulting in adoption placement declined 75%.[178] Placement declined in all racial groups, but the most dramatic change was in placement by white mothers, dropping from 19.3% in the period from 1952 to 1972 to only 3.2% during the time from 1982 to 1988.[179] There are now large numbers of prospective adoptive parents unable to adopt. In 1988 there were an estimated 3.3 people seeking to adopt for every actual adoption.[180]

The decline in the number of unmarried women placing their children with other families through adoption is due to a number of changes in

---

[174] *See* TEX. FAM. CODE ANN. § 161.103(a)(1) (Vernon Supp. 2000). As good source for information about domestic and adopted international law can be found on the Cornell website at <www.secure.law.cornell.edu/topics/adoption.html>.

[175] *See* Division of Reproduction Health, National Center for Chronic Disease Prevention and Health Promotion, *Achievements in Public Health, 1990-1999: Family Planning* (Dec. 3, 1999) (visited Oct. 9, 2000) <ftp://ftp.cdc.gov/pub/Publications/mmwr/wk/mm4847.pdf> ("Although pregnancy and childbearing rates for adolescent women have declined since 1991, the proportion of adolescent women who are unmarried at the time of giving birth has increased from 15% in 1960 to approximately 75% in 1998.") (footnotes omitted); *see also* Mosher & Bachrach, *supra* note 154, at 1 ("Only 4% of births in the United States in 1940 were to unmarried women, compared with 11% in 1970 and 31% in 1993.").

[176] *See* National Adoption Information Clearinghouse, *Placing Children for Adoption* (last modified Aug. 2, 2000) <http://www.calib.com/naic/pubs/s_place.htm> ("The proportion of teens placing their children for adoption has declined sharply over recent decades.").

[177] *Id.*

[178] *See id.* (citing Christine A. Bachrach et al., *Relinquishment of Premarital Births: Evidence from the National Survey Data,* 24 FAM. PLAN. PERSP. 27, 27–32, 48 (1992)) ("From 1952 to 1972, 8.7% of all premarital births were placed for adoption. From 1973 to 1981, this percentage fell to 4.1%. From 1982-1988, it fell further to 2%.").

[179] *See id.* During the same time period, placement by black mothers fell from 1.5% between 1952 to 1972 to .2% from 1973 to 1981 and returned to 1.1% from 1982 to 1988. *See id.*

[180] *See* Kathy S. Stolley, *Statistics on Adoption in the United States*, 3 ADOPTION 26, 37 (Spring 1993).

society. One of these changes is the reluctance of pregnancy counselors to discuss adoption as an option. A 1984 University of Illinois study found that over forty percent of those who identify themselves as "pregnancy counselors" in professional settings do not present adoption as an option to their clients.[181] "An additional [forty] percent provide inaccurate or incomplete information . . . ."[182] When presented with adoption, the same study found that thirty-eight percent of the women receiving counseling chose adoption.[183]

Many teens are reluctant to consider adoption because of concern that the adoptive parents are not capable of loving the child as much as birth parents can.[184] They fear that both they and their children will suffer psychological problems from adoption.[185] Girls are uncertain about who would adopt their baby and whether these strangers will be good parents.[186] Most of these fears are unfounded.

Studies have shown that children adopted as infants have as good or better mental health than children raised in an intact family.[187] They perform as well or better academically, seek psychological counseling no

---

[181] *See* Patrick F. Fagan, *Promoting Adoption Reform: Congress Can Give Children Another Chance* (May 6, 1996) <http://www.heritage.org/library/categories/healthwel/bg1080.html> (citing Edmund Mech, *Orientations of Pregnancy Counselors Toward Adoption*, University of Illinois (1984)).

[182] *Id.*

[183] *See id.*; *see also* Fredrica Mathews-Green, *Pro-Life Dilemma: Pregnancy Centers and the Welfare Trap*, 78 POLICY REVIEW (July–Aug. 1996) <www.policyreview.com/jul96/green.html>.

> According to the National Council for Adoption, a 1991 study found that pregnant, unmarried teens who were counseled in a program that mentioned adoption to every client were seven times more likely to choose it. When the teen's parents were involved in counseling, they were six times more likely to choose adoption. Teens asked to compare adoption with single parenting were also six times more likely to choose adoption.

Id.

[184] *See* Bethany Christian Services, *Adoption Myths: 8 Misunderstandings About Adoption* (visited Oct. 7, 2000) <www.bethany.org/pregnant/6a.htm>; *cf. In re* Doe (II), 19 S.W.3d 346, 358 (Tex. 2000) ("[Jane Doe 1] further testified that she would worry that the baby would have an unsuitable environment or that the adoptive parents would not provide the proper love or care.").

[185] *See* Bethany Christian Services, *Adoption Myths: 8 Misunderstandings About Adoption* (visited Oct. 7, 2000) <www.bethany.org/pregnant/6a.htm>.

[186] *See id.*

[187] *See* Fagan, *supra* note 181. *But see* David M. Brodzinsky, *Long-Term Outcomes in Adoption*, 3 ADOPTION 153 (Spring 1993).

more frequently, and have no greater behavioral problems than children who are raised by their birthparents.[188] This may be due, in part, to the fact that adoptive parents tend to be older, better off economically, and less likely to divorce.[189]

As to the parenting abilities of the adoptive parents, the National Adoption Information Clearinghouse suggests that the adoption process itself provides substantial safeguards to insure that people who adopt will be well situated to care for a child.[190]

> Prospective adoptive parents are carefully screened and give a great deal of information about themselves. They are visited in their home several times by a social worker and must provide personal references. They are taught about the special nature of adoptive parenting before the adoption takes place. By the time an agency has approved adoptive parents for placement, they have gotten to know them very well, and feel confident they would make good parents. This does not promise that they will be perfect parents, but usually decent people who really want to care for children.[191]

These precautions can be confirmed by the girl through careful inquiry of the adoption agency or by professionally arranging the adoption and in cases of "semi-open" or "open adoption," by the minor becoming acquainted with the adoptive parents herself.

In a semi-open adoption, the birth mother may select adoptive parents by reviewing information about the families provided by an adoption agency or professional. She may meet with the parents, exchanging only first names. This differs from an open adoption, in that with an open adoption, the birth mother and adoptive parents will have full information about each other's identities and may agree that the birth mother will continue to have some involvement with her child, even after the adoption.[192] In a closed adoption, the identities of the birth mother and the

---

[188] *See* Bachrach et al., *supra* note 178, at 27–48.

[189] *See* Fagan, *supra* note 181.

[190] *See* National Adoption Information Clearinghouse, *Are You Pregnant and Thinking about Adoption?* (visited Oct. 20, 2000) <http://www.calib.com/naic/pubs/f_pregna.htm#should_I>.

[191] *Id.*

[192] Relinquishment of parental rights may be ineffective where an adoption agency fails to assist a birthmother in creating a legally enforceable right to visit the child after placement if the agency knows that the birthmother has conditioned her relinquishment upon her ability to visit

adoptive parents are kept secret from each other.[193] Texas allows all three forms of adoptions.[194]

Fears of post-adoption regret are, perhaps, the most difficult to accurately respond to. It is true that women who place their children with other families often experience a sense of loss.[195] Yet after the initial period of sadness, many are happy and secure in the knowledge that their children are loved and growing up in good homes.[196] On average, women who place their children through adoption are of higher socioeconomic status than those who choose to parent their child alone. Women choosing adoption typically have higher educational goals and come from intact families that are supportive of the adoption decision.[197] Placing the child for adoption allows the minor who has decided to continue her pregnancy the opportunity to avoid prematurely assuming the responsibilities of parenthood, while respecting personal convictions about the status of *in utero* human life.

Before authorizing a minor to obtain a secret abortion, courts must confirm that the minor has been adequately informed of her options in continuing the pregnancy. She should know that resources are available that will insure she receives adequate care during her pregnancy and assistance in raising the child afterwards. In light of the research suggesting a bias against adoption by pregnancy counselors, it is particularly important that judges make sure that minors seeking to avoid parental notification understand that adoption is a viable option for many women and that these minors have received accurate information about continuing a pregnancy and placing a child with another family.

---

the child after he or she has been placed for adoption. *See* Vela v. Marywood, 17 S.W.3d 750, 760–61 (Tex. App.—Austin 2000, pet. filed). For an example of an agency that provides all three types of adoptions, see Adoption Access, Inc. <http://www.adoptionaccess.com>.

[193]Some women who have chosen to participate in a closed adoption change their minds years later. The Texas Department of Health (TDH) operates an adoption registry to facilitate contact between birthparents and adult adoptive children in cases where both parties wish to renew contact. Information about this registry and other registries in Texas can be found on the TDH website at <http://www.tdh.state.tx.us/bvs/car/car.htm>.

[194]Chapter 162 of the Texas Family Code contains the requirements and procedures governing adoption in Texas. An informative listing of advantages and disadvantages of each type of adoption can be found at <http://www.bethany.org/pregnant/>.

[195]*See* National Adoption Information Clearinghouse, *The Impact of Adoption on Birth Parents* (visited July 8, 2000) <http://www.calib.com/naic/Pubs/f_impact.htm#experience>.

[196]*See* Planned Parenthood Federation of America, Inc., *What If I'm Pregnant?* (visited Sept. 5, 2000) <http:// www.plannedparenthood.org/WOMENSHEALTH/whatifpregnant.htm>.

[197]*See* Stolley, *supra* note 180, at 32.

c. Emotional and Psychological Aspects of Abortion

A minor who can show that she has consulted with a healthcare provider, understands the risks of the particular type of abortion that she seeks at her particular stage of pregnancy, and has given knowledgeable and thoughtful consideration to the alternatives to abortion, must establish two more elements in order to obtain a judicial bypass of parental notification based upon being mature and sufficiently well informed. The final requirements of the *Doe* decision are that the girl establish that she is "aware of the emotional and psychological aspects of undergoing an abortion" and "that she has considered how this decision might affect her family relations."[198]

Like adoption, abortion is often accompanied by a sense of loss and sadness. At the committee hearings involving Senate Bill 30, the legislative committees heard other bills that proposed requiring parental consent for minors and informed consent for adult women. All of these bills were supported by testimony regarding post-abortion complications and regret.[199] Among the most poignant was the testimony of Ms. Linda Gartman before the Texas Senate Human Services Committee.[200]

> I became depressed, and in 1991 my daughter was having her first baby, this is my grandbaby and she invited me to see the sonogram, she was 12 weeks pregnant. I couldn't believe my eyes, I'd never seen a sonogram, I wanted to be

---

[198] *In re* Doe, 19 S.W.3d 249, 256–57 (Tex. 2000).

[199] *See Hearings on Tex. S.B. 27 Before the Senate Human Servs. Comm.*, 76th Leg., R.S. 9–10 (Mar. 10, 1999) (statement of Hal Wallis, M.D.) (transcript available from Senate Staff Servs. Office); *Hearings on Tex. S.B. 65 Before the Senate Human Servs. Comm.*, *supra* note 130, at 16–17 (statement of Linda Gartman) (transcript available from Senate Staff Servs. Office); The Parental Notification Act: *Hearings on Tex. S.B. 30 Before the Senate Human Servs. Comm.*, *supra* note 35, at 4–5 (statement of Dee Dee Alonzo) (transcript available from Senate Staff Servs. Office) ("I didn't know anything about the risks of abortion. I did not know of the depression and grief I was to experience, to say nothing of the emotional trauma I was to undergo."); *id.* at 2–3 (statement of Teresa Stanton Collett) (testifying in support of Senate Bill 30); *id.* at 6 (statement of Veronica Moore) (testifying in support of Senate Bill 30); *id.* at 16, 17 (statement of Terry Moore) (testifying in support of Senate Bill 30); *id.* at 3–4 (statement of Teresa Connolly) (testifying in support of Senate Bill 30); *id.* at 4–5 (statement of Becky Norrell) (testifying in support of Senate Bill 30); *Hearings on Tex. H.B. 623 Before the House Comm. on State Affairs*, *supra* note 32, at 13–17 (statement of Veronica Moore) (tapes available from the Office of the House Comm. Coordinator and content is from private transcripts of those tapes); *id.* at 23–24 (statement by Michael Love); *id.* at 25 (statement by Leslie French).

[200] *Hearings on Tex. S.B. 65 Before the Senate Human Servs. Comm.*, *supra* note 130, at 4–5 (statement by Linda Gartman) (transcript available from Senate Staff Servs. Office).

> happy for her, and to be excited for her, and I was in shock, I couldn't believe my eyes, couldn't believe what I was seeing, it was a tiny baby, complete body, had everything it needed except time in the womb. It was fully developed, it was doing flips inside her womb. It was precious, I could see her silhouette of her face. And I had to, I had to be happy, but I wanted to run out of there screaming. And inside I've been screaming ever since. I was depressed for years, I hated myself, my self-esteem went down, I wanted to die. Abortion is not an easy choice. There are circumstances for it and we have the right to choose. We certainly need to have all the facts, and we need the truth up front, so that we can make that choice, and make sure that, that's what we wanna do.[201]

The long-term emotional and psychological harm testified to by Ms. Gartman and others are the subject of intense debate. Many studies suggest that post-abortion reactions can be quite severe, but abortion providers insist that the studies are flawed methodologically.[202]

A 1995 medical text on induced abortion describes the extent and cause of emotional harm in the following manner.

> In the USA, it is estimated that 20% of women suffer from severe feelings of loss, grief and regret. These feelings may progress to anger (at herself and at her partner), or to depression and even obsession. These feelings are more likely to arise in women who: lack social support; whose decision to terminate the pregnancy is in conflict with their family or their religious beliefs; who feel they were pressurized into having an abortion; who have abortion because of fetal anomaly; and who are very young or have a very late abortion.[203]

---

[201] *Id.* at 16; *see also supra* note 131 and accompanying text.

[202] Compare the summary of research and bibliographies prepared by the Elliot Institute, found at <http://www.afterabortion.org>, with the information provided by the National Abortion Federation at <http://www.prochoice.org/>.

[203] Anna Glasier, *Counseling for Abortion, in* MODERN METHODS OF INDUCING ABORTION 112, 117 (David T. Baird et al. eds., 1995); *see also* Jo Ann Rosenfeld, *Emotional Responses to Therapeutic Abortion*, 45 AM. FAM. PHYSICIAN 137, 138 (1992) ("Teenagers who do not tell their parents about their abortion have an increased incidence of emotional problems and feelings of guilt."). Additional sources are collected and discussed in Thomas R. Eller, *Informed Consent*

Of the six indicia listed in the passage quoted above, at least two indicators will be present in every case involving a minor seeking judicial bypass. She will be young and, if successful in obtaining the bypass, she will be eliminating at least one major source of social support—her parents. Also, it is very likely that her decision is in conflict with the beliefs of her family.

Another medical text on abortion techniques identifies the risk factors for psychiatric illness following an abortion to include prior or concurrent psychiatric illness, coercion, genetic or maternal medical indications, lack of social supports, paralyzing ambivalence, and advanced gestational age.[204] In discussing the impact of youth on the psychological impact of abortion, the authors write:

> In the United States, the proliferation of state laws mandating parental involvement in the abortion decisions of unmarried women under the age of majority reflects an assumption that youth is a barrier to decision-making about pregnancy, thereby increasing the risk of a poor postabortion outcome. Adolescents, on average, do have less well developed decision-making skills than adults; they are less realistic about, and less interested in, the impact of current behaviors on future circumstances. However, no evidence suggests that this relative immaturity results in poorer decisions or poorer outcomes than those of adults.
>
> Adolescents are more likely than adults to see things in black and white; they may be more likely to consider abortion murder, for example. One survey indicates that some adolescents fear surgical abortion will decrease or end their fertility. Adolescent behavior may be driven more by fears of the immediate reactions of parents to the pregnancy than by realistic assessments of the demands of parenthood. Therefore adolescents are more likely to delay abortion decisions until later in pregnancy, when it is

Civil Actions for Post-Abortion Psychological Trauma, 71 NOTRE DAME L. REV. 639 (1996). For cases involving claims of psychological injury, see *Eidson v. Reproductive Health Services*, 863 S.W.2d 621 (Mo. Ct. App. 1993), and *Showery v. State*, 678 S.W.2d 103 (Tex. App.—El Paso 1984, writ ref'd).

[204] *See* Carol J. Rowland Hogue et al., *Answering Questions About Long Term Outcomes, in* A CLINICIAN'S GUIDE TO MEDICAL AND SURGICAL ABORTIONS 217, 225 (Maureen Paul et al. eds., 1999).

> more difficult and expensive to obtain abortions and when the procedure is more complex, risky, and stressful.[205]

The assertion that "no evidence" suggests poorer outcomes for adolescents than those experienced by adults is belied by the authors' own observations in the second paragraph and misrepresents the research published to date.[206] Nonetheless, it is possible that a woman who maturely, freely, and thoughtfully arrives at the decision to terminate her pregnancy and who has no emotional, social, or moral conflict over the decisions made, after the initial period following the abortion, will experience no more adverse psychological effects than occasional regret that she could not give birth to the child at the time of her unplanned pregnancy.

d. Affect on Family Relations

In addition to determining whether the girl is aware of the emotional and psychological aspects of undergoing an abortion, the court must inquire as to whether the minor "has considered how this decision might affect her family relations."[207] This is sensible in light of the widespread agreement that women who are conflicted about their decision or who lack social support are most likely to suffer emotionally or psychologically from an abortion. Although the Court has yet to elaborate on this requirement, in her concurrence in *In re Doe,* Justice Owen expressed her view of what should be required:

> I would require a minor to demonstrate that she has thoughtfully considered the potential impact on her relationships with her parents and other family members if they learn now or sometime in the future that she has had an abortion. She should also exhibit some consideration of how this decision may impact her future relationships, such as those she may have with a husband or future children. A minor should also have considered the impact that continuing her pregnancy would or might have on these relationships.[208]

---

[205] *Id.* at 223–24 (footnotes omitted).

[206] *See id.*

[207] *In re* Doe, 19 S.W.3d. 249, 256–57 (Tex. 2000).

[208] *Id.* at 265.

Testimony before the Texas Senate Human Services Committee illustrated the wisdom of Justice Owen's concern for the impact of postabortion revelation of the pregnancy and abortion. In her testimony before the Texas Senate Human Services Committee, Margaret Romberg Carter told the story of her secret abortion as a teenager and her parents' discovery of it years later:

> I could not bring myself [at age seventeen] to go and discuss my being pregnant with my parents, even though I was raised in a very, very loving family, very supportive family . . . . [W]hen I did tell my father, he looked at me, and this is extremely hard because I love my dad to death, but he looked at me and said, did you not come and tell us because you thought that I would beat you. And I came apart, that thought really didn't cross my mind but I guess maybe somewhere in the back of my mind it was there.[209]

This testimony confirms three important points. First, the witness acknowledged that she was raised in a very loving and supportive family, yet refused to voluntarily involve her parents. Second, she described the pain felt by both parent and adult-child when the secret abortion is revealed, even when the revelation occurs sixteen years after the fact.[210] Finally, this testimony alluded to the phantom fear of rejection or violence that may be experienced, even by girls who have loving and supportive parents. The Texas Supreme Court has expressly stated that such phantom fears do not justify excluding parents from knowing of their daughter's decision to obtain an abortion.[211]

In evaluating whether minors are mature and sufficiently well informed to avoid parental notification, Texas case law requires the minor makes several showings. While often summarized as three showings,[212] when each requirement is reduced to its elements, there are six things that the minor must establish in order to obtain an order finding that she is mature

---

[209]*Hearings on Tex. S.B. 27, 30, 65, 83 Before the Senate Human Servs. Comm.*, *supra* note 92, at 21 (statement of Margaret Romberg Carter) (transcript available from Senate Staff Servs. Office).

[210]*See id.* The witness was 33 at the time she testified.

[211]*See In re* Doe 2, 19 S.W.3d 278, 282 (Tex. 2000). "We note, however, that a minor's generalized fear of telling her parents does not, by itself, establish that notification would not be in the minor's best interests." *Id.*

[212]*See id.* at 281; *In re* Doe 3, 19 S.W.3d 300, 300–03 (Tex. 2000) (per curiam) (Gonzales, J., concurring); *In re* Doe 4 (II), 19 S.W.3d. 337,339 (Tex. 2000).

and sufficiently well informed to avoid parental notification. She must show that: (1) her decision to obtain an abortion is "not the product of impulse," but the result of "careful consideration of the various options available to her and the benefits, risks, and consequences of those options;" (2) she has consulted with a healthcare provider; (3) she understands the risks associated with the particular method of abortion to be performed at the particular stage of her pregnancy; (4) she understands and has given careful consideration to the alternatives to abortion and their implications; (5) she is aware of the emotional and psychological aspects of undergoing an abortion; and (6) she has considered how this decision might affect her family relations.[213] Each of these elements is designed to insure the well-being of Texas minors. By adhering to these requirements, Texas courts enhance the chances that only those girls who fully understand and have adequately considered the potential consequences of each response to an unplanned pregnancy are found to be sufficiently mature and well informed to consent to an abortion without the advice and involvement of a parent.

B. Best Interest of the Minor

In cases where a minor is unable to establish that she is sufficiently mature and well informed to make the decision alone, judicial bypass of parental notification may still be obtained if it is established that parental notification is not in the best interest of the girl.[214]

1. Presumption in Favor of Parental Involvement

The negative phrasing of this ground for judicial bypass is due to the general requirement of the Parental Notification Act that a parent be notified prior to the performance of an abortion on a minor.[215] This requirement is consistent with the strong presumption throughout Texas law that parental involvement is required in decisions regarding minor children.[216] As early as 1872, the Texas Supreme Court described parents' right to direct the care and upbringing of their children as "a universal law of nature, recognized by society, and enforced by governments."[217] A little

[213]*In re Doe*, 19 S.W.3d at 255–57.

[214]*See* TEX. FAM. CODE ANN. § 33.003(i) (Vernon Supp. 2000).

[215]*See id.* § 33.002(a)(1)(A).

[216]*See* McKinney v. Noble, 37 Tex. 731, 732 (1873); Wiley v. Spratlan, 543 S.W.2d 349, 352 (Tex. 1976); Act of May 26, 1997, 75th Leg., R.S., ch. 1225, § 3(b), 1997 Tex. Gen. Laws 4691, 4692.

[217]*McKinney*, 37 Tex. at 732.

over one hundred years later, in 1976, the court stated, "The natural right which exists between parents and their children is one of constitutional dimensions."[218] This understanding of parents' rights is shared by the Texas Legislature, as evidenced by the 1997 adoption of House Bill 425, which forbids state agencies from "adopt[ing] rules or policies or tak[ing] any other action which violates the fundamental right and duty of a parent to direct the upbringing of the parent's child."[219]

An important aspect of the parental right to direct the upbringing of children is the right to make decisions regarding their medical treatment. This is recognized as both a matter of state and federal law.[220] While Texas statutes permit minors to make a limited number of medical decisions without parental involvement,[221] the authority of parents to make

---

[218] *Wiley*, 543 S.W.2d at 352.

[219] Act of May 26, 1997, 75th Leg., R.S., ch. 1225, § 3(b), 1997 Tex. Gen. Laws 4691, 4692. Many legislators expressed support for Senate Bill 30 on the basis of the natural right of parents to direct the upbringing of their children. Representative Suzanna Gratia Hupp's comments represent some of the legislators' feelings:

> [Over] the last few weeks, I have been bombarded with phone calls and literature from both the pro-life and the pro-choice movements. And quite frankly, that amazes me. Because in my mind at least this bill has absolutely nothing to do with abortion. You could strike out abortion and substitute wart removal for all I care. It's got nothing to do with it. It has everything to do with a parent's right and responsibility. Most of you know I am a chiropractor. It amazes and floors me that as a chiropractor, I cannot do a school physical without a parent's consent form. I could be charged with assault and battery for doing a school physical without a parent's consent. Not a sibling's consent, not an aunt's consent, not a grandfather's consent, but a parent's consent for a school physical. As a mother, I believe the state should do everything within its power to put those rights and those parents' responsibilities back into the hands that God and nature intended them to be in.

Debate on substitute for Tex. S.B. 30 on the Floor of the House, 76th Leg., R.S. 8 (May 19, 1999) (statement of Representative Susanna Gratia Hupp) (tapes available from the Office of the House Comm. Coordinator and content is from private transcripts of those tapes).

[220] *See* TEX. FAM. CODE ANN. § 151.003(a)(6) (Vernon 1996) (stating that a parent of a minor child has "the right to consent to the child's marriage, enlistment in the armed forces of the United States, medical and dental care, and psychiatric, psychological, and surgical treatment"). The federal law regarding this issue is addressed in Parham v. J.R., 442 U.S. 584, 625 (1979) (recognizing the traditional authority of a parent to direct the psychiatric treatment for a minor child, over the minor's objection).

[221] *See* TEX. FAM. CODE ANN. § 32.003 (Vernon 1996).

decisions relating to the medical care of their minor children is the generally accepted rule in Texas jurisprudence.[222]

The Supreme Court of the United States described the foundation of this general rule in *Parham v. J.R.*:

> Our jurisprudence historically has reflected Western civilization concepts of the family as a unit with broad parental authority over minor children. Our cases have consistently followed that course; our constitutional system long ago rejected any notion that a child is "the mere creature of the State" and, on the contrary, asserted that parents generally "have the right, coupled with the high duty, to recognize and prepare [their children] for additional obligations." Surely, this includes a "high duty" to recognize symptoms of illness and to seek and follow medical advice. The law's concept of the family rests on a presumption that parents possess what a child lacks in maturity, experience, and capacity for judgment required for making life's difficult decisions. More important, historically it has recognized that natural bonds of affection lead parents to act in the best interests of their children.[223]

The accuracy of the Court's observation that parents most often act in the best interest of their children was affirmed by the testimony of witnesses appearing before the Texas legislative committees considering the Parental Notification Act.

2. Evidence that Parents Respond Reasonably

The Senate and House Committees heard numerous witnesses and received written testimony from others regarding the reaction of parents to the news of their minor daughters' pregnancies. While most speakers relied on their own stories, or stories of friends or family, some of the strongest evidence that parents respond reasonably and compassionately

---

[222]Two exceptions to this proposition exist. *See* TEX. FAM. CODE ANN. § 32.001 (Vernon 1996) (stating that alternative family members are authorized to provide consent upon a showing that the parent cannot be contacted and has not given actual notice to the contrary); O.G. v. Baum, 790 S.W.2d 839, 841 (Tex. App.—Houston [1st Dist.] 1990, no writ) (limiting parental authority where the parent has unreasonably refused to consent to life-sustaining care).

[223]*Parham*, 442 U.S. at 602 (citations omitted) (quoting Pierce v. Society of Sisters, 268 U.S. 510, 535 (1925)). The United State Supreme Court reiterated its support of the constitutional dimension of parental authority in Traxel v. Granville. 120 S. Ct. 2054 (2000).

came from supporters of other bills and opponents of the Parental Notification Act, Senate Bill 30.

Dr. Abby Myring, a licensed family therapist in Dallas, appeared before the House State Affairs Committee to urge approval of House Bill 5.[224] In support of her argument for including a "counselor bypass to parental involvement"[225] she shared two stories from her practice. The first case involved a sixteen-year-old patient that became pregnant, and wanted Dr. Myring to help her without telling the patient's parents. Dr. Myring was successful in persuading the teenager to tell her parents, who "eventually helped [the patient] come to the right decision for her."[226]

The second story involved a seventeen-year-old college freshman who found herself pregnant after having sex while intoxicated. She was uncertain whether she had consented to the act of sexual intercourse, but she was certain she did not want to continue the pregnancy. Without consulting her parents, she had an abortion. Two weeks after the abortion, a concerned friend told the girl's parents of the events "and the parents very wisely brought her into therapy and treatment to help her with the traumatizing effects she had from this abortion."[227]

In both cases, the parents reacted to the unwelcome news of their daughters' pregnancies by providing much-needed support. This was the pattern in almost every story told involving parents who had been informed of their daughters' situations.[228]

---

[224]*See Hearings on Tex. H.B. 1073 Before the House Comm. of State Affairs*, 76th Leg., R.S. 19–21 (Apr. 19, 1999) (statement of Abby Myring) (tapes available from the Office of the House Comm. Coordinator and content is from private transcripts of those tapes).

[225]*Id.* at 20.

[226]*Id.* at 19.

[227]*Id.* at 20.

[228]*See id.*; *see also Hearings on Tex. S.B. 27, 30, 65, 83 Before the Senate Human Servs. Comm.*, *supra* note 92, at 6 (statement of Veronica Moore) (transcript available from the Senate Staff Servs. Office); *Hearings on Tex. H.B. 1073 Before the House Comm. on State Affairs*, *supra* note 224 (statement of Michael Love) (tapes available from the Office of the House Comm. Coordinator and content is from private transcripts of those tapes); *id.* at 25 (statement of Leslie French).

The one exception, a story of abuse related to parental knowledge of a teen pregnancy, was presented by Dr. Dave Kittrell, an obstetrician and gynecologist who performs abortions. "I once had a patient tell me that she was afraid to tell her dad about her pregnancy because when her older th—older sister got pregnant, he broke her arm." *Hearings on Tex. S.B. 27, 30, 65, 83 Before the Senate Human Servs. Comm.*, *supra* note 92, at 10, 11 (statement of Dave Kittrell, M.D.) (transcript available from Senate Staff Servs. Office).

However, Dr. Kittrell's credibility was brought into question by his testimony regarding the harmful effects of abortion restrictions. "In the [c]ountry of Brazil where [abortion] is illegal and

Dr. Patricia Handley, a family practitioner in Austin, Texas, appeared to oppose Senate Bill 30.[229] She told two stories to support her position that the unintended adverse consequences of delayed abortion would outweigh any benefits from enactment of the proposed act.[230] The first was the story of a teenage patient whose mother had insisted that the daughter obtain birth control pills.[231] A few years later the patient appeared complaining of a sore throat, only to discover that she was pregnant.[232] Dr. Handley encouraged the girl to tell her parents.[233] "I thought this was sort of a novel idea, but in fact it is a much bigger deal to her parents now that they're helping raise and clothe the two-year old."[234] While no additional details about the parents' response are provided, it is clear that their support and concern for their daughter and grandchild continue even today.

The second example she gave was her personal story:

> I was a sexually active 16-year-old who was concerned regarding pregnancy and, you know, I went out of state to talk to a cousin as opposed to telling my mother. I didn't have any fears for my life or concern or any fears for repercussion, but I went to very great lengths to avoid [telling a parent].[235]

---

the physician's license is removed, there are over a million women a year in that country who die due to illegal abortions, so if there is a desire and a market, [abortion] will occur [regardless of legal restrictions]." *Id.* at 15.

Research revealed no study supporting Dr. Kittrell's assertion. In 1997, researchers from John Hopkins University Population Information Program reported estimates of 6000 maternal deaths per year due to post-abortion complications for all of Latin America. *See Care for Postabortion Complications: Saving Women's Lives*, 25 POPULATION REP. L. 1, 4 (1997). A 1999 study published by the Alan Guttmacher Institute, a research institute affiliated with Planned Parenthood, estimates that 1.444 million abortions a year occur in Brazil. Relying on statistics from the World Health Organization the authors estimate that these illegal abortions result in 288,700 hospitalizations for abortion complications. *See* Stanley K. Henshaw et al., *The Incidence of Abortion Worldwide*, 25 FAM. PLAN. PERSP. 30, tbl. 3 (Jan. 1999).

229 *Hearings on Tex. H.B. 1073 Before the House Comm. on State Affairs, supra* note 224 (statement of Patricia Handley) (tapes available from the Office of the House Comm. Coordinator and content is from private transcripts of those tapes).

230 *See id.*

231 *See id.*

232 *See id.*

233 *See id.*

234 *Id.*

235 *Id.*

This testimony is interesting in its candor regarding the reason that teens avoid involving their parents in decisions about their unplanned pregnancies. Contrary to the claims of opponents of parental involvement laws, most teens want secret abortions not because they realistically fear any harm by their parents, but because they fear disappointing their parents.[236] Foregoing the guidance and aid provided by the vast majority of parents whose daughters experience unplanned pregnancies is a heavy price to pay to merely avoid the expression of parental disappointment.

The underlying assumption of the Texas Parental Notification Act is that parents will react responsibly. This assumption claims no lesser pedigree than the observations of the United States Supreme Court.

> As with so many other legal presumptions, experience and reality may rebut what the law accepts as a starting point; the incidence of child neglect and abuse cases attests to this. That some parents "may at times be acting against the interests of their children" . . . creates a basis for caution, but is hardly a reason to discard wholesale those pages of human experience that teach that parents generally do act in the child's best interests. *The statist notion that governmental power should supersede parental authority in all cases because some parents abuse and neglect children is repugnant to American tradition.*[237]

---

[236]*See* Texas Family Planning Association, *Voluntary Survey of Minors Seeking Abortion Care*, submitted in support of testimony by Peggy Romberg, Hearing before the Senate Human Services Committee, Mar. 10, 1999.

Some of the reasons minors stated for not involving a parent:

> "Because I was too scared to tell anyone and I was against the procedure until it was my problem."
>
> "I did not involve my parents because they are unreasonable. My dad would've tried to put my boyfriend in jail."
>
> "My parents have high expectations for me."
>
> "They would not take it well."

Id.; *see also supra* text accompanying note 203, at 4. Published studies confirm that adolescents who seek to avoid parental involvement are often concerned about parental disappointment. *See* Griffin-Carlson & Mackin, *supra* note 92.

[237]Parham v. J.R., 442 U.S. 584, 602–03 (1979) (emphasis added) (citations omitted).

The testimony before both Texas legislative committees, on the whole, confirms the wisdom and necessity of parental involvement.[238] The Legislature intended the vast majority of pregnant minors have the benefit of parental guidance and assistance. This is evidenced by the requirement that minors overcome the presumption of parental involvement by affirmatively showing that parental notification is not in their best interest.

3. Factors in Assessing the Best Interest of the Minor

The Texas Supreme Court addressed the proper standard for determining when parental notification is not in a minor's best interest in *In re Doe 2*.

> To determine whether notification would not be in the minor's best interests, the trial court should weigh the advantages and disadvantages of parental notification in the minor's specific situation. Although the best interests determination necessarily involves evaluating whether notification could lead to abuse of the minor, that the

[238]In addition to the testimony presented at the hearing, members of Senate Human Services Committee reviewed a 1989 memo prepared by the Minnesota Attorney General, which states that "after some five years of the statute's operation, the evidence does not disclose a single instance of abuse or forceful obstruction of abortion for any Minnesota minor." *Hearings on Tex. S.B. 27 Before the Senate Human Servs. Comm., supra* note 199, at 23 (statement by Senator Florence Shapiro) (transcript available from the Senate Staff Servs. Office) (referring to a statement of the Minnesota Attorney General Opinion). The plaintiffs in *Hodgson v. Minnesota*, 497 U.S. 417 (1990) also conceded that there was no evidence of any increase in medical complications which could be attributed to the law. *See* State of Minnesota Office of the Attorney General, *Background Briefing Concerning the Minnesota Parent Notification Law*, at 3.

Testimony on the Massachusetts' experience with its parental consent law revealed a similar absence of unintended, but harmful, consequences. Ms. Jamie Sabino, chair of the Massachusetts Judicial Consent for Minors Lawyer Referral Panel, could identify no case of a Massachusetts' minor being abused or abandoned as a result of the law. *See Hearings on Tex. H.B. 1073 Before the House State Affairs Comm., supra* note 224 (statement by Jamie Sabino, M.D.) (tapes available from the Office of the House Comm. Coordinator and content is from private transcripts of those tapes). In response to questioning, she also testified that there had been no increase in the number of illegal abortions in Massachusetts since the enactment of the statute in 1981. *See id. But see Hearings on Tex. S.B. 27 Before the Senate Human Servs. Comm., supra* note 199 at 24, 26 (statement by Kate Mclaughlin) (transcript available from the Senate Staff Servs. Office) (referring to unidentified study indicating that "minors seeking illegal abortions to avoid the parental consent laws is now the number one cause of death from abortions"). The author of this article has diligently searched medical, social science, and legal literature and is unable to locate any article or even a reference to such an article, suggesting that this is the case in the United States, despite the fact that a reputable study with such findings would be worthy of national media attention.

> Legislature included the potential for abuse as a separate reason for granting a bypass makes it clear that the best interests determination encompasses a broader concern for the minor's welfare. In *Holley v. Adams*, the court developed a list of non-exhaustive factors for determining a minor's best interests. Four of these factors are relevant when adapted to the parental notification context, and a trial court should consider them in determining best interests: (1) the minor's emotional or physical needs; (2) the possibility of emotional or physical danger to the minor; (3) the stability of the minor's home and whether notification would cause serious and lasting harm to the family structure; and (4) the relationship between the parent and the minor and the effect of notification on that relationship. An additional factor that courts in other jurisdictions have considered is whether notification may lead the parents to withdraw emotional and financial support from the minor. This list is not exhaustive, and in making the best-interests determination the trial court should consider all relevant circumstances. We note, however, that a minor's generalized fear of telling her parents does not, by itself, establish that notification would not be in the minor's best interests.[239]

In fulfilling the Court's direction to weigh advantages and disadvantages of parental notification, it is important to consider the benefits of parental involvement identified in case law and the legislative record.

4. Medical Benefits Achieved through Parental Involvement

The United States Supreme Court has identified three specific medical benefits from involving parents in the decisions of minors to obtain abortions. First, as the Court has observed, parental involvement is essential to insuring an accurate medical history.

> The medical, emotional, and psychological consequences of an abortion are serious and can be lasting; this is particularly so when the patient is immature. An adequate medical and psychological case history is important to the physician. Parents can provide medical and psychological data, refer the physician to other sources of medical

[239] *In re* Doe 2, 19 S.W.3d 278, 282 (Tex. 2000) (footnotes omitted).

> history, such as family physicians, and authorize family physicians to give relevant data.[240]

As with any other surgical procedure, a full and complete medical history is a prerequisite to optimum care before, during, and after an abortion. At a minimum, such a history requires a statement of current health, a past history of medical conditions that may require further evaluation, a history of any bleeding disorders, a statement of current symptoms of respiratory illness, medications and allergies, as well as a description of all prior surgical procedures and any reactions to anesthetics.[241] Past psychological or psychiatric history is also important in assessing the risk of severe emotional distress related to obtaining an abortion.[242] Courts considering applications by minors seeking to avoid parental notification should not lightly disregard the benefit of parental input in assuring an accurate medical history prior to the performance of an abortion.

Similarly, in determining the best interest of the minor, courts should consider the superior ability of parents to evaluate and select appropriate healthcare providers.

> In this case, however, we are concerned only with minors who, according to the record, may range in age from children of 12 years to 17-year-old teenagers. Even the latter are less likely than adults to know or be able to recognize ethical, qualified physicians, or to have the means to engage such professionals. Many minors who bypass their parents probably will resort to an abortion clinic, without being able to distinguish the competent and ethical from those that are incompetent or unethical.[243]

[240]H.L. v. Matheson, 450 U.S. 398, 411 (1981) (footnotes omitted); *accord* Ohio v. Akron Ctr. for Reprod. Health, 497 U.S. 502, 518–19 (1990).

[241]*See* D. Scott Poehlmann & Bruce Ferguson, *Medical Evaluation and Management, in* A CLINICIAN'S GUIDE TO MEDICAL AND SURGICAL ABORTION 53, 53 (Maureen Paul et al. eds., 1999).

[242]*See* Jo Ann Rosenfeld, *Emotional Responses to Therapeutic Abortion*, 45 AM. FAM. PHYSICIAN 137, 138 (1992) ("Teenagers who do not tell their parents about their abortion have an increased incidence of emotional problems and feelings of guilt."). Additional sources are collected and discussed in Thomas R. Eller, *Informed Consent Civil Actions for Post-Abortion Psychological Trauma*, 71 NOTRE DAME L. REV. 639 (1996). For cases involving claims of psychological injury, see *Eidson v. Reproductive Health Services*, 863 S.W.2d 621 (Mo. Ct. App. 1993), and *Showery v. State*, 678 S.W.2d 103 (Tex. Civ. App.—El Paso 1984, pet. ref'd).

[243]Bellotti v. Baird, 443 U.S. 622, 641 n.21 (1979) (plurality opinion) (*Bellotti II*).

The concern of the United States Supreme Court in distinguishing competent and ethical abortion providers is well justified.

According to the Texas Department of Health, the vast majority of induced abortions are performed in abortion clinics.[244] Unlike many private physicians' offices, these providers offer only one option in responding to an unplanned pregnancy, abortion. In an ongoing federal lawsuit regarding recent changes in Texas licensing requirements, physicians who provide abortions as a part of their general obstetrical practice described abortion clinics as insensitive to the emotional needs of their patients,[245] prone to becoming profit-motivated,[246] and subject to "the cattle herd mentality."[247] The Texas Parental Notification Act was intended, in part, to protect minors from impulsive decisions unduly influenced by those who advocate only one response to unplanned pregnancies—that response being abortion.[248]

In laying out Senate Bill 30 for the Senate Human Services Committee, the senate sponsor summarized the question before the committee in these terms: "Members, the question before you is a very simple one, who should be involved in this most important decision making for our children. The parents that love them and have raised them, or a person who will financially profit from the decision to abort."[249] Before the House State Affairs Committee, the house sponsor identified the same concern: "There is the direct conflict of interest between what is best for the girl and the financial benefit of that, of that, person providing the abortion, and the parental involvement or the judicial bypass eliminates that conflict of interest."[250] Parental involvement protects the minor from

---

[244]*See* Texas Department of Health, Bureau of Vital Statistics, *Table 37: Induced Terminations of Pregnancy by Facility and Length of Gestation—1998* (visited July 8, 2000) <http://www.tdh.state.tx.us/bvs/stats98/ANNR_HTM/98t36_38.HTM> (The vast majority, 81.4% of resident abortions, were performed in abortion clinics. Seventeen and one-half percent were performed in physicians' offices, 0.9 % in hospitals and ambulatory surgery centers.).

[245]*See* Women's Med. Ctr. v. Archer, No. H-99-3639, at 13 (S.D. Tex. Dec. 29, 1999) (mem.) (summarizing the testimony by Dr. Fred Hansen).

[246]*See id.* at 16.

[247]*Id.* at 20 (summarizing the testimony of Dr. Tad Davis).

[248]*In re* Doe (II), 19 S.W.3d 346, 388 (Tex. 2000).

[249]*Hearings on Tex. S.B. 27 Before the Senate Human Servs. Comm.*, *supra* note 199, at 19 (statement of Senator Florence Shapiro) (transcript available from the Senate Staff Servs. Office).

[250]*Hearings on Tex. H.B. 1073 Before the House Comm. on State Affairs*, supra note 224 (statement by Representative Dianne Delisi) (tapes available from the Office of the House Comm. Coordinator and content is from private transcripts of those tapes); *see also id.* at 15 (statement by Veronica Moore); *id.* at 28 (statement by Ms. Martinson) ("If you have the

potential overreaching by abortion providers by insuring that the minor receives counsel from at least one person who knows the minor intimately and who seeks her best interest above all other considerations.

The third medical benefit from parental involvement recognized by the United States Supreme Court is the enhanced ability of parents to respond promptly to any signs of post-abortion complications.[251] While it is often claimed that abortion is one of the safest surgical procedures performed today, the actual rate of many complications is simply unknown.[252] This is because some of the most serious complications are delayed and only detected during the follow-up visit; yet, only about one-third of all abortion patients actually keep their appointments for post-operative checkups.[253] Absent parental notification, hemorrhaging may be mistaken for a heavy period and severe depression as typical teenage angst.[254]

Parental involvement enhances the medical care received by minors dealing with unplanned pregnancies. Once notified, parents can provide much needed information on the medical history of the minor. They more fully comprehend the risks attendant to various treatment plans and can advise the minor as she tries to evaluate her options. In cases where the

---

physician who earns $400 per abortion, as the confidant for this teenager, you've got the fox in the hen house."); *Hearings on Tex. S.B. 16, 17, 30, 65, 83 Before the Senate Human Servs. Comm.*, 76th Leg., R.S. 4–5 (statement by Becky Norrell) (transcript available from the Senate Staff Servs. Office).

[251] *Accord* Powers v. Floyd, 904 S.W.2d 713, 718 (Tex. App.—Waco 1995, writ denied) (stating that disclosure of the risks associated with abortion to the parent is preferable since disclosure may be "severely disturbing" to the minor); *see* Ohio v. Akron Ctr. for Reprod. Health, 497 U.S. 502, 519 (1990).

[252] *See* Henshaw, *supra* note 39, at 20. "The abortion reporting systems of some countries and states in the United States include entries about complications, but these systems are generally considered to underreport infections and other problems that appear some time after procedure was performed." *Id.*

[253] *See id.*

[254] Members of the Texas Senate Human Services Committee heard compelling testimony by Veronica Moore concerning the psychological harm suffered by her 15-year-old daughter after obtaining a secret abortion upon the urging of her 19-year-old boyfriend.

> Not one night since February 20th have passed that there has not been a nightmare or a 2:30 a.m. scream by my daughter. She has been diagnosed now with depression and now even borderline anorexic . . . . No one from the state came when Danaca needed to be fed, to be walked to the bathroom, to be dressed, to have her hair combed, to assist me, I still had to do it all on my own.

Hearings on Tex. S.B. 27 Before the Senate Human Servs. Comm., *supra* note 199, at 6 (statement of Veronica Moore) (transcript available from the Senate Staff Servs. Office).

minor decides to obtain an abortion prior to informing her parents, parental notification is still important since parents can play an active role in selecting the abortion provider and in monitoring the well being of the minor post-operatively. Courts should weigh all of these medical benefits in determining whether it is in the best interest of the minor to obtain a secret abortion.

5. Protection Against Ongoing Victimization

In addition to the medical benefits arising from parental involvement, requiring parental notification advances the safety of teens, many of whom are pregnant due to criminal acts. Section 22.011 of the Texas Penal Code characterizes sexual intercourse with a person under the age of seventeen as sexual assault.[255] In cases where the actor is within three years of age of the victim and the victim is over the age of fourteen, the statute recognizes an affirmative defense to prosecution for consensual acts.[256] Where the victim is under fourteen, the age difference is greater than three years, or the act is non-consensual, it is characterized as aggravated sexual assault which is a felony under section 22.021.[257]

National studies reveal that "[a]lmost two thirds of adolescent mothers have partners older than 20 years of age."[258] In a study of over 46,000 pregnancies by school-age girls in California, researchers found that "71%, or over 33,000, were fathered by adult post-high-school men whose mean age was 22.6 years, an average of 5 years older than the mothers . . . . Even among junior high school mothers aged 15 and younger, most births are fathered by adult men 6-7 years their senior. *Men aged 25 and older father more births among California school-age girls than do boys under age 18*."[259] Other studies confirm that many teenage pregnancies are the result of sexual exploitation of minors by men who are substantially older.[260]

---

[255]*See* TEX. PEN. CODE ANN. § 22.011 (Vernon 1994 & Supp. 2000).

[256]*See id.*

[257]*See id.* § 22.021(e).

[258]American Academy of Pediatrics Committee on Adolescence, *Adolescent Pregnancy—Current Trends and Issues: 1998*, 103 PEDIATRICS 516, 519 (1999). This document is also available on the worldwide web at <http://www.aap.org/policy/re9828.html>.

[259]Mike A. Males, *Adult Involvement in Teenage Childbearing and STD*, LANCET, July 8, 1995, at 64 (emphasis added).

[260]*See id.* (citing H.P. Boyer & D. Fine, *Sexual Abuse as a Factor in Adolescent Pregnancy and Child Maltreatment*, 24 FAM. PLAN. PERSP., 1992, at 4; H.P. Gershenson et al., *The Prevalence of Coercive Experience Among Teenage Mothers*, 4 J. INTERPERS. VIOL. 204 (1989); *see also* D.J. Taylor et al., *Demographic Characteristics in Adult Paternity for First Births to*

While no comparable comprehensive study of Texas teen pregnancy exists, it is relatively easy to calculate the approximate number of minors who were impregnated by an act of sexual assault. In 1998, the Texas Department of Health reported 26,627 pregnancies by Texas teens.[261] If the statistical profile of Texas partners of pregnant teens mirrors that of California, 18,905 of these pregnancies are the result of criminal conduct.

These statistics were personalized for Texas legislators by the testimony of Ms. Dee Dee Alonzo.[262] Ms. Alonzo testified before the Senate Human Services Committee in support of Senate Bill 30, the bill enacting chapter 33 of the Texas Family Code.[263] At age sixteen, she was seduced by her high school teacher.[264] When she became pregnant, he persuaded her to have a secret abortion.[265] She went to the clinic alone, obtained the abortion her seducer had paid for, and returned to continue the abusive relationship for another year.[266] Had Ms. Alonzo's parents known of her pregnancy, they could have intervened and stopped the continuing criminal assault of their daughter.[267]

While physicians and other professionals are required to report sexual assault, there is no substitute for parental involvement. Many abortion providers and some physicians oppose any reporting requirement and refuse to comply. This opposition is evident from recent statements of the Texas Medical Association, Planned Parenthood for the Texas Capital Region, and the Texas Family Planning Association. These groups oppose

---

Adolescents Under 15 Years of Age, J. ADOLESCENT HEALTH, Apr. 1999, at 251 (finding that adult fathers, responsible for 26.7% of births to very young adolescents, were a mean of 8.8 years older than the mother).

[261]*See* Texas Department of Health, Bureau of Vital Statistics, *Table 14B: Reported Pregnancies, Births, Fetal Deaths, and Abortions, Women Age 13-17—Texas, 1998* (last modified June 20, 2000) <http://www.tdh.state.tx.us/bvs/stats98/ANNR_HTM/98t14b.htm>.

[262]*See* The Parental Notification Act: *Hearings on Tex. S.B. 30 Before the Senate Human Servs. Comm.*, *supra* note 35, at 4–5 (transcript available from the Senate Staff Servs. Office).

[263]*See id.*

[264]*See id.* at 4.

[265]*See id.*

[266]*See id.*

[267]*See id.* "No matter what their reaction would have been, they were my parents and they were adults, and they did love me, it would not have been a secret and the man would have been exposed." *Id.* A similar incident involved another Texas high school student impregnated by her teacher. This is revealed in the settlement related to injuries she suffered during the abortion of her pregnancy. *See* Clement v. Riston, No. B-131,033, settlement reported in Jury Verdict Research, Research, LRP Pub. No. 65904 available on LEXIS-NEXIS; *cf.* Patterson v. Planned Parenthood, 971 S.W.2d 439, 447 (Tex. 1998) (Gonzales, J., concurring) (describing the sexual abuse of a young girl that resulted in two pregnancies and two secret abortions).

a requirement that recipients of state family planning funds show a good faith effort to comply with state reporting requirements of sexual abuse.[268] In determining the best interest of the minor, courts should consider the risk that orders permitting secret abortions often will enable adult men to continue their sexual abuse of Texas minors, with little hope of any intervention.

6. Limiting State Intervention in the Family

In addition to achieving the medical and safety benefits related to parental notification, the Act's presumption in favor of parental involvement protects the necessary discretion that parents must have in raising their children. The Texas cases regarding the constitutional stature of this discretion are well summarized in the concurring opinion of *Patterson v. Planned Parenthood, Inc.*

> [The Texas courts have] strongly affirmed the ancient and well-established right of parents to guide and direct the decisions of their minor children. "The natural right which exists between parents and their children is one of constitutional dimensions." "The child is not the mere creature of the state; those who nurture him and direct his destiny have the right, coupled with the high duty, to recognize and prepare him for additional obligations." Only a generation ago, this Court recognized the fundamental importance of parental rights in reaffirming the doctrine of parental immunity:
>
> We trust that it is not out of date for the state and its courts to be concerned with the welfare of the family as the most vital unit in our society. We recognize that peace, tranquility and discipline in the home are endowed and inspired by higher authority than statutory enactments and court decisions. Harmonious family relationships depend on filial and parental love and respect which can neither be created nor preserved by legislatures or courts. The most we can do is to prevent the judicial system from being used to disrupt the wide sphere of reasonable discretion which is necessary in order for parents to properly exercise

[268]*See* Scott S. Greenberger, *Health-care Groups Worry Law Will Harm Sexually Active Teens*, AUSTIN AMERICAN-STATESMAN, May 1, 2000, at A1.

their responsibility to provide nurture, care, and discipline for their children.[269]

The insight expressed in this last sentence is particularly relevant to interpretation of the judicial bypass provisions of chapter 33. Absent narrow construction of the judicial bypass, the judicial system will be used, as it is already being used,[270] to routinely disrupt the reasonable discretion necessary for responsible parenting.

7. Consideration of Whether Abortion is in the Minor's Best Interest

In *In re Doe 2*, the court did not discuss the question of whether an abortion was in a minor's best interest, leaving the impression that abortions should be automatically granted if notification was not in the minor's best interest.[271] The court articulated several factors that a trial court should consider in assessing a minor's claim that parental notification would not be in her best interest.[272] Yet, as Justice Owen notes in her concurring opinion, none of these factors go to the question of whether it is in the best interest of this particular minor to obtain an abortion.[273] Limiting the inquiry to only considering whether parental notification is in the best interest of the minor risks partially emancipating the minor and then abandoning her to "her rights."

No medical procedure is entirely risk free.[274] This fact, compounded by the unique character of abortion, imposes a heavy responsibility upon courts exercising their *parens patriae* power to authorize an immature or ill-informed minor to consent to a secret abortion.[275] To suggest that courts

---

[269]*Patterson*, 971 S.W.2d at 447 (Gonzales, J. concurring) (citation omitted) (quoting in turn: Wiley v. Spratlan, 543 S.W.2d 349, 352 (Tex. 1976); Pierce v. Society of Sisters, 268 U.S. 510, 535 (1925)).

[270]*See In re* Doe 3, 19 S.W.3d 300, 315 (Tex. 2000) (per curiam) (Hecht, J., dissenting). "[P]arental notification cases have completely exhausted the Court's resources for the past three weeks, and no relief is in sight." *Id.* at 318.

[271]19 S.W.3d 278 (Tex. 2000).

[272]*See id.* at 282.

[273]*See id.* at 285–86 (Owen, J., concurring).

[274]*See supra* text accompanying note 98–103.

[275]*See* Planned Parenthood v. Casey, 505 U.S. 833, 852 (1992) (plurality opinion).

> Abortion is a unique act. It is an act fraught with consequences for others: for the woman who must live with the implications of her decision; for the persons who perform and assist in the procedure; for the spouse, family, and society which must confront the knowledge that these procedures exist, procedures some deem nothing

could authorize such action only after inquiring as to whether a parent should be notified is to suggest that courts are free to secretly intervene in the natural and constitutionally-protected relationship of parent and child and usurp the natural prerogative of parents to make medical decisions for their child, and then irresponsibly desert the immature minor to make a decision the court has already determined she is ill-equipped to make. This result is not required under a fair reading of the Parental Notification Act or federal constitutional law and cannot be an accurate understanding of the Texas Supreme Court's view of the law.[276]

There was intense debate surrounding the question of who should be entitled to authorize parental bypass.[277] Proponents of permitting other

---

> short of an act of violence against innocent human life; and, depending on one's beliefs, for the life or potential life that is aborted.

Id.

[276] Should a court determine that parental notification is not in the best interest of the minor and that an abortion is also not in her best interest, the court would have some duty to insure the continuing well-being of the minor by referral to the appropriate governmental agencies providing assistance to minors in crisis. An example of where a court could reasonably determine that obtaining a secret abortion would not be in the best interest of a minor would be where the minor has delayed acknowledging her pregnancy until the fifth or sixth month of pregnancy, and the medical risks of abortion equal or exceed those attendant to childbirth. *See* Henshaw, *supra* note 39, at 20 (stating that mortality rates for abortions performed at 16-20 weeks is 9.3%, and 12% for those performed after 20 weeks compared to a mortality rate of 6.5% due to complications attendant to pregnancy and childbirth).

[277] Representative Phil King stated:

> From a larger policy standpoint, and we talk a lot about what state policy should be, I think that this amendment dramatically interferes with the traditional parent/child relationship that we have established not only in the Texas Family Code, but in the Texas laws both in statute and in case law at large. What we're doing with this is saying that a third party, be they well intended or not, that a third party can step in between a parent and their child without first having made any showing whatsoever that there is something wrong with the relationship between the parent and the child. We're allowing others to step in between mom and daughter taking that right of parenthood away from mother without first having had there be any evidence whatsoever that mother is not a good mother and that father is not a good father and I think that's wrong and I think that's bad policy. We do that in a courtroom daily. Courts in Texas have the authority to deal with parent/child relationships. Most of the lawyers in here have spent more time than they ever want to think about dealing with parent/child suits. That's what courts do. It's not a great way to do it. The judicial bypass is not an easy of [sic] perfect method, but I think from a policy standpoint that it is the only thing that we can do as a legislative body. Otherwise, otherwise [sic], I think we are stepping in between parents and children, taking mom out of the picture

relatives, licensed counselors, or clergy members to authorize a minor to consent to a secret abortion repeatedly challenged the qualifications of judges to make such a unique and difficult decision.[278] The decision to emancipate a minor is not unique and has been a subject of judicial

> and dad out of the picture with absolutely no evidence whatsoever that mom is not a good mom and dad is not the best one to help in that decision.

Debate on Tex. S.B. 30 on the Floor of the House, 76th Leg., R.S. 8–9 (May 19, 1999) (tapes available from the Office of the House Comm. Coordinator and content is from private transcripts of those tapes). *See, e.g., id.* (exchange between Representatives Patricia Gray and Arlene Wohlgemuth); *id.* (exchange between Representatives Phil King and Joe Deshotel); *id.* (exchange between Representatives Helen Giddings and Arlene Wohlgemuth).

[278]*See id.* (May 22, 1999) (statement from Representative Wilson).

> I know a lot of judges and I'm going to tell you I'd be scared to death for a 12- or 13-year old to go to someone I know. (interruption) Hold on, let me ask you a question, you asked me a question. I would feel much more comfortable if a teenager went to an individual who was a man or woman of the cloth for counseling and guidance on this issue than I would be some of the people who have been elected judges in this state.

Id.; *see also id.* (exchange between Representatives David Swinford and Senfronia Thompson):

> THOMPSON: But don't you think that you're putting the judge in a more tenable position than you would a clergy?
>
> SWINFORD: Well, one thing about it, the judge's duty is entirely different than the clergy's duty. The judge's duty is talking about the law and we're making the law here. The clergy's duty is talking about souls, about relationships and about family. You know, Ms. Thompson, in the Ten Commandments that Moses brought down from on top of the mountain one of those is honor your father and mother.
>
> THOMPSON: I didn't know that Moses did the Ten—did he do that?
>
> SWINFORD: And anything that we do to get where we're interfering with that in any way we're doing the wrong thing.
>
> THOMPSON: Mr. Swinford, wouldn't you agree that a lot of our judges are elected by special interest groups?
>
> SWINFORD: Oh I don't know. Probably.
>
> THOMPSON: And don't you think they're not free to exercise judicial discretion when called upon particularly in situations like this?
>
> SWINFORD: Well, you know I would be, if I was a judge, I would really dislike this bill because I'd hate to make that decision. But he's got a different thing to do than a minister. A minister is to take care of the flock.

Id.; *see also id.* (statement by Representative Ken Yarbrough) (expressing concern that experienced judges will decline to hear bypass cases from fear of political consequences).

decisions in Texas for over one hundred years.[279] Certainly child custody cases have long required courts to assess the best interest of minors.[280] Yet, there are no proposals that the authority exercised in either of these types of judicial proceedings be shared with a minor's relatives, professional counselors, or clergy. Rather, what proponents of additional bypasses relied upon in their arguments for inclusion of other decision makers is the unique nature of the abortion decision and the tremendous responsibility undertaken by those deciding that the best interest of an immature minor will be served by authorizing her to obtain an abortion, unbeknownst to her parents. In the end, it was in recognition of the awesome responsibility undertaken when authorizing a minor to obtain a secret abortion that the Legislature limited this bypass to only those abortions judicially authorized.[281]

United States Supreme Court precedent supports the conclusion that it is constitutionally permissible to require that courts answer both the question of whether parental notification is not in a minor's best interest and in those cases where it is not, the question of whether the girl's best interests are served by obtaining a secret abortion. In *H.L. v. Matheson*, the Court established that a state may require parental notification for immature minors seeking an abortion.[282] While it is an open question whether judicial bypass is even required in parental notification laws,[283] there is no doubt that a state acts constitutionally in limiting bypass to only

---

[279]*See, e.g.*, Trammell v. Trammell, 20 Tex. 406, 417 (1857) (stating that the marriage of male minors does not result in emancipation).

[280]*See, e.g.*, Legate v. Legate, 87 Tex. 248, 28 S.W. 281, 283 (1894).

[281]*See Hearings on Tex. H.B. 623 Before the House Comm. on State Affairs*, *supra* note 32 (exchange between Chairman Wolens and Representative Marchant) (tapes available from the Office of the House Comm. Coordinator and content is from private transcripts of those tapes).

[282]450 U.S. 398, 409 (1981).

[283]*See* Lambert v. Wicklund, 520 U.S. 292, 295 (1997) (per curiam). "We declined to decide [in *Ohio v. Akron Ctr. for Reprod. Health*, 497 U.S. 502, 510 (1990),] whether a parental notification statute must include some sort of bypass provision . . . ." *Id.* The United States Court of Appeals for the Fifth Circuit has never ruled on this question, and there is a split of authority among the circuits that have. The most recent and thorough opinion on the issue held that bypass was not required in all notification statutes. *See* Planned Parenthood v. Camblos, 155 F.3d 352, 373 (4th Cir. 1998). However the United States Courts of Appeals for the Sixth, Seventh, and Eight Circuits have ruled to the contrary. *See* Akron Ctr. for Reprod. Health v. Slaby, 854 F.2d 852, 869 (6th Cir. 1988), *rev'd sub nom. on other grounds* Ohio v. Akron Ctr. for Reprod. Health, 497 U.S. 502 (1990); Indiana Planned Parenthood Affiliates Ass'n v. Pearson, 716 F.2d 1127, 1132 (7th Cir. 1983); Planned Parenthood v. Miller, 63 F.3d 1452, 1460 (8th Cir. 1995).

mature minors and immature minors who can establish that abortion is in their best interest.

C. Likely to Result in Physical, Sexual, or Emotional Abuse

In cases involving immature or inadequately-informed minors for whom the court has determined it is not in the minor's best interest to avoid parental involvement, the Parental Notification Act also authorizes courts to grant judicial bypass in cases where notification of a parent may lead to physical, sexual, or emotional abuse of the minor.[284] *In re Doe 3* involved the review of a minor's claim that parental notification would lead to physical or emotional abuse.[285] The Texas Supreme Court, unable to arrive at a common definition of "emotional abuse," disposed of the appeal through a per curiam opinion.[286]

Statements during the House of Representatives debate regarding Senate Bill 30 provide insight into the legislative understanding of the circumstances that would justify bypassing parental involvement in a minor's decision to obtain an abortion. While there are multiple references to cases involving incest or physical beatings, there are only two examples given for bypassing parental involvement on the basis that notification may lead to physical, sexual, or emotional abuse of the minor. In discussing a proposed amendment to the bill, Representative Giddings stated:

> I know we have provisions in this bill for abused girls when abuse is suspected or detected to get help, but there are cases where the abuse is not known. I don't know how many of you might be aware that there are two high-profile cases in the Dallas area in the last year. One where a mother married and the young girl that was the daughter, 14 years old was forced to enter into a contract to have a daughter for her stepfather as a part of the marriage. Fortunately, that was discovered and that man is in prison and so is that mother. Additionally, we had a case where a mother had a Norplant put into the arm of her child so that

---

[284] *See* TEX. FAM. CODE ANN. § 33.003(i) (Vernon Supp. 2000).

[285] 19 S.W.3d 300 (Tex. 2000) (per curiam).

[286] *See id.* at 300–01.

the father could have sex with that child without fear of pregnancy.[287]

Her examples were referred to several times by other legislators and indicate the general understanding of the type of circumstances that would result in judicial bypass of parental notification due to abuse.[288] The Texas Supreme Court's interpretation of what would constitute adequate evidence of potential physical, sexual, or emotional abuse sufficient to justify bypassing parental notification should be informed by the gravity of the situations discussed during the legislative process.

The Texas Parental Notification Act did not introduce the phrase "physical, sexual, and emotional abuse" into the lexicon of Texas lawyers. This phrase had well-defined statutory meanings provided in section 261.001 of the Texas Family Code before the passage of Senate Bill 30.[289] The terms had been used repeatedly in Texas appellate opinions.[290] The vast majority of Texas cases authorizing any interference with the parent-child relationship involve claims of both emotional abuse and physical or sexual abuse, and there appears to have been little uncertainty concerning what constituted each of these forms of abuse.[291] The phrase "emotional abuse" had been used without additional definition or internal reference in at least three other statutes dealing with minors in the Family Code,[292] as well as in two additional statutes in the Human Resources Code.[293]

---

[287]Debate on Tex. S.B. 30 on the Floor of the House, 76th Leg., R.S. 11 (May 19, 1999) (tapes available from the Office of the House Comm. Coordinator and content is from private transcripts of those tapes).

[288]*See id.* (May 21, 1999) (statement by Representative Ron Clark) (giving the example "Look the parent is abusive, the parent, in Ms. Giddings' case is selling the child, we need a judicial bypass."); *cf. id.* (May 22, 1999) (statement by Representative Arlene Wohlgemuth) (opposing clergy bypass because of inadequate protection for girls like the victims in Ms. Giddings' examples).

[289]TEX. FAM. CODE ANN. § 261.001 (Vernon Supp. 2000).

[290]*See, e.g.*, State Farm Gen. Ins. Co. v. White, 955 S.W.2d 474, 475 (Tex. App.—Austin 1997, no writ); Rodriguez v. State, No. 05-95-01356CR, 1997 WL 527843, at *3–4 (Tex. App.—Dallas 1997, pet. ref'd).

[291]*See generally In re* J.J., 911 S.W.2d 437 (Tex. App.—Texarkana 1995, writ denied); *In re* L.S., 748 S.W.2d 571 (Tex. App.—Amarillo 1988, no writ); Clark v. Clark, 705 S.W.2d 218 (Tex. App.—Dallas 1985, writ dism'd).

[292]TEX. FAM. CODE ANN. §§ 32.004(a)(3), 107.052(c), 162.005(c) (Vernon 1996).

[293]TEX. HUM. RES. CODE ANN. §§ 42.059(a), 40.069(a) (Vernon 2000).

Nonetheless, in *In re Doe 3*, members of the Texas Supreme Court offered not one, but two new definitions of emotional abuse.[294] Justice Gonzales, joined by Chief Justice Phillips, looked to the definition of abuse governing elderly protective services and offered a definition of emotional abuse as "unreasonable conduct causing serious emotional injury."[295] The opinion does not explain why this definition, crafted as a measure of misconduct involving the interaction of adults, is superior to the definition designed specifically to be applied to the interaction of adults with minors.

Justice Enoch, joined by Justices Baker, Hankinson, and O'Neill, provided even less guidance in determining the parameters of emotional abuse.[296] He rejected the clear definition contained in section 261.001 as inapplicable because the Parental Notification Act does not specifically refer to it in section 33.003(i), although he acknowledged the use of section 261.001 in section 33.008 of the Act regarding a physician's duty to report abuse.[297] In place of the relatively objective criteria found in the statutory definition, "injury to a child that results in an observable and material impairment in the child's growth, development, or psychological functioning,"[298] Justice Enoch suggested, "Abuse is abuse; it is neither to be trifled with nor its severity to be second guessed."[299] The opinion fails to identify any advantage in using this non-defining definition over the comparative clarity of the existing statutory definition of emotional abuse. Lower courts attempting to decide bypass cases in accordance with the law, rather than personal predilection, find more guidance in the statutory direction to consider "observable and material impairment" than in the mere adjectives "unreasonable" and "serious" found in the definition of Justice Gonzales,[300] or in the refusal to provide any definition found in the opinion authored by Justice Enoch.[301]

In addition to providing clear guidance to the lower courts, using the existing statutory definition of emotional abuse facilitates compliance with Texas statutes requiring reports of abuse or suspected abuse. Currently any person having cause to believe that a minor has suffered harm as the result

---

[294] 19 S.W.3d 300, 303–05 (Tex. 2000) (per curiam) (Gonzales, J., concurring); *id.* at 306–08 (Enoch, J., concurring in part and dissenting in part).

[295] *Id.* at 304 (Gonzales, J., concurring).

[296] *See id.* at 306–09 (Enoch, J., concurring in part and dissenting in part).

[297] *See id.* at 308.

[298] *See* TEX. FAM. CODE ANN. § 261.001(1)(A) (Vernon Supp. 2000).

[299] *In re Doe 3*, 19 S.W.3d at 307 (Enoch, J., concurring in part and dissenting in part).

[300] *See id.* at 304 (Gonzales, J., concurring).

[301] *See id.* at 306–09 (Enoch, J., concurring in part and dissenting in part).

of abuse must report that belief to appropriate state officials for investigation.[302] The standard is even higher for licensed professionals, for they must not only report reasonable belief of past abuse, but must also report any reasonable belief of future abuse.[303] The state's concern to insure the protection of children is so strong that it even trumps the interests underlying testimonial privileges, including the privileges of physician-patient and attorney-client.[304]

Expression of this concern is continued in the Parental Notification Act by its reporting requirements regarding both past and future abuse.[305] The record is clear that the Texas Legislature intended to protect minors who may be endangered by revealing to a parent their pregnancy or intent to obtain an abortion. The mechanism chosen for this protection was the reminder to professionals involved in bypass cases of their reporting duties, with specific emphasis on the circumstances that appeared to be most common from the legislative testimony. There was substantial testimony concerning the large number of minors' pregnancies resulting from sexual assault by unrelated parties.[306] Similarly there were repeated expressions of concern to protect the unique vulnerabilities of children who are the victims of incest.[307] For these reasons, the Act contains specific provisions requiring the reporting of these patterns of conduct.[308] The inclusion of these provisions does not change, nor was it intended to change, the general reporting obligations of professionals under section

---

[302]*See* TEX. FAM. CODE ANN. § 261.101(a) (Vernon Supp. 2000).

[303]*See id.* § 261.101(b).

[304]*See id.* § 261.101(c).

[305]*See id.* § 33.008 (Vernon Supp. 2000) (stating that a physician's duty is to report and the Department of Protective and Regulatory Services' duty is to assist minors in applying for judicial bypass where it is appropriate due to evidence of abuse); *id.* § 33.009 (stating that the duty of the court, guardian ad litem, and attorney ad litem is to report sexual crimes committed against the minor).

[306]*See* The Parental Notification Act: *Hearings on Tex. S.B. 30 Before the Senate Human Servs. Comm.*, *supra* note 35, at 4–5 (statement of Dee Dee Alonzo) (testifying in support of Senate Bill 30) (transcript available from the Senate Staff Servs. Office) ("I didn't know anything about the risks of abortion. I did not know of the depression and grief I was to experience, to say nothing of the emotional trauma I was to undergo."); *id.* at 2–3 (statement by Teresa Stanton Collett) (testifying in support of Senate Bill 30); *id.* at 3–4 (statement by Teresa Connolly) (testifying in support of Senate Bill 30); *id.* at 6 (statement by Veronica Moore) (testifying in support of Senate Bill 30); *id.* at 16–17 (statement by Terry Moore, M.D.) (testifying in support of Senate Bill 30).

[307]*See supra* text accompanying notes 288–89.

[308]*See* TEX. FAM. CODE ANN § 33.009 (citing TEX. PEN. CODE ANN. § 25.02 (prohibited sexual conduct)).

261.101 of the Texas Family Code. To suggest otherwise is to abandon some of the most vulnerable Texans to the continuing degradation and harm of abuse.[309]

In order to insure compliance with the general reporting duties placed upon the judges, lawyers, and other professionals involved in a judicial bypass case, it is important to have clear and objective definitions of the various forms of abuse. Section 261.001 of the Family Code provides such definitions.[310] Without such clarity and objectivity, the general reporting requirement becomes an invitation to engage in witch hunts that lead to an unnecessary consumption of state resources in pursuit of questionable or even specious reports.

The Parental Notification Act specifically refers to the definitions of abuse contained in section 261.001 of the Texas Family Code.[311] The legislative record expresses support of the protection of minors who are the victims of abuse. It also expresses support for parental involvement in the vast majority of cases where a pregnant minor seeks an abortion. What is at issue is defining the circumstances where parental involvement should not occur, and the statute is clear on that issue. Notification should not occur in those rare circumstances where: (1) the minor is mature and sufficiently well informed to make the decision to have an abortion without parental involvement; (2) parental notification is not in the best interest of the immature or ill-informed minor and her best interest is served by obtaining an abortion; and (3) where parental notification may lead to physical, sexual, or emotional abuse of the minor.[312] Certainly in the last

---

[309] *See* Manning v. Hunt, 119 F.3d 254, 273 (4th Cir. 1997). In disposing of a constitutional challenge to a reporting duty imposed in the North Carolina parental consent statute, the court stated:

> Appellants would have a judge, who is sworn to uphold the law, withhold vital information regarding rape or incest which would allow state authorities to end the abuse, protect the victim, and punish the abuser. Not only would Appellants' position prevent the judge from helping the victim seeking the abortion, but it would prevent the judge from helping other juveniles in the same household under the same threat of incest. This Court does not believe that the Constitution requires judges to be placed in such an untenable position. . . . Appellants' position would instead afford protection to rapists and perpetrators of incest. This can only serve the interests of the criminal, not the child.

Id.

[310] *See* TEX. FAM. CODE ANN. § 261.001 (Vernon Supp. 2000).

[311] *See id.* § 33.008.

[312] *See id.*

two circumstances, where the court is exercising its *parens patriae* power, the paramount concern must be the well-being and protection of the minor. This is only served by clear definitions of abuse that insure both the immediate protection of the minor and long-term intervention to assure her continuing safety. Section 261.001 of the Family Code provides such definitions, and this section should be the standard whereby Texas courts determine whether potential abuse exists that justifies bypassing parental notification of a minor's intention to obtain an abortion.

V. CONCLUSION

As the United States Supreme Court has acknowledged, parents are in the best position to guide their children through difficult decisions.[313] This is true not only because of the superior experience, perspective, and judgment they bring to problems as adults, but also because of their commitment to the protection and care of their offspring. The resources they command in terms of personal experience with healthcare providers, knowledge of negotiating governmental or private assistance programs, and financial wherewithal simply enhance the much needed emotional support that their daughters need when facing a crisis pregnancy.

In contrast, the pregnant girl often underestimates the support she would receive from her parents, while exaggerating the potential for anger and rejection. Often she experiences rejection from her sexual partner who wants no part of the consequence of their actions. She may mistakenly believe that "going it alone" or "taking care of it by herself" are signs of maturity and independence, when too often that attitude is merely evidence of her refusal to acknowledge her situation to her parents and others she cares about.

Courts should be reluctant to allow girls to avoid parental involvement. Parents have a moral and constitutional right to direct the care of their minor children, and the vast majority of girls benefit from their parents' involvement. Only in cases where a minor has established that she has carefully and knowledgeably considered all options in dealing with her unplanned pregnancy and arrived at the reasoned conclusion that abortion is the best response, or in those few cases where the courts determine that notification of the immature or ill-informed girl's parents is not in her best interest and obtaining an abortion is in her best interest, should the courts

---

[313]*See* Planned Parenthood v. Danforth, 428 U.S. 52, 103 (1976) (Stevens, J., concurring in part and dissenting in part). *See, e.g.*, Planned Parenthood v. Casey, 505 U.S. 833, 895 (1992).

allow the minor to circumvent parental notification. In determining whether notification of a parent may lead to physical, sexual, or emotional abuse, Texas courts should look to existing statutory definitions of these terms, rather than distort Texas jurisprudence by introducing alternative and ill-defined meanings crafted merely to achieve the result of permitting minors to obtain secret abortions.

The judicial bypass process, as structured in the Texas Parental Notification Act, has the potential to become the exception that swallows the rule. Its short time limits, skewed procedural rules, and difficult substantive questions require extraordinary effort by judges who take seriously their responsibility to determine whether the girl is entitled to judicially bypass the involvement of a parent in her decision to obtain an abortion. Careful study of the statutory scheme and court rules, thoughtful selection of attorney and guardian ad litems, rigorous examination of the evidence presented to insure that the minor has established all of the required elements of her claim to judicial bypass, and carefully articulated reasoning supporting the decision to grant or deny judicial bypass will enhance the prospect that the Texas experience with judicial bypass will prove to be neither an insurmountable roadblock nor an express train to the abortion clinic.

VI. APPENDIX

The following annotated list of questions to be asked at a judicial bypass hearing is offered in an attempt to insure that judicial bypass proceedings in Texas involve meaningful review of the issues before the court.

A. Preliminary Questions for All Applicants

Do you understand the difference between truth and falsehood? What is the difference? Give me an example of a true statement. Give me an example of a false statement.[314]

How old are you? When is your birthday?[315]

Have you previously filed an application to avoid notification of your parents of your intention to obtain an abortion?[316] If so, when and where

[314]Minors are not qualified to testify absent a court determination that they understand the obligation to testify truthfully. *See* TEX. R. EVID. 601(a)(2).

[315]This information is contained in the application, but a simple opening question may help ease the tension the girl may be feeling. Also, since the application may be signed by someone other than the minor, it is important to obtain her answers to the questions on the application.

did you file that application? Do you know the name or number of the case? Do you have a copy of that application or any orders the court entered? How did the court rule on your application?[317]

How did you learn that you were pregnant? Has a doctor or other health professional confirmed that you are pregnant through a pregnancy test and internal examination?[318]

Please describe the circumstances surrounding your becoming pregnant. Was this your first act of sexual intercourse? Did you want to have sex? Were you forced to have sex?[319]

---

[316]This information is also required on the application, but may have been answered by someone signing on behalf of the minor. It is desirable to obtain her answer to this question.

[317]While no authority directly holds that res judicata applies to prior applications during the pregnancy, dicta from other jurisdictions assumes the applicability of this doctrine. *See* Orr v. Knowles, 337 N.W.2d 699, 704 (Neb. 1983). Certainly the goals of the doctrine, prevention of inconsistent judgments, promotion of judicial economy and efficiency, and preservation of the sanctity of judgments is desirable in this context and would support the application of res judicata to such proceedings. *Cf.* Sysco Food Servs., Inc. v. Trapnell, 890 S.W.2d 796, 801, 803 (Tex. 1994). The ability of the court to raise and apply res judicata sua sponte has been acknowledged by the United States Court of Appeals for the Fifth Circuit. *See United Home Rentals, Inc. v. Texas Real Estate Comm'n*, 716 F.2d 324, 330 (5th Cir. 1983). "This failure to assert res judicata as a defense does not determine the issue, however, since in the interest of judicial economy res judicata may properly be raised by a district court sua sponte, particularly where both actions are brought in the courts of the same district." *Id.* at 330 (citing Boone v. Kurtz, 617 F.2d 435, 436 (5th Cir. 1980)).

[318]*See* TEX. PARENTAL NOTIFICATION R. 2.5 cmt. 4. "Before performing an abortion, the provider should: [c]onfirm your pregnancy with a pregnancy test and internal examination, even if that has been done elsewhere; [t]est your blood for anemia and RH factor; and [i]nform you about other tests you will need." National Abortion Federation, *Having an Abortion? Your Guide to Good Care* (visited Sept. 17, 2000) <http://www.prochoice.org/pregnant/goodcare.htm>. The confirmation of the pregnancy is very important in light of reported cases of abortion procedures being preformed on non-pregnant women. *See, e.g.*, Clair v. Reproductive Health Servs., 720 S.W.2d 793 (Mo. Ct. App. 1986); Holtzman v. Samuel, 495 N.Y.S.2d 583 (Sup. Ct. 1985); Shkolnik v. Nyquist, 399 N.Y.S.2d 482 (App. Div. 1977); Pennsylvania Cas. Co. v. Simopoulos, M.D., Ltd., 369 S.E.2d 166 (Va. 1988).

[319]The statute requires reporting of sexual abuse. *See* TEX. FAM. CODE ANN. § 261.101(a) (Vernon Supp. 2000); *see also* TEX. PARENTAL NOTIFICATION R. 2.5 cmt. 5. The Texas Parental Notification Rules provides:

> Under [Parental Notification] Rule 2.5(b), once a court concludes that an application should be granted on a single ground, it need not address other grounds. But in addressing any ground, the court should attempt to ascertain, among other factors, whether the pregnancy resulted from sexual assault, sexual abuse, or incest. The legislative history of Chapter 33, Family Code, indicates that one of the principal purposes of the statute was to screen for sexual crimes and abuse of minors so as to protect them against further victimization.

Do you know who the father is? How old is he?[320]

Are you related to the father?

Were you using any form of contraception at the time?[321]

Were you using drugs or alcohol when you had sex? If so, who provided the drugs or alcohol?[322]

How far along in the pregnancy do you think that you are? Why do you think that? Has the doctor told you how many weeks pregnant you are?[323]

How do you feel about having an abortion?

TEX. PARENTAL NOTIFICATION R. 2.5 cmt. 5.

Claims that reporting abuse compromises the minor's anonymity have met with little success in the courts. In *Hodgson v. Minnesota*, the court upheld a Minnesota statute that required notification to both parents of the minor's intention to have an abortion unless the minor's doctor reported that she was the victim of abuse or neglect or obtained certification through a judicial bypass that required reporting of sexual abuse. 497 U.S. 417 (1990). In *Manning v. Hunt*, the court provided a thorough discussion of this issue, emphasizing that a contrary "position would instead afford protection to rapists and perpetrators of incest. This can only serve the interests of the criminal, not the child." 119 F.3d 254, 273 (4th Cir. 1997) (upholding a North Carolina statute).

[320]*See* TEX. PEN. CODE ANN. § 21.11(a)(2) (Vernon Supp. 2000). In a study of over 46,000 pregnancies by school-age girls in California, researchers found that

> 71%, or over 33,000, were fathered by adult post-high-school men whose mean age was 22.6 years, an average of 5 years older than the mothers. . . . Even among junior high school mothers aged 15 and younger, most births are fathered by adult men 6-7 years their senior. Men aged 25 and older father more births among California school-age girls than do boys under age 18.

Males, *supra* note 259, at 64. Other studies have found that most teenage pregnancies are the result of predatory practices by men who are substantially older. *See id.* (citing Boyer & Fine, *supra* note 260, at 4–11, 19); Gershenson et al., *supra* note 260, 203–08.

[321]Several courts have considered the purposeful failure to use contraception a sign of immaturity. *See, e.g.*, H.B. v. Wilkinson, 639 F. Supp. 952, 956–58 (D. Utah 1986).

[322]*See Hearings on H.R. 3682 Before the House Subcomm. on the Judiciary*, 105th Cong. 58 (1999) (statement of Joyce Farley) (stating that her teenage daughter was provided alcohol and raped when she passed out). This statement may be found at <http:// www.house.gov/judiciary/ 22460.htm>.

[323]*See supra* text accompanying notes 125–30.

B. *Questions to Ascertain Whether the Minor is Mature and Sufficiently Well Informed to Make the Decision to Have an Abortion Performed Without Notifying Either of the Minor's Parents, the Minor's Managing Conservator, or the Minor's Legal Guardian, as the Case May Be*

Are you attending school currently? What grade are you in? What kind of grades do you make in school? Have you missed any classes this year? Why have you been absent?[324]

What are your plans for the future?

Have you ever used drugs or alcohol? Have you ever received a ticket for driving under the influence or while intoxicated? Do you use drugs or alcohol currently?

Have you discussed your pregnancy with anyone?[325] If so, who? How old are they? What did you discuss? Did you receive any advice? What was that advice?[326]

Do you have a job? Have you ever had a job?[327]

Do you live with one or both of your parents? If you live with one, which parent do you live with?

If you do not live with a parent, do you live with any adult? If so, who do you live with, and what is your relationship to that person or persons?[328]

Has anyone promised you anything if you have an abortion? If so, who was it? What did he or she promise you?

Has anyone threatened you if you continue your pregnancy? If so, who was it? What did he or she threaten to do?

Is this your first pregnancy? If not, when were you last pregnant? How did you handle the prior pregnancies?[329]

Have you seen pictures of the development of a fetus throughout a pregnancy?[330] Would you like to opportunity to see such pictures or

---

[324]*See supra* text accompanying notes 159–67.

[325]*See, e.g.*, Arnold v. Board of Educ., 880 F.2d 305, 312–14 (11th Cir. 1989).

[326]*See generally In re* Doe, 19 S.W.3d 249, 256–57 (Tex. 2000).

[327]*See generally In re* Anonymous 2, 570 N.W.2d 836, 839 (Neb. 1997) (explaining that it is proper to consider a minor's prior work experience and independent handling of personal finances as some evidence of maturity).

[328]Minor's prior experience of living away from home is some evidence of maturity. *See, e.g.* H. B. v. Wilkinson, 639 F. Supp. 952, 955 (D. Utah 1986); *In re Anonymous 2*, 570 N.W.2d at 839.

[329]*See In re* Doe I, 566 N.E.2d 1181, 1184 (Ohio 1990) (holding that the trial court properly denied judicial bypass to a minor who had a prior abortion less than a year ago and a second child who was fathered by a different man).

possibly the development of your fetus through a special device called a sonogram?[331]

Do you have a regular or family doctor? If so, have you discussed your pregnancy with him or her? Have you discussed your decision to obtain an abortion with him or her? Do you plan to have your regular doctor perform the abortion? If not, why not?[332]

Have you informed the father of your pregnancy?

Did he offer to marry you?[333]

If you have told the father of your decision to have an abortion, how did he respond?

Did the father offer you any assistance in dealing with this pregnancy? Do you know that he is required to provide child support to help you if you have his child?[334]

Are you aware that there are people and groups who will help you obtain medical care, housing, and other things you need to continue your pregnancy?[335]

Have you spoken with anyone about the possibility of continuing the pregnancy? If so, who did you talk with? Describe the conversation for me. What was their advice? What do you think about their advice?

---

[330]*See generally* Planned Parenthood v. Casey, 505 U.S. 833 (1992) (plurality opinion).

[331]The use of ultrasonography is medically required prior to terminating pregnancies clinically estimated to be more that fourteen weeks from the last menstrual period. *See* NATIONAL ABORTION FEDERATION, CLINICAL POLICY GUIDELINES 13 (1999). Ultrasonography is also used in first and second trimester abortions to verify intra-uterine pregnancy and the gestational age of the fetus and to locate and aid in the removal of fetal parts, as well as to confirm that the uterus is empty and intact at the end of the abortion process. *See id.*

[332]*See generally In re* Anonymous, 655 So. 2d 1052, 1054 (Ala. Civ. App. 1995) (minor's having had pregnancy test done at hometown clinic prior to visiting abortion clinic is some evidence of maturity).

[333]*See* Ohio v. Akron Ctr. for Reprod. Health, 497 U.S. 502, 508 (1990).

[334]*See In re* Doe, 19 S.W.3d 249, 256 (Tex. 2000); *supra* text accompanying notes 168–73. *See generally* Children's & Parent's Rights Assoc. v. Sullivan, 787 F. Supp 724 (N.D. Ohio 1991).

[335]*See* Planned Parenthood v. Casey, 505 U.S. 833, 883 (1992) (plurality opinion).

> In short, requiring that the woman be informed of the availability of information relating to fetal development and the assistance available should she decide to carry the pregnancy to full term is a reasonable measure to ensure an informed choice, one which might cause the woman to choose childbirth over abortion. This requirement cannot be considered a substantial obstacle to obtaining an abortion, and, it follows, there is no undue burden.

Id.

Have you been around babies much? In what setting? Have you babysat before or have you cared for other children?

Have you spoken with anyone about placing your baby with another family through adoption? If so, who have you spoken with? How do you understand adoption to work? Do you understand that Texas allows open adoption, which means that you can select the future parents of your child, meet with them, and even require them to allow you to continue to visit your child after the adoption?[336]

Would you like [more] information about adoption?

Do you know how much the abortion will cost? Does this price include the costs of lab work? Anesthetic? Other medications or prescriptions? Your follow-up exam?[337]

How will you pay for the abortion? How will you pay for any follow-up care that may be required?

Have you, or anyone on your behalf, made any payments toward the cost of the abortion? If so, will the abortion provider refund your money if you decide to continue the pregnancy and have the baby?

[If someone else has paid the abortion fee] Why did [your friend] make the initial payment toward the abortion?

Where will you have the abortion? How far is this from your home?

What have you been told about your recovery period following the abortion?

How will you get to the clinic on the day of the abortion?

Where will you go after you leave the clinic to recuperate? How will you get there?

Have you been informed of the risks of abortion? What risks do you understand to exist?[338]

Have you been informed of the method to be used for your abortion? If so, what method does the provider plan to use?[339]

After an abortion, there may be symptoms of a post-abortion complication. Do you know what these are? What are they?

---

[336]*See supra* text accompanying notes 174–81.

[337]"In some facilities, the fee covers everything; in other facilities, it doesn't. Therefore, asking 'How much does the abortion cost?' may not give you all the information you need." National Abortion Federation, *Having an Abortion? Your Guide to Good Care* (visited Jan. 24, 2000) <http://www.prochoice.org/pregnant/goodcare.htm>.

[338]*See In re* Anonymous 2, 570 N.W.2d 836, 839 (Neb. 1997) (stating that a minor's inability to articulate risks associated with abortion evidenced a lack of perspective, experience, and judgment necessary to make the decision to obtain an abortion without parental involvement).

[339]*See supra* text accompanying notes 122–34.

After all abortions women will experience some bleeding. Usually it is minor, but in some cases the bleeding can be quite severe.[340] Heavy bleeding is called hemorrhaging, and is one of the most serious complications of an abortion.[341] Have you been told this?

Often, after surgeries, patients experience infection. Left untreated, infection can be very serious, and can even lead to death.[342] Have you been told this?

In some cases, the abortion is incomplete. This means either that the pregnancy continues or all of the products of the pregnancy (fetus, placenta, etc.) are not removed.[343] Have you been told this?

In some cases, a doctor pokes a hole in the uterus of the woman during the abortion.[344] Depending upon the size and location of the hole, this can be quite serious.[345] Have you been told of this risk?

---

[340]The National Abortion Federation defines excessive bleeding as saturation of more than one pad per hour for more than three hours. *See* NATIONAL ABORTION FEDERATION, CLINICAL POLICY GUIDELINES 32 n.17 (1999).

[341]*See id.*; *see also* Evans v. Mutual Assur., Inc., 727 So. 2d 66 (Ala. 1999) (discussing a dispute between a physician and the malpractice carrier regarding coverage for the death of an 18-year-old girl from hemorrhaging induced by abortion).

[342]*See* Stubblefield & Grimes, *supra* note 116, at 310.

> The risk of death from postabortion sepsis [or infection] is highest for young women, those who are unmarried, and those who undergo procedures that do not directly evacuate the contents of the uterus. . . . A delay in treatment allows the infection to progress to bacteremia, pelvic abscess, septic pelvic thrombophlebitis, disseminated intravascular coagulopathy, septic shock, renal failure, and death.

Id.; *cf.* Sherman v. District of Columbia Bd. of Med., 557 A.2d 943 (D.C. 1989).

> Dr. Sherman placed his patients' lives at risk by using unsterile instruments in surgical procedures and by intentionally doing incomplete abortions (using septic instruments) to increase his fees by making later surgical procedures necessary. His practices made very serious infections (and perhaps death) virtually certain to occur. Dr. Sherman does not challenge our findings that his misconduct was willful nor that he risked serious infections in his patients for money.

Id. at 945.

[343]*See* Showery v. State, 678 S.W.2d 103, 105 (Tex. App.—El Paso, 1984, writ ref'd); *cf.* United States v. Sherman, 150 F.3d 306 (3d Cir. 1998) (perjury charge for false statements regarding malpractice claim from 16-year-old girl's death due to physician's practice of performing incomplete abortions in order to require second procedure).

[344]*See* Reynier v. Delta Women's Clinic, 359 So. 2d 733 (La. Ct. App. 1978). "All the medical testimony was to the effect that a perforated uterus was a normal risk, but the statistics given by the experts indicated that it was an infrequent occurrence and it was rare for a major blood vessel to be damaged." *Id.* at 738.

In a few cases, women have had their bowels or bladder injured during the abortion.[346] Have you been told of this risk?

If any of these problems occur, a second surgery is often required to fix the problems which can be corrected.[347] Have you been told this?

In rare cases, women have died from abortions. In Texas, the Department of Health has confirmed that a woman in San Antonio[348] and a woman in Houston have died from complications from abortions.[349] Have you been told that death can occur?

There is some evidence that abortions increase women's risk of breast cancer.[350] Have you been told this? Have you discussed any history of breast cancer in your family with the doctor who will perform the abortion?

Are you currently taking or supposed to be taking any prescription drugs? If so, why were the drugs prescribed? Have you told the abortion provider that you are taking or supposed to be taking these drugs?

Do you or any member of your immediate family have a history of allergic reactions to any drugs? Have you told the abortion provider of this history?

Has a doctor or counselor ever diagnosed you as having depression or any other psychological or psychiatric condition?

Have you ever received psychological or psychiatric counseling? Are you still receiving counseling? Have you discussed your pregnancy or possible abortion with your counselor?

[If the minor has never received counseling] Have you ever wanted counseling and been unable to get the help you wanted?

345Untreated, a perforated uterus may result in an infection, complicated by fever, endometriosis, and parametritis. *See* Stubblefield & Grimes, *supra* note 115, at 310.

346See National Abortion Federation, *Fact Sheet: Safety of Abortion* (1999) (visited Jan. 24, 2000) <http://www.prochoice.org/facts/safety.htm>.

347*See id.*

348*See* Loydean Thomas, *ME's Office Verifies Teen Died From Legal Abortion*, SAN ANTONIO EXPRESS NEWS, Apr. 24, 1997, at 1B.

349Twenty/Twenty: A Woman's Right, A Woman's Risk Question of Safety at Some Abortion Clinics (ABC television broadcast, Mar. 8, 1999), *available in* 1999 WL 6790574; *Woman's Death After Abortion Under Scrutiny Ambulance Questioned*, ST. LOUIS POST-DISPATCH 01A, Apr. 29, 1997, *available in* 1997 WL 3338869.

350*See generally* John Kindley, *The Fit Between the Elements for an Informed Consent Cause of Action and the Scientific Evidence Linking Induced Abortion with Increased Breast Cancer Risk*, 1998 WIS. L. REV. 1595 (1998).

Have you ever had any suicidal thoughts or feelings? Have you ever attempted suicide or threatened to commit suicide?[351]

After an abortion, a woman may experience strong feelings about her decision. She may wonder if she made the right decision. Some women who describe these feelings find that they go away with time. Others find them so overwhelming they need help in dealing with their feelings.[352] Have you been told of this risk?

Have you ever had surgery? If so, when and what type? Did you experience any complications from that surgery?

---

[351]At least one study has found a significant statistical increase in suicide following termination of pregnancy by abortion. "The suicide rate after an abortion was three times the general suicide rate and six times that associated with birth . . . . [T]he rate [for women following a live] birth was 5.9 per 100,000; . . . following miscarriage was 18.1; [and following] abortion was 34.7." *See* Mika Gissler, *Suicides After Pregnancy in Finland 1987-1994: Register to Linkage Study*, 313 BRIT. MED. J. 1431, 1433 (1996). These results are consistent with an earlier American survey of teenaged girls, in which researchers at the University of Minnesota found that the rate of attempted suicide in the six months prior to the study increased ten fold—from 0.4% for girls who had not aborted during that time period to four percent for teens who had aborted in the previous six months. *See* B. GARFINKLE ET AL., STRESS, DEPRESSION AND SUICIDE: A STUDY OF ADOLESCENTS IN MINNESOTA (Minneapolis: University of Minnesota Extension Service 1986). These statistics are particularly troubling when considered in the conjunction with the fact that suicide is the third leading cause of death among teens in the United States. *See* National Mental Health Association, *Teen Suicide Fact Sheet* (visited July 8, 2000) <http://www.nmha.org/infoctr/factsheets/82.cfm> ("Each year, almost 5,000 young people, ages 15 to 24, kill themselves. The rate of suicide for this age group has nearly tripled since 1960, making it the [third] leading cause of death in adolescents and the second leading cause of death among college age youth.").

This question is particularly important if the minor is enrolled in an alternative high school. A national report on health risks of teens enrolled in alternative high schools reveals that 43.2% of the girls enrolled in alternative high schools were or had been pregnant. Of all girls in alternative high schools, 20% had attempted suicide within the past twelve months, with a higher incidence among white teens than other ethnic groups, and a higher incidence among younger girls, grades 9-11, than older females, grade 12. *See* Jo Anne Grunbaum et al., *Youth Risk Behaviors Surveillance*, National Alternative High School Youth Risk Survey, United States, 1998 (visited June 24, 2000) <http://www.cdc.gov/epo/mmwr/preview/mmwrhtml/ss4807a1.htm>.

[352]*See* Eidson v. Reproductive Health Servs., 863 S.W.2d 621, 622–26 (Mo. Ct. App. 1993); Showery v. State, 678 S.W.2d 103, 109 (Tex. App.—El Paso 1984, writ ref'd). "Teenagers who do not tell their parents about their abortion have an increased incidence of emotional problems and feelings of guilt." Jo Ann Rosenfeld, *Emotional Responses to Therapeutic Abortion*, 45 AM. FAM. PHYSICIAN 137 (1992); *see also* Thomas R. Eller, *Informed Consent Civil Actions for Post-Abortion Psychological Trauma*, 71 NOTRE DAME L. REV. 639 (1996).

Have you ever received anesthesia? Local or general? Have you had any adverse reactions? Have you been told of the risks that accompany the use of the anesthesia the doctor plans to use?

Have you received the Texas Department of Health brochure on parental notification?[353]

Have you met the physician that will perform the abortion? If you have not met the doctor, do you know the name of the doctor who will perform the abortion?

Is the doctor licensed to practice medicine in Texas?[354]

Does the doctor have "admitting privileges," the ability to have a hospital accept his or her patients at a nearby hospital, no more than twenty minutes away?[355]

If you plan to use an abortion clinic, have you called the Texas Department of Health to determine if the clinic you are considering using is licensed?[356] Does the clinic have any history of licensing violations?[357]

---

[353]The Texas Department of Health Bureau of Vital Statistics is the lead group regarding the publication of the teen booklet on Senate Bill 30 concerning parental notification for minor's abortions. Their website is located at <http://www.tdh.state.tx.us/bvs/>. Click on "Induced Abortions" at the bottom of the page to reach links to the online version of the educational booklet, as well as to the Texas Supreme Court rules and the actual language of the legislation. For the latest state data concerning abortions, see <http://www.thd.state.tx.us/bvs/stats98/annrpt.htm>. Any questions regarding the educational booklet or requests for hardcopies should be directed to Richard Bays at richard.bays@tdh.state.tx.us.

[354]*See* National Abortion Federation, *Having an Abortion? Your Guide to Good Care* (visited June 24, 2000) <http://www. prochoice.org/pregnant/goodcare.htm>.

[355]*See id.*

[356]*See* TEX. HEALTH & SAFETY CODE ANN. § 245.023 (Vernon Supp. 2000).

> The department on request shall make the following information available to the public:
>
> (1) the status of the license of any abortion facility;
>
> (2) the date of the last inspection of the facility, any violation discovered during that inspection that would pose a health risk to a patient at the facility, any challenge raised by the facility to the allegation that there was a violation, and any corrective action that is acceptable to the department and that is being undertaken by the facility with respect to the violation; and
>
> (3) an administrative or civil penalty imposed against the facility or a physician who provides services at the facility, professional discipline imposed against a physician who provides services at the facility, and any criminal conviction of the facility or a physician who provides services at the facility that is relevant to services provided at the facility.

Is there an adult that will accompany you to the clinic? What is your relationship with that person? Will that person stay at the clinic or doctor's office during the procedure? Will that person stay with you after you leave the clinic or office?

If something happens to you during the abortion, does the abortion provider know whom to notify? Whom should they notify?

If you experience any problems after the abortion, how will you obtain medical assistance?

Are you aware that, other than emergency care, if you need medical attention because of post-abortion complications your parents will have to consent to the follow-up care?

Have you arranged for a check-up after the abortion to make sure that you are recovering properly?[358]

Are there any questions you have about your pregnancy or the abortion procedure that you have not asked your doctor? Are there any questions your doctor did not answer? Did you understand the doctor's answers to your questions?[359]

Is there anything that would change your mind about continuing or terminating this pregnancy?

Id. Additional provisions protect the identity of callers who inquire about particular clinics, as well as the identity of abortion clinic employees. *See id.*

[357]*See id.*; *see also Twenty/Twenty: A Woman's Right, A Woman's Risk Question of Safety at Some Abortion Clinics* (ABC television broadcast, Mar. 8, 1989), *available in* 1999 WL 6790574.

[358]*See* National Abortion Federation, *Fact Sheet: What is a Medical Abortion?* (visited June 24, 2000) <http://www.prochoice.org/facts/medab.htm>.

> Because there is no way to know for sure that the abortion is complete without an examination by a health care professional, *keeping appointments with the clinic for follow-up care is very important!* In addition, a woman must report any problems she has during the medical abortion to a health care professional.

Id.

> Even if you feel fine afterwards, it's very important to return for an exam within a few weeks to make sure the abortion is complete and there are no hidden problems. It is best to go to the same facility, but if you have traveled a long distance, they can help you make arrangements to have the follow-up exam closer to home.

National Abortion Federation, *Having an Abortion? Your Guide to Good Care* (visited June 24, 2000) <http://www. prochoice.org/pregnant/goodcare.htm>.

[359]National Abortion Federation, *Having an Abortion? Your Guide to Good Care* (visited June 24, 2000) <http://www.prochoice.org/pregnant/goodcare.htm>.

Do you anticipate being sexually active after the conclusion of this pregnancy? If so, how will you avoid becoming pregnant again?[360]

Do you understand that the only way you can guarantee not becoming pregnant again is to avoid having sex?[361]

C. Questions to Determine Whether Notifying Either of the Minor's Parents, the Minor's Managing Conservator, or the Minor's Legal Guardian, as the Case May Be, Would Not Be in the Minor's Best Interest

Has anyone suggested that you should not involve your parents in your decisions about this pregnancy?[362] Who was that? Why do you think this suggestion was made?

Describe your relationship with your father.

Describe your relationship with your mother.

Why do you want to have an abortion without one of your parents [or guardian or conservator] knowing?

How do your parents usually respond when you do things that displease or upset them? Give me an example.

How do you think they would react if you were to tell them that you are pregnant?

How do you think they would react if you were to tell them that you wanted an abortion?

How do you think they will react if they discover that you had an abortion without telling either of them?

Many times parents know more about their children's medical history than the children themselves know. Have you considered this in making your decision to not involve your parents?[363]

---

[360]*See* William Hatcher, *Abstinance: Not Having Sexual Intercourse* (visited July 1, 2000) <http://www.emory.edu/wltsc/med/famplan/abstinence.htm>.

[361]*See* TEX. EDUC. CODE ANN. § 28.004(a)(3) (Vernon 1996).

[362]*See* Arnold v. Board of Educ., 880 F.2d 305, 313 (11th Cir. 1989) (holding that a 42 U.S.C. § 1983 action was permissible when the plaintiffs alleged that school officials encouraged white girls to continue their pregnancies and black girls to obtain abortions).

> Coercing a minor to obtain an abortion or to assist in procuring an abortion and to refrain from discussing the matter with the parents unduly interferes with parental authority in the household and with the parental responsibility to direct the rearing of their child. This deprives the parents of the opportunity to counter influences on the child the parents find inimical to their religious beliefs or the values they wish instilled in their children.

Id.

Many times parents know how to go about selecting a competent physician. Have you considered this in making your decision to not involve your parents?

Many young people overestimate the negative response of their parents to the news that their daughter is pregnant or wants to have an abortion.[364] Have you considered this in your decision to not involve your parents?

Have you considered asking another adult to help you tell your parents that you are pregnant or that you want to have an abortion? If so, why did you not choose to do this?

D. *Questions to Aid in Determining Whether Notifying Either of the Minor's Parents, the Minor's Managing Conservator, or the Minor's Legal Guardian, as the Case May Be, May Lead to Physical, Sexual, or Emotional Abuse of the Minor*

Have either of your parents ever hit you or physically hurt you in anyway? Describe what happened. What caused your parent to do this? Did your other parent know this happened? Did anyone else—like a relative, friend, teacher, school counselor, minister, priest, or rabbi—know this happened?

Have either of your parents ever touched you or allowed another person to touch you in a sexual way? What happened? Did your other parent know this happened? Did anyone else—such as a relative, friend, teacher, school counselor, minister, priest, or rabbi—know this happened?

Have either of your parents ever emotionally abused you? What happened? Did your other parent know this happened? Did anyone else—

---

[363]*See* Ohio v. Akron Ctr. for Reprod. Health, 497 U.S. 502, 518 (1990); H.L. v. Matheson, 450 U.S. 398, 400 (1981) (upholding a Utah notice statute that required the physician to notify the parents because the physician could often obtain a better medical history of the minor from her parents and was in the best position to provide full medical information to the parents so that the parents could provide good medical advice to their child).

[364]*See* Griffin-Carlson & Mackin, *supra* note 92, at 4 (discussing a study of 439 clients age 21 or under of five abortion clinics in metropolitan Atlanta).

> In the present study, when [nonconfiders were] asked why they did not discuss their abortion decision with parents, the clients gave four basic responses: fear of rejection, fear of disappointing parents, wanting to spare parents the problem, and wanting to handle the problem by themselves. When [confiders were] asked why they chose to confide in parents, they most often said: they needed money; they needed emotional support; it was the parents' right to know.

Id.

such as a relative, friend, teacher, school counselor, minister, priest, or rabbi—know this happened?

Is there any incident involving either of your parents that leads you to believe that you will suffer harm from telling them that you are pregnant or that you intend to have an abortion? What happened? Did anyone else—like a relative, friend, teacher, school counselor, minister, priest, or rabbi—know this happened?

THE PREGNANT CHILD'S RIGHT TO SELF-DETERMINATION

*Katheryn D. Katz**

I. INTRODUCTION

This Article examines the constitutional parameters of reproductive autonomy, particularly as they pertain to a pregnant minor's access to abortion. Both the United States Supreme Court's jurisprudence in this area and the effect of laws designed to curtail the access of unmarried pregnant minors to safe and legal abortions are surveyed. Also discussed are the current efforts at the federal level to impose national parental involvement requirements when minors seek access to contraceptives or abortion. Finally, a new standard for addressing a minor's constitutional claims to reproductive freedom is proposed.

As soon as the Supreme Court announced its decisions in *Roe v. Wade*[1] and *Doe v. Bolton*,[2] invalidating most existing abortion laws,

---

* Professor of Law, Albany Law School of Union University. B.A., University of California at Berkeley; J.D., Albany Law School of Union University. The author is grateful to Robert Begg, Robert Emery, Nancy Lenahan, and Tara Moffet for their invaluable research assistance.

[1] 410 U.S. 113 (1973). *Roe* determined that state criminal abortion statutes prohibiting abortions at any stage of pregnancy except to save the life of the mother are unconstitutional and summarized the various stages with which the state statutes must comply to afford due process to the pregnant individual. *See id.* at 164-65. The Court stated:

> [P]rior to approximately the end of the first trimester, the abortion decision and its effectuation must be left to the medical judgment of the pregnant woman's attending physician. . . .
>
> [S]ubsequent to approximately the end of the first trimester, the State . . . may . . . regulate the abortion procedure in ways that are reasonably related to maternal health. . . .
>
> For the stage subsequent to viability, the State . . . may . . . regulate, and even proscribe, abortion except where it is necessary, in appropriate medical judgment, for the preservation of the life or health of the mother.

Id.

[2] 410 U.S. 179 (1973). *Doe* invalidated, as violative of due process, provisions of a Georgia law which required that (1) an abortion be performed in a licensed hospital; (2) two physicians other than the physician performing the abortion approve the procedure; and (3) the physician's decision to perform the abortion be approved by a committee of at least three hospital staff members. *See id.* at 184, 192-201. The Court also invalidated the residency

anti-abortion activists unleashed a firestorm of activity seeking either to outlaw abortion entirely by constitutional amendment or to restrict access to abortion through legislative proposals. The legislative activity has continued unabated since 1973 and much of it has been productive.[3] Two of the most successful efforts have been measures aimed at the least powerful categories of pregnant females—poor women and unmarried minors. Congress and many state legislatures enacted prohibitions on the use of public funds for the abortion expenses of poor women[4] and states targeted unmarried pregnant minors' access to abortion through the enactment of parental notification and consent laws.[5] State parental involvement statutes are now widespread.[6] The laws typically provide criminal penalties for the physician who performs an abortion upon a minor without the requisite parental notification or consent.[7] The Supreme Court has upheld parental involvement statutes where

requirement for women who sought an abortion under Georgia law as violative of the Privileges and Immunities Clause of Article IV of the Constitution. *See id.*

[3] *See generally* JAMES RISEN & JUDY L. THOMAS, WRATH OF ANGELS: THE AMERICAN ABORTION WAR (1998) (tracing the way in which the abortion issue has defined American politics since *Roe v. Wade*).

[4] *See, e.g.*, Webster v. Reproductive Health Servs., 492 U.S. 490, 511 (1989) (upholding state law prohibiting public employees and public facilities from being used to facilitate abortions unless necessary to save a woman's life); Harris v. McRae, 448 U.S. 297, 326 (1980) (upholding congressional refusal to reimburse states for abortions necessary to preserve woman's health and relieving states from the obligation to fund medically necessary abortions for which federal reimbursement is unavailable); Beal v. Doe, 432 U.S. 438, 447 (1977) (holding that a "refusal to extend Medicaid coverage to nontherapeutic abortions is not inconsistent with Title XIX"); Maher v. Roe, 432 U.S. 464 (1977) (holding that the Equal Protection Clause does not require that a state participating in Medicaid pay for nontherapeutic abortions even though the state funds childbirth expenses); Poelker v. Doe, 432 U.S. 519, 521 (1977) (upholding states' refusal to fund or facilitate nontherapeutic abortions for poor women); Committee to Defend Reprod. Rights v. Myers, 625 P.2d 779, 798-99 (Cal. 1981) (holding that restrictions on abortion funding violated privacy rights, due process, and equal protection under the state constitution); Women of the State v. Gomez, 542 N.W.2d 17, 19 (Minn. 1995) (deciding, under strict scrutiny and pursuant to privacy provisions of the Minnesota Constitution, that a "pregnant woman . . . cannot be coerced into choosing childbirth over abortion by a legislated funding policy"); Right to Choose v. Byrne, 450 A.2d 925, 934-35 (N.J. 1982) (finding that the statutory restrictions violate the fundamental right to control one's body and destiny, a right protected by the equal protection provisions of the New Jersey Constitution); Planned Parenthood Ass'n v. Department of Human Resources, 663 P.2d 1247, 1261 (Or. Ct. App. 1983) (holding that the rule limiting state medical assistance was a violation of the privileges and immunities clause of the Oregon Constitution), *aff'd*, 687 P.2d 785, 793 (Or. 1984); Women's Health Ctr. of W. Va., Inc. v. Panepinto, 446 S.E.2d 658, 667 (W.Va. 1993) (finding a violation under the state constitution where the state failed to act neutrally with regard to the right to terminate a pregnancy).

[5] *See infra* notes 191-251 and accompanying text (discussing state constitutional law regarding parental consent and notice statutes).

[6] *See* Planned Parenthood v. Casey, 505 U.S. 833, 899-900 (1992) (explaining the parental consent jurisprudence).

[7] *See, e.g.*, N.C. GEN. STAT. § 90-21.10 (1997).

they provide for bypass procedures by which the young woman may petition a third party decision-maker and demonstrate that she is mature enough to decide whether to terminate her pregnancy.[8] If she is found to be immature, she still must be given the chance to demonstrate that an abortion is in her best interest.[9] Therefore, when a minor chooses to terminate her pregnancy, the state may, consistent with the United States Constitution, place the abortion decision in the discretion of a judge or some other government official as well as her physician.[10] If she is immature and unemancipated, arguably there is no constitutional necessity of a bypass procedure for a parental notification law.[11]

More recently, anti-abortion forces succeeded in having two pieces of anti-abortion legislation introduced in Congress.[12] Both federal proposals are directed at a minor's ability to obtain an abortion. One, entitled the Child Custody Protection Act (CCPA), makes it a federal crime for a non-parent to take a pregnant minor across state lines to obtain an abortion for the purpose of avoiding laws requiring the involvement of parents in abortion decisions.[13] In effect, this proposal will give extraterritorial force to state laws that mandate parental involvement in the minor's abortion decision. The other proposal, the Putting Parents First Act (PPFA), requires minors to get parental consent for abortion referrals or contraceptives obtained at any facility receiving federal funds, thus reversing years of public health policy.[14]

Parental involvement statutes are not the only legal means used to try to deny or limit a minor's access to abortion. A recent North Carolina case involved a civil suit for assault and battery against a physician and clinic for performing an abortion upon a sixteen-year-old who had forged her mother's signature on a consent form and stated that she was seventeen on a patient information record.[15]

---

[8] *See infra* notes 66-190 and accompanying text (discussing various Supreme Court decisions); *see also infra* notes 285-99 and accompanying text (critiquing parental involvement laws).

[9] *See infra* notes 127-46 and accompanying text.

[10] *See infra* notes 158-68 and accompanying text.

[11] *See* H.L. v. Matheson, 450 U.S. 398, 409 (1981) (noting that a requirement of parental notice is constitutionally sound).

[12] *See infra* notes 13-14 and accompanying text.

[13] *See* H.R. 3682, 105th Cong. (1998).

[14] *See* S. 2380, 105th Cong. (1998).

[15] *See* Jackson v. A Woman's Choice, Inc., 503 S.E.2d 422, 424-26 (N.C. Ct. App. 1998) (affirming the trial court's decision that abortion providers do not have an affirmative duty to determine the validity of a written parental consent).

The plaintiffs, the girl and her parents, alleged that the defendants intentionally or negligently inflicted emotional distress upon the girl and her parents; they sought compensatory and punitive damages.[16] The appellate court affirmed the trial court's order dismissing the complaint, agreeing that there had been compliance with the parental consent law,[17] and that the abortion providers had no affirmative duty to determine the validity of the purported written consent.[18] Other states, however, have included requirements in their parental consent laws that are intended to prevent forgery of the parent's signature.[19] Louisiana, for example, has adopted a law requiring parental consent to be notarized.[20] Until the courts invalidated South Dakota's parental involvement statute, it provided that parents of a minor, upon whom an abortion had been performed that was not in compliance with the statute, could sue the physician for treble damages and be awarded punitive damages in the amount of $10,000.[21]

---

[16] *See id.* at 423 (explaining the allegations).

[17] *See id.* at 426. Chapter 90 of the General Statutes of North Carolina contains a section entitled "Parental or Judicial Consent for Abortion," which embodies North Carolina's consent law for abortions performed upon minors. N.C. GEN. STAT. § 90-21.7 (1997). Section 90-21.7(a) states:

> No physician licensed to practice medicine in North Carolina shall perform an abortion upon an unemancipated minor unless the physician or agent thereof or another physician or agent thereof first obtains the written consent of the minor and of: (1) A parent with custody of the minor; or (2) The legal guardian or legal custodian of the minor; or (3) A parent with whom the minor is living; or (4) A grandparent with whom the minor has been living for at least six months immediately preceding the date of the minor's written consent.

Id. § 90-21.7(a). Subsection (b) of section 90-21.7 permits a minor seeking an abortion to petition the court for a waiver of the parental consent requirement, and section 90-21.8 sets forth the procedure and requirements for obtaining the waiver. Section 90-21.10 provides criminal sanctions for performing an abortion upon a minor in violation of the parental or judicial consent law:

> Any person who intentionally performs an abortion with knowledge that, or with reckless disregard as to whether, the person upon whom the abortion is to be performed is an unemancipated minor, and who intentionally or knowingly fails to conform to any requirement of Part 2 of this Article shall be guilty of a Class 1 misdemeanor.

Id. § 90-21.10.

[18] *See Jackson*, 503 S.E.2d at 426 (holding that the trial court was correct in finding that defendants had not violated the statute). The appellate court also found that section 90-21.4 provides immunity to the defendant physician and that the girl's actions "in presenting the forged consent and in giving her own informed consent to the procedure were a bar to her claims for assault and battery and negligent infliction of emotional distress." *Id.* at 424.

[19] *See, e.g.*, LA. REV. STAT. ANN § 40:1299.35.5 (West 1999).

[20] *See id.* (requiring "[a] notarized statement signed by the mother, father, legal guardian, or tutor of the minor" or a court order).

[21] *See* Planned Parenthood v. Miller, 63 F.3d 1452 (8th Cir. 1995) (holding that, as to that portion of the law, potential for civil liability for a good faith mistake would chill the willingness of health care providers to perform abortions, thus imposing an impermissible burden

Although supporters of parental involvement laws claim that they are justified by the need for parental wisdom and counsel when an unmarried minor faces an undesired pregnancy, there are anti-abortion activists who do not hesitate to take action when the parents' decision is to permit an abortion. In Michigan, a state that bans almost all abortions past twenty-four weeks, a twelve-year-old Detroit girl who had been impregnated by her older brother was taken into state custody when authorities learned that the parents planned to take her out of state for a late term abortion.[22] The court originally granted a petition preventing the parents from carrying through with their arrangements for medical assistance.[23] The judge eventually relented and returned her to her parents custody after her doctor argued that the pregnancy could imperil her physical and mental health, and a psychologist testified that a Hindu who had a non-marital child would be considered an outcast, unfit for marriage.[24] Abortion opponents offered the family money if the girl would continue the pregnancy, and stated that the girl's age and alleged incest did not sway them from their position.[25] "The best interests of the young mother would be served by delivering this child alive," stated Erin Wilson of Right to Life of Michigan.[26]

The parents of a pregnant girl's sexual partner may also seek to play a role in the abortion decision.[27] In a notorious Nebraska abortion prevention case, the parents of a male who had impregnated a fifteen-year-old girl learned of her appointment at an abortion

---

upon the minor female's right to an abortion). *But see* OHIO REV. CODE ANN. §§ 2919.12-.13, .15-.17 (Anderson 1996) (providing for criminal liability, civil liability, and medical decertification).

22 *See* Suzanne Siegel & Bill Roy, *Youth, Incest—and Abortion: A 12-year-old's Pregnancy Puts an Issue into Stark Relief*, NEWSWEEK, Aug. 10, 1998, at 52 (noting that the removal of the girl from the parents' custody was justified on the grounds of negligence, specifically that the parents should not have allowed the girl and her brother to share a bedroom).

23 *See id.* (noting that family court authorities were "tipped-off" that the family was taking the girl out of Michigan to obtain the abortion).

24 *See id.*

25 *See id.*

26 *Id.* The judge returned custody to the parents, thereby permitting them to take the girl to Kansas where the pregnancy was terminated. *Id.* After the petition was withdrawn, the prosecutor in the case said that "[w]e wanted to make sure she wasn't being rushed out of town by parents who were embarrassed." Talibah L. Chikwendu, *View from the Cheap Seats: Family Business*, BALT. AFRO-AMERICAN, Aug. 7, 1998, at A4.

27 *See, e.g.*, David Stout, *Woman Who Took Girl for Abortion is Guilty in Custody Case*, N.Y. TIMES, Oct. 31, 1996, at A15 (discussing the role of the mother who took her son's pregnant thirteen-year-old girlfriend across state lines for an abortion and was subsequently found guilty of custodial interference).

clinic, and interfered with the abortion decision made by the pregnant girl and her family.[28] The partner's mother obtained a letter from a physician (who had not examined the girl) stating that an abortion at twenty-three weeks could be risky.[29] Shortly after midnight, three police officers with possession of the letter took the girl from her parents' home.[30] She was detained in police custody for thirty-six hours and then sent to a foster home.[31] The police initiated judicial proceedings to determine whether she was in danger or neglected.[32] When the police determined that she was twenty-seven weeks pregnant, they released her after her parents promised in a court hearing that they would not obtain an abortion for her without a court order.[33] In fact, the girl and her family decided against an abortion when they realized the advanced stage of her pregnancy.[34] Four years later the girl's family settled the lawsuit they had filed against the ex-boyfriend's family and local officials for interfering with the family's decision concerning the pregnancy.[35]

In addition to the state-created obstacles to abortion, pregnant minors face the same shortage of abortion providers that adult women face. Abortion, although one of the fundamental aspects of reproductive freedom, is increasingly unavailable to poor and disadvantaged women.[36] Clinic violence, harassment, and social stigma has led to a marked shortage of physicians willing to perform abortions.[37] Approximately eighty-four percent of American counties have no abortion provider.[38] Further, there are fewer trained providers, and doctors who are willing to perform abortions

---

[28] *See* Veronica Rosman, *Suit Settled in Detainment over Abortion*, OMAHA WORLD-HERALD, May 12, 1998, at 11.

[29] *See id.*

[30] *See Abortion Prevention Case Finally Settled Neither Side Talking: The Wake of Heated Lawsuit and Resolution*, ROCKY MOUNTAIN NEWS, May 17, 1998, at A25.

[31] *See id.*

[32] *See* Rosman, *supra* note 28, at 11.

[33] *See id.*

[34] *See id.*

[35] *See id.*

[36] As of 1993, there were no abortion providers in 84% of the counties in the United States. *See* Tamar Lewin, *Number of U.S. Abortions Dipped to 13-Year Low in '92, Study Says*, L.A. DAILY NEWS, June 16, 1994, at N1 (relating statistics from a study by the Alan Guttmacher Institute); *see also* Charlotte Rutherford, *Reproductive Freedoms and African-American Women*, 4 YALE J.L. & FEMINISM 255, 281-82 (1992) (discussing the harmful impact of parental involvement laws on African-American women).

[37] *See* RISEN & THOMAS, *supra* note 3, at 342.

[38] *See* Tamar Lewin, *Fewer Abortions Performed in U.S.*, N.Y. TIMES, June 16, 1994, at A1.

are becoming scarce outside of urban areas.[39] For example, when the constitutionality of South Dakota's parental notice statute was challenged, the court noted that the physician who was involved in the challenge was the only doctor who performed abortions in the state.[40] There is such a paucity of medical school education and training in abortion procedures that the accrediting authorities have had to promulgate a requirement that hospitals training residents in obstetrics and gynecology include abortion skills in their programs.[41] Critics charge, however, that hospitals now provide so few abortions that doctors in training will have difficulty learning the necessary procedures.[42]

Driven by political and financial considerations, many hospitals have gradually withdrawn from providing abortions, a change that critics charge leaves "abortions outside the protective aura of established medical centers, creating delays for women who need abortions and leaving the independent clinics ever more susceptible to violence."[43] The isolation of abortion services in free standing clinics has lead to life-threatening delays in finding abortion providers for women who rely on hospitals for their medical care, as well as made it easier for anti-abortion groups to identify and to beleaguer doctors and patients.[44] In fact, in some states there is as few as *one* provider of abortion services.[45] The mergers that are taking place between private or municipal hospitals and Catholic hospitals mean not only that abortion services are no longer avail-

---

39 *See id.*

40 *See* Planned Parenthood v. Miller, 63 F.3d 1452, 1461 (8th Cir. 1995) (discussing the confidentiality issue surrounding the fact that doctors are not widely available, noting that "[i]n a state where there is only one doctor who performs abortions, the minor's decision to seek an abortion would be revealed merely by the [disclosure of the] name of the reporting physician").

41 *See* James Barron, *More Prospective Obstetricians Will Be Taught Abortion Skills*, N.Y. TIMES, Feb. 15, 1995, at A1 (noting that "the percentage of obstetric and gynecology residency programs that require first trimester abortion training has declined to 12 percent, half of what it was in 1985").

42 *See* Elisabeth Rosenthal, *Finances and Fear Spurring Hospitals to Drop Abortions*, N.Y. TIMES, Feb. 20, 1995, at A1 (noting that only about one-third of residency programs in New York offer abortion training).

43 *Id.*

44 *See id.* (attributing many of the hospital cut-backs to picketing and violence of anti-abortion protesters).

45 *See id.* (quoting the chairman of the Department of Obstetrics and Gynecology at Montefiore Medical Center, one of the few hospitals in New York performing abortions, as saying, "[t]he hospital is the last place you want to be providing these services"); *see also* DEBORAH L. RHODE, SPEAKING OF SEX: THE DENIAL OF GENDER INEQUALITY 204 (1997) (noting that by the mid-1990s, "[t]wo states had only one provider").

able, but family planning and sterilization services are also disappearing.[46]

My primary purpose is to examine the tension between parental rights and adolescent autonomy, particularly reproductive autonomy. Accordingly, I address the constitutional boundaries of parental control and the evolution of minor's reproductive rights.[47] I also consider the conflicts generated by a tradition of governmental limitations on a minor's self-determination imposed in the guise of protecting the minor and upholding the authority of parents.[48] I conclude that the analysis used to determine the breadth of a pregnant minor's right to seek an abortion is fatally flawed, emphasizing as it does the impact of an abortion, rather than the impact of pregnancy, childbirth, and an unwanted child on the young woman.[49]

II. THE PREGNANT MINOR'S CLAIM OF REPRODUCTIVE LIBERTY

A. *Supreme Court Jurisprudence Concerning a Minor's Reproductive Liberty*

1. General Principles Concerning Minors and the Constitution

The Supreme Court's jurisprudence on a minor's abortion decision must be understood within the basic framework of a child's constitutional rights. Since the middle of the twentieth century the Court has consistently recognized as a general principle that the Bill of Rights and the Fourteenth Amendment protect minors, and not just adults, from unjustified state action.[50] Nevertheless, when

[46] *See id.* (noting statements made by an abortion rights activist to the effect that Catholic and municipal hospitals, as well as medical schools, having succumb to political pressure, are avoiding abortion issues because "'[i]t's such a hot potato'"); *see also* Alissa J. Rubin, *Abortion Providers at Lowest Mark Since '73*, L.A. TIMES, Dec. 11, 1998, at A45 (attributing a drop in abortion providers to "increasing numbers of hospital mergers that, in many cases, have involved the takeover of nonprofit hospitals by Catholic hospitals which will not allow abortion services").

[47] *See infra* notes 50-251 and accompanying text.

[48] *See infra* notes 252-99 and accompanying text.

[49] *See infra* notes 300-24 and accompanying text.

[50] *See* Planned Parenthood v. Danforth, 428 U.S. 52, 74 (1976) ("Minors, as well as adults, are protected by the Constitution and possess constitutional rights."); Goss v. Lopez, 419 U.S. 565, 572-76 (1975) (finding that a minor has the right to procedural due process in a temporary school suspension situation); Breed v. Jones, 421 U.S. 519, 528-29 (1975) (holding that a minor is protected against double jeopardy and noting that the Court has consistently made "applicable in juvenile proceedings constitutional guarantees associated with traditional criminal prosecutions"); Tinker v. Des Moines Indep. Community Sch. Dist., 393 U.S. 503,

that abstract principle is applied to concrete cases, it is apparent that there are countervailing, limiting principles. The Court has made clear that there are some activities of children that may be subject to state regulation to a greater degree than those of adults.[51] The state may even punish or seek to curtail conduct of adults that would be unobjectionable or even constitutionally protected were children not involved.[52]

Accordingly, the Court has reinforced the state's power to curtail the rights of minors where it acts in the guise of a protector of minors from their lack of capacity to fend for themselves.[53] The Court has reiterated in a number of cases that the constitutional rights of minors are not coextensive with those of adults by reason of "the peculiar vulnerability of children; their inability to make critical decisions in an informed, mature manner; and the importance of the parental role in child rearing."[54] Thus, "the State is entitled to adjust its legal system to account for children's vulnerability and

---

506 (1969) (upholding the First Amendment rights of expression of students in a school environment); *In re* Gault, 387 U.S. 1 (1967) (holding that a minor has the right to a notice of charges, counsel, confrontation and cross-examination of witnesses, and the privilege against self-incrimination in a juvenile delinquency proceeding); *id.* at 41 (holding that the Fourteenth Amendment requires that minors be notified of their right to counsel); *id.* at 55 (holding that "the constitutional privilege against self-incrimination is applicable in the case of juveniles as it is with respect to adults"); Prince v. Massachusetts, 321 U.S. 158, 165-66, (1944) (upholding a minor's right to free exercise of religion but recognizing also the state interest as *parens patriae* which both restricts parental control and regulates a child's activities).

[51] *See, e.g.*, Schall v. Martin, 467 U.S. 253, 274 (1984) (upholding state's preventive detention scheme for juveniles accused of delinquency); McKeiver v. Pennsylvania, 403 U.S. 528, 545-51 (1971) (finding due process does not require jury trials for juveniles accused of delinquency); *Prince*, 321 U.S. at 170 (upholding state's labor law prohibiting children from selling articles on the street, as "the power of the state to control the conduct of children reaches beyond the scope of its authority over adults").

[52] *See, e.g.*, Denver Area Educ. Telecomm. Consortium, Inc. v. FCC, 518 U.S. 727 (1996) (finding a compelling interest in protecting children from exposure to patently offensive materials and thus justifying upholding a section of the Cable TV Consumer Protection and Competition Act of 1992 authorizing cable operators to refuse to carry leased access programming depicting sexual activities or organs in a patently offensive manner); New York v. Ferber, 458 U.S. 747 (1982) (treating child pornography as beyond First Amendment protection); Ginsberg v. New York, 390 U.S. 629 (1968) (holding that a state may have a variable definition of obscenity in order to limit the availability of sexual materials to minors). *But cf.* Sable Communications, Inc. v. FCC, 492 U.S. 115 (1989) (invalidating a complete congressional ban on "Dial-a-Porn" because less restrictive measures were available to protect children).

[53] *See, e.g.*, *Prince*, 321 U.S. at 168 ("The state's authority over children's activities is broader than over like actions of adults.").

[54] Bellotti v. Baird, 443 U.S 622, 634 (1979) [hereinafter *Bellotti II*] (Powell, J., plurality); *see* Planned Parenthood v. Danforth, 428 U.S. 52, 74 (1976) (holding that Missouri's parental consent statute was invalid because a state may not give a minor's parents a blanket veto over the minor's abortion decision).

their needs for 'concern, . . . sympathy, and . . . paternal attention.'"[55] The freedom of children is seen as validly limited as to those decisions having "potentially serious consequences," since "minors often lack the experience, perspective, and judgment to recognize and avoid choices that could be detrimental to them."[56]

The other general constitutional principle undermining minors' independence is the deference given to family autonomy—deference that has been a persistent hallmark of the Court's jurisprudence on the family from 1923 to the present.[57] The Supreme Court's understanding of the family is that the protection of liberty under the Due Process Clause includes parental authority to raise their children as they see fit.[58] Although there is general agreement on the Court that children are not beyond the protection of the Constitu-

---

[55] *Bellotti II*, 443 U.S. at 635 (Powell, J., plurality) (quoting McKeiver v. Pennsylvania, 403 U.S. 528, 550 (1971) (Blackmun, J., plurality)).

[56] *Id.*; *see* American Academy of Pediatrics v. Lungren, 940 P.2d 797, 840 (Cal. 1997) [hereinafter *Lungren III*] (Kennard, J., concurring), *vacating* 912 P.2d 1148 (1996). In her concurring opinion, Justice Kennard stated:

> Our laws have established various age restrictions for voting, driving motor vehicles, purchasing alcoholic beverages, and the like. Because individuals mature at different rates, these age limits are a necessarily inexact and therefore arbitrary measure of maturity, but they have nonetheless been accepted as constitutionally valid for most purposes. But not for all.

Id. The extent to which the State of California has stretched the holdings of the U.S. Supreme Court is exemplified through the following list of adult rights denied to minors, as well as additional responsibilities imposed upon those same minors: the denial of the right to purchase tobacco, CAL. PENAL CODE § 308(b) (West 1988 & Supp. 1998); the duty to attend school, CAL. EDUC. CODE § 49100 (West 1993); the obligation to abide by curfews not imposed on adults, CAL. PENAL CODE § 647(e) (West 1988 & Supp. 1998); the inability to consent to medical and dental procedures without parental notification and/or consent, CAL. FAM. CODE § 6910, 6911, 6922 (West 1994 & Supp. 1998), CAL. PENAL CODE § 11171 (West 1992); the inability to undergo voluntary sterilization, CAL. FAM. CODE § 6925(b)(1) (West 1994 & Supp. 1998); the inability to obtain a permanent tattoo, even with parental consent, CAL. PENAL CODE § 653 (West 1988); restrictions concerning the donation of any part of his or her body in the event of death, CAL. HEALTH & SAFETY CODE § 7150.5 (West 1970 & Supp. 1998); and the inability to use a tanning facility without parental consent, CAL. BUS. & PROF. CODE § 22706(b)(3)-(4) (West 1997); *see In re* Nancy C., 105 Cal. Rptr. 113, 120 (Ct. App. 1972) (upholding the constitutionality of a curfew imposed only on minors).

[57] *See, e.g.*, Meyer v. Nebraska, 262 U.S. 390, 399 (1923) (interpreting the Fourteenth Amendment's guarantee of liberty to include "the right of the individual to . . . marry, establish a home, and bring up children"); Pierce v. Society of Sisters, 268 U.S. 510, 535 (1925) ("The child is not the mere creature of the State; those who nurture him and direct his destiny have the right, coupled with the high duty, to recognize and prepare him for additional obligations.").

[58] *See* Wisconsin v. Yoder, 406 U.S. 205, 235 (1972) (holding that state compulsory education beyond eighth grade burdened Old Order Amish parents' free exercise of rights, thus entitling parents to withdraw their children from public schools upon completion of the eighth grade, but relying heavily upon findings that the Amish have "a long history as a successful and self-sufficient segment of American society" and that they "convincingly demonstrated the sincerity of their religious beliefs").

tion, the Court has never viewed children as fully sovereign individuals who have rights to dignity and personhood.[59] The Court's conception of the family as the institution by which society "inculcate[s] and pass[es] down many of [its] most cherished values, moral and cultural,"[60] is seen as requiring "that constitutional principles be applied with sensitivity and flexibility to the special needs of parents and children."[61] To the extent that children's interests are protected at the expense of their parents' authority, the protection is usually manifested by giving some other adults decision-making authority rather than through recognition of the minors' right to control important facets of her life.[62]

The Court's protection of the parental role in transmitting values has been both praised and condemned. Professor Peggy Davis, for example, has presented family liberty as entailing "the right of every individual to affect the culture and embrace, act upon, and advocate privately chosen values."[63] On the other hand, Professor Barbara Woodhouse has described the foundational decisions protecting parental autonomy as "constitutionalizing a patriarchal notion of parental rights," viewing children as parental property, and permitting the use of children as "conduit[s] for the parents' religious expression, cultural identity, and class aspirations."[64] Others have rejected the concept of parental rights in its entirety as antithetical to the principle that no one is entitled to control the life of another.[65]

---

59 *See, e.g.*, Schall v. Martin, 467 U.S. 253 (1984) (upholding New York's preventive detention plan for juveniles accused of delinquency).

60 Moore v. City of East Cleveland, 431 U.S. 494, 503-04 (1977).

61 *Bellotti II*, 443 U.S. 622, 634 (1979) (Powell, J., plurality).

62 *See id.* (discussing a child's general "inability to make critical decisions in an informed, mature manner").

63 Peggy Cooper Davis, *Contested Images of Family Values: The Role of the State*, 107 HARV. L. REV. 1348, 1371 (1994).

64 Barbara Bennett Woodhouse, *"Who Owns the Child?":* Meyer *and* Pierce *and the Child as Property*, 33 WM. & MARY L. REV. 995, 1113-14 (1992); *see* Barbara Bennett Woodhouse, *A Public Role in the Private Family: The Parental Rights and Responsibilities Act and the Politics of Child Protection and Education*, 57 OHIO STATE L.J. 393, 396-97 (1996) (summarizing recent legislative proposals that would limit the state's authority to protect children and would recognize parental autonomy as a fundamental right).

65 *See, e.g.*, James G. Dwyer, *Parents' Religion and Children's Welfare: Debunking the Doctrine of Parents' Rights*, 82 CAL. L. REV. 1371, 1372-73 (1994) (challenging the notion of parental rights in their entirety and offering a substantial revision of the law governing child rearing—that children's rights, and not the parents' rights, should serve as the basis for protecting the legal interests of children).

2. The Special Case of Abortion

The Supreme Court has issued at least nine decisions dealing with minors' access to abortion without ever satisfactorily explaining the reasons why a minor's right to seek termination of her pregnancy is not co-extensive with that of an adult woman who faces an unwanted or dangerous pregnancy.[66] A woman's interest in determining whether she will continue a pregnancy has been described as a "fundamental right to self-determination,"[67] "among the 'choices central to personal dignity and autonomy.'"[68] Furthermore, a woman's choice rests on the "moral fact that a person belongs to himself and not . . . to society as a whole."[69] The Court has not offered a persuasive rationale for denying an unmarried pregnant minor the same right to control her body and the concomitant right to define her "*own* concept of existence, of meaning, of the universe, and of the mystery of human life."[70]

The first abortion decision to reach the Supreme Court after *Roe v. Wade* was *Planned Parenthood v. Danforth*,[71] in which the plaintiffs challenged several provisions of a Missouri statute regulating various aspects of abortion. The Supreme Court struck down, among other things, a provision that required parental consent before an unmarried minor could have an abortion during the first twelve weeks of her pregnancy unless the abortion was necessary to preserve her life.[72] The State sought to defend the statute by arguing that minors "properly may [be] subject[ed] . . . to more strin-

---

66 The United States Supreme Court has addressed the validity of parental notice and consent provisions in abortion statutes in the following decisions: Lambert v. Wicklund, 520 U.S. 292 (1997); Planned Parenthood v. Casey, 505 U.S. 833 (1992); Ohio v. Akron Ctr. for Reprod. Health, 497 U.S. 502 (1990) [hereinafter *Akron II*]; Hodgson v. Minnesota, 497 U.S. 417 (1990); City of Akron v. Akron Ctr. for Reprod. Health, 462 U.S. 416 (1983) [hereinafter *Akron I*]; Planned Parenthood Ass'n v. Ashcroft, 462 U.S. 476 (1983); H.L. v. Matheson, 450 U.S. 398 (1981); *Bellotti II*, 443 U.S. 622 (1979); Bellotti v. Baird, 428 U.S. 132 (1976) [hereinafter *Bellotti I*]; Planned Parenthood v. Danforth, 428 U.S. 52 (1976); *see* Zbaraz v. Hartigan, 763 F.2d 1532 (7th Cir. 1985), *aff'd by an equally divided court*, 484 U.S. 171 (1987).

67 Rust v. Sullivan, 500 U.S. 173, 216 (1991) (Blackmun, J., dissenting); *see* Dwyer, *supra* note 65, at 1409.

68 *Casey*, 505 U.S. at 851 (1992); *see* Dwyer, *supra* note 65, at 1409.

69 Thornburgh v. American College of Obstetricians & Gynecologists, 476 U.S. 747, 777 n.5 (1986) (Stevens, J. concurring) (quoting Charles Fried, *Correspondence*, 6 PHIL. & PUB. AFF. 288, 288 (1977)), *overruled in part by Casey*, 505 U.S. at 833.

70 *Casey*, 505 U.S. at 851 (1992) (emphasis added); *see Dwyer*, *supra* note 65, at 1409.

71 428 U.S. 52 (1976).

72 *See id.* at 74 (invalidating section 3(4) of Missouri House Bill 1211 requiring parental consent before an unmarried minor could obtain an abortion).

gent limitations than are permissible with respect to adults."[73] Furthermore, the State pointed out that the government is prohibited from unreasonable or unwarranted interference with parental discretion and that, since the physician would not perform the abortion without parental consent prior to the statute's passage, the measure imposed no additional burden upon the physician.[74]

The district court in *Danforth* found the State's interest "in safeguarding the authority of the family relationship" to be a compelling basis for the parental consent measure.[75] The Supreme Court, however, agreed with the district and circuit courts that had concluded that parental consent statutes could not withstand constitutional scrutiny.[76] The Court stated that the right to decide whether to terminate a pregnancy does "not mature and come into being magically only when one attains the state-defined age of majority."[77] Given the unique nature and consequences of the abortion decision, the Court held that a provision giving any third party a blanket veto over the decision to abort is necessarily unconstitutional when measured by the *Roe v. Wade* guidelines.[78] The *Roe* decision stressed that "the abortion decision and its effectuation must be left to the medical judgment of the pregnant woman's attending physician."[79] Thus, Missouri lacked "the constitutional authority to give a third party an absolute, and possibly arbitrary, veto over the decision of the physician and his patient."[80]

---

[73] *Id.* at 72 (citing McKeiver v. Pennsylvania, 403 U.S. 528 (1971); Prince v. Massachusetts, 321 U.S. 158 (1944)).

[74] *See id.* at 73 (citing Wisconsin v. Yoder, 406 U.S. 205, 213 (1972); Pierce v. Society of Sisters, 268 U.S. 510, 518 (1925); Meyer v. Nebraska, 262 U.S. 390, 401 (1923)).

[75] *See* Planned Parenthood v. Danforth, 392 F. Supp. 1362, 1370 (E.D. Mo. 1975) (stating that there is a compelling basis because, "[t]he requirement of parental consent in section 3(4) of House Bill 1211 does not single out the abortion procedure, since it is the practice of hospitals and physicians to require that a minor's parent consent to other surgical treatment as well").

[76] *See Danforth*, 428 U.S. at 74 (citing Poe v. Gerstein, 517 F.2d 787, 792 (5th Cir. 1975); Wolfe v. Schroering, 388 F. Supp. 631, 636-637 (W.D. Ky. 1974); Doe v. Rampton, 366 F. Supp. 189, 193 (D. Utah 1973); State v. Koome, 530 P.2d 260, 262 (Wash. 1975)). The *Danforth* Court, based on these cases, decided that the states "may not impose a blanket provision . . . requiring the consent of a parent or person *in loco parentis* as a condition for abortion of an unmarried minor." *Id.*

[77] *Id.*

[78] *See id.* at 75 (stating that section 3(4) violates *Roe v. Wade* because "it imposes a special-consent provision, exercisable by a person other than the woman and her physician").

[79] Roe v. Wade, 410 U.S. 113, 164 (1973).

[80] *Danforth*, 428 U.S. at 74.

The *Danforth* Court, however, did not employ strict scrutiny in analyzing the parental consent measure.[81] Instead of requiring that the state demonstrate a compelling necessity, the Court required only that the State establish a "significant state interest in conditioning an abortion on the consent of a parent or person *in loco parentis* that is not present in the case of an adult."[82] Nevertheless, the Court rejected the view that the State's asserted interests in safeguarding the family unit and preserving parental authority justified the consent statute: "Any independent interest the parent may have in the termination of the minor daughter's pregnancy is no more weighty than the right of privacy of the competent minor mature enough to have become pregnant."[83]

The *Danforth* Court, however, did not preclude all parental involvement measures, indicating that there are minors who are incapable of giving effective consent for termination of their pregnancies.[84] A concurrence by Justice Stewart, joined by Justice Powell, adumbrated what later became the Court's doctrine concerning parental involvement statutes.[85] After noting that the parental consent provision's primary constitutional deficiency was "its imposition of an absolute limitation on the minor's right to obtain an abortion,"[86] he noted that *Bellotti v. Baird* (*Bellotti I*),[87] decided the same day, indicated:

> [A] materially different constitutional issue would be presented under a provision requiring parental consent or consultation in most cases but providing for prompt (i) judicial resolution of any disagreement between the parent and the minor, or (ii) judicial determination that the minor is mature enough to give an informed consent without parental concur-

---

[81] *See id.* at 74-75 (noting that "the State has somewhat broader authority to regulate the activities of children than of adults," therefore applying a "significant state interest" analysis).

[82] *Id.* at 75.

[83] *Id.*

[84] *See id.* at 75 (stating that the invalidation of section 3(4) "does not suggest that every minor, regardless of age or maturity, may give effective consent for termination of her pregnancy").

[85] *See id.* at 89-92 (Stewart, J., concurring) (proposing that parental approval not be an absolute condition upon the minor's right).

[86] *Id.* at 90.

[87] 428 U.S. 132 (1976) (discussing the requirement of consent before performing an abortion on an unmarried woman under age 18).

> rence or that abortion in any event is in the minor's best interest.[88]

His concurrence, as well as the concurrence and dissent of Justice Stevens, emphasized the gravity of the abortion decision and the pregnant minor's need for "mature advice and emotional support."[89] Despite its guarded holding, the *Danforth* decision led to immediate invalidation of many first generation parental consent laws.[90]

The Court ruled in *Bellotti I* that the constitutionality of a Massachusetts statute requiring both parents of an unmarried pregnant minor consent to her abortion should not be determined until the Supreme Judicial Court of Massachusetts construed the statute.[91] In *Bellotti I*, however, the Court reiterated its view that a pregnant minor may be too immature to make an independent judgment concerning the termination of her pregnancy.[92]

In the interval between *Bellotti I* and *Bellotti v. Baird*, 443 U.S 622 (1979) (*Bellotti II*), the Court was faced with a challenge to New York's ban on the distribution of contraceptives to minors under sixteen years of age.[93] In *Carey v. Population Services International*,[94] eight justices agreed that the New York statute was invalid, but the Court could not agree on the standard by which it should scrutinize legislation where the procreative rights of minors were at issue.[95] A plurality led by Justice Brennan concluded that

---

88 *Danforth*, 428 U.S. at 90-91 (Stewart, J., concurring) (outlining how the parental consent requirement could be drafted to remove the absolute condition).

89 *Id.* at 91 (Stewart, J., concurring); *see id.* at 103 (Stevens, J., concurring in part and dissenting in part) (stating that, assuming the abortion decision "is the most important kind of a decision a young person may ever make, that assumption merely enhances the quality of the State's interest in maximizing the probability that the decision be made correctly and with full understanding of the consequences of either alternative").

90 *See* Steven F. Stuhlbarg, Note, *When Is a Pregnant Minor Mature? When Is an Abortion in Her Best Interests? The Ohio Supreme Court Applies Ohio's Abortion Parental Notification Law:* In re Jane Doe 1, *566 N.E.2d 1181 (Ohio 1991)*, 60 U. CIN. L. REV. 907, 910 n.15 (1992) (listing post-*Danforth* decisions invalidating parental consent laws).

91 *See Bellotti I*, 428 U.S. at 151 (remanding the matter to the Supreme Judicial Court of Massachusetts for prompt interpretation of the statute).

92 *See id.* at 147 (stating that the Court was "concerned with a statute directed toward minors, as to whom there are unquestionably greater risks of inability to give an informed consent").

93 *See* Carey v. Population Servs. Int'l, 431 U.S. 678 (1977) (determining the constitutionality of a statute criminalizing the distribution of contraceptives to minors under 16).

94 *See id.*

95 *See id.* at 692 (plurality opinion) ("The question of the extent of state power to regulate conduct of minors not constitutionally regulable when committed by adults is a vexing one, perhaps not susceptible of precise answer."). Justice White supported the result because he believed that the State had not demonstrated that the ban measurably contributed to the deterrent purposes of the statute, namely discouraging young persons from engaging in promiscuous sexual intercourse. *See id.* at 702 (White, J., concurring).

the prohibition on distribution of nonprescription contraceptives to persons under sixteen, as applied, cannot be justified as a permissible regulation of minors' morality in furtherance of the State's policy against promiscuous sexual intercourse among the young.[96] The Court did not find the State's ends illegitimate; rather, the means used did not serve those ends.[97] The plurality reiterated that "the right to privacy in connection with decisions affecting procreation extends to minors as well as to adults."[98] Citing *Danforth* on the unconstitutionality of the State's efforts to impose "a blanket prohibition, or even a blanket requirement of parental consent, on the choice of a minor to terminate her pregnancy,"[99] the plurality concluded that the prohibition on the distribution of contraceptives was foreclosed *a fortiori*.[100] The plurality also noted that the abortion decision more clearly implicates "[t]he State's interests in protection of the mental and physical health of the pregnant minor, and in protection of potential life . . ." than does the decision to use a nonhazardous contraceptive.[101] Although he concurred in the judgment, Justice Powell rejected the rationale that, minors have a fundamental right to make reproductive decisions on the basis that respect for parental authority demands otherwise.[102] In fact, he opined that it was constitutionally permissible for the state to encourage "adolescents to seek the advice and guidance of their parents before deciding whether to engage in sexual intercourse."[103] Furthermore, the Court could not agree on the meaning of its precedents regarding the privacy rights of adults.[104]

In *Bellotti II*, the Court addressed the Massachusetts statute, requiring two-parent consent for a minor's abortion, after it had been

---

[96] *See id.* at 693 (plurality opinion) (stating the right to privacy involving procreation extends to both minors and adults).

[97] *See id.* at 695 (noting the skepticism as to whether limiting the means of obtaining contraceptives serves to discourage a minor's sexual behavior).

[98] *Id.* at 693.

[99] *Id.* at 694.

[100] *See id.*

[101] *Id.*

[102] *See id.* at 703-05 (Powell, J., concurring) (disagreeing with the plurality view that a compelling state interest is required to regulate the procreative choices of minors).

[103] *Id.* at 709.

[104] *Compare id.* at 688 n.5 (noting that the Court has never answered the question of whether the Constitution prohibits state statutes from regulating sexual behavior among adults), *and id.* at 694 n.17 (same), *with id.* at 718 n.2 (expressly disagreeing with the proposition that the Court has not answered this question, noting that "[w]hile we have not ruled on every conceivable regulation affecting such conduct the facial constitutional validity of criminal statutes prohibiting certain consensual acts has been 'definitively' established").

construed by the state's high court.[105] The statute provided for a judicial bypass but remained unconstitutional since it required that notice of any judicial proceeding be given to the minor's parents.[106] Justice Powell noted, in his plurality opinion, that typically, a state may impose parental notice and consent qualifications "on a minor's right to make important decisions."[107] The abortion decision, however, "differs in important ways from other decisions" a minor may face.[108] Among the distinguishing characteristics is the fact that the pregnant minor cannot postpone the abortion decision since the possibility of a legal abortion exists for a short period of time.[109] Furthermore, a pregnant minor faces a "potentially severe detriment" that is "not mitigated by her minority."[110] She typically lacks valuable attributes such as financial stability, education, and maturity—resources that an adult would be more likely to bring to a situation of unwanted motherhood.[111] Moreover, motherhood typically is an emancipating event which terminates the legal disabilities of minority.[112] Justice Powell concluded that "there are few situations in which denying a minor the right to make an important decision will have consequences so grave and indelible."[113] Thus, despite the traditional right of parents to direct their child's upbringing,[114] the Supreme Court held that any absolute parental right to be consulted about, much less veto, their child's decision to abort, is strictly foreclosed.[115]

In dicta, the *Bellotti II* plurality set forth four criteria for a constitutional bypass provision.[116] The bypass provision must: (1) al-

---

105 *See Bellotti II*, 443 U.S. 622 (1979) (Powell, J., plurality).

106 *See id.* at 646-48 (agreeing with the district court's recognition that such an imposition may result in a parent impeding on the minor child's right to go to court).

107 *Id.* at 640.

108 *Id.* at 642.

109 *See id.* (pointing out that a minor's options exist for only a limited time after conception).

110 *Id.*

111 *See id.* (noting that a pregnant minor is at a greater disadvantage than an adult in the same situation).

112 *See id.* (recognizing that becoming a parent gives rise to certain legal responsibilities, in effect conferring immediate adult status on the mother despite her young age).

113 *Id.*

114 *See id.* at 637 (stating that an "important justification for state deference to parental control over children is that '[t]he child is not the mere creature of the State; those who nurture him and direct his destiny have the right, coupled with the high duty, to recognize and prepare him for additional obligations'" (quoting Pierce v. Society of Sisters, 268 U.S. 510, 535 (1925))).

115 *See Bellotti II*, 443 U.S. at 643 (Powell, J., plurality) (holding that a blanket provision, which requires the consent of the parent, is not allowed).

116 *See id.* at 643-44 (plurality opinion).

low the minor to bypass the consent requirement if she establishes that she is mature enough and well enough informed to make the abortion decision independently; (2) allow the minor to bypass the consent requirement if she establishes that the abortion would be in her best interests; (3) ensure the minor's anonymity; and (4) provide for expeditious bypass procedures.[117]

Although the Court discussed the alternative procedure in terms of a judicial proceeding, the state is not required to provide a judicial, rather than an administrative, forum.[118] In fact, as Justice Powell noted, there is much to be said for a less formal proceeding than those identified with courts of general jurisdiction.[119] Furthermore, the Court has never held that parental consent is constitutionally required; it has held only that parental consent requirements that have a bypass procedure are constitutionally permissible.

Notwithstanding the fact that *Bellotti II* invalidated the parental involvement statute, the decision's detailed discussion of the requirements for a valid law led to a marked increase in state enactments of parental consent or notification laws.[120] The constitutionality of such a course was soon borne out. *City of Akron v. Akron Center for Reproduction Health* (*Akron I*)[121] is the only post-*Bellotti II* decision to invalidate a parental involvement law.[122] Akron had enacted a city ordinance requiring that a minor under fifteen obtain either her parent's written consent or a court order to have a legal abortion.[123] The Supreme Court rejected the city's argument that the juvenile courts would construe the law in a manner consistent

[117] *See id.* (plurality opinion); *see also Akron II*, 497 U.S. 502, 519 (1990) (concluding that Ohio's parental notification statute did not impose an undue burden on a minor seeking an abortion based on a four prong test of constitutionality).

[118] *See Bellotti II*, 443 U.S. at 643 n.22. States providing for an administrative bypass include Connecticut, Maine, Maryland, and West Virginia. *See* CONN. GEN. STAT. ANN. § 19a-601 (West 1997); ME. REV. STAT. ANN. tit. 22, § 1597-A (West 1964 & Supp. 1998); MD. CODE ANN., HEALTH-GEN. II § 20-103 (1996); W. VA. CODE § 16-2F-3 (1998).

[119] *See Bellotti II*, 443 U.S. at 643 n.22.

[120] *See* Burneatta Bridge, Comment, *Parent Versus Child:* H.L. v. Matheson *and the New Abortion Litigation*, 1982 WIS. L. REV. 75, 87. Massachusetts enacted a law providing that a judge first make a decision about the minor's maturity and then address the abortion question only for those minors who are too immature to make the decision themselves. It was upheld in *Planned Parenthood v. Bellotti*, 641 F.2d 1006 (1981) (finding that the statute satisfied the Supreme Court's directives which were promulgated in *Bellotti II*).

[121] 462 U.S. 416 (1983), *overruled by* Planned Parenthood v. Casey, 505 U.S. 833 (1992).

[122] *See* Bridge, *supra* note 120, at 87-89 nn.70-71 (listing the states which enacted parental involvement laws after the Supreme Court handed down *Bellotti II*, as well as the decisions which struck many of the statutes down).

[123] *See Akron I*, 462 U.S. at 422 n.4 (citing the Akron ordinance).

with the *Bellotti* doctrine so as to constitute a bypass procedure, noting that the governing statutes in juvenile courts neither mentioned abortion nor gave the juvenile courts the authority to inquire into a minor's maturity.[124] The *Akron* Court stated that "it is clear that Akron may not make a blanket determination that *all* minors under the age of 15 are too immature to make [the] decision [to have an abortion] or that an abortion never may be in the minor's best interests without parental approval."[125] The same day that the Court decided *Akron*, however, *Planned Parenthood v. Ashcroft*[126] upheld a parental consent statute that contained a judicial bypass procedure. Thus, the forecast in *Bellotti II* that such a statute would be sustained became reality.

In *Ohio v. Akron Center for Reproductive Health* (*Akron II*),[127] the Court had an opportunity to address the adequacy of a judicial bypass procedure in light of its five previous decisions entailing either parental notification or consent in the abortion context.[128] The Ohio statute in question made it a crime for a physician or other person to perform an abortion on an unmarried, unemancipated woman under eighteen unless the physician personally gave notice to one of the girl's parents, or in some circumstances, to other relatives before performing the abortion.[129] The statute also provided for a judicial bypass, requiring the minor to prove by clear and convincing evidence: (1) that she has enough information and maturity to make an intelligent decision; (2) that there exists a pattern of physical, emotional, or sexual abuse by one of her parents; or (3) that notice is not in her best interests.[130] Justice Kennedy's opinion relied on the "principal opinion" in *Bellotti II*, namely Justice Powell's concurrence.[131] Justice Kennedy's adoption of Justice Powell's four requirements led him to the conclusion that the Ohio scheme

---

124 *See id.* at 441 ("[W]e do not think that the Akron ordinance, as applied in Ohio juvenile proceedings, is reasonably susceptible of being construed to create an 'opportunity for case-by-case evaluations of the maturity of pregnant minors.'" (quoting *Bellotti II*, 443 U.S. at 643, n. 23)).

125 *Id.* at 440.

126 462 U.S. 476 (1983).

127 497 U.S. 502 (1990).

128 *See id.* at 510 (listing the five cases).

129 *See id.* at 507 (describing the circumstances under which the doctor may alert relatives other than the parents).

130 *See id.* at 508 (explaining the bypass requirements).

131 *See id.* at 515-16.

did "not impose an undue, or otherwise unconstitutional, burden on a minor seeking an abortion."[132]

In addition to challenges to the bypass procedures based on the requirements of *Bellotti II* and its progeny, the appellees sought additional criteria for constitutional bypasses.[133] They asked the Court to invalidate the "constructive authorization" provisions since those provisions did not require an affirmative order permitting the abortion when a court fails to act on the minor's complaint.[134] The appellees also challenged the statute's requirement that the minor had to prove her maturity or best interest by clear and convincing evidence.[135] They contended that "when a State seeks to deprive an individual of liberty interests, it must take upon itself the risk of error."[136] Finally, the appellees argued that the pleading requirements, namely that the minor must choose from three different forms depending upon which of the grounds for a bypass she intended to use, "create[d] a trap for the unwary."[137]

The Court, however, refused to extend the *Bellotti II* criteria and found no infirmities in the Ohio scheme.[138] The Court relied on the State's representation that a physician could "obtain certified documentation from the juvenile or appellate court that constructive authorization has occurred" and stated that an additional "safety net" was not required.[139] The Court again turned to *Bellotti II* to reject the challenge to the statute's requirement that the minor herself prove with clear and convincing evidence her maturity or best interests, stating that *Bellotti II* indicates that the minor

---

132 *Id.* at 519.

133 *See id.* at 514-15 (discussing the additional criteria).

134 *See id.* at 515 (noting that the appellees want this provision revised to provide that a court order be issued giving the physician the "go-ahead" to act).

135 *See id.* at 516-17 (holding that the clear and convincing standard does not place an unconstitutional burden on the minor).

136 *Id.* at 515 (citing Santosky v. Kramer, 455 U.S. 745, 755 (1982)).

137 *Akron II*, 497 U.S. at 516. Among the objectionable features of the notification law were the fact that the minor had to sign the complaint form—rather than using initials or a pseudonym—unless she had counsel, that the State's employees might unlawfully disclose the girl's identity, and that the procedure could take up to 22 days. *See* Akron Ctr. for Reprod. Health v. Slaby, 854 F.2d 852, 861-69 (6th Cir. 1988) (analyzing and affirming the lower court's holding on those issues). The Sixth Circuit affirmed the district court's finding that the statute had six constitutional defects, including the clear and convincing standard, the pleading requirements, and the physician's personal obligation to give notice to one of the parents. *See id.*

138 *See Akron II*, 497 U.S. at 514-20 (rejecting three specific challenges to the Ohio scheme put forth by the appellees in their facial challenge to the statute).

139 *Id.* at 515.

may be required to prove such facts in a bypass procedure.[140] The higher burden of proof was "acceptable" when the procedure was *ex parte* with "no one oppos[ing] the minor's testimony."[141]

The *Akron II* Court did not determine whether, under its precedents, due process mandates a bypass procedure for a parental notification statute, since the statute at issue had such a procedure and was consistent with its precedents.[142] Justice Kennedy stated that "it is a corollary to the greater intrusiveness of consent statutes that a bypass procedure that will suffice for a consent statute will suffice also for a notice statute."[143]

Only four Justices, however, joined that portion of Justice Kennedy's opinion, stating that the Ohio law constituted "a rational way to further [legitimate] ends."[144] The plurality also stated: "A free and enlightened society may decide that each of its members should attain a clearer, more tolerant understanding of the profound philosophic[al] choices confronted by a woman who is considering whether to seek an abortion," a decision which will affect "her own destiny and . . . dignity, and the origins of the other human life . . . within the embryo."[145] A consequence of *Akron II* has been that some physicians fearing criminal liability have required parents to come to the clinics, identify themselves, and sign a notarized statement.[146]

Most of the Supreme Court's decisions involving challenges to parental consent or notification have been facial challenges. *Hodgson v. Minnesota*,[147]—a companion case to *Akron II*—was a dispute in which the district court had made extensive factual findings concerning the operation of Minnesota's two-parent notification statute.[148] The statute provides that, "with certain exceptions, . . . no

---

[140] *See id.* at 515-16 (rejecting the appellees reliance upon *Santosky v. Kramer*, 455 U.S. 745 (1982), in which the Supreme Court held that the preponderance of the evidence standard used in a New York parental rights termination proceeding violated the Due Process Clause).

[141] *Id.* at 516.

[142] *See id.* at 510 (citing the five relevant cases upon which the Court relied).

[143] *Id.* at 511 (noting parenthetically the difference between notice and consent statutes in that the former do not bestow "veto power" over an abortion decision of a minor).

[144] *Id.* at 520.

[145] *Id.*

[146] *See* John F. Hagan, *State's Parental Notification Law Being Put to Judicial, Practical Test*, THE PLAIN DEALER, Nov. 18, 1990, *available in* 1990 WL 4628874 (explaining that this "extra precaution" was to protect physicians performing abortions at clinics because the law was "so new").

[147] 497 U.S. 417 (1990).

[148] *See* Rachael N. Pine, *Speculation and Reality: The Role of Facts in Judicial Protection of Fundamental Rights*, 136 U. PA. L. REV. 655, 694-97 (1988) (criticizing the district court's

abortion shall be performed on a woman under 18 years of age until at least 48 hours after both of her parents have been notified."[149] There is no exception "for a divorced parent, a noncustodial parent, or a biological parent who never married."[150] The statute imposes criminal liability on an individual who performs an abortion in violation of its terms and civil liability in an action brought by any person who was not properly notified.[151] The requirement was challenged as imposing additional trauma on the minor and causing delays that increased the health risk of the procedure.

Hodgson was the first of the Court's parental involvement decisions to focus on a two-parent notification provision. Among the findings of the district court was the following: that the statute "had particularly harmful effects on both the minor and the custodial parent when the parents were divorced or separated."[152] Additionally, it was found that forced notification did not result in reestablished relationships between the minor and absent parent, but rather, often created disappointment in the minor and situations in which the custodial parent reacted to the forced notification with "'anger, resentment and frustration at the intrusion of the absent parent,'" as well as fear that his or her custody rights will be threatened or that intra-family violence will result.[153] Moreover, two-parent notification had harmful effects on families in which the minor lives with both parents, particularly those in which "violence is a serious problem."[154] In fact, the district court found, family communication was actually impaired in those families where violence was a concern since the minor may simply go to court rather than inform either parent.[155] Despite these detriments, a fractured

---

opinion in *Hodgson v. Minnesota*, 648 F. Supp. 756 (D. Minn. 1986), for the failure of its conclusions of law to follow its finding of fact and for misinterpreting the Supreme Court's opinion in *Planned Parenthood Ass'n v. Ashcroft*, 462 U.S. 476 (1983)). Rachael Pine was an attorney for the *Hodgson* petitioners. *See Hodgson*, 497 U.S. at 421 (listing Rachael Pine as contributing on the brief of Janet Benshoof, attorney for petitioners).

[149] *Hodgson*, 497 U.S. at 422.

[150] *Id.* at 424-25. Justice Stevens, writing for the Court, noted that "Minnesota['s] statute is the most intrusive in the Nation" because it is the only state—of the thirty-eight which require some form of participation by the minor's parents—to specifically mandate that both parents of the pregnant woman consent to the abortion. *Id.* at 425 n.5 (discussing the varying requirements from state to state for a woman who seeks an abortion).

[151] *See id.* at 426 & nn.6-8 (providing the text of relevant portions of the statute).

[152] *Id.* at 438.

[153] *Id.* (quoting Hodgson v. Minnesota, 648 F. Supp. 756, 769 (D. Minn. 1986)).

[154] *Hodgson*, 497 U.S. at 439.

[155] *See id.* at 440 (recognizing also the situation in which the minor would only tell one parent, placing that parent in what the Court describes as a "torturous ordeal" of explaining

Supreme Court, after invalidating the two-parent requirement, upheld both the two-parent notification requirement with a judicial bypass and the forty-eight hour waiting period.[156] With good reason, the Fourth Circuit Court of Appeals has described the decision as almost incomprehensible.[157]

In its penultimate pronouncement on parental consent and notice, *Planned Parenthood v. Casey*,[158] the Court considered, among other provisions, the parental consent measure of the Pennsylvania abortion statute.[159] The statute provides that, except in a medical emergency, the informed consent of at least one parent (or guardian) is required before an unemancipated minor may obtain an abortion.[160] The statute also provides a judicial bypass procedure, if neither parent gives consent, upon a finding that the young woman is sufficiently mature or that an abortion would be in her best interests.[161] The joint opinion stated:

> Our cases establish, and we reaffirm today, that a State may require a minor seeking an abortion to obtain the consent of a parent or guardian, provided that there is an adequate judicial bypass procedure. . . . Under these precedents, in our view, the one-parent consent requirement and judicial bypass procedure are constitutional.[162]

The *Casey* decision, of course, has relevance far beyond the context of the minor's abortion decision. The less exacting undue burden standard has long been used in the context of the minor's abortion rights.[163] *Casey* altered the constitutional analysis for adult

why the second parent should not be notified, thus forcing the parent to reveal potentially embarrassing family history).

156 *See id.* at 496-97 (Kennedy, J., concurring).

157 *See, e.g.*, Planned Parenthood v. Camblos, 155 F.3d 352 (4th Cir. 1998). "The Court in *Hodgson* was so fractured as to render its opinions collectively all but impenetrable, with five different Justices filing opinions variously concurring and dissenting in other opinions and parts of other opinions . . . ." *Id.* at 364; *see* Pine, *supra* note 148, at 694-97 (discussing the foundation for the district court's opinion in *Hodgson* and noting that it understood Supreme Court precedent to mean that it and all courts should disregard the facts of a particular minor's abortion rights case in determining its outcome).

158 505 U.S. 833 (1992).

159 *See id.* at 899.

160 *See id.* (articulating the statutory provisions).

161 *See id.* (describing the situation in which judicial bypass is appropriate).

162 *Id.* (citing *Akron I*, 462 U.S. 416, 440 (1983), *overruled by* Planned Parenthood v. Casey, 505 U.S. 833 (1992); *Akron II*, 497 U.S. 502, 510-19 (1989); Hodgson v. Minnesota, 497 U.S. 417, 461 (1990), and *Bellotti II*, 443 U.S. 622, 643-44 (1979)) (internal citations omitted).

163 *See Bellotti II*, 443 U.S. at 644-47 (adopting the undue burden standard); *see also supra* notes 105-17 and accompanying text (discussing the *Bellotti II* Court's plurality decision and the four criteria set forth for a judicial bypass).

women by rejecting the trimester framework of *Roe v. Wade* and substituting the undue burden standard for all abortion issues.[164]

At the same time that the *Casey* Court upheld the parental notification statute, it struck down as an undue burden a spousal notification statute governing a married woman's abortion.[165] It did so even though the law exempted medical emergencies and reported cases of fear of bodily injury at the hand of their husbands.[166] The holding was justified by the prevalence of and impact of unreported physical and psychological spousal abuse as well as the fear of provoking child abuse.[167] There is no question that child abuse is a pervasive problem in our society.[168] Why should a minor have to report or prove parental abuse in order to avoid parental notification or consent? As difficult as it is for women who are in a situation of spousal abuse to seek help or take steps to end the situation, surely the circumstances are much more onerous for a minor who is dependent upon her parents. Even when there is no past abuse, the revelation of the daughter's pregnancy may provoke an explosive reaction from the parents.

One particularly egregious case is that of a thirteen year old Idaho girl who became pregnant after repeated rapes by her father.[169] Since Idaho does not provide abortion funding for women, the girl and her mother remained in Idaho while seeking the money to enable them to travel to Oregon where individuals and organizations were willing to provide the necessary financing for an abor-

[164] *See Casey*, 505 U.S. at 878 (recognizing that such a standard is not adopted without dissention). "Before viability, the State's interests are not strong enough to support a prohibition of abortion or the imposition of a substantial obstacle to the woman's effective right to elect the procedure." *Id.* at 846.

[165] *See id.* at 887-95 (laying out the district court's findings of fact regarding the effect of the spousal notification requirement upon marital relationships).

[166] *See id.* at 887 (summarizing other ways in which a woman may side-step the spousal notice requirement and the implication for a physician who performs an abortion without receiving a properly certified statement).

[167] *See id.* at 892-94 (relying upon the district court's findings and stating such results "reinforce what common sense would suggest," that women who are frequent victims of abuse would be loathe to inform their spouse of a decision to seek an abortion).

[168] *See* Council on Ethical and Judicial Affairs, American Medical Association, *Mandatory Parental Consent to Abortion*, 269 JAMA 82, 83 (1993) (noting the approximately 1.5 million cases of child abuse and neglect which occur yearly).

[169] *See* Margie Boule, *An American Tragedy*, PORTLAND OREGONIAN, Aug. 27, 1989, *available in* 1989 WL 6837685.

tion.[170] When the father learned of his daughter's intention to get an abortion, he shot and killed her.[171]

The Court sustained a parental notification statute without a by-pass provision in the case of an unemancipated minor living at home with her parents.[172] In *H.L. v. Matheson*,[173] the Court rejected an unmarried fifteen-year-old girl's challenge to a Utah statute requiring a physician to notify, if possible, parents of a minor seeking an abortion.[174] Although the plaintiff's physician concluded that an abortion was in her best medical interests, the physician would not proceed without notifying her parents.[175] Chief Justice Burger, writing for the Court, held that: (1) the plaintiff lacked standing to challenge the statute on its face on the ground of overbreadth;[176] and (2) as applied to an unemancipated minor girl living with and dependent upon her parents and making no claim or showing as to her maturity or as to her relations with her parents, the statute was narrowly drawn to protect only those interests and did not violate any guarantees of the Constitution.[177] Recognizing the traditional authority of parents over the rearing and welfare of their children, the Court concluded that the statute was reasonably calculated to promote family integrity, encourage parental consultation, and allowed parents the opportunity to provide essential medical and other information to the physician.[178] Justice Burger

---

170 *See id.* (reporting that a doctor and an anesthesiologist offered to donate their services, but that the Adams's also needed assistance with everything from money for the procedure to bus fare).

171 *See id.* (noting that the girl died at once and that her father was left in a coma after shooting himself).

172 *See* H.L. v. Matheson, 450 U.S. 398 (1981).

173 *See id.*; *see also The Supreme Court, 1980 Term—Parental Notification Prior to Abortions for Immature Minors:* H.L. v. Matheson, 95 HARV. L. REV. 142 (1981) (discussing the *H.L. v. Matheson* decision); Cynthia J. Oberg, Note, *Not While You Live in My House: The Supreme Court Upholds Mandatory Parental Notification of the Dependent Minor's Abortion Decision in* H.L. v. Matheson, 13 U. TOL. L. REV. 115 (1981) (arguing that an unemancipated minor's ability to have an abortion may be further restricted as a result of the *Matheson* decision).

174 *See Matheson*, 450 U.S. at 413 (affirming the holding of the Supreme Court of Utah and recognizing that "the statute plainly serves important state interests").

175 *See id.* at 400 (reciting the relevant portion of the Utah statute, which required the physician to notify the parents before proceeding with the abortion).

176 *See id.* at 405-06 (declining to address the argument that the statute is overbroad because the appellant never alleged she, or her class, is mature and emancipated in contrast to the statute).

177 *See id.* at 407-13 (discussing the privacy issues which the appellant alleged were at stake and explaining the right of the State to require notification when the pregnant minor is immature and unemancipated).

178 *See id.* at 411 (noting that a legitimate state interest is served by protecting these important considerations).

also made the astonishing statement that "[i]f the pregnant girl elects to carry her child to term, the *medical* decisions to be made entail few—perhaps none—of the potentially grave emotional and psychological consequences of the decision to abort."[179]

Despite the holding in *Matheson*, many states with parental notification laws also provide for a bypass procedure rather than running the risk of the statute being found facially unconstitutional.[180] Nevertheless, the uncertainty created by the lack of specific direction from the Supreme Court on one-parent notification statutes without bypass in *Hodgson* has emboldened some states to enact single-parent notice or consent laws with no bypass procedure.[181] South Dakota, for example, enacted such a law, only to have it struck down in federal court.[182] Since the result in *Hodgson* is open to varying interpretations, some courts have treated the question of whether a bypass procedure is required as unsettled.[183]

In the Court's latest parental notification decision, *Lambert v. Wicklund*,[184] it was held that a judicial bypass provision allowing

179 *Id.* at 412-13.

180 The following states have enacted one-parent notification statutes with bypass procedures: Delaware, DEL. CODE ANN. tit. 24, §§ 1783-1784 (1997); Georgia, GA. CODE ANN. §§ 15-11-112, -114 (1994); Illinois, 750 ILL. COMP. STAT. 70/15-25 (West Supp. 1998); Kansas, KAN. STAT. ANN. § 65-6705 (1992 & Supp. 1998); Maryland, MD. CODE ANN., HEALTH-GEN. § 20-103 (1996); Nebraska, NEB. REV. STAT. § 71-6901, -6903 (1996); Nevada, NEV. REV. STAT. § 442.255 (1996); Ohio, OHIO REV. CODE ANN. § 2151.85 (Anderson 1994), *id.* § 2919.12 (Anderson 1996); and West Virginia, W. VA. CODE § 16-2F-3, -4 (1998). The constitutionality of the Illinois one-parent notice statute was challenged in *Hope Clinic v. Ryan*, 995 F. Supp. 847 (N.D. Ill. 1998), but the federal court hearing the case awaited the state high court's adoption of bypass procedures under the statute. *See id.* at 861-62. The Illinois Supreme Court, however, refused to do so, explaining in a letter to the Illinois Attorney General that "'[t]he U.S. Supreme Court has not considered a single-parent notice statute without a bypass, but the clear implication of Hodgson [v. Minnesota, 497 U.S. 417 (1990)] is that such a statute would be constitutionally allowed.'" *See* Darryl Van Duch, *Ill. Abortion Tiff Stalemates Law: High Court Stalls New Parental Involvement Statute*, NAT'L. L.J., Feb. 12, 1996, at A6 (reporting that the "Illinois Supreme Court and the South Dakota attorney general have dug in at the front lines in a skirmish over laws that require parental involvement in the abortion decision").

181 Utah has a single-parent notification statute with no judicial bypass procedure. UTAH CODE ANN. § 76-7-304 (1995). The only exception to the parental notification requirement is in the case of a serious medical emergency. *See* UTAH CODE ANN. § 76-7-315 (1995 & Supp. 1998). Notably, New Mexico has enacted a parental *consent* statute without a judicial bypass procedure. *See* N.M. STAT. ANN. § 30-5-1, -5-3 (Michie 1994).

182 *See* Planned Parenthood v. Miller, 63 F.3d 1452, 1468 (8th Cir. 1995) (holding that the provision of the South Dakota statute requiring parental notification without a judicial bypass procedure was unconstitutional on its face).

183 *See, e.g.*, Planned Parenthood v. Camblos, 155 F.3d 352, 384 (4th Cir. 1998) (ruling that a bypass to notice did not have to comply with all of the requirements of *Bellotti II*, 443 U.S. 622 (1979)).

184 520 U.S. 292 (1997) (per curiam).

waiver of the notice requirement if notification was not in the minor's best interest was sufficient to protect the minor's right to abortion.[185] The Montana statute at issue provides:

> If the court finds by clear and convincing evidence that *any* of the following three conditions are met, it must grant the petition and waive the notice requirement: (i) the minor is "sufficiently mature to decide whether to have an abortion"; (ii) "there is evidence of a pattern of physical, sexual, or emotional abuse" of the minor by one of her parents, a guardian, or a custodian; or (iii) "the *notification* of a parent or guardian is not in the best interests of the [minor]."[186]

The *Lambert* Court addressed only the issue of whether the notification requirement must be waived if the "court determines that notification—not the abortion itself—is not in the minor's best interests."[187] The Court found no "constitutionally significant distinction," particularly since the challenge was to the face of the statute and not to the statute as applied.[188]

In sum, parental notice or consent statutes clearly will pass federal constitutional muster when they meet the requirements first set out in *Bellotti II*. Arguably, parental notice statutes do not have to provide a judicial bypass, at least for unemancipated, immature minors. At the same time, the Court has recognized that laws providing for parental involvement in the minor's abortion decision must not "unduly burden" the right to seek an abortion.[189] This recognition has led the Court to require states to provide access to an alternative decision-maker, such as a judge, when the state imposes parental notice and consent conditions on the minor's abortion decision.[190] Unquestionably, this is a compromise position between according minors the right to make their own decisions concerning continuation of a pregnancy and according parents or guardians unchallenged authority to determine that the pregnancy

---

185 *See id.* at 297 (comparing the Montana statute to the Ohio parental notification statute which was upheld in *Akron II*, 497 U.S. 502 (1990), and noting the two are "indistinguishable in any relevant way").

186 *Lambert*, 520 U.S. at 294 (summarizing the requirements for a judicial bypass under the Montana statute, MONT. CODE ANN. § 50-20-212 (1997)).

187 *Id.* at 297 (citing Glick v. McKay, 937 F.2d 434, 439 (9th Cir. 1991)).

188 *Id.* at 298.

189 *See supra* notes 184-86 and accompanying text (discussing recent case law regarding parental involvement in a minor's abortion decisions).

190 *See* Hope Clinic v. Ryan, 995 F. Supp. 847 (N.D. Ill. 1998) (striking down Illinois' parental notification statute as unconstitutional because it did not provide for a judicial bypass procedure).

must be continued to term. What the Court has never satisfactorily explained is the reason why a minor has, by reason of her age, less of an interest in her bodily integrity, her future, and her life than adult women possess.

B. State Constitutional Law

The constitutional law of reproductive rights is not limited to Supreme Court decisions interpreting the Federal Constitution. Since the Supreme Court has consistently upheld parental notice and consent statutes so long as they comply with the requirement of a bypass procedure, the only hope for a successful constitutional challenge to the concept of parental involvement in a minor's abortion decision lies in state constitutional provisions.[191] Under the ruling in *In re T.W.*,[192] the Florida Supreme Court was the first state high court to find that a state constitution's right of privacy provision gave a pregnant minor broader rights of self-determination than the Federal Constitution.[193]

The story of T.W.'s odyssey through the Florida court serves as an illustration of, among other things, the role played by individuals who have no interest in or concern about the minor herself. T.W.'s "uncontroverted testimony" established:

> that she was a high-school student, participated in band and flag corps, worked twenty hours a week, baby-sat for her mother and neighbors, planned on finishing high school and attending vocational school or community college, had ob-

191 There have been recent successful challenges to particular features of parental involvement statutes in the federal courts. *See, e.g.*, Causeway Medical Suite v. Ieyoub, 109 F.3d 1096 (5th Cir. 1997) (modifying Louisiana's parental notification statute to provide that a minor who demonstrates she is mature and well-informed, or that an abortion would be in her best interests, "may" rather than "shall" receive judicial authorization for an abortion, and holding that the vesting of discretion as to whether to grant permission with the juvenile court violates the Due Process Clause); *Hope Clinic*, 995 F. Supp. at 862 (holding Illinois' Partial-Birth Abortion Ban unconstitutional because it requires a physician to obtain parental consent before performing almost every abortion procedure on a minor, but does not provide a judicial bypass procedure); Memphis Planned Parenthood, Inc. v. Sundquist, 2 F. Supp. 2d 997 (M.D. Tenn. 1997) (stating that for purposes of determining the right to a preliminary injunction, Tennessee's notice of appeal provision for its parental involvement act, requiring an appeal of the juvenile court's decision denying a minor's petition for a bypass within 24 hours of the decision, is likely to impose an unconstitutional burden on the rights of a minor seeking an abortion).

192 551 So. 2d 1186 (Fla. 1989).

193 *See* Charlene Carres, *Legislative Efforts to Limit State Reproductive Privacy Rights*, 25 FLA. ST. U. L. REV. 273, 282-83 (1998) (discussing the effect of *Webster v. Reproductive Health Servs.*, 492 U.S. 490 (1989), on the *In re T.W.* decision).

served an instructional film on abortion, had taken a sex education course at school, would not put her child up for adoption, and had discussed her plans with the child's father and obtained his approval. She informed the court that due to her mother's illness, she had assumed extra duties at home caring for her sibling and that if she told her mother about the abortion, "it would kill her."[194]

Nevertheless, the trial court agreed with the guardian ad litem, whom it had appointed for the fetus, that the judicial bypass was vague and made no provision to controvert the testimony of the minor.[195] Therefore, parental consent had to be obtained in every case and T.W.'s petition was denied.[196] The District Court of Appeal, finding the bypass provisions to be so vague as to permit arbitrary denial of the petition, declared the entire statute invalid and quashed the order requiring parental consent.[197] The guardian ad litem appealed and unsuccessfully sought to block the abortion; nevertheless, "T.W. lawfully ended her pregnancy."[198]

Despite the arguable mootness of the parental consent issue, the Florida Supreme Court accepted jurisdiction because the questions raised were "of great public importance and . . . likely to recur."[199] As a preliminary matter the court found that it was clearly improper to appoint "a guardian ad litem for the fetus."[200] On the issue of a minor's right of privacy, the court held that under the state constitution a pregnant minor has the same right of privacy as an adult woman facing an unwanted pregnancy.[201]

Since *T.W.*, the high courts of both California and Massachusetts have upheld challenges to their parental involvement laws. In *American Academy of Pediatrics v. Lungren (Lungren III)*,[202] ten

---

194 *In re T.W.*, 551 So. 2d at 1189.

195 *See id.* (noting that the trial court denied T.W.'s petition for waiver of parental consent under the judicial bypass provision).

196 *See id.*

197 *See id.*

198 *Id.*

199 *Id.* (dismissing the mootness argument even though T.W. had already obtained an abortion).

200 *Id.* at 1190.

201 *See id.* at 1193 (concluding that because "[m]inors are natural persons in the eyes of the law" and "[t]he right of privacy extends to '[e]very natural person,'" they have the right to choose an abortion, just like an adult woman).

202 940 P.2d 797 (Cal. 1997) [hereinafter *Lungren III*]. This decision has a tortured procedural history. In 1996, the California Supreme Court upheld the constitutionality of the 1987 parental-consent law. *See* American Academy of Pediatrics v. Lungren, 912 P.2d 1148, 1170 (Cal. 1996) [hereinafter *Lungren II*] (reversing two lower courts that had found the

years after California enacted a mandate that a pregnant minor secure either parental consent or judicial authorization before obtaining an abortion, a divided California Supreme Court held that the statute infringed upon the pregnant minor's fundamental constitutional privacy interest under the California Constitution.[203] In fact, the court observed that an abortion can be a more significant issue for a pregnant minor than for an adult woman, and "'unwanted motherhood may be exceptionally burdensome for a minor.'"[204] Using heightened scrutiny,[205] the court held that, although the State's interests in protecting the health of minors and in fostering the parent-child relationship were extremely important interests rising to the level of "compelling interests"[206] for purposes of constitutional analysis under the privacy provision of the state constitution, the infringement was not necessary to further those interests.[207] The court noted: "No one would doubt the value to a pregnant minor of wise and caring parental guidance and support as she confronts a decision that will affect the rest of her life, assuming such support is available and the minor is willing to seek it."[208] The consent law, however, "has its most significant impact in those instances in which a pregnant minor is too frightened or too embarrassed to disclose her condition to a parent (or to a court)."[209]

Chief Justice Ronald George's majority opinion encapsulates the reasons why parental involvement laws undermine the very ideals

---

state's statute requiring minors to get parental consent for an abortion, or petition a juvenile court for authorization, unconstitutional). After the 1996 decision, however, two members of the majority retired, and the new judges appointed to fill the vacancies supported the 1996 minority in requesting a rehearing. *See* Tim Golden, *Abortion Law Is Overturned in California*, N.Y. TIMES, Aug. 6, 1997, at A12 (stating that Justice Ming Chin, one of the two new justices appointed by Governor Pete Wilson, even voted with the majority in *Lungren III*).

203 *See Lungren III*, 940 P.2d at 847 (finding that the California "parental consent law seriously invades the privacy interests of minors").

204 *Id.* at 815 (quoting *Bellotti II*, 443 U.S. 622, 642 (1979)).

205 *See id.* at 819 (noting the court's use of the "compelling interest" standard). Under the right of privacy provision of the California Constitution, "a statutory intrusion upon an autonomy privacy interest of such a fundamental nature may not be justified simply by showing that the statute serves a legitimate 'competing interest' sufficient to justify an impingement upon a 'less central' privacy interest." *Id.* at 819 (quoting Hill v. National Collegiate Athletic Ass'n, 865 P.2d 633, 653 (Cal. 1994)).

206 *Id.* (noting that the "compelling interest" standard was called for under the California constitutional privacy clause).

207 *See id.* at 829 (asserting that the California statute would actually "impede" the state's interest rather than serve it).

208 *Id.* at 800.

209 *Id.*

they purport to serve.[210] The court first noted a series of California statutes that expressly allow minors to make independent decisions concerning their own medical care and assailed the parental consent provision for making abortion an exception.[211] Although the State professed that its intervention protected the pregnant minor's health through the parental consent requirement, it nevertheless permitted the pregnant minor to make decisions about the complications of a high-risk pregnancy or the adoption of an unwanted child.[212] The court was also skeptical of the law's protective function since the testimony of experts called by the plaintiffs demonstrated the consent requirement "was likely to be detrimental both to the health of such minors and to their family relationships."[213] The court was concerned with the prospect of the parental involvement requirement "lead[ing] those minors who are too frightened or ashamed to tell their parents . . . about their condition . . . to terminate their pregnancy through a dangerous self-induced or back-alley abortion."[214] Alternatively, the minor might "postpone action until it is too late safely to terminate [the] pregnancy," leaving her with no choice except to "endure the increased physical, emotional, and psychological risks posed by an unwanted full-term pregnancy and birth."[215]

Justice Joyce Kennard, in concurrence, submitted that a consent law might still be valid for girls under fourteen, who might be too immature to take responsibility for a decision concerning whether to bear a child.[216] If the girl is too immature to make the decision concerning abortion, how can becoming a mother be good for her or the child? For those who suggest that adoption is the easy answer, how can a minor give valid consent to such a life-altering decision

---

210 *See id.* at 827 (noting that the "imposition of a parental consent or judicial authorization requirement is likely to impair, rather than protect, the health of pregnant minors who do not wish to bear a child").

211 *See id.* (noting that it is difficult to reconcile the contention that parental consent is necessary in the abortion decision to protect the health of the minor with the fact that "over the past 30 years the [California] Legislature has enacted a series of statutes authorizing minors, *without parental consent*, to obtain medical care related to . . . *sexually transmitted diseases*, *rape*, and *sexual assault*").

212 *See id.* at 826-27 (discussing two California laws, one that authorizes a minor to obtain medical care concerning her pregnancy and one that authorizes the minor to decide whether or not she will give her child up for adoption).

213 *Id.* at 828.

214 *Id.* at 827.

215 *Id.*

216 *See id.* at 832 (Kennard, J., concurring) (advising that minors fourteen years of age and younger are too immature to give consent to an abortion).

as the surrender of a baby for adoption? It is not a satisfactory reply to say that states permit even very young girls to give valid consent to adoption.

Planned Parenthood League v. Attorney General,[217] involved a challenge solely on state constitutional grounds to the statutory requirement that, with certain exceptions, a pregnant unmarried minor may not obtain an abortion unless both parents consent or a judge authorizes the medical procedure.[218] The plaintiffs averred that the requirement both on its face and in operation violated due process, equal protection, and the equal rights provisions of the Massachusetts Declaration of Rights.[219] Since there was no specific pregnant minor or class of pregnant minors involved, the court ruled only on the question whether the provision "without justification . . . unavoidably creates undesirable delay and emotional tensions that burden a minor's constitutional right to choose."[220] The court rejected the broad attack on the parental consent requirement, holding that "[a] minor does not have the same freedom to act on her constitutional right to choose to have an abortion as does an adult woman."[221] The court did, however, hold that the two-parent consent requirement lacked "sufficient justification to overcome the burden that . . . [it] place[d] on the minor's constitutional right to choose."[222] The court mentioned specific instances—such as where the father has impregnated his minor daughter—in which the two-parent consent requirement applies without any justification for the burden it imposed.[223] Although the burden imposed might be less onerous in other instances, the court concluded that the requirement was unconstitutional in every instance.[224]

---

217 677 N.E.2d 101 (Mass. 1997) (holding that the Massachusetts parental consent law violated the due process clause of the Massachusetts Constitution).

218 *See id.* at 102. Section 12S of chapter 112 of the General Laws of Massachusetts states that "[i]f a pregnant woman is less than eighteen years of age and has not married, a physician shall not perform an abortion upon her unless he first obtains both the consent of the pregnant woman and that of her parents, except as hereinafter provided." MASS. GEN. LAWS ch. 112, § 12S (1998).

219 *See Planned Parenthood League*, 677 N.E.2d at 102.

220 *Id.*

221 *Id.* at 103 (rejecting plaintiff's "broad attack" on the parental consent requirement of section 12S).

222 *Id.* at 107.

223 *See id.* (concluding that in such situations the parental consent requirement may have an effect adverse to the State's purported interest of protecting the welfare of the minor).

224 *See id.* (declaring its compliance with the Supreme Court decision in *Hodgson v. Minnesota*, 497 U.S. 417, 450 (1990), where the Court held that requiring the notification of both parents "does not reasonably further any legitimate state interest").

The fact that the Supreme Court of the United States had upheld a two-parent notification statute with a judicial bypass in *Hodgson v. Minnesota*[225] was not dispositive. The Massachusetts court noted that "[p]arental consent may be constitutionally required not to satisfy any interest of the parent but [rather] to protect the minor's best interests."[226] Accordingly, the purpose of parental consent is met by the one parent consent with a judicial bypass, and there is no justification for the additional burden imposed by a two-parent consent requirement. In sum, the Massachusetts court held that the parental consent and judicial approval requirements did not violate the due process or equal protection provisions of the state constitution, but that the two-parent requirement did in fact violate due process.[227]

Not every state constitutional challenge to a parental involvement law has been successful. In *Pro-Choice Mississippi v. Fordice*,[228] the Mississippi Supreme Court addressed the validity of the state's requirement of two-parent consent to an unemancipated minor's abortion.[229] A federal court, analyzing the provision's validity under the Federal Constitution, had previously determined that the two-parent consent requirement did not unduly burden a minor's right to seek an abortion.[230] After the federal constitutional challenge failed, a new group of plaintiffs brought suit in state

---

225 *See supra* notes 147-57 and accompanying text (discussing *Hodgson* and noting the Fourth Circuit's pronouncement that this case is almost incomprehensible).

226 *Planned Parenthood League*, 677 N.E.2d at 108 (stating that the process of obtaining the consent of both parents or in the alternative, a judicial bypass, "imposes delay and emotional stress on . . . [the] minor").

227 *See id.* at 109.

228 716 So. 2d 645 (Miss. 1998).

229 *See id.* at 647-48 (detailing the background of challenges to this provision). The United States District Court for the Southern District of Mississippi enjoined enforcement until the Mississippi Supreme Court could promulgate rules on parental consent waiver hearings, and stayed proceedings awaiting the outcome of a number of United States Supreme Court rulings. *See id.* at 648. In 1992, the same federal district court held that the rules governing appeals from consent waiver proceedings were unduly restrictive and impaired the minor's access to abortion. *See id.* The Fifth Circuit, however, found the abortion statutes were constitutional under *Bellotti II*, 443 U.S. 622 (1979), and *Hodgson v. Minnesota*, 497 U.S. 417 (1990). *See* Barnes v. Mississippi, 992 F.2d 1335, 1338-39 (5th Cir. 1993) [hereinafter *Barnes II*] (discussing *Bellotti II* and *Hodgson*); *id.* at 1341 (concluding that "[t]he Mississippi statute is facially constitutional"); *id.* at 1337 (noting that the provision was the subject of a facial challenge in federal court, brought in 1986 by a number of physicians, health clinics and reproductive rights organizations); *see also* MISS. CODE ANN. §§ 41-41-51, 41-41-63 (1972 & Supp. 1998).

230 *Barnes II*, 992 F.2d at 1341 ("[A] statute requiring the consent of a second parent, combined with an adequate judicial bypass mechanism, does not place an 'undue burden' on a minor's right to seek an abortion.").

court, contending that certain Mississippi abortion laws, including the two-parent consent requirement for the unemancipated minor's abortion, violated rights guaranteed by the Mississippi Constitution of 1890, "including the right to privacy, the right of bodily integrity, the right to make medical decisions free from governmental interference, freedom of conscience, the right to due process of law, and the right to safety."[231] The plaintiffs also argued that the two-parent consent law (and the mandatory delay/state mandated information law applying to all females seeking abortions) violated the right to free speech and the guarantee against vague punitive laws.[232]

At the trial court level, the chancellor determined that the state constitution provided for the right to an abortion under its article protecting the right to privacy.[233] Nevertheless, she granted the state's motion for summary judgment after finding that all of the challenged provisions of the abortion law were constitutional.[234] The Mississippi Supreme Court agreed that abortion is protected under the privacy provision of the state constitution, stating "that autonomous bodily integrity is protected under the right to privacy . . . [and] [p]rotected within the right of autonomous bodily integrity is an implicit right to have an abortion."[235] The court, however, rejected the contention that a higher standard of review is mandated when the court determines whether the state's abortion laws violate the state, rather than the federal, constitution.[236] The plaintiffs argued for a "compelling interest" standard; the state contended that the "undue burden" standard was sufficient.[237] The court noted that in other cases involving privacy rights it had required the state to prove a compelling interest of "great and imminent public danger."[238] However, viewing the abortion issue as

---

231 *Fordice*, 716 So. 2d at 649.

232 *See id.* The right to free speech is guaranteed by Article III, section 13 of the Mississippi State Constitution, and Article III, section 14 protects against vague punitive laws. *See* MISS. CONST. art. III, §§ 13, 14.

233 *See Fordice*, 716 So. 2d at 649 (noting the prior history of the case).

234 *See id.*

235 *Id.* at 653.

236 *See id.* at 654-55 (noting plaintiff's argument that the state may apply a stricter standard for state constitutional review but ultimately "approv[ing] the chancellor's decision to apply an undue burden analysis in this case").

237 *See id.* The plaintiffs relied on various Mississippi cases which held that a strict scrutiny standard is appropriate in cases involving the right to privacy. *See id.* at 654. The court, however, cited Supreme Court cases such as *Planned Parenthood v. Casey* and *Roe v. Wade*. *See id.* at 654-55.

238 *Id.* at 654 (citing *In re* Brown, 478 So. 2d 1033, 1040 (1985)).

more complex than other privacy issues, it adopted the *Casey* decision's undue burden standard solely for laws restricting abortion.[239]

The plaintiffs made every available argument against the parental consent requirement: that abortion is safer than childbirth for minors; that minors have the cognitive ability to give fully informed consent; that other provisions of the state's law allow minors to give consent for all medical procedures regarding pregnancy except abortion; that an unemancipated minor may consent to surgical and medical treatment if the minor is able to understand and appreciate the procedure; and that a minor may give medical consent for her own child and that a minor may consent to adoption, a step that "has at least as much impact on a mother's emotional and family welfare as the decision to obtain an abortion."[240] They also argued that the law did not serve the state's interests because minors simply will not involve their parents if they do not want to; instead, they will go out of state to obtain an abortion, or delay the abortion to the point that there is a greater risk of medical complications.[241] If the girl is from an abusive family, the law puts her in a dangerous position.[242] They contended that the judicial proceeding did not cure the difficulties inherent in the law.[243] Many minors are either unwilling or unable to navigate the court system, which forces them "to reveal intimate information in a stressful and humiliating setting."[244] Nevertheless, having declined to give privacy interests regarding abortion more searching scrutiny under the state constitution, the court had little trouble finding the Mississippi two-parent consent law combined with a judicial bypass procedure to be valid.[245]

---

239 *Id.* at 655 ("[Courts] are placed in the precarious position of both protecting a woman's right to terminate her pregnancy before viability and protecting unborn life. In an attempt to create a workable framework out of these diametrically opposed positions, we adopt the well reasoned decision in *Casey* . . . .").

240 *See id.* at 657 (outlining the plaintiffs' support for the position that the "legislature's selective approach to parental involvement" is indicative of "the lack of a compelling state interest").

241 *See id.*

242 *See id.* ("Plaintiffs claim that required parental consent jeopardizes the health and well-being of young women, because it can cause a minor to delay the abortion or put herself in a dangerous position if she is from an abusive family.").

243 *See id.*

244 *Id.*

245 *See id.* at 660 (concluding, after rejecting all of the plaintiff's arguments, that "Mississippi's parental consent law passes the undue burden test for determining state constitutionality").

The Mississippi court relied completely on federal precedents rather than following *In re T.W.* and *American Academy of Pediatrics v. Lungren* (*Lungren I*),[246] as urged by the plaintiffs.[247] The court noted that both Florida and California had, in the cases cited, invalidated parental consent provisions under explicit right to privacy clauses, whereas there is only an inferred right to privacy in the Mississippi Constitution.[248] Accordingly, the court found that the two-parent consent law served a legitimate interest in protecting the health of minors and ensuring that their abortion decisions are well-informed.[249] The court also opined that it is parents rather than physicians or clinic workers who "can provide the emotional and moral support that a minor needs in making the important decision of whether to have an abortion."[250] Any problems with abusive parents the court deemed cured by the judicial bypass.[251]

C. *Congressional Proposals to Curtail Minors' Reproductive Rights*

The Child Custody Protection Act (CCPA) would make it a federal crime for a non-parent to take a pregnant minor across state lines to obtain an abortion in order to avoid laws in her home state requiring the involvement of parents in abortion decisions.[252] It has already passed the House of Representatives[253] and is expected to be voted upon in the Senate in 1999.[254] This new federal offense is punishable by both fines and imprisonment and contains no exemption for relatives, such as grandparents or adult siblings. The law also provides for a civil action on behalf of the minor's "parent or

---

246 32 Cal. Rptr. 2d 546 (1994) [hereinafter *Lungren I*]; *see supra* notes 192-201 and accompanying text (discussing *In re T.W.*).

247 *See Fordice*, 716 So. 2d at 658 (noting plaintiff's argument, based primarily on those two cases, that the state constitutional analysis requires a stricter standard than the federal analysis).

248 *See id.* at 659.

249 *See id.* at 660.

250 *Id.*

251 *See id.* ("The judicial bypass cures any burden in cases where the minor is at risk due to an abusive home environment or simply has no real need for parental advisement on the issue.").

252 *See* H.R. 3682, 105th Cong. § 2401(c) (1998).

253 *See* H.R. REP. NO. 105-605, at 24 (1998).

254 *See* S. 1645, 105th Cong. (1998). It has already passed the Senate Judiciary Committee. *See* S. REP NO. 105-268 (1998). The Senate began consideration of the bill on September 16, 1998, but failed to invoke cloture. *See Status of Senate Bills*, [1997-1998] Cong. Index (CCH), at 21,034.

[legal] guardian who suffers legal harm from a violation of [this statute]."[255]

The CCPA's supporters argue that the Act is necessary to prevent older men who have impregnated young girls from taking them across state lines for abortions to hide the evidence of their misdeeds.[256] It is quite evident, however, that its true purpose is to deny access to abortion services to young, pregnant women. Since the chances of enacting a ban on all abortions are slim to nonexistent, particularly because it would take a constitutional amendment to do so, abortion opponents have concentrated on smaller measures involving issues which have popular appeal, such as parental rights in their children's upbringing.[257]

The CCPA raises difficult issues concerning the meaning of our federal system of government and its dual sovereignty. State laws that would seek to interdict their citizens from traveling to other jurisdictions to obtain abortions would raise serious constitutional questions about our "commitments to national union and national citizenship" and arguably would be "barred by the citizenship clause of the fourteenth amendment, the commerce clause, and the privileges and immunities clause of article IV of the Constitution."[258] If Congress acts, however, there are issues of whether the Privileges and Immunities Clause or the right to travel doctrine limit the actions of Congress.[259] The fact that minors are involved may well change the analysis, since minors do not have the same

---

255 H.R. 3682, 105th Cong. § 2401(c) (1998).

256 *See* H.R. REP. NO. 105-605, at 9-10 (noting the fact that "[t]he majority of teenage girls who become pregnant are impregnated by adult men" and that most girls who obtain abortions are accompanied by their boyfriends when the parents are unaware of the pregnancy).

257 *See* Carl Weiser, *Abortion Politics Alive and Lively on Capitol Hill*, GANNETT NEWS SERV., July 19, 1998, *available in* 1998 WL 5630949 ("[B]y concentrating on parental rights, anti-abortion lawmakers have found [a] cause[ ] that resonate[s] publicly."); *see also* Juliet Eilperin, *2 Lawmakers Seek to Add Nuances to Emotional Abortion Debate*, WASH. POST, June 21, 1998, at A2 ("Rather than demanding a wholesale repeal of abortion, opponents have focused on partial-birth abortion and parental consent laws because they resonate with a broader audience.").

258 Seth F. Kreimer, *The Law of Choice and Choice of Law: Abortion, the Right to Travel, and Extraterritorial Regulation in American Federalism*, 67 N.Y.U. L. REV. 451, 451 (1992).

259 *See id.* at 511 (noting that Article IV entitles Americans "to move from state to state, and to take advantage of . . . local privileges and immunities"). *But see* Stephen B. Presser, *Avoiding Restrictions on Abortions for Minors, Congressional Testimony*, May, 21, 1998, *available in* 1998 WL 12760452 ("This Bill is an important step in reinforcing Federalism and in reinforcing self-government.").

freedom of movement as adults.[260] In upholding suspicionless random urinalyses of student athletes , the Court wrote:

> Traditionally at common law, and still today, unemancipated minors lack some of the most fundamental rights of self-determination—including even the right of liberty in its narrow sense, *i.e.*, the right to come and go at will. They are subject, even as to their physical freedom, to the control of their parents or guardians.[261]

Another troubling aspect of the CCPA is whether its enactment violates principles of federalism by encroaching upon the states' traditional supremacy in the area of morals legislation. Given that Congress has no sweeping authority to enact legislation providing for the general welfare, there is some question concerning the constitutional authority of Congress to enact a criminal statute prohibiting conduct traditionally within the police powers of the states.[262] It is true that, until 1995, the Supreme Court's jurisprudence upheld federal enactments reaching purely intrastate activity so long as the federal enactments were remotely linked to the Interstate Commerce Clause's grant of Congressional authority to regulate commerce among the several states.[263] However, a recent Supreme Court decision, *United States v. Lopez*,[264] has called into doubt the Court's modern recognition of broad congressional authority to enact laws dealing with issues traditionally within the states' domain.[265] In *Lopez*, the Court held that the federal Gun-Free School Zones Act of 1990, which made it a federal offense to

---

260 Vernonia Sch. Dist. 47J v. Acton, 515 U.S. 646, 654 (1995) (noting that unemancipated minors lack some fundamental rights).

261 *Id.*

262 *See* United States v. Lopez, 514 U.S. 549, 567 (1995) (recognizing that "[t]he possession of a gun in a local school zone is in no sense an economic activity that might . . . affect any sort of interstate commerce").

263 *See* Heart of Atlanta Motel, Inc. v. United States, 379 U.S. 241, 261 (1964) (holding that inns and hotels that cater to interstate guests are within the power of regulation by the Commerce Clause of the Constitution); Katzenbach v. McClung, 379 U.S. 294, 304-05 (1964) (holding that Congress is within its power to regulate restaurants serving food, a substantial portion of which has moved through interstate commerce); Wickard v. Filburn, 317 U.S. 111, 125 (1942) (noting that even if an activity is local, it may still "be reached by Congress if it exerts a substantial economic effect on interstate commerce"); Champion v. Ames, 188 U.S. 321, 363 (1903) (holding that the transportation of lottery tickets from one state to another constitutes interstate commerce and thus such activity may be regulated by the federal government).

264 514 U.S. 549 (1995).

265 *See id.* at 567 (finding that to uphold the government's contentions would force the Court to make too many inferences and would "convert congressional authority under the Commerce Clause to a general police power of the sort retained by the States").

possess a firearm within a school zone, lacked any connection to interstate commerce.[266] Consequently, Congress lacked the authority to legislate concerning local gun safety.[267]

Lopez does not offer a complete answer to the question of whether Congress has the power to criminalize the act of taking a pregnant minor across state lines to seek an abortion. There is another strand of Supreme Court Commerce Clause jurisprudence recognizing the power of Congress to protect interstate commerce from contagion even though the perceived harm was local.[268] Accordingly, the Court has upheld federal enactments prohibiting the interstate transportation of lottery tickets,[269] and the carrying of obscene literature and articles designed for indecent and immoral use across state lines.[270] The Court has also treated the movement of people as interstate commerce, upholding the federal Mann Act's ban on the transportation of women in interstate or foreign commerce for "an 'immoral purpose.'"[271]

The Court later upheld the Mann Act's application to the transportation of plural wives by their polygamous husbands across state lines in an opinion which linked plural marriage to prostitution and other forms of commercialized vice.[272] Although "the regulation of marriage is a state matter," that fact alone did not "make the Mann Act an unconstitutional interference by Congress with the police powers of the States."[273] The Court reiterated that "[t]he power of Congress over the instrumentalities of interstate commerce is plenary; it may be used to defeat what are deemed to be immoral practices; and the fact that the means used may have 'the quality of police regulations' is not consequential."[274]

---

266 *See id.* at 551 (holding that "the Act exceeds the authority of Congress '[t]o regulate Commerce . . . among the several States'" (quoting U.S. CONST. art. I, § 8, cl. 3)).

267 *See id.*

268 *See* Asbell v. Kansas, 209 U.S. 251, 257 (1908) (noting the power of Congress to pass legislation "to control the interstate movement of cattle liable to be afflicted with a communicable disease").

269 *See* Champion v. Ames, 188 U.S. 321, 363 (1903) (deciding that carrying lottery tickets from state to state constitutes interstate commerce).

270 *See* United States v. Orito, 413 U.S. 139, 143 (1973) (holding that "the Government has a legitimate interest in protecting the public . . . by preventing such material from entering the stream of commerce").

271 Cleveland v. United States, 329 U.S. 14, 17 (1946); *see* White-Slave Traffic (Mann) Act, ch. 395, 36 Stat. 825 (1910) (codified as amended at 18 U.S.C. §§ 2421-2424 (1994)).

272 *See Cleveland*, 329 U.S. at 19 ("These polygamous practices have long been branded as immoral in the law.").

273 *Id.*

274 *Id.*

However, even if Congress has the power under the Commerce Clause to enact such legislation, there are still unresolved issues under the Privileges and Immunities Clause and the right to travel doctrine. Moreover, the activity sought to be regulated by the CCPA proposal involves a minor's right to abortion, a right that has been protected, although in a limited way, under the Due Process Clause of the Fourteenth Amendment.[275]

Senator John Ashcroft's proposed legislation, the Putting Parents First Act of 1998, would require minors to obtain parental consent for abortion referrals or contraceptives in any facility receiving federal funds.[276] Senator Ashcroft has been quoted as saying that "[p]arents must not be reduced to the status of mere bystanders when their children are facing these difficult decisions."[277] Since the vast majority of health clinics, schools, and hospitals receive federal funds, at least in the form of Medicaid, the bill arguably imposes a new national parental consent requirement not only for a minor's access to an abortion, but also for any access by a minor to contraceptives available at a health facility.[278] This proposal flies in the face of long-standing federal policy concerning family planning services. Presently, both Title X of the Public Health Service Act of 1970[279] and Medicaid (Title XIX of the Social Security Act of 1965)[280] mandate the confidential provision of contraceptive services to all those who seek them regardless of marital status or age. Furthermore, the proposal undermines public health policies that seek to encourage adolescents to protect themselves from unwanted or premature parenthood and sexually transmitted diseases. Many states have medical consent laws that permit minors to obtain con-

[275] *See* U.S. CONST. amend. XIV, § 1.

[276] *See* John Ashcroft, *Ashcroft Bill Affirms Role of Parents in Critical Choices by Their Children*, GOV'T PRESS RELEASES, July 28, 1998, *available in* 1998 WL 7325975.

[277] Weiser, *supra* note 257.

[278] *See* Ashcroft, *supra* note 276 (noting that the Putting Parents First Act reaffirms the parental role of assisting children in making choices concerning abortion and contraception).

[279] *See* Family Planning Services and Population Research Act of 1970, 42 U.S.C. § 300 (1994); *see also* Planned Parenthood Fed'n v. Heckler, 712 F.2d 650, 651 (D.C. Cir. 1983) (holding that regulations requiring parental consent for prescribing contraceptives were inconsistent with the congressional purpose in enacting Title X); New York v. Heckler, 719 F.2d 1191, 1196-97 (2d Cir. 1983) (recognizing that the Health and Human Services regulation under Title X of the Public Health Services Act, mandating notice within 10 days to parents of unemancipated minors obtaining prescription contraceptives, was invalidated as inconsistent with the statutory purpose of making family planning available to sexually active adolescents and preventing teen pregnancies).

[280] *See* Social Security Amendments of 1965, 42 U.S.C. § 1396 (1994).

traceptive services without parental participation.[281] There is little reason to believe that ending confidentiality will discourage teenagers from engaging in sexual activity as studies indicate that most teenagers have been active for nearly a year before obtaining family planning services.[282] While there are policy reasons to protest this measure, so long as it is tied to a spending bill, it is probably within the bounds of congressional authority as the Court has greatly expanded federal authority by upholding conditions of compliance with congressional dictates in spending bills,[283] even though they require the sacrifice of protected rights.[284]

III. CRITIQUE OF PARENTAL INVOLVEMENT LAWS

Parental involvement laws are designed to deter minors from exercising the right to choose to terminate a pregnancy rather than to police the medical profession.[285] Nevertheless, one of the least remarked upon features of parental involvement statutes is their intrusion upon medical judgment. A common feature of these laws is the use of the criminal law to prevent physicians from exercising their medical judgment concerning the minor's termination of her pregnancy without involving either parents or other adult decisionmakers.[286] Unlike the California Supreme Court, which has found that parental consent is not necessary when considering a physician's capability to determine whether a minor has the capacity to consent to the procedure,[287] the Supreme Court has operated on an unstated assumption that the physician will behave in an un-

281 *See, e.g.*, VA. CODE ANN. § 54.1-2969(D)(2) (Michie 1998) (deeming minors to be adults for purposes of consenting to medical or health services in the case of birth control).

282 *See* Sharon Pomeranz, *Condoms Overturned on Appeal: Teens Stripped of Their Rights*, 4 AM. U. J. GENDER & L. 219, 240 (1995) (citing to various studies).

283 *See* South Dakota v. Dole, 483 U.S. 203, 211-12 (1987) (upholding federal legislation that conditioned states' receipt of highway funds on their willingness to enact laws prohibiting persons less than twenty-one years of age from purchasing or possessing alcoholic beverages, stating "we conclude that encouragement to state action . . . is a valid use of the spending power").

284 *See, e.g.*, Rust v. Sullivan, 500 U.S. 173, 203 (1991) (upholding restrictions on abortion related speech for recipients of federal funds).

285 *See* Planned Parenthood v. Camblos, 155 F.3d 352, 355 (4th Cir. 1998) (noting that the parental notice statute "respects the fundamental interests of responsible parents in the rearing and in the educational, moral, and religious development of their children").

286 *See id.* at 355 (discussing the portion of Virginia's parental notice statute that prohibits a physician from performing an abortion on an unemancipated minor unless notice is given to one of the minor's parents).

287 *See Lungren III*, 940 P.2d 797, 828 (Cal. 1997) (noting that "physicians are well qualified to determine a minor's capacity").

ethical or unprofessional manner in this context.[288] In fact, in *Bellotti II*, the implicit assumption was made explicit when the Court stated that even seventeen-year-olds

> are less likely than adults to know or be able to recognize ethical, qualified physicians, or to have the means to engage such professionals. Many minors who bypass their parents probably will resort to an abortion clinic, without being able to distinguish the competent and ethical from those that are incompetent or unethical.[289]

Justice Stewart, speaking of a "girl of tender years" has also denigrated the counseling available, stating that "[i]t seems unlikely that she will obtain adequate counsel and support from the attending physician at an abortion clinic, where abortions for pregnant minors frequently take place."[290] This same statement can be made about parents, although the Court prefers to think that the reaction of parents is "compassionate and supportive."[291] The irony surrounding all of this lies in the distrust of physicians treating abortion-seeking minors, whereas when adult women are involved, the Court has deferred so markedly to medical judgment.[292] *Roe v. Wade* and its progeny have established that the state may mandate that the abortion provider be a licensed physician.[293]

The judges who hear minors' petitions for bypasses of parental participation in abortion decisions have a great deal of discretion under the Supreme Court's jurisprudence regarding parental involvement statutes.[294] Thus, judges are free to make rulings based on unarticulated factors, including jurists' views of adolescent

---

288 *See Bellotti II*, 443 U.S. 622, 641 (1979) (stating that "[i]t seems unlikely that [the minor] will obtain adequate counsel and support from the attending physician at an abortion clinic"). While adult input into any medical decision is necessary, no state licenses minors to practice medicine. Arguably, there is a conflict of interest between the provider and the patient, particularly if money is involved, but that is true with every medical service and procedure, unless the provider is acting *pro bono*.

289 *Id.* at 641 n.21.

290 Planned Parenthood v. Danforth, 428 U.S. 52, 91 (1976) (Stewart, J., concurring).

291 *See Bellotti II*, 443 U.S. at 640 n.20 (noting the high desirability of compassionate and supportive parental involvement in a minor's abortion decision).

292 *See* Planned Parenthood v. Casey, 505 U.S. 833, 895 (1992) (noting that although the assumption is that "minors will benefit from consultation with their parents," the Court "cannot adopt a parallel assumption about adult women").

293 *See, e.g.*, Connecticut v. Menillo, 423 U.S. 9, 11 (1975) (per curiam) (holding that the state may prosecute a non-physician for performing an abortion).

294 *See* Tamar Lewin, *Parental Consent to Abortion: How Enforcement Can Vary*, N.Y. TIMES, May 28, 1992, at A1 (comparing the extent of enforcement and judicial willingness to approve abortions under various state statutes requiring either parental notice or consent prior to commencing the procedure).

sexuality, the need for babies to supply the adoption market, the protection of fetal life, or assumptions about parental wisdom and benign control.[295] Furthermore, the members of the Supreme Court that support parental involvement laws have turned a blind eye to a number of truths. One is that parental notification is tantamount to a parental veto in many cases. A second truth is that parental involvement statutes are not primarily about the well-being of the pregnant minor or even about her parents' authority; rather, they represent a means of curtailing abortion in a way that has proven to be politically feasible. Third, minors in general have the ability to make reasonable decisions.[296] Fourth, minors also have the ability to make moral judgments. A fifth truth is that parents do not always act in the best interests of their children, particularly on an issue such as abortion where there may be deep divisions about its morality and justification. Sixth, the best interest standard, so widely used when dealing with children, is an amorphous, indeterminate standard particularly susceptible to the judge's biases and predispositions.[297] While an overwhelming majority of pregnant minors do consult with their parents, those who do *not* know their family situation far better than the judge or other third party decision-maker.[298] Seventh, parental involvement statutes do not promote the interests of minors and do not result in better family communication or a more reasoned decision-making process.

Furthermore, there is no way for the State to guarantee that parents will make the decision or counsel their daughters in ways that comport with her best interests. The late Judge Nanette Dembitz observed that mothers who opposed their daughters' abortions have

---

[295] *See, e.g.*, *Casey*, 505 U.S. at 895 (noting that minors benefit from consultation with their parents when dealing with abortion decisions); *see also* Carey v. Population Servs., Int'l, 431 U.S. 678, 702 (1977) (White, J., concurring in part and concurring in the result) (noting the beneficial aspects of deterring young people from engaging in sex).

[296] *See generally* Donald N. Bersoff & David J. Glass, *The Not-So Weisman: The Supreme Court's Continuing Misuse of Social Science Research*, 2 U. CHI. L. SCH. ROUNDTABLE 279, 302 n.134 (1995) (discussing scientific literature disputing states' view of adolescent incompetence); Maggie O'Shaughnessy, Note, *The Worst of Both Worlds?: Parental Involvement Requirements and the Privacy Rights of Mature Minors*, 57 OHIO ST. L.J. 1731, 1733-34 (1996) (noting that evidence indicates "minors exhibit adult-level reasoning" in making a decision about their pregnancy).

[297] *See Bellotti II*, 443 U.S. at 655-56 (Stevens, J., concurring) (contending that the best interests standard provides little guidance and judges' decisions are necessarily reflective of societal and cultural values, a fact "fundamentally at odds" with the right to privacy).

[298] *See* Tamar Lewin, *Study Finds Most Parents Know About Daughters' Abortion Plans*, N.Y. TIMES, Oct. 21, 1992, at A16 (noting the results of a study of 1500 teenage girls living in jurisdictions that did not have either a parental consent or notice statute which found that 61% of their parents knew about the abortion in advance).

> expressed a vengeful desire to punish the daughter for her sexual activity by making her suffer [an] unwanted child, a fervor to impose a religious conviction the mother has failed to instill in her daughter, a hope of caring for her daughter's baby as her own because of an inability or unwillingness to bear another child herself, a defensive or resentful attitude because *she* bore illegitimate children without seeking or being able to secure an abortion, or a general distaste for abortion.[299]

IV. RECONCEPTUALIZING MINORS' ABORTION ISSUES

In holding that parental involvement in a young woman's abortion decision is constitutionally permissible, the Supreme Court has focused on the need for parental guidance and support, as well as the need to uphold parental authority and control over their offspring.[300] It has ignored the reality that "[t]here is a very thin line between counsel and coercion, especially when they originate from a relationship as special as that of parent-child."[301] Factors such as guilt, loyalty, and fear may dictate the minor's decision. Assuming, therefore, that a notification requirement is tantamount to giving parents the power to veto their daughter's abortion decision, what has not been made clear is the nature or source of the interest parents have in forcing their daughter to continue her pregnancy to term. Likewise, if a judicial bypass is involved, what is the State's interest?

The father of the fetus, one of the people with the closest link to the fetus, does not have an interest sufficient to override the wishes of the pregnant female concerning the termination of the pregnancy.[302] Not only does the father not have a right to veto the woman's decision, he also does not have the right to be notified of her choice.[303] Whether anyone has an affirmative right to procreate

[299] Nanette Dembitz, *The Supreme Court and a Minor's Abortion Decision*, 80 COLUM. L. REV. 1251, 1255 (1980).

[300] *See Bellotti II*, 443 U.S. at 637-39 (noting that the guiding role of parents justifies the limits placed on the constitutional rights of minors).

[301] *In re* Mary P., 444 N.Y.S.2d 545, 548 (Fam. Ct. Queens County 1981).

[302] *See* Planned Parenthood v. Danforth, 428 U.S. 52, 69 (1976) ("[S]ince the State cannot regulate or proscribe abortion during the first stage, . . . the State cannot delegate authority to any particular person, even the spouse, to prevent abortion during that same period.")

[303] *See* Planned Parenthood v. Casey, 505 U.S. 833, 887-98 (1992) (explaining in detail why a requirement for notification would be unduly burdensome to the woman).

is a matter of debate.[304] It is beyond debate, however, that there is no recognized right to have grandchildren. In fact, in recent years some states have acted to discourage the birth of children to unwed pregnant minors by imposing financial responsibility on the parents of the minor who bears the child.[305] The United States Congress followed suit by allowing states to impose financial responsibility for children born to an unwed minor upon the grandparents.[306]

In *H.L. v. Matheson*,[307] the Court ruled that although a "blanket, unreviewable power of parents to veto their daughter's abortion" is unconstitutional, a "'mere requirement of parental notice'" is valid as to immature minors.[308] The Court relied on its abortion funding jurisprudence and concluded that the State is not required to "fine-tune" its statutes in order to promote abortion—that the state action encouraging childbirth is "'rationally related to the legitimate governmental objective of protecting potential life.'"[309] It is perverse to grant to the state a greater interest in the fetal life of a pregnant minor than to an older, pregnant female who is better able to withstand the pregnancy and childbirth and the rigors of unwed motherhood.

The State has a "legitimate interest" in the health of a pregnant woman.[310] Parents also have a recognized interest in their children's health and well-being.[311] However, it is difficult to see how forcing a minor daughter to go through pregnancy and childbirth fosters the daughter's health. The risks of childbirth are much greater for the young mother than are the risks associated with

---

304 *See, e.g.*, Katheryn D. Katz, *The Clonal Child: Procreative Liberty and Asexual Reproduction*, 8 ALB. L.J. SCI. & TECH. 1, 40-47 (1997) (discussing the parameters of reproductive liberty).

305 *See, e.g.*, WIS. STAT. ANN. § 49.90(1)(a)(2) (West 1997 & Supp. 1998) (requiring the parent of a dependent under the age of 18 to provide care to the child of such dependent "to the extent that the dependent person is unable to do so").

306 *See* Personal Responsibility and Work Opportunity Reconciliation Act of 1996, Pub. L. No. 104-193, § 373, 110 Stat. 2105, 2255 (1996); *see also* Susan Frelich Appleton, *When Welfare Reforms Promote Abortion: "Personal Responsibility," "Family Values," and the Right to Choose*, 85 GEO. L.J. 155 (1996) (discussing the effect of welfare reform on abortion).

307 450 U.S. 398 (1981).

308 *Id.* at 409. The Court was guided by its precedent regarding parental consent and notice statutes. *See id.* at 407-10; *see also Bellotti II*, 443 U.S. 622, 649 (1979); Planned Parenthood v. Danforth, 428 U.S. 52, 90-91 (1976) (Stewart, J., concurring); *Bellotti I*, 428 U.S. 132, 145, 147 (1976).

309 *Matheson*, 450 U.S. at 413 (quoting Harris v. McRae, 448 U.S. 297, 325 (1980)).

310 *See* Roe v. Wade, 410 U.S. 113, 163 (1973).

311 *See, e.g.*, Parham v. J.R., 442 U.S. 584, 600 (1979) (involving the admittance of children to a state mental hospital); Wisconsin v. Yoder, 406 U.S. 205, 213-14 (1972) (concerning Amish parents who declined to send their children to school after the eighth grade).

abortion but the law shields the daughter's decision to maintain the pregnancy from the parent's control.[312] Not only do most states allow the pregnant minor to seek medical treatment regarding the pregnancy without parental notification and consent, but also there is no reported decision in which parents have been able to enlist the aid of the courts in directing the unwilling minor to have an abortion.[313] In fact, there are only two reported cases in which a parent sought to use a court's jurisdiction over delinquent or incorrigible minors to force a minor daughter to have an abortion.[314]

One of these cases was decided solely on statutory grounds. In a ruling that antedated *Roe v. Wade*, a Maryland appellate court reversed a trial judge's order in a juvenile delinquency proceeding mandating that a pregnant sixteen year old submit to an abortion.[315] The Maryland Court of Special Appeals held that, although the evidence supported the finding that Cindy Lou was a minor in need of supervision, the juvenile court had exceeded its powers in seeking to compel Cindy Lou to submit to medical procedures relative to termination of her pregnancy.[316]

In *In re Mary P.*,[317] the court rejected the mother's petition to have her fifteen year old pregnant daughter declared a person in

---

[312] *See* Hodgson v. Minnesota, 497 U.S. 417, 461-78 (1990) (Marshall, J., dissenting) (criticizing parental notification law as underinclusive for not requiring parental notice for pregnancy and childbirth due to their far greater risks); *Lungren III*, 940 P.2d 797, 826-27 (Cal. 1997) (questioning the rationale of a California law requiring parental or judicial involvement in a minor's abortion decision in order to ensure her physical and emotional health even while California permits the minor to decide whether to continue a pregnancy, whether to obtain medical care in continuing that pregnancy, and whether to give up a child for adoption, all without parental consent). Of note, however, is the court's warning that minors fourteen years of age and younger are too immature to give consent to an abortion. *See id.* at 832.

[313] *See* J. Shoshanna Ehrlich, *Journey Through the Courts: Minors, Abortion and the Quest for Reproductive Fairness*, 10 YALE J.L. & FEMINISM 1, 27 n.114 (1998) (noting that 27 states gave minors the authority to obtain prenatal care and services without parental consent); Jennifer R. Kramer, Note, *Adolescents, Abortion and Amendments: Choices After* American Academy of Pediatrics v. Lungren, 33 U.S.F. L. REV. 133, 142 (1998) (noting that minors may give their children up for adoption without parental consent). By implication, the law allows a minor to consent even to a caesarian section. *See* Catherine Grevers Schmidt, *Where Privacy Fails: Equal Protection and the Abortion Rights of Minors*, 68 N.Y.U. L. REV. 597, 636 (1993) ("Many states, having recognized that requiring parental involvement in sensitive health issues often discourages minors from seeking treatment, grant minors the power to consent to treatment for substance abuse, mental health care, venereal disease, and prenatal care, including caesarian sections.").

[314] *See infra* notes 315-21 and accompanying text.

[315] *In re* Smith, 295 A.2d 238, 241-45 (Md. Ct. Spec. App. 1972) (explaining that the lower court had found the minor to be in need of supervision and a danger to herself and others).

[316] *See id.* at 245-46 (finding that the legislative intent emancipated a female minor over age sixteen from her parent's control in matters of emergency).

[317] 444 N.Y.S.2d 545 (Fam. Ct. Queens County 1981).

need of supervision in order to force compliance with the mother's demand that the daughter submit to an abortion.[318] Instead, the court issued an order of protection against the mother, mandating that the mother not interfere with the daughter's decision to carry the child to term.[319] The *Mary P.* court reasoned that "if the right to abort is within the zone of privacy protected by the fourteenth amendment, the right to give birth exists there as well," and further stated that "[i]t should be beyond question that the decision to give birth is 'fundamental' and 'implicit in the concept of ordered liberty.'"[320]

The *Mary P.* court's reasoning concerning the role of parental counseling, if applied to the decision to seek an abortion rather than to continue the pregnancy, suggests that the minor's decision to abort should be given equal protection:

> [A] minor's decision on whether or not to abort is of such far reaching consequence and sensitivity as to cry out for the understanding counsel of parents who care. And yet, such counsel must originate from the premise that it is the child who has the ultimate right to decide. Children are not the chattel of their parents. Rather, they are citizens in their own right, endowed with certain fundamental freedoms of which they may not be divested by parental fiat.[321]

Unfortunately, the entire structure of constitutional analysis is based primarily on notions of capacity to consent to an abortion and secondarily, on the need to uphold parental authority. Within that framework, courts weigh and measure a minor's privacy rights against the need to protect children from their immaturity and vulnerability.[322] Even as to those minors who are fully able to under-

---

[318] *See id.* at 546-47 (noting that Mary was due in about six months and had repeatedly stated that she wanted to carry the pregnancy to term).

[319] *See id.* at 547-48 (stating that the order of protection would protect her constitutional right to give birth).

[320] *Id.* at 547 (quoting Palko v. Connecticut, 302 U.S. 319, 325 (1937)).

[321] *Id.* at 548 (citing Planned Parenthood v. Danforth, 428 U.S. 52, 91 (1976) (Stewart, J., concurring)).

[322] *See generally* Hodgson v. Minnesota, 497 U.S. 417, 444 (1990) (balancing the interests of the minor, the parents, and the family unit); *Bellotti II*, 443 U.S. 622, 633-39 (1979) (laying out three specific justifications for the Court's consistent policy of defining the rights of minor's differently from those of adults); *In re* Smith, 295 A.2d 235, 245 (Md. Ct. Spec. App. 1972) (implying that if at least one of the five conditions set forth in a Maryland statute defining when a minor is able to consent is established, then the minor has the capacity to make decisions regarding her pregnancy); *In re Mary P.*, 444 N.Y.S.2d at 547 (citing *Bellotti II* for the proposition that a "state may deny an abortion to a child where she lacks sufficient maturity . . . [and] the abortion would not serve her best interests").

stand the consequences of and weigh alternatives to abortion, it is constitutionally permissible that the state require an adult to determine whether the young woman should be allowed to choose to terminate her pregnancy without parental involvement.[323] The entire focus is on the abortion and its consequences for the minor. When parental involvement statutes are challenged as unconstitutional, it is clear that the petitioning minor has the burden of proof and must convince the court by clear and convincing evidence that her parents need not or should not be involved.[324]

Imagine, instead, a scheme to protect young women facing the decision of whether to terminate a pregnancy which mandates that *those who oppose* the minors' choice, whether parent or judge, demonstrate with clear and convincing evidence that bearing a child is in the girl's best interests, medically and psychologically, and comports with her value system and religious beliefs. Perhaps then these difficult decisions would be made in the best interests of the young woman rather than in the best interests of the parents or the judge. Perhaps then the young woman will not be viewed as someone who has no right to self-determination, whose body can be conscripted as a means of expression for the views and beliefs of others.

---

323 *Bellotti II*, 443 U.S. at 642-44 (1979) (finding a parental consent requirement to be valid so long as an alternative procedure for authorization is made available).

324 *See generally Hodgson*, 497 U.S. at 427 (requiring, under the Minnesota statute, that the minor prove she is "'mature and capable of giving informed consent to the proposed abortion,' or that an abortion without notice to both parents would be in her best interest").

WHY CRIMINALIZE CHILDREN? LOOKING BEYOND THE EXPRESS POLICIES DRIVING JUVENILE CURFEW LEGISLATION

*Deirdre E. Norton**

INTRODUCTION

Juvenile curfew laws are popular throughout the United States.[1] Their popularity exploded in the 1990s when legislatures enacted more than one thousand new juvenile curfew laws and governments revived existing curfew laws that had long been dormant.[2] The express public policy rationales offered by legislatures in support of curfews sustain the enormous popularity of these laws. The most common rationales are: reducing juvenile crime rates; reducing the victimization of juveniles; and reinforcing parental authority.[3] While curfew proponents tout all of these policy rationales, none of these rationales has been proven to result from the imposition of curfews.[4] In fact, both the efficacy and the constitutionality of curfew laws have been challenged.[5] Since curfews are backed by popular support, these

---

* J.D. 2000, New York University School of Law. I would like to thank Professor K. Anthony Appiah for our brainstorming sessions and for supervising this note, Professor Bryan A. Stevenson for his guidance and inspiration, and my family for their unwavering support.

1. Brian Privor, *Dusk 'til Dawn: Children's Rights and the Effectiveness of Juvenile Curfew Ordinances*, 79 B.U. L. REV. 415, 421 (1999). For example, both recent presidential contenders, Vice President Al Gore and Governor George W. Bush, publicly supported the use of juvenile curfews. *See* Clay Robinson, *Bush Signs "Tough Love" Juvenile Crime Bill; Punishment Boosted for Young Offenders*, HOUSTON CHRON., June 1, 1995, at A29 (supporting juvenile crime bill which would authorize counties to enact curfew ordinances); Katharine Q. Seelye, *Gore's Plan for Success in 2000: Wide Array of Specific Positions*, N.Y. TIMES, July 29, 1999, at A1 (supporting Federal anti-gang law that would set curfews on specific gang members).

2. Craig Hemmens & Katherine Bennett, *Out in the Street: Juvenile Crime, Juvenile Curfews, and the Constitution*, 34 GONZ. L. REV. 267, 272 (1998/99); Tona Trollinger, *The Juvenile Curfew: Unconstitutional Imprisonment*, 4 WM. & MARY BILL RTS. J. 949, 961 (1996).

3. *See, e.g.*, CHARLOTTESVILLE, VA., CODE § 17-7 (1998); D.C. CODE ANN. § 6-2181(e) (2000); *see also* Hemmens & Bennett, *supra* note 2, at 270.

4. *See* discussion *infra* Part III.A.

5. *See infra* Part I.B.

issues are only addressed after the curfews have gone into effect, if at all.

Although the express policy rationales may be responsible both for the groundswell of public support and for providing sufficient grounds for the adoption of many curfew laws, additional conscious or unconscious motivations may lurk beneath their surface. It is possible, for example, that some curfews are a reaction to the public's fear of juveniles and are considered the most effective method of getting children off the streets and out of sight. Lawmakers may also mistakenly believe that curfews assist certain segments of society in properly disciplining their children.

By observing the totality of the circumstances surrounding juvenile curfews, we may discover that other implicit policies actually drive the popularity of juvenile curfew legislation. We may also discover discriminatory effects. These implicit policies and discriminatory effects should be expressly considered when drafting curfew legislation. For example, some juvenile curfew legislation is enacted with the express purpose of reducing gang activity.[6] However, while reducing this is a valid and desirable policy motivation, the implicit policies and discriminatory effects of legislation must also be considered, and curfew laws carefully tailored and enforced so that every child who may fit the supposed profile of a gang member does not get swept up in the criminal justice system.[7]

This note suggests that there are at least two ways in which we may uncover whether implicit policies drive the modern resurgence of juvenile curfew laws. First, an examination of the history of curfew laws in the United States indicates that these laws often arose out of oppressive and discriminatory motivations. It is therefore necessary to critically review different types of past curfew laws to assess whether similar insidious goals may actually motivate modern juvenile curfews. Second, a consideration of the enforcement and effects of modern juvenile curfew laws—to the extent that these results are predictable—provides insight into the policies guiding their enactment. But before delving into the history and effects of curfew laws

6. *See* Privor, *supra* note 1, at 420 (noting that Washington, D.C.'s curfew was passed in response to increase in juvenile violence and gang activity); *see also* U.S. DEP'T OF JUSTICE, YOUTH GANG PROGRAMS AND STRATEGIES 24 (2000) (on file with the *New York University Journal of Legislation and Public Policy*) (noting that aggressive curfew enforcement was one of three express strategies used in Antigang Initiative in Dallas, Texas).

7. *See infra* Part III.C.1. Note that the need to tailor curfew laws derives from the experience with curfews held invalid, on constitutional challenges, for overbroadness. *See infra* notes 17, 52-57, and accompanying text.

in order to reveal the implicit policies on which they may be based, this note will summarize the modern legal state of affairs in the area of juvenile curfew law.

I
Modern Juvenile Curfew Laws in the United States

A. *The Average Juvenile Curfew Law*

There is no national juvenile curfew law. Rather, juvenile curfew laws exist in major cities and small municipalities scattered throughout the United States. According to a 1995 study of the seventy-seven most populous cities in the United States,[8] 77% of them impose juvenile curfews. Only 56% of these curfew laws were long-standing, and the other 44% were enacted in the early nineties.[9] Since the 1995 study, more of the cities surveyed have enacted juvenile curfews.[10] Furthermore, many small towns across the nation are either enforcing long-dormant curfew laws or scrambling to enact new ones.[11]

Juvenile curfew legislation creates status offenses by criminalizing activities of minors that would be legal if undertaken by adults. The typical juvenile curfew law sets a time during which it is a misdemeanor for any person under a particular age to be outside his or her home.[12] Some curfew laws apply to an entire city, whereas others are enacted in "hot spots"—areas of a city where there is more crime—because regulation of these areas is considered particularly necessary.[13]

Curfew laws nearly always contain exceptions specifying those situations in which it is appropriate for a minor to be out past curfew.[14] The exceptions may include emergencies, running errands for

8. William Ruefle & Kenneth Mike Reynolds, *Curfews and Delinquency in Major American Cities*, 41 Crime & Delinq. 347, 353 (1995) (including in study all U.S. cities with 1992 population of more than 200,000).

9. "Long-standing" defined as enacted prior to 1990. *Id.* at 354.

10. Of the eighteen cities Ruefle & Reynolds listed as not having juvenile curfews, nine have since enacted curfews (Los Angeles, Washington, D.C., Charlotte, Tulsa, Pittsburgh, Anaheim, Louisville, Lexington-Fayette, and Jersey City). D.C. Code Ann. § 6-2181 (2000); Ruefle & Reynolds, *supra* note 8, at 353; *see also* U.S. Conference of Mayors, A Status Report on Youth Curfews in America's Cities: A 347-City Survey 1 (1997) (on file with the *New York University Journal of Legislation and Public Policy*), *available at* http://www.usmayors.org/uscm/news/publications/curfew.htm [hereinafter U.S. Conference of Mayors].

11. Hemmens & Bennett, *supra* note 2, at 272.

12. *See, e.g.*, D.C. Code Ann. § 6-2182 (2000).

13. *See infra* Part III.C.2.

14. Privor, *supra* note 1, at 454.

a parent, or coming to or from work, school, or religious events.[15] In order to survive a First Amendment challenge to the statute, some legislators have drafted curfew laws to include additional exceptions, such as permitting attendance at any civic or responsibly-sponsored event.[16] Legislators must use caution when adding exceptions, however, because a broadening of the statute may lead to a challenge for vagueness.[17]

After defining the offense and exceptions thereto, the statute then names the penalty for a curfew violation.[18] The penalties vary, and include the imposition of fines or community service not only for the juvenile offender, but also often for the parent or any other adult who enables the curfew violation.[19] Additional penalties may even include mandatory parenting classes for the offender's parents.[20] Given the variety of possible penalties for curfew violations, it becomes apparent that the ordinances are far-reaching and have the potential to do extensive damage to some families. For example, with some fines reaching $500,[21] curfew penalties could create a financial burden for middle and lower-income families.

B. *Constitutional Challenges*

Though many of the challenges to juvenile curfews have been made in state courts due to the local nature of curfew laws,[22] there have also been a number of constitutional challenges to juvenile curfew laws in federal courts, beginning with the 1975 case of *Bykofsky v. Borough of Middletown*,[23] brought in the Middle District of Pennsylvania.[24] The federal circuit courts are currently split on the issue of juvenile curfews, with some upholding the statutes as constitutional and others striking them down for violating the constitutional rights of

15. *See, e.g.*, D.C. CODE ANN. § 6-2183(b) (2000).
16. *See* Hutchins v. Dist. of Columbia, 188 F.3d 531, 547 (D.C. Cir. 1999).
17. *See id.* at 546-57.
18. *See, e.g.*, D.C. CODE ANN. § 6-2183(c) (2000).
19. *See, e.g.*, *id.* § 6-2183(d) (2000); 720 ILL. COMP. STAT. ANN. 551/1(c) (West 2000); MONT. CODE ANN. § 7-32-2302(3) (1999).
20. *See, e.g.*, D.C. CODE ANN. § 6-2183(d)(2) (2000).
21. *See, e.g.*, *id.* § 6-2183(d)(1) (2000).
22. *See, e.g.*, A.C.L.U. v. City of Albuquerque, 992 P.2d 866, 875 (N.M. 1999) (holding state constitution preempted city from enacting juvenile curfew ordinance that established criminal sanctions against children when such behavior was lawful if committed by adults); Sale *ex rel.* Sale v. Goldman, No. 27315, 2000 WL 989874, at *1 (W. Va. July 19, 2000).
23. 401 F. Supp. 1242 (M.D. Pa. 1975), *aff'd mem.*, 535 F.2d 1245 (3d Cir. 1976), *cert. denied*, 429 U.S. 964 (1976).
24. *See* Hemmens & Bennett, *supra* note 2, at 297.

minors and parents.[25] Business owners affected by the curfews have also joined some of the challenges.[26]

Most constitutional challenges look to the First and Fourteenth Amendments for support. The common First Amendment arguments are that curfew laws violate minors' rights to free assembly, speech, and religion by limiting the hours after which minors may not leave their homes.[27] The Fourteenth Amendment challenges often rely on due process and equal protection principles.[28] Under the Due Process Clause, parents argue that curfew laws violate their substantive due process right to raise their children free from government interference.[29] Minors also assert a substantive due process challenge based on their personal liberty interest in freedom to travel.[30] Finally, the equal protection arguments challenge the fact that curfew laws treat minors differently than adults.[31]

While children are afforded rights under the Constitution, the Supreme Court has declared that these rights need not be co-extensive with the constitutional rights of adults.[32] In several instances, the Supreme Court has upheld the constitutionality of laws aimed at children that would have been unconstitutional if applied to adults.[33] For example, in *Bellotti v. Baird*, the Supreme Court outlined three reasons why laws aimed at children should receive different consideration: (1) children are particularly vulnerable; (2) children possess a limited ability to make critical decisions in an informed and mature manner;

25. *See infra* notes 46-52 and accompanying text.

26. *See Hutchins*, 188 F.3d at 534. Business owners are often affected by curfews because statutes may provide penalties against them for doing business with minors in violation of the curfew. *See, e.g.*, CHARLOTTESVILLE, VA., CODE § 17-7(e) (1998); D.C. CODE ANN. § 6-2183(a)(3) (2000) ("The owner, operator, or any employee of an establishment commits an offense if he or she knowingly allows a minor to remain upon the premises of the establishment during curfew hours."). *See also City of Albuquerque*, 992 F.2d at 868-70 (holding business owner had standing to challenge juvenile curfew even though not charged with violation).

27. *See, e.g.*, Hodgkins v. Goldsmith, No. IP99-1528-C-T/G, 2000 WL 892964, at *7 (S.D. Ind. July 3, 2000).

28. *See infra* Part III.C.3.

29. *See, e.g.*, Schleifer v. City of Charlottesville, 159 F.3d 843, 852 (4th Cir. 1998).

30. *See, e.g.*, McCollester v. City of Keene, 586 F. Supp. 1381, 1384-85 (D.N.H. 1984).

31. *See City of Albuquerque*, 992 F.2d at 875.

32. *See* Tinker v. Des Moines Indep. Cmty. Sch. Dist., 393 U.S. 503, 514-15 (1969) (Stewart, J., concurring) (declaring that First Amendment rights of minors are not co-extensive with those of adults); Ginsberg v. New York, 390 U.S. 629 (1968) (holding children do not have same First Amendment rights as adults).

33. *See, e.g.*, *Ginsberg*, 390 U.S. at 639-40 (prohibiting sale of obscene material to minors); Prince v. Massachusetts, 321 U.S. 158 (1944) (prohibiting minors from selling merchandise in public places).

and (3) the parental role is very important in child rearing.[34] There have, however, been a number of cases where, in the interest of parental autonomy or the constitutional rights of the children, the Court has stricken laws targeting the behavior of minors.[35] As a result, the constitutional limits of the rights of minors are not clear, and this area of the law remains somewhat unpredictable.

Whether a law can withstand a constitutional challenge depends, in part, on the level of scrutiny with which the court reviews the law. The standard of review for constitutional challenges to curfews depends on whether the court finds that the rights asserted by minors and their parents are, in fact, fundamental.[36]

As citizens of the United States, minors are accorded fundamental rights of which they cannot be stripped merely because they are minors.[37] Although the rights of minors are not necessarily co-extensive with those of adults, it is clear that the protections of the Bill of Rights and the Fourteenth Amendment extend to minors.[38] Furthermore, in the context of juvenile curfews, several courts have recognized the fundamental right of minors to freedom of movement.[39] The important right of a citizen to move about freely has been recognized by the Supreme Court as one of the "amenities of life" that society holds dear.[40] Justice Marshall recognized this fundamental right to

34. Bellotti v. Baird, 443 U.S. 622, 634 (1979).

35. *See, e.g.*, Wisconsin v. Yoder, 406 U.S. 205 (1972) (holding that state cannot compel school attendance law for all minors); Pierce v. Soc'y of Sisters, 268 U.S. 510 (1925) (striking law requiring children to attend public school); Meyer v. Nebraska, 262 U.S. 390 (1923) (striking law prohibiting children from receiving education in any language other than English).

36. *See* Plyler v. Doe, 457 U.S. 202, 216-17 (1982) (holding when fundamental rights of citizens are abridged by law, usual judicial deference is misplaced and strict scrutiny must apply).

37. *See Tinker*, 393 U.S. at 511 (holding that minors are "persons" under United States Constitution and possess fundamental rights which state must respect).

38. *See* Planned Parenthood v. Danforth, 428 U.S. 52, 74 (1976) (extending Fourteenth Amendment privacy interest to minors); *In re* Gault, 387 U.S. 1, 13 (1967) (extending due process in criminal cases to minors).

39. *See* Nunez v. City of San Diego, 114 F.3d 935, 944-45 (9th Cir. 1997); Qutb v. Strauss, 11 F.3d 488, 492 (5th Cir. 1993); Johnson v. City of Opelousas, 658 F.2d 1065, 1072 (5th Cir. 1981); McCollester v. City of Keene, 586 F. Supp. 1381, 1384-85 (D.N.H. 1984).

40. Papachristou v. City of Jacksonville, 405 U.S. 156, 164 (1972); *see also* Aptheker v. Secretary of State, 378 U.S. 500, 520 (1964) (Douglas, J., concurring) ("[F]reedom of movement is the very essence of our free society, setting us apart. Like the right of assembly and the right of association, it often makes all other rights meaningful—knowing, studying, arguing, exploring, conversing, observing and even thinking. Once the right to travel is curtailed, all other rights suffer, just as when curfew or home detention is placed on a person."); United States v. Wheeler, 254 U.S. 281, 293 (1920) (citations omitted) ("In all the States from the beginning down to the

freedom of movement in his dissent over the Court's denial of certiorari in *Bykofsky*.[41] There he argued that this freedom is protected by the Due Process Clause of the Fourteenth Amendment and that any statute attempting to abridge this freedom must survive strict scrutiny.[42]

Those who oppose the notion that curfew laws implicate the fundamental rights of minors question whether minors have the right to control the time during which they are free to be outside their homes.[43] By casting the issue as a matter of the rights of minors, curfew proponents hope courts will be persuaded that it is acceptable to abridge these rights to meet legitimate state goals. However, the issue does not concern only the rights of minors, but also the rights of parents to make decisions for their children. Family autonomy is basic to the nature of freedom and is considered a basic concept of ordered liberty.[44] Thus, parents also often invoke the strict scrutiny standard based on the view that curfews interfere with the substantive due process right to parental autonomy.[45] However, although there appear to be grounds for giving curfews the highest level of review, the Supreme Court has not ruled on the issue and the circuit courts remain divided.

The results of suits in the circuit courts challenging the constitutionality of juvenile curfew laws reflect the unpredictability in this area of law. The Fourth,[46] the Fifth,[47] and, most recently, the D.C.[48] Circuits have upheld juvenile curfew laws challenged on constitu-

adoption of the Articles of Confederation the citizens thereof possessed the fundamental right, inherent in citizens of all free governments, peacefully to dwell within the limits of their respective States, to move at will from place to place therein, and to have free ingress thereto and egress therefrom . . . .").

41. *See* Bykofsky v. Borough of Middletown, 429 U.S. 964 (1976) (Marshall, J., dissenting).

42. *Id.* at 964-65.

43. *See, e.g.*, Hutchins v. Dist. of Columbia, 188 F.3d 531, 536-39 (D.C. Cir. 1999).

44. *See* Palko v. Connecticut, 302 U.S. 319, 325 (1937) (holding that rights at essence of ordered liberty are protected by Fourteenth Amendment from state interference); *see also* Moore v. City of East Cleveland, 431 U.S. 494, 499 (1977) (declaring that right to parental autonomy in decisionmaking is based on principle that family sphere is something that should be free from state interference).

45. *See, e.g.*, *Hutchins*, 188 F.3d at 540 (declining to apply strict scrutiny due, in part, to holding that fundamental right of parents to make decisions for children is not implicated by curfew law); Hodgkins v. Goldsmith, No. IP99-1528-C-T/G, 2000 WL 892964 (S.D. Ind. July 3, 2000) (recognizing but not deciding whether curfew impinged on fundamental right of parents).

46. *See* Schleifer v. City of Charlottesville, 159 F.3d 843 (4th Cir. 1998).

47. *See* Qutb v. Strauss, 11 F.3d 488 (5th Cir. 1993).

48. *See Hutchins*, 188 F.3d. at 531.

tional grounds. The Fourth Circuit case, *Schleifer v. City of Charlottesville,* sought an appeal to the Supreme Court, but the Court denied certiorari in early 1999.[49] The Supreme Court also denied certiorari to a Third Circuit case, *Bykofsky v. Borough of Middletown*, over a strong dissent from Justice Marshall, who argued that the Supreme Court should speak on the issue of juvenile curfew laws and the impact they have on thousands of towns.[50]

The Sixth Circuit has not heard a juvenile curfew case since *Cox v. Turley* in 1974.[51] *Cox* was not a challenge to the curfew law itself, but rather alleged that a minor's Fourth, Eighth, and Fourteenth Amendment rights were violated when he was arrested for a curfew violation and locked up for five days with the adult prisoners without being allowed to call his parents to notify them of his arrest. However, while the Sixth Circuit ruled in favor of the minor in this case, the curfew law itself remained intact.[52]

In fact, the Ninth Circuit is the only circuit court in recent years to strike down a juvenile curfew law. In *Nunez v. City of San Diego*, the Ninth Circuit reversed the district court's ruling and held a San Diego curfew ordinance unconstitutional.[53] Although its curfew was originally enacted in 1947, San Diego adopted a city resolution in 1994 to begin aggressive enforcement of the ordinance.[54] Using the *Bellotti* standards, the Ninth Circuit performed a strict scrutiny analysis, holding intermediate scrutiny improper when assessing the fundamental rights of minors.[55] The Court found the ordinance (1) unconstitutionally vague in violation of the First Amendment;[56] (2) not narrowly tailored enough to satisfy equal protection rights;[57] and (3) violative of parents' fundamental right to rear their children absent undue government interference.[58]

Although a strict scrutiny analysis has been applied in some curfew cases, many courts continue to apply a rational basis or intermedi-

49. Schleifer v. City of Charlottesville, 526 U.S. 1018 (1999).

50. *Bykofsky*, 429 U.S. at 965 (Marshall, J., dissenting) ("The question squarely presented in this case, then, is whether the due process rights of juveniles are entitled to lesser protection than those of adults. The prior decisions of this Court provide no clear answer.") (citation omitted).

51. Cox v. Turley, 506 F.2d 1347 (6th Cir. 1974).

52. *See id.* at 1355.

53. Nunez v. City of San Diego, 114 F.3d 935 (9th Cir. 1997).

54. *Id.* at 938-39.

55. *Id.* at 945-46.

56. *Id.* at 940.

57. *Id.* at 949.

58. *Id.* at 951-52.

ate scrutiny test to constitutional challenges to juvenile curfew laws.[59] A reason for rational basis scrutiny is the fact that age has not yet been held to be a suspect class meriting strict scrutiny,[60] and many courts are unwilling to accept the argument that minors have a fundamental right to travel.[61] The split among the circuits regarding the appropriate level of scrutiny will continue until the Supreme Court addresses the issue.

The applied standard of review does not, however, constitute the bottom line in constitutional curfew law analysis. Although the application of strict scrutiny makes it less likely that a curfew law will survive,[62] it does not render survival impossible. For example, in *Qutb v. Strauss*, the Fifth Circuit applied a strict scrutiny analysis to the juvenile curfew law in question, yet the law was upheld.[63] The court held that the curfew was narrowly tailored to serve the government's compelling interest in reducing juvenile crime and protecting minors.[64]

C. Discrimination Challenges

Whether the test is rational basis, intermediate, or strict scrutiny, the government's stated policy interests in curfew laws are always considered valid. Implicit policy rationales that may spur some of the curfew legislation are seldom discussed in federal court opinions. Challenges to the laws on a basis other than age have not yet reached the circuit courts.[65] Studies have shown, however, that minority youth disproportionately bear the brunt of juvenile curfew enforcement.[66] However, the racial issues that may play an underlying role in the enactment and enforcement of curfew legislation rarely are addressed in judicial opinions, particularly when a sound opinion can be drafted on other grounds.

For example, in *Kolender v. Lawson*, the Supreme Court upheld the striking of a California loitering law for unconstitutional vague-

59. *See* Hemmens & Bennett, *supra* note 2, at 294-95.

60. *See Nunez*, 114 F.3d at 944 ("Because age is not a suspect classification, distinctions based on age are subject to rational basis review.").

61. *See* Hemmens & Bennett, *supra* note 2, at 294-95; *see also supra* notes 40-42 and accompanying text.

62. *See, e.g.*, Johnson v. City of Opelousas, 658 F.2d 1065, 1072-74 (5th Cir. 1981).

63. Qutb v. Strauss, 11 F.3d 488, 494 (5th Cir. 1993).

64. *Id.*

65. If there has been a discrimination-based challenge on any basis other than age, this is not apparent in the federal circuit court opinions on curfew laws.

66. *See infra* Part III.C.

ness.[67] The law stated that suspicious persons could be stopped by the police and forced to identify themselves.[68] The plaintiff in the case had been stopped and forced to identify himself fifteen times over the course of two years.[69] The Court found this law unconstitutionally vague because it failed to inform citizens in a clear manner of how to comply, and it led to arbitrary enforcement.[70] The Court, however, failed to mention that the plaintiff was a black man with dreadlocks and that he had been stopped fifteen times while strolling through white neighborhoods.[71] Thus, while race was a factor in the case, the Court's opinion does not mention this fact.

The role race plays in motivating juvenile curfew laws is similarly unclear because the courts are legitimately able to decide cases challenging these laws on other grounds. Furthermore, because a plaintiff may need to establish discriminatory intent and not merely discriminatory effect in order to successfully challenge a law on discrimination grounds, plaintiffs may see the attempt at proving legislative intent to discriminate as futile unless the proverbial smoking gun can be found in the legislative record. Additionally, because curfews are primarily passed as municipal ordinances, legislative history may be difficult to find. Thus, whether because parties fail to raise the issue or because courts fail to recognize it, judicial opinions rarely acknowledge the discriminatory effects of curfew laws. Although there is a tendency to look to the courts to address the potential ramifications of legislative motivations, these issues should be discussed at the policy level, when the justifications for the laws are being expressed.

Even when the popular media addresses curfew laws, the discriminatory aspects of those laws receive little attention.[72] Political endorsements often tout the express policy rationales but do not venture beyond them.[73] Even most legal studies of curfews focus on constitutional aspects of curfews and address little in the way of their discriminatory effects.

67. Kolender v. Lawson, 461 U.S. 352, 353 (1983).
68. *Id.*
69. *Id.* at 354.
70. *Id.* at 361.
71. *See* Sheri Lynn Johnson, *Race and the Decision to Detain a Suspect*, 93 YALE L.J. 214, 230 (1983).
72. *See, e.g.*, Eloise Salholz et al., *Blacks and Cops: Up Against a Wall*, NEWSWEEK, May 11, 1992, at 52 (illustrating discussion of black distrust of law enforcement with picture of curfew violators); *Washington Police Begin to Enforce 1995 Curfew*, N.Y. TIMES, Sept. 12, 1999, at 30 (noting that A.C.L.U. legal director anticipated that curfew's enforcement may be "discriminatory").
73. *See, e.g.*, Hemmens & Bennett, *supra* note 2, at 272 & n.2.

Though important, constitutional arguments are not the critical issues to the thousands of children and parents affected by juvenile curfew laws each year. Every curfew law enacted in this country should certainly not be condemned for having a discriminatory intent and producing discriminatory effects. Nor is popular support for curfews found only among whites or members of the upper class.[74] However, legislatures must address the likely eventuality that small segments of the population will bear the brunt of the enforcement efforts made to ease the minds of those who favor curfew laws.

When arguing in favor of curfew laws, proponents proclaim intent to reduce juvenile crime and victimization. Rarely, however, do they discuss the history of curfew laws in order to critically assess their potential utility. Society should remember that curfews have traditionally been created by the upper class as a method to control the movements of the lower classes.[75] Curfews may therefore constitute a preemptive strike against an entire segment of the population presumed to have a propensity to commit crimes.

II
Types of Curfew Laws

Although nighttime juvenile curfews are the most popular type of curfew in the United States,[76] other types of curfews exist. Emergency curfews, for example, are implemented for brief periods of time in the interest of public safety, often during natural disasters or social protests.[77] Furthermore, past curfews have not only targeted juveniles but a variety of other populations. These curfews have a long and unpleasant history and have often been motivated by emotions—distrust, disrespect, discrimination, and hate—that have no place in lawmaking.

A. Gender-Based Curfews

In the recent past, fear for women's safety led to laws restricting their behavior. For example, Eastern Kentucky University imposed a curfew on all female freshmen as late as the 1970s.[78] After their

74. *Id.* at 275.
75. *See* Curfew.org, A Brief History of Curfews, *at* http://www.curfew.org/history/ (last modified Sept. 20, 2000); *see also* Hemmens & Bennett, *supra* note 2, at 279.
76. U.S. Conference of Mayors, *supra* note 10, at 1 (noting that four out of five of surveyed cities had nighttime curfew); *see also* Hemmens & Bennett, *supra* note 2, at 273.
77. *See* Trollinger, *supra* note 2, at 951.
78. 475 F.2d 707, 708 (6th Cir. 1973).

freshman year, however, female students could avoid the curfew and regulate their own hours if they: (1) maintained a "C" average and remained free of academic or social probation; (2) paid a fifteen dollar fee each semester; and (3) if they were under twenty-one, obtained written parental consent.[79] There were no curfew restrictions applicable to male students.[80]

In *Robinson v. Board of Regents of Eastern Kentucky University*, a female student challenged the curfew, arguing that it was unconstitutional because it violated the Equal Protection Clause of the Fourteenth Amendment.[81] The Sixth Circuit upheld the district court's decision that a curfew that imposes restrictions on women does not constitute an equal protection violation.[82] The court reasoned that sex-based classifications are often upheld and explained that equal protection does not require identical treatment.[83] The curfew regulation survived the Sixth Circuit's rational relation test because the state interest in the discriminatory statute was safety: Women are more likely to be attacked and less likely to defend themselves.[84] The Sixth Circuit's safety justification which permitted curfews targeting women effectively kept some young women under lock and key as a precaution against the improper behavior of men.

Gender-based curfews, however, only reinforce improper behavior rather than create incentives for lawfulness. Selective curfew laws criminalize otherwise lawful behavior and punish individuals for their status as potential crime victims. Like gender-based curfew laws, juvenile curfew laws similarly aim to protect those who would be crime victims. However, as in the previous example, these laws punish potential victims rather than aggressors. Furthermore, rather than seeking to create a safer environment for all citizens, curfew laws aimed at potential victims demonstrate that lawmakers have succumbed to fear. Fearing for the safety of some, legislators attempt to shield potential victims at the victim's expense. However, if these potential victims choose to leave their homes in violation of a curfew law, not only must they fear their aggressors, but also criminal prosecution.

79. *Id*. at 708-09.
80. *Id.* at 709.
81. *Id.*
82. *Id.*
83. *Id.* at 710.
84. *Id.* at 711.

B. Race-Based Curfews

The United States has also imposed race-based curfews. In order to demonstrate that discrimination and fear motivated the enactment of the laws, it is important to note that these types of curfews often applied to free blacks as well as to slaves. This fear led to laws allowing blacks to travel freely only during the daytime, when whites could observe them.[85]

In *Jennings v. Washington*, Mary Jennings challenged the ten dollar fine assessed against her for violating the city of Washington's curfew law.[86] Jennings argued that the city's power to restrain and prohibit the meetings of free persons of color did not include the power to prohibit their being outside after ten o'clock at night.[87] The court disagreed and held that the curfew was a valid exercise of the power to "restrain and prohibit the nightly and other disorderly meetings of slaves, free negroes, and mulattoes."[88]

The curfew at issue in *Jennings* did carve out some exceptions which allowed those who were subject to the law to be out past curfew. For example, in *Brown v. Robertson,* an 1843 case, Charles Brown, a free black man, challenged his arrest and detention for a curfew violation because he claimed to be exempt from the statute.[89] The curfew statute read, in pertinent part:

> [N]o free black or mulatto person shall be allowed to go at large through the city of Washington, at a later hour than ten o'clock at night, excepting such free black or mulatto persons have a pass from some justice of the peace or respectable citizen, or be engaged in driving a cart, wagon, or other carriage.[90]

Brown challenged his prosecution under the law because, at the time of his arrest, he was in the employ of Sen. Daniel Webster.[91] The court rejected Brown's argument, holding that he had to prove to the police officer at the time of arrest that he was out with the permission of Senator Webster: establishing that fact in court was too late.[92]

Curfews on free blacks and slaves were clear acts of discrimination. This could be expected, however, considering the state of affairs between blacks and whites in mid-nineteenth century America. The

85. Hemmens & Bennett, *supra* note 2, at 279.
86. 13 F. Cas. 547 (C.C.D.C. 1838) (No. 7,284).
87. *Id.*
88. *Id.*
89. 4 F. Cas. 426 (C.C.D.C. 1843) (No. 2,027). Brown also challenged the authority of the city to impose the curfew. *Id.*
90. *Id.* at 426 n.2.
91. *Id.* at 427.
92. *Id.*

use of curfews as a way to exercise control over a minority feared by a majority is instructive, however, in the modern American resurgence of juvenile curfews because the focus of curfew laws may not have shifted entirely from race to age. Today's curfew laws may disparately affect minority youth.[93] If today's juvenile curfews are enacted with knowledge of this discriminatory effect, such curfews could in fact be considered to reflect a discriminatory policy.

C. Ethnicity-Based Curfews

Perhaps the most famous (or infamous) ethnicity-based curfew in America was the curfew imposed on all Japanese, and alien Germans and Italians during World War II.[94] Although the curfew was imposed on persons from all three countries, the law focused on those of Japanese ancestry in the Pacific military region.[95] The curfew affected approximately 100,000 people of Japanese descent.[96] Several Americans of Japanese ancestry challenged the law in federal court, but the Supreme Court upheld the curfew law as a valid exercise of military power.[97]

This curfew exemplifies how an acceptable explicit policy (military exigency) may in fact mask an implicit, discriminatory policy. Under the War Powers Clause, President Roosevelt in his capacity as Commander in Chief signed an executive order granting powers to the Secretary of War and certain military commanders, including General DeWitt who oversaw Military Area Number One encompassing California, Oregon, Washington, and Arizona.[98] General DeWitt instituted a number of laws through public proclamations, including the curfew at issue.[99]

DeWitt's Public Proclamation No. 3 imposed a curfew on alien Germans and Italians and all Japanese from 8:00 P.M. to 6:00 A.M. every day.[100] In *Hirabayashi v. United States* (*Hirabayashi I*), Gordon Kiyoshi Hirabayashi, an American citizen of Japanese descent, challenged his arrest and prison sentence for violating the curfew.[101] Hirabayashi argued that the curfew constituted

93. *See infra* Part III.
94. *See generally* Hirabayashi v. United States, 320 U.S. 81, 88 (1943).
95. *Id.*
96. *See* Hirabayashi v. United States, 828 F.2d 591, 596 (9th Cir. 1987).
97. *See, e.g.*, Korematsu v. United States, 323 U.S. 214, 217 (1944); *Hirabayashi*, 320 U.S. at 102.
98. *Hirabayashi*, 320 U.S. at 85-88.
99. *Id.* at 86-88.
100. *Id.* at 88.
101. *Id.* at 83-85.

unconstitutional discrimination under the Fifth Amendment.[102] The Court held, however, that the curfew was a lawful delegation of legislative power to a military commander.[103] Furthermore, the Court refused to substitute its judgment regarding military necessity for that of DeWitt, in effect deferring to military commanders in times of national emergency.[104]

In *Hirabayashi I*, the Court paid lip service to legal precedent against discrimination, stating, "[d]istinctions between citizens solely because of their ancestry are by their very nature odious to a free people whose institutions are founded upon the doctrine of equality. For that reason, legislative classification or discrimination based on race alone has often been held to be a denial of equal protection."[105] The government also conceded in its oral argument before the Court in *Korematsu* that if the orders had been based on racist precepts, they would be invalid.[106] However, the Court explained that although racial classifications are usually irrelevant, they will not preclude a military commander's determination that such classifications are necessary for national defense purposes.[107]

The *Hirabayashi I* decision can be seen as a lengthy attempt by the Court to charge that the curfew did not concern race, but national defense. The Court itself gave several reasons for the need to target all persons of Japanese ancestry. For example, the Court stated that experience has taught that in times of war, those with an ethnic affiliation to the enemy are a greater source of danger than others.[108] Furthermore, the Court explained that the poor treatment of Japanese by white Americans in the past may have "been [a] source[ ] of irritation and may well have tended to increase [Japanese-Americans'] isolation, and in many instances their attachments to Japan and its institutions."[109] Instead of using the examples of poor treatment of Japanese-Americans as a red flag for the possible discriminatory intent behind the curfew law, the Court used these examples to argue that those of Japanese ancestry posed a national threat.

The Court revealed much of its anti-Japanese prejudice in its opinion, implying that all people of Japanese descent, although Ameri-

102. *Id.* at 83.
103. *Id.* at 104-05.
104. *Id.*
105. *Id.* at 100.
106. *See Hirabayashi*, 828 F.2d 591, 600 (9th Cir. 1987) (discussing *Korematsu*, 323 U.S. at 214).
107. *See Hirabayashi*, 320 U.S. at 100.
108. *See id.* at 101.
109. *Id.* at 98.

cans, remained foreign because "social, economic and political conditions . . . have intensified their solidarity and have in large measure prevented their assimilation as an integral part of the white population."[110] In explaining the threat posed by Japanese Americans, the federal district court trial judge also stated, "They are shrewd masters of tricky concealment among any who resemble them."[111] Perhaps these negative stereotypes did not attach to Americans of Italian and German descent because they could more easily physically assimilate with whites, thereby causing white Americans to be more forgiving of their particular ethnic affiliations.

More than forty years after his conviction and sentence under the emergency curfew, Hirabayashi was back in federal court challenging his conviction (*Hirabayashi II*).[112] Hirabayashi presented new evidence supporting his claim that the curfew law was based on racial discrimination, not military exigency: the sole copy of General DeWitt's report drafted to explain the basis of the curfew and exclusion orders.[113] The orders were, in fact, based on racial stereotypes, and the War Department had not only rewritten the report to change the materially offensive aspects but had also attempted to destroy all copies of DeWitt's original report.[114]

This new evidence supported the arguments from Hirabayashi's 1943 briefs to the Supreme Court that the law was based on discriminatory motives, not military emergency. Despite the concealed report, a federal court held that although Hirabayashi's exclusion was a violation of due process, the curfew was not a significant infringement on freedom. Therefore, it reasoned that the Supreme Court would have upheld the curfew conviction despite the racial basis of the order.[115] However, the Ninth Circuit reversed and held that the curfew order should be vacated.[116] The Ninth Circuit also noted that a plethora of reports and articles had condemned these laws as unjust because they were in fact based on race.[117]

The importance of *Hirabayashi I* and the *writ of coram nobis* granted in *Hirabayashi II* is critical. First, these cases demonstrate how a law can be supported by express policy justifications and embraced by the public, while concealing insidious policy justifications

110. *Id.* at 96.
111. United States v. Hirabayashi, 46 F. Supp. 657, 661 (W.D. Wash. 1942).
112. Hirabayashi v. United States, 627 F. Supp. 1445 (W.D. Wash. 1986).
113. *Hirabayashi*, 828 F.2d at 593.
114. *Id.* at 598.
115. *Hirabayashi*, 627 F. Supp. at 1457.
116. *Hirabayashi*, 828 F.2d at 608.
117. *Id.* at 593.

that, if expressed, might invalidate the law. Second, the length of time it took to vacate Hirabayashi's convictions demonstrates that even when it seems obvious that an insidious implicit policy drives legislation, proving that fact in court may be extremely difficult. In fact, had an archival researcher not discovered the smoking gun in DeWitt's original report, all of the historical condemnations of the wartime curfew still would not have led the courts to vacate Hirabayashi's convictions. Thus, without more than speculation and statistics regarding the implicit policy rationales driving juvenile curfew laws, there may be no immediate relief for those affected by them.

Italian-Americans also included in the executive order at issue in the *Hirabayashi* cases likewise received no legal relief since no federal challenges to the curfew were brought by any of the 50,000 Italians affected by the curfew.[118] While the Italian-American community's injuries cannot be quantified, the Wartime Violation of Italian American Civil Liberties Act was recently signed into law by President Clinton. This Act formally acknowledges the injustices, including curfews, that were perpetuated against Italian-Americans during World War II.[119]

The fact that Italian-Americans still clamor for recognition of the wrongs perpetuated against them because of their ethnicity indicates that discriminating curfew laws leave deep scars that persist throughout lifetimes. For Italian-Americans, the ill-effects felt by parents during World War II were passed on to their children who now seek symbolic reparations.[120] Likewise, the ill-effects of discriminatory juvenile curfew laws may also be passed on to an alarming number of children of those arrested for curfew violations.

III
Effects of Modern Juvenile Curfew Laws

A. *Juvenile Curfews May Not Attain Express Public Policy Goals*

Even where legislatures intend juvenile curfew laws to be applied neutrally, the enforcement of the curfews may result in minority youths being disproportionately targeted and criminally charged. Consider how curfew laws function. If a juvenile is stopped because

118. Wartime Violation of Italian American Civil Liberties Act, H.R. 2442, 106th Cong. § 2(2) (1999) (enacted Nov. 7, 2000).

119. *Id.*

120. *See generally Wartime Violation of Italian American Civil Liberties Act: Hearing on H.R. 2442 Before the Subcomm. on the House Constitution of the Comm. on the Judiciary*, 106th Cong. (1999) (statements of Reps. Charles T. Canady, Eliot Engel, and Rick Lazio).

he or she is out past curfew, that juvenile will either be punished for violating the curfew or, if he or she has a legitimate excuse for violating the curfew which falls under the curfew's express exceptions, that juvenile will be sent home. Therefore, in deciding whether to punish or to free the juvenile, enforcers have considerable latitude in deciding whether to enforce the curfew. We may query, then, whether the laws function satisfactorily such that they can be equally applied to all juveniles regardless of race, ethnicity, or social status.[121] If the laws are not implemented in an evenhanded manner, the express public policy goals may not be achieved.

The express public policy goals of curfews are, as previously mentioned, reducing juvenile crime, reducing juvenile victimization, and enhancing parental authority.[122] Whether the curfew laws successfully meet stated policy goals is a point of contention between proponents and opponents of curfew legislation.[123] For example, one may argue that if curfew laws achieve these goals when applied primarily to minority youths, then by extension minority youths may in fact be a group in need of regulation: If enforcing curfews against minority youths prevents crime, then minority youths must have been committing the targeted crimes; if enforcing curfews against minority youths reduces juvenile victimization, then minority youths may be most in need of protection; if enforcing curfew laws against minority youths enhances parental authority, then the parents of minority children may most need government assistance in exercising authority at home. This view, however, contrasts with the facially neutral laws, as those laws imply that all children, regardless of race, gender, ethnicity, or class, need protection.

If curfew laws are in fact enforced disproportionately against minorities, that does not mean that white children are above the law, nor does it mean that they escape its enforcement altogether. Instead, it signifies that white juveniles as a group feel the effects of the law less than they would if the laws were enforced in an evenhanded manner. If the law is consistently and predictably implemented in a discriminatory manner without achieving any of the express public policy rationales, it demonstrates a likelihood that discriminatory enforcement is an implicit policy behind the law.

Some argue that a discriminatory effect does not evidence a discriminatory intent. To mount a successful challenge to discriminatory curfew enforcement, the Supreme Court requires that a plaintiff estab-

---

121. *See infra* Part III.C.
122. *See supra* note 3 and accompanying text.
123. *See infra* notes 126-32 and accompanying text.

lish discriminatory intent, not just discriminatory effect.[124] However, legislatures may offer relief from discriminatory effects without evidence of intent.[125] Once a law's effects have been studied and disseminated, this knowledge should be incorporated to indicate lawmakers' intent. If known effects were not part of the intent, then the curfew law would be amended or abandoned in an attempt to avoid discrimination. When legislatures, made aware of curfews' discriminatory effects, gloss over or ignore them, these effects must be considered part of the policy driving the laws' enactment.

There is a paucity of studies showing the actual enforcement and effects of curfew laws on a national scale.[126] Data is available at the local level, however,[127] and legislators considering the implementation of a curfew law should review this information. A critical look at some of the available data reveals the disparate effect these laws have on different segments of society. For example, police enforcing the much publicized New Orleans juvenile curfew law arrest black youths at a rate nineteen times higher than white youths.[128] Vincent Schiraldi, director of the Center of Juvenile Justice argues that, "If middle-class white kids were arrested at 19 times the rate of African-American youths, there would be no debate over the effectiveness of the New Orleans curfew, because there wouldn't be a New Orleans curfew—period."[129]

The Justice Policy Institute's study examining the effects of the impact of juvenile curfews in California showed a slightly more hopeful picture. Evidence indicated that authorities in most counties even-handedly enforced curfew laws.[130] In four of the largest California counties, however, relatively minor discrepancies existed: police arrested black and Latino youths for curfew violations 2 to 8.4 times

---

124. *See* United States v. Armstrong, 517 U.S. 456, 465 (1996) (finding presumption that law enforcement acts in unbiased manner, absent clear and convincing evidence of discriminatory effect and discriminatory purpose).

125. *See* Bray v. Alexandria Women's Health Clinic, 506 U.S. 263, 273 n.4 (1993).

126. *See, e.g.*, Hemmens & Bennett, *supra* note 2, at 276; Ruefle & Reynolds, *supra* note 8, at 361.

127. *See infra* notes 128-38.

128. Vincent Schiraldi, *No Panacea: While Violating the Rights of Youths, The D.C. Curfew Won't Bring Down Juvenile Crime*, LEGAL TIMES, Sept. 27, 1999, *available at* WL 9/27/1999 Legal Times 23; *see also* Privor, *supra* note 1, at 417 (stating that New Orleans' curfew is most restrictive in America).

129. Schiraldi, *supra* note 128.

130. MIKE MALES & DAN MACALLAIR, THE IMPACT OF JUVENILE CURFEW LAWS IN CALIFORNIA 14 (Report by Justice Policy Institute of the Center on Juvenile and Criminal Justice, 1998) (on file with the *New York University Journal of Legislation and Public Policy*), *available at* http://www.cjcj.org/jpi/curfew.html.

more often than white youths.[131] Interestingly, while the study revealed relatively evenhanded enforcement, it also concluded that "curfew enforcement does not reduce youth crime over time for any racial/ethnic group on a statewide basis."[132]

The inefficacy of curfew laws calls into question whether, considering their discriminatory effects, juvenile curfew laws are worth legislatures' efforts.[133] No study has proven conclusively that enactment or enforcement of juvenile curfew laws achieves any of the laws' express policy goals.[134] For example, New Orleans officials claimed that their curfew led to a thirty-eight percent reduction in juvenile crime.[135] The empirical data, however, failed to support the city's claimed success.[136] Furthermore, when an overall drop in crime coincides with the implementation of a juvenile curfew law, it is difficult to determine whether the overall drop in crime or the curfew is responsible for reduced juvenile crime rates. Even if the juvenile crime rate for New Orleans did decrease, however, such a decrease does not necessarily constitute proof of the curfew law's effectiveness because other factors may have contributed to this decrease. Specifically, in addition to its curfew, New Orleans implemented many other programs, such as recreational centers, jobs, camps, and an increased police force.[137] Proclamations of curfew success may fail to take into account these and other factors that help to reduce juvenile victimization and crime rates. Furthermore, the implementation of a curfew to reduce juvenile crime rates seems misplaced because some studies show that the majority of juvenile crime occurs between three and eight P.M.,[138] hours unaffected by most juvenile curfews. Therefore, the implementation of a juvenile nighttime curfew does not target the time of day when most juvenile crime occurs.

There is also little evidence that juvenile curfew laws reduce the victimization of juveniles. Many children are abused and victimized in their own homes. Juvenile curfew laws may in fact increase victimization of some children, faced with the choice of being home during a parent's abusive rage or alcoholic haze, or being on the street and

---

131. *Id.*
132. *Id.* at 8.
133. *See infra* Part III.C.
134. *See* Hemmens & Bennett, *supra* note 2, at 269 ("While it is unclear whether juvenile curfews are effective in reducing crime, it is clear that they are being readily embraced by communities across the country.") (citations omitted).
135. Privor, *supra* note 1, at 467.
136. *Id.* at 467-68.
137. *Id.*
138. Schiraldi, *supra* note 128.

subject to a possible curfew violation and the resulting legal and personal consequences. Finally, the policy goal of increasing parental authority is not one a statistical study can quantify. The debate continues as to whether juvenile curfews in fact increase or decrease parental authority in the eyes of children since children may perceive that parents are no longer able to make basic child-rearing decisions. In effect, curfew laws conclusively achieve none of the express policy goals put forth in support of their enactment. Therefore, one may query whether a more insidious implicit discriminatory policy drives the enactment of these laws.

B. Discrimination in Drafting

Although appearing neutral on its face, a curfew law may, in fact, be drafted to have a discriminatory effect on a particular group of children. For example, a curfew law disproportionately affects minority youths whose cultural traditions leave them more susceptible to the effects of the facially neutral law. Implicit restrictions on black leisure have long existed in American law.[139] Thus, although the curfew implies that it will affect all children equally, certain cultural customs such as gathering at later hours may force some children to choose between violating the curfew or violating their own cultural norms.[140]

The curfew laws also have a discriminatory effect on children from lower socio-economic backgrounds. Children in large cities with curfews disproportionately tend to be minorities.[141] Furthermore, disallowing poor children to leave the home may itself be more restrictive than disallowing wealthier children from so doing, for wealthier children may have backyards, porches, or basements.[142] The Washington, D.C. curfew may have attempted to alleviate this problem in some way by creating a curfew exception if the juvenile is on the

139. *See, e.g.*, Regina Austin, *"Not Just for the Fun of It!": Governmental Restraints on Black Leisure, Social Inequality, and the Privatization of Public Space*, 71 S. CAL. L. REV. 667, 676-78 (1998) (discussing facially neutral laws, including curfews, with discriminatory impacts).

140. *See id.*

141. *See, e.g.*, Jessie McKinnon & Karen Humes, U.S. CENSUS BUR., THE BLACK POPULATION IN THE UNITED STATES 2 (1999) (finding that majority of blacks live in central cities of metropolitan areas), *available at* http://www.census.gov/prod/2000pubs/p20_530.pdf.

142. *See* Austin, *supra* note 139, at 678.

sidewalk in front of his or her home.[143] However, this is allowed only so long as neighbors do not complain.[144]

Curfew laws also disproportionately affect poorer juveniles because those juveniles may be more likely to have part-time jobs. Although many curfew laws create an exception for juveniles traveling to or from work, this still disproportionately affects working children. For example, if a police officer observes a person who appears to be in violation of the curfew ordinance, the officer has the right to question that suspect and determine whether he or she is affected by the curfew law. If the curfew law affects the suspect, the officer must then determine whether that child should be punished for a violation or whether he or she falls under one of the law's exceptions. In the case of the juvenile coming home from work at night, that juvenile bears the burden of explaining to a police officer why he or she is on the street and bears the risk that the police officer may not believe him or her. It is important to note that the more exceptions a juvenile curfew contains, the more discretion police officers may exercise.[145]

C. *Discrimination in Enforcement*

The politics behind the imposition of a curfew may enjoy popular support, but practical enforcement issues are often sorted out only after a curfew law has been enacted. Depending on the size of a city, universal enforcement of a juvenile curfew law may not be economically feasible. Therefore, large cities utilize three main techniques to enforce curfews: (1) regular enforcement (officers enforce curfew laws as any other law); (2) regular enforcement augmented by crackdowns by special curfew units; or (3) saturation.[146] Saturation is generally used in response to public outrage over increased violence, or used to increase police regulation for brief periods (such as the summer months).[147] Enforcement itself may lead to discriminatory effects, as distrust between members of different racial, ethnic, religious, and economic backgrounds often exists in the United States. This burden of distrust may fall on juveniles.

143. D.C. CODE ANN. § 6-2183(b)(1)(F) (2000).

144. *Id.*; *see also* Hutchins v. Dist. of Columbia, 188 F.3d 531, 547 (holding that neighbors' right terminate sidewalk privilege does not unconstitutional impair juvenile's rights).

145. Trollinger, *supra* note 2, at 1001 ("Vague language and inadequate standards vest in law enforcement officers unconfined discretion, unconstitutionally authorizing discriminatory and selective enforcement.").

146. Ruefle & Reynolds, *supra* note 8, at 352.

147. *Id.*

1. Racial Profiling

The realities of racial profiling were for years ignored, but recently such profiling, or the crime of "DWB" ("Driving While Black") has gained national attention both in the popular press and in scholarly work.[148] It is now widely conceded that black and Latino motorists are stopped at a much higher rate than their white counterparts.[149] For example, New Jersey's own internal audits showed that during a three year period, eighty-four percent of people arrested on the New Jersey Turnpike were members of minority groups.[150] The practice of racial profiling may similarly affect minority youths in the area of juvenile curfews.

With the prevalence of curfew laws, police officers have a legitimate pretext for stopping young drivers who appear to be black or Latino. Just as minority drivers are generally stopped disproportionately, minority juveniles may be stopped more frequently in a legitimate effort to enforce curfew laws or under that pretext. One may wonder what difference this makes, since all the juvenile must do is convince the police officer that he or she is not violating the curfew. However, all youths should bear the brunt of the curfew laws equally. Indeed, making certain children more frequent targets of the law will increase the levels of distrust of the criminal justice system and broaden the divide between white and minority children's experiences and consciousness.[151] Furthermore, some cities have raised the stakes. For example, with the express intent of reducing gang activity, one Illinois town passed a law allowing police officers to seize the car of any teenager out past curfew.[152]

Controlling gang activity is, of course, a valid public goal. However, the act of targeting gangs itself is replete with racial connotations. If the curfew is explicitly aimed at gangs dominated by minority youths from inner cities, the law may not be enforced in neighborhoods where gang activity is not present. Additionally, the

148. *See, e.g.*, David A. Harris, *The Stories, the Statistics, and the Law: Why "Driving While Black" Matters*, 84 MINN. L. REV. 265, 269 & n.17 (1999) (citing polls that show that majority of whites believe that blacks suffer from police racism).

149. *Id.* at 266-67 (using examples from Ohio to show that "Driving While Black" is not urban phenomenon).

150. *See* David Barstow & David Kocieniewski, *Records Show New Jersey Police Withheld Data on Race Profiling*, N.Y. TIMES, Oct. 12, 2000, at A1; *see also* Harris, *supra* note 148, at 267 ("Sophisticated analyses of stops and driving populations in [New Jersey and Maryland] showed racial disparities in traffic stops that were 'literally off the charts.'") (citation omitted).

151. *See* Harris, *supra* note 148, at 269-70 (describing pretextual traffic stops as phenomenon "common to blacks, but almost invisible to whites").

152. *Crime Prevention: Lights Out*, ECONOMIST, Sept. 18, 1999, at 30.

police may only stop children who fit race-based profiles of gang members.[153] It may appear that the curfew applies to all youths. However, when a curfew specifically targets a segment of the population traditionally made up of minority youths, other juveniles rarely share the burden of the law.

2. *Hot Spots*

In an effort to enforce juvenile curfew legislation, municipalities may target specific enforcement areas. In such situations, the curfew law has often been enforced infrequently or not at all, and suddenly an *ad hoc* enforcement team begins to enforce the curfew in a particular neighborhood.[154] Such a development usually occurs in response to a sudden increase in crime or community complaints, or to control a statistically high crime neighborhood, or "hot spot."[155]

Often, however, other unstated motives are at play. In *Ashton v. Brown*, a race-based curfew enforcement case presented in a Maryland state court, a nineteen-year-old and a sixteen-year-old sued the city of Frederick, challenging the constitutionality of the city's curfew and seeking damages for their detention.[156] The Frederick curfew applied to youths under eighteen who were out "during the nighttime hours."[157] The court record revealed that the enforcement of the curfew was generally limited to occasional arrests by individual officers,[158] but that police instituted a curfew crackdown aimed at "the Rainbow," a local club that attracted a predominantly black clientele.[159] The city contended that the crackdown was aimed at all four establishments on a particular block. However, the police concentrated their efforts on the Rainbow and detained no minors from any other establishment. In the end, all twenty-eight people detained were black.[160]

The *Ashton* plaintiffs claimed that white teenagers had never been "rounded up in such a manner" although they also congregated

153. *See, e.g.*, Note, *Juvenile Curfews and Gang Violence: Exiled on Main Street*, 107 HARV. L. REV. 1693, 1698 (1994) ("[Y]oung Hispanic males who match police profiles of gang members [ ] suffer frequent police stops and questioning.").
154. *See* Ruefle & Reynolds, *supra* note 8, at 352, 359.
155. For example, Denver, Phoenix, and Orlando have curfews that are restricted to hot-spots. *Id.* at 352. These target area curfews survived court challenges. *Id.*
156. Ashton v. Brown, 660 A.2d 447, 452-53 (Md. 1995).
157. *Id.* at 452.
158. *Id.* at 453 n.6.
159. *Id.* at 452.
160. *Id.* at 453. *But see id.* at 453 n.4 (noting police claimed that only twenty-five of twenty-eight arrestees were African-American).

past curfew hours.[161] The police chief admitted that the only other similar curfew crackdown had taken place in the mid-1980s and had also targeted an establishment predominantly frequented by blacks.[162] The plaintiffs argued that even if the curfew ordinance might be considered valid, the actions of the police constituted "a *de facto* policy" of subjecting black people to disparate treatment.[163] While the high court of Maryland struck the ordinance for being unconstitutionally vague, it noted that a lower court can avoid addressing the plaintiffs' claims of racial discrimination, although raised in the briefs and clearly a factor in the motivation of the police.[164]

The failure of the courts generally to address racial discrimination claims in this context demonstrates a nationwide reluctance to speak about race.[165] The fact that the police can target a minority group for curfew enforcement, and then refuse to address the racial issues inherent in the case, reflects the nation's tendency to ignore racial issues.

3. *Fourth Amendment*

The description of the detention of the plaintiffs in *Ashton* reflects the larger implications of juvenile curfew laws. The nineteen-year-old plaintiff, Vanessa Brown, should not have been affected by the curfew ordinance, which applied to individuals younger than eighteen.[166] However, as she was walking on a public street in the direction of the Rainbow, Brown was photographed, handcuffed, and searched, including being subjected to a "pat-down" of her entire body.[167] The police detained her for forty minutes on a police bus stationed outside of the Rainbow.[168] The lower courts held that the police had probable cause to arrest Brown, and, therefore, that any search or seizure incident to arrest was lawful.[169] The Maryland Court

161. *Id.* at 453.
162. *Id.* at 453 n.6.
163. *Id.* at 454.
164. *Id.* at 455.
165. *See supra* notes 67-72 and accompanying text.
166. Also illustrated by *Ashton* is the fact that not only minors, but also youthful-looking adults may be subject to police detention under the pretext of curfew laws. A person may be stopped if police have a reasonable suspicion that a person falls under the curfew law. Thus, police enforcing a juvenile curfew law have the authority to stop any adult who may be mistaken for a teenager. It is likely that the burdens of these laws will be disproportionately felt by minorities, even those whose age excludes them from the law. *See supra* Part III.C.1.
167. *Ashton*, 660 A.2d at 453.
168. *Id.*
169. *Id.* at 460.

of Appeals held, however, that even if the arrest was proper under the Fourth Amendment for probable cause, the arrest violated Brown's due process rights because the arrest was based on an unconstitutional ordinance.[170]

Ashton illustrates several additional problems that arise from the enactment of curfew laws. First, curfew laws may weaken the Fourth Amendment rights of juveniles. Maryland's supreme court refused to address this problem because the curfew was held to be unconstitutional under the Fourteenth Amendment. However, when a curfew ordinance is valid and police frisk or search a juvenile stopped for a potential curfew violation, that search may constitute a valid exercise of police power or an unconstitutional violation of the juvenile's Fourth Amendment rights. The courts are split on this issue,[171] as the Supreme Court has provided no guidance on the Fourth Amendment in the context of juvenile curfews. However, several federal district courts have upheld curfews in the face of Fourth Amendment challenges, holding that the Fourth Amendment right to be free from unreasonable search and seizure is properly limited by the governmental power to criminalize certain forms of behavior.[172]

If a curfew allows for the arrest of a juvenile as opposed to merely requiring an escort home, police will more likely be able to perform a search incident to arrest.[173] However, until the arrest or in cases in which the arrest is not authorized, the police must adhere to the same Fourth Amendment requirements that apply to adults:[174] no detention without reasonable suspicion of criminal activity, and no frisks unless a reasonable fear of imminent danger exists.[175] Curfew laws, however, allow police to eliminate the required reasonable suspicion of criminal activity by simply criminalizing the act of being outside the home. This establishes a pretext for police to detain and

170. *Id.* at 461.

171. *Compare* Schleifer v. City of Charlottesville, 963 F. Supp. 534, 551 (W.D. Va. 1997); Waters v. Barry, 711 F. Supp. 1125, 1138 (D.D.C. 1989); *with* L.A.F. v. State, 698 N.E.2d 355, 355-56 (Ind. Ct. App. 1998).

172. *See* Peckman v. City of Wichita, No. 00-1065-JTM, 2000 WL 1294422, at *4 (D. Kan. Aug. 15, 2000) (holding that policy of taking curfew violators into custody does not violate Fourth Amendment); *see also* Waters v. Barry, 711 F. Supp. 1125, 1137-38 (D. D.C. 1989).

173. See, for example, the arrest of Vanessa Brown in *Ashton*. *See supra* notes 167-70 and accompanying text.

174. *See, e.g.*, *In re* People, 506 P.2d 409, 411 (Colo. App. 1973).

175. *See, e.g.*, L.A.F. v. State, 698 N.E.2d 355, 355-56 (Ind. Ct. App. 1998) (holding search of minor detained for curfew violation violated Fourth Amendment because no evidence of reasonable belief that minor was armed and dangerous was presented).

search youth.[176] Again, this may result in discriminatory effects because enforcement officers disproportionately stop minority youths.[177]

The effects of curfews therefore include increased searches and seizures of minority youths and their property. An abrogation of the Fourth Amendment rights of the many juveniles affected by curfew laws may result. Courts have held that some searches incident to curfew violations' arrests are unreasonable. For example, in *In re People*, the Colorado Court of Appeals held that although the curfew violation was itself valid, the search was invalid because of its exploratory nature.[178] Furthermore, the search did not constitute a valid inventory search because the juvenile was not to be incarcerated; he was merely being detained until his parents picked him up.[179] However, other courts may find differently.

Curfew ordinances themselves generate the most juvenile arrests in the United States, more than all violent juvenile crimes combined.[180] With over 140,000 curfew arrests in 1996, up 116% from 1994,[181] such ordinances obviously affect a large number of families. When considering the possibility that any number of these children will be frisked, society must question whether a status crime justifies such invasions and whether curfews really meet the express policy goals.

CONCLUSION

As this note has indicated, the express policy goals of juvenile curfew laws enacted throughout the United States have not been consistently achieved. Furthermore, the documented existence of discrimination in the criminal justice system means that curfew laws are likely to disparately affect minority juveniles, as well as juveniles of lower socio-economic classes. Therefore, while the benefits of curfew

176. While frisks are generally reserved for those situations in which a police officer believes he or she is in imminent danger, some statutes authorize frisks of curfew violators. *See, e.g.*, N.C. GEN. STAT. § 14-288.10(b) (2000).

177. *See supra* Part III.C.; *see also* Benjamin Weiser, *U.S. Detects Bias in Police Searches: Prosecutors and Mayor's Office in Talks on Racial Profiling*, N.Y. TIMES, Oct. 5, 2000, at A1 (noting that analysis of New York City street searches found pattern of racial profiling).

178. *See In re People*, 506 P.2d at 412.

179. *See id.*

180. Jason Ziedenberg, *Curfew Violation—A Useless Statutory Crime*, WASH. POST, Sept. 15, 1999, at A24. Ziedenberg is a policy analyst at the Justice Policy Institute in Washington, D.C.

181. *See Youth Curfews Fizzle Under Microscope: First Comprehensive Study of Juvenile Curfews Finds No Reduction in Youth Crime*, JUSTICE POLICY INSTITUTE, *at* http://www.cjcj.org/jpi/curfewpr.html (last visited Nov. 14, 2000).

laws remain in dispute, their ill effects for particular segments of society are a virtual certainty.

Discriminatory enforcement is not unique to curfews, and legislatures have yet to find a meaningful solution to this problem in the criminal justice system. Legislative caution must be exercised in the area of juvenile curfews because a disenfranchised segment of the population is the target of these laws. The disparities in law enforcement require that legislators make critical assessments of their stated reasons for enacting curfew legislation in order to ascertain whether the stated goals are in fact the true basis for these laws. This proposition is a difficult one because legislators may be apprehensive of a potential backlash if they express doubt as to the efficacy of curfews.

In order to consider these issues fully, legislators must first critique their own motives. They must ask themselves tough questions, the answers to which they may fear. In the modern politically correct era, legislators may feel stifled and unable to have a truly free discussion about the racial, ethnic, and class differences that factor into the enactment of curfews for fear that a comment may be taken out of context, or used against the legislator in a political campaign. However, legislators must begin to discuss these issues because they inevitably bear responsibility for the negative effects of the curfew laws they enact.

The distinct possibility that the unfortunate practice of racial profiling will affect juveniles in the context of curfew laws, combined with the oppressive history of the use of curfews, creates a responsibility on the part of legislatures to be particularly critical of curfew legislation. Responsibility does not mean, however, that curfew laws should not be enacted. Rather, legislators must consider carefully the potential discriminatory, detrimental effects of a curfew law prior to its enactment. This may be accomplished in a variety of ways. Rather than looking only to statistics, legislatures could seek out feedback from those constituents most likely to bear the brunt of the proposed curfew in order to get a sense of the relationship between those citizens and the police.

Given the tremendous number of children and families swept up in the criminal justice system through juvenile curfew laws, consideration must also be given to the history of curfew laws. Curfew laws have traditionally been used to establish social control over and to oppress particular groups with limited political power. This history must be examined as a possible indicator of the policies driving the current vogue of juvenile curfew laws in the United States.

If proponents of curfew laws truly desire to meet their stated policy objectives, legislatures and communities should implement programs that have been proven to correlate with a drop in juvenile crime. The decision to criminalize behavior through curfews rather than to create proactive solutions to nocturnal juvenile activity, such as supervised recreation or employment, contributes to the perceived need for curfew laws. In passing curfew laws, legislatures create an offense which, being responsible for the most juvenile convictions in the nation, increases statistics indicating rising juvenile crime. As juvenile crime rate statistics increase, so does the public perception of the need for juvenile curfew laws.

Until researchers conduct more studies and legislators further discuss both the questionable efficacy and the possible discriminatory effects of curfew laws, popular support for curfews is likely to continue. The prevalence of curfew laws in the United States, which shows no sign of declining, manifests an unflagging desire to meet the express policy goals of decreasing juvenile crime, decreasing juvenile victimization, and increasing parental support. However, legislators owe a duty to juveniles and parents alike to ensure that the proclaimed benefits of curfew laws are supported by factual evidence. Without proof of the efficacy of curfews, legislators, academics, and the general public must look beyond the express policy goals and be cognizant and critical of the implicit policies and potential discriminatory effects of modern juvenile curfew laws.

Go to the Mall with My Parents?? A Constitutional Analysis of the Mall of America's Juvenile Curfew*

I. Introduction

The Mall of America (the "Mall"), located in Bloomington, Minnesota, could only exist in the United States. With 4.2 million square feet of gross building area,[1] it is the largest retail and entertainment center in the country.[2] Since its opening on August 11, 1992, the Mall has become a tremendous tourist magnet for Americans and foreign visitors alike.[3] The Mall is a living, breathing monument to American consumerism and to the collective fulfilled desire for a shopping experience that is as convenient, all-encompassing, and as efficient as possible. Convenient is certainly the operative word as the Mall contains infant care facilities, a high school, a college, a United States Post Office, a

---

* Author's note: Shortly before this comment was published, a decision from the Minnesota Court of Appeals, adverse to the central thesis of this comment, was handed down. *See* Minnesota v. Wicklund, No. C7-97-1381, 1998 WL 156240 (Minn. Ct. App. Apr. 7, 1998). The court of appeals, reversing the trial court, held that the free speech provision of article I, section 3 of the Minnesota Constitution does not apply to the Mall of America. Nevertheless, this comment argues for an expansion of the state's protections of individual liberties under article I, section 16 of the Minnesota Constitution.

1. *See* PUBLIC RELATIONS DEP'T, MALL OF AMERICA, AT A GLANCE (1996) [hereinafter AT A GLANCE]. Unless otherwise stated, all of the Mall's promotional materials, as well as two 1996 press releases, are based on promotional material provided by the Mall of America. The promotional material consisted of nine glossy 8 ½ x 11" sheets that detailed the Mall's variety of offerings (i.e. "Tourism" and "Restaurants & Nightclubs"); three brochures: "Map and Directory," "Dining and Entertainment Guide," and "The Place for Fun in Your Life;" and two press releases dated September 4, 1996 and October 8, 1996. The information packet was requested in early October 1996 and was received on October 11, 1996. An updated information package was received on October 20, 1997, and references to the 1997 information are noted herein.

2. *See* PUBLIC RELATIONS DEP'T, MALL OF AMERICA, DESTINATION PLANNING GUIDE, 1997-1998, 2 (1997) [hereinafter DESTINATION PLANNING GUIDE].

3. Over 190 million people have been to the Mall since its opening. *See* AT A GLANCE, *supra* note 1. Visitors from outside a 150 mile radius account for greater than 30% of the Mall's visitors. *See id.* International visitors account for 6%. *See* PUBLIC RELATIONS DEP'T, MALL OF AMERICA, TOURISM (1996) [hereinafter TOURISM]; AT A GLANCE, *supra* note 1.

bank, a hotel, a dental clinic, and a myriad of other non-shopping services.[4] Not only do the 520 shopping stores[5] under one roof provide for an efficient one-stop shopping experience, but the Mall has other types of attractions—including entertainment and dining—for practically every taste.[6]

Not surprisingly, teenagers frequent the Mall of America. Like their counterparts around the country, Minnesota teens regularly go to the Mall on weekend evenings. Estimates hold that between two and three thousand teenagers frequent the Mall of America on both Friday and Saturday evenings.[7] Many, if not most, go to the Mall because there is little else to do in the community on weekend evenings and because the Mall is a good place to see and be seen.[8] Due to its size, the Mall is thus faced with a proportionately larger group of teen visitors than are other malls across the nation.

Mall of America management initiated a number of creative solutions to handle teen conduct-related issues.[9] However, after

---

4. *See* PUBLIC RELATIONS DEP'T, MALL OF AMERICA, MAP AND DIRECTORY (1996) [hereinafter MAP AND DIRECTORY]; DESTINATION PLANNING GUIDE, *supra* note 2. For a detailed discussion of the services the Mall offers its visitors, see *infra* text accompanying notes 107-13.

5. *See* AT A GLANCE, *supra* note 1.

6. Youth entertainment includes Knott's Camp Snoopy, LEGO Imagination Center, and StarBase Omega. *See* PUBLIC RELATIONS DEP'T, MALL OF AMERICA, FAMILY FUN (1996) [hereinafter FAMILY FUN]. For further information on these amusements, as well as adult and family-oriented attractions, see *infra* text accompanying notes 97, 115-19.

7. *See* Robyn Meredith, *Big Mall's Curfew Raises Questions of Rights and Bias*, N.Y. TIMES, Sept. 4, 1996, at A1.

The importance of teen spending in United States commerce is evidenced by the fact that teenage spending in the United States is estimated at over $100 billion. *See* Leyla Kokmen, *Hang Time—Mall of America Withdraws Welcome Mat to Teens Who Gather on Weekends*, CHI. TRIB., Sept. 15, 1996 (citing a study conducted by Teenage Research Unlimited). *See also* Chuck Haga, *Minnesota Megamall's Effort to Subdue Teen Rowdiness Raises Issues of Fairness and Racial Bias*, THE CHRISTIAN SCI. MONITOR, Oct. 9, 1996.

8. *See* Meredith, *supra* note 7, at B9.

9. The Mall instituted a Youth Liaison Program in January 1995. *See* Public Relations Dep't, Mall of America, Press Release (Sept. 4, 1996) [hereinafter September Press Release]. In this program, security officers work with teens both inside and outside the Mall. *See id.* The officers are casually dressed when they visit schools to discuss appropriate behavior at the Mall. *See id.* They also volunteer at youth community organizations. *See id.* In April 1996, the Mall instituted the Mighty Moms Program. *See id.* It consists of twenty women who work with security officers in handling conflicts between disruptive teenagers and Mall security. *See* Neal Karlen, *Tapping 'Mom Power' to Police a Huge Mall*, N.Y. TIMES, Dec. 19, 1996, at C2. The Mighty Moms are able to diffuse tense situations and are highly effective at combating ugly confrontations between mall security and teens. *See id.* The Mall has also hired ten Dedicated Dads to serve the same function. For a further discussion of

a small eruption of gun violence in which teens were both the perpetrators and the victims,[10] Mall management initiated more drastic measures. Thus, on October 4, 1996, the privately-owned Mall[11] instituted a juvenile curfew termed a Parental Escort Policy; the goal of this policy was to reduce the number of unaccompanied teenagers at the Mall on weekend nights.[12] Under the policy, guards are posted at the Mall's twenty-three entrances and deny access after 6 p.m. on Friday and Saturday nights to anyone who is under the age of sixteen and not in the company of an adult twenty-one years of age or older.[13] The adult must exercise control over the teens in his or her care.[14] Mall security has the discretion to decide whether the group of teens is too large to be controlled by its escort.[15] The Mall's management states that it instituted the curfew as a preventative measure in order to

---

these Mall programs, see *infra* text accompanying notes 176-78.

10. In June 1996, Nancy A. Bordeaux and her family were visiting the Mall when a teenager pointed his gun at her sixteen year old son Felix. *See* Meredith, *supra* note 7, at B9. The gun-toting youth mistakenly thought Felix was a member of a rival group that he was chasing through the Mall. *See id.*

A widely reported incident occurred in 1993 in the Camp Snoopy Amusement Park. One group of male teenagers approached another group and demanded that a thirteen year old boy in the second group give them his jacket. *See* Bob Greene, *What to Do When Trouble Shows Up? Easy, Call Mom,* CHI. TRIB., May 7, 1996. There was a gunfight and three of the teenagers were shot. *See id.* These are the two most widely news reported incidences of gun violence.

11. The owners of the Mall are Triple Five Corp., Melvin Simon & Assoc., and the Teacher's Insurance & Annuity Ass'n. *See* AT A GLANCE, *supra* note 1.

12. *See* September Press Release, *supra* note 9. "Mall of America will implement a Parental Escort Policy effective October 4, 1996, to reduce the growing number of unsupervised youth at the Mall on weekend nights." *Id.*

13. *See id.* Mall security will also conduct sweeps throughout the Mall between 6 p.m. and closing to ask for identification from teenagers who entered the Mall prior to 6 p.m. *See id.*

14. One adult may escort up to 10 children ages 15 and younger. *See* DESTINATION PLANNING GUIDE, *supra* note 2.

When teenagers throughout the country were surveyed by various newspapers regarding their thoughts on the Mall's juvenile curfew, the overwhelming majority felt that the curfew was unfair and too restrictive. One Minnesota teen's response to the Parental Escort Policy was succinct: "[I]t would stink. If you came here with your mom, you'd have to go to Linens 'N Things. And you wouldn't have any independence." Sally Apgar, *Escort Policy for Youths Considered by Megamall,* MINNEAPOLIS-ST. PAUL STAR-TRIB., June 20, 1996. Added another teen, "[T]his is where we go to get away from our parents." *Id.*

"Teen-age shoppers who were interviewed recently said they would not be caught dead with their parents at the Mall of America, the biggest mall in the country and the coolest spot in town." Meredith, *supra* note 7, at A1.

15. *See* September Press Release, *supra* note 9.

avoid future teen violence.[16] Mall management was further concerned for the safety of innocent bystanders, as it desires to maintain a safe atmosphere for all who patronize the Mall.[17]

The effect of the policy has been to drastically curtail teenagers' right of assembly on Mall premises. Thus, the curfew raises many constitutional issues that are not easily answered.[18] This comment mainly addresses the issue of whether the privately owned Mall of America is so accessible to the public as to be deemed a public space for state action purposes. If so, the next inquiry must be whether state and federal constitutional rights should be granted at the Mall and, if so, to what extent. The issue is an interesting one because both sides have strong constitutional and emotional arguments and because a teen assembly right on mall property is a relatively new concept.[19] Between Mall management's right to control its property and the teenagers' right to assemble at the Mall lies a delicate balance. This comment

16. Mall visitors and store owners have lodged complaints regarding the "gangs" of teenagers who stand in large groups in certain areas of the Mall on weekend evenings. However, according to Mall Spokeswoman Teresa McFarland, the main reason the curfew was instituted was to combat violence and promote a safe atmosphere. *See* Telephone Interview with Teresa McFarland, Spokeswoman for the Mall of America (Oct. 31, 1996) [hereinafter McFarland Interview].

17. *See id.*

18. Other issues of significance which can only be tangentially covered by this comment include: 1) whether the Mall has a *right to exclude* such a broad class of people; and 2) whether by doing so the Mall is effectively discriminating against the disproportionately large number of minority teens who go to the Mall on weekend evenings. *See infra* note 279. *See generally* Apgar, *supra* note 14.

19. While the Mall of America's juvenile curfew received national news coverage, it was based on two lesser-known pre-existing curfews. *See id.* One was the curfew at the Asheville Mall in Asheville, North Carolina, enacted in 1993. *See id.* The Asheville curfew affects teenagers younger than 16 who are at the mall from 6-9 p.m. on Saturday evenings. *See id.* According to a spokeswoman for the mall, the curfew was imposed due to "an alarming trend of violent, aggressive, disturbing, lewd behavior that was getting worse. And we didn't want to get a reputation as a bad place to come on a Saturday night." *Id.* (quoting Mary Evans). In February 1994, the Patrick Henry Mall in Newport News, Virginia, became the second mall to impose such a curfew after teenagers were found with guns and clubs. *See id.* The curfew proved highly effective with incidents reportedly dropping by 80%. The types of incidents were not elaborated upon. *See id. See also* Lauren Beckham, *Teen Rap Shopping for a Hangout—Malls Consider Evening Curfews to Curtail Crime,* BOSTON HERALD, Oct. 14, 1996; The Associated Press, *Weekend Curfew at Mall of America Protested by Some,* SAN DIEGO UNION-TRIB., Oct. 6, 1996.

The Newport News curfew was retracted after it achieved its purpose. *See* McFarland Interview, *supra* note 16. The Asheville curfew, while similarly effective, has not been retracted. *See id.* Ms. McFarland stated that she regards the Mall of America curfew as akin to the Asheville curfew, therefore establishing the Parental Escort Policy as permanent Mall policy. *See id.*

analyzes one set of factors at work in that balance, and, while it respects the Mall owners' rights, it leans in favor of a constitutional right for teenagers to assemble at the Mall.

Thus, this comment challenges the constitutionality of the Mall of America's Parental Escort Policy although no cause of action has yet been filed against the Mall regarding the implementation of this curfew. Indeed, the Minnesota chapter of the ACLU has stated that it will not challenge the curfew because Minnesota constitutional law is not favorable to its cause of action.[20] However, the Minnesota Supreme Court has not yet decided upon the application of First Amendment[21] principles to privately-owned shopping malls. Based upon an examination of Minnesota statutory and case law, there is a strong argument to be made for the unconstitutionality of this curfew under existing Minnesota law.[22] This comment argues that while the Mall of America has a recognized interest in promoting safety on its premises, the breadth of its curfew constitutes a taking of the teenagers' freedom of assembly rights. Before the Mall implemented the Parental Escort Policy, a number of other alternatives already existed that would have made the Mall a safer environment without infringing on any one group's rights.[23] An in-depth analysis of Minnesota individual liberties protections provides strong authority for supporting teenager assembly rights at the Mall.

Beginning in 1968 with *Amalgamated Food Employees Union v. Logan Valley Plaza, Inc.*,[24] the United States Supreme Court

20. *See* Meredith, *supra* note 7, at B9. Kathleen Milner, legal counsel for the Minnesota Civil Liberties Union, stated that "Minnesota does not apply First Amendment principles to shopping malls." *Id.*

However, other ACLU attorneys take a more activist approach to challenge the curfew. Chris Hansen, a senior staff counsel at the Manhattan ACLU, stated that the curfew "infringes on the rights of young people .... We don't object to the mall setting up rules of behavior, but we do object ... to punishing the good kids for the behavior of kids that aren't behaving." Meredith, *supra* note 7, at B9. Similarly, John Roberts, executive director of the Massachusetts chapter of the ACLU, has stated that "[m]alls are private property .... But in the instance of the Mall of America, I think it is a punishment of the innocent based on the fact that some kids act up and act out. It just seems like one of these overkill measures that sweeps way too broadly." Beckham, *supra* note 19.

21. U.S. CONST. amend. I. The text of the amendment states that "Congress shall make no law respecting an establishment of religion, or prohibiting the free exercise thereof; or abridging the freedom of speech, or of the press; or the right of the people peaceably to assemble, and to petition the Government for a redress of grievances." *Id.*

22. *See* discussion *infra* Part IV.

23. *See* discussion *infra* Part V.

24. 391 U.S. 308 (1968).

has resolved four First Amendment challenges against finding any federal constitutional right to free speech in the settings of privately-owned shopping centers or malls.[25] In addition to the United States Supreme Court, numerous state courts have considered the issue of First Amendment free speech rights with regard to petitioning and leafleting at privately-owned shopping centers.[26] However, the right of a shopping center to exclude a certain class based solely on age is an issue of first impression. Malls across the country are watching to see if the Mall of America's curfew succeeds, and, if it does, they may institute their own juvenile curfews.[27] Were the Mall's curfew successfully challenged, the outcome could have an impact on malls throughout the United States.

This comment presents one framework for analyzing the constitutionality of a private shopping mall curfew while simultaneously applying this analysis to the Mall of America's curfew. Depending on factors unique to each situation, the emphasis on the issues will vary. Part II examines the application of First Amendment free speech principles in private shopping centers in order to: 1) establish the backdrop for the proposed challenge; and 2) draw a correlation between free speech rights and assembly rights on private property. A line of United States Supreme Court cases that have addressed the issue of First Amendment free speech rights in private shopping centers will thus be analyzed in order to determine the Court's stance on the application of such protections in private shopping malls. The most recent in this line of cases is *PruneYard Shopping Center v. Robins*[28] which held that state constitutions may afford individuals First Amendment type-rights in privately-owned shopping centers so long as the restrictions do not constitute a taking or otherwise violate the Federal Constitu-

25. *See* PruneYard Shopping Ctr. v. Robins, 447 U.S. 74 (1980); Hudgens v. NLRB, 424 U.S. 507 (1976); Lloyd Corp. v. Tanner, 407 U.S. 551 (1972); Amalgamated Food Employees Union, 391 U.S. at 308.

26. *See* discussion *infra* notes 84-86 (regarding state court decisions).

27. *See, e.g.*, Karl Vick, *Area Malls Watching Curfew and Wondering What's in Store for Them*, WASH. POST, Sept. 18, 1996, at A13; Lisa Peterson, *Malls in Jersey in No Hurry to Chase Teens—Minnesota Curfew Draws Their Interest*, NEWARK STAR-LEDGER, Oct.9, 1996; *Curfew Begins at Mall of America*, WIS. STATE J., Oct. 5, 1996; Chet Fuller, *Curfew Targets Teenagers at Minnesota Mall*, ATLANTA J. & CONST., Oct. 21, 1996; Meredith, *supra* note 7, at A1.

28. 447 U.S. at 81.

tion.[29] *PruneYard* held that First Amendment rights in private shopping centers may be enlarged under state constitutions.[30] It did not limit those rights to the freedom of speech.[31] Because *PruneYard* applied to all First Amendment individual liberties, it must, therefore, include the right of assembly.

Post-*PruneYard* state court decisions concerning free speech rights at shopping malls turn on the outcome of four questions: 1) Is the nature of the mall such that in essence it is a public space?; 2) What does the respective state constitution provide in the manner of First Amendment type-rights?; 3) How have those state provisions been interpreted?; and 4) How should they be interpreted in the immediate context?[32] Thus, Part III answers the first question by taking a detailed look at the Mall of America itself. After an examination of the Mall's establishments and its self-promotion, it will be argued that the privately-owned Mall serves as the new Bloomington downtown and is in all respects except for ownership a public space. Analogous decisions in state courts have created free speech rights at shopping centers based on findings that many larger malls have come to resemble, or in fact usurp, the role of the traditional downtown area.[33] Based upon this determination, courts have declared these private centers or malls to be so essentially public in nature as to require the protection of certain individual liberties on their premises. Therefore, courts have held that private mall owners' rights to prohibit certain speech must fall to the invitees' First Amendment rights, although reasonable restrictions on the place and timing of the speech are permitted.[34]

Part IV examines the Minnesota Constitution and its interpretation by the Minnesota Supreme Court with regard to its protection of individual liberties. While the Minnesota Supreme Court has never decided an individual liberty challenge in the context of a shopping mall, it has consistently read the state constitution broadly to provide for the protection of individual liberties not enumerated

29. *See id.*

30. *See id.*

31. "[N]either appellants' federally recognized property rights nor their First Amendment rights have been infringed by the California Supreme Court's decision recognizing a right of appellees to exercise state-protected rights of expression . . . ." *Id.* at 88.

32. *See infra* text accompanying notes 84-86.

33. *See* discussion *infra* notes 148-61.

34. *See id. See also* discussion *infra* notes 84, 86.

therein.[35] Minnesota's Human Rights Act[36] is another source to be examined in its application to this cause of action.

Part V argues that the curfew's breadth removes it from the sphere of a reasonable regulation on private property, and other methods to address the Mall's safety concerns are proposed.

Finally, Part VI presents affirmative defenses that would likely be raised by the Mall of America in support of its Parental Escort Policy. These include the Mall's strong interest in promoting a safe environment and that dismantling the Parental Escort Policy would result in a taking of private property. The safety factor is a very strong argument in favor of the curfew. The Mall is responsible for the safety of all of its patrons, shopkeepers, and personnel. Nevertheless, the Mall can protect these persons by employing other protective devices (as discussed in Part V) rather than an across-the-board juvenile curfew. By implementing the juvenile curfew, the Mall crossed the line between a welfare and safety measure and a denial of access rights to a group it has made every effort into bring to its premises.

II. First Amendment Rights in Privately Owned Shopping Centers

In a number of cases concerning the right to distribute literature, petition, or solicit signatures on private property, the United States Supreme Court has firmly held that there is no *federal* constitutional protection of First Amendment[37] free speech rights on such property.[38] However, the route the Court has taken to arrive at the current standing has not been without its detours. A brief history of the five major cases[39] that have shaped this area of the law provides the background for an analysis of how the Mall of America's curfew fits into this historical continuum.

The line of cases starts with *Marsh v. Alabama*,[40] which was the first case to recognize free speech rights on private property.[41]

35. *See* discussion *infra* notes 202-60.

36. MINN. STAT. ANN., §§ 363.01-.20 (West 1991 & West Supp. 1998).

37. U.S. CONST. amend. I.

38. *See supra* note 25 and accompanying text.

39. *See* PruneYard Shopping Ctr, v. Robins, 447 U.S. 74 (1980); Hudgens v. NLRB, 424 U.S. 507 (1976); Lloyd Corp. v. Tanner, 407 U.S. 551 (1972); Amalgamated Food Employees Union v. Logan Valley Plaza, Inc., 391 U.S. 308 (1968); Marsh v. Alabama, 326 U.S. 501 (1946).

40. 326 U.S. at 501.

41. *See id.* at 512 (Reed, J., dissenting).

The private property in *Marsh* was Chickasaw, Alabama, a company town owned by the Gulf Shipbuilding Corporation having "all the characteristics of any other American town."[42] The homes, shops, streets, and even sewer systems were company owned.[43] Grace Marsh was convicted of criminal trespass[44] after she attempted to distribute religious literature on a downtown Chickasaw sidewalk.[45] When she appealed her criminal trespass conviction, the Court was asked to decide if her free speech rights took precedence over Gulf's property rights, and the Court held that they did.[46]

The Court's analysis was two-fold. First, the Court conducted a detailed fact-finding of the nature of the town.[47] Placing substance over form, the Court's aim was to discern whether the town was essentially private or public property, regardless of ownership.[48] Relying on the fact that the town's business district was accessible to any individual wishing to enter, the Court held Chickasaw to be essentially no different from any non-company-owned town.[49] The Court then balanced the private property interests of the Gulf Corporation with the First Amendment rights of those who entered Chickasaw. The Court found that the more the town invited, welcomed, and served as any other town, the more it lost its ability to prohibit constitutionally protected behavior.[50] Justice Black, writing for the majority, stated that

42. *Id.* at 502.

43. *See id.* at 502-03.

44. Ms. Marsh was arrested in violation of title 14, section 426 of the 1940 Alabama Code after she was warned that she could not distribute literature without a permit. *See id.* at 503-04. Furthermore, she was informed that she would be unable to obtain a permit. *See id.* at 503. When Ms. Marsh refused to leave the sidewalk, she was arrested under this code provision which "makes it a crime to enter or remain on the premises of another after having been warned not to do so." *Id.* at 504.

45. *See Marsh*, 326 U.S. at 503.

46. *See id.* at 508-09.

47. *See id.* at 502-03.

48. *See id.* at 504-09.

49. *See id.* at 503. The Court stated: "In short the town and its shopping district are accessible to and freely used by the public in general and there is nothing to distinguish them from any other town and shopping center except the fact that the title to the property belongs to a private corporation." *Id.*

50. *See Marsh*, 326 U.S. at 506. Similarly, the Mall of America is open to all who wish to enter. *See generally* PUBLIC RELATIONS DEP'T, MALL OF AMERICA, THE PLACE FOR FUN IN YOUR LIFE (1996) [hereinafter THE PLACE FOR FUN]. Shopping hours are from 10 a.m. to 9 p.m. Monday through Saturday, and 11 a.m. to 7 p.m. on Sunday. *See id.* Entertainment and summer hours are extended. *See id.* The Mall is closed two days of the year: Thanksgiving and Christmas Day. *See id.*

"[o]wnership does not always mean absolute dominion. The more an owner, for his advantage, opens up his property for use by the public in general, the more do his rights become circumscribed by the statutory and constitutional rights of those who use it."[51] When balancing a property owner's rights against those of the freedoms of press and religion, the latter occupies a "preferred position."[52] Thus, the First Amendment, as applied through the Fourteenth, was held to apply to Chickasaw and to permit Ms. Marsh to distribute religious literature in downtown Chickasaw.

Twenty-two years later, the Court again considered the issue of free speech rights on private property in *Amalgamated Food Employees Union v. Logan Valley Plaza, Inc.*[53] Here, for the first time, the Court was deciding a freedom of speech issue within the context of a shopping center. Logan Valley Mall prohibited as trespass picketing on its premises.[54] When this prohibition was challenged, the Court held that the Logan Valley Mall was as open and accessible to the general public as the *Marsh* Chickasaw business district.[55] Authoring the majority opinion, Justice Marshall wrote that

> [w]e see no reason why access to a business district in a company town for the purpose of exercising First Amendment rights should be constitutionally required, while access for the same purpose to property functioning as a business district

51. *Marsh,* 326 U.S. at 506.

52. *Id.* at 509. The Court stated: "As we have stated before, the right to exercise the liberties safeguarded by the First Amendment 'lies at the foundation of free government by free men' and we must in all cases 'weigh the circumstances and . . . appraise the . . . reasons . . . in support of the regulation . . . of [those] rights.'" *Id.* (quoting Schneider v. State, 308 U.S. 147, 161 (1939)).

53. 391 U.S. 308, 309 (1968).

54. *See id.* at 311. Weis Markets and Sears Roebuck and Co. were the two companies occupying Logan Valley Plaza. *See id.* at 310. A sign was posted by Weis on the outside of its store prohibiting "trespass or soliciting by anyone other than its employees on its porch or parking lot." *Id.* at 311.

55. *See id.* at 315. The court noted that

> [i]t is clear that if the shopping center premises were not privately owned but instead constituted the business area of a municipality, which they to a large extent resemble, petitioners could not be barred from exercising their First Amendment rights there on the sole ground that title to the property was in the municipality.

Id.

should be limited simply because the property surrounding the 'business district' is not under the same ownership.[56]

Building upon *Marsh,* the Court held that Logan Valley Mall could not exclude those members of the public wishing to exercise their First Amendment rights *as long as* those rights are exercised in a manner consonant with the property's purpose.[57] The Court did affirm the private property owner's right to regulate First Amendment rights so long as any restrictions were reasonable in nature.[58]

The Court limited the *Logan Valley* holding four years later in *Lloyd Corp., Ltd. v. Tanner.*[59] Here, for the first time, the Court was strictly dealing with a mall situation as opposed to the company town in *Marsh* or the shopping center in *Logan Valley.* The mall at Lloyd Center was a privately owned, multi-level building containing stores and parking facilities and surrounded by public sidewalks and streets.[60] However, the Court did not find that the Center lost its private character due to its size,[61] holding that the public invitation to come to the Center *must* be compatible

56. *Id.* at 319. Extending this argument to the Mall of America situation is the focus of Part III of this comment. It is the intention of this comment to prove that the Mall of America functions in much the same way as a downtown business district. Thus, as the Majority exalts substance over form in *Logan Valley,* so should the Mall's essentially public character be of greater importance than its private ownership.

57. *See id.* at 319-20. The *Logan Valley* picketers were stationed outside the Weis supermarket and sought to inform customers that the supermarket's employees were non-union. *See id.* at 311. They were located in the parcel pickup area and the adjacent parking lot and posed no interference with customers entering or leaving the store. *See id.*

In *Logan Valley*, the Court refused to answer the question whether picketing would be allowed if it *was not* directly related to the property's purpose. *See id.* at 320, n.9.

58. *See Logan Valley*, 391 U.S. at 320. Therein, the Court recognized the emergence of the shopping center in relation to changing demographic trends: "The large-scale movement of this country's population from the cities to the suburbs has been accompanied by the advent of the suburban shopping center, typically a cluster of individual retail units on a single large privately owned tract." *Id.* at 324. Perhaps nothing reflects this shift better than the creation and popularity of the Mall of America.

59. 407 U.S. 551 (1972).

60. *See id.* at 554-56. Indeed, the Court placed emphasis on the nature of the mall and its societal role through the Court's in-depth discussion of the mall's attributes. *See id.* at 554. It must also be remembered that the year was 1972, when malls were still relatively new in the United States. The Mall of America was built 20 years later, and the public's attitude towards malls has evolved and changed with the growth of the shopping giant.

61. *See id.* at 369. The Court declared:

> Nor does property lose its private character merely because the public is generally invited to use it for designated purposes . . . . The essentially private character of a store and its privately owned abutting property does not change by virtue of being large or clustered with other stores in a modern shopping center.

Id.

with the purposes of the stores therein.[62] Because defendant Tanner went to the mall to distribute handbill invitations to a meeting protesting the Vietnam War, his speech was unprotected because it did not have a direct relationship to the center's purposes. Therefore, over a lengthy dissent authored by Justice Marshall,[63] it appeared that *Lloyd* left *Logan Valley* applicable only to situations in which the speech involved purposes consonant with the purposes of the mall itself.

Four years after *Lloyd,* the Supreme Court completed its evisceration of *Logan Valley* in *Hudgens v. NLRB.*[64] *Hudgens* held that *Logan Valley* did not survive *Lloyd* in any form and was, therefore, overruled by *Lloyd.*[65] The issue in *Hudgens* was whether striking union members had a right to picket in front of one of their employer's retail stores located in a shopping mall.[66] Relying on *Lloyd* for the proposition that privately owned shopping malls retain their private natures, the *Hudgens* Court held that First Amendment free speech principles were not applicable in a privately owned shopping mall.[67] The Court stated:

> [I]f the respondents in the *Lloyd* case did not have a First Amendment right to enter that shopping center to distribute handbills concerning Vietnam, then the pickets in the present case did not have a First Amendment right to enter this shopping center for the purpose of advertising their strike against the Butler Shoe Co.[68]

---

62. Unlike the picketers in *Logan Valley,* the handbillers in *Lloyd* had alternative areas available where they could relay their message. The Court noted that Lloyd Center was surrounded by public sidewalks that many Center patrons had to cross on their way to the Center. *See id.* at 556. Therefore, "[i]t would be an unwarranted infringement of property rights to require [the center's owners] to yield to the exercise of First Amendment rights under circumstances where adequate alternative avenues of communication exist." *Id.* at 567.

Picketing, demonstrating, distributing handbills, soliciting, and petitioning at the Mall of America are permissible with the prior written consent of the Mall's management. *See* Mall of America, Conduct Code (1996).

63. The *Lloyd* decision was 5,4. Justice Marshall, author of the *Logan Valley* majority opinion, wrote the *Lloyd* dissent in which Justices Brennan, Douglas, and Stewart joined.

64. 424 U.S. 507 (1976).

65. *See id.* at 518. The court declared that "[w]e make clear now, if it was not clear before, that the rationale of *Logan Valley* did not survive the Court's decision in the *Lloyd* case." *Id.*

66. *See id.* at 509.

67. *See id.* at 520-21.

68. *Id.*

The Court so held even though there was a connection between the picketing and one of the stores in the mall, a linkage that was absent in *Lloyd*.[69]

Most recently, the United States Supreme Court further clarified its *Lloyd* holding in *PruneYard Shopping Center v. Robins*.[70] PruneYard was a large shopping mall in California[71] whose owner sought to prohibit high school students from gathering signatures protesting a United Nations resolution on mall property.[72] The California Supreme Court upheld the students' right to petition in the mall under the California Constitution.[73] Relying on a line of California cases[74] and interpreting *Lloyd* not to prohibit the California Constitution from providing greater protections than the First Amendment, the California Supreme

69. Justice Marshall noted in his dissent that *Lloyd* preserved the right to picket when the picketing is related to the purpose of the property and when other alternatives for communicating the desired message are unavailable. *See Hudgens*, 424 U.S. at 540.

70. 447 U.S. 74 (1980).

71. Again, the United States Supreme Court placed emphasis on the fact-finding of the lower court in determining the nature of the mall. The Court reiterated the finding of the California Supreme Court that approximately 25,000 people congregated daily at the mall as a result of advertising and "the lure of a congenial environment." *Id.* at 78.

72. *See id.* at 77. Appellees were a number of high school students who set up a card table in the mall's central courtyard and who attempted to solicit support for their opposition to a resolution against "Zionism." *See id.*

73. *See* Robins v. PruneYard Shopping Ctr., 592 P.2d 341, 347 (Cal. 1979).

74. In so doing, the California Supreme Court cleared up any confusion regarding its own stance on free speech rights on public property. In *Diamond v. Bland*, 477 P.2d 733 (Cal. 1970), the court permitted free speech rights in a privately owned shopping center. After the U.S. Supreme Court decision in *Lloyd*, the court reversed *Diamond I* in *Diamond II*. *See* Diamond v. Bland, 521 P.2d 460 (Cal. 1974), *cert. denied*, 419 U.S. 885 (1974). Justice Mosk wrote a lengthy dissent in *Diamond II* in which he compared the shopping center in question to a downtown area in which citizens are granted free speech protections. *See id.* at 468. In *Robins v. PruneYard*, the court was presented with two questions: 1) whether *Lloyd* provided federally protected private property rights such that state constitutions were preempted from providing greater free speech rights on private property; and 2) if not, whether the California Constitution affirmatively protects free speech rights at shopping centers. *See Robins*, 592 P.2d at 342. Answering the first question, the court held that *Lloyd* was a First Amendment issue and that references to the Fifth and Fourteenth Amendments only applied to the state action question. *See id.* at 344. The court read nothing in *Lloyd* to preempt states from construing their own constitutions more broadly than the Federal Constitution. *See id.* at 346. Answering the second question, the court held that the California Constitution provided greater free speech protections than the First Amendment and that these protections extend to a private space whose purposes and uses cause it to function as a public arena. *See id.* at 347. The court was influenced by Justice Mosk's *Diamond II* dissent holding that the shopping center in question, while privately owned, was so public in nature that it constituted a public space worthy of free speech protections. *See id.* at 347.

Court granted the students the right to solicit signatures and distribute handbills under the California Constitution.[75] This ruling was highly significant because it granted certain free speech rights in privately owned shopping malls, a right the federal government was unwilling to provide.

The United States Supreme Court affirmed this holding. The Court stated that while the Federal Constitution does not protect free speech rights in shopping centers and malls,[76] it does provide a floor of individual liberties protections that state constitutions can build upon but never go below.[77] Indeed, the Supreme Court held that *Lloyd* did not limit states from construing their own constitutions more expansively than the Federal Constitution with regard to individual liberties.[78] Article 1, section 2 of the California Constitution states that "[e]very person may freely speak, write and publish his or her sentiments on all subjects, being responsible for the abuse of this right. A law may not restrain or abridge liberty of speech or press."[79] The Supreme Court of California interpreted this provision to allow a right of "speech and petitioning, reasonably exercised, in shopping centers even when the centers are privately owned."[80] Responding to the mall owner's argument that allowing the students to petition on his property amounts to a Fifth Amendment taking of private property without compensation, the United States Supreme Court held that the right to exclude others was not essential to the use of the property. The Court stated: "There is nothing to suggest that preventing appellants from prohibiting this sort of activity will unreasonably impair the value or use of their property as a shopping center."[81]

---

75. *See Robins*, 592 P.2d at 347.

76. *See PruneYard*, 447 U.S. at 81.

77. *See id.* The purpose of this analysis is to lay the groundwork for arguing for the right to freedom of assembly at the Mall of America under the Minnesota Constitution. This comment argues that *PruneYard* was intended to extend to all First Amendment type rights including the right to assemble. For older Supreme Court precedent holding that state constitutions may provide a source of greater individual liberty rights than their federal counterpart, see *Oregon v. Hass*, 420 U.S. 714 (1975) and *Cooper v. California*, 386 U.S. 58 (1967).

78. *See PruneYard*, 447 U.S. at 81. The Court stated: "Our reasoning in *Lloyd*, however, does not *ex proprio vigore* limit the authority of the State to exercise its police power or its sovereign right to adopt in its own Constitution individual liberties more expansive than those conferred by the Federal Constitution." *Id.*

79. CAL. CONST. art. I, § 2.

80. *Robins*, 592 P.2d at 347.

81. *PruneYard*, 447 U.S. at 83.

Since no specific harm could be proven by permitting the students access to solicit signatures and distribute information, the Court determined that free speech rights under the California Constitution outweigh private property rights under the Fifth Amendment.[82] Thus, under *PruneYard,* the current status of the law is that states may use their own constitutions to build upon First Amendment protections on private property, but state constitutions can never provide fewer rights than those already granted under the Federal Constitution.[83]

PruneYard subsequently bred much state litigation regarding whether state constitutions provided broader free speech rights than those granted under the Federal Constitution in the privately owned property context. In the early 1980s, a number of courts found in favor of free speech rights.[84] The tide began to change in the mid-eighties,[85] and in the nineties the courts have been

---

82. *See id.* The United States Supreme Court affirmed the mall's right to impose reasonable regulations to insure that the exercise of free speech rights did not interfere with the mall's regular business operations. *See id.* Similarly, the Mall of America does have a Conduct Code in place for this same purpose.

83. *See id.*

84. *See* Commonwealth v. Tate, 432 A.2d 1382 (Pa. 1981) (holding that when balancing free speech and private property rights, a college could not totally prohibit leafleting on campus); Alderwood Assoc. v. Washington Envtl. Council, 635 P.2d 108 (Wash. 1981) (permitting the collection of signatures at a mall as the mall was functioning as the new downtown). *See also* Batchelder v. Allied Stores Int'l, Inc. 445 N.E.2d 590 (Mass. 1983) (holding that a candidate for political office had a right to petition at a shopping center based on state election laws); State v. Schmid, 423 A.2d 615 (N.J. 1980) (discussed in Part III); State v. Shack, 277 A.2d 369 (N.J. 1971) (discussed in Part III). For a detailed analysis of state court decisions before 1986, see John A. Ragosta, *Free Speech Access to Shopping Malls Under State Constitutions: Analysis and Rejection,* 37 SYRACUSE L. REV. 1 (1986).

85. *See* Fiesta Mall Venture v. Mecham Recall Comm., 767 P.2d 719 (Ariz. Ct. App. 1988) (declaring that the Fiesta Mall did not constitute the downtown area rather than considering whether the mall met the state action requirement that would allow for signature solicitations); Cologne v. Westfarms Assoc. 469 A.2d 1201 (Conn. 1984) (holding that nothing in the Connecticut Constitution supported free speech rights in a privately owned mall to allow for the solicitation of signatures in support of the proposed ERA Amendment); Woodland v. Michigan Citizens Lobby, 378 N.W.2d 337 (Mich. 1985) (declaring that the Michigan Constitution did not prevent private mall owners from restricting First Amendment rights with regards to the solicitation of signatures at shopping malls); Shad Alliance v. Smith Haven Mall, 488 N.E.2d 1211 (N.Y. 1985) (upholding a privately-owned shopping mall's prohibition against leafleting based on a finding of no state action at the mall); Western Pa. Socialist Workers 1982 Campaign v. Connecticut Gen. Life Ins. Co., 515 A.2d 1331, 1337 (Pa. 1986); Commonwealth v. Tate, 432 A.2d 1382 (Pa. 1981) (holding that the mall was not a downtown district and that political speech at a private mall was not protected speech under the Pennsylvania Constitution); Southcenter Joint Venture v. National Democratic Policy Comm., 780 P.2d 1282 (Wash. 1989) (holding a state action requirement implicit in the state constitution and that the solicitation of political contributions at a privately owned mall was

almost evenly split.[86] In December 1994, the New Jersey Supreme Court issued a detailed decision on this subject.[87] Due to the similarity of the facts of the New Jersey case to the issues surrounding the Mall of America, that case provides the most persuasive authority to be used as a point of comparison with Minnesota caselaw. However, before embarking on an application of *PruneYard* to Minnesota Constitutional law and the Mall of America, it is necessary to analyze the features of the Mall itself. The point of departure for an analysis of freedom of assembly rights at the Mall of America lies in the nature of the Mall. Since state constitutions apply to state action,[88] it must be argued and established that the Mall functions not as private property but as a public space. Courts that have found free speech rights at malls have done so based first upon the nature of the mall as a "downtown" area, and based secondly, in conjunction with state First

---

thus prohibited as the state constitution established rights between the people and their government rather than between people and people, and thus reversing *Alderwood's* holding that Washington's free speech provision protected speech on private property); Jacobs v. Major, 407 N.W.2d 832 (Wis. 1987) (holding that the Wisconsin Constitution's free speech protections did not extend to private property in an action brought by an antinuclear dance troupe which wanted to perform at a private shopping mall). *See also* State v. Felmet, 273 S.E.2d 708 (N.C. 1981) (upholding the prohibition of petitioning in the parking lot of a privately owned shopping mall).

86. For cases granting free speech rights in privately owned shopping malls, see *Westside Sane/Freeze v. Ernest W. Hahn, Inc.*, 274 Cal. Rptr. 51 (1990) (following *PruneYard* and permitting leafleting at a privately owned mall); *Bock v. Westminster Mall Co.*, 819 P.2d 55 (Colo. 1991) (allowing political leafleting at a mall due to the state's financial interest in the mall which constituted state action and triggered free speech protections under the Colorado Constitution, but stating that under *PruneYard* it was unnecessary to find state action when a state constitution is more protective of free speech than the Federal Constitution, as the majority believed to be the case with the Colorado Constitution and declaring the mall the new downtown and public forum); *New Jersey Coalition Against War in the Middle East v. J.M.B. Realty Corp.*, 650 A.2d 757 (N.J. 1994) (discussed at length in Part III).

Those cases supporting private property owner's rights to prohibit free speech include *Citizens for Ethical Gov't, Inc. v. Gwinnet Place Assoc.*, 392 S.E.2d 8 (Ga. 1990) (holding that the Georgia Constitution did not protect petitioning on private property); *Eastwood Mall, Inc. v. Slanco*, 626 N.E.2d 59 (Ohio 1994), *cert. denied*, 513 U.S. 933 (1994) (holding that the Ohio Constitution's free speech guarantees were no broader than the First Amendment) and *Charleston Joint Venture v. McPherson*, 417 S.E.2d 544 (S.C. 1992) (holding that the South Carolina Constitution's free speech provisions provided no more free speech protections than the Federal Constitution).

87. *See New Jersey Coalition*, 650 A.2d at 757.

88. For a fuller explication of the state action requirement, see LAURENCE H. TRIBE, AMERICAN CONSTITUTIONAL LAW § 18-1, at 1688-1720 (2d ed. 1988).

Amendment-type provisions.[89] Following is a detailed analysis of the Mall of America as public arena.

III. Is the Mall of America the New "Downtown"?

The Mall of America is the largest retail and entertainment complex in the United States.[90] From its opening in 1992, there have been over 190 million visits to the Mall with weekly visits ranging from 600,000 to 900,000 depending on the season.[91] The Mall is located only five minutes from the Minneapolis/Saint Paul International Airport,[92] a convenient location because over thirty percent of the Mall's visits are made by people from outside a 150 mile radius.[93] Even foreigners make the Mall of America a stop on their itineraries, if not a focal point, as evidenced by the fact that international visitors account for six percent of the Mall's patrons.[94] Indeed, the Mall has become such a tourist attraction in the six years since its opening that citizens of each of the fifty states and over two dozen nations have visited it.[95] As amazing as it may seem, the Mall attracts more visits annually than Disney World

---

89. Beginning with *Marsh v. Alabama*, 326 U.S. 501 (1946) the United States Supreme Court spent a good deal of time analyzing the nature of the place where the free speech rights were being asserted. *See id.* at 502-03. A detailed fact-finding of the situation was important to determine the nature of the space itself, be it a company owned town *(Marsh)*, shopping center *(Logan Valley)*, or mall *(Lloyd Corp.*, *Hudgens* and *PruneYard)*. State courts, therefore, place much emphasis on the nature of the shopping center or mall in question when deciding whether to find for free speech rights at these locations.

90. *See* AT A GLANCE, *supra* note 1.

91. *See id.*

92. *See id.*

93. *See* TOURISM, *supra* note 3. In 1994 alone, more than 22,000 people in the United States participated in a same-day, low-cost airfare package on Northwest Airlines that brought them to the Mall for one shopping day. *See id.* A continuous bus service leaves every half hour from the airport going to the Mall. *See id.*

94. *See id.*

95. *See id.* As Mall literature proudly states, people from the following countries have been to the Mall: Australia, Austria, Brazil, Canada, China, England, France, Finland, Germany, Guam, Hong Kong, India, Indonesia, Ireland, Israel, Italy, Japan, Kuwait, Mexico, the Philippines, Russia, Saudi Arabia, Singapore, Spain, Sweden, Taiwan and Thailand. *See id.* Over 30,000 organized tour groups and over 800 Japanese groups have visited the Mall. *See id.* In order to accommodate many of these guests, the Mall of America Grand Hotel is located on the premises. *See* THE PLACE FOR FUN, *supra* note 50. A second hotel, the Doubletree Grand Hotel at Mall of America, is located across the street from the Mall and advertises itself as the "official hotel across from the Mall." MAP AND DIRECTORY, *supra* note 4.

and the Grand Canyon *combined*.[96] Clearly, the Mall has established itself in the American iconographic landscape.[97]

The Mall complex itself is awesome both in its grandness and by the attention to detail which went into its design. The Mall encompasses 4.2 million square feet[98] with a gross leaseable retail space of 2.5 million square feet.[99] The rest of the space is allotted for entertainment.[100] The Mall is so vast that a walk around one of its four level covers a distance of .57 miles.[101] The Mall has four national chain anchor stores: Bloomingdales, Macy's, Nordstrom's, and Sears; and five-hundred twenty smaller stores located amongst the anchors.[102] The Mall is in the shape of a square, and there are four "streets"[103] connecting the anchors stores in which the smaller stores are located. Each of the four "streets" has a distinct and separate character.[104] The Mall of America's promo-

96. *See* September Press Release, *supra* note 9. Justice Black's *Marsh v. Alabama*, 326 U.S. 501 (1946), majority opinion is thus recalled that "[t]he more an owner, for his advantage, opens up his property for use by the public in general, the more do his rights become circumscribed by the statutory and constitutional rights of those who use it." *Id.* at 506. While the context in which these words were written pertained to a company-owned town, they are not limited to company-owned towns only. They do in fact have significant bearing on the Mall of America. The owners of the Mall have made their property as accessible to the public as possible, and the Mall should fall within the *Marsh* penumbra of public places, regardless of private ownership.

97. After a visit to the Mall of America, the columnist Molly Ivins wrote, "[g]reat Caesar's armpit! Sweet suffering catfish! Holy gamoly! I have been to the pyramids of America. I have seen the cathedral of commerce. Our Parthenon, our Coliseum, our Chartres. I have been to the Mall of America, the world's largest shopping mall." PUBLIC RELATIONS DEP'T, MALL OF AMERICA, QUOTABLES (1996) [hereinafter QUOTABLES].

98. In order to grasp how large the Mall of America actually is, consider the following facts: the Mall can hold 32 Boeing 747s; it is as large as seven Yankee Stadiums; Moscow's Red Square can fit into the Mall five times, as can 20 of St. Peter's Basilicas in Rome. *See* PUBLIC RELATIONS DEP'T, MALL OF AMERICA, FUN FACTS & QUOTABLES (1996) [hereinafter FUN FACTS & QUOTABLES].

99. *See* AT A GLANCE, *supra* note 1. Gross leasable area is the total floor space available for merchants. *See id.* Occupancy as of March 1995 was at 93.5%. *See id.*

100. *See* John Sprenkle & Michael Tubridy, *Mall Openings Continue at Moderate Pace*, INTERNATIONAL COUNCIL OF SHOPPING CENTERS RES. Q., Summer 1996, at 13.

101. *See* FUN FACTS & QUOTABLES, *supra* note 98.

102. *See* THE PLACE FOR FUN, *supra* note 50. The Mall literature states, "[t]here are stores to fit every budget from discount to moderate to upscale . . . ." *Id.* These include specialty stores and national retail chain stores such as Filene's Basement, B. Dalton Books, Banana Republic, Ann Taylor, and Eddie Bauer Home Collection. *See id.*

103. *See* PUBLIC RELATIONS DEP'T, MALL OF AMERICA, USER FRIENDLY (1996) [hereinafter USER FRIENDLY].

104. *See id.* East Broadway, which connects Bloomingdale's and Sears, is modeled with chrome to provide a futuristic look. South Avenue, the "street" between Macy's and Bloomingdale's, is described as a "chic, sophisticated shopping avenue" while the West

tional information states: "It is . . . one of the most user friendly architectural designs in the country."[105]

In addition to the shopping, the Mall attracts adults to its entertainment and nightlife. The Mall contains nine nightclubs, a fourteen-screen movie theater, an eighteen-hole miniature golf course, a sports bar, a comedy club, and a wide variety of restaurants.[106] In order to accommodate adults who visit the Mall with small children, the Mall offers four family rooms designed for infant care.[107] Not only do these rooms provide space to feed and change babies, but they also contain microwaves for heating bottles and vending machines that sell baby needs.[108]

Parents can enroll their teenagers in the Metropolitan Learning Alliance, which is a high school located in the Mall.[109] Adults can earn a college degree from the National College, the first college campus located in a shopping mall.[110] Courses include accounting, marketing, human resources, computer, and business.[111] The College offers its classes during the day, at night, and on Saturdays.[112] Other conveniences for families and adults include a bank, a post office, a health and dental clinic, seven ATM machines sites, a copy center, a hotel/car rental information phone, four Mall of America Guest Service Centers, and two travel offices.[113] The Mall of America's promotional materials include one fact sheet entitled "User Friendly" which details all of the conveniences located in the Mall. In addition to the amenities already listed, the Mall contains forty-four escalators and seventeen elevators and is

---

Market is modeled on a European railway station. *See id.* Lastly, the North Garden is designed in the manner of a park containing gazebos and trellises. *See id.*

105. *Id.*

106. *See* PUBLIC RELATIONS DEP'T, MALL OF AMERICA, RESTAURANTS & NIGHTCLUBS (1996) [hereinafter RESTAURANTS & NIGHTCLUBS]; PUBLIC RELATIONS DEP'T, MALL OF AMERICA, THE PLACE FOR FUN IN YOUR LIFE (1997). The range of restaurants consists of everything from the trendy Planet Hollywood and a Rainforest Café to the more upscale Napa Valley Grille and California Café. *See* RESTAURANTS & NIGHTCLUBS, *supra.*

107. *See* PUBLIC RELATIONS DEP'T, MALL OF AMERICA, FAMILY FUN (1996) [hereinafter FAMILY FUN].

108. *See id.*

109. *See* USER FRIENDLY, *supra* note 103.

110. *See* PUBLIC RELATIONS DEP'T, MALL OF AMERICA, CELEBRATING 5 YEARS OF BRINGING THE WORLD TO MINNESOTA! (1997) [hereinafter CELEBRATING 5 YEARS].

111. *See id.*

112. *See id.*

113. *See id.* Not to be forgotten is the Chapel of Love. Over 1000 couples have been married at the Mall of America since 1994. *See* PUBLIC RELATIONS DEP'T, MALL OF AMERICA, FUN FACTS & QUOTABLES (1997); CELEBRATING 5 YEARS, *supra* note 110.

handicapped accessible. The Mall provides over 20,000 free parking spaces, and no vehicle parked on any one of the parking ramps is farther than three hundred feet from one of the Mall's twenty-three entrances.[114]

While there are numerous stores and attractions for adults and families, the Mall has made a concerted effort to attract youth. There are a variety of attractions and stores in the Mall which are intended to bring young people to the Mall complex. In the center of the Mall is Knott's Camp Snoopy, a seven-acre family theme park, which is the largest indoor theme park in the United States.[115] Knott's Camp Snoopy contains seventeen rides, nine eating places, shopping, and various other forms of entertainment.[116] That the park is oriented toward older youth as well as young children is evidenced by the rides inside the park: a log chute, a roller coaster, and a "multisensory Mystery Mine Ride."[117] Mall literature distinguishes these rides from those intended for youngsters; such rides include the Li'l Shaver roller coaster, Americana Carousal, and the Balloon Race.[118] Restaurants in the park such as the Hormel Food Court and Kemp's Cookies and Cream are oriented toward all age groups while the fast food eateries in the east wing are heavily frequented by teenagers.[119] Other youth attractions at the Mall include Star-Base Omega, an interactive laser game in which players are trained and outfitted in special gear, and Tempus Expeditions, a shopping center that provides an adventure-filled learning experience. The Mall also contains such teenage-oriented stores as a super sports store, a Tekno Comix interactive entertainment store, a holograms store, and a "junkyard" selling "grunge" clothing.[120]

---

114. *See* DESTINATION PLANNING GUIDE, *supra* note 2.

115. *See id. See also* FAMILY FUN, *supra* note 107.

116. *See id.* Also of interest is the 1.2 million gallon walk-through aquarium and the LEGO Imagination Center. *See* AT A GLANCE, *supra* note 1. Described as "an enormous LEGO showplace designed as a three-level fantasy LEGO factory," it is a place in which "[v]isitors are welcome at any time to come in and play with LEGO bricks and Duplo blocks at no cost." FAMILY FUN, *supra* note 107.

117. *See* PUBLIC RELATIONS DEP'T, MALL OF AMERICA, KNOTT'S CAMP SNOOPY (1996) [hereinafter KNOTT'S CAMP SNOOPY].

118. *See id.*

119. *See id.*

120. *See* PUBLIC RELATIONS DEP'T, MALL OF AMERICA, UNIQUE & INNOVATIVE RETAILERS (1996) [hereinafter UNIQUE & INNOVATIVE RETAILERS].

The Mall's concerted effort to welcome and invite teenagers to its premises is relevant to the teenagers' use of the Mall. Referring to the mall managements in *New Jersey Coalition,* the New Jersey Supreme Court stated that "[t]he issue is whether defendants' actual conduct, the multitude of uses they permitted and encouraged, including expressive uses, amounted to an implied invitation and, if so, the nature and extent of that invitation."[121] Little if any doubt exists that the Mall of America openly welcomed all teenagers to its premises and that the extent of this invitation, by its very nature, included activities other than those enumerated herein.

These are the highlights of some of the most popular attractions at the Mall of America. What can hopefully be learned from this information is that the Mall of America is a massive, all-encompassing structure. As previously stated,[122] almost all of the preceding information comes from the Mall of America's promotional literature. The Mall advertises itself as any other profit-making endeavor would: by accentuating the positives.[123] Hence, the promotional materials include a detailed separate listing of all conveniences offered at the Mall, a listing of all family activities, and a listing of the restaurants and nightclubs on the premises. The Mall aims to please everybody and advertises as such.[124] Once the Mall has so invited and catered to the public, the question presents itself whether it then is deemed a public space for First Amendment purposes.

An appropriate place to begin this inquiry is the Mall's literature itself. In one of its brochures entitled "The Place for Fun in Your Life," the Mall management states that the Mall was

---

121. New Jersey Coalition Against War in the Middle East v. J.M.B. Realty Corp., 650 A.2d 757, 772 (N.J. 1994).

122. *See supra* note 1 and accompanying text.

123. The Mall uses numerous superlatives in its promotional material, i.e. "the nation's largest retail and entertainment center," USER FRIENDLY, *supra* note 103; "Knott's Camp Snoopy, Mall of America's lively centerpiece, is the largest indoor family theme park in the nation . . . ." KNOTT'S CAMP SNOOPY, *supra* note 117. "[W]hat sets Mall of America apart from typical shopping malls is its unique range of retail, offering quality, variety and value, from luxury to the basics . . . ." UNIQUE & INNOVATIVE RETAILERS, *supra* note 120. "Mall of America is host to some of the finest eating establishments—all under one roof . . . ." RESTAURANTS & NIGHTCLUBS, *supra* note 106.

124. Indeed, a poll taken from November 27 to December 3, 1995, revealed that 70% of Mall shoppers combine a trip to the Mall with a visit to Knott's Camp Snoopy or the Mall's nightclubs and bars. Sally Apgar, *Minnesota Poll,* MINNEAPOLIS-ST. PAUL STAR-TRIB., Dec. 10, 1995.

"[d]esigned as *a city within a city*."[125] By naming the four wings of the Mall "streets", the Mall refers to itself in terms of a downtown area. "While the Mall's extensive skylight system allows the visitors to feel as though they're outdoors, it's guaranteed perfect weather and 70 degrees!"[126] Proof that Mall management wants the Mall to be considered a self-contained city is evidenced by the following quote from the Mall's promotional packet:

> Yet the most striking thing about the mall is that [it] seems to be providing what American cities themselves—at least the downtown shopping districts of American cities—once provided: a bright, vibrant, secure-feeling atmosphere where crowds of people congregate day and night, an immaculate and thriving shopping area where thousands of people—more than 600,000 during an average week—can spend time browsing, dining or going to the theater, a clean and well-run place that, while one is inside it, seems to be the center of things.[127]

Not only does Mall management consider the Mall to be an indoor city, but the contents of the Mall are the type found in a city. In the Mall, one may: enroll one's teenager in school; get a college degree; go to the health or dental clinic; make a bank transaction; go to the post office; dine at any number of restaurants; go to the movies or a nightclub; and shop to satisfy basically every need. Evidence that the Mall is a rival "downtown" is exemplified by the fact that the year it opened, business in downtown Minneapolis was "off" approximately twenty percent; by August 1995, it had stabilized at eight to ten percent.[128]

Perhaps the most decisive evidence that the Mall of America functions as the new downtown comes from the people who live

---

125. THE PLACE FOR FUN, *supra* note 50 (emphasis added).

126. CELEBRATING 5 YEARS, *supra* note 110.

127. QUOTABLES, *supra* note 97 (quoting Bob Greene, columnist of *The Chicago Tribune*).

128. *See* Sally Apgar, *It's a Megamall World After All*, MINNEAPOLIS-ST. PAUL STAR TRIB., Aug. 11, 1995, at 1A [hereinafter *It's a Megamall World*]. Other factors, such as the renovation of other large shopping centers, may have also contributed to the decline. However, as one area retail consultant stated in a 1995 interview: "[P]eople from out of the city who used to go downtown now go to the Mall of America." *Id.* Indeed, a telephone poll taken by *Star-Tribune*/WCCO-TV over November 27 to December 3, 1995, found that of 1,018 adults polled, 18% who shop at the Mall of America shop in downtown St. Paul less than in years past. The poll also found that downtown St. Paul, along with two other shopping centers, was losing the most customers to the Mall of America. *See* Sally Apgar, *Confounding Critics, Mall Displays Staying Power*, MINNEAPOLIS-ST. PAUL STAR-TRIB., Dec. 10, 1995, at 1B [hereinafter *Confounding Critics*].

with the Mall on a daily basis. Larry Carlson, a Minneapolis retail consultant, states that "[t]here are people who will shoot me for saying it, but the mall is serving as a new downtown."[129] One Mall patron has said that "[s]ometimes I go [to the mall] for entertainment. But mostly I go for shopping because everything you need is right in the mall. Downtown St. Paul is more spread out, so you have to go [sic] more places to find what you need."[130]

A. *Persuasive Precedent*—New Jersey Coalition Against War in the Middle East v. J.M.B. Realty Corp.

Precedent for recognizing the Mall of America as a functioning downtown can be found in numerous cases.[131] One of the most recent cases—*New Jersey Coalition Against War in the Middle East v. J.M.B. Realty Corp.*[132]—is also the most persuasive. In 1994, the New Jersey Supreme Court reversed a ruling denying access rights to a group of citizens desiring to conduct a leafleting campaign at ten privately-owned malls. The purpose of the leafleting was to protest United States intervention in the Middle East upon Iraq's invasion of Kuwait in 1990.[133] In a lengthy decision written by Chief Justice Wilentz, the court held that the nature of the malls was such that they functioned as public spaces and, therefore, they could not deny public free speech access.[134]

The court built its analysis on prior New Jersey caselaw, most specifically upon *State v. Schmid*.[135] *Schmid* held that a private

---

129. *It's a Megamall World*, *supra* note 128. The same article later states "[a]s Carlson and others see it, the Mall of America has become the new town square, the new downtown retail district of the Twin Cities. The combination of entertainment and retail has given people the wide variety of choices that they used to find only in downtown Minneapolis." *Id.*

130. *Confounding Critics*, *supra* note 128 (quoting Ann Scherman). The article states "[l]ike it or not, the megamall has become an integral part of the state's culture and shopping lives of many Minnesotans." *Id.* The article holds that the latest point of reference in Minnesota is the Mall of America, rather than Lake Woebegon of days of old. *See id.*

131. *See supra* notes 84, 86 and accompanying text.

132. 650 A.2d 757 (N.J. 1994).

133. *See id.* at 762.

134. *See id.* at 783. The court did hold that the malls could impose reasonable time, place, and manner restrictions on the leafleting. *See id.* For similar provisions, see *Westside Sane/Freeze v. Ernest W. Hahn, Inc.*, 274 Cal. Rptr. 51, 59 (1990); *Bock v. Westminster Mall Co.*, 819 P.2d 55, 63 (Colo. 1991); *Batchelder v. Allied Stores Int'l, Inc.* 445 N.E.2d 590, 591 (Mass. 1983); *Commonwealth v. Tate*, 432 A.2d 1382, 1390 (Pa. 1981); *State v. Schmid*, 423 A.2d 615, 630 (N.J. 1980).

135. 423 A.2d at 615.

university could not unreasonably deny the exercise of political speech to anyone who walked onto campus.[136] Princeton University, although a private institution, invited the public onto its premises to such an extent that the property was deemed public for constitutional purposes, and state free speech principles were held to apply.[137]

Thus, by granting a speech right on private property under the New Jersey Constitution, the New Jersey Supreme Court established a standard to determine when public use necessitates accompanying constitutional obligations. The standard is three-pronged: (1) What is the normal use of the property?; (2) What is the extent and nature of the public's invitation to use it?; and (3) What is the purpose of the expressional activity in relation to both

---

136. *See id.* at 633. Chris Schmid, who was not a Princeton student, was charged with trespass on private property after he distributed and sold United States Labor Party political materials on campus. *See id.* at 616.

137. *See id.* at 631. In contrast, in 1993 a New Jersey court upheld a criminal trespass ban on leafleting on a campus that was not held to be open to the public. *See* State v. Guice, 621 A.2d 553 (N.J. Super. Ct. Law Div. 1993). The Superior Court of New Jersey held that Stevens Institute of Technology, a much smaller institution than Princeton University, made a deliberate attempt to maintain the private nature of its campus, and thus its prohibition against leafleting was upheld. *See id.* at 556.

The New Jersey Supreme Court has a history of expansively protecting individual free speech rights over those of private property owners. In *State v. Shack*, 277 A.2d 369 (N.J. 1971), the unanimous court held that a private property owner who employs and houses migrant farm workers may not deny the workers the right to receive government visitors wishing to provide them with medical and legal advice. The Court did not support this holding under *Marsh* because it did not find a direct correlation between a migrant camp and the business district of Chickasaw, Alabama. *See id.* at 371. Nor did the court base its reasoning upon the New Jersey trespass statute (two government workers were charged with trespass when they entered a camp and refused to leave until they had a private audience with one of the migrant workers), nor upon the Sixth Amendment right to counsel. *See id.* at 371-72.

Rather, the court held that New Jersey law does not provide the owner of private property with the right to bar access to government services meant for migrant workers. *See id.* The court chose to ground its holding upon this basis rather than on constitutional considerations because doing so provided the migrant workers with a broader rights base. *See id.* at 372. As the court stated, "[a] decision in nonconstitutional terms is more satisfactory, because the interests of migrant workers are more expansively served in that way than they would be if they had no more freedom than these constitutional concepts could be found to mandate if indeed they apply at all." *Id.* Based on the fact that these laborers had little, if any, access to such information, the court held it to be in their best interests to meet with the state workers. *See id.* at 371-72. Private property rights are not absolute, and the rights and needs of the migrant farm workers outweighed the property owner's right to bar access to his property. *See id.* at 373. The court made a point of stating that the property owner is under no obligation to open his property to the general public. *See id.* at 374. Thus, traveling salesmen or solicitors were not guaranteed entry onto his land unless barring them would deny the migrant workers access to needed items. *See id.*

its private and public use?[138] Considering *Schmid, New Jersey Coalition* held that "[t]his 'multi-faceted' standard determines whether private property owners may be required to permit, subject to suitable restrictions, the reasonable exercise by individuals of the constitutional freedoms of speech and assembly."[139]

B. The First and Second Prongs of the Schmid *Test*

The *Schmid* test applies to the Mall of America situation because the New Jersey Supreme Court explicitly states that the test is to be employed to protect rights of speech *and* assembly.[140] After articulating the test, the *Schmid* court stated that "[t]his is a multi-faceted test which must be applied to ascertain whether, in a given case, owners of private property may be required to permit, subject to suitable restrictions, the reasonable exercise by individuals of the constitutional freedoms of speech *and assembly.*"[141] In *Schmid,* the primary issue concerned the scope of free speech.[142] However, the court explicitly stated its intention to also apply this test to assembly issues. The New Jersey Supreme Court, applying this test in *New Jersey Coalition* fourteen years after *Schmid* was decided, reiterated the intent that assembly rights were to be included in the rights granted protection under the *Schmid* test.[143] The court in *New Jersey Coalition* stated that it would decide the case based on constitutional and common law grounds;[144] common law "lays a foundation that would vindicate the exercise of speech and assembly rights in this setting."[145] The court then conducted an analysis of New Jersey common law and, from this analysis, held that free speech rights should be granted at the shopping malls; however, reasonable restrictions of this right would be allowed.[146]

---

138. *See Schmid,* 423 A.2d at 630.

139. *See New Jersey Coalition,* 650 A.2d at 761. Similarly, in *PruneYard,* the United States Supreme Court, while concerned with a free speech issue, held that its ruling covered First Amendment rights, thus encompassing the freedom of assembly. *See* PruneYard Shopping Ctr. v. Robins, 447 U.S. 74, 81 (1980).

140. *See Schmid,* 423 A.2d at 630.

141. *Id.* (emphasis added).

142. *See supra* note 134 and accompanying text.

143. *See New Jersey Coalition,* 650 A.2d at 761.

144. *See id.* at 777.

145. *See id.*

146. *See id.* at 783. It must be noted that the New Jersey Constitution provides a fundamental right of free speech while the Minnesota Bill of Rights does not enumerate a right to assemble. While this makes it easier for the New Jersey Supreme Court to ground

This precedent for recognizing assembly rights as one of the rights protected by the *Schmid* test weighs strongly in favor of recognizing this right in a mall setting. Because this comment advocates using the *Schmid* test as the standard against which the Mall's Parental Escort Policy must be measured, it is of primary importance that the test encompasses the right of assembly. Further, *New Jersey Coalition* is the case most akin in scope to the Mall of America cause of action. As it is argued that the *New Jersey Coalition* precedent (for finding the New Jersey malls to be public arenas) is strongly persuasive with regard to the Mall of America,[147] the New Jersey Supreme Court's recognition that the *Schmid* test encompasses assembly rights should also be very persuasive.[148] Once recognized as such, the Minnesota courts can rely on their common law tradition of extending individual liberties to decide whether that tradition should be extended to encompass assembly rights at malls. The *Schmid* test encompasses the right to assemble on private property, the issue in question at the Mall of America, and will thus be applied herein.

A comparison of the New Jersey Supreme Court's findings in *New Jersey Coalition* with the situation at the Mall of America assists in the determination of whether the Mall of America should be deemed a functioning downtown. Under the first and second *Schmid* prongs (which were jointly considered in *New Jersey Coalition),* the court conducted a detailed fact-finding into the normal use of the private property on which the restrictions were imposed. In *New Jersey Coalition*, the defendants were ten very large enclosed shopping centers,[149] nine of which were regional

---

its decision, the lack thereof should not hinder the Minnesota Supreme Court. Again, an argument can and should be made under article I, section 16 of the Minnesota Bill of Rights for a right of peaceful assembly. *See* discussion *infra* Part IV.

147. *See* discussion *infra* notes 148-61.

148. The Supreme Court of Pennsylvania cited *Schmid* in deciding a case of petition rights on a college campus. *See* Commonwealth v. Tate, 432 A.2d 1382 (Pa. 1981). In holding that a private Pennsylvania college must allow peaceful leaflet distribution (although certain restrictions were allowed), the court cited the recent *Schmid* decision holding that freedoms of speech and assembly apply to the distribution of political materials at Princeton University. *See id.* at 1390. After citing *Schmid,* the court stated that being "[m]indful of both this Commonwealth's great heritage of freedom and the compelling language of the Pennsylvania Constitution, we likewise hold that, in certain circumstances, the state may reasonably restrict the right to possess and use property in the interests of freedom of speech, assembly, and petition." *Id.*

149. At various times the opinion refers to them as both shopping centers and as malls. With the exception of Woodbridge Center, the defendants were all, as their names suggest,

centers.[150] The regional centers each had from 93 to 244 tenants including department stores, restaurants, banks, entertainment venues, travel agencies, hair salons, doctor's offices, and parking facilities that held from 3,075 to 9,000 vehicles.[151] With gross leasing areas ranging from 300,000 to 1,000,000 square feet, each of these regional malls is considerably smaller than the Mall of America, with its gross leasing area of 4.2 million square feet.[152] Each of the ten malls permitted non-shopping activities on its property; some involved community and political speech.[153]

The court continued its factual analysis by examining statistical information regarding the place of the mall in American life. Citing statistics from shopping center authorities, the court tracked the growth of the shopping center and the simultaneous decline of many downtown shopping districts.[154] The court was so persuaded by its findings that it held that "[r]egional and community shopping centers significantly compete with and have in fact significantly displaced downtown business districts as the gathering point of citizens, both here in New Jersey *and across America*."[155] Asserting that shopping malls have become an integral part of the American landscape, the court found that malls have evolved to the point where the larger ones serve as the new downtowns.[156]

Considering the public's invitation to use the property (the second *Schmid* prong), the court found that the contents of the mall and the easy access to them justified the holding that the private property was dedicated to public use.[157] The *New Jersey Coalition* court could have been referring to the Mall of America when it held that "there is no property more thoroughly 'dedicated' to public use than these regional and community shopping centers,

---

malls: The Mall at Short Hills, Cherry Hill Mall, Hamilton Mall, Monmouth Mall, Quakerbridge Mall, Livingston Mall, The Mall at Mill Creek, Riverside Square, and Rockaway Townsquare.

150. The tenth, a community center, was smaller in size and had less variety of stores than the regional centers. Despite this fact, the court included it in its holding. The gross leasable area of a community center ranges from 100,000 to 300,000 square feet. *See New Jersey Coalition*, 650 A.2d at 763-74.

151. *See id.*

152. *See supra* notes 98-99 and accompanying text.

153. *See New Jersey Coalition*, 650 A.2d at 764.

154. *See id.* at 766-68.

155. *Id.* at 766 (emphasis added).

156. *See id.*

157. *See id.* at 771-72.

a public use so pervasive that its all-embracing invitation to the public necessarily includes the implied invitation for plaintiff's leafleting."[158] The court based this holding equally upon: (1) the nature of the stores in the malls and (2) the public invitation to come the malls.[159]

The Mall of America has established its reputation as a complex that caters to almost every need and interest imaginable. In doing so, it has made a concerted effort to welcome people of all ages to its premises in order that they may partake of all that it has to offer. Like the malls in *New Jersey Coalition,* the Mall of America opened its doors not only for shopping and entertainment purposes, but for the by-products thereof: the space that provides places to sit down, relax, talk, or simply roam. Indeed, the New Jersey Supreme Court noted that malls are intentionally designed to provide breathing space to make them more attractive.[160] Such space is intended to provide an additional reason for going to the mall. This is to be distinguished from a strip-shopping center which provides neither shelter from inclement weather nor the multitude of places on which to sit down and relax. The court held that such "non-retail uses, expressive and otherwise, underline the all-inclusiveness of defendant's invitation to the people."[161] Since the malls act as a community gathering place, the court held that they could not unreasonably prohibit community activities on their premises.[162]

Predating *New Jersey Coalition* is older precedent recognizing free speech rights at privately-owned shopping centers or malls.[163] Based on this precedent, and in particular the similarities between the malls at issue in *New Jersey Coalition* with the Mall of America,

158. *See New Jersey Coalition,* 650 A.2d at 771-72.

159. *See id.* at 773-74. "The multiplicity of uses reflects the intention to bring the entire community—its citizens and its activities—into the center. The uses and invitation, in effect, reconstitute the community, conveniently, under one roof." *Id.*

160. *See id.* at 773.

161. *Id.*

162. *See id.*

163. *See* Bock v. Westminster Mall Co. 819 P.2d 55, 62 (Colo. 1991) (holding that "we are also persuaded that the Mall functions as the equivalent of a downtown business district"); Alderwood Assoc. v. Washington Envtl. Council, 635 P.2d 108, 117 (Wash. 1981) (holding that "[t]he shopping center now performs a traditional public function by providing the functional equivalent of a town center or business block"); Robins v. PruneYard Shopping Ctr. 592 P.2d 341, 347 (Cal. 1979); Batchelder v. Allied Stores Int'l, Inc., 445 N.E.2d 590, 591-92 (Mass. 1983). The latter two cases place substantial emphasis on the nature of the mall in question.

there is a secure basis for asserting that the Mall of America functions as a Bloomington/Minneapolis downtown district. The third prong of the *Schmid* test—the compatibility of the free speech exercised with the use of the property—is necessary to complete the analysis. This prong is in fact the most important prong for analysis purposes. While the normal use of the property and the nature of the public's invitation to use it [164] are relatively easily analyzed, the third prong is the decisive prong of the analysis: what is the nature of the teenagers' actions at the Mall, and can those actions be protected under the state constitution? It has been shown in Part II that no federal First Amendment rights exist on private property. However, a right such as freedom to assemble at the Mall of America may be granted by the Minnesota Constitution. Numerous issues must be considered in granting such a right, the most important of which is the nature of the teenagers' actions at the Mall.

C. The Third Prong of the Schmid *Test—The Nature of the Teenagers' Presence at the Mall on Weekend Evenings*

"The main issue is they [teens] yell and use abusive language and for the most part don't respect authority," said Teresa McFarland. "The majority of the kids don't act that way but the small percentage who do ruin it for the rest."[165]

The purpose of the expressional activity in relation to both the Mall's private and public use goes to the heart of the curfew.[166] Beginning with the basic facts, anywhere from 2,000 to 3,000 teenagers go to the Mall of America on weekend evenings, and the majority of the teens are black.[167] Weekend nights are the only time when large groups of black teenagers visit the Mall.[168]

---

164. *See supra* Part III.

165. Apgar, *supra* note 14.

166. The last prong of the *Schmid* test was discussed separately and in great length by the court. As this prong concerns constitutional considerations of First Amendment type rights, it is perhaps the most weighty of the three prongs.

167. *See* Meredith, *supra* note 7; Karl Vick, *Mall and Order in Minnesota,* WASH. POST, Sept. 18, 1996, at 1A (stating that "the Mall of America prides itself on its good relations with the community, and although management flatly refuses to say so, most of the young people gathering on weekend nights are black").

168. *See* Meredith, *supra* note 7 (quoting Marcus Wilson, an eighteen year-old who frequents the Mall of America). Yusef Mgeni, President of the Urban Coalition in the Twin Cities, has said that most teenagers who go to the Mall on weekend nights are low income, young people of color. Telephone Interview with Yusef Mgeni, President of the Urban Coalition in the Twin Cities (Sept. 25, 1996).

While most of the teens go to the Mall to "hang out," some do exercise their shopping power.[169] The Mall of America has repeatedly stated that it considered and then implemented the curfew because the large groups of teenagers disturbed other shoppers and tenants and posed a possible safety hazard.[170] Indeed, the behavior exhibited by some of the teens can only be described as obnoxious. Numerous incidents have occurred of teens chasing each other throughout the Mall, loudly using foul language, and even spitting over the railings at shoppers below.[171] Groups congregate at Knott's Camp Snoopy, the rotunda, and the East Broadway entrance.[172] Other groups block store entrances, and this intimidates many Mall shoppers.[173] They often dress in

---

169. *See* Meredith, *supra* note 7. Teenagers choose to congregate along the railings where they can talk and watch other teens. *See id.* Some shop and are the main customers of certain Mall stores. *See id.*

170. In June 1996, Teresa McFarland stated that "[w]e are dealing with too many unsupervised kids here who are acting disorderly, causing commotions, intimidating guests and preventing mall merchants from doing business." Apgar, *supra* note 14. Teresa McFarland has further stated that 80 percent of Mall stores support the juvenile curfew. *See* Beckham, *supra* note 19.

Ms. McFarland has also stated:

> Well, we've seen a very sharp increase in the number of kids that have been coming to the mall on the weekend nights, and within that a growing percentage of kids are acting up, they're at times getting into fights, we've found weapons on kids, we've had both kids and other guests that have been injured. Now nothing has been serious, but this policy is a pro-active attempt of poten—to—to prevent the potential for something more serious to happen.

Interview with Teresa McFarland, Spokeswoman for the Mall of America (Oct. 6, 1996) (NBC television broadcast).

However, as the store manager of the Nature Company stated, "[t]here are tons of good kids out there who are being punished by this . . . [a]nd I think it's going to affect our traffic." Haga, *supra* note 7, at 4 (quoting Linda Korenby).

171. *See* Meredith, *supra* note 7.

172. *See* Kimberly Hayes Taylor, *Mighty Moms Make Mark at Megamall*, MINNEAPOLIS-ST. PAUL STAR-TRIB., Apr. 27, 1996.

173. *See id.*

> On Saturday nights, large groups of young people have begun to congregate. No one likes to use the word "gangs," and in our racially sensitive times mall officials are reluctant to discuss the racial tensions inherent in what has gone on. But it has been reported that problems arise when, according to the *Minneapolis Star-Tribune*, the young people begin "blocking store entrances, intimidating other shoppers and sometimes walking in groups that swell to 50 people."

Greene, *supra* note 10. The Conduct Code handed out to teenagers entering the Mall includes the provision that "[a]ppropriate non-offensive attire, including shirts and shoes, must be worn." Mall of America, Conduct Code (1996).

what is assumed to be gang-related apparel, which further frightens some Mall shoppers.[174]

Prior to the curfew, the Mall had a Conduct Code in place[175] and Mall guards were required to ask teenagers in groups of three to keep moving.[176] However, while the Mall has its own security staff, management decided something more needed to be done to deal with the number of unsupervised teens. Thus, they originally implemented three new methods: (1) added security; (2) a Youth Liaison Program; and (3) the Mighty Moms.[177] The Mighty Moms program has been very successful. It consists of nineteen mothers, eighteen of whom are black, who are present at the Mall on weekend evenings and serve to diffuse confrontations between Mall security and the teens.[178] Often a yelling match erupts

---

174. Paul T. Barnes, a shopkeeper at the Mall, has stated that on weekend nights many of his older customers are scared away by the teenagers who congregate outside his store, "70 percent of them under the age of 20 and minority and wearing gang-related apparel . . . . [A] lot of people are not used to seeing large numbers of kids and large numbers of minority kids." Meredith, *supra* note 7.

Mall management has presented no evidence that fewer people have visited the Mall since the gun-related incidences. An issue that presents itself is whether Mall management intended the curfew not only to keep out the few violent teens, but also to provide an atmosphere more conducive to shoppers who feel intimidated by the large number of minority teens at the Mall. The Mall could have banned the violent and disruptive teenagers to achieve the first goal. With only a handful of gun related incidences, it surely is practical to provide Mall security, and especially security posted at Mall entrances, with pictures and names of the violent teens, in order that they can be recognized and refused entrance to the Mall. The Mall firmly denies a motive for implementing the Parental Escort Policy other than keeping the Mall environment safe. *See* Meredith, *supra* note 7 (quoting both Teresa McFarland and Virgil Heatwole). Such an analysis into the Mall's motives is beyond the scope of this comment, but the issue is raised for further inquiry.

175. The Conduct Code of the Mall of America is a small, 5 ½ x 8 ½" piece of paper with seven bullet headings that serve as the rules. The headings cover everything from disorderly conduct, loitering, and picketing, to attire and the disallowance of pets. At the bottom of the paper, in smaller print, is the information regarding the Parental Escort Policy. It includes the information necessary for obtaining a Minnesota State Identification Card which allows teenagers without driver's licenses or passports to provide acceptable identification.

176. *See* Taylor, *supra* note 172.

177. *See* September Press Release, *supra* note 9.

178. As one newspaper article states, the Mighty Moms have a good rapport with the teens because "the 'moms' say they can speak the same language. They may use the same words as security officials, but with a different tone, a gentler touch." Taylor, *supra* note 172. The Mighty Moms are paid $20 per hour for five hour shifts and are trained, as they say, in "verbal judo." *See* Karlen, *supra* note 9. While security and police handle violent incidences at the Mall, the Moms "are especially effective in heading off incidents that can be defused better with a friendly chat than with a badge." *Id.* The fact is, most kids will listen to a mom. Not only is there less authority tension between the Mighty Moms and the teenagers, but there is less (if any) racial tension as well.

between a teen (or group of teens) and Mall security when the teens are forced to leave the Mall due to a conduct violation. At this point, or before tempers rise, the Mighty Moms will step in, talk with the teens, and help them accept the guards' decision while lending the unhappy teens a sympathetic ear.[179]

While the Mighty Moms have been very successful, Mall management believed further action was necessary to cope with what they perceived to be a potential safety risk. Hence, they instituted the Parental Escort Policy. In a September 4, 1996 press release, the Mall's stated rationale behind the policy was to "reduce the growing number of unsupervised youth at the Mall on weekend nights."[180] Mall management obviously believed that parental supervision of anyone younger than sixteen would lead to a safer Mall atmosphere.[181] As previously discussed, serious violent incidents have already occurred at the Mall; two involved guns.[182] While no by-standers were hurt, the Mall management implemented the policy because, in its own words, "the risk of a serious incident continues to increase."[183] Indeed, before the policy was put into effect, the Mall Conduct Code was violated numerous times every weekend.[184] The weekend after the escort policy was implemented, the Mall's press release stated that fewer rules were violated, there were no fights between kids, and more families came to the Mall.[185]

Are the purposes of teen assembly compatible with the uses of the property? The answer to this question depends on which teens are referred to. For the teens who misbehave and are violent, the answer is a resounding no. The Mall of America was never intended to be a baby-sitter for rowdy Minnesota teens who have no other place to go. While the Mall serves numerous

---

179. When teens are asked to leave the Mall, they are escorted to the transportation center where they are put on a bus that will take them home. *See* Taylor, *supra* note 172.

180. September Press Release, *supra* note 9.

181. Due to the fact that many unsupervised kids go to the Mall of America, the Mall management states that it is "committed to controlling this situation by asking parents or guardians to be accountable for the actions of children in their care." *Id.* Virgil H. Heatwole, a Mall manager, has said that he "hoped the policy would result in children bringing their parents to the mall. 'I think society itself, we need to look at where parents are today.'" Meredith, *supra* note 7.

182. *See supra* note 10 and accompanying text.

183. September Press Release, *supra* note 9.

184. *See* Public Relations Dep't, Mall of America, Press Release (Oct. 8, 1996) [hereinafter October Press Release].

185. *See id.*

purposes, many teens who go to the Mall and gather in large groups on weekend evenings do not partake in either the activities offered or the shopping. Rather, by their presence, they intimidate some people who go there to shop, be entertained, or both. Also, storekeepers have complained that teens do a good deal of shoplifting on weekend nights, further eroding Mall consumerism.[186] The Mall's owners do have an interest in protecting their investment, and the presence of the rowdy and violent teens does pose a threat to the reputational value of the Mall.

These arguments persuasively establish that violent teenagers and teenagers who continually misbehave should be denied Mall access. However, the arguments do not overcome the fact that the vast majority of teens present at the Mall on weekend evenings *do* act in accordance with the purposes of the Mall and pose no safety threat. While the Mall would arguably prefer its patrons to participate in the activities it offers, like a downtown district it has opened its space to people who may only want to hang-out. Indeed, as *New Jersey Coalition* states, the public's invitation to the mall property "is not just an invitation to shop, but to do whatever one would do downtown, *including doing very little of anything.*"[187]

Once it has so opened its doors, the Mall of America should not be allowed to close them without greater justification. The fact that some shoppers are intimidated by large groups of teens at the Mall on weekend evenings does not justify the implementation of an across-the-board juvenile curfew. Indeed, as the United States Supreme Court has held, "mere public intolerance or animosity cannot be the basis for abridgment of these [free assembly and association] constitutional freedoms."[188] The Court so held in 1971 when it struck down a Cincinnati ordinance making it illegal for three or more people to assemble on a sidewalk and conduct themselves "in a manner annoying to persons passing by."[189] As in the Mall of America situation, a charge was also made that the

186. *See* Sally Apgar, *Megamall's Plan for Required Escorts Praised, Assailed,* MINNEAPOLIS-ST. PAUL STAR-TRIB., June 21, 1996, at 1B.

187. New Jersey Coalition Against War in the Middle East v. J.M.B. Realty Corp., 650 A.2d 757, 761 (N.J. 1994) (emphasis added). The court further stated that the malls have "substantially displaced the downtown business districts as the centers of commercial *and social activity.*" *Id.* at 767 (emphasis added).

188. Coates v. City of Cincinnati, 402 U.S. 611, 615 (1971).

189. *Id.* at 611.

ordinance was enforced disproportionately:[190] "[A]nd such a prohibition, in addition, contains an obvious invitation to discriminatory enforcement against those whose association together is 'annoying' because their ideas, their lifestyle, or their physical appearance is resented by the majority of their fellow citizens."[191] Due to the fact that the majority of the teens who are at the Mall on weekend evenings are black and the patrons are white, the appearance of a discriminatory motive in implementing the curfew is present. The teens speak and dress differently from the older adults at the Mall, and it is their appearance and speech which older people find intimidating. If some Mall patrons feel intimidated by seeing the large groups of black teens at the Mall, such feelings do not justify a prohibition on the teenager's access to the Mall.[192]

Furthermore, the Mall has not stated or implied that fewer people go to the Mall due to teen misbehavior, and no statistics have shown that the Mall's revenues have decreased following the teen shooting incidents. As Mall spokeswoman Teresa McFarland has said, most of the teens at the Mall are well behaved. She stated: "We have a lot of unsupervised young people on Saturday nights . . . . [T]hey should be supervised by parents or other adults, but they aren't. *Most are good kids. But a small percentage* won't follow any mall rules or obey any authority figures . . ."[193] Bob Lutz, the Bloomington police chief, has stated that "[m]ost of the trouble with teens is rowdy behavior and bad language, but nothing criminal."[194] He also says claims of gang activity are overblown: "Gang activity isn't running when you're supposed to walk or swearing."[195] The Mall has even been called safer than the streets.[196] By May 7, 1996, the Mall had let it be known that a juvenile curfew was under consideration. Lottie Dixon, one of the

---

190. *See id.* at 616, n.6. For one allegation that Mall of America employees hand out the Mall rules to black youth more often than to white youth, see Meredith, *supra* note 7.

191. *Coates*, 402 U.S. at 616.

192. *See* TRIBE, *supra* note 88, § 15-18, at 1409 (stating that "[i]f simply finding another's appearance or habits offensive to hear, see, or think about were enough to justify exclusionary regulation, rights of personhood and indeed of expression would be at an end").

193. Greene, *supra* note 10 (emphasis added).

194. Apgar, *supra* note 186.

195. *Id.* Further, on September 18, 1996, after the gun-related incidents had occurred, Chief Lutz stated: "[L]et's be clear . . . we're talking about non-criminal conduct by a bunch of snotty-nosed kids." *See* Vick, *supra* note 167.

196. *See* Taylor, *supra* note 172.

Mighty Moms, was quoted in the *Minneapolis-St. Paul Star-Tribune* as follows: "[T]he mall, she said, is much safer than the streets."[197]

In concluding the *Schmid* third prong analysis, this comment does not argue that all teens should be allowed in the Mall of America. Those who have displayed violent behavior, whether teens or adults, should not be allowed in the Mall. Those who have repeatedly broken the Mall's Conduct Code do not deserve to be in the Mall. But this comment does not advocate denying access rights to all teens when only a small number misbehave. To stereotype all teens as undeserving to be in the Mall is not simply grossly unfair but, this comment argues, violative of their assembly rights. Little justification can be found in informing the well-behaved teens that they are not welcome at the Mall unless accompanied by an adult. As the Mall management itself has said, the majority of the teens at the Mall on weekend evenings are well-behaved. Some of them do shop while they are there, and the curfew has actually hurt some storekeepers who cater to a younger clientele.[198] Indeed, many storekeepers and customers say that the policy doesn't work because teens who enter the Mall before 6 p.m. and who are not rowdy do not get checked for identification by Mall security.[199]

The Mall specifically encourages teens to come to its premises by catering to their entertainment and shopping needs.[200] The fact that most of the teens choose to just 'hang-out' on the premises is in no way incompatible with the Mall's purposes. *New Jersey Coalition* reiterated that the more a private property owner opens his/her property to the public, the "more do his rights become circumscribed by the statutory and constitutional rights of those who use it."[201] The question then arises whether an argument can be made under existing Minnesota constitutional and statutory law for recognizing teenagers' assembly rights at the Mall.

---

197. *Id.*

198. For example, Claire's, an accessory store that caters to young girls, now has less weekend business as its shoppers go to other area malls where they do not need escorts. *See* Preeti Gupta, *Mall Workers Give Mixed Reviews to Curfew*, MINNEAPOLIS-ST. PAUL STAR TRIB., July 7, 1997, at 6B. *See also* Apgar, *supra* note 186.

199. *See* Gupta, *supra* note 198.

200. *See supra* text accompanying notes 115-19.

201. New Jersey Coalition Against War in the Middle East v. J.M.B. Realty Corp., 650 A.2d 757, 775-76 (N.J. 1994) (quoting Marsh v. Alabama, 326 U.S. 501, 506 (1946)).

IV. Does Minnesota Law Protect Freedom of Assembly Rights on Private Property?

A. *The Minnesota Constitution and Caselaw*

There is no affirmative grant of freedom of assembly rights on private property in the Minnesota Constitution. Furthermore, unlike the Federal Constitution, the Minnesota Constitution has no express provision granting freedom of assembly rights whatsoever.[202] There is very little Minnesota caselaw on the subject of assembly rights. However, none of these cases approximate the cause of action contemplated by this comment. In 1939, the Minnesota Supreme Court in *State v. Winkels*[203] struck down an overbroad assembly statute, while in *State v. Hipp*[204] the state upheld the current unlawful assembly statute. The statute in *Hipp* has little bearing on the teenagers' cause of action as the statute is meant to provide police action after the fact and the Parental Escort Policy is a preventative measure. The language of the statute states that

> [w]hen three or more persons assemble, each participant is guilty of unlawful assembly, which is a misdemeanor, if the assembly is: (1) With intent to commit any unlawful act by force; or (2) With intent to carry out any purpose in such manner as will disturb or threaten the public peace; or (3) Without unlawful purpose, but the participants so conduct themselves in a disorderly manner as to disturb or threaten the public peace.[205]

The *Hipp* court upheld the constitutionality of the statute by refusing to find it vague or overbroad.[206] The third case, *State v. Johnson*,[207] is only tangentially related to assembly rights. *John-*

---

202. *See* U.S. CONST., amend. I.

203. 283 N.W. 763 (Minn. 1939). The statute which was struck down provided that

> [w]henever three or more persons, having assembled for any purpose, shall disturb the public peace by using force or violence to any other person or to property, or shall threaten or attempt to commit such disturbance, or to do an unlawful act by the use of force or violence, accompanied with the power of immediate execution of such threat or attempt, they shall be guilty of a riot.

Id. at 764.

204. 213 N.W.2d 610 (Minn. 1973).

205. MINN. STAT. ANN. § 609.705 (West 1987).

206. *See Hipp*, 213 N.W.2d at 614-15.

207. 163 N.W.2d 750 (Minn. 1968).

son was concerned with whether the defendants' had breached the peace in violation of a state ordinance by gathering in downtown Minneapolis to protest the Vietnam War.[208] The court held that the police officer's attempt to maintain order by arresting them was within the bounds of the ordinance and did not abridge the defendants' rights of free speech and assembly.[209] The case was decided in favor of the defendants, however, when the court found that there was insufficient evidence to prove that those arrested had actually violated the ordinance.[210]

Thus, there is very little upon which to base an affirmative right for teenager assembly rights in the existing Minnesota assembly caselaw.[211] However, a court may grant a specific individual liberty by considering the circumstances leading up to a cause of action and using its own precedent as a guide to the type of individual rights previously recognized. Minnesota caselaw provides a rich history of protecting individual liberties that were unimaginable to the writers of the Minnesota Bill of Rights. By working within this rich tradition and recognizing the need for affirmative assembly rights, there exists a strong argument for the creation of an affirmative assembly right under the Minnesota Constitution.[212]

Article I, section 16, of the Minnesota Constitution holds that "[t]he enumeration of rights in this constitution shall not deny or impair others retained by and inherent in the people."[213] Actions

---

208. *See id.* at 751.

209. *See id.* at 754-55.

210. *See id.* at 755.

211. While a detailed analysis of federal decisions dealing with assembly rights is necessary for a more complete argument, such analysis is beyond the scope of this comment. Indeed, while the First Amendment of the United States Constitution provides that Congress shall not abridge the peoples' freedom to assemble, similar to the Minnesota Supreme Court, the United States Supreme Court has heard relatively few cases regarding freedom of assembly.

One United States Supreme Court case bearing on the Mall of America situation is *Coates v. City of Cincinnati*, 402 U.S. 611 (1971). In *Coates*, the Court struck down a Cincinnati ordinance making it a criminal offense for "three or more persons to assemble . . . on any of the sidewalks . . . and there conduct themselves in a manner annoying to persons passing by, or occupants of adjacent buildings." *Id.* at 611 n.1. The Court held the ordinance void for vagueness, as "[c]onduct that annoys some people does not annoy others." *Id.* at 614. For a further discussion of *Coates*, see *supra* text accompanying notes 187-90.

212. Although this comment forcefully argues for a right of teenager assembly based on article I, section 16 of the Minnesota Constitution, the Minnesota courts may look to other jurisdictions to help them in their determination of whether such a right ought to be granted.

213. MINN. CONST. art. I, § 16.

for the recognition of individual liberties have been successfully brought, in whole or in part, under this clause.[214] The Minnesota Supreme Court has liberally interpreted this clause, thus providing constitutional protection for individual liberties not specifically enumerated in the state constitution.[215] Based on the state supreme court's liberal reading of the Minnesota constitution as granting protection for unenumerated individual liberties, it would be in keeping with this reading for the court to recognize teenagers' assembly rights at the Mall of America.

It has been established that under federal law there exist no First Amendment protections at privately owned malls; however, *PruneYard* affirmed states' rights to interpret their constitutions as providing more individual liberty protections than the Federal Constitution.[216] The Minnesota Supreme Court has actively utilized its state constitution as a fertile source of individual rights protections.[217] In 1985, the Minnesota Supreme Court expressly recognized this utilized power in *State v. Fuller*,[218] a decision which has been heavily relied upon. The *Fuller* court stated that "[i]t is axiomatic that a state supreme court may interpret its own state constitution to offer greater protection of individual rights than does the federal constitution."[219] Following is an analysis of the Minnesota Supreme Court's interpretation of its state Bill of Rights. This analysis will show that the Minnesota Supreme Court has consistently placed a high premium on individual liberties by supporting their protection through an expansive reading of the state Bill of Rights. By its nature, this survey cannot be conclusive

---

214. *See* discussion *infra* notes 230-54.

215. *See* discussion *infra* notes 230-54.

216. *See* PruneYard Shopping Ctr. v. Robins, 447 U.S. 74 (1980).

217. *See In re* Welfare of E.D.J., 502 N.W.2d 779 (Minn. 1993); State v. Hershberger, 462 N.W.2d 393 (Minn. 1990); State v. Gray, 413 N.W.2d 107 (Minn. 1987); State v. Fuller, 374 N.W.2d 722 (Minn. 1985).

218. 374 N.W.2d at 722.

219. *Id.* at 726. The court went on to state that:

> Indeed, as the highest court of this state, we are independently responsible for safeguarding the rights of [our] citizens . . . . State courts are, and should be, the first line of defense for individual liberties within the federalist system. This, of course, does not mean that we will or should cavalierly construe our constitution more expansively than the United States Supreme Court has construed the federal constitution. Indeed, a decision of the United States Supreme Court interpreting a comparable provision of the federal constitution that, as here, is textually identical to a provision of our constitution, is of inherently persuasive, although not necessarily compelling, force.

Id. at 726-27 (citations omitted).

as to how the Minnesota Supreme Court would rule if the Mall of America's curfew was to be challenged. Rather, it first provides the background for one avenue of analysis the court may utilize in this hypothetical cause of action; secondly, it resolves the issue in a manner consistent with precedent in honoring heretofore unrecognized individual liberties protections.[220]

Unlike the Federal Constitution, the Minnesota Bill of Rights is placed first in the Minnesota Constitution. At least one commentator has noted that this is perhaps as strong an indication as any of Minnesota's commitment to the protection of individual liberties.[221] The Minnesota Bill of Rights contains seventeen separate sections enumerating the rights granted therein.[222] However, while it enumerates separate rights, the Bill of Rights is not meant to be exclusive. As previously stated, article I, section 16 of the Minnesota constitution reads: "The enumeration of rights in this constitution shall not be construed to deny or impair others retained by and inherent in the people."[223] Regarding the interpretation of this provision, the Minnesota Supreme Court held in *Thiede v. Town of Scandia Valley*[224] that while the state constitution "specifically recognizes the right to 'life, liberty or property' . . . [it] does not attempt to enumerate all 'the rights or privileges secured to any citizen thereof.'"[225] Thus, as far back as 1944, the Minnesota high court held it unlawful for the state to

220. Because this cause of action is of first impression anywhere, this background into Minnesota caselaw can do no more than provide the history of the Minnesota Supreme Court's stance regarding individual liberties issues and argue for continued expansive protection in the case of teenagers' assembly rights at the Mall of America. While it will be proven that the Minnesota Supreme Court has consistently broadly interpreted article I, section 16 of its Bill of Rights, this author is well aware that such liberal interpretations may not necessarily translate to an extension of these holdings to the issue at the Mall of America. *See* Fiesta Mall Venture v. Mecham Recall Comm., 767 P.2d 719, 721 (Ariz. Ct. App. 1988); Southcenter Joint Venture v. National Democratic Policy Comm., 780 P.2d 1282, 1286 (Wash. 1989).

221. *See* Fred L. Morrison, *An Introduction to the Minnesota Constitution*, 20 WM. MITCHELL L. REV. 287, 299 (1994) (providing a detailed history of the Minnesota Constitution and a framework for raising state claims under the Minnesota Bill of Rights).

222. *See* MINN. CONST. art. I, §§ 1-17. Of special interest to this comment are article I, section 2 (Rights and Privileges); article I, section 13 (Private Property for Public Use); and article I, section 16 (Freedom of Conscience).

223. MINN. CONST. art. I, § 16.

224. 14 N.W.2d 400 (Minn. 1944).

225. *See id.* at 405.

forcibly remove an alleged pauper and relocate him against his will.[226] The court held that a property owner cannot be forcibly removed from his land and placed in a legal settlement for poor relief reasons even though, in the past, a state statute allowed such state action.[227] Rather, the individual's right to be free from this restraint on his liberty took precedence over the asserted state interest.

Since *Thiede,* the Minnesota Supreme Court has continued to interpret its constitution broadly to afford rights not expressly enumerated therein. Indeed, *Thiede's* support of unenumerated rights, coupled with *Fuller's* recognition that the Minnesota Constitution may offer more rights than the Federal Constitution, has proved to be a powerful one-two punch for the support of individual liberties under Minnesota constitutional law. For example, citing both *Fuller* and *Thiede,* the Minnesota Supreme Court has held that while no express right of privacy is enumerated under its constitution, one exists and is recognized by the Minnesota Constitution.[228] In *State v. Gray*, the court was faced with a constitutional challenge to a state sodomy statute. The defendant argued that the statute infringed on his right of privacy to have consensual, for-hire homosexual sex. Holding otherwise, the court decided that while the state constitution *does* recognize an unenumerated right of privacy, the court would not extend that right to commercial sex.[229] The court did not decide whether the sodomy statute was unconstitutional when prostitution was not involved. Thus, while the defendant in *Gray* lost, all Minnesotans

---

226. *See id.* at 406. The court held that town supervisors who continue to unlawfully remove a pauper from his home will be personally liable for actual and punitive damages stemming from the removal. *See id.* at 407-08.

227. Noting that a man's home is his castle, the court held this concept to be older than the Magna Carta and embedded in both the Declaration of Independence and in the Bill of Rights of the Federal *and* Minnesota Constitutions. *See id.* at 405.

228. *See* State v. Gray, 413 N.W.2d 107 (Minn. 1987).

229. *See id.* at 114. The Minnesota Supreme Court recognized the federal right of privacy enunciated in *Griswold v. Connecticut*, 381 U.S. 479 (1965) and extended this right to the Minnesota Constitution. *See Gray,* 413 N.W.2d at 111. One year before the *Gray* decision, the United States Supreme Court had decided *Bowers v. Hardwick*, 478 U.S. 186 (1986), holding that federal guarantees of privacy rights do not encompass the right to engage in homosexual sex. By the time Mr. Gray's case reached the Minnesota Supreme Court, he was preempted from arguing under the Federal Constitution. Although he may have chosen to argue under federal law if able to do so (were *Bowers* not yet decided), his argument under the Minnesota Constitution had the lasting effect of providing Minnesotans with a recognized right of privacy under their own state Bill of Rights. This right is clear and distinct from a correlative right under the Federal Constitution.

won as the right to privacy was recognized under Minnesota law.[230] The court specifically held that Minnesotans' right to privacy under their state constitution equaled that under the Federal Constitution; nevertheless, no specific sections of the Minnesota Constitution were cited to support this conclusion.[231]

The Minnesota Supreme Court has also expanded its constitution's individual liberties protections in the area of criminal law, providing more safeguards to the accused with regard to searches and seizures than does the Fourth Amendment. In *In re Welfare of E.D.J.*,[232] the court declined to adopt the United States Supreme Court's Fourth Amendment seizure definition in *California v. Hodari D.*[233] *Hodari* held that a seizure only occurs when physical force is used to restrain a person's movements or when a person physically submits to a show of police authority.[234] This definition was significantly narrower than the Minnesota concept of seizure. Minnesota had been applying the *Mendenhall/Royer* approach[235] as consistent with the state constitution. Under the *Mendenhall/Royer* approach, a seizure occurs when a reasonable person in the defendant's shoes would have concluded that s/he was

---

230. In *Gray*, the court stated:

> [A] comparison of the Minnesota Bill of Rights with the federal constitutional provisions upon which the right of privacy is founded shows that the rights protected by the Federal Constitution are also protected by the Minnesota Bill of Rights. Accordingly, it is our opinion that there does exist a right of privacy guaranteed under and protected by the Minnesota Bill of Rights.

Gray, 413 N.W.2d at 111. The court went on to state that the scope of this right extends only to fundamental rights. *See id.*

For a comprehensive history of privacy rights under the Minnesota Constitution, see Michael K. Steenson, *Fundamental Rights in the "Gray" Area: The Right of Privacy Under the Minnesota Constitution,* 20 WM. MITCHELL L. REV. 383 (1994).

231. The court anchored its right to privacy in its state Bill of Rights one year later in *Jarvis v. Levine*, 418 N.W.2d 139 (Minn. 1987). Mr. Jarvis was a mental patient committed against his will. *See id.* at 140-41. He successfully challenged the forcible administration of neuroleptic drugs to him in non-emergency situations. *See id.* at 148. The state supreme court held that the forcible administration of the drugs violated his privacy rights anchored in article I, sections 1, 2, and 10 of the state constitution. *See id.* at 148. The court stated that "[a]lthough judicial recognition of a constitutional right of privacy in Minnesota may be relatively recent, the protection of bodily integrity has been rooted firmly in our law for centuries." *Id.* at 148-49.

232. 502 N.W.2d 779 (Minn. 1993).

233. 499 U.S. 621 (1991).

234. *See E.D.J.*, 502 N.W.2d at 781. In *Hodari*, the Court held that under the Fourth Amendment, "[a]n arrest requires *either* force (as described above) *or,* where that is absent, *submission* to the assertion of authority." *Hodari*, 499 U.S. at 626.

235. *See* Florida v. Royer, 460 U.S. 491 (1983); United States v. Mendenhall, 446 U.S. 544 (1980).

not free to leave and walk away from the police in such a situation.[236] E.D.J. was a juvenile who was standing with two adults on a known drug-trafficking street corner.[237] As a police car approached, the three began walking in the opposite direction. The vehicle stopped behind them, and the officers ordered them to stop walking.[238] As the two men stopped, E.D.J. kept walking, dropped something, and eventually turned around. E.D.J. was later arrested for possession of crack cocaine obtained from a search and seizure.[239] The state supreme court reversed E.D.J.'s district court conviction and refused to adopt the *Hodari* approach.[240] Instead of applying the pre-*Hodari*, *Mendenhall/Royer* approach articulated above, the court "exercis[ed its] independent authority to interpret [its] own state constitution . . . ."[241] As a result, the court held that E.D.J. was seized by the police and that the stop was illegal because the police were unable to articulate a sufficient basis for the stop.[242]

One of the most frequently cited cases for an individual liberties protection argument under the Minnesota Constitution is *State v. Hershberger*.[243] In *Hershberger*, the Supreme Court of Minnesota held that a Minnesota Statute requiring the use of a Slow Moving Vehicles ("SMV") sticker on Amish buggies violated article I, section 16 of the Minnesota Constitution.[244] In addition to declaring that the enumerated rights of the constitution were not all inclusive,[245] the court noted that section 16 provided highly detailed freedom of religion protections.[246] The Amish had stated

---

236. *See E.D.J.*, 502 N.W.2d at 782 (setting forth the Minnesota Supreme Court's full articulation of the *Mendenhall/Royer* standard).

237. *See id.* at 780.

238. *See id.*

239. *See id.*

240. *See id.* at 783.

241. *E.D.J.*, 502 N.W.2d at 783.

242. *See id.*

243. 462 N.W.2d 393 (Minn. 1990).

244. *See id.* at 399.

245. *See id.* at 398 (citing State v. Fuller, 374 N.W.2d 722, 726 (1985)).

246. *See id.* The entire text of article I, section 16 provides:

Freedom of Conscience; no preference to be given to any religious establishment or mode of worship.

The enumeration of rights in this constitution shall not deny or impair others retained by and inherent in the people. The right of every man to worship God according to the dictates of his own conscience shall never be infringed; nor shall any man be compelled to attend, erect or support any place of worship, or to maintain any religious or ecclesiastical ministry, against his consent; nor shall

that their religious beliefs forbade the use of such symbols.[247] Realizing that the proposed use of the sticker was for safety purposes, it was suggested that the Amish use reflective tape and red lanterns which would not violate their religious tenets.[248] The Minnesota Supreme Court agreed and held that the Amish could use the tape and lanterns instead of the SMV stickers. However, on certiorari to the United States Supreme Court, the case was remanded to the state high court for a determination under the compelling state interest/least restrictive means test.[249]

On remand, the Minnesota Supreme Court held that the state statute violated this test.[250] While public safety had to be served, the court believed that, under the Minnesota Constitution, public safety could be balanced with religious freedom to produce a result that would satisfy both. "Thus, while the terms 'compelling state interest' and 'least restrictive alternative' are creatures of federal doctrine, concepts embodied therein can provide guidance as we seek to strike a balance under the Minnesota Constitution between freedom of conscience and the state's public safety interest."[251] The court went on to recognize that religious freedoms have traditionally been treated with high respect by the court.[252] In deference to this history, and in light of the fact that the state never proved that white reflective tape and red lanterns were inadequate safety precautions, the court held that the law violated the state constitution.[253]

Furthermore, there exists no explicit right in the Minnesota Constitution to grant criminal defendants the right to consult with an attorney before submitting to an intoxilizer test, but the Minnesota Supreme Court granted this right in *Freidman v.*

> any control of or interference with the rights of conscience be permitted, or any preference be given by law to any religious establishment or mode of worship; but the liberty of conscience hereby secured shall not be so construed as to excuse acts of licentiousness or justify practices inconsistent with the peace or safety of the state, nor shall any money be drawn from the treasury for the benefit of any religious societies or theological seminaries.

MINN. CONST. art. I, § 16.

247. *See Hershberger*, 462 N.W.2d at 395.

248. *See id.* at 399.

249. *See* Minnesota v. Hershberger, 495 U.S. 910 (1990).

250. *See Hershberger*, 462 N.W.2d at 399.

251. *Id.* at 398.

252. *See id.*

253. *See id.* at 399.

Commissioner of Public Safety.[254] The court has also held that the Minnesota Constitution requires juries of twelve in all criminal cases.[255] Although the United States Supreme Court had held that juries of less than twelve are allowed in certain non-capital criminal offenses, the Minnesota Supreme Court held that the intent of the framers of the state constitution was to require twelve jurors even in misdemeanor and gross misdemeanor cases.[256] In granting this right, the court held that it "must remain independently responsible for safeguarding the rights of our own citizens and for insuring that the intent of the people of Minnesota in adopting our constitution is continued forward."[257]

Hershberger, Fuller, Gray, E.D.J., Friedman, Hamm, and *Jarvis* all form a strong basis upon which a claim for a teenagers' right to assemble at the Mall of America can be established. As has been shown, Minnesota began a trend towards basing individual liberties protections in its state constitution with *Thiede*.[258] The Mall of America situation is unique in that, unlike the other cases herein discussed, this situation could only occur in Minnesota. That this situation is uniquely Minnesotan in nature and ought to be determined under Minnesota law can be most forcibly argued under *Jarvis v. Levine*.[259] Deciding a mental patient's right under the Minnesota Constitution to refuse the administration of neuroleptic drugs in nonemergency situations, the Minnesota Supreme Court held that "[w]e are faced with the rights of persons committed to Minnesota institutions, pursuant to Minnesota law, by the courts of this state. Given the significant state law issues involved, we feel it is imperative to assume our obligation to be 'independently responsible for safeguarding the rights of [our] citizens.'"[260]

This reasoning is most persuasive in the Mall of America situation as there is only one Mall of America, and Minnesota is in

254. 473 N.W.2d 828, 837 (Minn. 1991).

255. *See* State v. Hamm, 423 N.W.2d 379 (Minn. 1988).

256. *See id.* at 381 (citing Williams v. Florida, 399 U.S. 78 (1970)). The Minnesota Supreme Court focused on the fact that article I, section 6 of the state constitution states that "[i]n all criminal prosecutions the accused shall enjoy the right to a speedy and public trial by an impartial jury . . . ." MINN. CONST. art. I, § 6. Additionally, article I, section 4 guarantees that "[t]he right of trial by jury shall remain inviolate . . . ." *Id.* § 4.

257. *Hamm*, 423 N.W.2d at 382.

258. Thiede v. Town of Scandia Valley, 14 N.W.2d 400, 405 (Minn. 1944).

259. 418 N.W.2d 139 (Minn. 1988). *See also supra* note 231 and accompanying text.

260. *Id.* at 147 (quoting State v. Gray, 413 N.W.2d 107, 111 (Minn. 1987)).

the unique position of being home to what is undoubtedly the world's most famous shopping mall. Thus, while other states have malls that are facing problems with rowdy teenagers,[261] the Mall of America, while not the first to implement a juvenile curfew,[262] is the largest and most well-known of the country's malls to have done so. Only the Mall of America has two to three thousand teenagers arriving at its doors on weekends nights, and only the Mall of America has the funds and manpower to deal with the situation on this scale.[263] Finding a teen right of assembly at the Mall would have a lasting effect on both teenagers' rights and rights of assembly in Minnesota. It would also serve as persuasive authority to other states in which mall managements are considering implementing such a curfew. The Mall of America is so well-known and there is such widespread interest in it that when it imposed the curfew, the decision was deemed newsworthy enough to be written about in national newspapers across the country.[264] Surely a decision striking down the curfew as unconstitutional would receive similar coverage and, thus, other mall managements would be aware of it.

In order to make a constitutional argument for teenagers' freedom of assembly rights at the Mall, the Minnesota Supreme Court must ground such a right in the Minnesota Constitution. As has been shown in *Gray* and its progeny, the court is willing to extend individual liberties protections to those not enumerated in the constitution under article I, section 16.[265] Safeguarding the rights of Minnesota citizens by assessing their evolving needs can best be effectuated by granting an affirmative right to freedom of

261. Teresa McFarland states that she has taken calls from malls across the country asking her how the Mall of America deals with unsupervised youth. *See* Taylor, *supra* note 172. *See also* Kokmen, *supra* note 7; *Mall Execs Veto Curfews,* LONG ISLAND BUS. NEWS, Oct. 28, 1996, at 24; Peterson, *supra* note 27 (discussing teen problems at local malls as well as the reticence on the part of the mall owners and lack of need to impose a curfew); Vick, *supra* note 167.

262. *See supra* note 19 and accompanying text.

263. *See* Meredith, *supra* note 7. The Mall's revenue was $675 million in 1994 alone. *See It's a Megamall World, supra* note 128. Some of these monies could have been used to hire more guards and install metal detectors. These are relatively simple safety precautions which could easily be put in place and might obviate the need for the juvenile curfew.

264. For example, when the Mall announced that it was considering a juvenile curfew, the news made the front page of *The New York Times* and was written about in *The Washington Post* and *The Chicago Tribune*, arguably three of the most respected newspapers in the United States. *See supra* notes 7, 27 and accompanying text.

265. *See supra* notes 229-32 and accompanying text.

assembly at privately owned shopping malls that serve as public downtowns. The court will do well to recognize the Mall of America as a public arena and, as such, a place where First Amendment-type freedoms should not to be denied. Once such a right is grounded in the Minnesota Constitution, then the question becomes whether the state's purpose can be achieved by using any less intrusive methods.

B. *Statutory Basis—The Minnesota Human Rights Act*

As has been mentioned, there are many methods by which the Mall of America's Parental Escort Policy can be challenged. While this comment focuses mainly on the constitutional challenge to freedom of assembly rights, other approaches may achieve greater success. One of the alternative arguments, based on the Minnesota Human Rights Act (the "Act"), is briefly discussed because it adds a statutory basis to the constitutional and caselaw analysis discussed above.

The Act was most recently revised by the Minnesota Legislature in 1980.[266] The provision most applicable to the Mall situation is section 363.03(3) which deals with public accommodations. Section 363.03(3) provides that it is "unfair discriminatory practice: (1) to deny any person the full and equal enjoyment of the goods, services, facilities, privileges, advantages, and accommodations of a place of public accommodation because of race, color, creed, religion, disability, national origin, marital status, sexual orientation, or sex . . . ."[267] In the definitional section of the Act, a place of public accommodation is defined as "a business, accommodation, refreshment, entertainment, recreation, or transportation facility of any kind, whether licensed or not, whose goods, services, facilities, privileges, advantages or accommodations are extended, offered, sold, or otherwise made available to the public."[268] Clearly, the Mall of America satisfies the Act's definition of a place of public accommodation. With 520 stores and numerous restaurants, clubs, entertainment facilities, and even a hotel, the Mall qualifies as such a place. Additionally, its goods are extended, offered, and sold to the public at large.

266. *See* MINN. STAT. ANN. §§ 363.01-20 (West 1991) (Minnesota Human Rights Act).
267. *Id.* § 363.03(3)(a)(1).
268. *Id.* § 363.01(33) (1991).

Once held that the Mall of America is a place of public accommodation under the Minnesota Human Rights Act, it must be determined whether the Mall's Parental Escort Policy falls within the scope of the public accommodations provision. On its face, it appears that it does not. The provision mentions nothing about age. The Parental Escort Policy, serving as a curfew at the Mall of America, is based solely on an age requirement.[269] In order for the Minnesota Supreme Court to apply the Act to the Parental Escort Policy, the court would have to determine that the list enumerated in the Act is not exclusive. To take such action is not beyond the bounds of the state supreme court's authority. Indeed, as has been shown, the Minnesota Supreme Court has a tradition of granting individual liberty protections not enumerated in the state constitution. Furthermore, the Act itself states that "[t]he provisions of this chapter shall be construed liberally for the accomplishment of the purposes thereof."[270] The main purpose of the Act is "to secure for persons in this state, freedom from discrimination."[271]

In one of the first cases in which a cause of action was brought under the Minnesota Human Rights Act, the supreme court, in *United States v. McClure*,[272] discussed the long history of the Minnesota anti-discrimination laws and the place they hold for the people of the state. In 1897, 1905, 1943, 1965, and 1980, the Minnesota Legislature showed a continued commitment to fighting discrimination by revising and broadening its anti-discrimination law.[273] As the court recognized, Minnesota's first anti-discrimination law in 1885 preceded the anything-but "separate but equal" Jim Crow laws and was much more egalitarian than those laws.[274] The court then found that the United States Jaycees served as a place of public accommodation and, as such, could not continue granting unequal membership privileges to its male and female

269. An action against the Mall of America for racial discrimination is a strong claim under the Act. *See infra* note 279 and accompanying text.

270. MINN. STAT. ANN. § 363.11.

271. *Id.*. § 363.12.

272. 305 N.W.2d 764 (Minn. 1981). Based on the Minnesota Human Rights Act, the court held that the Jaycees served as a place of public accommodation. *See id.* at 774. Therefore, based on the Act's nondiscrimination provision relating to sex, the court held that the organization could not grant fewer membership privileges to its female members than those granted to its male members. *See id.*

273. *See id.* at 765-68.

274. *See id.* at 766-67.

members.[275] The court engaged in an in-depth analysis of whether the Jaycees, a national organization, served as a place of public accommodation.[276] Using criteria from other jurisdictions, the court determined that the Jaycees, a nonselective group with an uncapped membership, did serve as a place of public accommodation.[277]

The same logic should be applied to the Mall of America's curfew. The court should construe the statute liberally to consider age as a factor under the Act. Due solely to the teenagers' age, they are denied certain access to the Mall of America. The Minnesota Supreme Court in *United States Jaycees* noted that Minnesota's human rights laws have grown more inclusive with each revision.[278] An argument can and should be made for realizing the intent behind this legislation by expanding the Act's protections to include age discrimination. An analysis into the Minnesota Supreme Court's interpretations of legislative acts, be those interpretations strictly literal or broad in scope, would be necessary in making this argument. Such analysis is beyond the scope of this comment, but it is hoped that this comment succeeds in laying the foundation for the myriad constitutional and statutory challenges that may be brought against the Parental Escort Policy.[279]

---

275. *See id.* at 774.

276. *See id.* at 768-72.

277. *See United States Jaycees*, 305 N.W.2d at 768-72.

278. *See id.* at 765-68.

279. Indeed, this comment is narrow in scope compared to the number of approaches that can be taken in challenging the curfew. Again, the focus of this comment is to lay the foundation in arguing for an individual liberty right of teenager assembly under the Minnesota Constitution. However, there are numerous ways of challenging the validity of the juvenile curfew. Following is a very brief overview of three alternative arguments for challenging the Mall of America's Parental Escort Policy.

First, one of the strongest arguments which can be made is that the Parental Escort Policy discriminates against black youth who only frequent the Mall in such large numbers on weekend evenings. *See* Apgar, *supra* note 186; Meredith, *supra* note 7. While Mall management has stated that it implemented the curfew as a colorblind measure, the effect of the curfew undeniably affects black youth in greater numbers. *See id.* (noting President of the Minneapolis Urban League, Gary Sudduth's outcry upon the curfew's implementation). Under the Federal Constitution, a discriminatory motive, and not just a discriminatory effect, must be found in order for the cause of action to succeed. *See* Mayor of Washington, D.C. v. Davis, 426 U.S. 229 (1976). However, such a finding is not necessary under all state laws. Hence, it would be worth studying further the Minnesota Human Rights Act and state caselaw to determine whether a discriminatory motive must be present or whether a discriminatory impact is sufficient for a finding of discrimination. If the curfew is found to be discriminatory, as the evidence indicates, the next question is whether the stated non-discriminatory intent is sufficient to sustain it in light of the discriminatory impact or whether

V. Alternatives

After the New Jersey Supreme Court in *New Jersey Coalition* had granted petitioners the right to leaflet at the defendants' malls, the court stated:

> There is concern, understandable concern, about the possibility of confrontation, disturbance, and even violence—concerns not just for business, but for the safety and security of people at the premises. Freedom of speech has always had this potential, controversy being part of its nature. Defendants' fears are not fanciful, but this is hardly a novel problem. This country, and its cities, and more to the point, its downtown business districts, have successfully dealt with it and lived with it for centuries.[280]

The court stated that the speech right granted—that of distributing leaflets—was not likely to result in harm to the

---

the curfew is a pretext for discrimination.

Secondly, a due process argument under the Minnesota Constitution Rights and Privileges Clause, should be explored. *See* MINN. CONST. art. I, § 2. The first sentence of that provision states that "[n]o member of this state shall be disfranchised or deprived of any of the rights or privileges secured to any citizen thereof, unless by the law of the land or the judgment of his peers." *Id.*

In conjuction with a Minnesota due process claim, an argument may be made under the state curfew regulations. Minnesota has a curfew regulation establishing that "a county board may adopt an ordinance establishing a countywide curfew for unmarried persons under 18 years of age . . . ." MINN. STAT. ANN. § 145A.05(7)(2) (West Supp. 1997). An argument may be made analogizing the Mall of America's Parental Escort Policy to municipal curfews across the country. A number of the curfews have been invalidated due to the broadness of their scope. By contrast, many of the curfews that have been upheld are more narrowly tailored. An analogy can be made to the Mall of America situation by arguing that its curfew is overboard and that the result desired by Mall management can be achieved with more narrowly tailored means. *See* discussion *infra* Part V.

Third, a federal Fourteenth Amendment due process argument can also be raised in conjunction with this state argument. *See* U.S. CONST. amend. XIV, § 1. Under the Federal Constitution, teens are not granted equal rights as compared to adults. *See* Bellotti v. Baird, 443 U.S. 622 (1979), *reh'g denied,* 444 U.S. 887 (1979). However, in a number of state cases challenging local municipal juvenile curfew laws under both state and federal law, state courts have been closely divided on whether juvenile curfews deny teens assembly and association rights. Depending on whether the state court viewed teen assembly rights as fundamental or as somewhat less, the courts used either heightened scrutiny or the rational basis test to determine the constitutionality of a municipal curfew. *See In re* J.M., 768 P.2d 219 (Colo. 1989); Deerfield v. Greenberg, 550 N.E.2d 12 (Ill. App. Ct. 1990); People v. Chambers, 360 N.E.2d 55 (Ill. 1976); City of Maquoketa v. Russell, 484 N.W.2d 179 (Iowa 1992); Brown v. Ashton, 660 A.2d 447 (Md. Ct. Spec. App. 1992); Bykofsky v. Middletown, 401 F. Supp. 1242 (M.D. Pa. 1975), *cert. denied,* 429 U.S. 964 (1976).

280. New Jersey Coalition Against War in the Middle East v. J.M.B. Realty Corp., 650 A.2d 757, 782 (N.J. 1994).

shopping centers or to the people inside them because that right was "the least intrusive form of free speech and the easiest to control."[281] The right this comment advocates, that of teen assembly, is arguably higher up on the "intrusiveness" scale. There is a justified concern about future violence in the Mall of America; however, there are practical alternatives to the juvenile curfew and very strong public policy reasons why the Mall should use them before turning to the Parental Escort Policy. The alternatives, discussed herein, are less intrusive than the Parental Escort Policy and may perhaps be even more effective in preserving the Mall as a safe environment for all who enter. The two most prominent public policy reasons for repealing the Parental Escort Policy are: (1) to repair relations with the black community, and (2) to repair relations with teen shoppers in general, a group with great spending power and which has been alienated by the Mall's policy.

The first and most important reason for the Mall to reconsider its policy is to regain the trust of the black community. Even before the juvenile escort policy was implemented, members of the black community believed that the Mall discriminated against low-income black youth.[282] These allegations were based on arguments that Mall security discriminately handed-out the Mall's Conduct Code more often to black youth as compared to white youth; additionally, security allegedly approached more groups of black teens than white teens.[283] Mall management has steadfastly

---

281. *Id.*

282. *See supra* note 167 and accompanying text.

> Given the Mall's earlier attempt to restrict bus access to its site, we can only conclude that racism is playing a role here . . . . It seems to us that the Mall of America believes that children of color will not have a parent—or a car—readily available for their visit to the mall. Therefore, they believe, the new policy requiring the presence of a parent will reduce the number of non-white young people in the mall in the early evening.

Apgar, *supra* note 186 (quoting Gary Sudduth, President of the Minneapolis Urban League). *See also* Taylor, *supra* note 172 (stating that "[t]he mall has been getting criticism from members of the African-American community, who claim black youths are unduly harassed [by mall security]").

There have been at least two discrimination suits filed by African Americans against the Mall of America. First, three women filed a discrimination complaint against the Mall in 1996 after their teenage daughters had a scuffle with Mall security. *See* Taylor, *supra* note 172; Margaret Zack, *Cop Disciplined for Conduct in Megamall Arrest,* MINNEAPOLIS-ST. PAUL STAR-TRIB., May 4, 1996. The suit was settled for $200,000. Second, in October 1995, three different minority teens sued the Mall on their own behalf. *See* Taylor, *supra* note 172.

283. *See* Meredith, *supra* note 7. The article quotes Marcus Wilson, an 18 year-old black teen who goes to the Mall on weekend nights, who stated that Mall security tend to give him

held that its security implementation is colorblind,[284] but the introduction of the curfew, the practical effect of which is to keep large groups of black teens out of the Mall on weekend nights, has not convinced the black community that the curfew was not racially motivated. Indeed, the only time such large numbers of black teens go to the Mall is on weekend nights.[285]

It can and should be argued that the Mall has a responsibility to the community with which it has a symbiotic relationship. The community has given the Mall its business while the Mall has provided the surrounding area with thousands of jobs.[286] With the Mall's prominence in the Bloomington/Minneapolis community comes a responsibility to treat all those in the community with respect. Even before it had opened the Mall had gained national prominence, and the implementation of the Parental Escort Policy was national news.[287] By its very existence, the Mall of America has become the preeminent mall in America. With that reputation comes the responsibility of being a role model. It may not be a role the Mall management desired, but it has become the Mall's role nonetheless.[288] With the concern voiced by the Minneapolis Urban Coalition and the Urban League, the Mall would show its continuing commitment to social problems by recognizing the race issue and by effecting another policy that would not have such a disproportionate effect on the area's black youth. By implementing an alternative to the curfew that is more egalitarian in nature, the Mall would best effectuate this commitment and set an example which would be seen by the rest of the country.

The second reason for the Mall to rescind its Parental Escort Policy flows somewhat from the first. Malls across the country are watching the Mall of America's juvenile curfew to discern whether

---

a copy of the Conduct Code when he enters the mall; by contrast, white teenagers are rarely handed copies of the Code. *See id.*

284. *See* McFarland Interview, *supra* note 16.

285. *See* Meredith, supra note 7; Telephone Interview with Yusef Mgeni, President of the Urban Coalition in the Twin Cities (Sept. 25, 1996).

286. The Mall of America employs approximately 12,000 people. *See* AT A GLANCE, *supra* note 1.

287. *See supra* notes 7, 27 and accompanying text.

288. Famous people and places, such as the Mall of America, are closely watched by the media and the country at large. This should make them aware that their actions (or inaction) are observed and that they have the tremendous power of setting as good an example as a poor one.

such a policy is effective.[289] The Mall would set an example as to the treatment of all teenagers were it to end its policy of welcoming them on weekend evenings only with a parental escort. As one commentator has noted, the curfew might solve the Mall's problems, but it also "might unnecessarily damage its relationship with teens and reinforce negative stereotypes of them."[290] Teens do not have as many rights as adults do in this country, but the Mall would set an example as to how to treat teens with greater respect were it to institute an alternative to the curfew that would achieve similar results as the curfew. The best way to ask teens to act like responsible adults may be to treat them in a more adultlike fashion.[291]

This objective could perhaps be best effectuated if the Mall began using the state Unlawful Assembly and Disorderly Conduct statutes at its disposal.[292] Rather than denying access to a whole class of people, the vast majority of whom are innocent of any wrongdoing, the Mall should deny access to the few who display poor conduct. The Mall could replace the information about the Parental Escort Policy on the Conduct Code handout with a warning that state statutes will be used to keep violators off the premises. The statutes alone can in fact be used to keep perpetrators out of the Mall. As has hopefully been proven in this comment, the behavior of the majority of the teens is consistent with Mall policy. As the New Jersey Supreme Court in *New Jersey*

289. *See supra* notes 27, 261 and accompanying text.

290. *Teen Curfews—Paterson Should Think Twice Before Acting,* THE RECORD (Bergen County, N.J.), Sept. 12, 1996.

291. With the Parental Escort Policy, the Mall of America has effectively alienated many members of the teen population. While Mall management argues that most of the teens who go to the Mall on weekend nights do not go there for shopping, teens in general have a tremendous amount of spending power in this country. Were other malls across the country to follow the Mall of America's example, they could find themselves effectively closing off a large source of revenue. According to Teenage Research Unlimited, teenage spending in the United States is estimated at over $100 billion annually. *See* Kokmen, *supra* note 7. In the same article, Mark Schoifet, Spokesman for the International Council of Shopping Centers, states that "nobody in our industry wants to alienate this group . . . . They grow into adults, and they are the people you want as your loyal customers. Ninety nine point nine percent of kids are good kids . . . . But sometimes dealing with teenagers is a difficult dilemma for mall managers." *Id.*

292. *See* MINN. STAT. ANN. § 609.705 (West 1987) (Unlawful Assembly); *see also id.* § 609.72 (West Supp. 1997) (Disorderly Conduct). Under the disorderly conduct statute, one is guilty of disorderly conduct if one "engages in offensive, obscene, abusive, boisterous, or noisy conduct or in offensive, obscene, or abusive language tending reasonably to arouse alarm, anger, or resentment in others." *Id.*

Coalition states, simply "hanging around" the Mall is allowed.[293] It is only those who are violent who should not be allowed in the Mall.[294] The Mall would set an example that violent and disruptive behavior is not tolerated by having the offending teens arrested. Therefore, the violent teens, and the teens who congregate in large groups which act as a public nuisance, would be on notice that their behavior will not be tolerated by the Mall or by society. The latter group, which is the more prevalent group at the Mall, should not be banned. Rather, it is those groups that are especially large in number or loud in their behavior who should be asked to split up into smaller, less obtrusive groups. The failure to do so would result in arrest. While this sounds like a harsh remedy for teens who are only gathered in large groups, after such a remedy is imposed once, it is not likely to be necessary again. Using state statutes to police the Mall would perhaps be the most effective method of keeping violent teens out of the Mall while at the same time informing others that such behavior will not be condoned.

The Mall has repeatedly conceded that most of the kids who go to the Mall on weekend nights are good kids.[295] A safe environment need not be achieved at the expense of denying the well-behaved teens access to the Mall; this is the practical effect of the Parental Escort Policy. Nor will keeping the well-behaved teens from the Mall serve to make the Mall a safer environment. If safety is the Mall's objective, an effort should be made to at all times restrict permanent Mall access to the teenagers who have exhibited violent behavior on Mall premises. A violent incident may occur at 5 p.m. on a Saturday or perhaps 1 p.m. on a Wednesday when teenagers are on school vacation. Banning violent teens from the Mall altogether will have the lasting effect of making the Mall safer at all times rather than only on weekend evenings. Implementing this policy would require distributing pictures and names of violators to Mall security and instructing Mall security to deny access to those teens. Security should also be authorized to arrest as a trespasser any teen gaining access to the Mall who has been a perpetrator of a violent incident at the Mall. While this approach may seem difficult in practice, Mall security now requests

293. *See* New Jersey Coalition Against War in the Middle East v. J.M.B. Realty Corp., 650 A.2d 757, 773 (N.J. 1994).

294. The issue of prior restraint, while pertinent to this topic, is beyond the scope of this comment.

295. *See supra* notes 192-96 and accompanying text.

identification of all people thought to be under the age of sixteen. To request identification of those individuals thought to be perpetrators of Mall violence is far less intrusive than asking every teen for identification.[296]

Indeed, perhaps the most egalitarian method of insuring Mall safety would be the installation of metal detectors at each Mall entrance. This would have the effect of not only banning teens with weapons, but it would keep all persons with weapons out of the Mall. While this measure may sound harsh, suggestive of airport metal detectors and dangerous inner-city schools, metal detectors will do the best job of keeping all concealed weapons off Mall premises. If Mall patrons are concerned about their safety, they should tolerate the minor inconvenience of removing their keys and passing through the detector. The effect of using metal detectors would be to keep all weapons out of the Mall and not just those that teenagers carry. If a seventeen year-old were to bring a gun to the Mall, the teen would be denied entrance under this policy. Conversely, under the Parental Escort Policy, entrance would be granted once identification proving age over sixteen was shown.

Lastly, hiring more Mall security and strictly enforcing the Conduct Code would in all likelihood alleviate the problem of teen violence.[297] At least one other mall has found success by strictly enforcing its conduct code and ejecting violators for anywhere from thirty days to one year from mall premises.[298] Granted, no other mall can compare in size to the Mall of America, but most of the teens at the Mall of America do not pose a safety threat. As Mall spokeswoman Teresa McFarland herself has said, the majority of teens at the Mall are well-behaved, and it is the minority who spoil it for the majority.[299]

---

296. *See supra* note 291 and accompanying text. This editorial compares the Mall of America curfew with a proposed teen curfew in Paterson, New Jersey and suggests that both the Mall of America and Paterson can achieve their goals without imposing curfews. *See id.* The editorial recommends banning the teens who cause problems, rather than asking for identification from every teen attempting to enter the Mall. *See id.*

297. This alternative would be most effective if implemented in conjunction with other alternatives previously discussed.

298. *See* Peterson, *supra* note 27 (quoting David Groom, General Manager of the Monmouth Mall in Eatontown, New Jersey).

299. *See supra* note 192 and accompanying text.

Mall security already has an active community component in place with the Youth Liaison Program.[300] The Mighty Moms and Dedicated Dads also serve as an effective link to the community because the moms and dads live in the same areas as many of the teens. However, the Mall could do more within the community before implementing the curfew. One step should be working with community centers and perhaps religious organizations in order to provide alternatives to going to the Mall on weekend nights. Indeed, one reason so many teens go to the Mall of America may be that they have nowhere else to go in the Bloomington/Minneapolis area on weekend nights. The Mall could take the initiative to work with local groups to plan alternate, safe events for teenagers. As many of the teens go to the Mall on weekend nights only to be with one another, it is likely that they would be interested in another place that provided a space to relax with friends, especially one where they could comfortably hang-out in large groups. Since such a venue would welcome large groups of teens, this could become an attractive alternative for many Minnesota teens. Community centers and religious houses could offer their spaces on a rotating basis. Perhaps for a minimum entrance fee special events, such as a dance or a comedy night, would be offered.

VI. Affirmative Defenses

The strongest argument to be made by the Mall of America on behalf of the Parental Escort Policy is that the policy works to promote a safe environment.[301] The number of arrests at the Mall has decreased dramatically.[302] Once the Mall is determined to serve as a downtown area such that its actions constitute state action, the Mall will likely defend the policy by stating that the policy is in the best interests for the health, safety, and welfare of

300. *See supra* note 9 and accompanying text.

301. After the first weekend that the Parental Escort Policy was put into effect, Mall management stated that "[t]he policy is working exactly as we intended. More families came out to enjoy the mall and it was a safer atmosphere for everyone. This was the first weekend in memory where we didn't have a fight between kids." October Press Release, *supra* note 184.

302. From January through October 1996, 394 arrests were made at the Mall. From the time the Juvenile Curfew Policy went into effect through June 1997, there has been only one arrest. *See* Gupta, *supra* note 198.

Minnesota citizens. While the Mall should be concerned about safety, the fact that a safety interest is involved is not dispositive of the constitutionality of the action. As the Minnesota Supreme Court stated in *Hershberger,* "[m]erely because public safety is articulated as a competing interest in section 16, however, does not establish that interest as paramount."[303] In relation to the Mall of America, once the court determines that the curfew is state action, the question then becomes whether the state's interest in protecting the safety of its citizens at the Mall can be achieved in an equally effective method that is less violative of individual rights. The author of this comment is fully aware that teen assembly rights have not traditionally been of equal constitutional concern as freedom of religious expression,[304] search and seizure rights,[305] or the bodily integrity of the mentally ill.[306] While stretching the bounds of constitutional concern, this comment argues that the Minnesota courts can and should draw on their rich history of caselaw to require less restrictive alternatives before a right so fundamental as freedom of assembly is infringed. As best evidenced by *Hershberger,* as well as by *E.D.J.* and *Jarvis,* Minnesota places a high premium on individual liberties. The court would hopefully consider the previously discussed alternatives to the curfew and hold that the Mall's safety objective could be effectuated in such a way that would serve the goal of keeping the Mall safe for all its patrons without the need to resort to a Parental Escort Policy.

After the safety argument, the Mall's second line of defense may rely on article I, section 13 of the Minnesota Constitution which provides that "[p]rivate property shall not be taken, destroyed or damaged for public use without just compensation therefor, first paid or secured."[307] The United States Supreme Court addressed this argument in *PruneYard*, holding that the rights of free expression and petition did not amount to an unconstitutional taking under the Fifth Amendment Takings Clause.[308] The court stated that "[t]here is nothing to suggest that

303. State v. Hershberger 462 N.W.2d 393, 399 (Minn. 1990).
304. *See id.* at 393-400.
305. *See In re* Welfare of E.D.J., 502 N.W.2d 779 (Minn. 1993).
306. *See* Jarvis v. Levine, 418 N.W.2d 139 (Minn. 1988).
307. MINN. CONST. art. I, § 13.
308. *See* PruneYard Shopping Ctr. v. Robins, 447 U.S. 74, 83 (1980). *See also* U.S. CONST. amend. V.

preventing appellants from prohibiting this sort of activity will unreasonably impair the value or use of their property as a shopping center."[309] Indeed, the Mall of America did not state that the few gun-related incidents had in any way diminished the Mall's revenue. Thus, it cannot be argued that the implementation of the curfew has restored lost business to the Mall. The Mall stated that it had received complaints from shoppers that they found the large groups of teens to be intimidating, but again, the Mall had no statistics indicating that business was down due to the congregating teens. The Mall has not argued that it has lost business or revenue on account of the teenagers' actions, and this line of argument would in all likelihood fail when compared to the great benefit the Mall has obtained by making itself so accessible to the general public.[310]

VII. Conclusion

As one individual has said: "[N]o place can shut out the depressing realities of our new, uncivil society. If the promise of the Mall of America was to seal off the tumult of the outside world, that is a promise no enterprise can likely keep."[311]

A balance must be struck between respecting the Mall of America's need to maintain a safe environment and teenagers' right of assembly in the Mall. Mall of America's management has made many efforts to curb teen violence and teen congregating on Mall premises. Mall management has shown a commitment to dealing with this situation; however, further steps could and should have been taken before the Mall instituted its Parental Escort Policy. The policy is too broad in its scope and keeps out the many good teens in order to deny access to the few who misbehave. Under the Minnesota Constitution, a strong argument can be made for

309. *PruneYard*, 447 U.S. at 83.

310. A counterpart to the takings argument is that the Mall, as private property, has a right to exclude. An analysis of this argument is beyond the scope of this comment. However, it is worth noting that while the Mall does have a right to exclude in order to make its premises safer, it can achieve this goal by excluding only those teens who are violent and violate the Conduct Code, which is a class much narrower than those now affected under the Parental Escort Policy.

311. Greene, *supra* note 10.

recognizing teenagers' assembly rights at the Mall of America. It is intended that this comment serve as a starting point for bringing such a constitutional challenge.

Alysa B. Freeman

NOTES

CURFEW LAWS, FREEDOM OF MOVEMENT, AND THE RIGHTS OF JUVENILES

INTRODUCTION

In the early 1990s, the arrest rate for minors between the ages of ten and seventeen in the District of Columbia was the highest in the nation.[1] Teens from the age of fifteen to nineteen met violent deaths in Washington D.C. more frequently than in any other city in the nation.[2] Moreover, the problem was escalating. Between 1987 and 1995, the juvenile arrest rate "for aggravated assault increased by 89.8%, for murder by 157%, and for carrying a dangerous weapon by 282.7%."[3]

Concerned with these frightening statistics, the D.C. Council adopted a juvenile curfew ordinance.[4] Washington, D.C. was not the first city to do so. President Clinton advocated curfew laws as a measure to keep children safe,[5] and during the 1990s many cities have turned to curfew laws[6] in an effort to stem rising rates in juvenile crime.[7]

Litigation ensued, and the District of Columbia's curfew law began its journey through the federal judicial system. In *Hutchins v.*

---

[1] *See* Hutchins v. District of Columbia, 188 F.3d 531, 542 (D.C. Cir. 1999) (en banc) ("[T]he juvenile violent crime arrest rate for juveniles ages 10 to 17 was higher than that in any state and was more than three times the national average.") (citation omitted).

[2] *See id.*

[3] Hutchins v. District of Columbia, 144 F.3d 798, 810 (D.C. Cir. 1998), *rev'd on reh'g en banc*, 188 F.3d 531 (D.C. Cir. 1999).

[4] *See infra* note 278 and accompanying text.

[5] *See* THE WHITE HOUSE, MAKING OUR SCHOOLS AND COMMUNITIES SAFER (March 19, 1998) ("Because of the success of curfews in helping to fight juvenile crime and keeping children safe, the Clinton Administration has encouraged communities to adopt curfew policies.").

[6] *See* Mark Potok, *Teen curfews 'the norm' in more cities*, USA TODAY, June 26, 1995, at 1A (stating that since 1990 "53 cities have enacted a curfew ordinance; another 37 revised older laws").

[7] *See id.* at 1A ("The most common age for arrestees nationally is now 16, and an upcoming Department of Justice analysis reports that juveniles were behind 30% of the growth in violent crime between 1988 and 1992."); Patty Ryan, *Lights on, teens home*, THE TAMPA TRIB., July 16, 1995, at 1 ("Nationwide, arrests for juvenile violent crime shot up 67 percent in the nine years after 1984.").

District of Columbia,[8] the district court found the curfew unconstitutional on the ground that it impermissibly burdened minors' right to freedom of movement and interfered with a parent's right to control the activities of their children.[9] On appeal, a three-judge panel affirmed without agreeing on a rationale.[10] The D.C. Circuit agreed to rehear the case en banc and reversed, again unable to agree upon a rationale.[11]

This Note focuses on the central constitutional question posed by juvenile curfew laws and confronted by the D.C. Circuit Court of Appeals: whether a curfew violates a minor's[12] right to travel on public fora.[13] The question of whether a curfew law violates a minor's right to travel on public fora encompasses two issues: (1) whether a right to

---

[8] 942 F. Supp. 665, 680 (D.D.C. 1996), *rev'd on reh'g en banc*, 188 F.3d 531 (D.C. Cir. 1999).

[9] *See id.* at 680.

[10] Judge Rogers, writing for the court, argued that minors possess fundamental rights, but legislation burdening these rights should be subject to an intermediate standard of review. *See* Hutchins v. District of Columbia, 144 F.3d 798, 809-10 (D.C. Cir. 1998), *rev'd on reh'g en banc*, 188 F.3d 531 (D.C. Cir. 1999). Judge Tatel, on the other hand, argued that legislation burdening the rights of minors should be subject to a strict scrutiny standard of review. *See id.* at 826 (Tatel, J., concurring). Judge Silberman, in contrast, argued that minors have no fundamental right "to be unaccompanied on the streets at night." *Id.* at 828 (Silberman, J., dissenting).

[11] The plurality opinion in *Hutchins* held that: (1) juveniles do not have a fundamental right to be on the streets at night without adult supervision; (2) parents do not have a right to "unilaterally determine" if their children will roam the streets at night; and (3) even assuming that the curfew implicates the fundamental rights of both minors and adults, the curfew satisfies intermediate scrutiny. *Hutchins*, 188 F.3d at 538-48. Judge Edwards, concurring in part and concurring in result, found that the curfew law implicates the fundamental right of parents to control the "'care,' 'nurture,' 'upbringing,' 'management,' and 'rearing'" of their child, *id.* at 560, but the law survives intermediate scrutiny. *See id.* at 548-52. In contrast, Judges Wald and Garland, concurring in part and concurring in result, found that although the curfew law implicates the fundamental rights of both minors and parents, but in both instances survives intermediate scrutiny. *See id.* at 552. Judge Rogers, concurring in part and dissenting in part, found that the curfew law implicates a minor's fundamental right "to walk through public streets without thereby subjecting oneself to police custody," *id.* at 562, that intermediate scrutiny is the appropriate standard of review, and that the curfew law is unconstitutional under an intermediate scrutiny standard. *See id.* at 563-70. Judge Tatel, dissenting, found that the curfew law burdens the fundamental rights of both minors and parents, that in each case legislation that burdens those rights should be subject to strict scrutiny, and that the curfew law cannot survive strict scrutiny because of the burdens it places on parental rights. *See id.* at 562-70.

[12] Throughout the course of this Note, I will use the terms "juveniles," "minor," and "child" interchangeably to refer to those unemancipated persons who are under the age of 17.

[13] Many other constitutional challenges have been made against curfew laws, but they are beyond the scope of this Note. Among these challenges are: vagueness, freedom of movement, freedom of speech, freedom of association, freedom of assembly, and the Equal Protection Clause. *See* Bykofsky v. Borough of Middletown, 401 F. Supp. 1242, 1248 (M.D. Pa. 1975), *aff'd*, 535 F.2d 1245 (3d Cir. 1976) (holding that a curfew ordinance did not infringe on freedom of speech). These laws have also been challenged under the Fourth Amendment, and for violating a parent's right to freedom from undue government interference upon child rearing. *See, e.g.*, Schleifer v. City of Charlottesville, 963 F. Supp. 534, 538 (W.D. Va. 1997) (applying a rational basis test to uphold a curfew law against an undue influence claim because age is not a suspect class).

free movement exists; and (2) if such a right exists, does it protect juveniles to the same extent that it protects adults.

Part I of this Note considers whether a right to travel on public fora may be established by analogy to Supreme Court case law on the right to interstate travel. Part II sketches the struggle of the Supreme Court to find a standard of review for alleged burdens of juvenile rights. Part III analyzes the circuit split on the issue of intrastate travel and concludes that a right to travel on public fora exists as an aspect of substantive due process. Part III also concludes that courts confronting this issue should use an "undue burden" standard as a threshold inquiry when deciding whether to apply heightened scrutiny to alleged violations of this right. Part IV analyzes the three standards of review (strict scrutiny, intermediate review, and rational basis) that have been used by courts in dealing with juvenile rights and concludes that alleged infringements of rights held by juveniles that would be fundamental if held by adults merit intermediate scrutiny. Finally, Part V of this Note applies the "undue burden" test and the intermediate scrutiny standard of review to the District of Columbia curfew ordinance, and concludes that it is constitutional.

I. THE RIGHT TO INTERSTATE TRAVEL

"Once the right to travel is curtailed, all other rights suffer . . . ."[14]

Courts frequently rely on interstate travel case law to support the proposition that a fundamental right to intrastate travel exists.[15] Little in the way of argument, however, is offered to support this conclusion. Stating that "language in the decisions suggests that the right extends to purely local movement"[16] does not help the cause. A meaningful argument supporting this statement must identify both the source of such a right and the rationale underlying its existence.[17]

---

[14] Aptheker v. Secretary of State, 378 U.S. 500, 520 (1964) (Douglas, J., concurring).

[15] *See, e.g.*, Schleifer v. City of Charlottesville, 963 F. Supp. 534, 542-43 (W.D. Va. 1997), *aff'd*, 159 F.3d 843 (4th Cir. 1998) (relying in part on interstate travel case law); Bykofsky v. Borough of Middletown, 401 F. Supp. 1242, 1254-55 (M.D. Pa. 1975), *aff'd mem.*, 535 F.2d 1245 (3d Cir. 1976) (citing, *inter alia*, right to interstate travel cases).

[16] *Hutchins*, 188 F.3d at 561 (Rogers, J., concurring in part and dissenting in part).

[17] Thus, Judge Rogers is wrong when he argues in dissent that "there is no reason for this court to resolve the debate" about the source of the right to travel. *Id.* at 562 n.22. This would be true if the court was merely applying Supreme Court precedent, which it is not. Instead, Judge Rogers' opinion attempts to analogize interstate travel case law to an intrastate travel case. Claiming that the right to travel encompasses both rights, *see id.* at 560-62, the opinion makes a sweeping generalization that interstate and intrastate travel are the same without offering a reason why this is so—the logical fallacy of *dicto simpliciter*. Nor does the assertion that intrastate mobility is "important" because of "its utility and the implications of its denial," *id.* at 561, aid the argument. Despite its emotive appeal, this statement is irrelevant to the argument that a right of intrastate mobility is implied by the Supreme Court's interstate travel case law.

One of the problems with relying on interstate travel cases is the inability of the Court to agree upon a constitutional source for this right. Not surprisingly, the source of such a right (as well as its scope as developed in these cases) has clear implications for the viability of a right to travel on public fora by analogy. This Part reviews the various constitutional theories the Court has offered to support its interstate travel case law. It also assesses the prospects of each of these theories to serve as a springboard for an analogous right to travel on public fora.

The pedigree of the right to interstate travel is long and varied. The right to interstate travel first appeared in 1825 as an aspect of the privileges enjoyed by citizens of the United States under the Article IV Privileges and Immunities Clause.[18] Since this first mention, the right to travel has been variously described as residing within the ambit of the Commerce Clause, the Fourteenth Amendment Privileges or Immunities Clause, and as a right inferred from the structure of our Constitution.[19] In more recent years, this right has also been found to reside in the Due Process Clause.[20] However, on the whole, the Court has agreed to disagree on the specific source of this right.[21]

A. *Article IV Privileges and Immunities Clause*

Case law grounding the right to travel in the Article IV Privileges and Immunities Clause is rooted in 19th century case law.[22] In *Corfield v. Coryell*,[23] Justice Washington, while riding circuit, inti-

---

[18] *See* Corfield v. Coryell, 6 F. Cas. 546, 552 (C.C.E.D. Pa. 1823) (stating that the right of a citizen to pass through another state was protected by the Article IV Privileges and Immunities Clause).

[19] *See* Attorney General of New York v. Soto-Lopez, 476 U.S. 898, 902 (1986); Lutz v. City of York, 899 F.2d 255, 262-65 (3d Cir. 1990).

[20] *See, e.g.*, Kent v. Dulles, 357 U.S. 116, 125 (1958) ("The right to travel is a part of the 'liberty' of which the citizen cannot be deprived without due process of law under the Fifth Amendment.").

[21] *See Soto-Lopez*, 476 U.S. at 902 ("[I]n light of the unquestioned historic acceptance of the principle of free interstate migration . . . we have not felt impelled to locate this right definitively in any particular constitutional provision.") (citation omitted).

[22] *See, e.g.*, Corfield v. Coryell, 6 F. Cas. 546, 552 (C.C.E.D. Pa. 1823). *But see* Saenz v. Roe, 119 S. Ct. 1518 (1999). *Saenz* separates the "right to travel" into three components: (1) the right of a citizen to enter into another state; (2) the right of that citizen to be treated as a "welcome visitor" while in another state; and (3) if the citizen chooses to become a permanent resident of the state which they are visiting, the right to be treated like all other citizens of that state. *See id.* at 1525. The court did not identify the source of the first component of the right to travel. *See id.* The court held that the second component is "expressly protected" by the Article IV Privileges and Immunities Clause, while the third is governed by the Privileges or Immunities Clause of the Fourteenth Amendment. *See id.* at 1526.

[23] 6 F. Cas. 546 (C.C.E.D. Pa. 1823). The *Corfield* court held that a New Jersey statute, which prohibited non-residents from gathering shellfish within New Jersey's waters in a ship that was owned by a non-resident, was constitutional. *See id.* at 551-53.

mated that this clause was a source of fundamental rights.[24] Justice Washington broadly described these rights as those necessary for "the enjoyment of life and liberty,"[25] and included "[t]he right of a citizen of one state to pass through . . . any other state."[26]

This conception of the Article IV Privileges and Immunities Clause lasted for less than fifty years. In *Paul v. Virginia*,[27] the Court held that a corporate tax imposed by Virginia on foreign insurance companies was constitutional.[28] The *Paul* Court rejected the *Corfield* view that the Article IV Privileges and Immunities Clause was a source of implied fundamental rights in dicta.[29] The effect of the *Paul* dicta was to redefine the right to interstate travel as an anti-discrimination right embodied in principles of federalism.[30]

The Court embraced the *Paul* dicta in *Bray v. Alexandria Women's Health Clinic*.[31] Citing *Paul*, the Court observed that the right to interstate travel is protected against two types of obstacles: (1) "'the erection of actual barriers to interstate movement;'"[32] and (2) "'being treated differently' from intrastate travelers."[33] This formulation of the right to interstate travel is fully consistent with the anti-discrimination principle set forth in *Paul*.

---

[24] *See id.* at 551. ("We feel no hesitation in confining these expressions to those privileges and immunities which are, in their nature, fundamental; which belong, of right, to the citizens of all free governments . . . . ").

[25] *Id.*

[26] *Id.* at 552. In total, *Corfield*'s definition of fundamental rights includes "everything but the kitchen sink." JOHN HART ELY, DEMOCRACY AND DISTRUST 198 n.64 (1980).

[27] 75 U.S. (8 Wall.) 168 (1868).

[28] *See id.* at 177.

[29] *See id.* at 180 ("[T]he privileges and immunities secured to citizens of each State in the several States . . . are those privileges and immunities which are common to the citizens in the latter States under their constitution and laws by virtue of their being citizens."). In *Paul*, a man serving as an agent for an unlicensed corporation was indicted for violating a statute that forbade anyone from acting as an agent without a license. *See id.* at 169. A tax had to be paid in order to obtain a license. *See id.* The agent argued that the act violated the Article IV Privileges and Immunities Clause and the Commerce Clause. *See id.* at 170-72. The Court held that the Article IV Privileges and Immunities Clause did not apply because the corporation was not a citizen within the meaning of that clause. *See id.* at 177. Therefore, any discussion of the substantive scope of the rights conferred by that clause was pure dictum.

[30] *See* Lutz v. City of York, 899 F.2d 255, 262 (3d Cir. 1990) (recognizing the Article IV Privileges and Immunities clause as "a federalism-based antidiscrimination principle").

[31] 506 U.S. 263 (1993). Abortion clinics and organizations supporting those clinics sued to enjoin Operation Rescue from demonstrating in a manner that obstructed general access to those clinics. *See id.* at 266. The District Court granted injunctive relief under 42 U.S.C. § 1985 (3) (1992), whose ancestor was § 2 of the Civil Rights Act of 1871. *See id.* The precise issue before the Court was whether a federal cause of action had been stated by the alleged private conspiracy conducted by Operation Rescue to deprive individuals of their right to interstate travel and their right to an abortion. *See id.* at 268, 274, 277.

[32] *Id.* at 277 (quoting Zobel v. Williams, 457 U.S. 55, 60 n.6 (1982) and citing *Paul*, 75 U.S. (8 Wall.) at 180).

[33] *Id.* (quoting *Zobel*, 457 U.S. at 60 n.6 and citing *Paul*, 75 U.S. (8 Wall.) at 180).

There are two difficulties with applying by analogy the Article IV Privileges and Immunities Clause to the right to travel on public fora. First, language of the clause itself will not support a right to travel on public fora. The text of Article IV, Section Two of the Constitution states that "[t]he Citizens of each State shall be entitled to all Privileges and Immunities of Citizens in the several States."[34] As Professor Ely notes, "[t]his [is] an equality provision, intended to keep states from treating outsiders worse than their own citizens."[35] The clause does not speak to the duties owed by states to their own citizens. Therefore, the Privileges and Immunities Clause cannot be the source of any right to intrastate travel.

The second problem with trying to locate a right to travel on public fora under the Privileges and Immunities Clause is that the clause would have no security. As *Paul* made clear, this clause is violated only where a state denies to visitors the privileges that it bestows upon its own citizens.[36] If all citizens are treated equally, then the clause is not violated. Thus, a state could withhold the right to travel from both its own citizens and out-of-state visitors and still comply with *Paul*.

B. The Commerce Clause

The view that the right to travel is an aspect of the Commerce Clause originates in *Edwards v. California*.[37] *Edwards* involved a California penal statute that forbade a resident from knowingly aiding a nonresident in entering the state.[38] The Court relied on the Commerce Clause to strike down the statute, stating that "it is settled beyond question that the transportation of persons is 'commerce,' within the meaning of [the Commerce Clause]."[39] Thus, the question was whether a protectionist measure, designed to keep indigent nonresidents out of the state, violated the negative aspect of the Com-

---

[34] U.S. CONST. art. IV, § 2.
[35] ELY, *supra* note 26, at 23.
[36] *See* Paul, 75 U.S. (8 Wall.) 176-77.
[37] 314 U.S. 160 (1941).
[38] *See id.* at 165-66.
[39] *Id.* at 172 (citations omitted).

merce Clause.[40] Viewed from this perspective, the Court concluded without much difficulty that the statute was unconstitutional.[41]

Any attempt to apply the Commerce Clause right to interstate travel rationale by analogy to an asserted right to travel on public fora must fail. The "negative," or "dormant," Commerce Clause prevents a state from enacting protective legislation.[42] There are several problems, however, with analyzing intrastate travel restrictions such as curfew laws under such a doctrine. First, as the Court recognized in *Bray*, if the right to interstate travel is derived from the negative Commerce Clause, then "it could be eliminated by Congress."[43] Second, a curfew law applies generally to both in-state and out-of-state residents.[44] Therefore, there is no protectionist motive on the part of the state or municipality in enacting a curfew law.

Third, applying the dormant Commerce Clause to right to travel on public fora cases would skew the analysis of the courts by focusing on the wrong questions. People who oppose curfew laws do so because they don't like their travel restricted, not because Joe Oklahoma is upset that Tom Nebraska's business is benefiting from the regulation. Thus, application of the dormant Commerce Clause would skew the terms of the debate.

C. National Citizenship

In a concurring opinion in *Edwards v. California*,[45] Justice Douglas described the right to interstate travel as "an incident of *national* citizenship."[46] The Court has occasionally grounded the right to travel in a concept of national citizenship not tied to any specific constitutional provision. The first member of the Court to do so was

---

[40] As the *Edwards* Court stated, "[t]he issue presented in this case, therefore, is whether the prohibition embodied in [the statute] against the 'bringing' or transportation of indigent persons into California is within the police power of that State. We think that it is not, and hold that it is an unconstitutional barrier to interstate commerce." *Id.* at 173; *see also* Lutz v. City of York, 899 F.2d 255, 265 (3d Cir. 1990) ("*Edwards* . . . involved a statute prohibiting the importation of 'goods' perceived to produce unwanted local burdens . . . . [T]his is virtually per se unconstitutional.").

[41] *See Edwards*, 314 U.S. at 174 ("We think this statute must fail under any known test of the validity of State interference with interstate commerce.").

[42] *See* City of Philadelphia v. New Jersey, 437 U.S. 617, 624 (1978) (stating that the crucial issue under the dormant Commerce Clause is whether a law "is basically a protectionist measure, or whether it can fairly be viewed as a law directed to legitimate local concerns").

[43] Bray v. Alexandria Women's Health Clinic, 506 U.S. 263, 277 n.7 (1993).

[44] In fact, many current curfew laws provide an exception for interstate travel. *See, e.g.*, DALLAS, TEX., REV. ORDINANCES ch. 31, § 31-33(c)(1)(C) (1992); *see also infra* note 278 (setting out the terms of the District of Columbia curfew ordinance).

[45] 314 U.S. 160 (1941).

[46] *Id.* at 178 (Douglas, J., concurring) (emphasis in original). Justice Douglas believed that the right to interstate travel was firmly established as a right of national citizenship prior to the adoption of the Fourteenth Amendment. *See id.* at 179.

Chief Justice Taney in his dissenting opinion in the *Passenger Cases*.[47] Chief Justice Taney stated that "[w]e are all citizens of the United States; and, as members of the same community, must have the right to pass and repass through every part of if without interruption, as freely as in our own States."[48]

Chief Justice Taney's statement is a conclusion, not a constitutional argument. The Chief Justice did not make reference to anything in the text, structure, or history of the Constitution that suggests that a right to interstate travel exists. The Court bolstered Chief Justice Taney's statement in *Shapiro v. Thompson*.[49] *Shapiro* explained that the right to interstate travel results from the unity of "the nature of our Federal Union and our constitutional concepts of personal liberty."[50] This unity is not present when the issue is whether there is a right to travel on public fora.

The right to interstate travel recognized in *Shapiro* exists, in part, to prevent one state from excluding (or expelling) citizens of other states. Language in later decisions confirms that this was the purpose of the right to travel recognized in *Shapiro*. In fact, the right recognized by *Shapiro* is now described "more precisely, [as] the right of free interstate migration."[51] The "nature of our Federal Union" requires that citizens of the United States, as citizens of the United States, be free to relocate from one state to another if they so choose.

The right to travel on public fora does not implicate the "nature of our Federal Union." Intrastate travel restrictions do not prevent citizens from changing residences or implicate any other federalism-related concerns. By definition, these travel restrictions apply solely to travel within the state that enacted the legislation. Thus, there is no "unity" of interests between the "nature of our Federal Union" and constitutional concepts of individual liberty in an interstate travel case. Therefore, the right to interstate travel recognized by concepts of "national citizenship" provides a poor analogy for a right to travel on public fora.

D. Substantive Due Process

Kent v. Dulles[52] described the right to travel as "a part of the 'liberty' of which the citizen cannot be deprived without due process

---

47 48 U.S. (7 How.) 283 (1849).
48 *Id.* at 492 (Taney, C.J., dissenting).
49 394 U.S. 618 (1969).
50 *Id.* at 629.
51 Attorney General of New York v. Soto-Lopez, 476 U.S. 898, 902 (1986).
52 357 U.S. 116 (1958).

of law under the Fifth Amendment."[53] In *Kent*, citizens sued the Secretary of State after he refused to issue them passports.[54] Hence, the right to travel involved in *Kent* was the right to travel internationally. The Court held that the Secretary of State's action in denying passports on the basis of association was beyond the authority vested in the Secretary by Congress under the Immigration and Nationality Act of 1952.[55] Thus, *Kent* avoided the "important constitutional question[]" that would arise if Congress had authorized a restriction of "the citizens' right of free movement."[56]

Much of the discussion in *Kent* surrounding the right to travel concerned the social utility of visiting foreign nations.[57] *Kent* also cited the writings of scholar Zachariah Chafee extensively to reference both the right to migrate from one state to another and the right to travel abroad.[58] The citations, and other language in the opinion, suggest that the Court was analogizing the right to travel internationally to the right to travel interstate.[59]

The discussion of the right to travel offered in *Kent*, however, was dictum because the Court avoided the constitutional question by a narrow interpretation of the Immigration and Nationality Act of 1952. The Court returned to the *Kent* dicta in *Haig v. Agee*[60] and settled on a curious interpretation. *Agee* concerned an action brought by an ex-CIA agent challenging the revocation of his passport by the Secretary of State.[61] Agee argued that the act of revoking his passport impermissibly burdened his right to travel freely abroad.[62] The Court disagreed, stating that "the *freedom* to travel outside the United States must be distinguished from the *right* to travel within the United States."[63]

---

53 *Id.* at 125.

54 The Secretary of State refused to issue the passports because the plaintiffs would not file an affidavit concerning their alleged Communist party membership. *See id.* at 119-20.

55 *See id.* at 130.

56 *Id.*

57 *See id.* at 126. The Court emphasized that this right emerged in Anglo-Saxon law at the time of the Magna Charta. *See id.* (citing ZACHARIAH CHAFEE, THREE HUMAN RIGHTS IN THE CONSTITUTION OF 1787 (1st ed. 1936)).

58 *See id.* (citing CHAFEE, *supra* note 57, at 171-81, 197).

59 *See id.* The Court stated that "[f]reedom of movement across frontiers in either direction, and inside frontiers as well, was a part of our heritage. Travel abroad, like travel within the country, may be necessary for a livelihood." *Id.* Read in context, these sentences compare the right to interstate travel with the right to travel abroad.

60 453 U.S. 280 (1981).

61 *See id.* at 283-87.

62 *See id.* at 306.

63 *Id.* (emphasis in original).

Why these two rights must be distinguished is not entirely clear. *Agee* quoted from *Califano v. Aznavorian*,[64] wherein the Court recognized "the crucial difference between the freedom to travel internationally and the right of interstate travel."[65] *Califano* explained that the right to interstate travel is "virtually unqualified," whereas the right to travel abroad is "no more than an aspect of the 'liberty' protected by the Due Process Clause of the Fifth Amendment."[66] Yet, this statement is nothing more than a conclusion, and *Agee* offers no explanation as to why this is true. The only hint of a rationale for this disparate treatment comes from *Califano*, wherein the Court emphasized that, unlike the right to travel abroad, the right to interstate travel has been "recognized by this Court for over 100 years."[67]

If longevity (in terms of the number of years that a right is recognized by the Court) is the sole criterion for determining whether a right to travel is fundamental, then the right to travel on public fora is in trouble. The Court has never explicitly recognized this right. Just last term in *City of Chicago v. Morales*,[68] the Court declined to address the issue of whether such a fundamental right exists.[69] At the very least, *Agee* and *Morales* suggest that the Court is unwilling to extend the right to travel without some sort of independent justification explaining why the specific right asserted is fundamental.[70]

In sum, the Court's interstate travel decisions do not lend themselves to an easy analogy to the right to travel on public fora. Most of the decisions ascribe the right to interstate travel to a source that will not support such an analogy. While the Due Process Clause will support such an analogy, the tenor of the Court's opinions suggests that it will not recognize such a right without some sort of independent justification. Therefore, relying on interstate travel case law, without more, to support a right to travel on public fora is inappropriate.

---

[64] 439 U.S. 170 (1978).

[65] *Id.* at 176.

[66] *Id.* (quoting Califano v. Torres, 435 U.S. 1, 4 n.6 (1953)).

[67] *Id.* (citations omitted).

[68] 119 S. Ct. 1849 (1999).

[69] *See id.* at 1863 n.35 (basing decision on the statute being overbroad and therefore holding that "it is unnecessary to reach the question whether the . . . ordinance is invalid as a deprivation of substantive due process").

[70] Such a justification is explored later in this Note. *See infra* Part III (discussing the right to travel on public fora).

II. THE DEVELOPMENT OF JUVENILE RIGHTS

"Those who are still in a state to require being taken care of by others must be protected against their own actions as well as against external injury."[71]

The scope of juvenile rights under our Constitution remains uncertain to this day.[72] The rights of minors got off to an inauspicious start in this century,[73] but picked up steam during the Warren Court years.[74] However, despite occasional broad pronouncements,[75] the treatment of minors remains variable and uncertain.[76] Perhaps the best way to bring order to these decisions is to separate those that deal with procedure from those that deal with substantive liberty interests.

A. Juvenile Rights and Procedural Due Process

Starting with *In re Gault,*[77] the Court wrote a series of decisions that were designed to reform the juvenile system. However, the crossover relevance of these decisions to the substantive liberty interests of minors is probably minimal. These cases focused on the nature of the juvenile court system and its deficiencies, not the liberation of minors.

In re Gault held that the rights to notice of charges, counsel, and confrontation of accusers, as well as the right against compulsory self-incrimination and the right to cross-examine witnesses, apply to minors.[78] The Court emphasized the importance of the procedural safeguards required by the Due Process Clause, commenting that "these instruments . . . enhance the possibility that truth will emerge from the confrontation of opposing versions and conflicting data."[79]

---

71 J. MILL, ON LIBERTY 69 (Penguin Classics ed. 1974).

72 As Justice Marshall states in *Bykofsky v. Borough of Middletown*, 429 U.S. 964 (1976), "[t]he question squarely presented by this case . . . is whether the due process rights of juveniles are entitled to lesser protection than those of adults. The prior decisions of this Court provide no clear answer." *Id.* at 965 (Marshall, J., dissenting) (footnote omitted).

73 *See, e.g.*, Pierce v. Society of Sisters, 268 U.S. 510, 534 (1925) ("No question is raised concerning the power of the State . . . to require that all children of proper age attend some school . . . . ").

74 *See, e.g.*, Tinker v. Des Moines Indep. Community School Dist., 393 U.S. 503, 511 (1969) (holding that "[s]chool officials do not possess absolute authority over their students. Students in school as well as out of school are 'persons' under our Constitution.").

75 *See id.* (stating that students "are possessed of fundamental rights which the State must respect").

76 *See Bykofsky*, 429 U.S. at 965 (Marshall, J., dissenting) (stating that "[t]he prior decisions of this court provide no clear answer" to the question of whether the due process rights of minors are entitled to lesser protection than those of adults).

77 387 U.S. 1 (1967).

78 *See id.* at 33, 42, 57.

79 *Id.* at 21.

In sum, "procedure is to law what 'scientific method' is to science."[80] *In re Gault* rejected the argument that the civil nature of juvenile proceedings, which emphasize rehabilitation over punishment, made them exempt from the ordinary requirements of the Due Process Clause.[81] The Court explained that "[u]nder our Constitution, the condition of being a boy does not justify a kangaroo court."[82]

In re Winship[83] and *Breed v. Jones*[84] quickly followed *In re Gault*. The two cases applied the "guilt beyond a reasonable doubt" standard and Double Jeopardy Clause, respectively, to juvenile court proceedings. Both of the cases focused on the serious consequences of juvenile proceedings. *In re Winship* observed that "civil labels and good intentions do not themselves obviate the need for criminal due process safeguards in juvenile courts,"[85] because delinquency proceedings are "comparable in seriousness" to felony prosecutions.[86] In *Jones*, the Court again focused on the nature of juvenile proceedings, commenting that "in terms of potential consequences, there is little to distinguish an adjudicatory hearing such as was held in this case from a traditional criminal prosecution."[87] Neither of the cases purported to define the totality of the relationship between a minor and the state.

By way of contrast, in *McKeiver v. Pennsylvania*[88] the Court held that the Sixth Amendment right to trial by jury does not apply to delinquency proceedings.[89] A plurality of the Court recognized the failures of the juvenile court system,[90] but emphasized that imposing a right to trial by jury in a juvenile proceeding would turn it into an adversary hearing without advancing the fact-finding process.[91]

---

[80] *Id.*

[81] *See id.* at 27. The Court stated that:

> While due process requirements will, in some instances, introduce a degree of order and regularity to Juvenile Court proceedings to determine delinquency, and in contested cases will introduce some elements of the adversary system, nothing will require that the conception of the kindly juvenile judge be replaced by its opposite, nor do we here rule upon the question whether ordinary due process requirements must be observed with respect to hearings to determine the disposition of the delinquent child.

Id.

[82] *Id.* at 28.

[83] 397 U.S. 358 (1970).

[84] 421 U.S. 519 (1975).

[85] *In re* Winship, 397 U.S. at 365-66.

[86] *Id.*

[87] *Jones*, 421 U.S. at 530.

[88] 403 U.S. 528 (1971).

[89] *See id.* at 572.

[90] *See id.* at 545.

[91] As the plurality explained:

> The Court has refrained, in the cases heretofore decided, from taking the easy way with a flat holding that all rights constitutionally assured for the adult accused are to be imposed upon the state juvenile proceeding . . . .

With the sole exception of *McKeiver*, all of the procedural rights afforded to adults in criminal proceedings are available to juveniles in delinquency proceedings. The fact that the procedural rights of adults and minors are virtually the same, however, does not mean that the Court will readily conclude that the substantive rights of minors and adults are the same. In procedural due process case law involving the rights of minors, the Court has applied only those safeguards that it felt were necessary to enhance the trustworthiness of juvenile proceedings. In each case, the Court was concerned with the procedural fairness of the juvenile proceedings and did not attempt to equate the rights of minors in a general sense to those of adults. Therefore, these cases are not overly helpful when the issue is whether a juvenile has the same right to liberty as an adult.

B. Juvenile Rights and Substantive Liberty

The Court has recognized that a minor's substantive rights are not coextensive with those of adults. The Court first confronted this issue in *Prince v. Massachusetts*,[92] wherein the Court upheld Massachusetts' child labor laws against a constitutional challenge brought under the Equal Protection Clause and the First Amendment.[93] The child labor law prohibited minors under the age of twelve from selling newspapers or periodicals in any street or public place.[94] The Court observed that the statute would be unconstitutional if it applied to adults.[95] Then, in an oft-quoted passage, the Court remarked:

> The state's authority over children's activities is broader than over like actions of adults. . . . A democratic society rests, for its continuance, upon the healthy, well-rounded growth of young people into full maturity as citizens, with all that im-

---

> . . .
> The imposition of the jury trial on the juvenile court system would not strengthen greatly, if at all, the factfinding function, and would, contrarily, provide an attrition of the juvenile court's assumed ability to function in a unique manner.

Id. at 545-47.

92 321 U.S. 158 (1944).

93 *See id.* at 169-70. Mrs. Prince, who had legal custody of Betty Simmons (age nine) was a Jehovah's Witness who went door-to-door spreading her religious message. *See id.* at 162. Betty went out with Mrs. Prince and carried magazines which, from time to time, she had sold at the rate of five cents per copy. *See id.*

94 *See id.* at 160-61.

95 *See id.* at 167 ("Concededly a statute or ordinance identical in terms with Section 69, except that it is applicable to adults or all persons generally, would be invalid.") (citations omitted). The Court further stated that "the mere fact a state could not wholly prohibit this form of adult activity . . . does not mean it cannot do so for children." *Id.* at 168.

> plies. It may secure this against impeding restraints and dangers within a broad range of selection.[96]

The precise dimensions of the state's authority over children are still unclear. The Court has struggled over how to define the scope of a minor's rights in cases dealing with the First Amendment rights of minors, and those pertaining to a minor's right to privacy (including the right to obtain an abortion). While these cases do not suggest a precise test for determining the extent of a minor's substantive rights, a couple of general principles are clear. First, the Court has never started from scratch and asked whether a right that exists for adults exists at all for children. In each case, the Court assumes that minors have some constitutional protection. Second, the Court is more likely to show deference to a state law that regulates the conduct of minors.

In several cases dealing with restrictions on the First Amendment rights of minors, the Court has assumed that minors share many of the rights possessed by adults. As the Court declared in *Tinker v. Des Moines Independent School District*,[97] minors "are possessed of fundamental rights which the State must respect."[98] In each of these cases, the Court looked to the body of law it had already developed for adults, and asked whether minors should be treated differently.

Clearly, minors do enjoy a substantial degree of protection under the First Amendment. Thus, in *Tinker* the Court held that students had a right to wear black armbands in class in protest of the war in Vietnam.[99] *Tinker* emphasized that the classroom is quintessentially the "marketplace of ideas,"[100] and minors learn best through exposure to a plurality of ideas, rather than one authoritative account of the truth.[101]

---

[96] *Id.* The Court went on to state that:

> It is true children have rights, in common with older people, in the primary use of highways. But even in such use streets afford dangers for them not affecting adults. . . . What may be wholly permissible for adults therefore may not be so for children, either with or without their parents' presence.

Id. at 169.

[97] 393 U.S. 503 (1969).

[98] *Id.* at 511.

[99] *See id.* at 514.

[100] *Id.* at 512.

[101] *See id.* at 510-13. The school's decision to suspend students wearing armbands was based solely on the desire to avoid the controversy that would result from open opposition to the Vietnam War. *See id.* at 510. The Court found that this action was a form of viewpoint based discrimination. *See id.* at 512-13.

Viewpoint-based discrimination upon ideas is particularly repugnant to the Constitution in the arena of the First Amendment. *See generally* R.A.V. v. City of St. Paul, 505 U.S. 377 (1992). Moreover, as the Court noted in *Tinker*, "[t]he classroom is peculiarly the 'marketplace of ideas.' The Nation's future depends upon leaders trained through wide exposure to that robust exchange of ideas which discovers truth 'out of a multitude of tongues, [rather] than through any kind of authoritative selection.'" *Tinker*, 393 U.S. at 512 (quoting Keyishian v. Bd. of Regents, 385 U.S. 589, 603 (1967)).

The First Amendment rights of minors, however, do not extend to speech that borders obscenity. In *Ginsberg v. New York*,[102] the Court held that a state may adjust its statutory definition of obscenity for minors.[103] *Ginsberg* emphasized that "even where there is an invasion of protected freedoms 'the power of the state to control the conduct of children reaches beyond the scope of its authority over adults.'"[104] The Court recognized that the state "has an independent interest in the well-being of its youth."[105] The Court then upheld the statute, applying a rational basis test.[106]

Even at the borders of protected speech, however, the state must be careful not to prohibit too much. In *Erznoznik v. City of Jacksonville*,[107] the Court struck down a law that prohibited drive-in movie theaters from showing movies that contained any nudity.[108] One of the arguments advanced by the city in defense of the law was that the statute was a reasonable means of protecting minors from harm, citing *Ginsberg*.[109] The Court rejected the argument, stating that "[s]peech that is neither obscene as to youths nor subject to some other legitimate proscription cannot be suppressed solely to protect the young from ideas or images that a legislative body thinks unsuitable for them."[110] *Erznoznik* acknowledged, however, that there are some areas where a child "'is not possessed of that full capacity for individual

---

102 390 U.S. 629 (1968). The issue in *Ginsberg* was whether a state may adjust its definition of obscenity for minors. *See id.* at 631-32. A vendor was charged with selling "girlie" magazines to a 16 year-old boy. *See id.* The trial judge found that he had violated New York's criminal obscenity statute. *See id.* The statute defined material containing nudity as harmful to minors where it: "(i) predominantly appeals to the prurient, shameful or morbid interest of minors, and (ii) is patently offensive to prevailing standards in the adult community as a whole with respect to what is suitable material for minors, and (iii) is utterly without redeeming social importance for minors." *Id.* at 633.

103 *See id.* at 642-43.

104 *Id.* at 638 (citing Prince v. Massachusetts, 321 U.S. 158, 170 (1944)).

105 *Id.* at 640. The Court then quoted Chief Judge Fuld of the New York Court of Appeals, who stated that:

> [T]he knowledge that parental control or guidance cannot always be provided and society's transcendent interest in protecting the welfare of children justify reasonable regulation of the sale of material to them. It is, therefore, altogether fitting and proper for a state to include in a statute designed to regulate the sale of pornography to children special standards, broader than those embodied in legislation aimed at controlling dissemination of such material to adults.

People v. Kahan, 206 N.E.2d 333, 334 (1965).

106 390 U.S. at 641 ("The only question remaining, therefore, is whether the New York Legislature might rationally conclude, as it has, that exposure to the materials proscribed by [the obscenity law] constitutes such an 'abuse.'").

107 422 U.S. 205 (1975).

108 *See id.* at 216-17.

109 *See id.* at 212.

110 *Id.* at 213-14.

choice which is the presupposition of First Amendment guarantees.'"[111] The Court did not elaborate on what these areas include.

Another principle developed from the Court's case law concerning minors is that legislative classifications concerning minors should receive a greater degree of deference. The Court's right to privacy jurisprudence pertaining to minors demonstrates this principle. While the Court has been unable to agree on a standard of review to apply to classifications that burden a minor's rights, all of the cases show a greater degree of deference than the normal strict scrutiny standard of review that is applied to classifications burdening the rights of adults.

The Court has struggled to formulate a test for alleged infringements of a minor's right to privacy. In *Planned Parenthood v. Danforth*,[112] the Court considered the constitutionality of a parental consent provision in Missouri's abortion statute.[113] *Danforth* framed the test as "whether there is any significant state interest . . . that is not present in the case of an adult."[114]

The following year, the Court considered whether a state may prohibit the distribution of contraceptives to minors under the age of sixteen in *Carey v. Population Services International*.[115] A plurality of four applied the *Danforth* test. The plurality observed that this test is "apparently less rigorous than the 'compelling state interest' test applied to restrictions on the privacy rights of adults."[116] The plurality found the lower standard appropriate because: (1) a state has greater latitude to regulate the conduct of minors; and (2) minors have a lesser capacity for making important decisions.[117]

In *Bellotti v. Baird*,[118] a plurality elaborated on the reasons for treating cases dealing with the rights of minors differently from those concerning adults:

> We have recognized three reasons justifying the conclusion that the constitutional rights of children cannot be equated with those of adults: the peculiar vulnerability of children; their inability to make critical decisions in an informed, ma-

---

[111] *Id.* at 214 n.11 (citing Ginsberg v. New York, 390 U.S. 629, 649-50 (1968) (Stewart, J., concurring)).

[112] 428 U.S. 52 (1976).

[113] *See id.* at 52. The applicable section of Missouri's abortion statute required that, in the first twelve weeks of her pregnancy, the minor obtain the written consent of a parent or person *in loco parentis* if she is under 18 and unmarried unless the abortion was necessary to save the life of the mother. *See id.* at 58.

[114] *Id.* at 75.

[115] 431 U.S. 678 (1977).

[116] *Id.* at 693 n.15.

[117] *See id.*

[118] 443 U.S. 622 (1979).

ture manner; and the importance of the parental role in child rearing.[119]

Bellotti did not mention or apply the *Danforth* standard. In fact, this standard has been all but forgotten in the Court's later decisions. In *H.L. v. Matheson*,[120] the Court reviewed an abortion statute as it applied to a minor.[121] At the end of the opinion, the Court stated that the statute "plainly serves important state interests, is narrowly drawn to protect only those interests, and does not violate any of the guarantees of the Constitution."[122] Unfortunately, the Court did not elaborate on the test it was applying, and did not explain how the test was supposed to be applied or what the individual factors meant.

More recently, in *Hodgson v. Minnesota*,[123] the Court considered whether a state's two-parent notification provision, without a judicial bypass, violated the Constitution.[124] The Court again was confused by the question of what standard to apply. Justice Stevens and Justice O'Connor applied a rational basis test, citing *Ginsberg*.[125] Justice Marshall, joined by Justices Brennan and Blackmun, expressed the view that minority status does not affect the nature of the right itself, but only the state's interests.[126] A four-Justice plurality observed that, "[t]he law does not give to children many rights given to adults, and provides, in general, that children can exercise the rights they do have only through and with parental consent."[127] And while the plurality purported to apply some form of rational basis review, in actuality they looked much closer at the justifications for the statute than such a standard of review would imply.[128]

---

[119] *Id.* at 634. For an explanation of what the plurality might have meant by these factors, it is helpful to look at what it cited. When discussing a child's "peculiar vulnerability," the plurality discussed the procedure cases set forth above, including *In re Winship* and *In re Gault*. *See id.* When discussing the child's inability to make important, affirmative choices, the Court cited Justice Stewart's opinion in *Prince* and *Ginsberg*. *See id.* at 635-37. For a discussion of *Winship* and *Gault*, see *supra* notes 78-86 and accompanying text. For an explanation of *Prince* and *Ginsberg*, see *supra* notes 92-96, 102-06 and accompanying text.

[120] 450 U.S. 398 (1981).

[121] *See id.* at 398.

[122] *Id.* at 413 (footnote omitted).

[123] 497 U.S. 417 (1990).

[124] *See id.* at 424-25.

[125] *See id.* at 448-49.

[126] *See id.* at 464 ("Neither the scope of a woman's privacy right nor the magnitude of a law's burden is diminished because a woman is a minor. Rather, a woman's minority status affects only the nature of the State's interests.") (citations omitted).

[127] *Id.* at 482 (citation omitted).

[128] *See id.* at 483-501. Such justifications include the protection of a parent's right to participate in the child's upbringing, the fostering of parent-child relationships, and a general societal interest. *See id.* at 485-86.

III. THE RIGHT TO TRAVEL ON PUBLIC FORA

"If I choose to take an evening walk to see if Andromeda has come up on schedule, I think I am entitled to look for the distant light of Almach and Mirach without finding myself staring into the blinding beam of a police flashlight."[129]

There is no consensus among the lower courts regarding either the existence of a fundamental right to travel on public fora or the scope of such a right if it indeed exists. This Part offers a solution to that controversy.

For the most part, the circuit split does not stem from an underlying doctrinal disagreement. Rather, the underlying factual circumstances in the circuit cases show that in each case the court is responding to somewhat different concerns. The constitutional right to travel on public fora is properly understood as an aspect of substantive due process. This right is rooted in our nation's history and traditions, and deserves recognition as a fundamental aspect of the "liberty" protected by the Due Process Clause of the Fourteenth Amendment. Anxiety over the potential consequences of recognizing such a right can be dispelled by adopting a modified formulation of the "undue burden" standard set forth by the joint opinion in *Planned Parenthood v. Casey*[130] to determine which level of scrutiny to apply to alleged deprivations of this right.

A. *Circuit Split: Doctrinal Disagreement or Sloppy Rights Talk?*

The right to travel on public fora is frequently recognized by courts in general terms as a right to freedom of movement.[131] The failure of courts to describe this right precisely as a right to travel on public fora has led to a needless and superficial disagreement amongst the circuit courts over whether such a right exists.[132] The

[129] Papachristou v. City of Jacksonville, 405 U.S. 156, 164 n.6 (1972) (*quoting* Charles A. Reich, *Police Questioning of Law Abiding Citizens*, 75 YALE L.J. 1161, 1172 (1966)).

[130] 505 U.S. 833, 873-78 (1992) (stating that not every burden that makes a right more difficult to exercise is an infringement of that right and that the right is only violated if the state imposes an undue burden on its exercise).

[131] *See, e.g.*, Nunez v. City of San Diego, 114 F.3d 935, 944 (9th Cir. 1997) ("Citizens have a fundamental right of free movement, 'historically part of the amenities of life as we have known them.'") (citations omitted); Cole v. Housing Auth., 435 F.2d 807, 809 (1st Cir. 1970) ("[T]he right to travel is a fundamental personal right that can impinged only if necessary to promote a compelling governmental interest.") (footnote omitted). *But see* Lutz v. City of York, 899 F.2d 255, 268 (3d Cir. 1990) (recognizing a fundamental "right to travel locally through public spaces and roadways").

[132] *Cf.* Laurence H. Tribe & Michael C. Dorf, *Levels of Generality in the Definition of Rights*, 57 U. CHI. L. REV. 1057, 1067 (1990). As the authors explain:

> [A] right to be let alone cannot serve as a constitutional rule of decision. A right to be let alone while doing what? While harming others? Harming others in what way?

cases involve three distinct factual scenarios: (1) a "right to commute;"[133] (2) a right to receive public housing in the context of durational residency requirements;[134] and (3) a right to travel freely within a given jurisdiction, or a right to travel on public fora.[135]

1. Right to Commute

The first scenario involves an employment situation where constitutional rights may be waived by contract. Thus, it was unnecessary for the courts to consider and reject a broadly described right to freedom of movement.[136] Further, these residency requirements are not justified by a desire to discourage persons from migrating to a community, which is the purpose that *Shaprio v. Thompson*[137] found unconstitutional.[138]

Three of the four circuit courts that rejected an asserted right to intrastate travel did so in the context of a "right to commute." In *Wardwell v. Board of Education*,[139] the Cincinnati Board of Education adopted a resolution that required all teachers to establish residency in the school district within ninety days of starting employment.[140] In *Andre v. Board of Trustees*,[141] the Village of Maywood, Illinois adopted a resolution that required all administrative personnel and

> As determined by whom? These questions make clear the need for a less abstract formulation of the right at stake . . . .

Id.

[133] Andre v. Bd. of Trustees, 561 F.2d 48, 52-53 (7th Cir. 1977) (finding that residency requirement for municipal employment did not impermissibly burden plaintiffs' right to interstate or intrastate travel); Wardwell v. Bd. of Educ., 529 F.2d 625, 627 (6th Cir. 1976) (finding that there was no right to intrastate travel and upholding residency requirement for employment); Wright v. City of Jackson, 506 F.2d 900, 902 (5th Cir. 1975) (determining that there is no support for a fundamental Constitutional "right to commute" which would require a compelling governmental purpose).

[134] *See* King v. New Rochelle Mun. Hous. Auth., 442 F.2d 646 (2d Cir. 1971) (finding five year residency requirement for admission to public housing violated the Equal Protection Clause); *Cole*, 435 F.2d at 809 (finding that a two year residency requirement to qualify for subsidized housing violated the Equal Protection Clause).

[135] *See* Hutchins v. District of Columbia, 188 F.3d 531 (D.C. Cir. 1999) (en banc) (holding that because juveniles had no fundamental right to free movement, intermediate scrutiny was proper, and upheld a curfew law); *Nunez*, 114 F.3d at 944-46 (applying strict scrutiny to overturn curfew law); Smith v. Avino, 91 F.3d 105, 109 (11th Cir. 1996) (finding that a curfew imposed by a county after a hurricane was not unconstitutionally vague and the court upheld the restriction on travel); *Lutz*, 899 F.2d at 268-71 (applying intermediate scrutiny to uphold municipal cruising ordinance).

[136] *See Andre*, 561 F.2d at 53 (rejecting any right of intrastate travel outside of cases involving durational residency requirements).

[137] 394 U.S. 618 (1969).

[138] *See id.* at 629 ("[T]he purpose of inhibiting migration by needy persons . . . is constitutionally impermissible.").

[139] 529 F.2d 625 (6th Cir. 1976).

[140] *See id.* at 626.

[141] 561 F.2d 48 (7th Cir. 1977).

department heads to establish residency in Maywood within two years; all other personnel were given four years to comply.[142] Similarly, in *Wright v. City of Jackson*,[143] the City of Jackson, Mississippi passed a statute that required all civil service employees to maintain their domicile within the city limits during their period of employment.[144]

In each of these cases, the employees brought suit seeking to overturn the statutes that required them to live within the jurisdiction of their employment. In *Andre*, the court observed that under *Shapiro*, the fact of residency itself was distinct from the durational residency requirement, and that it was only the latter that is unconstitutional.[145] The purpose of a residency requirement is to assure that city employees live in the community where they work. Employees who are subject to such a restriction are all subject to it equally. Thus, no group is penalized for moving into the community "late."

More fundamentally, the difference between a residency requirement in the *Andre* sense and the durational residency requirement of *Shapiro* is the privity between the *Andre* employee and the government that passes the law. In *Andre*, *Wright*, and *Wardwell*, the persons affected were governmental employees who were getting paid for what they did. The residency requirement was merely a condition of their employment. Thus, they gave up their rights by bargaining for employment.[146] By way of contrast, *Shapiro* involved the eligibility of persons for welfare payments. There was no contract between these welfare recipients and the state.

2. *Durational Residency Requirements*

The decisions in *King v. New Rochelle Municipal Housing Authority*[147] and *Cole v. Housing Authority*[148] recognized a right to

---

142 *See id.* at 49.

143 506 F.2d 900 (5th Cir. 1975).

144 *See id.* at 901.

145 *See Andre*, 561 F.2d at 52 ("Bona fide residency requirements as continuing conditions of municipal employment rest upon footings significantly different from those of durational residency requirements.").

146 There is precedent for finding constitutional rights waived by signing a contract. *See, e.g.*, D.H. Overmeyer Co. v. Frick Co., 405 U.S. 174, 187 (1972) (holding that procedural due process rights may be waived by contract where such a waiver is made "voluntarily, intelligently, and knowingly . . . ."). However, such a waiver must be clear and must be made in circumstances that are not unconscionable. *See, e.g.*, Fuentes v. Shevin, 407 U.S. 67, 95-96 (1972) (holding that due process rights cannot be waived by an adhesion contract which stated that upon default a seller may repossess the merchandise).

147 442 F.2d 646 (2d Cir. 1971). The *King* court held that a five-year residency requirement for admission to public housing was unconstitutional under the Equal Protection Clause. *See id.* at 648.

intrastate travel in the context of durational residency requirements for public housing. These cases cannot be distinguished in any meaningful sense from *Shapiro*. The durational residency requirements in *King* and *Cole* were justified by the same purposes that *Shapiro* found unconstitutional. It would be surprising if the constitutionality of such an ordinance turned on the issue of whether it deterred migration by those living in another state, or deterred migration by both those living in another state *and* people seeking to relocate from a different city within the same state.

Such a result might be squared with *Shapiro* if the case was based solely upon principles of federalism and a notion of dual citizenship.[149] *Shapiro*, however, also rested on grounds of personal liberty.[150] Thus, to the extent that a durational residency requirement infringes on concepts of personal liberty, such a requirement may be unconstitutional when practiced only against citizens of the same state.[151] As the Second Circuit stated, within this context "[i]t would be meaningless to describe the right to travel between states as a fundamental precept of personal liberty and not to acknowledge a correlative constitutional right to travel within a state."[152]

3. Right to Travel on Public Fora

Three of the four circuits that have addressed the issue of whether there is a right to travel on public fora found such a right. The Ninth Circuit recognized this right in broad terms in a case involving a juvenile curfew law.[153] The Eleventh Circuit recognized this right in the context of an emergency curfew applicable to both chil-

---

[148] 435 F.2d 807 (1st Cir. 1970). *Cole* held that a two-year residency requirement for admission to public housing was unconstitutional under the equal protection clause. *See id.* at 813-14.

[149] *See, e.g.*, Slaughter House Cases, 83 U.S. 36, 77 (1872). Elaborating upon the meaning of the Fourteenth Amendment Privileges or Immunities Clause, the Court stated:

> Its sole purpose was to declare to the several States, that whatever those rights, as you grant or establish them to your own citizens, or as you limit or qualify, or impose restrictions on their exercise, the same, neither more nor less, shall be the measure of the rights of citizens of other States within your jurisdiction.

Id.

[150] As the *Shapiro* Court explained:

> This Court long ago recognized that *the nature of our Federal Union and our constitutional concepts of personal liberty unite* to require that all citizens be free to travel throughout the length and breadth of our land uninhibited by statutes, rules, or regulations which unreasonably burden or restrict this movement.

394 U.S. 618, 629 (1969) (emphasis added).

[151] A full exploration of this issue is beyond the scope of this Note.

[152] *King*, 442 F.2d at 648.

[153] *See* Nunez v. City of San Diego, 114 F.3d 935, 946 (9th Cir. 1997) (holding that the right of travel by children is fundamental and thus applying strict scrutiny analysis to a municipal juvenile ordinance).

dren and adults.[154] Finally, the Third Circuit recognized the "right to travel locally through public spaces and roadways" in the context of an anti-cruising ordinance.[155] Only the D.C. Circuit refused to recognize such a right.[156]

Judge Silberman's plurality opinion in *Hutchins v. District of Columbia*[157] subsumes a child's minority status into the definition of the right itself.[158] Judge Silberman justifies this choice on judicial restraint grounds. The more general the definition of the right is, the argument runs, the easier it is to extend the bounds of substantive due process.[159] Thus, to ensure against unlicensed judicial lawmaking, the right must be described at "the most specific level at which a relevant tradition protecting, or denying protection to, the asserted right can be identified."[160]

Ironically, in the context of a right to free movement, the opposite is true. As this Part demonstrates, the main reason why this right has not won universal approval is because it remains in abstract form and thus encompasses a wide range of interests (some of which should not enjoy fundamental right status).[161] Furthermore, incorporating a child's minority status into the definition of an asserted fundamental right is contrary to Supreme Court precedent.[162]

---

154 *See* Smith v. Avino, 91 F.3d 105, 109 (11th Cir. 1996) (holding that the right to travel may be temporarily limited or suspended in emergency situations).

155 Lutz v. City of York, 899 F.2d 255, 268-69 (3d Cir. 1990). The court held that one's right to move about town implicates the Due Process Clause. *See id.* at 268. However, the Court applied intermediate scrutiny, and not strict scrutiny, to the anti-cruising ordinance. *See id.* at 268-70.

156 *See* Hutchins v. District of Columbia, 188 F.3d 531, 538-39 (D.C. Cir. 1999) (en banc) (concluding, in a plurality opinion, that juveniles do not have a fundamental right, without adult supervision, to be on the streets).

157 188 F.3d 531 (D.C. Cir. 1999) (en banc).

158 *See id.* at 538 ("[W]e must ask not whether Americans enjoy a general right of free movement, but rather whatever are the scope and dimensions of such a right (if it exists), do minors have such a substantive right?").

159 *See id.* ("[T]he more general is the right's description, *i.e.*, the free movement of people, the easier is the extension of substantive due process.").

160 *Id.* (quoting Michael H. v. Gerald D., 491 U.S. 110, 127 n.6 (1988)). Justice Scalia, writing for the majority, took an approach to identifying and defining fundamental rights that has been subjected to harsh criticism. *See, e.g.*, Tribe & Dorf, *supra* note 132, at 1086 (arguing that Scalia's approach is not value-neutral, and that there is no one way to measure the appropriate level of generality for an asserted right).

161 One of the main problems with the approach taken by Justice Scalia in *Michael H*, *see supra* note 160 and accompanying text, is that it provides no criterion for achieving the proper degree of specificity. A definition may be narrow along one axis, yet broad along another. Thus, while my definition of the right to travel on public fora is more general in the sense that it includes minors, it is also more specific. Unlike a generalized right to free movement (which could be read to authorize travel anywhere), the right as I define it does not *prima facie* include a right to trespass on private property or gain unauthorized admittance to secure government buildings.

162 *See supra* Part II.B (tracing the Supreme Court's development of substantive rights for juveniles).

The Third Circuit found a fundamental "right to travel locally through public spaces and roadways" in the Due Process Clause.[163] The court conceded that "this bottom-line judgment is unquestionably ad hoc, to some extent."[164] The Third Circuit seemed terrified by the consequences of not finding such a right,[165] and felt that recognition of this right "is a judgment we are required to make."[166]

The right to move freely involved in scenario three above is of a different magnitude, if not a different kind, than the right implicated in scenario two. It is one thing to discourage a family from changing their residency, and quite another to discourage them from leaving their house at all. Therefore, it simply will not do to put both of these rights together into the general category of "freedom of movement."[167] While the one right could be described as the "right to migrate with intent to reside," the other must be described as the right to travel on public fora.[168]

B. *The Right to Travel on Public Fora*

The right to travel on public fora is a liberty interest that is protected by the Due Process Clause of the Fourteenth Amendment.[169]

---

[163] Lutz v. City of York, 899 F.2d 255, 268 (3d Cir. 1990).

[164] *Id.*

[165] *See id.* ("Under York's view, a state or local government could constitutionally prohibit all freedom of movement that does not involve interstate migration, interstate commerce, business between a citizen and the federal government, and (presumably) travel incident to otherwise protected activity.").

[166] *Id.*

[167] These two rights should also be kept separate because they draw upon separate histories. For a history of the right to migration, see CHAFEE, *supra* note 57, at 176-93 (describing the history of migratory freedom between the English colonies, the relevant language in the Articles of Confederation, and the rights' history since the adoption of our Constitution). The right to travel on public fora has its own common law history. *See infra* Part II.B.

[168] This latter right is developed more clearly below. *See infra* Part III.B.

[169] Perhaps no portion of the Court's jurisprudence has created more controversy than its forays into substantive due process. *See, e.g.*, Paul Brest, *The Fundamental Rights Controversy: The Essential Contradictions of Normative Constitutional Scholarship*, 90 YALE L.J. 1063, 1068-89 (1981) (canvassing various arguments for and against the legitimacy of fundamental rights). Many scholars have defended the Court's expansive decisions by arguing that certain moral principles underlie the abstract phrase "due process of law," and that these principles must be recognized and adhered to if our government is to be considered democratic. *See, e.g.*, Ronald Dworkin, *The Arduous Virtue of Fidelity: Originalism, Scalia, Tribe, and Nerve*, 65 FORDHAM L. REV. 1249, 1264 (1997) ("Majority rule is democratic only when certain prior conditions—the democratic conditions of equal membership—are met and sustained."); James E. Fleming, *Securing Deliberative Autonomy*, 48 STAN. L. REV. 1, 62 (1995) ("[D]ue process should secure a forward-looking antitotalitarian principle, criticizing historical practices that deny the promise of liberty . . . .") (citation omitted). Critics of the Court have argued that these decisions are anti-democratic and do not respect the Constitution's original meaning. *See* ANTONIN SCALIA, *Common-Law Courts in a Civil-Law System: The Role of the United States Federal Courts in Interpreting the Constitution and Laws*, *in* A MATTER OF INTERPRETATION: FEDERAL COURTS AND THE LAW 3, 41 (1997) ("Neither the text of such a document nor the intent of its framers (whichever you choose) can possibly lead to the conclusion that its only

Indeed, this liberty interest has always been protected from encroachment by the Due Process Clause. It is a mirror-like reflection of the historical meaning of due process; namely, "liberty from bodily restraint."[170] As such, it is a fundamental right that may not be abridged without demonstrating a compelling governmental interest.

1. The Magna Charta and English Common Law

"The phrase, 'life, liberty or property without due process of law' came to us from the English common law."[171] "Due process of law" is the rough equivalent of the phrase "by the law of the land" that appears in the thirty-ninth article of Magna Charta.[172] The latter phrase includes freedom from bodily restraint.[173] As one author explains, "[a]ltogether, it may be said that the history of the growth and development of the right of personal liberty is the main element in the history of early English constitutional law."[174]

Unsurprisingly, when Blackstone spoke of the rights of persons in his commentaries on the English law, he included "personal liberty." "[P]ersonal liberty consists in the power of loco-motion, of changing situation, or removing one's person to whatsoever place one's own inclination may direct; without imprisonment or restraint, unless by due course of law."[175] If the right to exercise one's "power

---

effect is to take the power of changing rights away from the legislature and give it to the courts."). The Court itself has responded to this conflict by stating that "[a]s a general matter, the Court has always been reluctant to expand the concept of substantive due process because guideposts for responsible decisionmaking in this unchartered area are scarce and open-ended." Collins v. Harker Heights, 503 U.S. 115, 125 (1992) (citation omitted).

In an effort to reconcile these competing visions of the judicial role, the Court has attempted to limit the liberties recognized as fundamental under the due process clause to those "which are, objectively, 'deeply rooted in this Nation's history and tradition.'" Washington v. Glucksberg, 521 U.S. 702, 720-21 (1997) (citation omitted). This inquiry is backward-looking and protects against short-term departures from historical practices. *See* County of Sacramento v. Lewis, 523 U.S. 833, 858 (1997) (Kennedy, J., concurring).

170 On several occasions, the Supreme Court confirmed that freedom from bodily restraint is at the core of the liberty protected by the due process clause. *See* Foucha v. Louisiana, 504 U.S. 71, 80 (1992) ("Freedom from bodily restraint has always been at the core of the liberty protected by the Due Process Clause . . . . ") (citing Youngberg v. Romeo, 457 U.S. 307, 316 (1982)); Ingraham v. Wright, 430 U.S. 651, 673-674 (1977) ("While the contours of . . . [the liberty interests protected by the Due Process Clause] have not been defined precisely, they have always been thought to encompass freedom from bodily restraint and punishment.").

171 Charles Warren, *The New "Liberty" Under the 14th Amendment*, 39 HARV. L. REV. 431, 440 (1926) (stating that under the common law, "liberty" meant simply liberty of the person or, in other words, the right to have one's person free from bodily restraint).

172 *See* Charles E. Shattuck, *The True Meaning of the Term "Liberty" in those Clauses in the Federal and State Constitutions Which Protect "Life, Liberty, and Property,"* 4 HARV. L. REV. 365, 372-73 (1891).

173 *See id.* at 375 (stating that in the American context, the term "liberty" entails freedom of the person from restraint).

174 *Id.* at 376.

175 1 WILLIAM BLACKSTONE COMMENTARIES *134.

of loco-motion" did not exist, "there would soon be an end of all other rights and immunities."[176]

This right was so important that it could not be revoked except in an emergency.[177] "'Next to a man's life the nearest thing that concerns him is freedom of his person ; for indeed, what is imprisonment but a kind of civil death?'"[178] In this sense, the right to personal liberty is an autonomy right that arises out of respect for the dignity of the person.

A government violated the right to personal liberty whenever a person was imprisoned without cause. Imprisonment was defined broadly, so that "[t]he confinement of the person, in any wise, is an imprisonment."[179] Thus, confining a person to the boundaries of his own home was an imprisonment, as was forcibly detaining him in the street.[180]

2. *Supreme Court Case Law*

This central meaning of the Due Process Clause (protecting a citizen's freedom from bodily restraint)[181] is so well understood that it is an afterthought in the Court's opinions. Beginning with *Meyer v. Nebraska*[182] and continuing through *Foucha v. Louisiana*,[183] the Court has consistently assumed that the Due Process Clause "encompass[es] freedom from bodily restraint and punishment."[184] Indeed, the Court has been "careful not to 'minimize the importance and fundamental nature' of the individual's right to liberty."[185]

A necessary corollary of this freedom from bodily restraint is the right of a citizen to "remove from one place to another according to inclination."[186] The ability to move about within a community is "simply another way of saying that you are not imprisoned."[187] Thus, "freedom of locomotion may well be treated as a part of freedom of

---

176 *Id.* at *134-35.

177 *Id.* at *135.

178 Shattuck, *supra* note 172, at 378 (quoting CARE'S ENGLISH LIBERTIES 185 (1721)).

179 BLACKSTONE, *supra* note 175, at 135.

180 *See id.*

181 *See* JACOBUS TENBROEK, THE CONSTITUTION AND THE RIGHT OF FREE MOVEMENT 6 (1955) ("In fact, though the word liberty in the due process clause has come over the years to be filled with much additional content, this meaning . . . is the primary and historical meaning.").

182 262 U.S. 390 (1923). The *Meyer* Court stated that "[w]ithout doubt, it denotes *not merely freedom from bodily restraint.*" *Id.* at 399 (emphasis added).

183 504 U.S. 71 (1992). The *Foucha* Court declared that "[f]reedom from bodily restraint has always been at the core of the liberty protected by the Due Process Clause from arbitrary governmental action." *Id.* at 80 (citation omitted).

184 Ingraham v. Wright, 430 U.S. 651, 673-74 (1977).

185 *Foucha*, 504 U.S. at 80 (quoting U.S. v. Salerno, 481 U.S. 739, 750 (1987)).

186 Williams v. Fears, 179 U.S. 270, 274 (1900).

187 TENBROEK, *supra* note 181, at 6.

restraint of the person."[188] This freedom has been recognized in the Court's dicta.

The Court's decisions holding loitering and vagrancy laws unconstitutional on vagueness grounds frequently allude to the existence of such a right. In *Papachristou v. City of Jacksonville*,[189] the Court stated that walking and strolling are "historically part of the amenities of life as we have known them."[190] Again, in *Kolender v. Lawson*[191] the Court observed that a loitering ordinance "implicates consideration of the constitutional right to freedom of movement."[192] Finally, in *City of Chicago v. Morales*[193] a plurality of the court declared that "[w]e have expressly identified this 'right to remove from one place to another according to inclination' as 'an attribute of personal liberty' protected by the Constitution."[194] The plurality did not consider whether this right would support a substantive due process challenge.[195]

The right to travel on public fora is also logically implied by the right to interstate travel itself, whose existence is no longer questioned.[196] At least prior to the 20th century and the invention of the airplane (and perhaps the 19th century and the invention of the locomotive engine), it is difficult to imagine how one could exercise their right to interstate travel without the use of public sidewalks and roadways. Even now, most people must use public streets and sidewalks to access airports. Thus, recognition of a right to interstate travel compels the recognition of a right to travel on public fora, lest the former right be reduced to a dead letter.

C. *The Right to Travel and an "Undue Burden"*

Restrictions on the right to travel on public fora that eliminate the utility of the right should be unconstitutional unless justified by a "compelling governmental interest." It does not follow, however, that all restrictions that incidentally burden this right need to satisfy this high threshold. As the Supreme Court has explained:

---

188 Warren, *supra* note 171, at 450. Warren stated that *William v. Fears* did not add, substantively, anything to the Due Process Clause. *See id.*

189 405 U.S. 156 (1972).

190 *Id.* at 164.

191 461 U.S. 352 (1983).

192 *Id.* at 358.

193 119 S. Ct. 1849 (1999).

194 *Id.* at 1857 (citation omitted).

195 *See id.* at 1863 n.35 ("[I]t [is] unnecessary to reach the question whether the . . .. ordinance is invalid as a deprivation of substantive due process.").

196 *See supra* Part I (tracing the development of the right to interstate travel).

> The authority of a municipality to impose regulations in order to assure the safety and convenience of the people in the use of public highways has never been regarded as inconsistent with civil liberties but rather as one of the means of safeguarding the good order upon which they ultimately depend.[197]

Thus, the question is how much of an impact must a regulation have before it is considered an infringement of a fundamental right.

The Third Circuit dealt with this issue in *Lutz v. City of York*.[198] The *Lutz* court proposed an "intermediate" standard of review for all alleged violations of the right to intrastate travel, relying on Supreme Court precedents in the arena of time, place, and manner restrictions on speech.[199] The court reasoned that "[i]f the freedom of speech itself can be so qualified, then surely the unenumerated right of localized travel can be as well."[200] The *Lutz* court recognized that content-

[197] Cox v. New Hampshire, 312 U.S. 569, 574 (1941).

[198] 899 F.2d 255 (3d Cir. 1990). The *Lutz* court framed the issue as follows: "We believe that reviewing all infringements on the right to travel under strict scrutiny is just as inappropriate as applying no heightened scrutiny to any infringement on the right to travel not implicating the structural or federalism-based concerns of the more well-established precedents." *Id.* at 269.

[199] *See id.* In applying intermediate scrutiny, the court held that the cruising ordinance "will be upheld if it is narrowly tailored to meet significant city objectives." *Id.* at 270.

[200] *Id* at 269. The Court gave two justifications for this analogy. First, the Court stated that not all "burden[s] on First Amendment rights [are] sufficiently serious to trigger heightened scrutiny." *Id.* at 270 n.41. This is true, but largely beside the point. Similar distinctions have been made in case law dealing with privacy rights as well. In *Zablocki v. Redhail*, 434 U.S. 374 (1978), the Court considered a Wisconsin statute which prevented parents who paid child support and who did not have custody of the child from marrying without court approval. *See id.* at 375. The Court observed that only regulations which "interfere directly and substantially with the right to marry" were subject to a strict scrutiny standard of review. *Id.* at 386-87. The *Zablocki* court then distinguished *Califano v. Jobst*, 434 U.S. 47 (1977), which involved a provision of the Social Security Act that cut off disability benefits to a person who married someone who was not separately entitled to benefits. *See id.* at 48. The Court distinguished *Califano* on the ground that the burden in *Zablocki* was more direct and substantial an interference with the right to marry. *See Zablocki*, 434 U.S. at 387 n.12 ("The statutory classification at issue here, [in contrast to *Califano*], clearly does interfere directly and substantially with the right to marry."). As one scholar has observed, "[t]he only reason for the more rigorous scrutiny applied in *Zablocki* is the fact that the burden on the right to marry in that case was more severe than it was in *Califano*." Alan Brownstein, *How Rights are Infringed: The Role of Undue Burden Analysis in Constitutional Doctrine*, 45 HASTINGS L.J. 867, 896 (1994). Thus, the fact that First Amendment jurisprudence has a mechanism for dealing with insubstantial burdens does not by itself justify this analogy.

Second, the *Lutz* court found the First Amendment analogy helpful because of the Supreme Court's forum analysis. *See Lutz*, 899 F.2d at 270 n.41. The court reasoned that, just as heightened scrutiny is appropriate in speech cases only where the forum is a public one, it is also appropriate in "localized" travel cases only where the forum is a public one. *See id.* This is true, but the same problem may be addressed by carefully describing the right. My description of the right to travel on public fora encompasses the fora that are considered by the Court to be public. Therefore, the analogy is unnecessary in this respect as well.

based restrictions on speech merit strict scrutiny,[201] but felt that the content-neutrality requirement in free speech cases had "no obvious analog in the travel context."[202]

Content-based restrictions on speech are treated differently from content-neutral restrictions because "content discrimination 'raises the specter that the Government may effectively drive certain ideas or viewpoints from the marketplace.'"[203] A regulation is content-neutral when it is justified not by hostility to the content of the speech, but by the "secondary effects" of the speech on the community.[204] As Professor Dorf explains, "[c]ontent-based regulations aim at the communicative impact of communicative activity, whereas content-neutral regulations merely have an adverse effect on communicative opportunity."[205] Thus, content-neutral regulations impose, at most, incidental burdens on core First Amendment values.

Missing from the *Lutz* test is a mechanism for distinguishing burdens on the right to travel on public fora that are incidental (such as traffic lights) from those that are direct (such as a curfew law). The *Lutz* test treats both categories of burdens identically. As a consequence, the *Lutz* test is both overprotective and underprotective.

The test is overprotective because it would require that traffic signals, stop signs, and right-of-way designations survive an intermediate standard of review. These regulations are meant to facilitate the right to travel, not burden it. They are necessary to keep the roadways safe. Without them, the right to travel as we know it would not exist because streets would be covered with traffic accidents. Cities should not be forced to prepare detailed analyses of the purposes of each stop sign to justify them. Unless the placement of traffic signals and the like causes a substantial disruption of a person's ability to travel, such burdens should not be subject to heightened scrutiny at all.

Lutz is also underprotective because it evaluates direct burdens on the right to travel on public fora under an intermediate standard of review. Traditionally, laws that directly burden a fundamental right must survive strict scrutiny by demonstrating that they are narrowly

---

201 *See id.* at 270 n.40 ("Only content-neutral restrictions are subjected to intermediate scrutiny in the public fora cases. Content-specific restrictions, by contrast, must survive strict scrutiny.") (citation omitted).

202 *Id.*

203 R.A.V. v. City of St. Paul, 505 U.S. 377, 387 (1992) (quoting Simon & Schuster, Inc., v. Members of the New York State Crime Victims Board, 502 U.S. 105, 116 (1991)).

204 *See* City of Renton v. Playtime Theatres, 475 U.S. 41, 47-48 (1986) (holding that a zoning ordinance that prohibited theaters from showing non-obscene pornographic films was content neutral because it was justified by the secondary effects of adult theaters on the community, including prostitution).

205 Michael C. Dorf, *Incidental Burdens on Fundamental Rights*, 109 HARV. L. REV. 1175, 1201 (1996).

drawn to serve a compelling governmental interest.[206] There is no compelling reason for treating the right to travel on public fora differently from all other fundamental rights.

The best method for distinguishing between those burdens that justify heightened scrutiny and those that do not is the "undue burden" standard adopted by a plurality in *Planned Parenthood v. Casey*.[207] This is a threshold inquiry.[208] Once an undue burden is found, the regulation is subject to strict scrutiny. If there is no "undue burden," then the regulation merely has to pass rational basis review. This mechanism eliminates the problems of overinclusion and underinclusion that are caused by the *Lutz* test.

A statute or regulation constitutes an undue burden where it "has the purpose or effect of placing a substantial obstacle in the path" of the exercise of the right.[209] Thus, the inquiry is whether a state or municipality has placed a substantial obstacle in the path of a person's right to travel on public fora. The right to travel on public fora is one of those rights that, as Professor Dorf explains, "presuppose[s] the existence of conditions such that a regulation that appears to burden a right could actually be consistent with the assumptions that define the right."[210] As the *Lutz* court observed, certain types of regulations are necessary for the right to travel upon public parks, sidewalks, and roadways to have meaning.[211] This right assumes that regulations providing for a right-of-way and other necessities for organized and orderly travel exist; otherwise, accidents occur and every hour ends

---

206 *See id.* at 1177-78 (distinguishing between strict level of scrutiny applied to laws that directly burden a fundamental right and more deferential scrutiny applied to laws that only incidentally burden a fundamental right).

207 505 U.S. 833 (1992). In *Casey*, the plurality evaluated the constitutionality of six separate provisions of the Pennsylvania abortion statute. *See id.* at 879-901. The plurality found the statute's definition of medical emergency, informed consent requirement, 24-hour waiting period requirement, parental consent requirement, and most of the record keeping and reporting requirements to be constitutional. *See id.* at 880-87, 899-901. The plurality found the spousal notification provision, and the portion of the reporting requirement which mandated that a woman failing to notify her spouse give a reason for that failure, to be unconstitutional. *See id.* at 887-98, 901.

208 *See* Brownstein, *supra* note 200, at 879-80. This author argues that the *Casey* plurality collapses the threshold standard with the strict scrutiny analysis in the context of abortion. This argument stems from the Court's understanding of the "right/infringement/justification interrelation," which assumes that there is no "sufficiently compelling interest" before viability that would warrant that level of interference with a woman's right to choose an abortion. *See id.*

209 *Id.* at 878 (quoting Planned Parenthood v. Casey, 505 U.S. 833, 877 (1992) (Scalia, J., concurring in part and dissenting in part)).

210 Dorf, *supra* note 205, at 1226.

211 As the *Lutz* court explained:

> [T]he right to travel cannot conceivably imply the right to travel whenever, wherever and however one pleases—even on roads specifically designed for public travel. Unlimited access to public fora or roadways would result not in maximizing individuals' opportunity to engage in protected activity, but chaos.

Lutz v. City of York, 899 F.2d 255, 269 (3d Cir. 1990).

up looking like rush hour. In other words, a right to travel assumes a right to orderly travel and not merely disjointed movement in an abstract sense.

Thus, a strict scrutiny standard of review should only apply to incidental burdens on the right to travel that do not facilitate its exercise and impose, in the words of *Casey*, a "substantial obstacle" in the path of the exercise of this right. This inquiry is objective and from the point of view of the individual traveller.[212] If such an obstacle does not exist, then rational basis review is warranted.

Under such a standard, *Lutz* is an easy case. An "anti-cruising" ordinance is clearly facilitative of the right to travel upon public streets. It has as its principal objective the removal of traffic congestion, which is necessary for orderly and efficient travel. The ordinance does not place a substantial obstacle in the way of anyone exercising their fundamental right to travel upon public streets. It merely requires persons to travel with some particular destination in mind, or, if not, that one at least wanders aimlessly rather than in circles.

Adopting such a standard with respect to all adults will secure a citizen's right to travel on public fora while minimizing unwarranted judicial interference with respect to the legitimate regulatory concerns of states and local governments. Assuming that the regulation does impose an undue burden, this Note now turns to the question of whether the same standard of review (e.g., strict scrutiny) should apply to the rights of juveniles.

---

[212] The Seventh Circuit, in *Hope Clinic v. Ryan*, 195 F.3d 857 (7th Cir. 1999), took a different position. Writing for the majority, Judge Easterbrook stated that:

> [O]ur best estimate is that 'undue' rather than 'burden' is the key word, and that 'undue' means not only 'substantial' (a small cost or inconvenience is not 'undue') but also that the burden must be undue in relation to the woman's interests, rather than undue in relation to the court's assessment of society's interests.

Id. at 874. Judge Posner, however, adopted the view that courts should conduct the inquiry from an objective standpoint. He accordingly stated that "if a statute burdens constitutional rights and all that can be said on its behalf is that it is the vehicle that legislators have chosen for expressing their hostility to those rights, the burden is undue." *Id.* at 881.

IV. FINDING A STANDARD OF REVIEW FOR JUVENILE RIGHTS

"But the word 'right' is one of the most deceptive of pitfalls; it is so easy to slip from a qualified meaning in the premise to an unqualified one in the conclusion. Most rights are qualified."[213]

The Supreme Court's confusing pronouncements on the issue of juvenile rights[214] forced the lower courts to deduce a standard of review to apply when considering the constitutional rights of minors under curfew laws. It should come as little surprise that the results have not been uniform. Much of the confusion revolves around the Court's opinion in *Bellotti v. Baird*.[215] Although the *Bellotti* plurality viewed its criteria as a rationale for treating the rights of minors differently in a general sense,[216] lower courts have latched onto this opinion as providing a test for whether or not the rights of minors should be treated differently.[217]

Many of these courts have applied the *Bellotti* factors to the right asserted.[218] Others have applied these factors to the nature of the government's interests.[219] None of the courts that have applied these factors to either prong of the analysis offered an elaborate or fully adequate justification for why they have applied *Bellotti*.

A. Fundamental Rights and the Strict Scrutiny Alternative

As noted above, no clear standard of review has emerged for analyzing the constitutional rights of juveniles. Many courts and com-

---

213 American Bank & Trust Co. v. Fed. Reserve Bank of Atlanta, 256 U.S. 350, 358 (1921).

214 *See supra* Part II (tracing Supreme Court development of juvenile rights).

215 443 U.S. 622 (1979).

216 *See supra* note 119 and accompanying text.

217 *See, e.g.*, Nunez v. City of San Diego, 114 F.3d 935 (9th Cir. 1997); Schleifer v. City of Charlottesville, 963 F. Supp. 534 (W.D. Va. 1997); Gaffney v. Allentown, Civ. No. 97-4455, 1997 U.S. Dist. LEXIS 14565 (E.D. Pa. Sept. 17, 1997); McCollester v. City of Keene, 586 F. Supp. 1381 (D.N.H. 1984); *In re* Appeal in Maricopa County, 887 P.2d 599 (Ariz. Ct. App. 1994); *In re* J.M., 768 P.2d 219 (Colo. 1989); City of Maquoketa v. Russell, 484 N.W.2d 179 (Iowa 1992); City of Panora v. Simmons, 445 N.W.2d 363 (Iowa 1989); Brown v. Ashton, 611 A.2d 599 (Md. Ct. Spec. App. 1992); Allen v. City of Bordentown, 524 A.2d 478 (N.J. Super. Ct. Law Div. 1987); Washington v. J.D., 937 P.2d 630 (Wash. Ct. App. 1997); *see also* Note, *Assessing the Scope of Minors' Fundamental Rights: Juvenile Curfews and the Constitution*, 97 HARV. L. REV. 1163, 1175-80 (1984) [hereinafter *Juvenile Curfews and the Constitution*] (arguing that courts should apply the *Belloti* criteria in assessing curfew ordinances to determine whether such ordinances serve any interests that are compelling for children).

218 *See, e.g.*, *Schleifer*, 963 F. Supp. at 541-42; *Gaffney*, 1997 U.S. Dist. LEXIS 14565, at *13-*14.

219 *See, e.g.*, *Nunez*, 114 F.3d at 945-46.

mentators continue to advocate a strict scrutiny standard.[220] Courts that advocate the use of a fundamental rights/strict scrutiny analysis for regulations burdening children typically do so with the caveat that children's rights may be burdened to a greater extent than those of adults.[221] Ordinarily, when a fundamental right or suspect class is burdened by a legislative classification, that classification is subjected to strict scrutiny and struck down unless the state has a compelling governmental interest and the legislation is narrowly tailored to further that interest.[222] However, proponents of fundamental rights for children do not argue that the strict scrutiny analysis should be applied in this form. Instead, they argue that courts should apply a "modified" form of strict scrutiny that recognizes interests that are "compelling for children."[223]

In order to determine which interests are compelling for children, courts and commentators that follow this mode of analysis have usually looked to *Bellotti v. Baird*.[224] The *Bellotti* plurality identified three factors which justify differential treatment for the constitutional rights of children: (1) a child's "peculiar vulnerability"; (2) a child's "inability to make critical decisions in an informed, mature manner"; and (3) the role of the parent in the development of the child.[225] Courts that afford minors fundamental rights then look to the *Bellotti*

---

[220] *See generally* Nunez v. City of San Diego, 114 F.3d 935 (9th Cir. 1997); *In re* Appeal in Maricopa County, 887 P.2d 599 (Ariz. Ct. App. 1994); City of Maquoketa v. Russell, 484 N.W.2d 179 (Iowa 1992); Brown v. Ashton, 611 A.2d 599 (Md. Ct. Spec. App. 1992); *see also* Susan M. Horowitz, *A Search for Constitutional Standards: Judicial Review of Juvenile Curfew Ordinances*, 24 COLUM. J. L. & SOC. PROBS. 381, 415 (1991) (arguing in favor of a form of strict scrutiny analysis which would recognize those state interests that are "compelling for children"); *Juvenile Curfews and the Constitution*, *supra* note 217, at 1171 (arguing that children's rights should be viewed as fundamental, and that courts should apply strict scrutiny to analyze constitutional challenges on the basis of those rights).

[221] *See, e.g.*, *Nunez*, 114 F.3d at 945 ("[M]inors' rights are not coextensive with the rights of adults because the state has a greater range of interests that justify the infringement of minors' rights.").

[222] *See, e.g.*, Adarand Constructors, Inc. v. Pena, 515 U.S. 200, 237 (1995) ("When race-based action is necessary to further a compelling interest, such action is within constitutional constraints if it satisfies the 'narrow tailoring' test . . . .").

[223] Horowitz, *supra* note 220, at 415. As another commentator explains:

> The principle of strict scrutiny for infringements of fundamental rights presupposes a universe of citizens equal under the Constitution; what qualifies as a compelling state interest does not ordinarily vary depending on which citizens are affected . . . . Thus, to recognize special interests surrounding one unique class of citizens—children—is to recognize the need for a unique form of strict scrutiny. Such a form of review would acknowledge compelling state interests that pertain only to children.

Juvenile Curfews and the Constitution, *supra* note 217, at 1171-72 (citation omitted).

[224] 443 U.S. 622 (1979).

[225] *Id.* at 634.

factors to ascertain if there is a compelling interest that justifies the curfew ordinances.[226]

This analysis improperly conflates concerns relevant to defining fundamental rights with those appropriate to ascertaining compelling governmental purposes. Fundamental rights are negative rights—they restrict the sphere of government action.[227] Compelling governmental interests, on the other hand, justify why the government has acted.[228] Whereas fundamental rights concern liberties retained by the people, compelling interests concern a government's need to act in a certain situation.[229]

A minor's vulnerability, or inability to make critical decisions, pertains to whether (or not) a child has a fundamental right, not whether the government has a compelling interest. Many fundamental rights stem from a personal interest in autonomy. As Professor Fallon explains:

> As beings who are capable of self-direction, we have an interest in being able to make decisions for ourselves and to act on those decisions that is sometimes independent of the interest in having the decision made that will be best for us in the sense of producing the greatest after-the-fact well-being.[230]

This interest, however, presupposes the capacity to act as a fully autonomous person.[231] Where this capacity is not fully present, this

---

[226] *See, e.g.*, *Nunez*, 114 F.3d at 945 ("The Bellotti framework enables courts to determine whether the state has a compelling interest justifying greater restrictions on minors than on adults.") (citations omitted); *In re* Appeal of Maricopa County, 887 P.2d 599, 606-07 (phrasing the issue as "whether a significant state interest not present in the case of an adult justifies infringing upon minors' fundamental rights"); City of Maquoketa v. Russell, 484 N.W.2d 179, 185-86 (Iowa 1992) (citing *Bellotti* to state that "an ordinance which restricts minors' rights to an extent greater than it restricts adults' rights may be sustained if the State or municipality demonstrates that it protects minors' peculiar vulnerability, accounts for their lesser ability to make sound judgments, and reflects society's deference to the guiding role of parents").

[227] *See* Erwin Chemerinsky, *Constitutional Scholarship in the 1990s*, 45 HASTINGS L.J. 1105, 1115 (1994) (distinguishing between rights, which are negative because they restrict what government can do, and interests, which involve justifications for why government has affirmatively acted).

[228] *See id.*

[229] *See id.*

[230] Richard H. Fallon, Jr., *Individual Rights and the Powers of Government*, 27 GA. L. REV. 343, 354 (1993) (footnote omitted).

[231] *See* David A.J. Richards, *Sexual Autonomy and the Constitutional Right to Privacy: A Case Study in Human Rights and the Unwritten Constitution*, 30 HASTINGS L.J. 957, 964 (1979). As this commentator explains, two critical assumptions underly all concepts of human rights: "first, that persons have the *capacity* to be autonomous in living their life [sic]; second, that persons are entitled, as persons, to equal concern and respect in exercising their capacities for living autonomously." *Id.* (emphasis in original).

interest (and *a fortiori* the constitutional rights that it supports) is diminished.

Saying that a minor is "vulnerable," or that he or she is unable to make critical decisions, is simply another way of stating that minors do not yet possess the capacity to act as fully autonomous persons. The lesser capacity of minors is well established in the law. As Professor Hafen observes, "it [is] of profound importance in all legal inquiries involving children that minors are presumed by all phases of the law (and by the culture reflected by our law) not to have the same basic capacities as adults."[232] In this vein, *Bellotti* merely reiterated what the common law already understood, which is that children do not possess the same capacity to act autonomously that adults have.[233]

Since minors do not possess this capacity, their rights are not fundamental in the same sense that adult rights are fundamental. This is not to say that a minor's rights have no value, or, even worse, that a minor has no rights. As Judge Rogers explained in *Hutchins v. District of Columbia*,[234] "minors and adults share basic rights, but these rights have less force when used by minors as shields against regulation."[235] Because the rights of minors have less force as shields against regulation, a strict scrutiny standard of review is inappropriate.

The foregoing discussion assumes that capacity is relevant to the definition and assertion of fundamental rights. A more radical approach to children's rights argues that capacity should not be relevant to the consideration of constitutional rights, and that children should be endowed with fundamental rights because they are powerless *vis-à-vis* the state.[236] The view that children should be afforded fundamental rights because they are powerless *vis-à-vis* the state seeks to equate children with historically oppressed groups, such as women and African Americans.[237]

---

[232] Bruce C. Hafen, *Children's Liberation and the New Egalitarianism: Some Reservations About Abandoning Youth to Their "Rights,"* 1976 BYU L. REV. 605, 646-47 (1976).

[233] *See supra* note 71 and accompanying text.

[234] 188 F.3d 531 (D.C. Cir. 1999) (en banc).

[235] *Id.* at 563.

[236] *See* Katherine Hunt Federle, *Children, Curfews, and the Constitution*, 73 WASH. U. L.Q. 1315, 1350 (1995) (describing the empowerment rights theory, under which fundamental rights would inhere in children because of their powerlessness as to the state). This argument may be taken as an attempt to classify minors as a "discrete and insular minority" within the meaning of *United States v. Carolene Products Co.*, 304 U.S. 144, 152-53 n.4 (1938) (suggesting that review of statutes targeted at constitutional rights of particular groups may be subjected to judicial scrutiny more exacting than the rational basis test). The Court rejected a similar argument made by senior citizens that they should enjoy status as a suspect classification because of their age. *See generally* Gregory v. Ashcroft, 501 U.S. 452 (1991).

[237] *See* Federle, *supra* note 236, at 1340-44 (comparing the experience of children to slavery and the civil rights movement).

The argument, for example, is that African-American slaves, like minors, were treated paternalistically by most whites.[238] Slaves were viewed much like children, and thus their relationship with their owner was seen to be similar to that of child to parent.[239] Looking back through the lens of history, it is clear "that the infantilization of African-Americans was nothing more than an attempt to control and oppress an entire race."[240] Similarly, rights theories that do not allow for children as rights-holders perpetuate "these traditions of power and dominance."[241] Thus, children must be afforded rights so that they can challenge the existing hierarchies and power structures.[242]

However, there are relevant differences between children and other oppressed social groups that make this analogy weak. First, the interests of the "power holders," or those institutions that perpetuate the existing hierarchies, are different. Whereas oppressors have an interest in maintaining oppression, those who preside over the lives of children have an interest in terminating the child's dependent condition.[243] Thus, to the extent that the motivations of the state are a concern, there is less likelihood of an illicit motive in the case of children.[244]

Furthermore, and perhaps more importantly, childhood is not a permanent state. In this sense, a child's lack of power is less permanent than that of a slave.[245] While a slave will always be a slave, a child will not always be a child. The slave's only remedy is to be bestowed with rights. The child has a further remedy—she may grow up.[246] In this sense, childhood is not an immutable characteristic, and children thus lack one of the features that have historically qualified a

---

238 *See id.* at 1343 (arguing that even though some slave owners had sexual relations with their slaves, these owners dared not treat them as equals for fear of sacrificing control over them).

239 *See id.* (describing the position held by many that slaves, like children, had reduced mental capacity and were thus dependent on their masters for guidance and protection).

240 *Id.* at 1344. The author continues to note that slaves were not seen as rights-holders, and the notion that slaves would have been able to exercise such rights was inconceivable to whites. *See id.*

241 *Id.*

242 *See id.* (arguing that the experience of African-American slaves demonstrates the impotence of rights that are incapable of challenging existing hierarchies).

243 *See* ONORA O'NEILL, *Children's Rights and Children's Lives, in* CHILDREN'S RIGHTS RE-VISIONED 38 (Rosalind Eckman Ladd ed. 1996).

244 *See* Laurence H. Tribe, *Childhood, Suspect Classifications, and Conclusive Presumptions: Three Linked Riddles*, 39 LAW & CONTEMP. PROBS. 8, 10 n.8 (1975) ("No adult, having once been a child, can with real conviction draw the line between "us" and "them" —the line that makes it at least plausible in other contexts to treat "them" as a special minority needing protection from politics.").

245 *See* O'NEILL, *supra* note 243, at 38.

246 *See id.* at 39.

group as a discrete and insular minority.[247] Therefore, a strict scrutiny standard of review is inappropriate.

B. The Need for Something More than Rational Basis Review

Only two courts hold that the appropriate standard of review is the rational basis test.[248] Their main argument is that a minor's liberty interest is circumscribed by his or her inability to exercise the right maturely.[249] Since minors are more vulnerable than adults, and because minors may commit delinquent acts due to their immaturity, the child's right to freedom of movement is not fundamental. Therefore, a rational basis standard of review is appropriate because no fundamental right is implicated.[250]

This argument has superficial appeal because it accurately describes the Court's two-tiered mode of analysis in due process cases. Either a regulation burdens fundamental rights and is subject to strict scrutiny, or it does not and is judged under rational basis review. In the end, however, this is not an adequate justification for evaluating statutes burdening a minor's rights under the same deferential standard that courts use when evaluating legislation that impacts economic rights.[251]

Clearly, children do not have substantive liberty rights in the same sense, and of the same scope, as adults.[252] There is a major logic gap, however, between this premise and the conclusion that rational basis review is required. The conclusion rests on the further premise

---

[247] Professor Federle challenges the relevance of these distinctions, commenting that "[a]ny form of oppression has negative consequences and should be intolerable in a rights-oriented society." Federle, *supra* note 236, at 1344 n.198.

[248] *See In re* J.M., 768 P.2d 219, 223 (Col. 1989); City of Panora v. Simmons, 445 N.W.2d 363, 368-69 (Iowa 1989).

[249] *See* In re *J.M.*, 768 P.2d at 223; *Simmons*, 445 N.W.2d at 369. This argument derives from the three factors enunciated by the plurality in *Bellotti v. Baird*, 443 U.S. 622, 634 (1979). *See supra* note 119 and accompanying text.

[250] *See* In re *J.M.*, 768 P.2d at 223 (concluding that a minor's "liberty interest in freedom of movement does not constitute a fundamental right" and accordingly stating that the curfew law at issue will be measured by "the rationality standard"); *Simmons*, 445 N.W.2d 363, 368-69 (Iowa 1989) ("[A] minor's right of intracity travel is not a fundamental right for due process purposes, and the ordinance need not meet a strict scrutiny test.").

[251] *See Juvenile Curfews and the Constitution*, *supra* note 217, at 1172 n.44 ("[T]he rights of children should not be subordinated to the will of the majority or limited purely for economic or efficiency reasons . . . .").

[252] *See* Schleifer v. City of Charlottesville, 963 F. Supp. 534, 540 (W.D. Va. 1997) ("Bending to the dictates of common sense, the Supreme Court [has] recognized that the behavior of minors may be constitutionally regulated more stringently than that of adults."); Nunez v. City of San Diego, 963 F. Supp. 912, 923 (S.D. Cal. 1995), *rev'd*, 114 F.3d 935 (9th Cir. 1997) ("The conclusion that minors possess a lesser right to free movement than adults corresponds with society's recognition that minors are more vulnerable to society's dangers than adults and that juveniles lack the ability 'to make critical decisions in an informed mature manner.'") (citation omitted); *see also supra* Part II (tracing judicial development of minors' rights).

that there is no middle ground between strict scrutiny and rational basis review. True, most due process cases fit neatly into a two-tiered scheme of review. This method, however, is not set in stone. The Court has already discarded it when analyzing cases under the Equal Protection Clause.[253] There is a similar need to discard the two-tiered mode of analysis when dealing with the rights of minors. As Justice Frankfurter observed, "[l]egal theories and their phrasing in other cases readily lead to fallacious reasoning if uncritically transferred to determination of a State's duty towards children."[254]

Analyzing all burdens on the rights of minors under a rational basis standard of review does not respect Supreme Court precedent.[255] It also fails to give minors the respect they deserve as persons possessed of rights under the Constitution[256] by requiring only that legislation respecting minors is not arbitrary, a requirement that all legislation must meet anyhow. Therefore, something more than rational basis review is required.

C. Intermediate Scrutiny: A Workable Compromise

We are left then with the task of defining the minor's relationship *vis-à-vis* the state in the constitutional sense. Strict scrutiny is not appropriate,[257] and neither is rational basis review.[258] What is needed is an approach that recognizes the significance of a minor's diminished capacity and greater vulnerability without dehumanizing its

---

253 As Justice Marshall stated:

> The Court apparently seeks to establish today that equal protection cases fall into one of two neat categories that dictate the appropriate standard of review—strict scrutiny or mere rationality. But this Court's decisions in the field of equal protection defy such easy categorization. A principled reading of what this Court has done reveals that it has applied a spectrum of standards in reviewing discrimination allegedly violative of the Equal Protection Clause.

San Antonio Indep. School Dist. v. Rodriguez, 411 U.S. 1, 98-99 (1973) (Marshall, J., dissenting).

What Justice Marshall intuitively recognized in 1973 is now plainly evident in the Court's jurisprudence. As Judge Michael recognized in *Schleifer*, "the presumption of equal treatment under the Constitution is somewhat diluted by the sliding scale of scrutiny employed by the Supreme Court, depending on the characteristics of the individual seeking constitutional protection." 963 F. Supp. at 541. For example, while the Supreme Court reaffirmed in *Adarand Constructors, Inc. v. Pena*, 515 U.S. 200, 238-39 (1995), that all race-based classifications are subject to strict scrutiny review, classifications that are based on gender are subject to an intermediate level of review. *See generally* United States v. Virginia, 518 U.S. 515 (1996).

254 May v. Anderson, 345 U.S. 528, 536 (1953) (Frankfurter, J., concurring).

255 *See supra* Part II (canvassing Supreme Court development of juvenile rights).

256 The Supreme Court has stated that "[c]onstitutional rights do not mature and come into being magically only when one attains the state-defined age of majority. Minors, as well as adults, are protected by the Constitution and possess constitutional rights." Planned Parenthood v. Danforth, 428 U.S. 52, 74 (1976) (citations omitted).

257 *See supra* Part III.A.

258 *See supra* Part III.B.

subject—an approach that is both internally coherent, and not so foreign to the field of constitutional law that it is rendered impossible to apply. As federal courts have increasingly come to recognize,[259] the proper standard of review in cases involving juvenile rights is intermediate scrutiny.[260]

An intermediate standard of review finds support in two of the court's opinions in cases dealing with abortion rights. First in *Planned Parenthood v. Danforth*,[261] and then again in *Carey v. Population Services International*,[262] the court flirted with an intermediate standard of review. In *Danforth*, the Court reviewed, *inter alia*, the constitutionality of a portion of the abortion legislation passed by Missouri that pertained to juveniles.[263] The Court stated that the question

---

[259] Several courts have applied an intermediate standard of scrutiny to juvenile rights. *See, e.g.*, Hutchins v. District of Columbia, 188 F.3d 531 (D.C. Cir. 1999) (en banc); Schleifer v. City of Charlottesville, 963 F. Supp. 534, 542 (W.D. Va. 1997); *see also* Peter L. Scherr, Note, *The Juvenile Curfew Ordinance: In Search of a New Standard of Review*, 41 WASH. U. J. URB. & CONTEMP. L. 163, 191 (1992) (advocating a form of intermediate scrutiny to be applied to evaluation of juvenile rights).

[260] The test that I am proposing is confined to purported infringements upon the substantive liberty interests of minors. Therefore, this test would not apply in determining the procedural rights of minors in the juvenile court system. *See generally* Breed v. Jones, 421 U.S. 519 (1975) (holding the Fifth Amendment's double jeopardy clause applicable to minors in juvenile court proceedings); McKeiver v. Pennsylvania, 403 U.S. 528 (1971) (holding that the Sixth Amendment right to trial by jury does not apply to minors in juvenile court proceedings); *In re* Winship, 397 U.S. 358 (1970) (holding that juveniles in a juvenile court proceeding are entitled to the protection of the proof beyond a reasonable doubt standard); *In re* Gault, 387 U.S. 1 (1967) (holding the constitutional rights of notice to charges, counsel, confrontation, and cross-examination, and privilege against self-incrimination applicable to juveniles in juvenile court proceedings).

Likewise, the First Amendment may present a special case. At least in the context of schools, there is greater reason to treat the First Amendment rights of juveniles as analogous to those of adults. The First Amendment encompasses a societal right to information in the form of ideas. As Justice Brandeis has stated:

> [The founding fathers] believed that freedom to think as you will and to speak as you think are means indispensable to the discovery and spread of political truth; that without free speech and assembly discussion would be futile; that with them, discussion affords ordinarily adequate protection against the dissemination of noxious doctrine; that the greatest menace to freedom is an inert people; that public discussion is a political duty; and that this should be a fundamental principle of the American government.

Whitney v. California, 274 U.S. 357, 375 (1927) (Brandeis, J., concurring) (footnote omitted). As has been recognized by the Court, "[t]he classroom is peculiarly the 'marketplace of ideas'" Tinker v. Des Moines Independent Community School District, 393 U.S. 503, 512 (1969) (quoting Keyishian v. Bd. of Regents, 385 U.S. 589, 603 (1967)). Since the interest recognized here is societal and not individual, a full exploration of the issue of First Amendment juvenile rights is beyond the scope of this Note.

[261] 428 U.S. 52 (1976).

[262] 431 U.S. 678 (1977).

[263] *See Danforth*, 428 U.S. at 72-75. The applicable section of the Missouri statute required that during the first 12 weeks of her pregnancy the minor must obtain the written consent of one parent or person *in loco parentis* of the woman if the woman was unmarried and under the age of eighteen years, unless the abortion is certified by a licensed physician as necessary in order to preserve the life of the mother. *See id.* at 58. The court held that "the State does not have the

was "whether there is any significant state interest . . . that is not present in the case of an adult."[264] A four-justice plurality applied the same standard in *Carey*,[265] observing that "[t]his test is apparently less rigorous than the 'compelling state interest' test applied to restrictions on the privacy rights of adults."[266] The plurality felt that this lesser degree of scrutiny was appropriate, both because of the greater degree of latitude that the states have when regulating the conduct of minors, and because the law presumes that minors have a lesser capacity "for making important decisions."[267] In each of these cases, the Court felt the asserted interest was insignificant, and therefore did not comment on how close the fit between the classification and the statute's purpose would have to be to satisfy the test. However, courts should require that the classification be "substantially related" to the statute's objectives.[268]

The requirement of a "significant," or important, governmental objective assures that minors will not be the subject of dehumanizing legislation.[269] The primary concern in reviewing legislation affecting juvenile rights,[270] which may be termed quasi-fundamental, should be in assuring that the legislation was drafted out of genuine concern for, and in furtherance of, a legislative purpose that is designed to protect

---

constitutional authority to give a third party an absolute, and possibly arbitrary, veto over the decision of the physician and his patient to terminate the patient's pregnancy." *Id.* at 74. The court found that an asserted state interest in safeguarding the family unity and parental authority was insufficient. *See id.* at 75.

[264] *Id.* at 75.

[265] *See Carey*, 431 U.S. at 691-99. The issue was the constitutionality of a nonprescription contraception distribution ban pertaining to all minors under the age of 16. *See id.* at 691-92. New York asserted an interest in discouraging sexual activity amongst the young. *See id.* at 694. The Court, however, did not take this interest seriously. *See id.* at 694-96. The Court, for example, found that "the State's interests in protection of the mental and physical health of the pregnant minor, and in protection of potential life are clearly more implicated by the abortion decision than by the decision to use a nonhazardous contraceptive," *id.* at 694, and that "there is substantial reason for doubt whether limiting access to contraceptives will [as the State contends], substantially discourage early sexual behavior." *Id.* at 695.

[266] *Id.* at 693 n.15.

[267] *Id.*

[268] The requirement of a "substantial relationship between the means chosen and the end asserted is one of the hallmarks of an intermediate standard of review." *See* L. TRIBE, AMERICAN CONSTITUTIONAL LAW §16-32 (2d ed. 1988).

[269] As Professor Tribe explains, more generally, it has become "obvious . . . that, as the Court's assessment of the weight and value of the individual interest escalates, the less likely it is that mere administrative convenience and avoidance of hearings or investigations will be sufficient to justify what otherwise would appear to be irrational discriminations." *Id.* § 16-32.

[270] I use the term juvenile rights here to refer to rights held by juveniles, which would be fundamental if held by adults. For lack of a better term, it is perhaps appropriate to refer to these rights of juveniles as quasi-fundamental rights. *Cf.* Plyler v. Doe, 457 U.S. 202, 244 (1982) (Burger, C.J., dissenting) (criticizing the Court's apparent recognition of public education as a quasi-fundamental right).

children.[271] The reason for this heightened standard of review, which is less than strict scrutiny but more rigorous than rational basis, lies in the recognition that children are persons under the constitution with rights,[272] but they are uniquely vulnerable and not always able to exercise their rights responsibly.[273]

Therefore, courts should evaluate alleged infringements of juvenile rights under an intermediate standard of review. The recognition of juvenile rights as quasi-fundamental suggests that they have value and are worthy of respect. However, it also signifies the uniqueness of the rights that juveniles possess and an understanding that their rights are not as full in scope as the rights of their adult counterparts. Furthermore, the requirement that a state demonstrate an important governmental interest explicitly recognizes the greater authority of the state to regulate juvenile rights.

The most important difference between this test and either strict scrutiny or the proposed "compelling for children" test lies in the fact that an intermediate standard allows for legislation as long as it is "substantially related" to the legislative goals. Strict scrutiny is usually fatal in fact.[274] While the inability of legislation to survive such review may be attributed in large part to the "compelling state interest" prong of the test, it is clear that the "least drastic means" element is important as well.[275] Thus, the greater latitude in means used that is afforded by this intermediate test is crucial if the Court is to fulfill its promise that "the power of the state to control the conduct of children reaches beyond the scope of its authority over adults."[276]

---

[271] As Professor Tribe explains, "[t]he 'establishment of prompt efficacious procedures to achieve legitimate state ends is a proper state interest worthy of cognizance in constitutional adjudication. But the Constitution recognizes higher values than speed and efficiency.'" TRIBE, *supra* note 268, §16-32 (citing Vlandis v. Kline, 412 U.S. 441, 458-459 (1973) (White, J., concurring)).

[272] As the *Danforth* Court explained, "[c]onstitutional rights do not mature and come into being magically only when one attains the state-defined age of majority. Minors, as well as adults, are protected by the Constitution and possess constitutional rights." 428 U.S. 52, 74 (1976).

[273] *See* Bellotti v. Baird, 443 U.S. 622, 634 (1979) (referring to the unique characteristics of children which justify special treatment including, *inter alia*, "the peculiar vulnerability of children" and a child's "inability to make critical decisions in an informed, mature manner").

[274] *See* TRIBE, *supra* note 268, § 16-6 ("When expressed as a standard for judicial review, strict scrutiny is . . . 'strict' in theory and usually 'fatal' in fact.") (footnote omitted).

[275] As one commentator explains, "[s]ome may argue that the 'less drastic means' element is not required in most cases. However, a close examination of the Court's analysis shows persistent consideration has been given to this element. The strict scrutiny standard has been almost impossible for lawmaking bodies to meet." Randall Fox, *Equal Protection Analysis: Laurence Tribe, The Middle Tier, and the Role of the Court*, 14 U.S.F. L. REV. 525, 526 n.4 (1980).

[276] Prince v. Massachusetts, 321 U.S. 158, 170 (1944).

V. JUVENILE RIGHTS AND CURFEW ORDINANCES

"The spontaneity of children in responding to invitation to play, without calculating the risk, is as well known as the sequence of the seasons or the regularity with which night follows day. It is not an imponderable, or a matter of speculation. It is simply fact."[277]

This Part of the Note applies the tests derived in Parts III and IV to juvenile curfew laws. These laws directly burden a minor's right to travel on public fora, and are subject to a heightened standard of review. Because the rights of minors are lesser in scope than those of adults, however, an intermediate standard of review is applied.

Following hearings, the District of Columbia Council unanimously adopted the Juvenile Curfew Act of 1995.[278] The curfew bans

---

[277] Jennings v. Glen Alden Coal Co., 87 A.2d 206, 212 (Pa. 1952) (Musmanno, J., dissenting).

[278] The text of the curfew law is set forth in an appendix to the District Court opinion. *See* Hutchins v. District of Columbia, 942 F. Supp. 665, app. A at 681-82 (D.D.C. 1996), *rev'd on reh'g en banc*, 188 F.3d 531 (D.C. Cir. 1999). In pertinent part, the curfew ordinance reads:

§ 6-2182 Definitions

For the purposes of this act, the term:

(1) "Curfew hours" means from 11:00 p.m. on any Sunday, Monday, Tuesday, Wednesday, or Thursday, until 6:00 a.m. on the following day, and from 12:01 a.m. until 6:00 a.m. on any Saturday or Sunday. During the months of July and August, the term "curfew hours" means from 12:01 a.m. until 6:00 a.m.

(2) "Emergency" means an unforeseen combination of circumstances or the resulting state that calls for immediate action. The term "emergency" includes, but is not limited to, a fire, a natural disaster, an automobile accident, or any situation that requires immediate action to prevent serious bodily injury or loss of life.

(3) "Establishment" means any privately owned place of business operated for profit to which the public is invited, including, but not limited to, any place of amusement or entertainment.

(4) "Guardian" means a person who, under court order, is the guardian of the person of a minor or a public or private agency with whom a minor has been placed by the court.

(5) "Minor" means any person under the age of 17 years, but does not include a judicially emancipated minor or a married minor.

(6) "Narcotic trafficking" means an act of engaging in any prohibited activity related to narcotic drugs or controlled substances as defined in the District of Columbia Uniform Controlled Substances Act of 1981 . . . .

(7) "Operator" means any individual, firm, association, partnership, or corporation that operates, manages, or conducts any establishment. The term "operator" includes the members or partners of an association or partnership and the officers of a corporation.

(8) "Parent" means a natural parent, adoptive parent or step-parent, or any person who has legal custody by court order or marriage, or any person not less than 21 years of age who is authorized by the natural parent, adoptive parent, step-parent, or custodial parent of a child to be a caretaker for the child.

(9) "Public place" means any place to which the public, or a substantial group of the public, has access, and includes, but is not limited to, streets, highways, and the

minors under the age of 17 from being in a public place without a parent, or adult supervision, during certain hours. These hours include 11:00 p.m. - 6:00 a.m. from Sunday night through Thursday morning, and from midnight to 6:00 a.m. Saturday and Sunday. The curfew law does not include minors who are "judicially emancipated" or married.[279]

A. *Is the Right to Travel Unduly Burdened?*

In *Hutchins v. District of Columbia*,[280] the District of Columbia asserted that the ordinance furthered important interests in the reduction of juvenile crime and victimization.[281] The government could argue that this regulation does not directly target a minor's interest in traveling on public fora. Rather, the ordinance is attempting to reduce

---

> common areas of schools, hospitals, apartment houses, office buildings, transport facilities, and shops.
> (10) "Remain" means to linger or stay or fail to leave the premises when requested to do so by a police officer or owner, operator, or other person in control of the premises.
> (11) "Serious bodily injury" means bodily injury that creates a substantial risk of death or that causes death, serious permanent disfigurement, or protracted loss or impairment of any bodily member or organ.
>
> § 6-2183 Curfew authority; defenses; enforcement and penalties.
> (a)(1) A minor commits an offense if he or she remains in any public place or on the premises of any establishment within the District of Columbia during curfew hours.
> . . .
> (b)(1) It is a defense to prosecution under this act that the minor was:
> (A) Accompanied by the minor's parent or guardian;
> (B) On an errand at the direction of the minor's parent or guardian, without any detour or stop;
> (C) In a motor vehicle, train, or bus involved in interstate travel;
> (D) Engaged in an employment activity pursuant to [the District of Columbia child employment act], or going to, or returning home from, an employment activity, without detour or stop;
> (E) Involved in an emergency;
> (F) On the sidewalk that abuts the minor's residence or that abuts the residence of a next-door neighbor if the neighbor did not complain to the Metropolitan Police Department about the minor's presence;
> (G) In attendance at an official school, religious, or other recreational activity sponsored by the District of Columbia, a civic organization, or another similar entity that takes responsibility for a minor, or going to, or returning home from, without any detour or stop, an official school, religious, or other recreational activity supervised by adults and sponsored by the District of Columbia, a civic organization, or another similar activity that takes responsibility for a minor; or
> (H) Exercising First Amendment rights protected by the United States Constitution, including free exercise of religion, freedom of speech, and the right of assembly . . . .

D.C. CODE ANN. §§ 6-2182, 2183 (Supp. 1999).

[279] *See supra* note 278.

[280] 188 F.3d 531 (D.C. Cir. 1999) (en banc).

[281] *See id.* at 541-42.

juvenile crime and victimization. Thus, the ordinance impacts upon the minor's right to travel on public fora only indirectly.

The problem with this argument is that it proves too much. Such an argument would almost always convert direct regulations into incidental burdens because "what renders the exercise of a right offensive to the majority has little to do with what renders the right valuable to the rightholder."[282] In other words, "it is usually possible to characterize the harm that a right's exercise causes in a way that does not target the right's value from the perspective of the rightholder."[283]

Here, the burden is not incidental in the usual sense because it applies only to conduct that is protected. The ordinance, while being concerned with juvenile crime and victimization, does not punish or seek to regulate any conduct associated with these two goals other than a minor's right to travel. The burden is thus direct in the sense that the means the legislature used to further its goals were solely concerned with restricting a minor's right to travel. Hence, the regulation is targeted to prevent a minor's exercise of the right to travel. As Judge Rogers observed, "[w]hatever else the curfew might be, it is not an incidental burden. The curfew . . . does not constrain specific types of movement, but with few exceptions bars all movement in public; it is not confined to a brief period, but extends for roughly 25% of the day."[284] Therefore, the curfew law is subjected to heightened scrutiny because it imposes a "substantial obstacle" on a minor's right to travel.

B. Curfew Laws and Intermediate Scrutiny

In order to pass the intermediate level of scrutiny applicable to an alleged infringement of a minor's quasi-fundamental right, the District of Columbia curfew law must be substantially related to significant state interests.[285]

1. Significant State Interests

The District of Columbia's interest in enacting its curfew law was "to protect the welfare of minors by reducing the likelihood that minors will perpetrate or become victims of crime and by promoting

---

282 Dorf, *supra* note 205, at 1222.

283 *Id.* at 1223.

284 *Hutchins*, 188 F.3d at 562 (Rogers, J., concurring in part and dissenting in part).

285 *See* Lalli v. Lalli, 439 U.S. 259, 265 (1978) (framing the intermediate scrutiny standard as whether the legislative classification is "substantially related to permissible state interests"); *see also supra* note 268 and accompanying text.

parental responsibility.'"[286] There should be no doubt that these interests are substantial.

The Court has long recognized that a state's interest in the well-being of its youth is compelling. In *New York v. Ferber*,[287] the Court stated that "a State's interest in 'safeguarding the physical and psychological well-being of a minor' is 'compelling.'"[288] In *Ginsburg v. New York*,[289] the Court recognized that society has an interest in assuring that children are "'safeguarded from abuses' which might prevent their 'growth into free and independent well-developed men and citizens.'"[290] This interest exists "even when the laws have operated in the sensitive area of constitutionally protected rights."[291]

Several lower courts have questioned whether a state or local government has an interest in enacting a curfew law that is "compelling for children."[292] The argument is that the state does not have an interest that is compelling for children because a minor is not "peculiarly vulnerable" to night-time crime, and "the decision to go outside during certain hours does not involve any critical decisions by minors."[293] As set forth above,[294] this approach is conceptually misguided because it equates a minor's capacity with the state's interest instead of with the scope of the minor's right. However, the argument also rests on a fundamental misunderstanding of precedent.

The decisions that hold that the state or local government does not have an interest in enacting a curfew law that is "compelling for children" rely on the three factors set forth in *Bellotti v. Baird*.[295]

The *Bellotti* plurality stated that "the Court has held that the States validly may limit the freedom of children to choose for themselves in the making of important, affirmative choices with potentially serious consequences."[296] Interpreting this portion of *Bellotti* to

---

286 *Hutchins*, 188 F.3d at 541-42 (quoting Globe Newspaper Co. v. Superior Court, 457 U.S. 596, 607 (1982)).

287 458 U.S. 747 (1982).

288 *Id.* at 756-57.

289 390 U.S. 629 (1968).

290 *Id.* at 640-41 (quoting Prince v. Massachusetts, 321 U.S. 158, 165 (1944)).

291 *Ferber*, 458 U.S. at 757.

292 *See, e.g.*, Waters v. Berry, 711 F. Supp. 1125, 1137 (D.D.C. 1989) (holding that the danger of nighttime violence is not peculiar to children and curfews may infringe on parental choice); Brown v. Ashton, 611 A.2d 599, 608-09 (Md. App. 1992). *But see* Nunez v. City of San Diego, 114 F.3d 935, 947 (9th Cir. 1997) (recognizing "that minors are more susceptible to the dangers of the night and are generally less equipped to deal with danger that does arise").

293 Brown v. Ashton, 611 A.2d 599, 609 (Md. App. 1992).

294 *See supra* Part IV (advocating the intermediate scrutiny standard for review of juvenile rights).

295 443 U.S. 622 (1979). For a discussion of *Bellotti*, see *supra* notes 224-26 and accompanying text.

296 *Id.* at 635.

require that the decision be a "critical" one[297] is simply wrong. How important must these choices be? In the next sentence, the *Bellotti* plurality explains that "minors often lack the experience, perspective, and judgment to . . . avoid choices that could be detrimental to them."[298]

In explaining what "choices that could be detrimental" means, the *Bellotti* plurality relied exclusively on the case of *Ginsberg v. New York*.[299] *Ginsberg* involved a minor's asserted right to choose whether to buy "so-called 'girlie' magazines."[300] The Court did not require proof that the purchase of these magazines could be detrimental. Rather, it was enough for the Court that "the growing consensus of commentators is that 'while these studies all agree that a causal link has not been demonstrated, they are equally agreed that a causal link has not been disproved either.'"[301] Hence, choices that are "important," or "could be detrimental," are choices that a rational person believes could harm a child, if there is no solid proof to the contrary. With respect to curfew laws, the Ninth Circuit's observation is on point: "[I]t [is] unexceptional for the City to conclude that minors are more susceptible to the dangers of the night and are generally less equipped to deal with danger that does arise."[302]

In sum, it is clear that a government has a significant interest in safeguarding the welfare of minors. This interest is present where the government enacts a curfew law, and nothing in *Bellotti* should be construed to the contrary. These curfew laws are constitutional when challenged on right to travel grounds if they are "substantially related" to this interest.[303]

2. *Curfew Laws and the "Substantial Relation" Requirement*

The substantial relation requirement does not require mathematical precision. "In the end, the precise accuracy of [the State's] calculations is not a matter of specialized judicial competence; and [courts] have no basis to question their detail beyond the evident consistency and substantiality."[304] The Court has emphasized that, "[i]t is unrealistic to expect either members of the judiciary or state officials to be well versed in the rigors of experimental or statistical technique."[305]

---

297 *Brown*, 611 A.2d at 609.
298 *Bellotti*, 443 U.S. at 635 (footnote omitted).
299 *See id.* at 636 (citing Ginsberg v. New York, 390 U.S. 629 (1968)).
300 *Ginsberg*, 390 U.S. at 631.
301 *Id.* at 642 (citations omitted).
302 Nunez v. City of San Diego, 114 F.3d 935, 947 (9th Cir. 1997).
303 *See supra* note 285 and accompanying text.
304 Lalli v. Lalli, 439 U.S. 259, 274 (1978).
305 Craig v. Boren, 429 U.S. 190, 204 (1976).

What is required is a fit between the governmental interests and the means chosen that is not unduly tenuous.[306] However, such a relationship does have to be empirical.[307]

The District of Columbia was confronted with evidence of an ever-increasing juvenile crime rate.[308] The evidence before the District Court included statistics, which stated that in 1992 the D.C. crime arrest rate for youths aged ten to seventeen was the highest in the nation.[309] D.C. also "had the highest violent death rate [in the nation] for teens ages 15 to 19 . . . ."[310] The D.C. Council also had before it statistics that showed a high number of incidents of violent crime in areas covered by the curfew.[311]

The D.C. Council reviewed evidence relating to the efficacy of juvenile curfew laws in other jurisdictions, which showed that after a juvenile curfew was enacted the number of juvenile arrests for violent offenses decreased.[312] A couple of jurisdictions had also experienced a reduction in juvenile victimization.[313] The Council heard evidence that "more than 50% of juvenile arrests took place during curfew hours."[314] The D.C. Council also utilized a statistical projection from the police chief on the anticipated effect of a curfew statute.[315]

---

306 *See Lalli*, 439 U.S. at 273 (stating that a court's constitutional inquiry into a state law "does not focus on the abstract "fairness" of a state law, but on whether the statute's relation to the state interests it is intended to promote is so tenuous that it lacks the rationality contemplated by the Fourteenth Amendment"). As the Fifth Circuit has explained:

> We will not . . . insist upon detailed studies of the precise severity, nature, and characteristics of the juvenile crime problem in analyzing whether the [curfew law] meets constitutional muster . . . . Federal courts have always been reluctant to question the potential effectiveness of legislative remedies designed to address societal problems.

Qutb v. Strauss, 11 F.3d 488, 493 n. 7 (5th Cir. 1993).

307 *See Lalli*, 439 U.S. at 274.

308 *See* Hutchins v. District of Columbia, 188 F.3d 531, 542 (D.C. Cir. 1999) (en banc).

309 *See id.* This rate was more than three times the national average. *See id.*

310 *Id.*

311 *See* Hutchins v. District of Columbia, 144 F.3d 798, 810 (D.C. Cir. 1998), *rev'd on reh'g en banc*, 188 F.3d 531 (D.C. Cir. 1999). The court continued:

> Further, elected representatives of Advisory Neighborhood Commissions ("ANCs") and other District residents testified before the D.C. Council about violence plaguing the streets, gunfire from early evening through early morning, children counting the new bullet holes every morning in the doors to their kindergartens, the worsening of teen violence, the gang victimization of youths, and murder becoming sport.

Id. at 810-11.

312 *See* Hutchins v. District of Columbia, 942 F. Supp. 665, 675 n.13, *rev'd on reh'g en banc*, 188 F.3d 531 (D.C. Cir. 1999) (stating that statistics from Dallas showed that the city recorded a 21.7% decrease in juvenile arrests for violent crimes); *Hutchins*, 144 F.3d at 812 (noting similar studies in New Orleans and San Antonio).

313 *See Hutchins*, 942 F. Supp. at 675 n.13 (noting that statistics from San Antonio showed a 60% decrease in juvenile victimization during curfew hours).

314 *Hutchins*, 188 F.3d at 544.

315 *See Hutchins*, 144 F.3d at 812. The Police Chief informed the D.C. Council, after the curfew law had been in effect for three months, "that '[t]he juvenile curfew has made a signifi-

The "substantial relation" requirement is satisfied by such a showing. Experiences of other cities with curfew laws are an important source of information that should not be disregarded "so long as whatever evidence the city relies upon is reasonably believed to be relevant to the problem that the city addresses."[316] As Judge Silberman, writing for the plurality in *Hutchins*, remarked, "it would be folly for any city not to look at experiences of other cities."[317]

The fact that some of the statistics used by the Council included 17-year-olds, who were not subject to the curfew, does not make the "fit" insubstantial. As the Supreme Court has explained, "[t]he 'precise accuracy of [the State's] calculations is not a matter of specialized judicial competence.'"[318] Additionally, "few statutory classifications are entirely free from the criticism that they sometimes produce inequitable results."[319] Crime deterrence is not the sole concern of those who pass a curfew law. The legislature also must consider the average maturity of the age group whose rights it inhibits.

Therefore, while it may well be that juveniles who are age seventeen commit a significant portion of juvenile crimes, the fact that this group of juveniles is excluded from the ordinance does not make the means insubstantially related to the ends of the curfew law. The presumably higher degree of maturity possessed by seventeen year-olds[320] justifies their exclusion from the curfew law.[321] The precise accuracy of this legislative determination is not a matter of "specialized judicial competence."

The fact that the Council was unable to discern the precise number of juvenile crimes that took place during curfew hours is also not determinative. The Council was presented with evidence that "more than 50% of juvenile arrests took place during curfew hours."[322] Under similar circumstances, the Fifth Circuit stated that "[a]lthough the city was unable to provide precise data concerning the number of juveniles who commit crimes during the curfew hours, or the number of

---

cant impact on the District's youth arrest rate,' noting a decrease of 39% in the arrest rate for more serious offenses and a 34% decrease over all." *Id.* at 814 n.28.

316 City of Renton v. Playtime Theaters, Inc., 475 U.S. 41, 51-52 (1986).

317 *Hutchins*, 188 F.3d at 544.

318 Lalli v. Lalli, 439 U.S. 259, 274 (1978) (quoting Matthews v. Lucas, 427 U.S. 495, 515 (1976).

319 *Id.* at 273.

320 17 year-olds, after all, are only one year removed from exercising the right to vote. *See* U.S. CONST. amend. XXVI.

321 The discussion in Part IV, *supra*, demonstrates that what justifies the differential treatment of minors is their comparative lack of capacity. When precisely this lack of capacity ends, or ceases to become determinative where it is still relevant, is a question without a clear answer. It is, however, a determination that should be made by the parents of the community through their council members, rather than by unelected federal judges.

322 Hutchins v. District of Columbia, 188 F.3d 531, 544 (D.C. Cir. 1999) (en banc).

juvenile victims of crimes committed during the curfew, the city nonetheless provided sufficient data to demonstrate that the classification created by the ordinance 'fits.'"[323] Because there is a sufficient fit between the means used by the District of Columbia and the goal of protecting juveniles from crime and victimization, the curfew is constitutional.

VI. CONCLUSION

More than eighty years ago, Justice Brandeis looked upon our system of government and remarked that "one of the happy incidents of the federal system [is] that a single courageous State may, if its citizens choose, serve as a laboratory; and try novel social and economic experiments without risk to the rest of the country."[324] The nation has been experimenting with the efficacy of curfew laws for the past ten years. Courts should not step in and stop this experiment. While a right to travel on public fora exists, the rights of minors have always been subject to certain burdens that a state could not place on the rights of adults. Unless cities panic and pass curfew laws without justification, these laws should survive constitutional scrutiny because they are substantially related to the significant government interest of protecting juveniles from crime.

BENJAMIN C. SASSÉ[†]

---

[323] Qutb v. Strauss, 11 F.3d 488, 493-94 (5th Cir. 1993).

[324] New State Ice Co. v. Liebmann, 285 U.S. 262, 311 (1932) (Brandeis, J., dissenting).

[†] With thanks to Professor Jonathan Entin for suggesting the topic, to Professor Ken Margolis for reviewing earlier drafts of this Note, and Cynthia Sassé for her helpful editorial suggestions.

NOTE

Constitutional Law: *Hutchins v. District of Columbia*: The Constitutional Dilemma over Juvenile Curfews

I. Introduction

When judges are required, in interpreting and applying legislation, to balance the interests of a political community with the constitutional rights of individuals, they find themselves in a precarious situation. On the one hand, they risk trespassing on the domain of the policy makers and overturning the legitimate will of the duly elected democratic majority. On the other hand, courts risk trespassing on the rights of the individual person. Although an unenviable task, judges usually succeed at balancing the competing interests when they uphold a guiding principle to be impartial; regard only the law inasmuch as it is divorced from outside concerns; and seek as much ideal justice as is possible in a pragmatic world.

The existence of unenumerated rights forms a proverbial "no man's land" between political will and civil liberties. Yet, constitutional jurisprudence insists that fundamental rights are present in the very spirit of the U.S. Constitution — unwritten, but every bit as vital as those expressly set forth in the Bill of Rights.[1] These include rights that perhaps the founders saw no need to list, believing them too evident to require formal protection. Or, perhaps the founders left these rights unwritten intentionally out of a belief that the matters of which they were part belonged more properly in the realm of politics. The necessity of recognizing these rights creates a dilemma that courts frequently face.

Among these unenumerated rights is a "right to movement." Although many courts have recognized the right to movement as fundamental, the U.S. Supreme Court has addressed the issue in only limited contexts.[2] The term "movement" means a multitude of things, including international, interstate, and intrastate travel; movement in the sense of mere locomotion; and freedom from state-created hindrances such as residency requirements, vagrancy ordinances, and police interrogation.[3] The few contexts in which the Court has addressed this right have never included municipal curfew ordinances,[4] and only rarely has any law restricted an otherwise law-abiding citizen's movement outright.[5] The Court has ruled in other

---

1. *See infra* text accompanying notes 115-22.

2. *See, e.g.*, Shapiro v. Thompson, 394 U.S. 618, 629 (1969) (declaring the right to interstate travel to be fundamental); Kent v. Dulles, 357 U.S. 116 (1958) (holding that the right to travel is a part of the constitutional liberty interest).

3. *See infra* text accompanying notes 132-57.

4. *See* Scott A. Kizer, Note, *Juvenile Curfew Laws: Is There a Standard?*, 45 DRAKE L. REV. 749, 753 (1997).

5. *See, e.g.*, Gomez v. Turner, 672 F.2d 134, 143 n.18 (D.C. Cir. 1982) ("That citizens can walk the

contexts that children are citizens enjoying the same fundamental rights as adults[6] and that a broad right to movement indeed exists.[7] While it may seem counterintuitive to suggest that minors have a fundamental right to be on the streets at night, there are legitimate circumstances implicated by juvenile curfews, not all of which are practical, and not all of which can be anticipated by statutory defenses. And, while a juvenile curfew ordinance may be valid on its face, the enforcement and application of the ordinance may extend beyond that which is permitted by constitutional standards.

This note analyzes the recent decision by the U.S. Court of Appeals for the D.C. Circuit in *Hutchins v. District of Columbia*,[8] which overturned the district court's injunction against the enforcement of Washington D.C.'s juvenile curfew law. This note compares the circuit court's reasoning with other court decisions regarding similar issues. Although *Hutchins* raised many constitutional issues, this note focuses on the freedom of movement issue and addresses the appropriate constitutional test for dealing with the rights of minors. Part II of this note briefly traces the history of curfews in America, and describes recent circuit court decisions regarding juvenile curfews. Part III examines the plurality and dissenting opinions of *Hutchins*. Part IV analyzes the *Hutchins* plurality opinion regarding a minor's right to movement in light of the reasoning of other federal appellate and district court opinions, arguing that the plurality erred in implying that a broader right to movement does not exist. Part IV also analyzes federal case law with regard to constitutional tests and the rights of minors. It argues that the *Hutchins* plurality correctly chose the "intermediate scrutiny" test but that the curfew ordinance was not substantially tailored to the District of Columbia's objective.

II. Juvenile Curfews v. Fundamental Rights in America

The word "curfew" comes to the English language from the Norman French *couvre feu*, or "cover the lamp," which is a phrase meaning colloquially "lights out."[9] Within the United States, curfews have met legal challenges almost since

---

streets, without explanations or formal papers, is surely among the cherished liberties that distinguish this nation from so many others."); King v. New Rochelle Mun. Hous. Auth., 442 F.2d 646, 648 (2d Cir. 1971) ("It would be meaningless to describe the right to travel between states as a fundamental precept of personal liberty and not to acknowledge a correlative constitutional right to travel within a state.").

6. *See* Planned Parenthood v. Danforth, 428 U.S. 52, 74 (1976) ("Constitutional rights do not mature and come into being magically only when one attains the state-defined age of majority. Minors, as well as adults, are protected by the Constitution and possess constitutional rights."); Tinker v. Des Moines Indep. Community Sch. Dist., 393 U.S. 503, 506 (1969) ("It can hardly be argued that either students or teachers shed their constitutional rights to freedom of speech or expression at the schoolhouse gate").

7. *See, e.g.*, Papachristou v. City of Jacksonville, 405 U.S. 156 (1972).

8. 188 F.3d 531 (D.C. Cir. 1999).

9. *See* Thistlewood v. Trial Magistrate for Ocean City, 204 A.2d 688, 690 (Md. 1964) (colloquial translation by the author). The first curfews in England may have been enacted under William the Conqueror in the eleventh century, although there may have been a curfew in Oxford as early as the reign of Alfred the Great in the ninth century. *See id.*

their inception.[10] In *Ex parte McCarver*, the Texas Court of Criminal Appeals overturned a curfew ordinance that prohibited anyone under the age of twenty-one from being on the streets after the bell at the town's Baptist Church had rung.[11] The court ruled that the ordinance was an unreasonable invasion of the rights of citizens to come and go as they please.[12] Thus began a century-long relationship between juvenile curfew ordinances and the American courts. Despite the longevity of this relationship, only in the last forty years have curfews enjoyed widespread popularity.[13] And, only the 1990s have witnessed a veritable "boom" in juvenile curfew enactments.[14] The reasons for this boom are obvious to most Americans. Juvenile crime rates from the end of the 1980s into the beginning of the 1990s soared.[15] The belief that removing juveniles from the streets at night would reverse this alarming trend motivated many large cities to enact juvenile curfew ordinances.[16] Smaller cities, even those without serious crime problems, saw merit in this movement and quickly followed suit.[17] The result today — most U.S. municipalities with substantial populations have some form of curfew ordinance.[18] Local governments in Oklahoma, not immune to such concerns, have enacted their own juvenile curfews in the state's largest municipalities.[19]

Not all juvenile curfew ordinances are created equal. Depending upon the level of restriction and the statutory defenses available, a court will be more or less inclined to find a constitutional violation.[20] An important U.S. Supreme Court

10. *See, e.g.*, *Ex parte* McCarver, 46 S.W. 936 (Tex. Crim. 1898).

11. *See id.* at 937.

12. The court declared in its ruling that the law is

> paternalistic and is an invasion of the personal liberty of the citizen .... No power exists at common law for the enactment of such an ordinance by a city government. It is arbitrary and does not apply to all persons alike. It makes criminal acts which in themselves are not criminal ....

Id. at 937.

13. *See* Brian Privor, *Dusk 'til Dawn: Children's Rights and the Effectiveness of Juvenile Curfew Ordinances*, 79 B.U. L. REV. 415, 419 (1999).

14. *See id.* at 419 n.19 (stating that "the 1990's will be remembered as a decade in which a 'curfew movement' swept across America") (quoting William J. Ruefle & Kenneth M. Reynolds, *Keep Them at Home: Juvenile Curfew Ordinances in 200 American Cities*, 15 AM. J. OF POLICE 63, 75-77 & tbls.1-2 (1996)).

15. *See id.* at 421 n.25 (stating that "the rate at which juveniles committed violent crimes increased nearly 43% from 1989 to 1993") (quoting from OFFICE OF JUVENILE JUSTICE & DELINQUENCY PREVENTION, U.S. DEP'T OF JUSTICE, JUVENILE OFFENDERS AND VICTIMS: 1997 UPDATE ON VIOLENCE 16 (1997)).

16. *See* Kizer, *supra* note 4, at 749-50.

17. *See* Privor, *supra* note 13, at 420.

18. *See id.*

19. *See, e.g.*, OKLAHOMA CITY, OKLA., CODE art. XV, § 30-423; TULSA, OKLA., CODE tit. 27, § 2800-06. These Oklahoma curfew laws are substantively identical to the Dallas, Charlottesville, and District of Columbia ordinances, which are discussed herein. *See infra* text accompanying notes 29-33, 41-45.

20. *Compare* Bykofsky v. Middletown, 401 F. Supp. 1242 (M.D. Pa. 1975) (finding that a curfew, where reasonable in its breadth, does not violate any fundamental rights or equal protection) *with* Waters v. Barry, 711 F. Supp. 1125 (D.D.C. 1989) (declaring a curfew invalid for overbreadth).

decision outlining a methodology for determining the constitutional validity of a law restricting the rights of juveniles generally is *Bellotti v. Baird*.[21] In *Bellotti*, the Court struck down a law restricting a minor's right to an abortion, stating, "a child, merely on account of his minority, is not beyond the protection of the Constitution."[22] Quoting from the 1967 decision, *In re Gault*, the Court continued, "whatever may be their precise impact, neither the Fourteenth Amendment nor the Bill of Rights is for adults alone."[23] These statements solidified the Court's previous pronouncements in the cases of *Tinker v. Des Moines Independent School District*[24] and *Planned Parenthood v. Danforth*.[25] The *Bellotti* Court, meanwhile, went on to declare three general factors differentiating the rights of minors from those of adults, including "the peculiar vulnerability of children; their inability to make critical decisions in an informed, mature manner; and the importance of the parental role in child rearing."[26] The resulting policy resembled a balancing test with constitutional parity between adults and juveniles except in narrowly justified circumstances.[27]

The Supreme Court has never ruled directly on the constitutionality of juvenile curfew laws.[28] However, in the past decade, four U.S. Circuit Courts of Appeals have issued important and far-reaching opinions on the matter. In 1993, the U.S. Court of Appeals for the Fifth Circuit overturned a district court ruling that held the curfew ordinance of Dallas, Texas, unconstitutional in *Qutb v. Strauss*.[29] The district court had ruled that the ordinance violated a minor's First Amendment right to associate by creating unconstitutional classifications in violation of the Equal Protection Clause of the Fourteenth Amendment.[30] The Fifth Circuit, noting the rule in *Bellotti*,[31] agreed that the Dallas curfew implicated the fundamental rights of minors and thus was subject to strict scrutiny review.[32] However, in a rare event in constitutional jurisprudence, the court held that the curfew satisfied both the compelling interest and narrow tailoring requirements of strict scrutiny analysis.[33]

21. 443 U.S. 622 (1979).

22. *Id.* at 633.

23. *Id.* (quoting *In re* Gault, 387 U.S. 1, 13 (1967)).

24. 393 U.S. 503, 506 (1969).

25. 428 U.S. 52, 74 (1976).

26. *Bellotti*, 443 U.S. at 634.

27. *See* Susan M. Horowitz, *A Search for Constitutional Standards: The Judicial Review of Juvenile Curfew Ordinances*, 24 COLUM. J.L. & SOC. PROBS. 381, 409 (1991) (arguing that the *Bellotti* standard should operate as a balancing tool to permit the review of juvenile laws as impinging on fundamental rights without discounting the right all together).

28. *See, e.g.*, Bykofsky v. Middletown, 429 U.S. 964 (1976) (denying a writ of certiorari in an appeal of a decision upholding a juvenile curfew law); *see also* Kizer, *supra* note 4, at 753.

29. 11 F.3d 488 (5th Cir. 1993).

30. *See id.* at 491.

31. *See id.* at 492 n.6. The court here suggests that the *Bellotti* rule does not affect the determination of whether juveniles possess fundamental rights or whether the constitutional test is different for juveniles. *See id.* Rather, the court indicates that, under *Bellotti*, laws affecting the fundamental rights of juveniles satisfy more easily the means/ends analysis, no matter the particular test. *See id.*

32. *See id.* at 492.

33. *See id.* at 496. *But cf.* Johnson v. City of Opelousas, 658 F.2d 1065, 1074 (5th Cir. Unit A Oct.

In 1997, the U.S. Court of Appeals for the Ninth Circuit struck down a curfew ordinance in *Nunez v. City of San Diego*.[34] In this case, a federal district court upheld San Diego's curfew ordinance, claiming that the burden imposed on the rights of minors was minimal and that the law was narrowly tailored to address a compelling interest.[35] The Ninth Circuit overturned the district court, ruling on the grounds that the curfew law was void for vagueness,[36] that it was not narrowly tailored to meet the City's objective,[37] that it was not a reasonable restriction on time, place, or manner of speech,[38] and that it violated the fundamental rights of parents to raise their children.[39]

In 1998, the U.S. Court of Appeals for the Fourth Circuit applied intermediate scrutiny to the curfew law of Charlottesville, Virginia, and upheld it as constitutional in *Schliefer v. City of Charlottesville*.[40] The curfew law of Charlottesville closely resembled the curfew law of Dallas.[41] The reasoning of the *Schliefer* court was much the same as the *Qutb* court, with the exception of the constitutional test employed.[42]

Finally, in 1999, the U.S. Court of Appeals for the D.C. Circuit, sitting *en banc*, reversed a divided panel of its own court, as well as the district court, and upheld the constitutionality of the District of Columbia's juvenile curfew law in *Hutchins*, the case that is the subject of this note.[43]

III. *Hutchins v. District of Columbia*

A. *Facts and Procedural History*

In September 1995, the District of Columbia formally adopted a juvenile curfew ordinance that prohibited minors from remaining "in any public place or on the premises of any establishment within the District of Columbia during curfew hours."[44] The law defined a minor as "any person under the age of 17 years," with the exception of a married or emancipated minor, and it set forth curfew hours as running from 11:00 p.m. to 6:00 a.m. beginning on any Sunday through Thursday until the next day and from midnight to 6:00 a.m. beginning on any Saturday or

---

1981) (same circuit declaring a curfew law in Opelousas, Louisiana, unconstitutional).

34. 114 F.3d 935 (9th Cir. 1997). The curfew ordinance in question had been enacted in 1947. *See id.* at 938.

35. *See generally* Nunez v. City of San Diego, 963 F. Supp. 912 (S.D. Cal. 1996), *rev'd*, 114 F.3d 935 (9th Cir. 1997). The district court relied on *Qutb* in applying a strict scrutiny analysis through the *Bellotti* lens. *See id.* at 923; *see also Qutb*, 11 F.3d at 492.

36. *See Nunez*, 114 F.3d at 943. The court was particularly concerned with the vagueness of the language, "loiter, wander, idle, stroll or play." *Id.* at 940.

37. *See id.* at 949.

38. *See id.* at 951.

39. *See id.* at 952.

40. 159 F.3d 843 (4th Cir. 1998).

41. *Compare* CHARLOTTESVILLE, VA., CODE § 17-7 *with* DALLAS, TEX., CODE § 31-33.

42. *See Schliefer*, 159 F.3d at 852.

43. Hutchins v. District of Columbia, 188 F.3d 531 (D.C. Cir. 1999).

44. D.C. CODE ANN. § 6-2183(a)(1) (1996).

Sunday.[45] Although the District's evidentiary support was sketchy, the "findings and purpose" of the law claimed that the District's Council had noticed an increase in juvenile violence and gang activity and that minors under the age of seventeen were "particularly susceptible" to the lure of crime and to being the victims of crime.[46] The law further stated that the Council was seeking to reduce the victimization of juveniles, reduce juvenile crime, and aid parents in carrying out their parental responsibilities.[47] The law, besides setting forth a broad restriction on minors' movement, created a number of defenses and exemptions designed to protect innocent or justified activities.[48] Some of these defenses included accompaniment by a parent, interstate travel, errand running at the behest of a parent, involvement in an emergency, and the exercise of "First Amendment rights . . . including free exercise of religion, freedom of speech, and the right of assembly."[49] The law punished parents and employers for knowingly permitting or negligently allowing a minor to violate the curfew.[50] The penalties included police detainment of the minor, a $500 fine, community service, and parenting classes for the minor's parents and guardians.[51]

Tiana Hutchins, her parents, a private business, and others sued the District of Columbia seeking to challenge the constitutionality of the curfew law and to enjoin the law's enforcement.[52] These plaintiffs charged that the law violated four constitutional principles, including equal protection of the law and the fundamental due process right to free movement,[53] the fundamental right of parents to raise their children free from state interference, unconstitutional vagueness, and the minors' rights to be free from unreasonable searches and seizures.[54] In October 1996, Judge Sullivan of the U.S. District Court for the District of Columbia ruled for the plaintiffs, granting summary judgment on the basis of the equal protection and due process claims, as well as the unconstitutional vagueness claim.[55] The district court held that the law violated the fundamental rights of movement and parental freedom and that the law was not narrowly tailored to a compelling interest under the correlative strict scrutiny analysis.[56] The District of Columbia appealed. A divided panel of the D.C. Circuit Court of Appeals affirmed the ruling in May 1998.[57] The circuit court,

---

45. *Id.* § 6-2182(1), (5).

46. *Id.* § 6-2181(a), (b).

47. *See id.* § 6-2181(e).

48. *See id.* § 6-2183(b).

49. *Id.* § 6-2183(b)(1)(H). *But cf.* City of Chicago v. Morales, 119 S. Ct. 1849 (1999) (holding that an anti-loitering ordinance designed to deter gangs was unconstitutionally vague and violated due process by deterring innocent and constitutionally protected behavior).

50. *See* D.C. CODE ANN. § 6-2183 (a)(2), (3) (1996).

51. *See id.* § 6-2183(c)(3), (d)(1), (2).

52. *See* Hutchins v. District of Columbia, 942 F. Supp. 665, 666 (D.C. Cir. 1996), *aff'd*, 144 F.3d 798 (D.C. Cir. 1998), *vacated and rev'd en banc*, 188 F.3d 531 (D.C. Cir. 1999).

53. Although not a state, the District of Columbia is subject to the Fourteenth Amendment through the doctrine of "reverse" incorporation. *See generally* Bolling v. Sharpe, 347 U.S. 497 (1954).

54. *See Hutchins*, 942 F. Supp. at 667.

55. *See id.* at 680.

56. *See id.*

57. *See* Hutchins v. District of Columbia, 144 F.3d 798 (D.C. Cir. 1998), *vacated rev'd en banc*,

vacating the panel's ruling, agreed to rehear arguments *en banc*.[58]

B. Issues and Holding of the Hutchins Plurality

The U.S. Court of Appeals for the District of Columbia Circuit, sitting *en banc*, reheard the arguments originally made by the plaintiff-appellees in the district court and subsequently found, in a plurality opinion, for the defendant-appellants on each issue. First, on the issue of the fundamental right to movement, the plurality ruled that such a substantive right does not exist beyond the narrow right to interstate travel. The U.S. Supreme Court had suggested a more general right only in dicta.[59] And, even if the right to movement did indeed exist, juveniles did not possess it.[60]

Second, on the issue of the fundamental right of a parent to raise a child, the plurality held that the curfew did not implicate such a right because whether a child is allowed outside the home at night is not an "intimate family decision[]."[61] The court then entertained the hypothesis that if the fundamental rights of children and parents were implicated, where children's issues are concerned, intermediate scrutiny would apply.[62] Consequently, according to the plurality the curfew could withstand such heightened scrutiny because it is substantially related to an important government interest.[63] As to whether the curfew law was unconstitutionally vague, the plurality found that the District could legitimately enforce and expect broad understanding of the language set forth in the curfew.[64] Finally, the plurality dispatched the claims that the curfew violated First and Fourth Amendment rights. Regarding the First Amendment, the plurality held that a challenge must first prove a facial violation of the First Amendment and that the statutory language at issue only implicated a potential violation.[65] Regarding the Fourth Amendment, the plurality held that giving a police officer discretion to make an arrest based on reasonableness does not violate due process because probable cause is the very definition of Fourth Amendment due process.[66]

C. Reasoning of the Hutchins Plurality

In addressing the fundamental right to movement and parental freedom claims, the *Hutchins* plurality began by distinguishing between procedural and substantive due process.[67] In describing the substantive right to movement, the plurality cited the U.S. Supreme Court decisions creating the fundamental right to interstate travel

---

188 F.3d 531 (D.C. Cir. 1999).

58. *See* Hutchins v. District of Columbia, 188 F.3d 531 (D.C. Cir. 1999).

59. *See id.* at 536-38 (referring to Papachristou v. City of Jacksonville, 405 U.S. 156, 164 (1972); United States v. Guest, 383 U.S. 745, 758 (1966); Kent v. Dulles, 357 U.S. 116, 126 (1958); and Williams v. Fears, 179 U.S. 270, 273 (1900)).

60. *See id.* at 538-39.

61. *See id.* at 541.

62. *See id.*

63. *See id.* at 541-46.

64. *See id.* at 546.

65. *See id.* at 548.

66. *See id.*

67. *See id.* at 536.

and then denied that those decisions lend any support to a broader right to movement.[68]

The plurality next acknowledged a small number of cases supporting a broader right to movement, but held that since those cases assert the right only in dicta, they were not controlling.[69] The plurality also suggested that because a broad right to movement must necessarily include international travel, and the regulation of international travel has been specifically declared constitutional, a fundamental right could not exist at all.[70] The plurality declined to accept the right to movement essays found in the "vagrancy cases"[71] as dispositive since the holdings of those cases went to different issues. The court conceded that there was substantial case law supporting a right to "intrastate" travel paralleling the right to travel interstate and that this might implicate a fundamental right in instances where a curfew is "draconian."[72] Finally, the plurality relied on a distinction between the rights of juveniles and those of adults.[73]

In addressing the fundamental right of parents to raise their children without government interference, the court was brief in its reasoning. The plurality outlined the cases establishing the right and then discussed a distinction between a "private realm of family life" and laws regarding public places.[74] The plurality also looked to the defenses to the curfew and found that parents still retain "*almost* total discretion" over their children's activities.[75] The plurality concluded its reasoning on this issue by stating that curfews do not infringe any recognized "intimate family decisions."[76]

The remainder of the plurality opinion divided the other claims into two categories. First, denying that the curfew implicated any fundamental right, the plurality considered the problem of deciding which constitutional test to use, as a hypothetical question.[77] Agreeing with case law on point, the plurality stated that juveniles do possess constitutional rights, but found that those rights are not coextensive with the rights of adults.[78] The plurality resolved the dilemma of which constitutional analysis to use by compromising the usual strict scrutiny test

68. *See id.* (citing Saenz v. Roe, 119 S. Ct. 1518 (1999); Zobel v. Williams, 457 U.S. 55, 79-81 (1982); Shapiro v. Thompson, 394 U.S. 618, 629-31 (1969); United States v. Guest, 383 U.S. 745, 758 (1966); and Edwards v. California, 314 U.S. 160, 173-74 (1941)).

69. *See id.* at 537.

70. *See id.*

71. *See id.* (referring to Papachristou v. City of Jacksonville, 405 U.S. 156, 164 (1972) and Kolender v. Lawson, 461 U.S. 352 (1983) as the vagrancy cases).

72. *Id.* at 538.

73. *See id.* at 539-41.

74. *Id.* at 540-41 (citing Pierce v. Society of Sisters, 268 U.S. 510 (1925); Meyer v. Nebraska, 262 U.S. 390 (1923)).

75. *Id.* at 545.

76. *Id.* at 541.

77. *See id.*

78. *See id.* (citing Planned Parenthood v. Danforth, 428 U.S. 52, 74 (1976), to support juvenile rights, but then contrasting this with Prince v. Massachusetts, 321 U.S. 158, 169 (1944) and Bellotti v. Baird, 443 U.S. 622, 633-39 (1979)).

and concluding that "something less than strict scrutiny — intermediate scrutiny — would be appropriate."[79] Intermediate scrutiny requires that a law be substantially related to the achievement of an important government interest.[80] The plurality reasoned that reducing juvenile crime and protecting minors from being victimized by crime were important objectives.[81]

Next, admitting that determining whether the curfew is substantially related to these objectives "is the more difficult question here,"[82] the plurality set forth a three-part analysis for identifying a substantial relationship. The plurality looked to: (1) "the factual premises upon which the legislature based its decision," (2) "the logical connection the remedy has to those premises," and (3) "the scope of the remedy employed."[83] Discussing the use of statistical and other sociological data by both the Council in enacting the law and the district court in striking it down, the plurality found that despite irregularities in the District's statistics, the government need only demonstrate a substantial relation between the law and the statistics.[84] The plaintiff-appellees' argument that the curfew should be confined to the high-crime areas of the district in order to substantially tailor the law to its objective was discarded as potentially racist or politically unpopular.[85] The plurality also noted that the defenses to the curfew helped narrow the scope of the law to more suspicious "nocturnal activities."[86]

D. Judge Rogers' Dissent

Hutchins had two dissenting opinions that differed mainly in the determination of which constitutional test to apply when dealing with the fundamental rights of minors.[87] The more cogent dissent by Circuit Judge Rogers had four parts. Parts I and II dealt with defining a fundamental right in general and defining the right to movement in particular. In addressing the plurality's methodology for defining fundamental rights, the dissent began by criticizing the narrow definition of the rights at issue.[88] Instead of defining a right "as the mirror-image of a particular burden," Judge Rogers admonished the plurality for not defining rights in a more abstract context.[89] Otherwise, according to Rogers' dissent, narrow definitions would result in stripping protection from constitutionally protected, disfavored conduct and tipping the scales against recognizing any right.[90] Second, and conversely, Judge Rogers argued that a narrowly defined right denies the recognition

79. *Id.*
80. *See id.*; *see also* Craig v. Boren, 429 U.S. 190, 197 (1976).
81. *See Hutchins*, 188 F.3d at 542.
82. *Id.*
83. *Id.*
84. *See id.* at 543.
85. *See id.* at 544.
86. *See id.* at 545.
87. *See id.* at 552, 570.
88. *See id.* at 552-54.
89. *Id.* at 554-55.
90. *See id.* at 555.

of an individual's interest against the "conventional wisdom."[91] Third, Judge Rogers asserted that although defining rights too broadly encourages improper subjectivity, defining rights too narrowly results in the same problem in reverse.[92] That is to say, a court might be too subjective in its attempt to restrict a proposed right. Judge Rogers claimed that since the plurality failed to proffer a methodology for defining rights, it left open the door to apply whatever standard the court might subjectively desire in the future.[93] Fourth, Judge Rogers criticized the application of an equal protection analysis to a fundamental rights issue. He asserted that the combining of the analyses resulted in a "blurring" of the tests so that it allowed the plurality to dispense with the equal protection claim, and, by extension, allowed the plurality to deny the recognition of the fundamental right.[94] Finally, Judge Rogers attacked the plurality's application of Justice Scalia's reductionist method for characterizing a fundamental right, pointing out that the approach has never garnered a majority on the Supreme Court.[95]

Judge Rogers' dissent continued by declaring that "there is no doubt that minors possess rights that are fundamental."[96] He reasoned that the corpus of juvenile and fundamental rights cases read together results, not in an absolution of such rights when applied to minors, but only in a dilution.[97] In defining the right to movement, his dissent distinguished the plurality's legitimate concern over extending a broad right to locomotion, which might serve to challenge even "trivial . . . impediments" such as traffic lights, from a vital liberty interest protecting a citizen from "police interference for mere [public] presence."[98]

Parts III and IV of Judge Rogers' dissent dealt with the means/ends analysis appropriate for juvenile rights issues. He began by agreeing with the plurality's application of intermediate scrutiny in dealing with the fundamental rights of minors.[99] While admitting that some juvenile curfews might survive intermediate scrutiny and stating without comment that the "curfew has legitimate ends," Judge Rogers claimed that the District's curfew was not substantially tailored to meet those ends.[100] First, he criticized the District's evidence as being "too broad" in that it included crimes and victimization by and of those who were not affected by the curfew.[101] Second, Judge Rogers found the evidence too narrow in that it failed to point out when juvenile crime and victimization occur.[102] He next demonstrated that over "90% of all juveniles do not commit any crimes," thus burdening a far

91. *Id.*
92. *See id.*
93. *See id.* at 556.
94. *Id.*
95. *See id.* at 557.
96. *Id.* at 558.
97. *See id.* at 558-59
98. *Id.* at 562.
99. *See id.* at 563.
100. *Id.* at 564.
101. *Id.* at 565.
102. *See id.*

larger class than might be necessary.[103] Judge Rogers distinguished the facts in the *Schliefer* case as having "sturdier evidence."[104] Finally, Judge Rogers claimed that "efficacy can be no substitute for constitutional scrutiny."[105] In other words, the curfew was not rendered constitutionally proper simply because the juvenile crime rate had declined; a curfew of adults or a juvenile curfew covering day and night would also reduce crime, yet they would both raise constitutional questions.[106]

IV. An Analysis of Hutchins

A. The Freedom of Movement as a Liberty Interest

Liberty is an ancient word. Its most basic and common meaning is "freedom."[107] It comes to the English language from the French *liberté*, and to the French from the Latin *libertas*.[108] Although its denotation in all three languages is the same, in American jurisprudence it has connotations all its own.[109] Liberty's mention in the Fourteenth Amendment is loaded with legalistic meaning; along with "life" and "property" it provides the foundation for the concept of substantive due process.[110] Liberty's etymology has arguably[111] given the Supreme Court the jurisprudential mandate to recognize the existence of broad, fundamental rights. These rights, in turn, have spawned the recognition of other rights within what has been termed the *penumbra* of the Bill of Rights.[112] When one of these rights is fully recognized and its sanctity threatened, the menacing state action will be subjected to the strictest of constitutional tests and will almost certainly fail.[113] The constitutional

---

103. *Id.* at 566.

104. *Id.* at 568.

105. *Id.* at 570.

106. *See id.*

107. *See* BLACK'S LAW DICTIONARY 664 (6th ed. 1990) (defining "freedom" as "[t]he state of being free; liberty; self-determination; absence of restraint; the opposite of slavery.").

108. *See* THE OXFORD-HACHETTE FRENCH DICTIONARY 470 (Marie-Hélène Corréard & Valerie Grundy eds., 2d ed. 1997); THE POCKET OXFORD LATIN DICTIONARY 251 (James Morwood ed., 1995).

109. *See, e.g.*, BLACK'S LAW DICTIONARY 918-19 (6th ed. 1990). There are no fewer than thirteen sub-definitions for "liberty" listed, including "personal liberty," which states, "The right or power of locomotion; of changing situation, or moving one's person to whatsoever place one's own inclination may direct, without imprisonment or restraint, unless by due course of law." *Id.*

110. U.S. CONST. amend. XIV, § 1. The Amendment states:

> All persons born or naturalized in the United States, and subject to the jurisdiction thereof, are citizens of the United States and of the State wherein they reside. No State shall make or enforce any law which shall . . . deprive any person of life, liberty, or property, without due process of law; nor deny to any person within its jurisdiction the equal protection of the laws.

Id.

111. *See, e.g.*, ROBERT BORK, THE TEMPTING OF AMERICA: THE POLITICAL SEDUCTION OF THE LAW 110-26 (1990).

112. *See* Griswold v. Connecticut, 381 U.S. 479, 483 (1965).

113. "Strict scrutiny" requires that a state action be narrowly tailored to a compelling state interest. *See* Plyler v. Doe, 457 U.S. 202, 217 (1982). *But cf.* Regents of the Univ. of Cal. v. Bakke, 438 U.S. 265, 362 (1978) (Brennan, J., concurring in part, dissenting in part) (stating that strict scrutiny does not mean simply "strict in theory, but fatal in fact.").

tests of strict scrutiny, intermediate scrutiny, and rational basis review collectively form the modern paradigm for constitutional review.[114] And, as entrenched as these tests are in constitutional methodology, it seems impossible to imagine that anything will replace them in the foreseeable future.

One of the fundamental rights that courts often recognize as being under the rubric of substantive due process is the fundamental right to movement.[115] This makes sense because a literal, layman's reading of the words, "deprive any person of . . . liberty"[116] tends to indicate a person in a state of imprisonment, or in some other analogous state of confinement. What is meant by "liberty" in this context would at least mean the inverse of confinement, which "deprivation" of liberty denotes.[117] Syllogistically, therefore, liberty means freedom from confinement, the synonym of free movement. On its face such a conclusion is clearer than this analysis would suggest. However, the clarity of this logical analysis becomes muddied when one confronts the problem of defining due process.

Before undertaking a critical analysis of *Hutchins*, it is important to have a basic framework for understanding the dual nature of the Due Process Clause of the Fourteenth Amendment. A denotation/connotation dichotomy proves useful in acquiring this cursory understanding because the courts have chosen to interpret due process along similar lines. A denotative reading of the Due Process Clause provides the basis for the concept of "procedural" due process. It means simply that a state actor must be fair and impartial in its application of the laws; it must follow established legal process owed to every person.[118] In this way, the literal reading of the words "deprive any person of . . . liberty"[119] does not create any unenumerated rights. However, the connotative reading of the word "liberty" in the Due Process Clause does lay a foundation for the recognition of many rights by way of the doctrines of incorporation and "substantive" due process.[120] Substantive due process rights are based on the connotations (i.e., the implicit and traditional meanings) of the term "liberty." Inherent in the American cultural understanding of the word "liberty" is the "absence of confinement" connotation described above, or

114. The three most common tests include: the "rational basis test" (a law must be rationally related to a legitimate governmental interest), *see, e.g.*, Williamson v. Lee Optical, 348 U.S. 483 (1955); the "intermediate scrutiny" test (a law must be substantially tailored to meet an important governmental interest), *see, e.g.*, Mississippi Univ. for Women v. Hogan, 458 U.S. 718 (1982); and the "strict scrutiny" test (a law must be narrowly tailored to a compelling governmental interest), *see, e.g.*, Roe v. Wade, 410 U.S. 113 (1973).

115. *See, e.g.*, Shapiro v. Thompson, 394 U.S. 618, 629-30 (1969) (finding the right to travel to be implicit in the concept of personal liberty); King v. New Rochelle Mun. Hous. Auth., 442 F.2d 646, 648 (2d Cir. 1971) (stating that the right to interstate travel has a corollary in intrastate travel).

116. U.S. CONST. amend. XIV, § 1.

117. *See, e.g.*, BLACK'S LAW DICTIONARY 298 (6th ed. 1990). *Cf. supra* note 107.

118. *See, e.g.*, Goldberg v. Kelly, 397 U.S. 254, 267-71 (1970) (defining the fundamental constitutional parameters for procedural due process).

119. U.S. CONST. amend. XIV, § 1.

120. *See, e.g.*, Palko v. Connecticut, 302 U.S. 319, 324-25 (1937) (establishing the doctrine of fundamental versus nonfundamental rights and the incorporation of fundamental rights in the Bill of Rights into the Due Process Clause of the Fourteenth Amendment).

its analog "free movement."[121] This particular connotation coincides with liberty's denotation, resulting in the possibility of confusion. However, the word does not uniquely mean one or the other, but both. The American concept of unenumerated rights being founded on the connotations of liberty,[122] this analysis suggests that foremost among any fundamental rights derived from the Fourteenth Amendment is a general right to movement.

B. The Fundamental Right to Movement in the Courts

The *Hutchins* plurality erred when it implied that a fundamental right to movement does not exist.[123] The Supreme Court has indeed found a fundamental right to movement implicit in the Fourteenth Amendment.[124] The fact that the Court has not heard a case implicating this right with regard to juvenile curfews does not mean that the general right does not continue to hold an important position in everyday American life. On the contrary, were it not for the fundamental right of movement, states could restrict even the most innocent aspects of daily travel; police could question a citizen's mere presence in public. Yet, few would doubt that such restrictions would be constitutionally prohibited. The right to movement is perhaps such an obvious aspect of personal liberty that the right has not been specifically recognized as needing formal protection. What rational political entity would ever legislate such a right away? Absent a compelling justification, such as a civil emergency, it is unlikely a law would ever be enacted that would similarly restrict the movement of adults who could, and surely would, vote the legislators out of office. Thus, the judiciary is unlikely to deal with such an issue given the systemic prohibitions present in a representative democracy with universal suffrage. Suffrage, however, is not truly universal. Besides mental incapacity and conviction of a felony, there is yet another prohibition to voting — age.[125] Minors, by definition, cannot vote. They are politically powerless in the truest sense of the phrase. Therefore, the judiciary must be extra sensitive to the fundamental rights of minors. In their capacity as the last defense of civil liberties, the courts should weigh carefully the public policy at stake and realize, from both an ethical and positivist standpoint,[126] that a repudiation of a right so intrinsic to the concept of a free society could substantially harm that society as a whole. This is especially true when the particular court happens to bear the moniker of "the second highest

121. In saying "American cultural understanding," the author is intending a purely legalistic reference, insofar as our legal tradition comes from the common law of England. *See* BLACK'S LAW DICTIONARY, *supra* note 109.

122. U.S. CONST. amend. XIV, § 1.

123. Hutchins v. District of Columbia, 188 F.3d 531, 536-38 (D.C. Cir. 1999).

124. *See, e.g.*, Shapiro v. Thompson, 394 U.S. 618 (1969).

125. U.S. CONST. amend. XXVI, § 1 ("The right of citizens of the United States, who are eighteen years of age or older, to vote shall not be denied or abridged by the United States or by any State on account of age.").

126. From the standpoint of both Kantian and utilitarian ethics it is morally wrong to pursue a policy that needlessly sacrifices the rights of autonomous, morally significant agents. For a brief and accessible explanation of the ethical implications involved, see generally JEFFRIE G. MURPHY & JULES L. COLEMAN, PHILOSOPHY OF LAW: AN INTRODUCTION TO JURISPRUDENCE 67-106 (1990).

court in the land."[127]

The foundation for a violation of the Equal Protection Clause is the prejudicial treatment by a state actor of a suspect class.[128] Prejudicial treatment can come in the form of a facially prejudicial law or the prejudicial application of an otherwise neutral law. A suspect class is any group of persons sharing an immutable trait whose special protection has been recognized by law. While curfew laws are facially prejudicial to minors, age is not a legally recognized classification for equal protection purposes.[129] However, based upon the analysis proffered by Judge Rogers,[130] an equal protection analysis is unnecessary. Rather, substantive due process may stand on its own where a fundamental right is at stake. The issue first demands a definition of the fundamental right. The analysis of a fundamental rights' branch of equal protection and that of a substantive due process claim is essentially the same.[131] Therefore, the underlying question remains, is movement a fundamental right?

The Supreme Court has defined "interstate" movement as a fundamental right. In *Shapiro v. Thompson*[132] the Court invalidated Connecticut, Pennsylvania, and District of Columbia laws that created a one-year residency requirement for recipients of welfare benefits.[133] The Court held that such statutory provisions violate a fundamental "freedom of travel" by discouraging poorer families from moving wherever they so choose within the country.[134] This seminal case engendered a series of subsequent federal court rulings that struck down temporal residency requirements for state benefits, all in the name of the fundamental freedom of interstate travel.[135]

Years earlier, in 1941, the Supreme Court addressed a similar issue in *Edwards v. California*.[136] When California enacted the "anti-okie" law, prohibiting the transportation of indigents and migrant workers into California, the Court struck it down as "void on its face and operat[ing] to deprive the appellant of liberty without due process of law and to deny him the equal protection of the laws."[137]

127. *See, e.g.*, Laura A. Smith, *Justiciability and Judicial Discretion: Standing at the Forefront of Judicial Abdication*, 61 GEO. WASH. L. REV. 1548, 1550 (1993).

128. *See, e.g.*, Korematsu v. United States, 323 U.S. 214 (1944) (holding that classifications based on race implicate the Equal Protection Clause).

129. *See* Massachusetts Bd. of Retirement v. Murgia, 427 U.S. 307, 313 (1976) (holding that age does not constitute a discrete and insular group for equal protection purposes).

130. *See* Hutchins v. District of Columbia, 188 F.3d 531, 552-70 (D.C. Cir. 1999).

131. *See, e.g.*, Shapiro v. Thompson, 394 U.S. 618 (1969) (utilizing the same strict scrutiny analysis triggered by the fundamental rights branch of equal protection as would be necessary under a substantive due process analysis).

132. *Id.*

133. *See id.* at 638-42.

134. *Id.* at 638.

135. *See, e.g.*, Edwards v. California, 314 U.S. 160 (1941); Lutz v. City of York, 899 F.2d 255 (3d Cir. 1990).

136. 314 U.S. 160 (1941).

137. *Id.* at 163.

More recently, in *Memorial Hospital v. Maricopa*,[138] the Court again dealt with a residency requirement for state benefits in a slightly more subtle context. When Arizona refused to provide county-funded, non-emergency medical care to a person prior to that person's establishment of a one-year residency, the Court refined the *Shapiro* ruling to strike down the residency requirement.[139] Because medical care was a necessity of life, the Court reasoned that to withhold it constituted an unconstitutional penalty on interstate travel.[140] In each of these cases and their progeny, the Court interpreted the right to travel interstate as both a fundamental right, deserving of strict scrutiny analysis, and a liberty interest, thereby applicable to all "persons" under the Fourteenth Amendment.

Furthermore, the Court has indicated a corollary between the fundamental right to interstate travel and the right to move about within a state. In *Papachristou v. City of Jacksonville*,[141] the Court struck down a municipal vagrancy ordinance as unconstitutionally vague.[142] Justice Douglas's reasoning clearly supported a general right to movement as implicit in the concept of personal liberty. However, the holding of the case did not recognize this right directly or as distinct from the vagueness theory.[143] Instead, the holding struck down the vagrancy ordinance as "void for vagueness, both in the sense that it 'fails to give a person of ordinary intelligence fair notice that his contemplated conduct is forbidden . . .' and because it encourages arbitrary and erratic arrests . . . ."[144] Without confronting curfews by name, Justice Douglas did condemn their purpose by stating:

> Persons "wandering or strolling" from place to place have been extolled by Walt Whitman and Vachel Lindsay. The qualification "without any lawful purpose or object" may be a trap for innocent acts . . . The difficulty is that these activities are historically part of the amenities of life as we have known them. They are not mentioned in the Constitution or in the Bill of Rights. These unwritten amenities have been in part responsible for giving our people the feeling of independence and self-confidence, the feeling of creativity . . . . They have encouraged lives of high spirits rather than hushed, suffocating silence.[145]

Although the Court has struck down broad restrictions to movement among and within the states, the Court has not upheld such restrictions anywhere. The paucity of Supreme Court precedent dealing with overt restrictions to movement is rather likely due to the uncommon existence of such restrictions.

---

138. 415 U.S. 250 (1974).
139. *See id.* at 269.
140. *See id.*
141. 405 U.S. 156 (1972).
142. *See id.* at 170-71.
143. *See id.* at 162.
144. *Id.*
145. *Id.* at 164.

Recent examples of U.S. Circuit Court rulings on the right to movement tend to blur the distinction between interstate and intrastate travel. In *Lutz v. City of York*,[146] the Third Circuit concluded that an unenumerated right to intrastate travel exists under substantive due process, even while holding that the particular "anti-cruising" law at issue did not violate it.[147] The *Lutz* court applied intermediate scrutiny to this right, drawing an analogy to the time, place, and manner doctrine of free speech jurisprudence.[148] The reasoning of the *Lutz* court was admittedly "*ad hoc*"[149] and encompassed numerous constitutional arguments. However, the court claimed that given the "rational continuum"[150] of substantive due process and the precedent of *Shapiro* and its progeny, the court had no choice but to recognize the basic right to travel as "implicit in the concept of ordered liberty" and "deeply rooted in the Nation's history."[151]

Recently, the Supreme Court addressed similar liberty issues in *City of Chicago v. Morales*.[152] In *Morales*, the Court struck down an anti-loitering ordinance enacted to deter gang activity as unconstitutionally vague.[153] Justice Stevens' opinion held that because the ordinance did not set forth a requirement that the prohibited conduct have a "harmful purpose,"[154] and because it prevented two or more persons from congregating where even one of them was a gang member (thus encompassing non-gang members) the ordinance was too broad.[155] Although the *Morales* majority did not invoke the fundamental right to movement *per se*, the same elements of unconstitutionality present in Chicago's failed ordinance existed in the District of Columbia's curfew. That is to say, the District's curfew did not require a harmful purpose on the part of juveniles and the ordinance applied to innocent juveniles as well as criminals; juveniles reasonably safe from crime as well as likely victims.[156] In finding such breadth unconstitutional, the *Morales* Court implicated the substantial tailoring requirement of the intermediate scrutiny analysis present in the *Hutchins* opinion and strongly suggested that the District's ordinance would not withstand this requirement.[157]

146. 899 F.2d 255 (3d Cir. 1990).

147. *Id.* at 270.

148. *See id.* at 269.

149. *See id.* at 268.

150. *Id.*

151. *Id.*

152. 527 U.S. 41 (1999).

153. *See id.* at 63-64.

154. *Id.* at 62-63.

155. *See id.*

156. *Compare* D.C. CODE ANN. § 6-2182 (5) (1996) *with* § 6-2183(a)(1) (stating that a minor is any unemancipated person under the age of 17 and that a minor commits an offense simply by remaining in a public place after curfew hours).

157. Based on the *Morales* reasoning, the District's curfew ordinance is too vague and unrelated to its purpose to pass constitutional muster in that it criminalizes the innocent. Taken another way, this means that the curfew ordinance is not substantially tailored to the District's objective.

C. Applying the Appropriate Constitutional Test

The *Hutchins* plurality was correct in applying the standard of "intermediate scrutiny" to the fundamental rights of minors. Minors have the same fundamental rights as adults.[158] The difference is that minors do not have these rights to the same extent as adults. What this difference translates into when making a constitutional analysis determines the level of review. For example, the *Tinker* case held that minors have the same extent of protection under the First Amendment right to free speech as do adults, subject to time, place, and manner restrictions.[159] Hence, minors, like adults, could expect a strict scrutiny analysis from a court hearing their claim of a free speech violation. However, the *Bellotti* case held that minors are subject to certain factors that serve to lessen the extent of constitutional protection for fundamental rights such as the right to have an abortion.[160] The distinction seems to lie in whether the fundamental right is enumerated or not. Where the right is enumerated, as in the right to free speech, minors have full constitutional protection commensurate with adults. Where the right is unenumerated, as in the privacy right to an abortion, special considerations seem to limit the extent of the constitutional protection of juveniles.

The factors articulated by the Supreme Court in *Bellotti* do not provide any blueprints for defining the extent of juvenile rights; neither do they provide much in the way of determining what level of review is appropriate for juveniles. Instead, the *Bellotti* factors simply provide justifications for why some juvenile rights should not extend to the level enjoyed by adults. Taking this way, courts are left with two options. On the one hand, a court may follow the example of the *Qutb* court and lower the government's threshold requirement for proving the relation of the means to the end.[161] In other words, a court may make it easier to prove "narrowly" or "compelling" under strict scrutiny analysis. Or, on the other hand, a court may follow the example found in *Schliefer* and *Hutchins* and simply take the level of heightened scrutiny down a notch, from strict scrutiny to intermediate scrutiny, when dealing with the fundamental rights of minors.[162] The latter surpasses the former in judicial efficacy for two reasons. First, it takes an entire step out of the analytical process. Instead of starting with strict scrutiny and then struggling with how to adapt the terms "compelling" and "narrowly tailored" to the *Bellotti* criteria, a court would simply apply intermediate scrutiny and keep the specifics of the *Bellotti* test out of the analysis completely. Second, a simpler analytical process leaves less room for subjectivity. The interpretations of the words "narrowly" and "compelling" are already sufficiently imprecise to allow for a high level of judicial

158. *See* Planned Parenthood v. Danforth, 428 U.S. 52, 74 (1976); Tinker v. Des Moines Indep. Community Sch. Dist., 393 U.S. 503, 511-12 (1969).

159. *See Tinker*, 393 U.S. at 505-06.

160. *See* Bellotti v. Baird, 443 U.S. 622, 634 (1979).

161. *See* Qutb v. Strauss, 11 F.3d 488, 492-94 (5th Cir. 1993).

162. *See* Hutchins v. District of Columbia, 188 F.3d 531, 535-36 (D.C. Cir. 1999); Schlieffer v. City of Charlottesville, 159 F.3d 843, 847 (4th Cir. 1998).

discretion. With the *Bellotti* factors available to modify these words, the potential for subjective interference from a judge's personal prejudices increases greatly.

The *Hutchins* plurality erred when it ruled that the District of Columbia's curfew ordinance was substantially tailored to meet its important objective. It would be wholly fruitless to argue that the District's objective of reducing juvenile crime and the likelihood of juvenile victimization was not at least important. Certainly it was important, and probably compelling as well. Few statements of purpose would invoke a greater sense of urgency than one such as, "we must save our children from becoming criminals and the victims of crime." However, a constitutional rights analysis under intermediate scrutiny also requires that the State's means be substantially tailored to its important objective.[163] The meaning of the word "substantially" is somewhat subjective, although a court must be as objective as possible. Yet, the word "substantial" does indicate a high standard. In high-crime areas of certain cities, a curfew ordinance such as the District of Columbia's would indeed be substantially related to the goal of preventing crime by and against minors. On its face, therefore, the District's curfew ordinance is constitutional. However, such an ordinance is unconstitutional where a less than substantial relationship exists between the curfew's application and the goal of preventing juvenile crime. An unconstitutional application would be the enforcement of a juvenile curfew in a city or distinguishable area of a city that does not have a juvenile crime or victimization problem. In *Hutchins*, the District failed to limit application of the curfew ordinance to the areas of the District with recognizable crime problems.[164] Therefore, the curfew ordinance in *Hutchins* was not substantially tailored to meet its important objective and the District's curfew ordinance should have failed the constitutional test.

The District of Columbia's curfew ordinance falls short of a substantial relationship by way of its overbreadth. Because the District is large and contains whole, definable suburbs and neighborhoods in which criminal activity by and against juveniles is not a problem, the ordinance as applied to these areas is unconstitutional. Conversely, there are certain areas of the District in which the curfew ordinance would be constitutional, in that therein exists a crime problem or potential for juvenile victimization. The *Hutchins* plurality countered this conclusion by claiming that to require limited application of the curfew ordinance to high juvenile crime areas of the District would be to invite accusations of judicial racism.[165] This claim, besides being presumptuous and dubious, is itself racist by implication. The *Hutchins* plurality betrayed two stereotypical assumptions: (1) the District's high-crime areas are home to members of a particular "race"; and (2) members of this race compose the majority of the District's juvenile criminals. Even if these assumptions are verifiable, the *Hutchins* plurality did not rely on any evidence.[166] In any case, no court may shirk its duty to uphold the law on the

---

163. *See, e.g., Hutchins*, 188 F.3d at 541.
164. *See id.* at 543-44.
165. *See id.*
166. *See id.*

basis of some speculative fear of political unpopularity. To do so recalls the disastrous undertones of *Scott v. Sandford*[167] and stands to lessen the public's expectation of impartiality from the courts.

V. Conclusion

Even if constitutional on its face, a juvenile curfew ordinance may still violate substantive due process where its application and enforcement does not comport with the limits demanded by accepted constitutional methodology. In *Hutchins*, the Council of the District of Columbia extended enforcement of a curfew ordinance to include areas of the District where crime by and against juveniles was too minimal to justify so drastic a restriction of the liberty interests of minors. In upholding the constitutionality of the curfew, the U.S. Court of Appeals for the D.C. Circuit correctly applied the intermediate scrutiny test for dealing with the fundamental rights of minors. However, the court erred by stating that to require stricter tailoring of the law would invite accusations of racism against the court. Such reasoning is unsupportable given the judicial duty to interpret the law impartially and according to the objective criteria set forth in controlling case precedent and established constitutional doctrine. The *Hutchins* court also erred in implying that a fundamental right to movement does not exist. This implication directly contradicts holdings and dicta from U.S. Supreme Court cases in which a general right to movement finds broad support.

The courts must always be careful in balancing the legitimate powers of state and federal actors against the restrictions imposed on state action by the substantive rights of individuals. Fundamentally stated, constitutional rights establish procedural and substantive limits to the exercise of political authority. When a court expands substantive rights out of some personal sense of justice or any subjective notion of natural law, this can result in an abrogation of legislative and political privilege. This is judicial activism. However, a court's restriction of rights for any of the same illegitimate reasons, through "reverse" judicial activism, is at least as egregious a violation of the judicial duty, but arguably more so given the essential nature of fundamental rights and their paramount importance in the American constitutional scheme.

William L. Foreman

167. 60 U.S. (19 How.) 393 (1856) ("The Dred Scott Case") (holding that persons of African descent could not sue in federal court because, at the time, they were not considered citizens of the United States).

Acknowledgments

Geimer, William S. "Juvenileness: A Single-Edged Constitutional Sword," Vol. 22 *Georgia Law Review* 949–973 (1988). Reprinted with the permission of the *Georgia Law Review*.

Hanisco, Christine, Note, "Acknowledging the Hypocrisy: Granting Minors the Right to Choose Their Medical Treatment," Vol. 16 *New York Law School Journal of Human Rights* 899–932 (2000). Reprinted with the permission of New York Law School.

Carey v. Population Services International, 431 U.S. 678–719 (1977).

Puzella, Carolyn, "Rights of Children: Abortion Rights of Minors, Parental Consent, and Parental Notification," Vol. 11 *Journal of Contemporary Legal Issues* 642–645 (2000). Reprinted with the permission of University of San Diego, School of Law.

Collett, Teresa Stanton, "Seeking Solomon's Wisdom: Judicial Bypass of Parental Involvement in a Minor's Abortion Decision," Vol. 52 *Baylor Law Review* 513–601 (2000). Reprinted with the permission of the *Baylor Law Review*.

Katz, Katheryn D., "The Pregnant Child's Right to Self-Determination," Vol. 62 *Albany Law Review* 1119–1166 (1999). Reprinted with the permission of the Albany Law School.

Deirdre E. Norton, "Why Criminalize Children? Looking Beyond the Express Policies Driving Juvenile Curfew Legislation," Vol. 4 *New York University Journal of Legislation & Public Policy* 175–203 (2000/2001). Reprinted with the permission of Fred B. Rothman & Co.

Alysa B. Freeman, "Go to the Mall with My Parents?? A Constitutional Analysis of the Mall of America's Juvenile Curfew," Vol. 102 *Dickinson Law Review* 481–538 (1998). Reprinted with the permission of Dickinson Law Review.

Sasse, Benjamin C., Note, "Curfew Laws, Freedom of Movement, and the Rights of Juveniles," Vol. 50 *Case Western Reserve Law Review* 681–728 (2000). Reprinted with the permission of the *Case Western Law Review*.

Foreman, William L., Note, "Constitutional Law: *Hutchins v. District of Columbia*: The Constitutional Dilemma Over Juvenile Curfews," 53

Oklahoma Law Review 717–735 (2000). Reprinted with the permission of the *Oklahoma Law Review.*

For Product Safety Concerns and Information please contact our EU
representative GPSR@taylorandfrancis.com
Taylor & Francis Verlag GmbH, Kaufingerstraße 24, 80331 München, Germany

www.ingramcontent.com/pod-product-compliance
Ingram Content Group UK Ltd.
Pitfield, Milton Keynes, MK11 3LW, UK
UKHW022114190926
475702UK00013B/1440

* 9 7 8 0 4 1 5 5 1 2 8 0 0 *